Praise for *The Plantagenets*

"A real life *Game of Thrones*, as dramatic and blood-soaked as any work of fantasy . . . Jones has opted for a bold narrative approach, anchored firmly upon the personalities of the monarchs. Fast-paced and accessible, *The Plantagenets* is old-fashioned storytelling and will be particularly appreciated by those who like their history red in tooth and claw." —*The Wall Street Journal*

"*The Plantagenets* is rich in detail and scene-setting. You can almost smell the sea salt as the *White Ship* sinks and hear the screams of the tortured at the execution grounds at Tyburn. . . . But there is a larger point: the Plantagenets' saga is the story of how English monarchs learned, or failed to learn, how to be kings, and how the English people, commoners and barons alike, learned how to limit their powers." —*USA Today*

"Outstanding. Majestic in its sweep, compelling in its storytelling, this is narrative history at its best. A thrilling dynastic history of royal intrigues, violent skullduggery, and brutal warfare across two centuries of British history." —Simon Sebag Montefiore, bestselling author of *Jerusalem: The Biography* and *Young Stalin*

"Jones has brought the Plantagenets out of the shadows, revealing them in all their epic heroism and depravity. His is an engaging and readable account . . . researched with exacting standards. The result is an enjoyable, often harrowing journey through a bloody, insecure era in which many of the underpinnings of English kingship and Anglo-American constitutional thinking were formed. . . . Jones brings the world of the court, the nobility, and battlefield alive, and it's compelling reading." —*The Washington Post*

"Some of the greatest stories in all of English history . . . rich in pageantry and soaked in blood." —Lewis Lapham, *Lapham's Quarterly*

"The single best one-volume general introduction to the Plantagenets ever written . . . Jones proves time and again that he's alive to the inherent drama of his subject. . . . The kings and queens seem larger than life because, one strongly suspects, life was larger while they were in it. They brawled and laughed and rode and loved and warred (and occasionally peaced) as though the world itself depended on what they did. And they were right about that." —*Open Letters Monthly*

"Jones, a protégé of David Starkey, writes with his mentor's erudition but also exhibits novelistic verve and sympathy. . . . This is a great popular history, whether you are au fait with the machinations of medievalism or whether the Magna Carta mystifies you. . . . *The Plantagenets* is proof that contemporary history can engage with the medieval world with style, wit, and chutzpah."

—*The Observer* (London)

"The risk with a long dynastic history is that it becomes just one damn thing after another, and the reader gets lost in the snowstorm of names and events. Jones avoids this with a combination of gripping storytelling and pin-sharp clarity. . . . *The Plantagenets* is a satisfying as well as an enjoyable read. There is no need for added goblins in this real life *Game of Thrones*."

—*The Literary Review*

"This action-packed narrative is, above all, a great story, filled with fighting, personality clashes, betrayal, and bouts of the famous Plantagenet rage. . . . Jones is an impressive guide to this tumultuous scene. . . . *The Plantagenets* succeeds in bringing an extraordinary family arrestingly to life."

—*The Telegraph* (London)

"A story filled with intrigue, murder, rebellion, military conflict (both internal and international), espionage, abdication, sexual shenanigans, and much more . . . Jones has provided a gripping overview of this exciting period. . . . Written in a lively narrative style, *The Plantagenets* is popular history at its best."

—*History in Review*

"A beautiful history . . . that frequently reads like a novel and can be opened to any chapter. . . . *The Plantagenets* is a brilliant and entertaining study of the roots of today's United Kingdom and its unwritten constitution."

—*Tampa Bay Times*

"Dan Jones's epic portrait of the medieval royals is a timely reminder that things haven't always been so rosy for those on the throne. The House of Plantagenet ruled England for more than two centuries, giving us eight generations of our best and worst kings and queens—and some bloody, brutal, and brilliant tales to match."

—*GQ*

"Jones has written a magnificently rich and glittering medieval pageant, guiding us into the distant world of the Plantagenets with confidence. This riveting history of an all-too-human ruling house amply confirms the arrival of a formidably gifted historian."
—*Sunday Telegraph* (London)

"They may lack the glamour of the Tudors or the majesty of the Victorians, but the Plantagenets are just as essential to the foundation of modern Britain. . . . The great battles against the Scots and French and the subjugation of the Welsh make for thrilling reading but so do the equally enthralling struggles over succession, the Magna Carta, and the Provisions of Oxford. . . . Written with prose that keeps the reader captivated throughout accounts of the span of centuries and the not-always-glorious trials of kingship, this book is at all times approachable, academic, and entertaining."
—*Booklist*

"An excellent book . . . *The Plantagenets* is a wonderful gallop through English history. Powerful personalities, vivid descriptions of battles and tournaments, ladies in fine velvet, and knights in shining armor crowd the pages of this highly engaging narrative."
—*Evening Standard*

"This is an exciting period and Jones describes it with verve. He has a keen appreciation of how power was seized and wielded by medieval monarchs, and the way they manipulated history, religion, and symbolism in the service of kingship. . . . Medieval history is enjoying its time in the sun again thanks to some excellent writers. Heaven be praised for that."
—*New Statesman* (London)

"The Plantagenets played a defining part in shaping the nation of England, and Dan Jones tells their fascinating story with wit, verve, and vivid insight. This is exhilarating history—a fresh and gloriously compelling portrait of a brilliant, brutal, and bloody-minded dynasty."
—Helen Castor, author of *She-Wolves: The Women Who Ruled England before Elizabeth*

"This is history at its most epic and thrilling. I would defy anyone not to be royally entertained by it."
—Tom Holland, author of *Rubicon: The Last Years of the Roman Republic*

Dan Jones is an award-winning historian of the Middle Ages. A graduate of Cambridge University, where he studied under David Starkey, he is the author of *Summer of Blood*, a history of the Peasants' Revolt of 1381, which was chosen by *The Independent* as Book of the Year. His four-part television series based on *The Plantagenets*, a number one bestseller in the UK and a *New York Times* bestseller, is currently in production and will be broadcast in 2015. He lives in London with his wife and two daughters.

The Plantagenets

The Warrior Kings and Queens
Who Made England

DAN JONES

PENGUIN BOOKS

For JJ, VJ, and IJ

PENGUIN BOOKS
Published by the Penguin Group
Penguin Group (USA) LLC
375 Hudson Street
New York, New York 10014

USA | Canada | UK | Ireland | Australia | New Zealand | India | South Africa | China
penguin.com
A Penguin Random House Company

First published in Great Britain by HarperPress,
an imprint of HarperCollins Publishers, 2012
First published in the United States of America by Viking Penguin,
a member of Penguin Group (USA) Inc., 2013
Published in Penguin Books 2014

THE LIBRARY OF CONGRESS HAS CATALOGED THE HARDCOVER EDITION AS FOLLOWS:
Jones, Dan, 1981–
The Plantagenets : the warrior kings and queens who made England / Dan Jones.—
[Revised edition].
pages cm
Includes bibliographical references and index.
ISBN 978-0-670-02665-4 (hc.)
ISBN 978-0-14-312492-4 (pbk.)
1. Plantagenet, House of.   2. Great Britain—History—Plantagenets, 1154–1399.
3. Great Britain—Kings and rulers—Biography.   4. Great Britain—Politics
and government—1154–1399.   I. Title.
DA225.J76 2013
942.030922—dc23
2012039998

Printed in the United States of America
10

Set in Adobe Jenson Pro
Maps by John Gilkes and Jeffrey L. Ward

For a sensible man ought to consider that Fortune's favor is variable and her wheel is ever turning.... [T]he Prince must take care, and always have imprinted on his mind the fact that although the merciful Creator ... is long-suffering and patient ... He is likewise severe in executing punishment and vengeance upon the stubborn and willful, and usually begins to exact that punishment here on earth.

—Gerald of Wales, *The Conquest of Ireland*

Contents

Contents

Contents

Contents

Plantagenet England

SCOTLAND

Glasgow • Edinburgh • • Berwick-upon-Tweed

Tweed

Carlisle •

Durham •

Scarborough •

Lancaster •

North Sea

York •

Irish Sea

Conwy

Dee

• Chester

Trent

Nottingham •

WALES

Severn

Leicester •

Norwich •

Kenilworth •

Wye

Hereford •

Avon

Northampton •

Cambridge •

Orwell

• Evesham

Gloucester •

Oxford •

Thames

London •

Cardiff •

Bristol •

Devizes •

Windsor •

Canterbury •
Dover •

• Glastonbury

Winchester •

Southampton • Portsmouth •

Exeter •

Isle of Wight

English Channel

FRANCE

0 Miles 50 100
0 Kilometers 100

The Plantagenet Empire in France at Its Peak, c. 1187

ENGLAND

Rhine

Calais

FLANDERS

Bouvines

Crécy

Barfleur

Rouen

VERMANDOIS

Reims

Seine

Caen

Falaise

Paris

CHAMPAGNE

NORMANDY

MAINE

BLOIS

ROYAL
DEMESNE

BRITTANY

Rennes

Le Mans

Nantes

ANJOU

TOURAINE

BERRY

BURGUNDY

Fontevraud

Chinon

Loire

POITOU

Poitiers

CHATEAU-
ROUX

BOURBON

La Rochelle

LA MARCHE

AUVERGNE

SAINTONGE

ANGOULÊME

LIMOUSIN

Territories held by
the French Crown

Plantagenet territories

Garonne

Bordeaux

PÉRIGORD

Lot

CAHORSIN

AGENOIS

Rhône

GASCONY

Avignon

ARMAGNAC

Toulouse

TOULOUSE

NAVARRE

ARAGON

0 Miles   50   100

0 Kilometers   100

CATALONIA

Barcelona

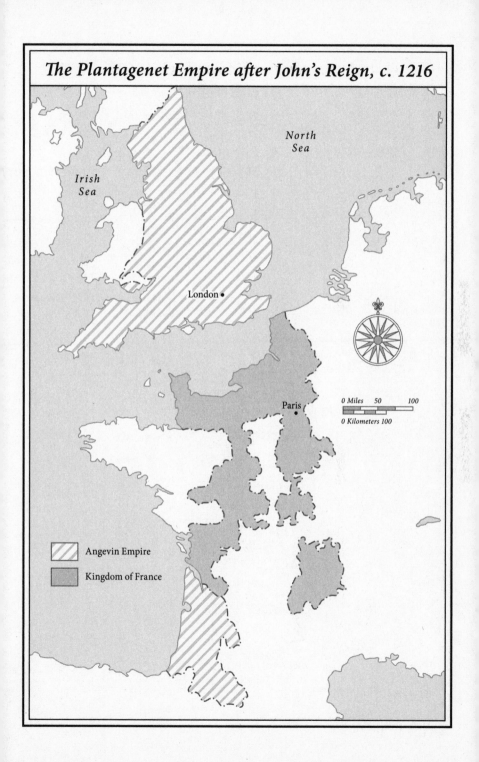

The Plantagenet Empire after John's Reign, c. 1216

North
Sea

Irish
Sea

London •

Paris •

0 Miles   50   100

0 Kilometers 100

Angevin Empire

Kingdom of France

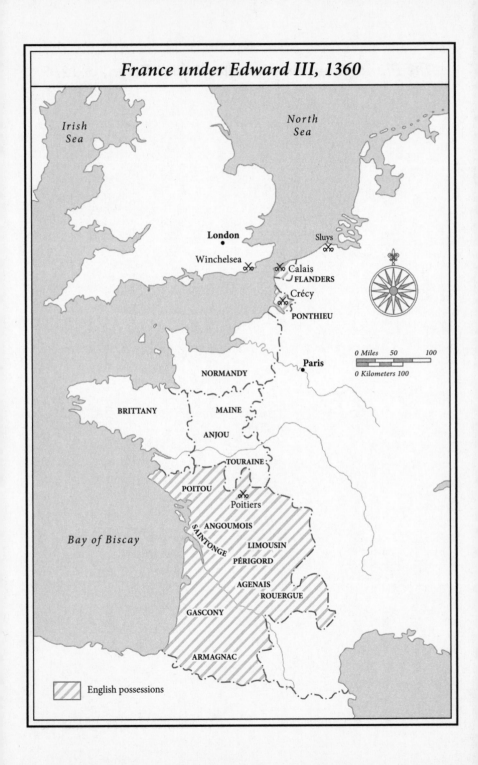

France under Edward III, 1360

Irish Sea

North Sea

London •

Winchelsea ⚔

Sluys ⚔

⚔ Calais
FLANDERS

⚔ Crécy

PONTHIEU

Paris •

NORMANDY

BRITTANY

MAINE

ANJOU

TOURAINE

POITOU

⚔
Poitiers

Bay of Biscay

ANGOUMOIS

SAINTONGE

LIMOUSIN

PÉRIGORD

AGENAIS

ROUERGUE

GASCONY

ARMAGNAC

0 Miles   50   100

0 Kilometers 100

▨ English possessions

Plantagenet Scotland

Elgin

Banff

Kildrummy

Aberdeen

Loch Ness

Stracathro

North Sea

Scone

Perth

Tay

Methven

St. Andrews

Dupplin Moor

Stirling Bridge

Dunfermline

Stirling Castle

Forth

Dunbar

Bannockburn

Halidon Hill

Clyde

Falkirk

Edinburgh

Berwick

Bothwell

Lanark

Norham

Tweed

Loudoun Hill

Roxburgh

Ayr

Alnwick

Annan

Dumfries

Caerlaverock

Neville's Cross

Carlisle

Cree

Stanhope Park

Irish Sea

Faughart

0 Miles 50

0 Kilometers 50

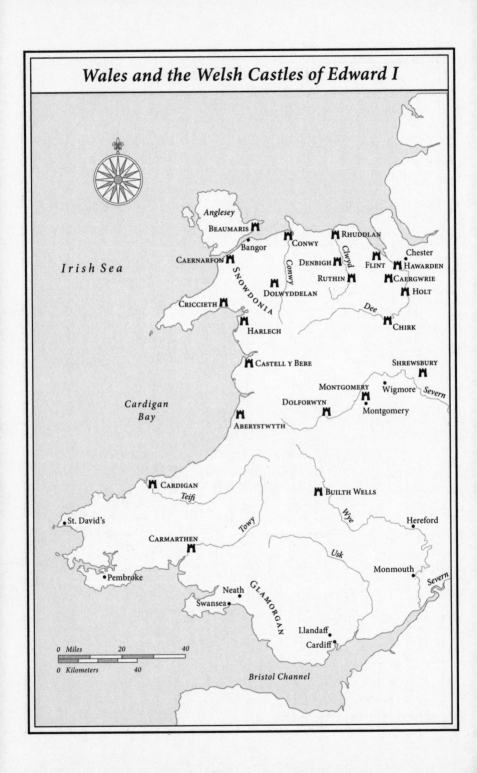

Wales and the Welsh Castles of Edward I

Irish Sea

Anglesey

BEAUMARIS

• Bangor

CAERNARFON

CONWY

RHUDDLAN

Clwyd

Chester

DENBIGH

FLINT

HAWARDEN

CAERGWRIE

RUTHIN

HOLT

Conwy

SNOWDONIA

DOLWYDDELAN

CRICCIETH

Dee

CHIRK

HARLECH

CASTELL Y BERE

SHREWSBURY

MONTGOMERY

• Wigmore

Severn

DOLFORWYN

• Montgomery

Cardigan Bay

ABERYSTWYTH

CARDIGAN

BUILTH WELLS

Teifi

• St. David's

Wye

• Hereford

CARMARTHEN

Towy

Usk

• Pembroke

• Monmouth

Severn

Neath •

GLAMORGAN

Swansea •

Llandaff •

Cardiff •

0 Miles   20   40

0 Kilometers   40

Bristol Channel

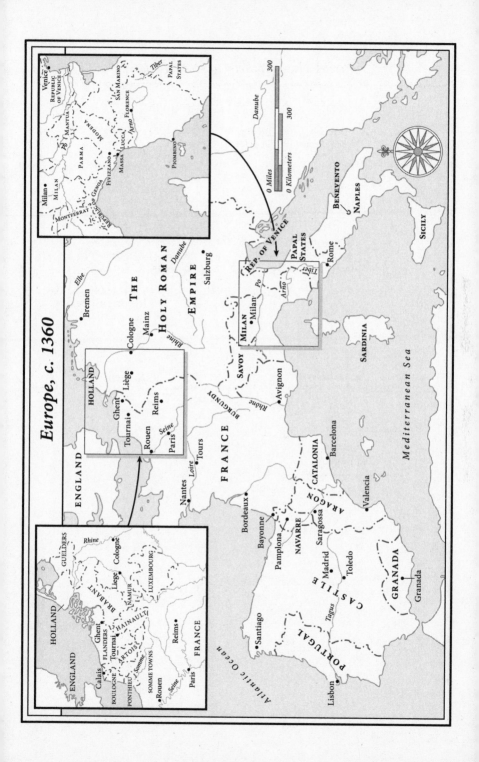

Europe, c. 1360

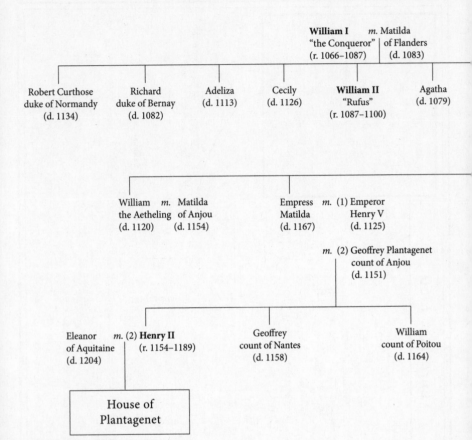

William I *m.* Matilda
"the Conqueror" of Flanders
(r. 1066–1087) (d. 1083)

Robert Curthose
duke of Normandy
(d. 1134)

Richard
duke of Bernay
(d. 1082)

Adeliza
(d. 1113)

Cecily
(d. 1126)

William II
"Rufus"
(r. 1087–1100)

Agatha
(d. 1079)

William *m.* Matilda
the Aetheling of Anjou
(d. 1120) (d. 1154)

Empress *m.* (1) Emperor
Matilda Henry V
(d. 1167) (d. 1125)

m. (2) Geoffrey Plantagenet
count of Anjou
(d. 1151)

Eleanor *m.* (2) Henry II
of Aquitaine (r. 1154–1189)
(d. 1204)

Geoffrey
count of Nantes
(d. 1158)

William
count of Poitou
(d. 1164)

House of
Plantagenet

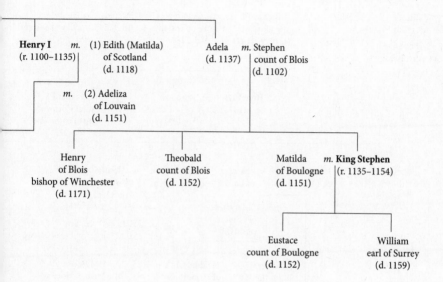

The Normans

Henry I *m.* (1) Edith (Matilda)   Adela   *m.* Stephen
(r. 1100–1135)   of Scotland   (d. 1137)   count of Blois
                    (d. 1118)   (d. 1102)

        m.   (2) Adeliza
               of Louvain
               (d. 1151)

Henry   Theobald   Matilda   *m.* **King Stephen**
of Blois   count of Blois   of Boulogne   (r. 1135–1154)
bishop of Winchester   (d. 1152)   (d. 1151)
(d. 1171)

                                      Eustace   William
                                      count of Boulogne   earl of Surrey
                                      (d. 1152)   (d. 1159)

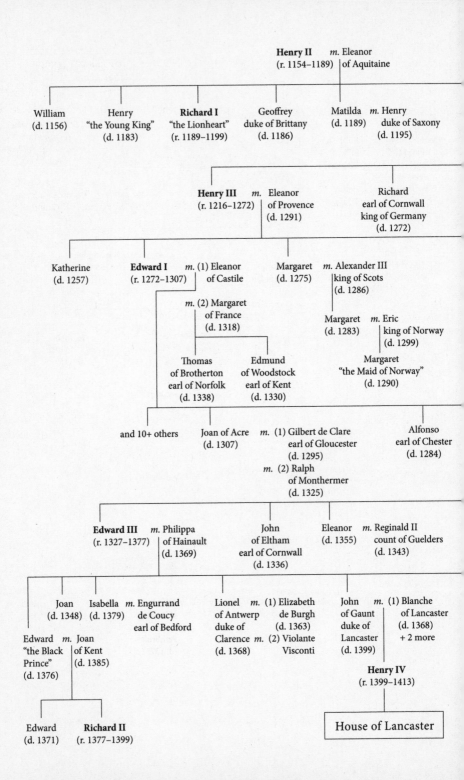

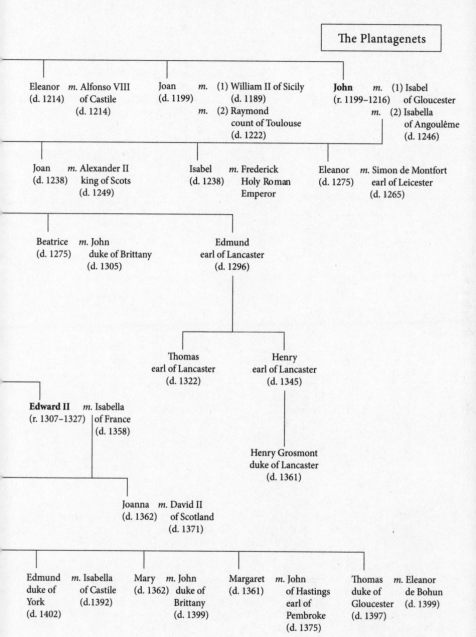

The Plantagenets

Eleanor *m.* Alfonso VIII
(d. 1214)   of Castile
          (d. 1214)

Joan   *m.* (1) William II of Sicily
(d. 1199)   (d. 1189)
        m. (2) Raymond
                count of Toulouse
                (d. 1222)

John   *m.* (1) Isabel
(r. 1199–1216)   of Gloucester
          m. (2) Isabella
                of Angoulême
                (d. 1246)

Joan   *m.* Alexander II
(d. 1238)   king of Scots
            (d. 1249)

Isabel   *m.* Frederick
(d. 1238)   Holy Roman
            Emperor

Eleanor   *m.* Simon de Montfort
(d. 1275)   earl of Leicester
            (d. 1265)

Beatrice   *m.* John
(d. 1275)   duke of Brittany
            (d. 1305)

Edmund
earl of Lancaster
(d. 1296)

Thomas
earl of Lancaster
(d. 1322)

Henry
earl of Lancaster
(d. 1345)

Edward II   *m.* Isabella
(r. 1307–1327)   of France
              (d. 1358)

Henry Grosmont
duke of Lancaster
(d. 1361)

Joanna   *m.* David II
(d. 1362)   of Scotland
            (d. 1371)

Edmund   *m.* Isabella
duke of   of Castile
York   (d.1392)
(d. 1402)

Mary   *m.* John
(d. 1362)   duke of
           Brittany
           (d. 1399)

Margaret   *m.* John
(d. 1361)   of Hastings
            earl of
            Pembroke
            (d. 1375)

Thomas   *m.* Eleanor
duke of   de Bohun
Gloucester (d. 1399)
(d. 1397)

French Kings, 1060–1422

House of Capet

Philip I	1060–1108
Louis VI	1108–1137
Louis VII	1137–1180
Philip II	1180–1223
Louis VIII	1223–1226
Louis IX	1226–1270
Philip III	1270–1285
Philip IV	1285–1314
Louis X	1314–1316
John I	November 15–20, 1316
Philip V	1316–1322
Charles IV	1322–1328

House of Valois

Philip VI	1328–1350
John II	1350–1364
Charles V	1364–1380
Charles VI	1380–1422

Preface

Who were the Plantagenets? The name was not used by any of the characters in this book to describe themselves, with the exception of one: Geoffrey count of Anjou, a handsome, belligerent redheaded young man born in 1113, who wore a sprig of yellow broom blossom in his hat and decorated his shield with lions. It was from the Latin name (*Planta genista*) of the broom that the name Plantagenet derived, while lions passant guardant became the heraldic symbol of English kingship, carried before vast armies from the chilly Lowlands of Scotland to the dusty plains of the Middle East. There is some irony here: Geoffrey never visited England, took scant direct interest in the affairs of the realm, and died in 1151, three years before his eldest son inherited the English Crown.

Nevertheless, Plantagenet is a powerful name. The kings who descended from Geoffrey ruled England for more than two centuries, beginning with Henry II, who inherited the Crown in 1154, and ending with Richard II, who was relieved of it by his cousin Henry Bolingbroke in 1399. They were the longest reigning English royal dynasty, and during their times were founded some of the most basic elements of what we today know as England. The realm's borders were established, as were its relationships with its neighbors—principally Scotland, Wales, France, and Ireland, but also the Low Countries, the papacy, and the Iberian states that eventually became Spain. Principles of law and institutions of government that have endured to this day were created in their essential forms—some deliberately, others either by accident or under duress. A rich mythology of national history and legend was concocted, and the cults of two national saints—Edward the Confessor and St. George—were established. The English tongue rose from an uncultured, rather coarse local dialect to become the language of parliamentary debate and poetic composition. Great castles, palaces, cathedrals, and monuments were raised; many of them still stand as testament to the genius of the men who conceived them, built them, and defended them against attack. Heroes were born, died, and became legends; so too were villains whose names still echo through the pages of history. (Some of those villains wore the crown.) Several of the most famous and dramatic battles in

European history were fought, at Bouvines and Bannockburn, Sluys and Winchelsea, Crécy and Poitiers. Military tactics were revolutionized between a Norman age, in which warfare was the art of siegecraft, and the dawn of the fifteenth century, during which pitched battles were commonplace and the English, with their brave men-at-arms and deadly mounted archers, were the scourge of Europe. By the end of the Plantagenet years, the English had begun to explore the art of war on the open seas. Naval tactics lagged some way behind tactics in the field, but by the middle of the fourteenth century something resembling an English navy could be deployed to protect the coasts and attack enemy shipping. It is undeniable that during the Plantagenet years many acts of savagery, butchery, cruelty, and stupidity were committed, but by 1399, where this book ends, the chilly island realm that had been conquered by William, the bastard of Normandy, in 1066 had been transformed into one of the most sophisticated and important kingdoms in Christendom. At its heart lay the power and prestige of the royal family.

That is the process described in this book, but this is also a book written to entertain. It is a narrative history, and it tells some of the great stories of England. They include the civil war between Stephen and Matilda; the murder of Thomas Becket by Henry II's knights; the Great War of 1173–1174; Richard I's wars against Saladin on the Third Crusade; the Barons' War against King John and the ratification of the Magna Carta; Henry III's hapless attempts to deal with the barons of a later age, including his brother-in-law and nemesis Simon de Montfort; Edward I's campaigns in Wales and Scotland; Edward II's peculiar romance with Piers Gaveston and his dismal abdication in 1327; Edward III's provocation of the Hundred Years War, in which he fought alongside his son the Black Prince and captured the king of France, and the subsequent institution of the Order of the Garter to celebrate England's new martial supremacy; the scourge of the Black Death; Richard II's heroism against Wat Tyler's rebels during the Peasants' Revolt of 1381, which was followed by Richard's tyranny and his final fall. These stories are exciting in their own right; they are also part of a historical canon that still, even in the cultural chaos of the twenty-first century, defines England as a nation and as a people. The Plantagenet kings did not just invent England as a political, administrative, and military entity. They also helped invent the *idea* of England, an idea that has as much importance today as it ever had before.

This is a long book, and it could have been longer still. For ease of reading I have divided the text into seven sections. Part I, "Age of Shipwreck," illustrates the dismal state to which England had sunk by the end of its period of Norman rule, which began under William the Conqueror and continued during the reigns of two of his sons, William Rufus and Henry I. After the death of the latter, a vicious and paralyzing civil war engulfed England and Normandy. It was fought between rival claimants, the Conqueror's grandson King Stephen and his granddaughter Empress Matilda, and it took nearly two decades to resolve it in favor of the latter. During that time England was effectively partitioned between two courts and two competing governments, leaving public authority splintered and the countryside a smoldering ruin, infested with mercenaries. Only with the accession of Matilda's son—her eldest child by Geoffrey Plantagenet, a disheveled, quick-tempered, but brilliant boy known as Henry FitzEmpress—was the realm reunited and restored to good governance. Henry FitzEmpress became Henry II, and through a combination of some good fortune, immense personal energy, and a great deal of military capability and hardheaded purpose, Henry set about establishing himself, and by association the English Crown, as the master of a patchwork of territories reaching from the borders of Scotland to the foothills of the Pyrenees.

The story of Henry II's rule over his vast dominions and their gradual, if unintended, coherence into a form of empire is the subject of Part II, "Age of Empire." It charts Henry's astonishing conquests, his catastrophic dispute with his onetime best friend Thomas Becket, and the king's struggles with his feckless children and extraordinary wife, Eleanor of Aquitaine, which some contemporaries believed were divine punishment for Becket's death. "Age of Empire" also explores Henry's revolutionary reforms of English law, justice, and bureaucracy, reforms that gave England legal processes and principles of government that endured for centuries.

Despite the feats and achievements of his astonishing reign, Henry II is one of the lesser-known Plantagenet kings. Not so his third son, Richard I, "the Lionheart," who inherited the Plantagenet empire in 1189, during the white heat of Europe's most enthusiastic crusading years. Richard, who spent a surprisingly small amount of time in England given the heroic status he achieved there within decades of his death, devoted his life to defending and expanding the horizons of Plantagenet power. This led him to conquests as far afield as Sicily, Cyprus, and the kingdom of Jerusalem during the Third Crusade, before he returned, via an expensive imprisonment in Germany, to fight for his inheritance against the French king Philip II, "Augustus." "Age of Empire" ends in 1204, when Richard's brother King John suffered a humiliating defeat to Philip, lost the duchy of Normandy, and disgraced his family's military legacy in a reign that was to influence relations between England and France for almost 150 years.

The repercussions of John's military failure are explored in Part III, "Age of Opposition." After the loss of Normandy, the kings of England were forced to live permanently in England, a state of affairs that brought John rapidly into conflict with his barons, churchmen, and Celtic neighbors. "Age of Opposition" begins during the dark days of John's reign, when military successes against Wales, Scotland, and Ireland were clouded by the unusual cruelty of a defective king. John's use and misuse of the sophisticated system of government bequeathed to him by his father provoked one of the greatest constitutional crises in English history. In 1215 England collapsed into a long civil war, at the heart of which lay a question: How could a realm discipline a tyrannical king? It was a question that a failed peace treaty known as the Magna Carta sought unsuccessfully to answer. The Magna Carta expressed some important principles of English government, and the great charter subsequently became a rallying cry to opponents of the Crown during the reign of John's son Henry III and the early career of his grandson Edward I. It was to the Magna Carta that all opponents of the Crown turned at moments of crisis for the rest of the thirteenth century. Chief among these opponents was a man called Simon de Montfort. Henry III's and Edward's wars with de Montfort eventually brought the "Age of Opposition" to a close.

Part IV begins in 1260, toward the end of the long period of intermittent civil war between Plantagenet kings and their barons. The royal hero of this time was Edward I, a tall and relentless king who was said to be so fierce that he once actually scared a man to death. Under Edward's belligerent leadership, the English were finally induced to cease fighting one another and turn their attentions on their neighbors Scotland and Wales. Edward I's brutal attempts to become the master not only of England but also of the whole of Britain are the subject of "Age of Arthur." The popularity of Arthurian tales and relic hunting increased as a new mythology of English kingship was explored. Edward cast himself as the inheritor of Arthur (originally a legendary Welsh king), who sought to reunite the British

Isles and usher in a great new age of royal rule. Despite flurries of outrage from his barons, who began to organize political opposition through the nascent political body known as parliament, Edward very nearly succeeded in his goals, and his influence over England's relations with Scotland and Wales has never entirely waned.

Edward I was undoubtedly one of the great, if not one of the more personally endearing, Plantagenets. His son Edward II was the worst of them on every score. In Part V, "Age of Violence," this book examines the desperate tale of a king who failed completely to comprehend any of the basic obligations of kingship and whose reign dissolved into a ghastly farce of failure in foreign policy, complete isolation of the political community, and murderous civil war. Edward's disastrous relationships with his favorites Piers Gaveston and Hugh Despenser the Younger wreaked havoc on English politics, as did the brutish behavior of Edward's cousin Thomas earl of Lancaster, who waged uncompromising war on the king until he was executed in 1322. Through Lancaster's belligerence and Edward's inadequacy, kingship was debased, degraded, and finally attacked by the king's own subjects; the pages of English history between 1307 and 1330 are stained with blood. Part V aims to explain how this came to be so and how the bloodshed was eventually brought to an end.

The greatest of all the Plantagenet kings was Edward III, who inherited the throne as a teenage puppet king under his mother and her lover Roger Mortimer. He soon shook off their influence, and the next three triumphant decades of his reign are described in Part VI, "Age of Glory." Under the accomplished generalship of Edward, his son the Black Prince, and his cousin Henry Grosmont, England pulverized France and Scotland (as well as other enemies, including Castile) in the opening phases of the Hundred Years War. Victories on land at Halidon Hill (1333), Crécy (1346), Calais (1347), Poitiers (1356), and Nájera (1367) established the English war machine, built around the power of the deadly longbow, as Europe's fiercest. Success at sea at Sluys (1340) and Winchelsea (1350) also gave the Plantagenets confidence in the uncertain arena of warfare on water. Edward and his sons deliberately encouraged a national mythology that interwove Arthurian legend, a new cult of St. George, and a revival of the code of knightly chivalry in the Order of the Garter. They created a culture that bonded England's aristocracy together in the common purpose of war. By 1360 Plantagenet kingship had reached its apotheosis. Political harmony at home was matched by dominance abroad. A new period of greatness beckoned.

Then, just as suddenly as it had arrived, English preeminence dissolved. Part VII charts just how rapidly fortune's wheel, a favorite medieval metaphor for the vicissitudes of life, could turn. After 1360 Edward's reign began to decay, and by the accession of his grandson Richard II in 1377 a crisis of rule had begun to emerge. Richard inherited many very serious problems. The Black Death, which ravaged Europe's population in wave after wave of pestilence from the middle of the fourteenth century, had turned England's economic order upside down. Divisions among the old king's sons led to a fractured foreign policy, while France, revived under Charles V and Charles VI, began to push the English back once more toward the Channel. But if Richard was dealt a bad hand, he played it diabolically. Plantagenet kingship and the royal court imported trappings of magnificence; the first great medieval English writers—Geoffrey Chaucer, John Gower, and William Langland—set to work. But Richard was a suspicious, greedy, violent, and spiteful king, who alienated some of the greatest men in his kingdom. By 1399 the realm had tired of him, and he was deposed by his cousin Henry Bolingbroke.

That is where this book ends. It would be perfectly possible, in theory, to have carried on. Direct descendants of Edward III continued to rule England until 1485, when Henry Tudor took the throne from Richard III at Bosworth. Indeed, the name Plantagenet first came into royal use during the Wars of the Roses, when in 1460 the Parliament Rolls record "Richard Plantaginet, commonly called Duc of York," claiming to be king of England. Thereafter Edward IV and Richard III awarded the surname to some of their illegitimate children—a nod to royalty outside the official family tree, whose use denoted a connection to an ancient and legendary royal bloodline.

I have defined England's Plantagenet years as being between the dates 1154 and 1400 for three reasons.

First, this was the only period of the English Middle Ages in which the Crown passed with general certainty from one generation to the next without any serious succession disputes or wars of dynastic legitimacy. With the exceptions of Arthur of Brittany and Prince Louis of France, who made hopeful but ultimately fruitless claims at the beginning and end of King John's torrid reign, there were no rival claimants to the English Crown during these years. The same cannot be said either for the Norman period that ended with King Stephen's reign or for the century following Richard II's deposition, when the Plantagenet dynasty split into its two cadet branches of Lancaster and York.

Second, I have chosen to write about the period 1154–1399 simply because it seems to me that this is one of the most exciting, compelling periods in the Middle Ages, during which some of the greatest episodes in English history took place. And third, I have limited this story to these years for reasons of practicality. Though I look forward to taking the story of the Plantagenets through to the grisly death of the dynasty under Henry Tudor, it was not possible to do so in a single volume light enough to read in bed. A second book will then complete the story.

This book has been a pleasure to write. I hope it is a pleasure to read too. A number of people have helped me write it. Nothing would have been possible without my peerless agent, Georgina Capel. I also want to thank Dr. Helen Castor for her extraordinary generosity, wisdom, and encouragement as we discussed almost every aspect of the book. Ben Wilson and Dr. Sam Willis helped with naval matters. Richard Partington offered useful advice about Edward III. Walter Donohue, Paul Wilson, and Toby Wiseman gave invaluable comments on the manuscript at different stages. Any errors are mine, of course. My editor, Joy de Menil, at Viking has been wonderfully enthusiastic about this book since the moment she first read it and has worked on the text with great care and skill. Likewise, my British editor at Harper Press, Arabella Pike, was patient and piercing with her observations and notes on the text. The staff at the British Library, London Library, National Archives, London Metropolitan Archives, and Guildhall Library have been exceptionally kind, as have the keepers, guides, and staff at the innumerable castles, cathedrals, and battlefields I have visited in the course of researching this journey through three centuries of European history.

Above all, however, I should like to thank Jo, Violet, and Ivy Jones, who have put up with my incessant scribbling and to whom it is only reasonable that this book is dedicated.

Dan Jones

PART I

Age of Shipwreck

(1120–1154)

It was as if Christ and his saints were asleep.

—*The Anglo-Saxon Chronicle*

The *White Ship*

The prince was drunk. So too were the crew and passengers of the ship he had borrowed. On the evening of November 25, 1120, nearly two hundred young and beautiful members of England's and Normandy's elite families were enjoying themselves aboard a magnificent white longship that bobbed gently to the hum of laughter in a crowded harbor at Barfleur, in Normandy. A seventy-mile voyage lay ahead across the choppy late-autumn waters of the Channel, but with the ship moored at the edge of the busy port town, barrels of wine were rolled aboard, and all were invited to indulge.

The prince was William the Aetheling. He was the only legitimate son of Henry I, king of England and duke of Normandy, and Matilda of Scotland, the literate, capable queen descended from the line of Wessex kings who had ruled England before the Norman Conquest. His first name, William, was in honor of his grandfather William the Conqueror. His sobriquet, Aetheling, was a traditional Anglo-Saxon title for the heir to the throne. William was a privileged, sociable young man, who conformed to the time-honored stereotype of the adored, spoiled eldest son. One Norman chronicler observed him "dressed in silken garments stitched with gold, surrounded by a crowd of household attendants and guards, and gleaming in an almost heavenly glory." He was pandered to on all sides with "excessive reverence" and was therefore prone to fits of "immoderate arrogance."

William was surrounded by a large group of other noble youths. They included his half brother and half sister Richard of Lincoln and Matilda countess of Perche, both bastard children from a brood of twenty-four fathered by the remarkably virile King Henry; William's cousin Stephen of Blois, who was also a grandson of William the Conqueror; Richard, the twenty-six-year-old earl of Chester, and his wife, Maud; Geoffrey Ridel, an English judge; the prince's tutor, Othver; and numerous other cousins, friends, and royal officials. Together they made up a golden generation of the Anglo-Norman nobility. It was only right that they traveled in style.

The *White Ship* belonged to Thomas Fitzstephen, whose grandfather Airard had contributed a longship to William the Conqueror's invasion fleet. Fitzstephen had petitioned the king for the honor of carrying the royal party safely back from Barfleur to the south coast of England. Henry had honored him with the passage of the prince's party, but with this duty came a warning: "I entrust to you my sons William and Richard, whom I love as my own life."

William was a precious charge indeed. He was seventeen years old and already a rich and successful young man. He had been married in 1119 to Matilda, daughter of Fulk V, count of Anjou and future king of Jerusalem. It was a union designed to overturn generations of animosity between the Normans and Angevins (as the natives of Anjou, a small but important province on the lower Loire, were known). Following the wedding, William had accompanied his father around Normandy for a year, learning the art of kingship as Henry thrashed out what the chronicler William of Malmesbury described as "a brilliant and carefully concerted peace" with Louis VI, "the Fat," the sly, porcine king of France. It was intended as an education in the highest arts of kingship, and it had been deemed effective. William had lately been described as *rex designatus* (king-designate) in official documents, marking his graduation toward the position of co-king alongside his father.

The highest point of William's young life had come just a few weeks earlier, when he had knelt before the corpulent Louis to pay homage as the new duke of Normandy. This semisacred ceremony acknowledged the fact that Henry had turned over the dukedom to his son. It recognized William as one of Europe's leading political figures and marked the end of his journey to manhood. A new wife, a new duchy, and the unstoppable ascent to kingship before him: these were good reasons to celebrate, and that was precisely what William was doing. As the thin November afternoon gave way to a clear, chilly night, the *White Ship* stayed moored in Barfleur, and the wine flowed freely.

The *White Ship* was a large vessel, capable of carrying several hundred passengers, along with a crew of fifty and a cargo of treasure. The Norman historian Orderic Vitalis called it "excellently fitted out and ready for royal service." It was long and deep, decorated with ornate carvings at prow and stern and driven by a large central mast and square sail, with oar holes along both sides. The rudder, or "steer-board," was on the right-hand side of the vessel rather than in the center, so the onus on the captain was to be well aware of local maritime geography; steering was blind to the port side.

A fair wind was blowing up from the south, and it promised a rapid crossing to England. The crew and passengers bade the king's vessel farewell sometime in the evening. They were expected to follow shortly behind, but the drinking on board the *White Ship* was entertaining enough to keep them anchored long past dark. When priests arrived to bless the vessel with holy water before her departure, they were waved away with jeers and spirited laughter.

As the party ran on, a certain amount of bragging began. The *White Ship* contained little luggage and was equipped with fifty oarsmen. The inebriated captain boasted that his ship, with square sail billowing and oars pulling hard, was so fast that even with the disadvantage of having conceded a head start to King Henry's ship, they could still be in England before the king.

A few on board started to worry that sailing at high speed with a well-lubricated crew was not the safest way to travel to England, and it was with the excuse of a stomach upset that William's cousin Stephen of Blois excused himself from the party. He left the *White Ship* to find another vessel to take him home. Dismayed at the wild and headstrong behavior of the royal party and crew, a couple of others joined him. But despite the queasy defectors, the drunken sailors eventually saw their way to preparing the ship for departure. Around midnight on a clear night lit by a new moon, the *White Ship* weighed anchor and set off for England. "She [flew] swifter than the winged arrow, sweeping the rippling surface of the deep," wrote William of Malmesbury. But the ship did not fly far.

Whether it was the effects of the celebrations on board, a simple navigational error, or the wrath of the Almighty at seeing his holy water declined, within minutes of leaving shore the *White Ship* crashed into a sharp rocky outcrop, which is still visible today, at the mouth of the harbor. The collision punched a fatal hole in the wooden prow of the ship. The impact threw splintered timber into the sea. Freezing water began to pour in. The immediate priority of all on board was to save William. As the crew attempted to bail water out of the *White Ship*, a lifeboat was put over the side. William clambered aboard together with a few companions and oarsmen to return him to the safety of Barfleur. It must have been a terrifying scene: the roar of a drunken crew thrashing to bail out the stricken vessel, combining with the screams of passengers hurled into the water by the violence of the impact. The fine clothes of many of the noble men and women would have grown unmanageably heavy when soaked with seawater, making it impossible to swim for safety or even to tread water. The waves echoed with the cries of the drowning.

As his tiny boat turned for the harbor, William picked out among the panicked voices the screams of his elder half sister Matilda. She was crying for her life, certain to drown in the cold and the blackness. The thought was more than William could bear. He commanded the men on his skiff to turn back and rescue her.

It was a fatal decision. The countess was not drowning alone. As the lifeboat approached her, it was spotted by other passengers who were floundering in the icy waters. There was a mass scramble to clamber to safety aboard; the result was that the skiff too capsized and sank. Matilda was not saved, and neither now was William the Aetheling, duke of Normandy and king-designate of England. As the chronicler Henry of Huntingdon put it, "instead of wearing a crown of gold, his head was broken open by the rocks of the sea."

Only one man survived the wreck of the *White Ship*, a butcher from Rouen who had boarded the ship at Barfleur to collect payment for debts and been carried off to sea by the revelers. When the ship went down, he wrapped himself in ram skins for warmth and clung to wrecked timber during the night. He staggered, drenched, back to shore in the morning to tell his story. Later on the few bodies that were ever recovered began to wash up with the tide.

King Henry's ship, captained by sober men and sailed with care and attention, reached his kingdom unscathed, and the king and his household busied themselves preparing for the Christmas celebrations. When the awful word of the catastrophe in Barfleur reached the court, it was greeted with dumbstruck horror. Henry was kept in ignorance at first. Magnates and officials alike were terrified at the thought of telling the king that three of his children, including his beloved heir, were what William of Malmesbury called "food for the monsters of the deep." Eventually a small boy was sent to Henry to deliver the news; he threw himself before the king's feet and wept as he recounted the tragic news. According to Orderic Vitalis, Henry "fell to the ground, overcome with anguish." It was said that he never smiled again.

The sinking of the *White Ship* was not just a personal tragedy for Henry I. It was a political catastrophe for the Norman dynasty. In the words of

Henry of Huntingdon, William's "certain hope of reigning in the future was greater than his father's actual possession of the kingdom." Through William the Aetheling's marriage, Normandy had been brought to peace with Anjou. Through his homage to Louis VI, the whole Anglo-Norman realm was at peace with France. All of Henry's plans and efforts to secure his lands and legacy had rested on the survival of his son. Now it was all in vain.

The death of William the Aetheling and the fortuitous survival of his cousin Stephen of Blois would come to throw the whole of Western European politics into disarray for three decades.

Hunt for an Heir

Henry I was, as one contemporary chronicler put it, "the man against whom no one could prevail except God himself." The fourth son of William the Conqueror, he enjoyed an exceptionally long, peaceful, and prosperous reign of thirty-five years, in which royal authority in England reached new heights. After his father's death in 1087, England and Normandy had been split apart. Henry ruthlessly reunited them. After snatching the English Crown following his brother William Rufus's death in 1100, he defeated another elder brother, Robert Curthose, at the battle of Tinchebrai in 1106 to seize control of Normandy and thereafter kept Robert imprisoned for nearly three decades at Cardiff Castle. Henry encouraged the intermingling of an Anglo-Norman aristocracy, whose culture and landholdings straddled the Channel. Meanwhile, in Queen Matilda he chose a wife who would bring the Norman and Saxon bloodlines together, to heal the wounds of the Conquest.

Henry was a great lawgiver and administrator. He created a sophisticated system of Anglo-Norman government, a vast improvement on anything known under the rule of his father, William the Conqueror, or his brother William Rufus. He granted the English barons a charter of liberties, which celebrated the laws of the last Saxon king, Edward the Confessor, guaranteed baronial rights, and set out some limits to royal power. He sent royal judges into the English shires on large judicial circuits, investigating crimes, abuses, and corruption and strengthening the Crown's role in local government. He reformed the royal treasury, setting up an exchequer to make accounts twice a year and drawing together the accounting systems of England and Normandy under a single treasurer. And he did much to secure Normandy's position on the Continent. Taken together, Henry's government was one of the most sophisticated bureaucratic machines in Europe since the Roman era. "In his time," said *The Anglo-Saxon Chronicle*, "no man dared do wrong against another; he made peace for man and beast." Yet for all of King Henry I's great triumphs, he failed in one vital task: he never managed to secure the future.

After William the Aetheling's tragic death, Henry I tried hard to father another legitimate son on whom he could settle his lands and titles. Queen Matilda had died in 1118, so in 1121 he married a nubile teenager, Adeliza of Louvain. Surprisingly for a man who had sired twenty-two bastard children, he was unable to impregnate his new wife. That left Henry with one, rather desperate option. Given that he could not groom as king any of his bastard sons (such as the extremely capable eldest, Robert earl of Gloucester), he decided that he would appoint as his heir his only other legitimate child, the empress Matilda.

When her younger brother died on the *White Ship*, Matilda was eighteen years old. She had been living in Germany for a decade, having been sent at the age of eight to marry Henry V, king of the Germans and Holy Roman Emperor, whose power reached from Germany to Tuscany. She had grown up in utmost splendor in the cities and palaces of central Europe, where she tasted the very heights of political power. Matilda served as regent when her husband was absent, stretched constantly between his large domains. She had twice worn her imperial crown at great ceremonial occasions in Rome, and as one of the most important women in Europe she kept the company of the most famous and influential figures of her age.

In 1125, however, the emperor died unexpectedly. Matilda had borne no children, so her political role in Germany was cut short. Henry I brought her straight back to England and told her of his new plan for the kingdom. She arrived with her title of empress and her favorite precious relic, the preserved hand of St. James, a souvenir from the imperial chapel. At the Christmas court of 1126 Matilda sat beside her father as his loyal barons came to swear an oath of allegiance to her as heir to the kingdom and duchy. This was an extraordinary measure, and both Henry and his barons realized it. The precedents for female rule in the twelfth century were very weak. Kingship was the role of a soldier, a judge, and a lawgiver. All these roles in the Middle Ages were inescapably male. A king asked a lot when he extracted from his people a promise that they would consent to be ruled by his daughter. Unfortunately, Henry had little other choice.

It was clear that Matilda would need a new husband to bolster her claim to succession. As he had with William the Aetheling, Henry now sought an alliance with the counts of Anjou. He contacted Fulk V and negotiated a marriage alliance between Matilda and Fulk's eldest son, Geoffrey. On June 17, 1128, the couple was married in the Norman-Angevin border town of Le Mans. The empress Matilda was twenty-six years old; her groom was fifteen. John of Marmoutier recorded that the marriage was celebrated "for three weeks without a break, and when it was over no one left without a gift."

On his wedding day Geoffrey of Anjou was a tall, bumptious teenager with ginger hair, a seemingly inexhaustible energy, and a flair for showmanship. His fair-skinned good looks earned him the sobriquet Le Bel. Tradition also has it that he liked to wear a sprig of bright yellow broom blossom (*Planta genista* in Latin) in his hair, which earned him another nickname, Geoffrey Plantagenet. John of Marmoutier later described him as "admirable and likable . . . he excelled at arguing . . . [and was] unusually skilled at warfare." A week before his marriage, he had been knighted by Henry I in Rouen. He was dressed in linen and purple, wearing double-mail armor with gold spurs, a shield covered in gold motifs of lions, and a sword reputedly forged by the mythical Norse blacksmith Wayland the Smith. As soon as the marriage was completed, Geoffrey became count of Anjou in his own right, as Fulk V resigned the title and left for the East, to become king of Jerusalem.

Despite all this, Matilda was underwhelmed. Geoffrey was eleven years her junior, and Normans saw Angevins as barbarians who murdered priests, desecrated churches, and had appalling table manners. A legend held that they were descended from Satan's daughter Melusine, who had married an Angevin count of old. She had revealed herself as a devil when forced to witness the Mass, flown out of a church window, and disappeared forever, but her fiendish blood still bubbled in the veins of her descendants. If this was legend from the distant ages, there was evidence closer to hand that the Angevin bloodline was dangerous. Geoffrey's great-grandfather Fulk III, "the Black," was notorious for his violence. He was said to have had his first wife burned at the stake in her wedding dress on discovery of her adultery with a goatherd, and his reputation as a perverted rapist and plunderer stretched from the shores of the Atlantic to the Holy Land.

Notwithstanding this checkered ancestry, Geoffrey Plantagenet had seemed to Henry I a necessary husband for his imperial daughter. The couple did not get along, but that was hardly the point. They argued and separated for the first years of their marriage, then settled down under Henry I's guidance and did their political duty. On March 5, 1133, at Le Mans, Matilda gave birth to their first son. The couple named him Henry, after the king whose Crown it was intended that he should inherit. The infant was baptized on Easter Saturday in Le Mans Cathedral and placed under the protection of St. Julian. But it would take more than a saint's protection to provide for the child's future. Within two years, everything that Henry I hoped for in his grandson would be cast into chaos and doubt.

The Shipwreck

In the last week of November 1135, Henry I and his entourage arrived at Lyons-la-Forêt in upper Normandy. The castle and the forest surrounding it had been a regular haunt of the Norman dukes for two centuries, and Henry arrived late on a Monday evening with the intention of enjoying himself the next day as his ancestors had, in the thrill of the hunt. Even at the age of sixty-eight the king remained vigorous and strong.

During the night he fell ill, and his condition worsened fast. By the end of the week it was apparent that the illness was extremely grave. According to a letter from the archbishop of Rouen, Henry "confessed his sins . . . beat his breast and set aside his animosities." On Sunday, December 1, after three days of absolution, prayer, and almsgiving, the archbishop anointed Henry with holy oil, whereupon the king expired.

Although many chroniclers noted the piety with which Henry I died, one of them, Henry of Huntingdon, recorded some gruesome details of the king's immediate afterlife. The royal corpse was "brought to Rouen, and there his entrails, brain and eyes were buried together." Then "the body was cut all over with knives and copiously sprinkled with salt and wrapped in oxhides to stop the strong pervasive stench, which was already causing the deaths of those who watched over it. It even killed the man who had been hired for a great fee to cut off the head with an ax and extract the stinking brain, although he had wrapped his face in linen cloths."

If this was the physical reality of Henry I's death, the political fallout was far worse. For even as Henry's embalmed corpse was transported to England for burial at Reading Abbey, a constitutional crisis that was to last for nearly two decades was brewing. This period is usually known as the Anarchy, but those who lived through it preferred to call it the Shipwreck. Henry's failure to provide for an adult male successor left the Anglo-Norman realm contested. Three times since his daughter Matilda's return from Germany—in 1126, 1131, and 1133—Henry I had caused his barons to swear that they would be loyal to her. But from the moment the old king died, his subjects began to abandon their promises.

In December 1135 Matilda's cousin Stephen of Blois was in Boulogne, the seat of his wife's family. As soon as he learned of his uncle's death, he crossed directly to England and went straight to London, where he had himself proclaimed king. Then, on December 22, he went to Winchester, where he seized the royal treasury and had himself anointed by the archbishop of Canterbury. He moved quickly to secure the support of the Anglo-Norman magnates on both sides of the Channel. With little hesitation or delay, they threw themselves behind him. The empress Matilda, Geoffrey Plantagenet, and their young family were suddenly disinherited.

The speed with which the barons and bishops of England and Normandy abandoned Matilda's claim speaks volumes about the nature of kingship in the twelfth century. Female rule had precedents—three decades earlier, Mathilde of Tuscany countess of Canossa had ruled in her own right in northern Italy—but they were scarce and unconvincing. Rumors flew around that Henry on his deathbed had absolved his barons from their oaths of allegiance to his daughter. They found willing ears. The prospect of being ruled by a woman was not an appealing one.

There was at that time a strong elective element to kingship. Without it, Henry I would never have been king. He had grabbed England and Normandy in 1100 and 1106 respectively, despite having an elder brother, Robert Curthose, with a superior claim in blood. Now history repeated itself. Stephen had no real claim under primogeniture to be king. For one thing, he had an elder brother, Theobald of Blois, whose blood claim was stronger than his. Yet as the son of William the Conqueror's daughter Adela, he was a credible candidate. He had been raised at Henry I's court with the king's sons and held an exalted position among the rest of the Anglo-Norman barons. He had narrowly avoided death alongside William the Aetheling by abandoning the *White Ship*, claiming an attack of diarrhea before it left harbor, and since then he had been one of Henry's favorites. He was a wealthy, powerful, charming, and courteous man in his early forties, and his wife Matilda's county of Boulogne was important to the English wool trade. His brother Henry of Blois bishop of Winchester was a powerful voice in the English Church and commanded the support of many of his fellow bishops. But perhaps most important of all, Stephen pounced fast to claim the throne in a power vacuum. "There was no one else at hand who could take the king's place and put an end to the great dangers threatening the kingdom," wrote the anonymous author of the *Gesta Stephani* (*The Acts of Stephen*).

All this contrasted sharply with Matilda. The empress was pregnant with her third child in December 1135 (after Henry's birth in 1133 a second son, Geoffrey, had been born in 1134; her third son, William, would be born in July 1136) and unable to move as swiftly as her cousin Stephen. Geoffrey, as an Angevin, was the object of much suspicion in Normandy and England, and Matilda's reputation was apparently not much better. According to Henry of Huntingdon, the empress "was lifted up to an insufferable arrogance . . . and she alienated the hearts of almost everyone." Although both her two sons—the two-year-old Henry and one-year-old Geoffrey—could claim more impressive royal blood than Stephen, there was little chance that a toddler would be acclaimed as a twelfth-century king simply by virtue of birthright. Matilda and Geoffrey had been engaged in a violent dispute with Henry I in the years before he died, as they attempted to claim the Norman border castles that the old king had promised as his daughter's dowry. The most they could do now was move to claim the disputed fortresses and bide their time while Stephen cemented his unlikely rule.

Stephen did not find the practice of kingship as easy as its acquisition. He relied on a small group of friends for advice and assistance and failed to impose himself on barons who resisted his authority. He lacked Henry's calculated ruthlessness and political intelligence and managed to alienate men who ought to have been his biggest supporters. Within three years Stephen's rule on both sides of the Channel had been severely rocked. From 1136 Geoffrey Plantagenet began to wage a war of conquest from Normandy's southern borders, which Stephen was ill placed to resist. All the king's attention was focused on England, where he lost the support, in quick succession, of Matilda's half brother Robert of Gloucester, the most powerful baron in the country; of his own brother Henry, the bishop of Winchester, whom he passed over for promotion to the see of Canterbury; and of Roger, the bishop of Salisbury, an experienced royal administrator whose followers and son were arrested in clear breach of Stephen's promise at his coronation not to molest the Church or its bishops.

Stephen's reign was, from the beginning, divisive. He was generous but not evenhanded in dispersing Henry I's carefully accumulated treasure. He lavished favors on friends like the twins Waleran and Robert de Beaumont at the expense of powerful established barons like Ranulf earl of Chester. The destabilizing effects of his arbitrary rule were exacerbated by Stephen's ill-advised attacks on the professional government Henry I had constructed.

He dismissed a number of prominent career administrators and attempted to run England through highborn military men, appointed by virtue of their rank.

If all this was highly disruptive, it was encouraging to Matilda. In 1138 Matilda's influential half brother Robert earl of Gloucester officially defected from Stephen's side. The following year, as Geoffrey Plantagenet continued his assaults on Normandy, Matilda appealed her case to Rome at the Second Lateran Council and invaded England; she allied herself with Gloucester and set up headquarters and a nascent alternative government in Bristol. A civil war had begun.

Matilda attracted a small but significant coalition of disaffected barons, including Brian FitzCount and Miles of Gloucester. Both were marcher lords, whose territorial bases lay in the wild borderlands between England and Wales. Miles had been a powerful official in the West Country during Matilda's father's reign. The effect of their defection was to split England in two. Miles launched attacks on royalist strongholds across England that Stephen was unable to crush, allowing Matilda's faction to grow in strength and confidence. Yet the empress was nowhere near powerful enough to defeat her cousin outright. The result was a prolonged period of war: each cousin claimed to be the rightful ruler of England, but neither could impress his authority over the whole realm.

In 1141 Matilda won her first significant victory. In late 1140 King Stephen had offended Ranulf earl of Chester by granting lands and castles that the latter coveted to his enemies. It had been enough to push him into armed opposition. Ranulf seized Lincoln Castle from a royal garrison, and in February 1141 Stephen was besieging the castle to attempt its recapture. Seizing his chance, Robert earl of Gloucester marched troops to Lincoln and attacked the royal army. In the pitched battle that followed, Stephen's troops were routed and the king was captured.

This should have been Matilda's moment. She assumed the novel title of "lady of the English" and attempted to arrange a coronation in London. Stephen's brother Henry bishop of Winchester was by now a papal legate, and he threw his weight behind the empress. Many of England's major barons, unwilling to save a regime of which they had long stood in doubt, abandoned the king and took to their estates. Yet the empress could not press home her advantage. She was opposed by spirited military defenses organized under Stephen's wife, swiftly managed to fall out with the bishop of

Winchester, and offended most of the magnates whom she encountered with her arrogance and haughtiness. As summer approached, the citizens of London rose against her when she refused to give the heavily taxed city any relief from the financial contributions she demanded to support her rule, and on June 24, 1141, they chased her out of the city. With her campaign now in disarray, Matilda tried to besiege Henry bishop of Winchester in his diocesan seat. In a disastrous battle, Robert earl of Gloucester was captured. In order to free her half brother, Matilda had no option but to arrange a prisoner swap. She released King Stephen. Her brief victory, which had lasted just under eight months, was undone.

By the fall of 1142 Matilda had been chased by Stephen's forces all the way to Oxford, and by late November she was besieged in her castle, with hope draining away. Far away across the Channel her husband was pushing on with a highly successful conquest of Normandy. Robert earl of Gloucester failed to persuade him to divert from the task to come rescue his beleaguered wife. The best Geoffrey would do was send three hundred knights and their nine-year-old son Henry.

As Christmas approached, Matilda was growing desperate. Rather than wait for her husband's knights, she placed her faith in her own resourcefulness. One snowy night she wrapped herself in a white cloak, slipped silently toward a postern door in the castle, crept out past the guards, and headed away toward the snowy fields. Her white camouflage, a ghostly cloak against the dark skyline, allowed her to trudge the eight miles or so to Abingdon without being captured. She walked the frozen landscape ready at any moment for the crunch of hooves in the snow to announce a search party sent to capture her. But it did not come. At Abingdon, she met with friends, who helped her on to the safety of the West Country. She was saved, and with her, the fight for the kingdom of England lived on.

This famous moment in the war was both providential for Matilda and disastrous for the realm of England. Now reinforced by fresh troops and encouraged by the near-miraculous escape of his half sister, Robert of Gloucester led the fight against Stephen's rule. But once again the war lapsed into violent stalemate. Stephen held the Crown, but he remained a weak king who could not command the loyalty of his Anglo-Norman barons. Matilda was more powerful than ever, but after the debacle of 1141 she was discredited in too many eyes to have any hope of conquest in her own name. The only decisive action was taking place in Normandy, where

Geoffrey Plantagenet was rapidly occupying a duchy that Stephen had visited only once during his whole reign. By 1144 Geoffrey had captured Rouen and been recognized as duke of Normandy, forcing those barons whose property bestrode the Channel into the impossible position of having to acknowledge two lords for the same estates.

Both England and, to a lesser degree, Normandy remained crippled by conflict. From 1142 England was firmly split between two courts—one under Stephen, nominally at Westminster and Winchester, and the other with Matilda, who ruled from Devizes in the southwest. The rule of law dissolved. With it went public order. The country, wrote the chronicler William of Newburgh, was "mutilated." With no adequate king in the north, King David I of Scotland ruled Westmorland, Cumberland, and Northumberland. England, which under Henry I had been wealthy, well governed, and stoutly defended at its borders, had now become a patchwork of competing fiefdoms of authority and power. "It was as if," wrote the author of *The Anglo-Saxon Chronicle*, "Christ and his saints were asleep."

Stephen and Matilda both saw themselves as the lawful successor of Henry I and set up official governments accordingly: they had their own mints, courts, systems of patronage, and diplomatic machinery. But there could not be two governments. Neither could be secure or guarantee that its writ would run; hence no subject could be fully confident in the rule of law. As in any state without a single, central source of undisputed authority, violent spoliation among the magnates exploded. Flemish mercenaries garrisoned castles and newly fortified houses the length and breadth of the country. Forced labor was exacted to help arm the countryside. General violence escalated as individual landholders turned to private defense of their property. The air ran dark with the smoke from burning crops, and people suffered intolerable misery at the hands of marauding foreign soldiers.

The chronicles from the time are full of records of the bleak days that accompanied the war. The author of the *Gesta Stephani* recorded one example: "[The king] set himself to lay waste that fair and delightful district, so full of good things, round Salisbury; they took and plundered everything they came upon, set fire to houses and churches, and, what was a more cruel and brutal sight, fired the crops that had been reaped and stacked all over the fields, consumed and brought to nothing everything edible they found. They raged with this bestial cruelty especially round

Marlborough, they showed it very terribly round Devizes, and they had in mind to do the same to their adversaries all over England."

Eventually, in 1148, Matilda left England. It may seem strange that she left a fight in which she had invested so much of her life, but after the decade she'd spent leading the Plantagenet cause, her work was done. Her children—Henry and his two younger brothers, Geoffrey and William— were growing up across the Channel. Matilda aimed to live out the remaining years of her life in comfortable retirement at the priory of Notre-Dame-du-Pré, a cell of the abbey of Bec at Quevilly, where across the Seine she could visit Rouen, the Norman capital that Orderic Vitalis described as a "fair city set among murmuring streams and smiling meadows . . . strongly encircled by walls and ramparts and battlements." The city owed her much, for her grim efforts to distract King Stephen on the English front had allowed Geoffrey Plantagenet to capture it. Now she intended to enjoy the view.

But England was not forgotten. Her eldest son was approaching his sixteenth birthday. It was time for him to take up the struggle, time for Henry FitzEmpress to try his hand at conquest.

Ambition

Henry FitzEmpress landed on the shores of Devon on April 13, 1149. It was his third visit to the fractured realm that he would have heard his mother tell him was his by birthright. He had seen the country in its bleakest hour in 1142, before Matilda's great escape from the snowy wastes of Oxford, and had subsequently stayed under the tutelage of his uncle Robert earl of Gloucester as England settled into its vicious stalemate. Henry spent fifteen months studying in Bristol, meeting the famous astronomer, mathematician, and Scholastic philosopher Adelard of Bath, who dedicated to the young man a treatise on the astrolabe. Then, from 1144, for reasons as much of safety as of political pragmatism, Henry had returned to his father, to help him secure his position as duke of Normandy. Now, on the verge of manhood and burning with ambition, he was returning to England to claim his birthright.

Henry was a strange-looking young man who could switch in seconds from bluff good humor to fierce anger. From his father, he had inherited his auburn complexion and tireless energy; from his maternal grandfather, a powerful domineering streak and a nose for an opportunity. Gerald of Wales left a vivid description of Henry later in life: "[He] was a man of reddish, freckled complexion, with a large, round head, gray eyes that glowed fiercely and grew bloodshot in anger, a fiery countenance and a harsh, cracked voice. His neck was thrust forward slightly from his shoulders, his chest was broad and square, his arms strong and powerful. His body was stocky, with a pronounced tendency toward fatness, due to nature rather than self-indulgence—which he tempered with exercise. For in eating and drinking he was moderate and sparing."

From the earliest age Henry was conspicuously brave, albeit rather reckless. When he made his second visit to England, in 1147, it had been not to study but to fight. Although he was only thirteen, he had managed to hire a small band of mercenaries to accompany him across the Channel, where he attempted to assist his mother's war effort. The arrival of this wild teenager had briefly terrified England: rumors spread that he had come with thousands of troops and boundless treasure. The truth had been closer to farce: Henry the teenager had barely been able to afford to pay his hired soldiers, who deserted him within weeks of their arrival. ("Weakened by sloth and idleness, overcome by poverty and want, they abandoned the noble youth," wrote William of Newburgh.) Stephen's reaction to Henry's teenage invasion was more amused than intimidated: he paid off Henry's mercenaries and sent him packing back to Normandy.

That the thirteen-year-old Henry had had the gall to attempt a solo invasion of England, however poorly executed, is testament to the time he had spent at his father's side on campaign in Normandy. Geoffrey Plantagenet had involved his son in government since at least 1144. Henry had seen how a long-term military campaign played out amid the complex, fractured politics of the French mainland. He knew that he was being groomed as duke of Normandy, and it may also have been suggested to him that he would be count of Anjou too. Henry spent hours on horseback following his father around Anjou and Normandy, learning to gallop at what would become legendary speed. (In later years his legs were bowed from the shape of the ever-present saddle.)

Twelfth-century France was divided into loose and shifting territories that owed little or no allegiance to any central authority, ruled across large swaths by noblemen who were little more than warlords. As he watched his tenacious and cunning father grind his way through the conquest of Normandy, Henry would have learned that political survival was a game of forestalling shifts of power, managing volatile relations between one's friends and enemies, and appealing to the right allies at the right time in order to further one's territorial objectives. In such a bewildering business, only the most devious and adept players survived.

In this game of feudal lordship, Henry knew that he had one huge advantage: he was the son of an empress, with a claim to the English throne. France contained many powerful dukes and counts, but there were only two kings: the king of England and the king of France. To be a major force on the Continent and to stand up to the new French king, Louis VII, who had succeeded to the throne in 1137, Henry knew that he must be more than just another powerful count or duke. He was "Henry, son of the daughter of King Henry [I] and right heir of England and Normandy."

When he arrived in England in 1149, Henry's first task was to establish himself as a credible successor to his mother's cause. It was not his natural home. He understood the English language, but he did not speak it. It was all very well having royal blood; now he needed to secure the recognition of his peers. Here the long days in the saddle paid off, as Henry rode north to be invested with knighthood by his uncle King David of Scotland. He was girded in Carlisle on Whitsunday 1149. Now, sporting the belt of knighthood, he decided to show England that he had the martial valor to match. On his way back south he attempted an attack on York. This was unsuccessful, and Henry had to flee to the Channel, harried all the way by royal attacks. The sixteen-year-old knight made his way to the southwest, relieved a siege of Devizes by Stephen's son Eustace, and skipped back to Normandy. If it was not an entirely fruitful mission, he had at least won over important allies and made his mark.

In 1150 Geoffrey formally invested Henry as duke of Normandy, a role he had already been affecting for some months. In August of the following year Henry gave homage for Normandy to King Louis VII of France, a ceremonial declaration of his ducal right and dignity. Then, in September, Geoffrey Plantagenet suddenly died. He was thirty-nine years old. According to John of Marmoutier, Geoffrey was returning from a royal council when he was taken "severely ill with a fever at Château-du-Loir. [He] collapsed on a couch. Then, looking into the future of his land and his people with the spirit of prophecy, he forbade Henry his heir to introduce the customs of Normandy or England into his own county [i.e., Anjou], nor the reverse." Then: "the death of so great a prince having been foretold by a comet, his body returned from earth to heaven."

It was an abrupt end to a highly eventful life. The eighteen-year-old duke of Normandy still had far to go if he wanted to realize the ambitions of his parents. The fight would be hard, but the rewards it promised were almost beyond imagination.

A Scandalous Wife

On May 18, 1152, at the cathedral in Poitiers, Henry duke of Normandy married Eleanor duchess of Aquitaine. Planned in haste and with the utmost secrecy, the ceremony was executed as quickly as possible. Like his father, Henry was marrying an older woman. Eleanor was twenty-eight years old, and he was a restless young soldier who had only just turned nineteen. His bride was almost impossibly glamorous, famous across Christendom for her unconventional beauty, her outspokenness, and her headstrong political views. Only two months earlier she had been queen of France, the wife of Louis VII. Their marriage had been annulled on the ground of consanguinity after Eleanor had provided the king with two princesses but no sons.

Henry's marriage to Eleanor of Aquitaine was one of the greatest coups of his life. For an ambitious young player in European politics, there could have been no more valuable bride. Eleanor brought wealth, power, and vast lands. Her duchy of Aquitaine was a vital part of the territorial reach of the French Crown, stretching down from the borders of Anjou to the Pyrenees. She was an experienced ruler and a wily political player. And the fact that she had recently been discarded by the French king only raised her value for a duke of Normandy intent on establishing his status as a preeminent French nobleman.

Eleanor's life story was already extraordinary. She was born in 1124, the eldest daughter of William X duke of Aquitaine and count of Poitou, a patron of the arts and an enthusiastic warrior, who alternated between quarreling with the papacy and making pious submissions to ecclesiastical authority. Her grandfather was William IX, "the Troubadour Duke," who was the greatest wit, poet, and songwriter of his age. He composed verse in the southern French language of Occitan, telling the stories of seduction, heroism, and courtly love that were part of the fabric of southern French life. The house of Aquitaine was formed in his image. William IX died in 1126, shortly after his granddaughter Eleanor's birth. Eleven years later Eleanor's father also died suddenly, while on pilgrimage to Compostela. His death left a thirteen-year-old Eleanor sole heir to one of the greatest inheritances in Europe.

Aquitaine was a large, sprawling, loosely governed territory that comprised more than a quarter of the territory of medieval France. It included the lordship of Gascony, the cities of Bordeaux and Bayonne, the counties of Saintonge, Angoulême, Périgord, Limousin, Auvergne, and La Manche. The dukes of Aquitaine looked north via the county of Poitou and south to the Spanish peninsula, where they had links with Navarre and Barcelona. It was a warm, fertile country, which traded in wine and salt via the Gascon ports on the Atlantic coast and had an important tourist industry, thanks to the fact that it controlled the pilgrimage roads to Compostela, as they converged on the few passes cutting through the Pyrenees. The duchy would provide a potentially huge source of wealth, power, and cultural influence to whoever could control it. Control came hard, however. Government sat very light in Aquitaine. Power and authority were subject to a patchwork of troublesome and rebellious lords whose fealty to the duke was seldom more than nominal. It was obvious to everyone that this was no place for a thirteen-year-old girl to rule. King Louis VI of France moved swiftly, and three months after her father's death, on July 25, 1137, Eleanor was married to his eldest son, the seventeen-year-old Prince Louis, at the cathedral in Bordeaux. This union with the heir to the French Crown brought Aquitaine under the protection of Paris. Then, just seven days after Eleanor's first marriage, her new father-in-law was dead. Eleanor became queen of France.

The feisty southern child queen quickly proved out of place in the frosty Parisian court. There was a marked difference between the cultures of the Île de France and Aquitaine. Even the languages were different: the langue d'oïl of the north contrasted sharply with the langue d'oc spoken by Eleanor and her large group of attendants. Eleanor was a worldly southerner who both captivated and terrified her new husband. While Louis VII conducted himself with austere piety, Eleanor embraced the splendor of queenship. She and her entourage dressed and behaved extravagantly and enjoyed a rich palace life that shocked her husband's closest attendants. Louis VII wore a habit and followed a frugal diet. According to William of Newburgh, Eleanor complained in later years that she had married "a monk, not a king."

From the start the marriage was profoundly dysfunctional, both personally and politically. Eleanor was capable, as the famous French abbot Bernard of Clairvaux wrote, of "taking a determined political stance." She pushed Louis into several unwise ventures, including a vicious war with the count of Champagne, provoked when her younger sister Petronilla had a rash fling with the count of Vermandois. Very swiftly Eleanor built a reputation for causing scandal and chaos. When she accompanied Louis on the Second Crusade in 1147, rumors flew up concerning almost every aspect of her participation. She was blamed (wrongly) for disastrous ambushes on the crusading forces and accused (falsely) of conniving—or sleeping with— her uncle Prince Raymond of Toulouse, the ruler of Antioch. Later chroniclers even spread the rumor that she had had an affair with Saladin and attempted to elope with him on a boat, an odd fantasy given that he was only ten at the time. On the way home from Jerusalem, Louis and Eleanor stopped at Tusculum to meet Pope Eugene III. He gave them marriage counseling and offered them a reconciliatory bed, draped with his own precious curtains.

It did not work. Although Eleanor bore Louis two children—Marie countess of Champagne was born in 1145 and Alix countess of Blois in 1150—it was clear by the early 1150s that the marriage was untenable. Perhaps they could have continued had Eleanor produced a male heir. But she did not. By the time of the Christmas court of 1151–1152, held deep in Eleanor's territory at Limoges, it was an open secret that the royal marriage would soon follow the path of many others before them. On March 21, 1152, an assembly of French bishops declared that Louis and Eleanor were related within the prohibited bounds of consanguinity, and their marriage was declared void. Eleanor would retain her duchy of Aquitaine, and Louis, like every other Capet since Philip I, would have his marriage annulled. It is hard to believe that Eleanor felt anything but relief.

This relief, however, would have been alloyed by the knowledge that she was as vulnerable at the age of twenty-eight as she had been on the day of her father's death. The unwed duchess of Aquitaine was back on the marriage market, with no shortage of bidders. In March 1152 she made a perilous journey through the Loire Valley from Beaugency to Poitiers, the principal seat of her duchy. Knowing that the countryside around her was fraught with danger, she moved with all possible haste. Already word was spreading that Eleanor was no longer the queen of France. Kidnappers were said to be pursuing her from two directions. According to a chronicler from Tours, both Theobald V count of Blois and Geoffrey Plantagenet the Younger (Henry's sixteen-year-old brother) were bent on waylaying Eleanor, hoping to abduct and force her into marriage.

But a decade and a half spent at court in Paris had taught Eleanor a thing or two about political survival. She realized that marriage was inevitable and necessary but was determined that it should be on her terms. So as she rode hard for Poitiers, giving the slip to her would-be abductors, she was thinking of the one man who would best secure her future. Henry Plantagenet duke of Normandy and count of Anjou and its neighboring counties of Maine and Touraine was in Lisieux, near the coast of Normandy, preparing an invasion of England, where he aimed to claim the Crown in his mother's name. Eleanor had met Henry the previous year, when he and his father had visited Paris for peace talks. It is possible that the unhappy queen and the ambitious would-be king had considered each other as potential future mates. Whether a formal agreement was made is unknown.

On arrival in Poitou, Eleanor sent a message to Henry, asking him with all urgency to come and marry her. Henry wasted no time, canceling all his plans for invading King Stephen's troubled realm. "The duke indeed allured by the nobility of that woman and by desire for the great honours belonging to her, impatient at all delay, took with him a few companions, hastened quickly over the long routes and in little time obtained that marriage which he had long desired," wrote William of Newburgh. So it was that Henry Plantagenet married Eleanor duchess of Aquitaine in a low-key ceremony at the cathedral of Notre-Dame-la-Grande in Poitiers on May 18, 1152. Their marriage ceremony was swift and discreet, but its aftershocks were no less massive.

The big loser was Louis VII. While he could not have expected Eleanor to take any other course of action, he would have expected her future spouse—as vassal—and Eleanor—as ex-wife—to seek his permission. They did not, and it rankled ever after. As Henry of Huntingdon put it, Henry's marriage to Eleanor was "the cause and origin of great hatred and discord between the French king and the duke." Eleanor's marriage to Henry transformed the map of France at a stroke. Henry's control of Normandy, Anjou, Maine, and Touraine was now fused with the giant duchy of Aquitaine. One man now theoretically controlled virtually the entire western seaboard of the kingdom of France and almost half the landed territory.

In seeking an annulment of his marriage to Eleanor, Louis had made an understandable decision for the future of the French Crown. In letting her fall into Henry Plantagenet's hands, he had committed an inexcusable blunder.

To add to the French king's woes, within months of her speedy marriage Eleanor was pregnant with a son, and Henry had revived his plans to conquer England. This not only made a mockery of Louis's inability to produce an heir with her but also threatened to sunder his daughters from any claim to the duchy of Aquitaine. A Plantagenet heir, who one day might conceivably rule Normandy, Anjou, and Aquitaine together, was on his way. Within two years that likely patrimony would grow to include the Crown of England.

Henry the Conqueror

Malmesbury, in Wiltshire, was a wretched little town, as sorely treated as any in England during the agonies of the civil war. Its walls and motte castle had been besieged at least three times during the civil war, and its people brutalized and plundered for many years. On a freezing January day in 1153 Henry Plantagenet stood outside its walls in a belligerent mood, preparing to destroy what little was left of the town. He had been blown ashore after a rough and dangerous winter crossing of the Channel. It was Epiphany, the eight-day festival when Christians celebrate the visit of the three kings to the infant Jesus. But Henry came not to pay homage but to overthrow the king, with an invading force of 140 knights and 3,000 infantry, armed to the teeth.

The author of the *Gesta Stephani* described the scene: "When a crowd of common people flew to the wall surrounding the town as though to defend it, [Henry] ordered the infantry, men of the greatest cruelty, whom he had brought with him, some to assail the defenders with arrows and missiles, others to devote all their efforts to demolishing the wall." The din would have been tremendous: the whiz of crossbow bolts, the screams of the fleeing townsfolk, and the crash of great rocks pitched up at the castle walls by the siege machines. Torrential rain and winds lashed besiegers and defenders alike; soaking mud clung to them all. Ladders were placed against the wall, and Henry's fierce mercenaries scaled them with ease. The townsfolk ran in terror to the church, seeking sanctuary with the resident community of monks. The mercenaries, having vaulted the walls, pursued them. If the chronicler is to be believed, the church was plundered, the monks and priests were butchered, and the altar was desecrated.

King Stephen had been expecting the invasion, but he had not foreseen an attack on Malmesbury. His royal forces were besieging the rebel town of Wallingford, and he had expected Henry to join him there in battle. Henry refused to be drawn. Stephen was obliged to go meet the invader. "It was a huge army with many barons, their banners glittering with gold, beautiful and terrible indeed," wrote Henry of Huntingdon. "But God, in whom alone is safety, was not with them." The weather was foul, and the men who marched with Stephen had little faith in their leader. "The floodgates of heaven opened and such bitter cold gusts of wind and pouring rain were driven into their faces that God himself seemed to be fighting for the duke. The king's army could barely hold their weapons or their dripping wet lances."

Drenched and demoralized, Stephen's army refused to fight. The civil war had dragged on long enough, and the conditions in which they were expected to relieve a siege were nothing short of treacherous. There was little promise of reward or advance in the battle, and Stephen now had a mutiny on his hands. "The king . . . retreated without effecting his purpose," wrote William of Newburgh. The first victory of the invasion had been won. Writing in retrospect, William of Newburgh noted that after Malmesbury "the nobles of [England] . . . gradually revolted to [Henry]; insomuch as that, by the augmentation of his power and the brilliancy of his successes, the fame of the duke . . . obscured the kingly title of his opponent." But it was not quite that simple. As he took stock of his position, Henry discovered a realm in a state of total war-weariness. It was his response to these conditions, as much as his military successes, that enabled him to make advances beyond those achieved by his mother.

One of the first things Henry realized was that the mercenaries he had brought with him inspired fear rather than trust. England was already teeming with hired foreign soldiers, and they were deeply resented by the people. "Being unable to endure their bestial and brutal presumption any longer, [the barons] suggested to the duke that he should allow [his mercenaries] to go home, lest on account of their shameful forwardness some calamity should befall him or his men by the vengeance of God," recorded the *Gesta Stephani*. Showing a flexibility of mind that was to serve him well in the future, Henry listened. He sent five hundred of his mercenaries back across the Channel to Normandy. As they sailed, a mighty storm blew up and drowned them all.

Instead of inflicting more war on an exhausted kingdom, Henry made peaceful overtures toward barons and bishops alike. Channels of negotiation with Stephen were opened, under the guidance of Archbishop Theobald of Canterbury and Bishop Henry of Winchester. And slowly the magnates came over to the young duke.

The most important baron to join Henry's cause was Robert earl of Leicester. He and his twin, Waleran, were among the elite of the Anglo-Norman nobility who had been loyal to Stephen for many years. That Leicester was a powerful landowner in the Midlands gave Henry a vital territorial advantage in the heart of England. But the earl also brought important personal qualities and experience to Henry's following and proved to be one of Henry's most trusted and reliable servants for the remainder of his life. He was in fact an excellent archetype for the sort of noble that Henry both attracted and needed. Leicester was in his late forties, literate, and well schooled. He had been brought up with William the Aetheling, and as children he and Waleran had been the young darlings of the European courts, debating for show with cardinals while they were still precocious youngsters. The twins had been loyal to Henry I and Stephen, but Stephen's inability to guarantee their lands in Normandy had chipped away at their political will.

Leicester embodied the complex position of any number of the Anglo-Norman magnates: torn between their Norman estates guaranteed by the Plantagenet duke of Normandy and the English lands theoretically protected by Stephen. The task for Henry was to convince more men like Leicester that he could protect their property in England as well as in Normandy, rather than subject it to further ruin and war. That, after all, was the underlying purpose of kingship. Henry spent the spring of 1153 on a vigorous publicity drive. After visiting Bristol and Gloucester, both bastions of support for his mother, he made his way through the turbulent Midlands, where an uneasy peace was kept by a patchwork of individual treaties between magnates. This land was the ultimate emblem of the failures of Stephen's reign. Public authority was nonexistent.

At the heart of Henry's new pitch was good lordship, not good generalship. Instead of ravaging lands, he held court around the country and invited the great noblemen to come to him in peace. Rather than burn crops, he issued charters guaranteeing the land and legal rights of the magnates—not only in England but in Normandy too. He indicated his commitment to judicial process by asserting that his grants of English lands were subject to legal ratification. Moving around England in a circuit that came to look more and more like a triumphant tour, he presented himself at every turn as a credible alternative king.

Yet battle could not entirely be avoided. In July 1153 Henry met Stephen at Wallingford, a town nestled inside a long bend in the Thames, southeast of Oxford and dangerously close to Westminster and London. Stephen had the castle—loyal to Henry—under siege. The area was sown with a series of smaller royal castles and ditchworks, built in a semipermanent ring of defense. Henry approached with an army to relieve the siege, but also with a sense that an end to the war was near.

King Stephen had been waiting. In early August he marched a splendid army out to meet the duke. Once again, as at Malmesbury, there was a general refusal to fight. In the words of the *Gesta Stephani*, "The leading men on both sides . . . shrank from a conflict which was not merely between fellow countrymen, but meant the desolation of the whole kingdom." Men were not tired of Stephen's rule per se; they were tired of war. "The barons, those betrayers of England . . . were unwilling to fight a battle, as they did not want either side to win," wrote Henry of Huntingdon. But these "betrayers of England" were men who had suffered nearly two decades of civil war and who realized that victory for either side in battle was likely to result in mass land confiscations and continued bitter divisions in the realm. The time for a cease-fire had arrived. Henry and Stephen agreed to talk. "The king and the duke had a conference alone together, across a small stream, about making a lasting peace," wrote Huntingdon. "The peace treaty was begun here, but not completed until another occasion." The terms of peace were growing obvious to both sides: Stephen would have to recognize Henry Plantagenet as his legal heir to the Crown and begin a process by which the deep wounds of their families' war could be healed. Only one major obstacle remained.

King Stephen's eldest son, Eustace IV count of Boulogne, had grown up knowing nothing but division and war. He had been told that he was a king in waiting and had been encouraged to fight for the sake of securing his Crown. Eustace had made it his business to see that the Norman chronicler Robert of Torigni's assessment that "almost all of the Normans thought that Duke Henry would rapidly lose all of his possessions" came true as rapidly as possible. To that end he had allied with Louis VII, whose sister Constance he had married, and Henry's own brother Geoffrey Plantagenet the Younger. Together they had contrived to wage war against the duke of Normandy wherever and whenever they could. Eustace stood to lose the most in any rapprochement between Stephen and Henry. His position was unusually weak.

An argument between Stephen and Pope Eugene III meant that in 1153 Eustace had not yet been anointed as co-king, in the manner that was now customary. This paved the way for an eventual peace in which Stephen could disinherit his sons (Eustace had a younger brother, William) and name Henry as his heir. After Wallingford that seemed more and more likely. According to the author of the *Gesta Stephani*, Eustace was "greatly vexed and angry because the war, in his opinion, had reached no proper conclusion." To give vent to some of this anger and frustration, he stormed eastward to Bury St. Edmunds, where he indulged in a bout of fairly pointless burning and pillaging. Alas, for the unfortunate Eustace, God—or perhaps St. Edmund—was on hand to punish the iniquitous. Shortly after his self-indulgent orgy of violence and rapine, Eustace fell ill. He died in early August 1153, just twenty-three years old. The cause was thought to be either rotten food or sheer grief, though some have suspected poison.

Eustace's death was heartbreaking to Stephen, who had lost his precious wife, Matilda, the previous year. Yet it was also providential, in that it opened the path for negotiations that would allow Duke Henry to take his place. The agreement took the form of a sort of legal fostering that would hand the Crown to the Plantagenet line and end the war for good. Stephen's second son, William, evidently more tractable than his elder brother, accepted a large landed settlement in recompense for abandoning any claim to the throne.

Discussions between the two parties took place throughout August, September, and October, overseen by Archbishop Theobald of Canterbury and King Stephen's brother Henry bishop of Winchester. In November 1153, at a conference in Winchester, a formal truce was agreed upon. Stephen formally adopted Henry as his son and heir. "What inestimable joy! What blessed day!" cheered Henry of Huntingdon. "The king himself received the young prince at Winchester with a magnificent procession of bishops and nobles through the cheering crowds." England could harbor its greatest hope of peace and prosperity under a single, unified, and universal royal authority since 1135.

The peace was sealed in a highly symbolic venue and ceremony. Winchester was the place where English kingship was sanctified: the old minster was the resting place of St. Swithun, the Anglo-Saxon bishop credited with numerous miracles, including the ability to restore broken eggs to wholeness, and of Saxon kings such as Eadwig, who, like Stephen, had ruled in war-torn times. The great men of the land gathered in the chill of the cathedral, to be addressed by King Stephen and Duke Henry.

What a pair they made. The sixty-one-year-old Stephen performed his role with dignity. "A mild man, and gentle, and good," was how the *Gesta Stephani* described him. Next to the impish, scruffy, twenty-year-old redhead, he seemed a relic of a departing generation. But he stood with grace and spoke to the congregation, uttering words that would have had his eldest son spinning in his grave.

"Know that I, King Stephen, appoint Henry duke of Normandy after me as my successor in the kingdom of England and my heir by hereditary right," Stephen said. "Thus I give and confirm to him and his heirs the Kingdom of England."

Henry made a similar statement. Then, in the presence of all his future nobles, he did homage to Stephen and received the homage of Stephen's younger son, William. It was an open and wholly visible representation of the new order of things. A new narrative of royal lineage had been publicly constructed. The legal chaos of a usurpation or deposition was avoided. Through sound military leadership and brilliant diplomacy, Henry had muscled his way into the line of succession.

The celebrations were lavish. Stephen swept into England's ancient capital with his newly adopted son. "[T]he illustrious young man was gloriously received in the city of Winchester, led by the king, with a glittering procession of bishops and famous men," wrote William of Newburgh. "Then the king took the duke to London, and there he was received with joy by an innumerable assembly of common people, with splendid processions." The truce of Winchester was formally sealed and distributed at Westminster. "Peace dawned on the ruined realm," wrote Henry of Huntingdon, "putting an end to its troubled night."

During the limbo that prevailed between Henry's acceptance as heir and Stephen's death, the old king agreed to act on the next king's advice. Together they began the long process of cleaning up the broken kingdom. There were three key tasks: suppressing violence and spoliation, ejecting the gangs of hired foreign mercenaries that had flooded the country, and leveling the castles that had sprung up since Stephen's accession. There were still extremist factions that disapproved of the peace process. At a meeting in Canterbury in March 1154, Henry was informed of a plot against his life by dissident Flemings. It was alleged that Stephen's son William knew about it. Judging that the situation in England was now stable enough to make his continued presence unnecessary and dangerous enough to justify his departure, Henry decided to return to Normandy. As Stephen went on progress to the north of England and busied his administrators with the task of circulating a new coinage, Henry left England that March, taking a discreet route to the Channel via Rochester and London.

In late October 1154 Henry was campaigning with Louis VII against rebellious vassals in the borderland region between Normandy and France known as the Vexin when news reached him that Stephen was dead. According to the chronicler Gervase of Canterbury, Stephen had been meeting with the count of Flanders on October 25, 1154, when he was taken ill. "The king was suddenly seized with a violent pain in his gut, accompanied by a flow of blood (as had happened to him before)," wrote Gervase. "After he had taken to his bed in [Dover Priory] he died." Stephen was buried in the Cluniac monastery in Faversham, Kent, alongside his wife, Queen Matilda, and his intemperate son Eustace.

Stephen died disconsolate. He was a man obsessed with royal dignity and ceremony, and his failure to freely anoint one of his sons as heir would have been compounded by the humiliation of losing the loyalty and support of his sworn nobles. But if his reign was a dismal failure, the peace that followed was a resounding success, negotiated well and upheld by the admirable will of the major magnates. Henry and Stephen had successfully created a vehicle to ensure the first peaceful transfer of royal power for nearly seventy years. When Henry came to England to claim his Crown in December 1154, it was at his leisure, knowing that he was wanted and implicitly accepted by the political community as king. His wife, Eleanor, arrived at his side; she had given birth to a son, William, in August 1153 and was now pregnant again, soon due to deliver. The succession, at last, seemed secure. Henry promised stability and a single, universal authority such as had been sorely missing for the last, miserable nineteen years. What was more, he had proven himself. There was sycophancy, no doubt, in Henry bishop of Huntingdon's invocation on the coming of the king, but there was real hope too: "England, long numbed by mortal chill, now you grow warm, revived by the heat of a new sun. You raise the country's bowed head, and with tears of sorrow wiped away, you weep for joy. . . . With tears you utter these words to your foster child: 'You are spirit, I am flesh: now as you enter, I am restored to life.'"

PART II

Age of Empire
(1154–1204)

A king who fights to defend his right
Has a better claim on his inheritance.
Struggle and largesse allow
A king to gain glory and territory.

—Bertran de Born

Births and Rebirth

Henry II was crowned at Westminster Abbey on December 19, 1154, with a heavily pregnant Queen Eleanor sitting beside him. Judging by her near-constant state of pregnancy and childbirth, which contrasted sharply with her time as queen of France, Eleanor had thrown herself enthusiastically into establishing a royal dynasty with Henry. The elderly archbishop Theobald of Canterbury performed the sacred ceremony, and the great bishops and magnates of England looked on. Henry was the first ruler to be crowned king of England, rather than the old form, king of the English. And the coronation brought with it a spirit of great popular optimism. "Throughout England, the people shouted, 'Long live the King,'" wrote William of Newburgh. "[They] hoped for better things from the new monarch, especially when they saw he possessed remarkable prudence, constancy and zeal for justice, and at the very outset already manifested the likeness of a great prince."

Henry's coronation charter addressed all the great men of the realm, assuring them that he would grant them all the "concessions, gifts, liberties and freedoms" that Henry I had allowed and that he would likewise abolish evil customs. He made no specific promises, and unlike his predecessor Stephen, he did not hark back to the "good laws and good customs" enjoyed by English subjects in the days of Edward the Confessor. But the charter mentioned specifically Henry's desire to work toward "the common restoration of my whole realm."

England found its new twenty-one-year-old king well educated, legally minded, and competent in a number of languages, although he spoke only Latin and the French dialects. He struck his contemporaries as almost impossibly purposeful, hunting and hawking and sweeping at a headlong pace through the forests and parks of his vast lands. Gerald of Wales described him as "addicted to the chase beyond measure; at crack of dawn he was often on horseback, traversing wastelands, penetrating forests and climbing the mountain-tops, and so he passed restless days. At evening on his return home he was rarely seen to sit down, either before or after supper. . . . [H]e would wear the whole court out by continual standing. . . ." And then: "He was a man of easy access, and condescending, pliant and witty, second to none in politeness . . . strenuous in warfare . . . very prudent in civil life. . . . He was fierce toward those who remained untamed, but merciful toward the vanquished, harsh to his servants, expansive toward strangers, prodigal in public, thrifty in private. . . . He was most diligent in guarding and maintaining peace, liberal beyond comparison in almsgiving and the peculiar defender of the Holy Land; a lover of humility, an oppressor of the nobility and a contemner of the proud."

Another famous description, by the court writer Walter Map, remarked upon many of the same characteristics. Henry was "blessed with sound limbs and a handsome countenance . . . well read . . . easy of approach . . . ever on his travels, moving in intolerable stages like a courier." He showed "very little mercy to his household which accompanied him. . . . [H]e had great experience of dogs and birds and was a very keen follower of hounds." Even when one allows for the flattery and platitudes native to courtiers' pen portraits, it was clear that the men who knew him found Henry a striking, energetic ruler.

From his earliest years Henry lived a peripatetic life. Although he invested heavily in magnificent castles and palaces, he rarely stayed anywhere for long. His traveling court was frequently described by visitors as disgusting: smelly and ratty, with the wine served so vinegarish that it had to be filtered through the teeth. Such were the living conditions of a man in perpetual motion. The chronicler Ralph de Diceto described an astonished Louis VII's opinion on Henry's ability to pop up anywhere and everywhere about his territories, without warning. It was as if he were flying rather than riding on horseback, said the French king. He was, said the twelfth-century biographer Herbert of Bosham, like a "human chariot, dragging all after him."

The king could hardly drag his young family about with him, though, and after the splendor of the coronation, the Plantagenets found they needed somewhere to live. Their first son, William, was little more than a year old at the time of his parents' coronation; a second son, Henry, was born on February 28, 1155. Both the boys and Eleanor required households while they were in the country. The enormous Anglo-Saxon palace of Westminster had deteriorated badly during the civil war and was now uninhabitable. So in 1155 the family moved to the royal palace of Bermondsey on the opposite bank of the Thames, to the south of the city of London.

From the palace, Eleanor was able to visit London as she pleased. She would have found the English capital a busy, ripe city: frantic with commerce and entertainment, jesters and jugglers, crime, filth, despair, and humanity. The Canterbury cleric and biographer William Fitzstephen wrote a famously wide-eyed description of the twelfth-century city:

[London] is fortunate in the wholesomeness of its climate, the devotion of its Christians, the strength of its fortifications, its well-situated location, the respectability of its citizens, and the propriety of their wives. Furthermore it takes great pleasure in its sports and is prolific in producing men of superior quality. . . . On the east side stands the royal fortress [i.e. the Tower of London], of tremendous size and strength, whose walls and floors rise up from the deepest foundations—the mortar being mixed with animal's blood. On the west side are two heavily fortified castles. Running continuously around the north side is the city wall, high and wide, punctuated at intervals with turrets, and with seven double-gated entranceways. . . .

Two miles from the city and linked to it by a populous suburb, there rises above the bank of that river the king's palace [of Westminster], a structure without equal, with inner and outer fortifications. . . . To the north there are tilled fields, pastures, and pleasant, level meadows with streams flowing through them, where watermill wheels turned by the current make a pleasing sound. Not far off spreads out a vast forest, its copses dense with foliage concealing wild animals—stags, does, boars, and wild bulls. . . .

Every morning you can find [people] carrying on their various trades, those selling specific types of goods, and those who hire themselves out as labourers, each in their particular locations engaged in their tasks. Nor should I forget to mention that there is in London, on the river bank amidst the ships, the wine for sale, and the storerooms for wine, a public cookshop. On a daily basis there, depending on the season, can be found fried or boiled foods and dishes, fish large and small, meat—lower quality for the poor, finer cuts for the wealthy—game and fowl (large and small). . . . Those with a fancy for delicacies can obtain for themselves the meat of goose, guinea-hen or woodcock—finding what they're after is no great chore, since all the delicacies are set out in front of them. . . . Middlemen from every nation under heaven are pleased to bring to the city ships full of merchandise.

This was a busy, lively, international city, and it must have kindled in Eleanor memories of Paris, the grandest city in northern Europe, with its own rivers, palaces, and rolling meadows, the site of her first experience of queenship. Something in London must have agreed with the queen, for during her first spell in England, Eleanor managed what she most manifestly had not when she was queen of France and gave birth to a rapid succession of healthy children. In September 1155, as soon as she had recovered from young Henry's birth, Eleanor was pregnant again: a girl, Matilda, was delivered in June 1156, named for the empress who had struggled so long to secure the Plantagenets' new realm.

Matilda's birth would have relieved some of the sadness Eleanor felt in June 1156, when William, her first son, died. The little boy was three years old. He was buried with dignity at the feet of his great-grandfather Henry I in Reading Abbey. It would have been a time of grief for the family. But child mortality was a fact even of royal life in the Middle Ages, and the best insurance against it was a large brood of children. Without pause or delay, two more boys were born: Richard, who was born at Oxford in September 1157, and Geoffrey, who came almost exactly a year later.

Henry, Matilda, Richard, and Geoffrey: by the end of 1158 Henry and Eleanor had four healthy children below the age of four. Three more children would survive to adulthood: Eleanor (born 1162), Joan (born 1165), and John (born 1167). A gap of four years, during which Henry was away from his wife, managing the farther reaches of his realm, separated the two bursts of procreation. During her husband's absence Eleanor played a prominent role in royal rule and ceremony, presented to councils of magnates with her young children and assuming the role of regent while Henry was away. When she traveled overseas with him—as they did in 1156, on a tour of Aquitaine, and again for a Christmas court in Normandy in 1158—she often took her children with her. For the most part, however, she remained in England, usually residing at palaces in Salisbury and Winchester.

When he was at home, Henry traveled frequently about his kingdom, addressing issues of government and diplomacy while finding time to indulge his great passion for the hunt. As he traveled, Henry grew familiar with the best locations both for government and for the chase. Very swiftly after his arrival, work began to transform the hunting lodges of Clarendon and Woodstock into full-blown palaces to match the sumptuous comfort of any in Europe. But all the palaces in the world could not answer the pressing question of the 1150s: How could the new king heal a country so deeply damaged by civil war? England had supplied Henry with what the chronicler Richard of Poitiers described as "the honor and reverence of his royal name." But this rich land, with its ports and towns, its hard-drinking, hardworking populace, and its ancient history, needed to be rescued from the doldrums. Henry would have to reimpose on his new realm the royal authority enjoyed by his grandfather Henry I. It amounted, effectively, to a mission of reconquest.

The realm was a shambles. Under Stephen royal revenue had fallen by two-thirds. Royal lands, castles, and offices had been granted away, often in perpetuity. The county farm, a staple royal income collected by the sheriffs, was running dismally low. Earldoms with semiregal powers proliferated, and in places the country was not only ungoverned but seemingly ungovernable. Relations between Church and Crown were at a stalemate following a long-running feud between Stephen and Archbishop Theobald over their respective jurisdictions. Fortresses built as the Normans had conquered South Wales had fallen into the hands of barons and native rulers. The far north of England was effectively ruled by the king of the Scots.

Henry's first task was to stamp out the few embers of rebellion. His coronation charter had deliberately avoided confirming any liberties or possessions that had been granted by Stephen, either to churchmen or to lay magnates. Anything granted since Henry I's reign was therefore held to be illegitimate, unless reconfirmed by the new king. He ordered the return to the Crown of all castles, towns, and lands that had been granted away under Stephen, followed by an abolition of the earldoms that Stephen had granted to his supporters. In many cases, confiscated lands were granted back to their holders, but Henry was sending a clear message: lordship now began with him, and everyone owed his position and possessions to the Plantagenet Crown.

At the same time, directly after Christmas 1154, Henry set in motion a rapid decommissioning program to enforce the destruction of illegal castles and the expulsion of foreign mercenaries. Castles packed with hired soldiers were the primary expressions of military power in the twelfth century, and the more that existed across the realm—particularly without royal sanction—the more violent and unstable society tended to be. As a result, hundreds of castles fell in a juddering demolition project during the course of 1155. The sound of falling timber was accompanied by a rush from the shores of Flemish soldiers, so despised by the chroniclers and ordinary people alike.

Henry had to take serious direct action against only a few of the magnates. William of Aumerle, who had cemented his position in Yorkshire so as to make it virtually untouched by royal influence, was deprived of his lands and of Scarborough Castle, the towering stone stronghold that sat on a headland, dominating sea approaches and the windswept northeast of the realm. Roger of Hereford, a Welsh marcher lord of the sort disinclined to obey royal authority, was persuaded to surrender castles at Gloucester and Hereford by the sensible mediation of his cousin Gilbert Foliot bishop of Hereford.

Henry of Blois bishop of Winchester—Stephen's brother—chose to flee the country rather than submit to his brother's successor. In doing so, he forfeited to Henry six castles. The only magnate who required serious military measures to be taken against him was Hugh Mortimer, lord of Wigmore Castle, who in the late spring clung to three castles in the Midlands and forced Henry to march an army against him. Even he was allowed to keep his lands after making a formal submission to Henry.

This was a lightning cleanup operation, undertaken in the spirit of reconciliation, not revenge, which owed a great deal to Henry's earlier successful diplomacy in establishing and prosecuting the terms of the peace of Winchester. That there was so little resistance to him and no threat of a serious rival for the throne demonstrated the broad appeal of Henry's strong, unified lordship. He was wielding the sword and the scales of justice like a king. This speed of reconciliation was a necessity, not a luxury, for England was only one part of the extensive Plantagenet domains.

In 1156 Henry was forced to leave England, to deal with a rebellion in Anjou led by his younger brother Geoffrey, who believed that under the terms of their father's will, Henry's accession as king of England ought to have triggered the handover of Anjou, Maine, and Touraine to Geoffrey. And indeed it was quite possible that this had been the elder Geoffrey Plantagenet's intention. There was no precedent for a single man to rule England, Normandy, and Anjou as one.

Henry had no intention of handing over the heartlands of his patrimony to his vexatious younger brother. Geoffrey had shown himself untrustworthy and disloyal when, in 1151, he had joined forces with Louis VII and Eustace to attack Henry's positions in Normandy. Giving Geoffrey lands that sat directly between Henry's duchy of Normandy and Eleanor's duchy of Aquitaine would be asking for trouble. It would also damage Henry's ambition to rule his extraordinary patchwork of territories under his own, direct sovereignty.

But Geoffrey had to be appeased. On February 2, 1156, a family conference was held in Rouen under the eye of the empress Matilda, who had been living in retirement in the Norman capital for nearly a decade and had not even crossed to England for Henry's coronation. Despite this, she was a regular confidante and counselor to her eldest son, teaching him, according to the chronicler Walter Map, to "spin out the affairs of everyone . . . never confer anything on anyone at the recommendation of any person, unless he had seen and learned about it." Under his mother's guidance, Henry met Geoffrey along with their youngest brother, William, and their aunt Sibylla countess of Flanders, to negotiate a deal. To isolate his brother diplomatically, Henry had performed homage to Louis VII for Normandy, Anjou, and Aquitaine in late January, and had sent an embassy to the newly elected pope, Adrian IV (the only Englishman ever to hold the title), to request release from the oath he had sworn to uphold his father's will. He was determined to hold on to Anjou, whatever the cost.

The peacekeeping efforts came, predictably, to nothing. Soon after the conference broke up, Geoffrey formally rebelled. The quarrel was resolved only later in the year, when the people of Nantes and lower Brittany elected Geoffrey their new count. It was a stroke of luck that found him a rich new territory to call his own and doused his disappointment at being, as he saw it, disinherited by his newly elevated elder brother.

A delighted Henry vouched for Geoffrey's election to this strategically useful new position. He paid off his brother's claim to a Plantagenet inheritance with the gift of a single border castle, Loudon, and a cash pension. This was an acceptable price to pay for quashing a distracting rift. Geoffrey's new position in Nantes extended the Plantagenet family enterprise farther downstream along the Loire and closer to the Breton seaboard— virtually the only piece of French coastline they did not already control.

This appeased Geoffrey until he rather conveniently died in 1158. But it also showed that for all his brilliance in pacifying his new kingdom, Henry would have to work with the unceasing effort of an Alexander or a Charlemagne if he wished to keep his vast Continental possessions from breaking apart.

L'Espace Plantagenet

The 1150s were a glorious decade for Henry. From a position of insignificance and insecurity in 1151, he had extended his power far and wide. The progress was relentless and impressive. In 1155 Pope Adrian IV gave Henry a blessing to expand his lordship in Ireland when he granted the papal bull *Laudabiliter*, exhorting Henry to reform the Irish Church. Henry did not act on *Laudabiliter* straightaway, but a principle had been established. In 1157 Henry took the homage of Malcolm IV of Scotland at Peveril Castle, regaining the northern border counties that had been usurped during the civil war and exchanging them for the earldom of Huntingdon, which was a traditional Scottish honor. That same year, Henry drove an army into Wales, aiming to reestablish the dominant position that had been established by his Norman ancestors. He was almost killed during an ambush in Ewloe Wood, near Flint, during one of the major military exercises of the campaign, and found the warlike Welsh as fierce an enemy as every one of his predecessors had. In the end the two great Welsh princes Owain of Gwynedd and Rhys ap Gruffydd of Deheubarth were persuaded to submit in the face of a massive show of military strength. This freed Henry in 1158 to use the threat of armed force to claim the county of Nantes in the name of his late brother, thus expanding his direct power into the duchy of Brittany. In the same year, he betrothed his eldest son, Henry, to Louis VII's daughter Margaret. The Vexin, a tiny but strategically vital portion of the borderlands between the Île de France and Normandy, was given as a dowry to be delivered on the celebration of the marriage.

Piece by piece, front by front, Henry was proving to all the princes and kings with whom he rubbed shoulders that the Plantagenets were a power to reckon with. As the 1150s drew to a close, Henry was the master of more territory than any of his ancestors could ever have dreamed of. But even that was not enough.

In the summer of 1159, a season when the sun beat mercilessly down on the southern valleys of France, a gigantic army rumbled toward the city of Toulouse. Inside the walls thirty-five thousand souls quaked with fear as they listened to the tread of foot soldiers, the thud and creak of warhorses and wagons, the blare of trumpets and drums, and the monstrous drag of siege engines. As the army marched, it left destruction in its wake. Cahors, Auvillars, and Villemur were ransacked and torched. Crops were burned, and property was plundered. The whole region of Toulouse contemplated a new scourge of the West. "Henry the second . . . terrifies not only the Provençals as far as the Rhône and the Alps," wrote the author and diplomat John of Salisbury. "[He] also strikes at the princes of Spain and Gaul through the fortresses he has destroyed and the peoples he has subdued."

The army with which Henry II crossed southern France in June 1159 was the largest he would ever raise. The cost for mercenaries in England alone exceeded nine thousand pounds, more than the previous year's entire royal income. The poet Stephen of Rouen wrote that Henry came with "iron, missiles and machines," while the Norman chronicler Robert of To-rigni called it "the military force of the whole of Normandy, England, Aquitaine and the other provinces which were subject to him." There was no doubt of his purpose: Henry came in conquest. His aim was to take Toulouse from its ruler, Count Raymond V, and add it to the duchy of Aquitaine. "The king was claiming the inheritance of his wife Queen Eleanor," wrote Torigni. But Henry was doing more than that. He was engaged in a wide-reaching campaign to assert his rights as overlord to a vast expanse of territory that stretched from the foothills of Scotland to the Pyrenees.

The army included many great nobles. His recently reconciled neighbor Malcolm IV of Scotland sailed south with a flotilla and joined Henry's army at Poitiers. Southern lords, including Raymond-Berengar IV count of Barcelona and Raymond Trencavel lord of Béziers and Carcassonne, joined in too, gleeful at the prospect of harassing a neighbor. And somewhere in the middle rode the churchman who had organized the campaign, Thomas Becket, chancellor of England and archdeacon of Canterbury, wearing helmet and hauberk, his armor gleaming in the sun. Becket had command of what is said to have been a personal troop of seven hundred knights. This figure is almost certainly an exaggeration; even so, we can be sure that he mustered a strong military force, particularly for a cleric.

The siege of Toulouse lasted from June to September 1159 and represented the height of Henry's ambitions in Europe during the early years of his reign. He had expended considerable time and effort reforming and securing the vast territories he had accumulated between 1149 and 1154. But he had no intention of making do with his lot. Toulouse marked the logical conclusion of a policy he developed following the pacification of England. He used armies, quite often massive armies, to encroach on territory on the fringes of his already extensive borders. He seemed to want to become not merely a king and a duke but an emperor.

In reality, his policy was more pragmatic than this suggests. Henry aimed to pursue all his rights, in all his capacities, at all times. There were occasions when he used military means and others when he used diplomacy. He drove hard to have his lordship recognized wherever he could do so, tidying up all the fraying parts of his huge network of territories by waging wars against the fringes. Toulouse was just another border region in which his authority was challenged. He was leading a war not so much of conquest as of recognition.

Toulouse, however, was a famously tough nut to crack. Eleanor of Aquitaine held a rather tenuous claim to the county via her paternal grandmother, Philippa, who had been passed over for inheritance in the 1090s. In 1141 Louis VII had attempted to invade in much the same manner as Henry did in 1159 but had been repulsed. That did not discourage Henry. He had a claim, the wherewithal to raise a large army, and momentum gained from his success against the Welsh and the Bretons.

No doubt, as John of Salisbury reported, the princes of Spain and Gaul remarked upon the size of the army Henry had assembled. But they would also have been skeptical of Henry's chances of success. Toulouse was a large city, well protected, positioned on a sharp bend in the Garonne, and divided into three fortified sections. The ancient Roman city was adjacent to a walled bourg that had sprung up rather later around the vast, beautiful Basilica of St.-Sernin. A wall ran around both these two areas, and between them and to the south lay the Château Narbonnais, a separate castle in which the city's ruler resided. It could not be parched into submission, because the river provided a constant supply of water and did not dry up during the summer.

For all the efforts of Henry's invading force, and all the misery they inflicted on the countryside and castles of the region, the skeptics were vindicated. As had happened to Louis in 1141, a king once again had thrown his might at the city defenses and found himself thwarted.

How did so huge a force fail to overrun a relatively tiny prize? Perhaps the liberal lordship of the counts of Toulouse was preferred to the clunking mastery suggested by Henry's invading force. Perhaps the city's natural defenses really did make it untakable. In any case, the decisive blow that finished Henry's campaign was struck in the early autumn of 1159, when he was caught unawares by the arrival in Toulouse of Louis VII.

Of all the lords in France it was Louis whom Henry had troubled the most during his expansions in the 1150s. The duke of Normandy's elevation to the rank of king made him a dangerous vassal for the Capetian Crown, one with military resources and a pedigree that far outstripped any other French nobleman's. This was most obviously a problem where the boundaries of the duchy of Normandy met French royal lands, in the area known as the Vexin. It was true that in 1156, in a ceremony of great pageantry and political symbolism, Henry had done homage to the French king, swearing to Louis that "I, King Henry, will safeguard the life, limbs and landed honor of the King of France as my lord, if he will secure for me as his *fidelis* my life and limbs and lands which he has settled on me, for I am his man." But Louis's feudal status would be worth nothing if he sat by and allowed Henry to conquer Toulouse, an area that he had nearly failed to bring within his own direct control. Moreover, Count Raymond was the French king's brother-in-law. To let him down would proclaim a very hollow lordship.

Louis arrived in Toulouse knowing that his mere presence at Count Raymond's shoulder would force Henry to consider very carefully whether he could afford to continue his campaign. Attacking Raymond alone was one thing; to take on Louis and Raymond together was an act of explicit aggression that would cause Henry untold problems farther north in Normandy and Anjou, areas he had been at pains to keep in good order. Furthermore, to take on Louis in an armed contest and lose would undermine the symbolic value of the whole Toulouse expedition.

Henry took counsel with his barons and his key advisers, including Becket. In the absence of a specific insult to his royal honor, the barons counseled that it was unacceptable to attack the French king. Becket protested, calling for an immediate assault on the city. He was outvoted and ignored. Henry gave up the fight. Claiming that he wished to spare the Capetian king and the city, he withdrew from Toulouse around the feast of Michaelmas.

The chronicler Roger of Howden called Toulouse Henry's "unfinished business." It was not quite a disaster, but it was undeniably a failure. The most profitable event of the campaign was tangential to the siege itself: William count of Boulogne, King Stephen's younger son, who had joined Henry on campaign, died on his way back to England in October 1159. His extensive English estates reverted to the Crown. Otherwise, all that could be said for an expensive summer spent hurling rocks at the walls of a city was that Henry had tested to the limit his capacity for wielding military power.

There was another cost to the failure of the Toulouse campaign. It brought into question for the first time the relationship between Henry and his closest counselor, the chancellor Thomas Becket.

Unholy War

In the summer of 1158, a year before he led Henry's troops to the walls of Toulouse, Thomas Becket rode at the head of an even grander procession into the city of Paris. Coming in peace, as the chancellor of England and servant of the English king, he radiated solemn magnificence and glory. Becket had been sent on an embassy to negotiate the betrothal of Henry's three-year-old son and namesake to Louis's baby daughter Margaret, creating a dynastic union between the two royal houses and securing the Vexin for the Plantagenets. It was appropriate that he should impress the French king with the wealth and dignity of his master.

Becket put on an extraordinary show. In private he was a rigorously pious man who scourged himself regularly, wore a hair shirt, ate frugally, and never took a mistress. But Henry's chancellor knew how to entertain a crowd. He swept into Paris with exotic gifts and lavish pageantry—dogs, monkeys, and a seemingly endless train of servants, all testifying to the English king's largesse and splendor. A vivid record was kept by William Fitzstephen, who accompanied Becket and saw it all firsthand:

> In his company he had some two hundred horsemen, knights, clerks, stewards and men in waiting, men at arms and squires of noble family, all in ordered ranks. All these and all their followers wore bright new festal garments. He also took twenty-four suits . . . and many silk cloaks to leave behind him as presents, and all kinds of parti-coloured clothes and foreign furs, hangings and carpets for a bishop's guest-room.
>
> Hounds and hawks were in the train . . . and eight five-horse chariots drawn by shire horses. On every horse was a sturdy groom in a new tunic, and on every chariot a warden. Two carts carried nothing but beer . . . for the French, who are not familiar with the brew, a healthy drink, clear, dark as wine, and finer in flavor. Others bore food and drink, others dorsals [dossals], carpets, bags of night attire and luggage in general. He had twelve sumpter horses and eight chests of table places, gold and silver. . . . One horse carried the plate, the altar furnishings and the books of his chapel. . . . Every horse had a groom in a smart turnout; every chariot had a fierce great mastiff on a leash standing in the

cart or walking behind it, and every sumpter beast had a long-tailed monkey on its back....

Then there were about 250 men marching six or ten abreast, singing as they went in the English fashion. At intervals came braces of staghounds and greyhounds with their attendants, ... then the men at arms, with the shields and chargers of the knights, then the other men at arms and boys and men carrying hawks.... Last of all came the chancellor and some of his friends....

Arrived in Paris ... he loaded every baron, knight, ... master, scholar and burgess with gifts of plate, clothing, horses and money.

It was a show fit for a king.

In 1158 Thomas Becket was fast becoming one of Henry II's closest friends and most trusted advisers. The king had found him working as a clerk in the service of Theobald archbishop of Canterbury. Theobald had admired the young man's ambitious capacity for hard work and had promoted him through his service until in 1154 Becket had become archdeacon of Canterbury. It was in this post that he became known to Henry, who was encouraged to think of Becket as a highly competent candidate for the post of English chancellor. In 1155, on Theobald's recommendation, Henry had placed Becket at the top of the English administration. Becket rose to the task. He excelled in royal service.

Twelfth-century government was still a scrappy, personal business. The courtier Walter Map has left us a dramatic but highly plausible image of Henry's court in full pelt: "Whenever [the king] goes out he is seized by the crowd and pulled and pushed hither and thither; he is assaulted by shouts and roughly handled; yet he listens to all with patience and seemingly without anger; until hustled beyond bearing[,] he silently retreats to some place of quiet." At the heart of such a throng, the king required a large and sophisticated system of household servants, clerks, diplomats, and administrators. It was this sort of loose organization over which Becket presided. Like the great royal servants of centuries to come—Henry VIII's chief minister Thomas Wolsey, or Elizabeth I's principal secretary William Cecil—Becket spared a charismatic monarch the strain of day-to-day government and turned his grand visions into reality.

Becket reached the height of his power around 1160, when he was just past forty and the king was approaching twenty-seven. The chancellor was a tall, pleasant-looking man with studied manners and cultivated skills in courtly conversation. His rise to power, wealth, and glory had been extraordinary. He had enjoyed a good education at Merton Priory in Sussex and a London grammar school—perhaps St. Paul's. But his progress through life was cut short when his merchant father's business premises burned down. He spent two years studying in Paris during his early twenties but never completed the full education in canon and civil law that distinguished any ambitious young medieval man of letters. All his life he would overcompensate for the sense of inferiority that lingered. What Becket lacked in intellectual finesse, he made up for with ambition. As well as chancellor, he was archdeacon of Canterbury, an important position in the English Church. He accumulated rich benefices everywhere from Kent to Yorkshire and kept in London a fine and luxurious household, to which several magnates sent their sons for an education.

With his pale skin, dark hair, and long nose, the chancellor could not have cut a more contrasting figure with the short, red-haired king, with his raw energy and ease in company more inborn than acquired. Becket set great store by values that meant very little to his king but that were essential to maintaining the dignity of kingship. According to Becket's biographer Fitzstephen, the chancellor "hardly ever dined without the company of sundry earls and bishops." He kept a fine table, with delicate foods served in fine vessels of gold and silver. He enjoyed all the lordly pageantry that bored the king, and Henry was happy for him to carry it out in his stead.

The king seems to have enjoyed the almost comical contrast between himself and his chancellor and occasionally poked fun at his friend. Fitzstephen recorded a famous story of Becket and Henry riding together through the wintry streets of London early in their friendship. The king pointed out a poor beggar shivering in the cold and remarked to his chancellor that it would be a fine thing to give him a thick, warm cloak. When Becket agreed that this would indeed be charitable, Henry grabbed him and forcibly ripped the fine scarlet and gray cape from his back, which he presented to the bewildered beggar. Becket did not share in the hilarity this caused among the royal attendants. But Henry always insisted on pricking his friend's pride when he could. He was known to ride into the chancellor's dinner hall, jump from his horse, and sit down to eat. The experience must have grated on Becket as much as it amused the king. Yet despite the irritations and the small indignities, Becket was Henry's friend, trusted servant, and confidant.

Most important, the king saw Becket as the bridge between two worlds: Crown and Church. All over Europe during the twelfth century, kings and their vassals were struggling with ecclesiastical authorities over questions of jurisdiction and authority. There were frequent clashes over the right to perform coronations or to appeal to papal rather than royal courts, the right of bishops to leave the country to attend conferences and that of kings to divorce their wives. Virtually every king in Europe had been or would be threatened with interdict (a sentence banning most church services and sacraments throughout a realm) or personal excommunication. Pope Eugene III had attempted to impose both penalties on King Stephen during a bitter argument about an appointment to the archbishopric of York. And Frederick I, "Barbarossa," the Hohenstaufen prince who had been elected Holy Roman Emperor and was the only king in Europe with more extensive territories than Henry, was excommunicated in 1160 during a war for legal supremacy with Pope Alexander III.

Henry knew that his plans for governing England would not please the papacy and the Church. He believed his rights as king were prejudiced by an overpowerful Church, which he was determined to bring into line. Building his empire was not just a matter of expanding borders. It was about defining and deepening the rights and powers of kingship within the realm. He did not wish to seize total dominion over the Church or to rule as king and priest combined. But he had exacting notions of royal prerogatives, and he intended to defend them.

On April 18, 1161, Archbishop Theobald died in his palace in Canterbury, after a long illness. He had lived past the grand old age of seventy and had been archbishop since 1138, when Stephen had appointed him. Henry saw an opportunity. He had plans that would require a pliable archbishop in the seat of Canterbury, chief among them his aim to have his eldest son crowned as king-designate. This was something Theobald had explicitly refused to do for King Stephen. Henry also wished to begin a process of redefining the boundaries of rights held by Crown and Church. It suited him to have an ally as English primate.

Becket struck Henry as the ideal candidate to replace Theobald. Frederick Barbarossa had used archbishop-chancellors—of Mainz and Cologne—to rule Germany and Italy. Henry resolved to do the same. Yet to many in the English Church, including the monks of Canterbury Cathedral who traditionally held the right to elect the archbishop, Becket's candidacy was a travesty. He was unfit for office on several grounds. He was essentially a secular figure with a second-rate academic record. He was no lawyer and certainly no theologian. He was a clear partisan of the Crown and had treated the Canterbury monks ungraciously during his service for Theobald. The monks were not alone in objecting. Henry's mother, the empress Matilda, also wrote strongly to discourage him from promoting his friend to archbishop.

None of this swayed Henry. The advantages of appointing Becket as a chancellor-archbishop far outweighed the laments that would rise from Canterbury. Henry wished to pass the kingdom of England to his eldest son, with Becket as his mentor and regent. The boy was nearly seven years old, at which age it was customary for young noblemen to leave their mothers' households and begin their education for manhood. In 1162 the king planned to put young Henry under Becket's tutelage. All the better that this should be in the household of an archbishop. On June 2, 1161, Becket was ordained a priest. The next day he was consecrated as archbishop.

In Henry's mind Becket's elevation was a triumph, but he soon discovered that there was a major flaw in his strategy. The flaw was not the reaction from others in the Church. It was Becket himself.

Despite the titles and gifts lavished on him by the king, Becket felt deeply inadequate as archbishop. Part of the reason for this lay in the fact that the English primate was traditionally a monk. Becket was marked very clearly as an outsider by his pale, nonmonastic dress. Having spent a lifetime learning how to be a great secular chancellor, he was now parachuted into a world where everything he stood for was despised. He was poorly educated in ecclesiastical terms and instantly disliked for his royal associations. He felt a painful need to prove himself worthy both to his new flock and to God himself. This prompted a sudden and violent change of outlook and attitude that dramatically and catastrophically reshaped his relationship with Henry.

Almost as soon as he became archbishop, Becket began to distance himself from royal policy. His very first action was to resign the chancellorship, protesting that he was "unfit for one office, let alone two." He then picked a fight over Church lands with several lay magnates, including the earl of Hertford and William Lord Eynsford, another Kentish landowner. He declared the day of his own consecration a new feast day—that of the Holy Trinity—and he sent a flurry of requests to Pope Alexander III, asking to strengthen the authority of Canterbury over the rival archbishopric of York. The trusted royal agent became—almost overnight—an opponent of the Crown. Henry had expected him to grease the cogs of royal policy within Church ranks. Instead, he was jamming his bony fingers into them. Becket became, for the rest of his life, a pompous, disagreeable, and obstreperous distraction from Henry's every effort at smooth governance.

Whatever the cause of Becket's conversion, it was remarked on with astonishment by contemporaries. The anonymous Battle Abbey chronicler unsurprisingly viewed it as a sort of glorious skin shedding, a spiritual transformation wrought by his elevation in status: "In him, as the common proverb has it, 'honours changed conduct,' but not, as with the conduct of nearly all men, for the worse, but day to day for the better. For he put off the old man who is created according to the world, and strove to put on the new man who is created according to God." Even William of Newburgh, a writer generally unsympathetic to Becket, was impressed: "Soon weighing up by pious and wise consideration what the burden of such a great honor might be, he was thus immediately changed in habit and manner, as one might say 'This is the hand of God' and 'This is the transformation of the hand of the Almighty.'"

Becket's switch from loyal Crown enforcer to prickly defender of Church rights had taken place with bewildering swiftness. At first Henry tolerated his friend's exasperating behavior from afar. He was too preoccupied with Norman affairs to concentrate fully on England. But once he returned from the Continent in January 1163, he was determined to push through a series of legal and governmental reforms that he thought were essential to improve law and order. The program of reforms he introduced in 1164 is now known as the Constitutions of Clarendon, for the royal hunting lodge where it was drawn up. The sixteen-point document is one of the most famous in English constitutional history, representing Henry's attempt to draw a clear line between the blurred jurisdictions of Church and royal authority. This was an area of bitter dispute, but the issue on which he chose to attack was that of criminous clerks—the term used for those clergymen who stole, raped, maimed, or killed.

Perhaps one in six Englishmen in the late twelfth century was technically a clergyman. While most were not and never would be priests, there were plenty in minor orders or who had entered the Church for an education and left to work for lay masters. Many parish priests were poorly educated and barely literate. Their lives would not have differed much from those of ordinary peasants. But clerical status bestowed great advantage if one fell foul of the law. The Church demanded the right to discipline criminous clerks but punishments were considerably lighter under canon law than under the secular criminal code. The Church would neither inflict trial by ordeal nor mutilate or execute the guilty. This allowed what was perceived by Henry to be a shameful number of crimes to go unpunished. To the king's mind, hawkish as it was about his royal rights, for criminous clerks to shelter beneath the broad cassock of the canon law was an egregious abuse and one that he was not prepared to tolerate.

To reduce a complex dispute to simple terms: Henry wanted criminous clerks tried in ecclesiastical courts to be stripped of their orders and returned to the secular powers for bodily punishment. This did not technically create a hierarchy of courts, but it would bring churchmen who committed crimes into what Henry thought was their rightful place of punishment. Becket meanwhile chose to resist every perceived intrusion into the Church's rights, at whatever political cost.

At the council of Woodstock in the summer of 1163, Becket quarreled with the king over the Church's payment of the sheriff's aid. This was a form of taxation, which was traditionally paid by landowners directly to their local sheriff, to help fund his peacekeeping duties in the county. Henry now wished to draw this revenue directly into the exchequer, bringing a large source of finance under central supervision and implicitly reminding the whole of England that it was from the wellspring of the king's direct authority that all other political power flowed. This was an accounting reform with political significance. It was probably not a wildly important issue to anyone but the sheriffs themselves, but the archbishop, cast in his new, self-appointed role of scrutineer of the Crown's reform program, objected. He informed the king that "it does not become your excellence to deflect something that belongs to another to your use" and added that the realm would not be "forced by law." This so infuriated Henry that he swore a great oath. According to Edward Grim, a contemporary who wrote a biography of Becket, Henry shouted at his archbishop: "By God's eyes! It shall be given as revenue and entered in the royal rolls: and it is not fit that you should gainsay it, for no one would oppose your men against your will."

But the archbishop faced him down. "By the reverence of the eyes by which you have sworn, my lord king, there shall be given from all my lands or from the property of the church not a penny." This was especially stubborn behavior from Becket, considering that he had very little personally to lose from the sheriff's aid reform. But it showed just how determined he was to prove himself in his new position and to thwart his sovereign's ambitious plans for reform.

Relations between the two former friends deteriorated further over the course of the summer. The issue of criminous clerks would not disappear. Henry had heard from his advisers that in the nine years since his coronation, more than one hundred murders and an untold number of other crimes had been committed by clerks who had gone unpunished by the royal courts. Although Becket tried to ward Henry off making any fundamental changes in the courts' jurisdictions by banishing and branding several criminous clerks and imprisoning others for life, it was not enough to convince the king that the matter could be left as it stood. On October 1, 1163, Henry summoned the spiritual magnates of the realm to a royal council at Westminster. He addressed his audience, demanding that they obey and observe the ancient customs of the realm. A heated legal debate broke out, in which royal and canon lawyers contested for supremacy. Henry asked the bishops to recognize that a criminous clerk, once found guilty in the Church courts, should be surrendered to the royal courts for bodily punishment. If they would not, then they must reveal whether or not they were prepared to abide by any of the "customs of England." Led by Becket, the bishops at Woodstock answered that they would observe England's customs "saving their order," a nonanswer that reserved the right to observe canon law above the laws of kings.

"In heated mood [the king] left London without notice, and with all his business unfinished and lawsuits left hanging," wrote Becket's close companion and biographer Herbert of Bosham. The next morning Henry demanded that Becket return all the castles granted to him during his chancellorship and removed his son from Becket's care. It was a spiteful gesture that tore the heart out of a decade-long friendship. Henry's view, later expressed in person, in a failed rapprochement at Northampton, was that the archbishop ought to stop preaching and remember that he owed everything to royal favor. "Were you not the son of one of my villeins?" he asked Becket. "You adhere and rely too much on the manner of your ascent." It was a piercing remark.

The breach at Westminster left bad feelings on both sides. Both men appealed to Pope Alexander. The pope, however, had more pressing troubles of his own and was in exile from Rome. He had quarreled with the Holy Roman Emperor, Frederick Barbarossa, and the end result had been papal schism. An antipope, Victor IV, now sat at Rome, while Alexander licked his wounds in Venice and other, less grand parts of the Italian peninsula. Alexander gently urged Becket to cooperate, as later did Gilbert Foliot bishop of London and Roger archbishop of York, several cardinals, and the respected Cistercian abbot Philip of Aumone. In November, according to Roger of Pontigny, "the archbishop, swayed by the advice of the lord pope and the cardinals and the words of this abbot and the others who came with him," agreed to submit to the king. He did so privately at Oxford. Henry summoned a great council to his hunting lodge and palace at Clarendon in late January 1164. He intended Becket's humiliation to be public and complete. Becket was uneasy and evasive but was manipulated, through a series of tantrums and dark threats from Henry, into declaring before the assembled magnates—barons, officials, and bishops—that he would uphold all the laws and customs of the realm, without condition.

Henry then sprang a trap. Rather than accept this moral victory, he pressed home his advantage and drove for binding, unambiguous supremacy. On January 29 the Constitutions of Clarendon were issued as a chirograph, a written form of lawmaking that implied permanence and universality. A copy was handed to Becket, a copy was kept for the king, and a third copy was filed in the royal archives for posterity. Becket was appalled. The document listed sixteen points, comprising the "customs" to which he had apparently assented the previous day. These included Henry's desired scheme for criminous clerks, a limitation on appeals to the papacy above the king's authority, and several broad statements asserting the primacy of royal courts over Church jurisdiction.

Browbeaten by the king to accept royal policy, Becket had placed the Church in a position of unprecedented submission and proved himself to be what he supposed everyone must all along have thought him, a royal patsy.

Tormented, Becket suspended himself from priestly duties and denounced the snare Henry had closed around him. He wrote to the pope, admitting what he had done and begging absolution. He was, said Herbert of Bosham, "unusually disquieted and gloomy." Great salty sobs racked his body as he bewailed his unfitness for office. His wild attempts to prove himself to his spiritual peers, to God, and to himself had come to nothing. He had wholly lost the king's goodwill, political support, and friendship, but he had not gained the favor of a greater lord. "I clearly see myself worthy to be abandoned by God and removed from the holy seat in which I was placed," he cried. Panicking, he wrote to Henry's enemy Louis VII for support and in the summer attempted unsuccessfully to flee to France.

Henry, meanwhile, was in a vindictive mood. In the autumn he summoned Becket to a council of the magnates in Northampton Castle. On October 6, 1164, Henry's former friend was accused of embezzlement committed during his term as chancellor. Becket again appealed to the pope. So did Henry. He aimed to have the archbishop deposed and denounced his appeal, for malicious effect, as being in breach of the Constitutions of Clarendon.

Faced with crimes against the Crown and against his own soul, Becket panicked. As judicial proceedings against him at Northampton were coming to a head, he declared that he refused to hear judgment pronounced, turned on his heel, and walked out of the room. He managed to flee the castle, and the next morning, as rain lashed from a leaden sky, the disgraced and sodden archbishop tramped from town with just four men to accompany him. He escaped England on November 2, 1164, when a desperate and dangerous Channel crossing in a small boat put him ashore in Flanders, where he set off to seek refuge with the king of France. He would not return to England for almost five years.

Succession Planning

Becket slipped out of England in a state of dejection, which very quickly gave way to fury. He made his home on French soil, at Pontigny Abbey. There he sat in wrathful indignation, writing letters of protest to the pope and complaining to anyone who would listen. He punished himself with a furious asceticism, as his companion Edward Grim recorded:

> From this time content with eating vegetables and coarser feasts and removing lighter things, he furtively withdrew certain delicacies from himself. . . . He would also lower himself into the stream which ran between the workshops of the monastery [i.e., Pontigny] where he would remain for longer than human fragility can take. The extent of bodily torment inflicted by the extreme cold in his efforts to purge himself of the stings of desire that seemed to dwell in him, was revealed by his consequent illness. . . . [H]e developed an abscess which festered as far as the inside of his throat, and grew into an ulcer. He suffered for a long time in this agony, with much trouble and sorrow, until after the extraction of two teeth he eventually recovered.

Letters written by Becket while he was staying at Pontigny betrayed a sense of high indignation that turned, the longer his exile lasted, into declamations of his own righteousness. He wrote long salvos against Henry II's key ministers, in particular the justiciar, Richard de Lucy, and Jocelin de Balliol, principal authors of the Constitutions of Clarendon. On Whitsunday 1166, at Vézelay, he preached a furious sermon pronouncing sentences of excommunication against a host of his enemies in England.

Yet his bark was much worse than his bite. Henry took a sporadic interest in Becket, but he was occupied constantly with a broad range of concerns across his different territories. As time passed, the affair with his archbishop became merely irksome. Henry just got on with things. He turned over the responsibilities of chancellor (albeit not the title) to Geoffrey Ridel. The new man was pointedly given Becket's old post of archdeacon of Canterbury. Henry continued to wage border wars against Louis and various of his own rebellious vassals. He threw himself into the conquest of Brittany, built alliances on the eastern and southern fringes of the Plantagenet dominions, from the Alps to the Norman kingdom of Sicily, coped with rebellions in Aquitaine, and pushed back French aggression around the fringes of Normandy. Despite the tirades that erupted from Becket's pen, the king of England, duke of Normandy and Aquitaine, and count of Anjou had better things to worry about in the late 1160s than his priggish former chancellor eating vegetables in the backwaters of France.

In September 1167 the empress Matilda fell ill and died. She was sixty-five. During the first thirteen years of Henry's reign she had proved a source of wise advice and a useful sounding board for policy—particularly toward the Holy Roman Empire, where she had spent her youth. On occasion she could play her part as the grande dame of Normandy, and she was approached with requests for counsel and mediation from the great men of Europe, including Louis VII, who acknowledged her authority in the affairs of Rouen. She had shown foresight by urging Henry not to promote Becket to Canterbury in 1162, and she was still playing stateswoman a few months before her death, attempting to reconcile her son with Louis as hostilities between the two kings mounted.

Matilda died surrounded by the monks of Bec, among whom she had lived during her long retirement. The brothers sewed her body into an oxhide and laid her to rest with lavish ceremony in recognition of the magnificent treasures she had showered upon their abbey church: two heavy gold crowns from Germany, portable altars made from marble and silver, and her own magnificent gold-trimmed imperial cape. She died as she had lived, the daughter, wife, and mother of three magnificent kings. Although two of her sons had predeceased her—Geoffrey in 1158 and William (who had died rather suddenly in 1164)—she left grandchildren poised one day to rule over the whole of Europe.

Matilda's death marked the passing of a generation. In 1168 Robert earl of Leicester also died. His defection to Henry's side in 1153 had marked a vital moment in the struggle to take the English Crown, and since 1154 he had served as cojusticiar of England. One by one the veterans of the civil war were passing. Henry's ambitions were maturing. According to John of Salisbury, in 1168 Henry exclaimed that "now at last he had secured the authority of his grandfather, who was king in his own land, papal legate, patriarch, emperor and everything he wished." He had his family, his kingdom, his security. It was time to think of the future.

Eleanor gave birth to her last surviving child in 1167. The boy, who was named John, brought the number of children to seven: four boys and three girls. Eleanor was forty-three at the time of John's birth. The significance of this reproductive feat was matched by her political achievement, for through these seven children, Henry could begin to unfold his dynasty across Europe. His children's futures were the future of his empire, and the arrangements he made for them would shape much of the Western world for the rest of the century.

The highest concern for Henry in the late 1160s was to establish a stable relationship with an increasingly belligerent Louis VII. In August 1165 the French king's third wife, Adèle of Champagne, finally produced a son, Philip. This long-awaited arrival of an heir to the house of Capet was greeted with jubilation in the streets of Paris, and a weight was lifted from Louis's shoulders. But if Philip's birth was a relief, it was also a catalyst. The French king was concerned for the future and had grown nervous at the thought that he would hand to his son a royal inheritance sharply diminished in its territorial scope and the prestige of its lordship. He began to look for ways to discomfit the English king wherever he could. Harboring Becket was one such move. Tit-for-tat military exchanges escalated in the border regions between their territories, and Louis had begun to encourage dissent among Henry's more troublesome subjects: the king of Scots, the Welsh princes dispossessed in 1157, and the Bretons who squirmed under Henry's aggressive conquest of their duchy. Louis's role as a focus for opposition to Henry's Continental lordship was not lost on the barons of Aquitaine, led by the count of Angoulême and the count of La Marche, both of whom flirted with the possibility of transferring their allegiance from the English king to the French.

It was perhaps appropriate, as a memorial to his mother, that the year after the empress's death Henry sent his eldest daughter, Matilda, to be married to Henry the Lion, duke of Saxony and Bavaria, thereby preserving the links between the English Crown and the German states. But with four brothers, this Matilda was not likely to be recalled from Germany to fight for England. In Henry II's plans, that honor belonged to his eldest son and namesake. In 1162 and 1163 young Henry had already received the homage of the English barons, the Scottish king, and the princes of Wales. His father's plan to have him crowned *rex designatus* had stalled thanks to the quarrel with Becket, because only the archbishop of Canterbury could crown an English king. Nevertheless, King Henry made it clear that he wished the boy to grow up to rule over the entire Plantagenet patrimony: England, Normandy, and Anjou.

Through a program of relentless military and diplomatic pressure that lasted the better part of a decade Henry II had succeeded in marrying his third son, Geoffrey, to Constance, the only daughter of Conan IV duke of Brittany. He then effectively forced the duke to abdicate, giving him the English earldom of Richmond and in return taking control of Brittany in Geoffrey's name. When he came of age, Henry decreed, Geoffrey was to rule as duke of Brittany, holding the duchy in feudal tenure from his eldest brother, who in turn would do homage for it to the king of France. Until the boy reached maturity, Henry would rule Brittany personally.

Of the first four children, that left just Richard. Of all of Henry's children, his second son was the closest to his mother, and it was therefore decided that he should inherit her part of the Plantagenet empire, the duchy of Aquitaine and county of Poitou. Eleanor, as she neared the end of her fertile years, harbored ambitions to return to Aquitaine and rule it as the duchess she had always been. With Richard by her side, that might be a possibility.

Aquitaine's independence still mattered greatly to King Louis because he had been deprived of its control when Eleanor married Henry in 1152. Henry proposed that Richard would hold Aquitaine directly from the French Crown, loosening its connection to the rest of Henry's dominions. To sugar the pill, Henry also proposed a strategic marriage between Richard and Louis's daughter Alice, who was born in 1160.

This plan was proffered to Louis at Montmirail, in Maine, at a conference held in January 1169. It was a generous settlement, both for Henry's sons and for Louis himself. Henry might have been an assiduous empire builder, but he had no intention that the great dominions he controlled should remain fully connected in perpetuity. The Plantagenet realm was not an empire in this truest sense—territories to be conjoined forever and ruled as one. After Henry's death, it was conceived as a federation, whose ties could be loosened or strengthened. With the partition that Henry proposed, the lasting effects of his reign would have been to unite Anjou with

England and Normandy, to consolidate central power somewhat in Aquitaine, and to alter the feudal relationship between Brittany and the French Crown. When Henry followed his mother to the grave, the clock would turn back to 1152.

This was some way from Louis's worst fears of a perpetual empire ruled from Rouen and Westminster that could outstrip its rival in Paris. Montmirail brought a truce between the kings and offered a new picture of future feudal relations. The conference had been preceded by much wearisome warfare: Henry had sent campaigns thundering through Brittany and Aquitaine in 1167 and 1168, crushing rebellions stirred up against his lordship. He had also ravaged lands belonging to Louis's vassals on the borders of Normandy and in Perche. Even in the twelfth-century world of near-constant siege and skirmish, hostilities had dragged on too long.

Montmirail might, under the right circumstances, have led to an unprecedented period of peace and concordance between the two kings. But there was one issue that could not be solved at the negotiating tables of the great French fortress. This was the case of Thomas Becket. Henry came face-to-face with his old friend at Montmirail for the first time since their great breach, brought together in the spirit of peace that pervaded the whole conference. Becket came to Henry under firm diplomatic pressure to apologize and resolve the damaging row that had dragged on for five years.

Unfortunately Becket showed Henry that he had in no way changed during his years in exile. Herbert of Bosham was present at the meeting, and described the scene in his biography of Becket:

> The archbishop was led before the kings, with . . . so great a crowd surrounding him and trying to speak to him. . . . The archbishop immediately in the first place prostrated himself at the king's feet. . . . But as soon as he had prostrated himself at his feet, the king immediately took hold of him and raised him up.
>
> Standing before the king then, the archbishop began humbly and zealously to solicit royal mercy toward the Church committed to him, though, as he said, an unworthy sinner. As is the custom of the just, in the beginning of his speech he found fault with himself and attributed the Church's great disturbance and harsh affliction solely to his own failings. And in the conclusion of his speech, he added: "Therefore, my lord, regarding the entire cause between you and me, I now submit

myself to your mercy and judgment in the presence of our lord king of France, and the bishops and nobles and others present here." But to the surprise of the king, the mediators and even his own men, he added: "—saving God's honor."

This was typical Becket. He had been warned at length by the mediators at Montmirail not to add such an inflammatory limiting clause to his apology. The phrase "saving our order" had been at the root of the violent arguments over the Constitutions of Clarendon in the first place, and Becket was fooling no one by amending it to "God's honor." As soon as he heard Becket's concluding words, Henry realized that nothing had changed. "The king took strong offense and burned with anger toward the archbishop, throwing many insults at him, condemning him a great deal, reproaching him more, inveighing against him, accusing him of being proud and haughty, forgetful of and ungrateful for the royal bounty lavished on him," wrote Herbert of Bosham, who noted that even the French king seemed weary of Becket's intransigence, asking him: "Lord archbishop, do you wish to be more than a saint?" The peace conference broke up with territorial plans well made, but with the estrangement between Becket and Henry II still wholly unresolved.

"Do you wish to be more than a saint?" These were prescient words indeed. After the failure to make peace at Montmirail, Henry and Becket tried again with another botched reconciliation at Montmartre in November 1169. This time Henry would not offer the archbishop the kiss of peace. Becket subsequently threatened to lay the whole of England under interdict and worked to gain papal backing for his threats. In the context of Henry's succession planning he was becoming more than just a nuisance.

In July 1170 Henry decided to act boldly. Crossing to England with his eldest son and a number of Norman bishops, he traveled to Westminster Abbey and had the younger Henry anointed king—*rex designatus*—by the archbishop of York, Roger de Pont l'Evêque. About ten other bishops witnessed the ceremony. When Becket learned of the outrageous breach of his privileges, he was incensed. After a short period of uneasy peace, on November 30, 1170, Becket crossed to England with the intention of disciplining the bishops who had partaken in the improper coronation. He preached fire from the pulpit in Canterbury Cathedral on Christmas Day, excommunicating virtually everyone he could recall who had ever wronged him.

Then he announced severe sentences against those who had taken part in Henry the Young King's coronation.

Word of Becket's provocative and unrestrained activities in England reached Henry at his Christmas court in Bures, in Lower Normandy. On receiving the news, he uttered a phrase now among the most infamous in history: "What miserable drones and traitors have I nurtured and promoted in my household who let their lord be treated with such shameful contempt by a lowborn clerk!" (This is often rendered incorrectly as "Will no one rid me of this troublesome priest?")

On December 29 four heavily armed men smashed through a side door to Canterbury Cathedral with an ax. The archbishop of Canterbury was waiting for them inside. They were angry. He was unarmed. They tried to arrest him. He resisted. They hacked the top of his head off and mashed his brains with their boots.

The four knights who murdered Becket seem to have believed that Henry wanted them to do so. It was a belief that spread in the shocked weeks and months following Becket's death. Henry, having recently fancied himself the greatest man in Europe and inheritor of Henry I, was suddenly a pariah. Not only the Church, but the whole of European society was outraged by the murder. It seemed likely that Pope Alexander, who refused to speak to an Englishman for a week after he received news of Becket's death, was ready to excommunicate Henry. Fortune's wheel turned sharply downward. Henry's position, built so carefully on political cunning and dynamic leadership, had exploded, thanks to a few words spoken in anger. Now under the most intense pressure of his political career, the best that the king could do was flee. He went to a corner of his empire where it was highly unlikely anyone would follow, Ireland.

Henry landed at Waterford, in Ireland, in October 1171. His time there proved a useful distraction, as it expanded the scope of his influence to the western limits of the British Isles and kept him conveniently away from the European spotlight.

The situation in Ireland was complex. Although Henry had been given permission to invade Ireland by Pope Adrian IV in 1155, he had never followed up the offer. But latterly, civil war had engulfed Ireland. The king of Leinster, Diarmait MacMurchada, had been deposed by a coalition of enemies under Rory O'Connor and forced into exile in England. Henry had granted Diarmait permission to recruit an invasion force from among the

Anglo-Norman barons, and Diarmait had used their support well, regaining his throne and handsomely rewarding the barons who had helped him. These included Richard FitzGilbert de Clare, the son of a former earl of Pembroke, whose nickname, Strongbow, became famous across Europe. Diarmait, Strongbow, and their allies were taking on the role of Irish colonizers and accruing to themselves the sort of autonomous power that Henry found irksome among men whom he considered his vassals and subjects. Strongbow in particular was a troubling figure. Tall, fair, and statesmanlike, he commanded respect and admiration from those (like the writer Gerald of Wales) who wrote about him. He had married Diarmait's daughter Eve, and when Diarmait died in May 1171, he inherited the lordship of Leinster and huge amounts of territory in southern Ireland.

Henry brought with him a large army and threatening siege equipment, but this was a show of strength, not a serious attempt to throw men like Strongbow out of Ireland. Henry was satisfied by the recognition of his authority and was pleased when all of Ireland's invading lords and a large number of the native princes submitted to him. Strongbow was stripped of his lands and titles and then regranted most of them as fiefs held explicitly from the English king. Lordship, and the pecking order of princes, was firmly established. Henry's tidy mind was satisfied.

Henry spent six months in Ireland in all, reorganizing jurisdictions and establishing his rights and prerogatives as high king. And as he busied himself, the horror that had engulfed Christendom following Becket's murder began to subside. Pope Alexander III thawed sufficiently to write to Henry, commending him for his efforts in Ireland. The pope told the Irish bishops that the English king was "our dearest son in Christ," who had "subjugated this barbarous and uncouth race which is ignorant of divine law," and demanded that they assist him as best they could. In spring 1172 Henry was sufficiently rehabilitated to return to the Continent for a reconciliatory meeting that produced a peace between king and Church, known as the Compromise of Avranches.

The compromise ended Henry's painful breach with the Church. It was a worldly agreement that decreed a concordat might in theory be made between church and state, while avoiding most of the bigger questions about how that could practically be achieved. Henry was obliged to drop his insistence that his English bishops observe the letter of the Constitutions of Clarendon, and there were some well-meaning clauses pertaining to crusading obligations. It allowed all parties to go about their business with face saved and conflict averted. Yet to some contemporaries, it seemed that Henry ought still to be punished for his harsh words over Christmas in 1170. And so it proved. Within a year of the Compromise of Avranches, divine punishment was visited on the king of England. According to *The Chronicle of Battle Abbey*, "the Lord's martyr, or rather the Lord, for his martyr, seemed to seek vengeance for the innocent blood." The punishment came from a quarter that hurt the Plantagenet king most of all: his family.

The Eagle's Nest

The rebellion that gripped the Plantagenet lands in 1173 was, on the heels of the Becket affair, the most serious crisis Henry faced during the course of his long reign. Apparently out of nowhere, Henry's wife and his three oldest sons rose in arms against the thirty-nine-year-old king. Together with a patchwork of allies that included some of the most powerful men in Christendom, the Plantagenet children raised men and garrisoned castles far and wide throughout their extensive territories. Henry, taken at first by surprise, soon realized that he faced united opposition from across Europe, galvanized by the involvement of his family. He was forced to fight on multiple fronts for more than a year as his network of territories threatened to collapse. He later likened the war to the experience of an eagle, pecked and destroyed by its own chicks.

The trouble began with Henry the Young King. In early 1173 young Henry was approaching his eighteenth birthday. He was on the cusp of manhood and married to Louis VII's daughter Princess Margaret. Henry was tall, blond, and good-looking, a skilled horseman with highly cultivated manners, a real fondness for the tournament, and a huge household of followers who egged on his chivalrous ambitions. He was a twice-crowned king, for his controversial coronation by Roger archbishop of York had been followed in August 1172 by a second ceremony in Winchester, presided over by Rotrou archbishop of Rouen, where his wife was crowned alongside him. On both occasions Henry had been anointed with chrism, an especially holy oil, and treated with extraordinary reverence in the company of vast numbers of knights. At one coronation banquet he had been personally served by his father. The young king reveled in his own magnificence and was widely seen as arrogant, greedy, feckless, and glib.

Despite his exalted position as his father's heir, the Young King was denied the real fruits of kingship. As he approached manhood, his access to landed revenue was strictly limited. Although he had been given many titles, he was never properly invested with the lands and revenues of his ostensible dominions. He was thus heavily in debt, the result of maintaining a lavish courtly lifestyle without the means to pay for it. And his pride was wounded. Henry II had been sixteen when the full duchy of Normandy was settled on him. At eighteen his eldest son had virtually nothing. His frustrations were fed enthusiastically by his father-in-law, Louis VII.

The breach between Henry and his father was triggered by arrangements for the six-year-old John's marriage. To provide for John, Henry II gave him a wedding gift of three castles: Chinon, Loudon, and Mirebeau. These fortresses were strategically important, lying between Anjou and Maine. Chinon in particular was an important center of Plantagenet power, a linchpin in what the Young King viewed as his rightful inheritance. All were part of the power bloc that young Henry felt he had been denied. Within days of the castles' being granted, a furious young Henry slipped away from his father's company and rode for the court of the French king. A rebellion had begun.

For Henry II to fall out with his eldest son was understandable, perhaps even inevitable. What was more surprising was that Richard (who was fifteen) and Geoffrey (fourteen) should also have joined the rebellion, riding from their mother's side at Poitiers to join Louis. "The sons took up arms against their father at just the time when everywhere Christians were laying down their arms in reverence for Easter," wrote the chronicler Ralph de Diceto. Public opinion pointed to Eleanor of Aquitaine as the person responsible for stirring up her younger sons to join the revolt against her husband. Henry himself seems to have believed it because he had the archbishop of Rouen write a letter to his wife reminding her of the duty to "return with your sons to the husband whom you must obey and with whom it is your duty to live."

Why Eleanor turned against her husband after such a long period of quiet loyalty remains to this day something of a mystery. It has been attributed to peevishness at having been discarded by her husband for his mistress Rosamund Clifford (a theory that has no basis at all in fact), or resentment at the influence of Henry II's mother, the empress Matilda (ludicrous because Matilda had died six years earlier). It is likely that the queen had a rather more substantial grievance.

In 1173 Eleanor was as politically disenchanted as her eldest son. During the first fifteen years of her marriage to Henry she had been occupied with producing children. Since John's birth in 1167 that period in her life had ceased, and she had resumed her role as duchess of Aquitaine, exercising political control over the great southern quarter of the dominions she had brought to her husband. Yet in 1173 she, like Henry the Young King, found her political role undermined. Even as she acted out her part as duchess of Aquitaine, Eleanor's independent control over her duchy was slowly being eroded. Ignoring his wife's prerogative, Henry had begun to dispose of parts of Aquitaine as he saw fit. He granted Gascony as their daughter Eleanor's dowry when she married the king of Castile. Then, when making a peace with Raymond count of Toulouse, he instructed the count to pay homage to Henry the Young King, who held no rights in Aquitaine. This told Eleanor that her husband had begun to see her duchy as subject to the Anglo-Norman Crown, rather than as an autonomous part of a broader Plantagenet federation. Like her eldest son, Eleanor began to feel that she had been granted a hollow crown. She chose to rebel to secure her rightful control over her lands.

Eleanor did not view Aquitaine's independence solely in the light of her own prestige. Its future independence was also a vital matter for her favorite son, Richard. Under Henry's succession plan, Richard was to become duke of Aquitaine. To that end he had been installed in 1170 as count of Poitou, the natural first post on the way to becoming duke. Eleanor had set up a regency council for Richard and took a keen interest in his political development. Would Richard, when he reached eighteen, be scavenging for scraps of real authority in the duchy that Eleanor was teaching him how to govern? This would have been an intolerable situation for both of them.

And so Eleanor began to contemplate a grand coalition with one man whom she would never have imagined siding with, her former husband, Louis VII of France. At the end of February she set out on horseback cross-country for Paris, where her three eldest sons were already ensconced with the French king.

For the second time in her life Eleanor rode in mortal danger across the French countryside. The chronicler Gervase of Canterbury tells us that Eleanor dressed in male costume as she headed from the castle of Faye-la-Vineuse, near Poitiers, in the direction of Chartres. Despite her disguise, she did not reach her destination. Eleanor was nearly fifty now and not as vigorous as the young woman who had evaded two suitors on her flight to Henry in 1152. She was recognized and arrested by Henry's agents and taken as a prisoner to Chinon Castle. When news leaked to the chroniclers of the day that the queen had been taken while dressed in male clothing, there was an outpouring of scandal and disbelief.

Eleanor was captured early, but she had already guided her sons into the French king's arms. When Henry II discovered their treachery, he sent messengers to Paris instructing the boys to quit their foolishness. The messengers found Henry the Young King in the company of Louis VII. When they asked him to return to his father, Louis VII interjected: "Who asks?"

"The king of England," came the reply.

Not so, retorted Louis, looking at the younger Henry. "The king of England is here."

Both sides prepared for a long fight. Louis VII and the Plantagenet boys attracted a wide coalition of the disgruntled to join them, many enticed by ridiculous promises of enrichment from Henry the Young King's realms. Louis had a special seal cut for him, and young Henry set about using it. The whole county of Kent was signed away, along with important territories in Mortain and Touraine and thousands of pounds of revenue. With such gifts on offer Philip count of Flanders, Matthew count of Boulogne, and Theobald count of Blois took up the cause enthusiastically.

In England they were supported by Robert earl of Leicester, son of the elder Robert who had served Henry II loyally as joint justiciar until his death a few years previously. Several northern earls and the bishop of Durham also joined the revolt, as did Hugh Bigod earl of Norfolk. Finally, the rebels recruited William the Lion, the king of Scotland since 1165, when he had succeeded his father, a man so hated by Henry II that the very mention of his name was once said to have sent Henry into spasms of rage as he thrashed about on the floor of his bedchamber, eating the straw from his mattress. William was promised all the lands that Malcolm IV had held in England during the Anarchy.

These gifts of land and sovereignty show how callow and limited was young Henry's real understanding of kingship. Throughout the Great War that raged during the following eighteen months, Henry the Young King served mainly as a puppet for Louis VII and those allies who wished to erode Plantagenet power. The first stage of the war took place during the summer of 1173. In May the rebels attacked towns in the Vexin, without success. In June and July they captured Aumale and Driencourt, where Matthew of Boulogne was hit by an arrow fired from the castle walls and killed. In July Louis and Henry the Younger besieged Verneuil, but the castle held out for long enough for Henry II to arrive with relief. The rebel troops fled, and Henry's men slaughtered their rear guard as they gave chase.

Meanwhile, in late June, the Scots attacked Northumbria. It was not an impressive campaign. They failed to capture the castles at Wark or Warkworth, ravaged the area around Newcastle-upon-Tyne without consequence, and engaged in a huge and bloody melee before the vast stone walls of Carlisle. The loyalist forces, led by the castellan Robert de Vaux, fought with valor and courage and seized from the Scots provisions and booty, which allowed them to withstand the subsequent siege. When news reached the Scots that a loyal army was approaching from the south under the justiciar, Richard de Lucy, they melted away to cause a minor nuisance elsewhere in the border region.

The rebels' strategy during 1173 was elementary and unsuccessful. They tried to open multiple fronts, dragging Henry II around and hitting him hardest when he was absent. Yet this played to Henry's greatest strength: moving at pace around his dominions, acting decisively, and deploying mercenaries with pinpoint accuracy to break resistance. He moved his troops around on punishing forced marches, at one point apparently crossing Normandy from Rouen to Dol in two days. He packed his armies with fearsome Brabanter mercenaries, costly but highly skilled, mobile, and vicious. Henry wrote that he favored them for their skills in battle, fearlessness on the attack, and ferocity exceeding that of wild beasts.

Henry's energetic tactics not only cowed his less resolute enemies but also exposed the French king as a bad general and a listless leader. This was quickly obvious, and Henry did his best to exploit it, offering his sons generous terms to lay down their arms during peace talks at Gisors. The talks were abandoned when Robert earl of Leicester, who had joined forces with the rebels, created a scene, drawing his sword and shouting obscenities at Henry. The king still had enough opponents across his vast domains for war to extend through the summer.

As hostilities continued on multiple fronts, Henry benefited from having highly competent subordinates across his lands. He had set up each of his territories under the administration of talented men who could operate the machinery of government in his absence. Unlike his sons and their allies, he had no need to bribe men to stick by his cause. Men like Richard de Lucy, the justiciar of England, supported their king out of loyalty and the bonds of service. Despite everything, the Church supported him too.

In September the focus of war moved to England, where the earl of Leicester and another rebel baron, Hugh Bigod, hired bands of Flemish weavers turned mercenaries and attempted to ravage England. They landed in Framlingham and attempted to move northwest through East Anglia toward the Midlands. As the hired soldiers tramped through the countryside, the flat, chilly plains rang with their battle songs.

No one who remembered the dark days of the Anarchy could have been pleased to see Flemings back in England. At Dunwich women and children hurled rocks at the rebel army. Richard de Lucy gathered a great deal of support from the English magnates, though it was said that they were still outnumbered four to one when battle was joined in the marshland at Fornham, near Bury St. Edmunds. But the loyalists won a resounding victory, scattering the earl's knights and leaving the mercenaries to be attacked by local people. Many of them drowned in the fenland bogs.

The winter was no season for warfare, and it brought the customary truces. But when spring broke in 1174, war resumed. This time the situation grew perilous in England. The king of Scots had regrouped during the winter, and his forces were swelling. The loyalists suffered a series of defeats at Northampton, Nottingham, and Leicester, while their hold on Northumbria was uncertain. To cap it all, Philip of Flanders had sworn on a holy relic that he would undertake a full-scale invasion of England by July. After repeated pleas from the English magnates, Henry finally left the Continent and sailed for England.

He put to sea in July 1174 at Barfleur, with a vast army of Brabanter mercenaries and members of his immediate family: the Young King's wife, Queen Margaret, and his children, Joanna and John. He also took with him a number of captives, including his own wife.

Conditions at sea were wild, with a rough wind and violent waves. When his sailors expressed concern, Henry stood before his entire crew and told them that if God wished him to be restored to his kingdom, he would deliver them safely to port.

God's will was at the top of Henry's mind. He arrived in Southampton with one object before he engaged in battle. It was perhaps the masterstroke of his entire campaign. Rather than head directly for East Anglia, where Philip of Flanders was mustering his forces, Henry made for Canterbury. Henry could be a stubborn man, but he was usually sensitive to others' perception of him. He knew that many people thought the Lord had rained rebellion and discord upon him in revenge for Becket's death. He also realized that while rebellion was tangled up with the cause of the blessed martyr Thomas, there could be no hope of peace.

Three days after his landing, Henry arrived in Canterbury determined to put on a show. Ralph de Diceto described the scene: "When he reached Canterbury he leaped off his horse and, putting aside his royal dignity, he assumed the appearance of a pilgrim, a penitent, a supplicant, and on Friday 12 July, went to the cathedral. There, with streaming tears, groans, and sighs, he made his way to the glorious martyr's tomb. Prostrating himself with his arms outstretched, he remained there a long time in prayer."

With the bishop of London looking on, Henry protested with God as his witness that he had not intended Becket's death but acknowledged that by his rash words he had inadvertently caused it. Diceto continued: "He asked for absolution from the bishops then present, and subjected his flesh to harsh discipline from cuts with rods, receiving three or even five strokes from each of the monks in turn, of whom a large number had gathered. . . . He spent the rest of the day and also the whole of the following night in bitterness of soul, given over to prayer and sleeplessness, and continuing his fast for three days. . . . There is no doubt that he had by now placated the martyr." Indeed he had. With this extraordinary show of public penance Henry had won the most important propaganda battle of the war. The chronicles buzzed with reports of this great king prostrate, half-naked, and bleeding as he was whipped in the harshest manner.

Far away from Canterbury, on the morning after King Henry's penance, William the Lion was resting, his helmet by his side as he ate breakfast. The Scottish king had renewed his attacks on the northern castles he had been promised in return for his complicity in the rebellion. Wark had withstood fierce blows with picks and siege irons, an assault with catapults, and an attempt to burn it down. William had sent forces against Carlisle and Prudhoe, also without success. As he breakfasted, he contemplated his next move, an attack on the formidable polygonal shell of the castle at Alnwick.

Then disaster struck. A band of Yorkshire knights who had been tracking the Scots from Prudhoe to Alnwick launched a surprise attack. A fierce battle broke out in which all the Scottish knights were either killed or captured. William the Lion was among those taken prisoner.

It was late at night, and Henry was in bed at Canterbury when he had the news of William's capture at Alnwick, brought by an exhausted messenger who had flogged his horses nonstop from the north to be first with the news. Brimming with joy, the king leaped out of his bed and roused all his barons to tell them the incredible news, thanking God and the martyr Thomas for his good fortune. With one fortunate event, the heart was ripped out of the rebellion.

With only the slightest military effort, Henry now consolidated his power in England, vanquishing his enemies in the Midlands and East Anglia. Those who were not subdued by force had surrendered to the old king by the end of July. On August 8, 1174, Henry was back in Barfleur. He had been away for less than a month.

During that time Louis, Henry the Young King, and Philip of Flanders had broken into Norman territory and besieged Rouen. Henry had gambled that he would be able to smash his way to a rapid victory in England before the citizens of Rouen gave in. The gamble had been rewarded. Now, confident of victory, he gathered another force, made up of fierce Welsh mercenaries as well as his trusted Brabanters. The French soon dropped their siege. Shortly afterward Louis VII sued for peace.

"Peace was restored after the kingdom's shipwreck," wrote Henry's treasurer, Richard FitzNigel. "The most powerful men who conspired . . . learned that it is difficult or impossible to snatch the club from the hand of Hercules." Henry's skill and good fortune as a general had allowed him to outflank the inferior French king and his own callow sons. He had survived the betrayal of his wife, Eleanor, who was now locked away in an English castle, probably at Salisbury. He could afford to be merciful to his sons when they sued for peace at Montlouis in 1174.

Having demonstrated his mastery at Montlouis, Henry allowed that everyone who had rebelled might have his lands and possessions back in the same state as a fortnight before the rebellion began. He endowed each of his sons with castles or revenue, although not the power that they craved, for Henry lived in justifiable fear of dispersing his lands before his death. The Young King received two castles in Normandy and fifteen thousand pounds of revenue from Anjou in return for confirming the wedding grants of border castles that had been made to John. Richard received two mansions in Poitou and half its annual revenues. Geoffrey received half of Brittany's annual revenues, and arrangements were made to formalize his marriage to Constance, the heiress to the duchy. Henry forbade his sons to ask for any more than he should choose to give them; then he sent Richard and Geoffrey off to Poitou and Brittany to stamp out the embers of the rebellion they had stirred up.

Henry reserved his real wrath for his wife. Eleanor had abused her position overseeing Richard's fledgling regency in Aquitaine. She had stirred her three eldest sons to rebellion with the same callousness as had her former husband in Paris. And she had rebelled against her sex and status. Eleanor was kept in courteous imprisonment, or palace arrest, in various southern English castles for the remainder of Henry's reign. She made a few appearances at court as the years passed, but she was never again trusted by Henry, who briefly attempted to secure papal approval for a divorce. This came to nothing, and Eleanor remained an exile from the duchy she loved, a punishment that could not have been more devastating.

The last significant rebel with whom Henry had to deal was William the Lion. If Eleanor received the most psychologically cruel treatment for her part in the rebellion, then William was punished with the harshest political terms. On December 1, 1174, he was forced to agree to the Treaty of Falaise. Sealed at York, this made William a personal liegeman of both Henry II and Henry the Young King, confiscated castles, and ordered the forced allegiance of the Scottish barons, bishops, and clergy to the English Crown and Church. The Scottish Crown was thus subordinated to England's, its dignity formally crushed.

But even in Scotland his retribution was limited, for Henry was interested less in revenge than in restoring regular government to his dominions. The peace at Montlouis showed Henry at his most astute. It was the high point of his entire reign.

Henry Triumphant

The Plantagenet court of the mid-1170s was uncommonly magnificent. Henry's victory in the Great War established him as the preeminent ruler in Europe. Louis VII had been roundly defeated. In 1177 the French king would sign a nonaggression pact at Ivry, recognizing that the French and English kings were "henceforth to be friends, and that each of us will to the best of his ability defend the other in life and limb." Henry's three eldest sons, who would form the next generation of European rulers, had been put to good use across their father's dominions, snuffing out the embers of their own revolt. The king of Scots had acknowledged Henry's supremacy in the humiliating Treaty of Falaise. In 1175 the king of Connaught, in Ireland, Rory O'Connor, agreed to the Treaty of Windsor, which confirmed Henry as feudal overlord of most of Ireland and allowed him two years later to nominate his young son John as high king of the whole country. It seemed that none of Henry's illustrious neighbors could compete with him. Even the emperor Frederick Barbarossa's fortunes paled by comparison: while the king of England basked in military triumph, the emperor lost a long-running war with the Lombard League in May 1176 and felt his power in southern Europe seriously diminished.

Everyone now looked to the king of England as the greatest ruler in Europe. His court received envoys and ambassadors from all over the Christian world: from Barbarossa, the emperor of Constantinople, the archbishop of Reims, the duke of Savoy, and the count of Flanders. The pope sent a legate, Cardinal Huguzon, who remained for several years and attempted to persuade Henry to support a revived European crusading movement by taking the cross, the term used for formally declaring an intention to join the Church's holy war. Even William the Lion was a regular visitor to the royal court and council. Henry was called on to arbitrate disputes between the great lords of southern Europe. There were prestigious offers of marriage for his two younger daughters. His eldest girl, Matilda, was already duchess of Saxony by virtue of her marriage in 1166 to Henry the Lion. Even greater prospects now beckoned for Matilda's sisters. In 1176 the king's youngest daughter, ten-year-old Joan, was sent to be married to

King William II of Sicily. The following year a fourteen-year-old Eleanor was married to Alfonso VIII king of Castile. The Plantagenets' influence was spreading to every corner of Europe.

If his international prestige was at its zenith, Henry also regained his authority in his own lands—especially in England—with astonishing speed and political intelligence. The two great aims of his reign had been to secure the frontiers of his empire and to deepen his authority within the areas he ruled. The Great War had left him largely triumphant over the enemies who had harassed his borders. From 1174 on his attention turned to the second aim.

The eruption of violence in 1173 had left England once again dotted with castles and fortifications occupied by the king's enemies. Just as during King Stephen's reign, these timber or stone garrisons with their fierce ramparts and deep ditches loomed against the skyline, proclaiming the local power of whichever lords kept them. To Henry, castles occupied without his explicit approval were affronts to his rule. According to Roger of Howden, in 1176 Henry "took every castle in England into his own hand." He expelled the castellans and placed his own men in charge. To stress the fact that this was a demonstration of his supreme public authority rather than a partisan act of revenge, Henry forced even his own most loyal servants, including Richard de Lucy, who had done so much to win the war in England, to give up their castles. Some were destroyed; others, redistributed to the great men of the land. The message was unmistakable: the authority by which the barons and bishops of England held castles and arms derived from one source only, the king.

Castles and their keepers had always been a vital matter to Henry. Since the Norman invasion castles had been the ultimate symbols of military authority. Henry spent heavily on them throughout his reign—at least twenty-one thousand pounds on rebuilding castles in England alone. He hastened the general movement in English castle building away from timber structures and toward more permanent and impregnable stone fortresses. Particularly extensive works were undertaken at Newcastle-upon-Tyne, Nottingham, Orford, Windsor, and Winchester. Improvements made to the stone keeps of castles in Scarborough and Bowes secured the border region with Scotland. The Norman chronicler Robert of Torigni noted that Henry's reign saw castles built "not only in Normandy but also in England, in the duchy of Aquitaine, in the county of Anjou, in Maine and Touraine."

But the jewel that glittered brightest among all of Henry's castle-building projects was at Dover, at the head of the soaring white cliffs that overlooked the sea approach to England from northwestern France. William the Conqueror had erected an earth-and-timber fortress on the site of an Iron Age hill fort. Henry's massive reconstruction of his great-grandfather's castle took twelve years to complete and cost nearly sixty-five hundred pounds, more than two-thirds of the total expenditure on English castles during the final decade of his reign. When Louis VII visited England for the first time, for a four-day expedition to Becket's shrine in August 1179, Dover Castle was the first thing the French king and his companion, Philip count of Flanders, saw. Before they left, Henry proudly took his guests on a tour of the building site. Louis was by now a frail fifty-nine-year-old, and Henry must have thoroughly enjoyed guiding his old adversary around the magnificent fortification. An imposing wall overlooked the cliffs and the sea approach, and work was beginning on a massive stone keep that would stand comparison with the great castles of his Continental empire: the Angevin fortresses at Loches, Loudon, Montbazon, Montrichard, and Beaugency and the great Norman works at Falaise, at Caen, and on the border with France.

Castle building was just one part of a wider drive on Henry's part to extend his authority in the 1170s. For besides being a soldier, Henry was an astute, legal-minded politician. Having consolidated his hold on his realm, he embarked on a decade of legal revolution that was to influence the government of England for generations to follow.

Henry's greatest piece of legislative work before the Great War had been the Assize of Clarendon, decreed in February 1166, which had brought the entire system of English criminal law beneath overarching royal control. Under the Normans, justice had been served by a patchwork of local courts and jurisdictions that answered variously to the king, his barons, and the Church. Now, in response to what Henry had seen as the lawlessness of the 1160s, the ultimate responsibility for dealing with robbery, homicide, theft, and the harboring of criminals was given to royal sheriffs and justices. Baronial and ecclesiastical courts still existed, but they were superseded throughout England by the king's law. A standard procedure for dealing with crime was introduced. Criminals were to be rooted out through juries of presentment—empaneled bodies, usually of twelve men, who were required to tell the sheriff or justice under oath all the crimes that had been committed in their local communities. The suspects were then tried by the ordeal of water, a ghastly ritual in which the accused was tied up and immersed in a pond, river, or lake. To sink was a sign of innocence, to float a sign of guilt, which would be punished by mutilation (cutting off the convict's right foot), banishment, or death. A guilty man's possessions would revert to the Crown.

Under the Assize of Clarendon, royal sheriffs were awarded the right to investigate crimes regardless of whether they would have to cross into great lords' private jurisdictions. "Let there be no one, within his castle or without his castle ... who shall forbid the sheriffs to enter into his court or his land," said the assize. This was a truly revolutionary measure, for with it the hand of royal justice reached, or aimed to reach, into every corner of England. The king's law now clearly trumped all other jurisdictions. Legally and judicially Henry had declared himself master of his own realm.

In 1176, after the rebellion, this idea was symbolically more important than ever. In January the Assize of Northampton reissued, modified, and strengthened the laws that had been made a decade earlier at Clarendon. The disruption caused by the Great War had led to increased disorder and crime. Punishments were therefore made harsher: those sentenced to mutilation would now lose their right hand as well as their right foot; those who survived the ordeal of water but were still suspected of felonies were banished regardless. To bring justice to the people, Henry and his advisers divided England into six judicial circuits, or eyres, and royal judges began a tour of the whole realm, designed both to restore England to order by punishing evildoers and criminals and to establish the king's law as the final and ultimate form of public authority. Crimes were investigated retrospectively to ensure that the royal justices could punish, in the words of the assize, "all offenses ... except minor thefts and robberies which were committed in time of war, as of horses, oxen, and lesser things."

At the same time as this reform of criminal law, Henry pushed a new royal prerogative in overseeing civil law. When word came back from his justices out on eyre that land dispossession was as great a problem as crimes against his subjects themselves, Henry decided to introduce a system by which land disputes could be quickly settled by appeal to the royal law. A new legal process known as the assize of novel disseisin put this into action. It allowed royal justices to question juries about contested lands. They asked whether a plaintiff had been unjustly disseised (i.e., dispossessed) of a piece of land; if the jurors found that he had, then the justices decided whether it was the defendant in the case who was to blame. The losing party was amerced—penalized with damages—for the loss he had caused.

In twelfth-century England land was power, and arbitrating land disputes between his greatest subjects was a vital function of the king. Now, in theory, all the land in England could be protected, contested, and recovered simply by purchasing a writ from the king's chancery. This would begin an action of novel disseisin, ultimately managed by the local sheriff. The writ was short and formulaic. The thirteenth-century legal writer Bracton recorded that devising the wording of the writ had caused Henry and his counselors many sleepless nights. If this was true—and it has the ring of truth about it—then it was with good reason. Royal law and royal officials were now indispensable to the functioning of political landed society not only when the royal magnates came into contact with the court but every day, at the county level. One of the king's most important roles, from the perspective of his barons, had been devolved to a simple bureaucratic machine. Disputes could be settled by an application to chancery, rather than by an appeal to the king in person—an invaluable development, given the vast size of the Plantagenet dominions and Henry's penchant for traveling around them relentlessly and at speed.

In 1178 the royal council (or curia regis) was reorganized. Instead of following the king wherever he went, hearing appeals for justice as they traveled, five members of the royal council were appointed to remain at Westminster, to hear legal cases full-time. This effectively became England's supreme court and would, in time, become known as the Court of King's Bench. The legal machinery of England was established, independent of King Henry II but exercising his full authority (and generating handsome fees for its services as it did so).

By 1179 further writs governing land law were available, and yet more of the king's traditional, personal legal role had devolved to a chancery mechanism. *Darrein presentment* established rights over appointments to Church benefices. *Mort d'ancestor* settled disputes over inheritances. The writ *de recto*, or writ of right, allowed lesser men who believed they had been denied justice by their local lord's private court to appeal to the royal court over his head. This writ had existed for some time, but now it too became formulaic and invested the sheriff as the leading authority for ensuring that justice was done at a county level. All this amounted to the start of a revolution in royal government.

So, as Henry settled his dominions after the throes of the Great War, England was slowly transformed. The castles that dotted the landscape, either occupied by the king's servants or licensed by him for their use, became potent symbols of the royal monopoly on military power in general. The Assize of Arms of 1181 encouraged the development of scutage, payments made by magnates in lieu of supplying troops and military service, which helped further demilitarize the English barons and defray the cost of hiring mercenaries. In the shires of England, the fingers of royal justice were suddenly everywhere. The power of the Crown was now firmly rooted in English soil.

In February 1182, on the cusp of his forty-ninth birthday, Henry held a great council at Bishop's Waltham, in Hampshire, where he announced that he had made his will. It was firmly nonpolitical. He had made bequests to the Knights Templar and Hospitaller and left five thousand silver marks to the religious houses of England and one thousand silver marks to those of Anjou. Two hundred gold marks were left to assist with the dowries of poor virgins in Normandy and Anjou. He commanded his four sons— Henry, Geoffrey, Richard, and John—to cause his will "to be firmly and inviolably kept; and whoever shall oppose or contravene it, may he incur the indignation and anger of Almighty God, and mine and God's malediction." The will made no provision for Eleanor, who remained under close guard.

Henry continued to travel far and wide across his lands, dividing his time mainly between England and Normandy. But in a sense he had completed his mission. The judicial reforms of the 1170s marked the last aggressive phase of his energetic rule. He had been in perpetual motion for more than three decades. It was time to consider his legacy. After 1182 Henry's thoughts were turning to the best way to turn over his vast territories to his sons. It was here that all his decades of triumph would dissolve, finally, into heartbreak.

A World on Fire

For all his inventiveness and natural vigor, by the time Henry II approached his fiftieth birthday in 1183 he was feeling old. A busy life had taken its toll. His legs, long bowed from a life in the saddle, now ached constantly. He had been kicked in the thigh by a horse in 1174, and the injury had left him with a wound—perhaps a fractured femur—that never properly healed. It affected his general health and slowed him down. He must have walked with a permanent limp. He still moved incessantly around his territories, but his travels were now interrupted by occasional bouts of illness. Although Henry was pressed by Rome to take up the cross and lead a new crusade to the East, it was becoming clear that he would do no such thing.

The world was moving on. King Louis VII had died, aged sixty, on September 18, 1180, after a long illness that ended in a series of paralyzing strokes. Louis's fifteen-year-old son had been crowned co-king a year before his death, and now he succeeded him as Philip II. Suddenly Henry had to negotiate treaties and make policy in consultation with a teenage boy rather than a man a decade older than himself. Philip was younger than all three of Henry's eldest sons and only a matter of months older than John. Henry seemed like a figure from another time. The whole of France would soon belong to these boys.

Henry the Young King was to be Philip II's new sparring partner. He too had been crowned as junior king, and he occasionally styled himself in charters as "king of England, duke of Normandy and count of Aquitaine, son of King Henry," while referring to his father as "of famous memory." Philip's full accession to the throne only sharpened his hunger.

Young Henry's practical experience of ruling was still virtually nonexistent. He was twenty-eight years old in February 1183 and, despite all his titles and his marriage to a Capetian princess, had very little actual power. In part because of this, he had developed little by way of political intelligence or military skill. He still struck many contemporaries as vain, shallow, and immature, with notions of grandeur but no understanding of the real business of kingship. The Young King devoted most of his time and energy to the tournament field. Along with Philip count of Flanders and Baldwin count of Hainault he was a regular on the glamorous European sporting circuit. The Young King spent exorbitant amounts of money styling himself as a dazzling chivalrous hero. His tournament captain was William Marshal, a man who had been his tutor until 1170 and was developing a reputation as one of the gallant knights in Europe. When Philip II was crowned at Reims in 1179, it was the Young King who represented the Plantagenets at the ceremony, carrying the Capetian Crown during the procession and bringing five hundred knights to the celebratory tournament that followed. Yet for all this finery, he knew how little real power he wielded. In frustration, he began to flex his muscles within his father's territories, with results that were embarrassing and almost calamitous.

During the late summer of 1182 the Young King renewed his demands to his father for what the chronicler Roger of Howden described as "some territory, where he and his wife might dwell, and from which he might be able to support knights in his service." The implication was that he wished to take formal possession of the duchy of Normandy. Henry refused. Just as he had in 1173, the Young King flew into a humiliated rage and took himself away to the French court, to ally himself defiantly with Philip II. It was only with repeated offers of an increased allowance that Henry II coaxed his son back and brought him to a family conference that was held immediately after Christmas. Henry presided over a meeting at Le Mans that included the Young King, his two eldest brothers, Richard and Geoffrey, and the duke of Saxony, who had recently been expelled from his duchy along with his wife, Henry's eldest daughter, Matilda.

Henry's aim at the meeting was to ensure that all three of his elder sons remained reconciled to his plans to divide the Plantagenet dominions for the future. That meant placating his eldest son with some sign of his exalted status without alienating the younger sons too much. Henry demanded that all the boys give him a solemn oath of their allegiance, before requiring Richard and Geoffrey to do homage to the Young King, for their respective duchies of Aquitaine and Brittany.

Richard refused. As duke of Aquitaine he owed homage to the king of France, not the king of England, and he had no intention of altering the status quo. He had spent most of the decade since the Great War establishing his preeminence in Aquitaine, honing his fine military brain in the ceaseless effort to stamp down the rebellious vassal lords of his mother's duchy. That task had lately grown far more difficult thanks to his eldest brother. The Young King had been making treacherous overtures to the barons of Aquitaine, insinuating that he could offer them better lordship than Richard and stirring up rebellion that his brother had to fight hard to keep in check. There was no love lost between Richard, whose education and upbringing under Eleanor's eye had honed the gifts of a naturally brilliant soldier, and his vain and posturing brother. At Le Mans their feud spilled over into bitter argument, and Richard stormed out of the conference and returned to Aquitaine to fortify his castles. The Young King sent his wife to safety in Paris, allied himself with Geoffrey, who was described memorably by Gerald of Wales as "overflowing with words, soft as oil . . . able to corrupt two kingdoms with his tongue; of tireless endeavor, a hypocrite in everything, a deceiver and a dissembler," and prepared to attack. Henry II could not stand by as two of his sons made civil war on the other and had little choice but to back Richard. Thus the old king celebrated his fiftieth birthday, on March 5, 1183, attempting to bring some order to what threatened to be a disastrous battle between the Plantagenet family's younger generation. Meanwhile Eleanor of Aquitaine, who was perhaps the only person who might have been able to effect a resolution, remained under close house arrest in England.

The Young King's conduct in the short war that ensued was appalling. He negotiated in bad faith with his father; had his servants attack diplomatic envoys; robbed townspeople, churches, and shrines throughout Aquitaine to pay for his mercenaries; and attempted—without much success—to raise the lords of Aquitaine in a general revolt against Richard's rule. Henry II and Richard hired soldiers and scrambled from town to town, keeping control of a dangerous situation as best they could.

Fate rather than strategy finally brought hostilities to a close. In early June, shortly after carrying out an attack on a church in Quercy, the Young King was struck down with dysentery. After a short and severe illness he died on June 11, in the southern town of Martel. Shortly before he died, the Young King asked William Marshal, his former tutor and tournament companion, to carry to Jerusalem the crusader's cross that he had recently taken. It was said that he also made a deathbed request that his mother's terms of imprisonment might be loosened. At the end of the month his body was brought for burial to Rouen. The world was rid of a glib and troublesome young man. The Young King had never been allowed to grow up, but he had shown precious few signs of wishing to do so. Even so, his death threw all of his father's carefully laid succession plans into disarray.

Once he had recovered from his grief, Henry began to plan a new future. In the autumn of 1183 he told Richard that he should now give up Aquitaine to his youngest brother, John. The implication was that Richard should step into the Young King's shoes as heir to England, Normandy, and Anjou and allow John to take over the inheritance of Aquitaine.

Richard adamantly refused. Aquitaine was his, and he was as unprepared to hand it over to his youngest brother as he had been to his eldest. By late 1184 Henry realized that his now eldest son was intractable. He let Richard return to Aquitaine and made preparations to send John to Ireland, to make good on his theoretical title of king. Meanwhile he gave consideration to a plan to promote Geoffrey to the Young King's inheritance, joining Brittany (of which Geoffrey was duke by his marriage to Constance) permanently to the Plantagenet patrimony and leaving Richard to his own devices in his beloved Aquitaine. Richard would not accept this either. He raised an army and raided Geoffrey's borders.

In frustration, Henry snapped. Finally he brought over from England the only person who he could reasonably say had a better right to Aquitaine than Richard himself. Queen Eleanor, who had been silently imprisoned for many years, was now brought briefly out of captivity to Henry's side, and the old king demanded that Richard surrender his duchy back to his mother. Practically, of course, this meant surrendering Aquitaine to Henry, for although Eleanor was momentarily freed from prison, she remained Henry's captive rather than his wife. Richard, however, was finally persuaded. He handed formal control of Aquitaine to his father, and for the next two years Henry avoided making any firm decisions on the future of his dominions.

Yet if the problem had been averted, it was hardly solved. Henry stalled and bided his time, working out questions of border security on the Continent that had arisen as a result of the Young King's death. But with neither Richard nor Geoffrey installed either as co-king or heir presumptive, Henry's grip on his succession remained weak.

In July 1186 fate intervened once more. In the spirit of disloyalty that was so widely ascribed to him by the chroniclers, Geoffrey had struck up a close friendship with Philip II, anticipating that the day might come when he would need the French king's support against his father or brothers. He was in Paris for the summer when he was badly injured in a tournament. On August 19 he died, probably of complications from his wounds. He was buried with great honor in the cathedral of Notre-Dame in Paris. It was said that King Philip was so wrought by grief that he attempted to throw himself into his friend's open grave.

Henry had now lost two adult sons. Although few mourned Geoffrey with the intensity of the French king—Roger of Howden called Geoffrey a "son of perdition" and a "son of iniquity"—Henry was now even more troubled than before. He could not countenance the obvious solution: making Richard his sole heir. Henry never seemed to believe that anyone—even the obviously talented Richard—could be his equal and hold together the vast conglomeration of lands he had assembled. Even when the patriarch of Jerusalem had traveled all the way to England in January 1185 and laid the keys to the Holy City, the Tower of David, and the Holy Sepulcher at Henry's feet, begging him to travel to the East and accept the title of king of Jerusalem, Henry had decided, after consulting his greatest barons, that he was better served defending his dominions in Europe than the Christian possessions under threat from Saladin. It was this dogged refusal to let go that had made Henry such a great ruler, but it would shortly be his undoing.

Geoffrey's death brought relations between Henry II and Philip II (who in time was known to his supporters as Philip Augustus) into a new phase. For the first six years of the young French king's reign, their relationship had been cordial. Henry had assisted in making peace between Philip and the count of Flanders. Philip had enjoyed close friendships with both Henry the Young King and Geoffrey. Now, though, the twenty-three-year-old Philip began to chafe at Henry's influence in France. Richard had been engaged to Philip's elder half sister Alice since 1161. She had been kept at Henry's court for the best part of twenty-five years, but a marriage had never been formalized. Politically Henry delayed the wedding for a time of his own dominance, at which the dowry extracted from Philip could be maximized. But there were also ugly rumors that Henry had seduced the girl himself.

From 1186 relations between the Plantagenet and Capetian crowns cooled sharply. Several important border wars broke out. Because Henry would not consent to Richard and Alice's marrying, the Vexin border country between France and Normandy, which was discussed as Alice's dowry, came back under dispute. Philip claimed to be overlord of Brittany, where

Geoffrey had left as his heirs two young girls and a baby boy called Arthur. There were mounting disputes in Berry and in the county of Toulouse, the scene of the great showdown between Henry and Louis VII in 1159. It was the first serious period of conflict between the English and French kings since 1173–1174.

Philip could not match Henry for wealth, experience, or military cunning, but in 1187 he began to explore other ways to discomfit his rival. The most obvious was through his son Richard. There were cracks in the relationship between the former duke of Aquitaine and his father, into which Philip began to thrust probing fingers. Henry's studious avoidance of settling the succession on Richard, and his growing enthusiasm for John, suggested that Richard's future role was far from settled. Richard was impatient to leave Europe and join the crusading movement to the East. He could not do so until his status as heir was confirmed.

In the summer of 1187 Philip attempted to strike up his third successive friendship with a Plantagenet prince. When Richard visited Paris, the French king plied him with all the charm he could muster. According to Roger of Howden, "Philip honoured Richard so highly that every day they ate at the same table and shared the same dishes; at night the bed did not separate them. The king of France loved him as his own soul and their mutual love was so great that the lord king of England was stupefied by its vehemence." Roger's comment about Richard and Philip sharing a bed has since been read as a reference to Richard's sexuality. It was not. Rather, it was an acknowledgment of the strong and sudden political friendship struck up between the young king of France and the Plantagenet heir presumptive. Philip played on Richard's fears of disinheritance and may even have suggested that Henry intended for Alice to marry John.

It worked. Richard returned from Paris to rejoin his father in Normandy, but as crusading fever gripped Europe and Richard's dreams of the Holy Land grew stronger, his relationship with his father grew ever more strained. Stoked by Philip's whispers, Richard began to believe, as Gervase of Canterbury put it, that "his father wished to defraud him of the succession to the kingdom, in that he intended, as rumor had it, to confer the crown of the kingdom on his younger son John." In November 1188 matters came to a head. War had broken out between Philip and Henry over Berry and Toulouse. At a bad-tempered peace conference held in Bonmoulins, in which Philip and Henry quarreled so bitterly that they almost came to blows, Richard demanded outright that his father assure him of his succession to the kingdom. Henry said nothing. "Then I can only take as true what previously seemed incredible," said Richard, according to Gervase of Canterbury. He knelt before Philip and did homage for Aquitaine and Normandy. It was a final, irreparable breach.

In January 1189 Henry fell into a lingering sickness, which lasted until Easter. From his sickbed he sent messages begging Richard to return to his side. But Richard would not be swayed and instead helped Philip launch border raids against his ailing father. When Henry recovered sufficiently to attend a peace conference at La Ferté-Bernard in early June, it once again broke up amid suspicions, fanned enthusiastically by Philip, that the old king still intended to name John as his heir.

Philip and Richard launched a surprise attack on the castle of La Ferté, which they seized along with all the other castles in the area. On June 12 they moved swiftly to attack Henry at his base in Le Mans, the town of his birth fifty-six years before.

Le Mans was unprepared for attack. As an emergency measure the town's defenders set fire to the suburbs, to try to stall the invaders. A wind blew up, pushing the fire back toward the town proper, and soon the whole of Le Mans was ablaze. Henry and his attendants retreated rapidly. Then, despite the heat of the summer and Henry's weakened state, they attempted a forced march north into Normandy.

As they marched, Henry did what he had never in his long life done before. He gave up. Ten miles from the border fortress of Alençon, he doubled back, sending the bulk of his escort on to Normandy, while he returned to Anjou. After a dangerous journey of two hundred miles through roads and countryside now overrun with Philip's men, Henry arrived before the imposing walls of Chinon Castle, one of the greatest fortresses not only in Anjou but in all the Plantagenet lands and one of Henry's favorite residences. By the time he was inside, he was totally drained. He lay in bed for the next fortnight, sickening daily, weakening ever more.

By the beginning of July, Maine had been overrun and Tours had fallen. Henry dragged himself out of bed to meet Philip face-to-face at Ballan, near Tours, on July 3. As Philip reeled off a long list of demands, which amounted to Henry's utter surrender and the confirmation of Richard as his heir in all lands on both sides of the Channel, the old king had to be held upright on his horse by his attendants. A hot day broke into a thunderstorm. Henry agreed to all of Philip's terms. Then, too weak to ride back to Chinon, he was carried home by his servants in a litter.

Back at Chinon, barely able to stand, Henry sent for a list of all his supporters who had gone over to Richard's side. The first name on the list, according to Gerald of Wales, was that of his favorite son, John. The grief and shock were too much for the old king to bear. He collapsed into his final sickness, hallucinating and raving. In one short moment of clarity he received Holy Communion at the castle chapel. Then, on July 6, 1189, he died.

Henry's astonishing life ended in misery. He had been betrayed by his wife and every one of his sons, had seen his birthplace reduced to smoldering rubble, and had suffered humiliation at the hands of a Capetian king more than thirty years his junior. But he had left his indelible stamp on all of France and the British Isles. Until his last years he had mastered every king, duke, and count who had tested him. He was perhaps the most famous man in Christendom. And his fame burned across the ages to follow. For Henry II, king of England, duke of Normandy and Aquitaine, count of Anjou, Maine, and Touraine, and lord of Ireland, had begun a dynasty that shaped the future of Europe for more than two centuries.

King Richard

Richard stood over his father's corpse in silence. He looked down at a face marked by nearly half a century of trouble and glory. Henry II had died a miserable death: abandoned and embittered. The last words he had spoken to Richard were a vicious hiss in his ear as the two men embraced following the humiliating peace at Ballan: "God grant that I may not die until I have my revenge on you." But God had granted no such thing. Since 1187 Richard, in alliance with Philip II, had taken much of his royal inheritance—Maine, Touraine, and many of the castles of Anjou—by force of arms. After Henry's death the rest passed to him by right of law.

Henry's corpse now lay in the abbey church of Fontevraud, the great monastic foundation in the hinterland between Anjou and the county of Poitou, the power base of the duchy of Aquitaine. As he stood vigil over his father, Richard would have heard his own heart beat in the cool of the nave. The church's arched ceilings and thick, cold columns soared high above him. Silent before his father's still body, this man of action could pause and reflect. As Richard stood at the head of the bier, he betrayed no emotion. He simply looked down at his once-restless father's motionless face, then turned on his heel and walked out. An epic reign was over. A new one—his own—had begun.

News had reached France in 1187 that Jerusalem had fallen to Muslim forces under Saladin, the fearsome and chivalrous Arab general whose military successes were the talk of the whole world. The whole of Outremer—the general term for the Christian states established in the Middle East after the First Crusade—faced being overrun by his armies. Richard had heard of great atrocities committed in Saladin's name: the brutal butchery of holy knights; the execution of great soldiers, including Reynaud of Châtillon, who had been slashed with a sword by Saladin himself before he was beheaded. He would have known of the Christian armies' disastrous defeat on July 4 in the battle of Hattin, in which Frankish soldiers had been slain in their thousands amid burning scrubland, their parched tongues cracking as they succumbed to the lethal attacks of Muslim archers. He would have been told of the misery of poor Christians sold into slavery in

North Africa. But most of all, he was troubled by the loss of the True Cross, the most holy relic in the kingdom of Jerusalem, which had been paraded at the head of every Christian army until it was captured by Saladin's armies at Hattin.

The Third Crusade appealed to Richard both as a soldier of Christ and as a Plantagenet prince. Richard shared the abhorrence of the infidel felt by every Christian who joined the crusading movement. But he was also aware that Sybil, the queen of Jerusalem, was a cousin, descended from Fulk V of Anjou, his father's grandfather. Sybil's husband, Guy de Lusignan, was a Plantagenet vassal. Crusading was therefore both a spiritual business and a family matter.

Richard was the first nobleman north of the Alps to take the cross in the autumn of 1187. His departure for the Holy Land had been delayed almost two years by his quarrels with his father. Dearly as he would have loved to have led the European charge, that honor had fallen to his brother-in-law William II king of Sicily, who had scrambled fifty ships and hundreds of knights as soon as the news of Jerusalem's fall had reached him. The elderly Frederick Barbarossa also sent troops to Outremer in 1188, his armies beginning their long march overland by way of the Danube. (It was on this mission that Barbarossa died, drowned while bathing in a river.) Richard could hardly bear to wait any longer. But he had two sorely pressing issues to settle before he could sew to his clothes a white cloth cross (denoting a crusader of the English kingdom; French crusaders wore red) and set off for the East. The first was his inheritance; the second, his relationship with Philip II. The two issues were closely entwined.

Richard was crowned on Sunday, September 13, 1189, in Westminster Abbey. It was only the second time since the Norman Conquest that a king had been succeeded, relatively smoothly, by his chosen son. Crowds turned out to glimpse a man of whom they would have seen almost nothing in the thirty-two years of his life. They were greeted by a tall, elegant figure, with reddish blond hair and long limbs: grander than his father, but with the same weather-beaten features earned by a life spent in the saddle. It would have been easy to imagine that this was the start of a glorious new age.

Richard processed to Westminster behind ranks of bishops and abbots, barons, knights, and the solemn officers of England. His favored lay nobles bore great golden swords and ceremonial scepters before him. The clergy were resplendent in purple copes and white robes. At the head of the procession was a great cross, and the abbey was lit with the bright flicker of candles. The rich, sickly smell of incense filled the early autumn air and left a trail behind the procession as it approached the abbey's inner chamber. Inside the abbey church, solemn hymns boomed. Richard walked up to the altar, watched on all sides by the greatest holy lords and magnificent barons of England.

Perhaps the proudest of them all was Eleanor of Aquitaine. To see Richard crowned king of England represented the apogee of his mother's ambition, fulfilling as it did a famous prophecy of Merlin: "The eagle of the broken covenant will rejoice in [her] third nesting." Immediately on Henry's death, her beloved son had released her from captivity and restored the lands and revenues that had been taken from her as punishment for the rebellion of 1173; even before he had arrived in England, Richard had sent a command that his mother, now aged sixty-six, should occupy a preeminent place in English government. She had spent the weeks preceding the coronation traveling around the country, holding court, and extracting oaths of allegiance from the great and good of the realm.

Before the altar Richard made three oaths. He swore on the Gospels and the relics of many saints that he would bear peace and honor and reverence toward God, the holy Church, and its ministers; that he would administer justice to the people; and that he would abolish bad laws and customs in favor of good. As he stood, stripped to his breeches and with his undershirt unsewn at his right shoulder, wearing sandals woven from golden cloth, this pious soldier must have reflected with special reverence on the first of his oaths. He was being anointed as God's hammer.

Richard held the scepter in his right hand and the royal rod in his left, while Baldwin archbishop of Canterbury anointed him with holy oil on his head, shoulders, and sword-bearing right arm. He was dressed in a consecrated linen cloth, cope, tunic, and dalmatic—the liturgical tunic, with wide sleeves that billowed around his arms. Then he was armed with the weapons of the Almighty: Baldwin gave him a sword with which he was to chastise those who did wrong to the Church, and two of his earls strapped to his feet golden spurs from the royal treasure.

Finally, when he had been cloaked, Richard was led up to the altar and publicly warned by the archbishop of the awesome responsibility of his kingship. Impatient, he answered that he quite understood. He grabbed the crown from its place on the altar, thrust it into Baldwin's hands, and motioned for the archbishop to place it on his head. "And so," wrote the chronicler Roger of Howden, "the crowned king was led to his throne."

England, like the rest of Christendom, was gripped by crusading fever. Preachers toured Europe, holding large recruitment rallies on holy festival days, enlisting the faithful in their thousands with the promise of remission of sins and eternal life for those who fell on campaign. It was no coincidence that areas known for their military character received especially close attention: Archbishop Baldwin made a grand tour of Wales, enlisting three thousand fierce Welsh soldiers, known for their devastating skill with the bow and lance. The thirteenth-century biographer of the great chivalrous knight William Marshal recorded the king's preparations:

> King Richard prepared, during his stay in England, a great fleet of ships to take him to the Holy Land. . . . There were many fine ships fortified with towers and magnificently equipped and manned by such worthy crews that they had no fear about putting up a stout defense against any galleys or hostile forces.
>
> Richard shipped so much silver and gold, so many furs of minever and gray squirrel, so much plate, so many splendid and expensive garments and arms of every kind, that no man who had seen them could have easily listed them one by one. There were no stores wanting: there were flitches of bacon, wines, wheat, flour and ship's biscuit in abundance . . . there was pepper, cumin, wax and spices and electuaries of the very best available. There were many other drinks and jellies and syrup, bows, crossbows and bolts, sharp-pointed and swift-flying.

Richard spent around fourteen thousand pounds in a single year from September 1189, ordering vast stockpiles of goods: fourteen thousand cured pig carcasses, sixty thousand horseshoes, huge numbers of cheeses and beans, thousands upon thousands of arrows. The mass of provisions and supplies required was paid for through a parallel exploitation of every conceivable source of royal revenue.

Before his death, Henry II had raised the enormous sum of one hundred thousand pounds through the Saladin Tithe: a tax of 10 percent on all movable goods enforced by threat of excommunication and collected by Templar and Hospitaller knights. But one hundred thousand pounds were only the beginning for Richard. He looked at the empire he had inherited and saw revenue streams where his father had not. Henry had generally balanced the profits that could be derived from the sale of office and royal favor against the need to offer stable government by competent royal servants. Richard was never so keenly bureaucratic. As Roger of Howden noted, "he put up for sale all he had: offices, lordships, earldoms, sheriffdoms, castles, towns, lands, everything." He did not sell his land so recklessly as to jeopardize its governance, but he sold it nevertheless. It was said that Richard joked he would sell London if he could find a buyer.

As England hummed with activity, Richard attended to politics. He met Philip II at Nonancourt after Christmas in 1189 and thrashed out a mutual defense pact. The French king was also committed to the crusade, but leaving Europe leaderless would demand a good deal of mutual trust. Richard and Philip swore not to attack each other's lands, to protect the goods of all crusaders, and to act in good faith toward each other. Their barons swore to keep the peace. But mutual suspicion smoldered. The two kings had seen enough of each other during Henry II's reign to know the limits of good faith.

The most difficult problem Richard faced in leaving his kingdom was what to do with his twenty-two-year-old brother John. Known as Jean sans Terre, or John Lackland, during their father's reign, John was now lord of Ireland and had been promised four thousand pounds of land in England. Richard fulfilled the promise. John was given a Norman title, count of Mortain, and awarded the earldoms of Derby, Nottingham, Cornwall, Devon, Somerset, and Dorset; numerous castles in the Midlands; and marriage to Isabel of Gloucester, heiress to Bristol, Glamorgan, and Newport. This was a massive power bloc with which John could easily threaten to destabilize government. Richard had never trusted his younger brother, and when making peace with his father, he had tried to insist that John should accompany him on crusade. Now he vacillated, first banning John from England outright and then relenting, probably on the advice of his mother. There was no easy way to solve the problem of John; leaving him with much land but no official power was the only solution he could muster.

Richard appointed a team of loyalists to govern in his absence. Eleanor was tasked initially with keeping a maternal eye on her youngest son. Administration in England was split between Hugh de Puisat bishop of Durham and William Longchamp bishop of Ely, whose jurisdictions were divided along the line of the river Humber. They were given clear instructions as to the government of the country but must have been apprehensive.

Henry II might have shown that a Plantagenet king could successfully spend more time out of England than inside it, but he had never been farther away than the southern coast of France.

Finally, with his armies mustered and provisioned and a huge fleet set to meet him in Marseille at the end of July 1190, Richard met Philip II in Burgundy. They swore an oath to share whatever plunder and gain they made equally. On July 4 the two kings set off for Jerusalem accompanied by their gigantic armies. At Lyon they split paths: the French king's contingent headed for Genoa, where a fleet was to be hired; Richard's men headed for Marseille. Ever mindful of his own romantic myth, Richard carried a sword that was purported to be Excalibur, King Arthur's legendary blade. He meant to put it to good use.

Hero of the East

In the midwinter of early 1191 Eleanor of Aquitaine and her young charge moved slowly through the freezing Alpine passes. They had been on the road for weeks. In the nights they slept in monasteries, and during the days they picked their way slowly through the steep countryside. They were carried in litters and traveled with a train of servants, but luxury on so difficult a journey was by its nature hard to come by. These were royal travelers, but the road ahead was full of hardship. They were heading over the mountains, down toward the plains of Lombardy, and on to Pisa.

Eleanor of Aquitaine had collected the girl, eighteen-year-old Berengaria of Navarre, from her family in the newly constructed castle-palace of Otile, near Pamplona, which towered over the baking plains of Navarre in northern Spain. She was taking Berengaria to meet her son Richard in order that they might be married. She had found a bride recorded by most chroniclers as more wise than beautiful but with an honest nature.

The girl's epic journey had been planned for several years, and it must have required much persuasion from Richard and his diplomats to persuade Sancho VI to entrust his young daughter to a long and dangerous journey, through many rival kingdoms and difficult terrain, in pursuit of a king heading for the world's most dangerous war zone. That she would be in the hands of his mother, the most famous and notorious woman in Europe, would have been as much a concern as a comfort.

Berengaria knew her marriage to Richard would be highly controversial. The English king was still engaged to marry Philip II's sister Alice, to whom he had been betrothed since they were children. Despite the widespread rumors that his father had seduced Alice, Richard was formally committed to marrying her. Only a handful of people in the whole of Christendom knew that his intentions lay elsewhere.

If Berengaria was nervous, she had at least the comfort of a traveling companion who had seen far worse. Eleanor, undimmed by the years, transacted diplomatic business as they traveled, including a meeting at Lodi, near Milan, with Frederick Barbarossa's son and successor, Henry VI. The young Berengaria would have been aware of the enhanced prestige that her marriage was bringing her; with her marriage to Richard she would be joining the highest reaches of a dynasty whose contacts and influence stretched from the German empire to Jerusalem.

After narrowly missing Richard at Pisa, Eleanor and Berengaria finally caught up with him in Sicily on March 30, 1191. He had been there for six months and had already had an eventful journey. His massive army had put ashore at Lisbon, in the kingdom of Portugal, where they had shown their zeal for holy war by raping women and plundering the land, before meeting Richard at Marseille and sailing on to Sicily. Richard had had his own adventures on his way down the Italian coastline and at one point was nearly stoned to death by a group of Neapolitan peasants whom he had berated for usurping the trappings of aristocracy by flying a hawk. When he reached Sicily, he took the liberty of conquering Messina, which owed its allegiance to Tancred king of Sicily, and flying the English flag above the city ramparts, thus ignoring his deal with Philip to split the spoils of war. The Messina strait now bristled with his heavy warships, much to the chagrin of the French king, who found the pomp in which his comrade traveled somewhat tiresome.

But if Philip was annoyed by Richard's high-handed military style, he was truly apoplectic when he learned of his plans to marry Berengaria of Navarre. Richard had kept his plans a tightly guarded secret until, in a humiliating exchange just days before his new bride's arrival, he finally told Philip that there would be no wedding to Alice. He cited his father's seduction of the girl, claiming she had borne him a bastard child. Philip had no choice but to accept that he had been strung along, probably for years. He accepted ten thousand marks in compensation for swallowing the shameful news that the marriage was off and, in a state of shock and rage, left Sicily several days before Berengaria's arrival.

Eleanor stayed in Sicily for three days, just long enough to greet her favorite son and her daughter Joan, the former queen of Sicily, who had been the prisoner of King Tancred until Richard had freed her during his conquest of Messina. Eleanor had not seen Joan since she had been sent away for marriage as a girl of eleven in 1177. But the reconciliation was brief. Business in England and Normandy, where John remained a worry to his elder brother, called Eleanor home. Joan took over the position as chaperone to Berengaria as the crusading party prepared to leave the island for the Holy Land, where the marriage ceremony was to be held.

The next staging post was supposed to be Crete, but a gale blew up at sea, splitting Richard's party. Around twenty-five ships were blown off course to Cyprus, an independent Greek territory ruled by the Byzantine "tyrant of Cyprus," Isaac Comnenus. The island was a vital staging point for the coastal cities of Outremer, but Comnenus was a wholly unreliable ruler. When several of Richard's ships were wrecked on the island's coast, the passengers were sorely mistreated by his subjects. Most offensive of all, there was an attempt made to capture the ship carrying Joan and Berengaria, as it waited at anchor off Limassol.

Richard landed at Rhodes on April 22 and received news of his sister's and fiancée's predicament. He determined that the Cypriots, like the Messinans, should be punished by conquest, regardless of the fact that Cyprus was a Christian state. On May 5 he stormed ashore at Limassol and fought a bloody street battle to capture the town. The Cypriots were beaten back to Famagusta on the east coast. To celebrate his victory, Richard married Berengaria of Navarre on May 12, in a ceremony in the Byzantine chapel of St. George in Limassol. The young queen was crowned by the Norman bishop of Evreux. The guests must have included Guy of Lusignan, erstwhile king of Jerusalem and Richard's retainer in his capacity as count of Poitou. It was undoubtedly one of the most extraordinary royal marriages and coronations in the history of the English Crown: a Navarrese teenager crowned queen of England by a Norman bishop in a Cypriot chapel, attended by émigré Jerusalemites. If ever there was an indication of the vast reach of the English Crown under the Plantagenets, this was it.

With the royal wedding concluded, Richard's army spent the next three weeks completing its conquest of Cyprus. Richard split his fleet in two and had it sail in opposite directions around the island. Everywhere they stopped the air would have filled with shrieks of terror, as men bearing the white cross of England's holy war stormed ashore to raid towns, capture castles, and board enemy ships. The main prize was Isaac Comnenus himself. The tyrant held out briefly, but when his beloved daughter was captured in the fortress of Kyrenia, his will to resist collapsed. He submitted to Richard with the sole request that his status should be respected and he should not be bound in irons. Richard, ever chivalrous, obliged. Comnenus was bound in specially struck silver manacles.

The Plantagenet empire now extended to the fringes of the Middle East. Richard wrote home to his English chancellor, William Longchamp: "We have subjected to ourselves the whole island of Cyprus with all its strong-points." He forced every Cypriot man to shave his beard and confirmed lo-cal laws and customs under his own officials' administration. But unlike his father, Richard was more concerned with hard cash than enduring over-lordship. With his conquest completed, he promptly sold the island to the Templars for one hundred thousand Saracen bezants.

From certain high vantage points on Cyprus, one could see the coast of Lebanon. The Holy Land now lay tantalizingly close. Richard wasted no time in setting sail. He arrived in Acre on June 8, 1191, to find that a siege had been going strong for more than a year. Philip II had reached Acre several months earlier, and his armies were camped to the east of the city, having recently joined the ranks of the Christian host, including the armies of the occupying Christians, the Germans, Pisans, and the rest. His great cata-pult Malvoisine (bad neighbor) was pitted against its equivalent on the Muslim side, Malcousine (bad cousin). Malvoisine was continuously dam-aged by enemy fire, but Philip simply had it rebuilt. The rumbling and crash-ing sounds as huge stones smashed into the city and buried themselves deep into the ground, followed by hailstorms of vicious arrows, would have terri-fied everyone within earshot.

As Richard approached by sea, he looked upon a city clouded in the dust of attritional warfare. It was as miserable a scene of human suffering as the mind can imagine. Dead horses and dead soldiers, stinking with dis-ease, were used as ballast by the Christians as they attempted to fill in the city moat for their siege engines.

There was no salvation here. Atrocity was rife. Christian women cap-tured an Egyptian galley crew and tortured them to death. Muslim leaders planned terror attacks on the Christian army, aiming to let loose hundreds of poisonous snakes among their camp. The French built giant siege ma-chines, and the Muslim defenders burned the machine operators alive with Greek fire. Starving German troops ate mule flesh. Trench diggers worked themselves to exhaustion and gagged as they dug in the hot pestilential air of the battlefield, thick with death. Prostitutes worked both sides in the seedy den of vice that sprang up in the Christian camp. The nearby sea bobbed with bloated human remains.

No sooner had Richard arrived than problems surfaced with the French. Far from presenting a unified Christian front against the infidel, all the ri-valries of Europe were imported to the Holy Land. Richard was vastly wealthier than Philip, and he brought with him well-paid soldiers hungry for success and plunder. He stoked Philip's ire by offering higher pay than the French king to uncontracted men.

Even without the siege warfare and infighting, Acre was a dangerous place to invaders. Within a week of setting up camp, Richard had fallen grievously ill with a scurvylike disease known as Arnaldia or Leonardie. His teeth and fingernails began to loosen, and his hair fell out in clumps. Yet Richard was a king in command of his own propaganda. Illness was personally debilitating, but it could not be allowed to stall the pace of his campaign. To maintain the momentum of the crusade, he sent messages to Saladin, requesting secret negotiations—and asking for peaches and ice to cool his raging fever. Saladin sent the fruit and rejected the requests to meet. A correspondence was maintained between the two leaders as he soon learned to respect this new leader of the Franks.

Illness kept Richard periodically debilitated during his crusading career, but he refused to be cowed. Early in July, as the Christians intensified their assault on Acre and the city's defenses nearly collapsed, he was carried onto the battlefield on a litter; he was covered in a gloriously regal silken quilt and carried a crossbow, which he fired at Muslim defenders from behind a screen, killing several and giving cheer to his own men. Acre's defenses were finally breached on July 5. Its fall owed equal parts to Philip's tenacious assault from the east and Richard's further battery from the north. The walls had been sapped with trenches, mined, smashed with heavy stones, scaled with ladders, and fired at with arrows for nearly two years, by thousands of forces, including almost every notable Christian aristocrat in the East, and the combined military might of the Plantagenet and Capetian empires, Pisans, Genoese, Danes, Germans, and assorted other pilgrim soldiers. That the city had held out so long was testament to the extreme valor of its Muslim defenders.

Before Acre fell, a deal that averted a bloody sack was hammered out between Saladin and the Christian kings. The crusaders allowed Acre's garrison to make an honorable submission and raised the flags of Richard and Philip—as the principal leaders of the assault—over the city with minimal further bloodshed. In return for this, Saladin agreed to pay a ransom of two hundred thousand dinars, to release nearly two thousand prisoners, and hand back the True Cross taken at Hattin. The bulk of the Egyptian galley fleet that was moored in the city harbor was captured, extending

Christian hegemony along the coasts of the Levant and virtually ending Muslim ambitions to spread their influence farther west in the Mediterranean. Outside the royal palace, Christians flocked into Acre, singing and dancing with joy after their long, nerve-shredding ordeal, and indulged themselves in the drinking dens and whorehouses of the city's grubbier quarters. But in victory lay the seeds of a disaster that would have serious implications back home. Although Acre fell to a joint attack, Richard, Berengaria, and Joan moved into the royal palace, where Richard tore down the livery of his ally Duke Leopold of Austria, who had been in the Holy Land since April and had been instrumental in the siege. Richard's arrogance infuriated both Duke Leopold and Philip, whose numerous slights at Richard's hands had made the crusade a catalog of humiliation.

In the days after Acre, the crusading movement received both a fillip and a blow. Philip II, driven by a cocktail of jealousy, homesickness, and exasperation, announced that he considered his crusading oath to have been served by the conquest of Acre. He was going home. This was generally seen to be an act of cowardice that undermined the dignity of the French Crown. In truth Philip was sick of being humiliated by Richard, latterly over a power struggle in which the two kings had backed opposite candidates for the kingdom of Jerusalem: Richard supported Guy de Lusignan, and Philip's candidate was Conrad of Montferrat.

The victory at Acre had come at a cost. Philip count of Flanders had died in the siege. This was a major loss to the European aristocracy in the East, but it was far more important in Europe. Flanders was the wool and cloth capital of Europe, a vastly wealthy corner of the world, which would transform French finances if parts of it could be brought within the royal demesne. Serving the glory of God in the East was one thing, but Philip was a Capetian at heart. His claim to the rich territory that the count of Flanders had left behind was more pressing. Pushing the claims of the French Crown in northwestern Europe appealed far more to the French king than playing second fiddle in the baking cesspit of the East. Philip left Outremer from Tyre on August 3 and sailed for France.

Richard was now the de facto commander of the Third Crusade. He had men, money, a vast fleet, and burgeoning prestige. He now also had almost full direction over military operations. According to the chronicler Richard of Devizes, Richard declared that having Philip around in the East was like being a cat with a hammer tied to its tail. With the hammer cut loose, the cat was free to run. Richard's stay in the region would earn him plenty of further glory, which he now had no obligation to share. Yet for every month he spent in the Holy Land, problems loomed larger back home.

Treachery

Geoffrey archbishop of York stared up, like every other visitor to Dover, at the great castle being built above the harbor. It was September 1191, and work had progressed since the late King Louis VII had toured the building site with Henry II. Now Geoffrey could look up at its imposing square keep and think of his father, who had spent a fortune building it into a statement of royal magnificence and a shrine to the secular power of the Plantagenet dynasty.

Geoffrey was a magnificent man himself. He was a military talent, a learned clerk, and half a Plantagenet prince. The illegitimate child of Henry II and a woman named Ykenai, whom the chronicler Walter Map tells us was a meretrix, or common harlot, he had built a career in the royal service and the Church, serving as his father's chancellor and risking his life fighting a brilliant campaign in the north during the Great War of 1173–1174. Now he was his brother Richard's second-highest ecclesiastic authority. A rich, powerful, and ambitious young man of royal blood was dangerous to have around the country with the king away and no direct heir yet produced. When Richard left for the Holy Land eighteen months earlier, he had made Geoffrey swear an oath to remain out of England for three years. Government had been left in the hands of William Longchamp, who combined the roles of bishop of Ely, papal legate, justiciar, and chancellor—as close to a figure of universal authority over government and Church administration as it was possible to create.

Now, allied with his half brother John, Geoffrey was breaking his oath. In Sicily Richard had given an indication that his nephew Arthur of Brittany should be heir to England in the event of his death. Arthur of Brittany was Richard's younger brother's son; his father, another Geoffrey, had been killed in a Paris tournament in 1186. When Richard left for Outremer, Arthur was around four years old. John, who was twenty-four, had reacted violently to his brother's choice of heir. Contravening his own oath, he had returned to England and seized the great castles of Nottingham and Tickhill and, assisted by William Longchamp's meager popularity, raised men against the chancellor. Longchamp, a Norman by birth and background, bore an overbearing style that set him at odds with the men he was attempting to govern. In talks aimed at resolving the dispute, John had bullied Long-champ into abandoning young Arthur of Brittany and recognizing him as England's heir.

When Geoffrey landed at Dover, he received a message from John warning him of impending danger. Word had leaked of his arrival, and Longchamp's agents were on their way to Dover to arrest him. He would be charged with entering the realm illegally and might well find himself imprisoned. In haste, Geoffrey fled through town and took refuge at St. Martin's Priory.

Longchamp's men laid siege outside the grounds of the priory, but after four days they lost patience and battered their way in to fetch their quarry. They found the archbishop of York by the altar. It was a safe place, a holy place. It was also, in the context of recent events, a highly symbolic place. In a scene disturbingly reminiscent of Becket's murder, the chancellor's men fell on Archbishop Geoffrey and bundled him out of the priory. He was dragged by his arms and legs through the streets of Dover, his head banging on the ground as he went. This was no doubt an uncomfortable experience for Geoffrey, but it was a political disaster for William Longchamp, who was now turned upon by virtually every churchman in England.

John's propagandists went into overdrive. Writers like Hugh of Nonant, who were loyal to John, derided Longchamp as an ape, a midget, a pervert, and a pedophile. He was accused of every vice and abomination that the medieval imagination could conjure. Meanwhile John prepared to take con-trol of London. When Longchamp attempted to prevent him from entering the city, the citizens barred the gates and denounced the chancellor as a traitor.

A triumphant John hauled Longchamp before the regency council, where Geoffrey of York leveled a series of accusations of financial impropriety and condemned the chancellor for involvement in his arrest. Longchamp's au-thority was all but destroyed. He was stripped of his office by the council, forced to hand over hostages for his castles, and thrown into Dover Prison for a week. When he was released, he was ruined and made his way as quickly as he could to Flanders. The council named John supreme governor of the realm. It was precisely the sort of situation that Richard had hoped to avoid.

Back in the Holy Land, Richard's crusade was going rather well. Despite dif-ficult conditions and his own illness, he had secured Acre and was managing to discomfit Saladin, albeit with the help of some highly unpleasant tactics. In August 1191 he massacred twenty-six hundred Muslim prisoners on a plain outside Acre. Shortly afterward the Christians marched south and took Jaffa, Jerusalem's port town. There were constant lines of communication open with Saladin, and the two leaders were beginning to test each other with diplomatic offers for a peace settlement. These included, most mischievously, an offer from Richard to marry his sister Joan to Saladin's brother, on condition that the brother convert to Christianity.

News of John's plot and sharp practice did not take long to fly east. In early April 1192, at Ascalon, Richard heard that his chancellor had been deposed. This was disturbing, but Richard had already made contingency plans and sent Walter of Coutances bishop of Lincoln back to mediate between John and Longchamp and play an active role in government as justiciar. At the end of May Richard received far more troubling news. He learned that John was plotting with Philip II of France. His envoy warned of "abominable treachery" and the potential loss of England. Only Eleanor was holding her son in check. Richard knew from personal experience what damage could be wrought when a prince of the blood allied with the Capetians. After all, he had done just that to his own father.

The kingdom of Jerusalem was only partly won, but the longer he stayed, the greater the chance he would return to find the kingdom of England reduced to rubble by his brother and half brother. A new campaign season was about to begin. It would have to be his last in Outremer. He would have one last opportunity for glory—one last chance to put Saladin back in his place—and then home, to Normandy and England.

In the middle of April 1192 the Italian nobleman Conrad of Montferrat received some wonderful news. After a long career spent fighting in the Holy Land he was to become king of Jerusalem. His long-running struggle against his chief rival, Guy of Lusignan, was over. Guy had relinquished his claim on Jerusalem in exchange for the lordship of Cyprus. Conrad was to be placed at the permanent head of the Christian community in Outremer, and he would bear responsibility for pushing on with the war against Saladin. It was a great honor, for which he had long hankered.

On the night of April 28 Conrad, still in a celebratory mood, went to supper at the home of Philip bishop of Beauvais. After a convivial evening Conrad rode home through the streets of Tyre, flanked by a pair of guards.

When he turned down a narrow street, he saw two men sitting on either side of the road. As he approached, they stood up and walked to meet him. One of them was holding a letter. Conrad was intrigued but did not dismount. He stretched down from his horse and reached out to take the letter. As he did so, the man holding the letter drew a knife and stabbed upward, plunging the blade deep into Conrad's body. The other man leaped onto the back of Conrad's horse and stabbed him in the side. Conrad slumped down, dead, from his horse. He had been nominal king of Jerusalem for less than a fortnight.

Conrad was murdered by two assassins sent by the mysterious Rashid ad-Din Sinan, known as the Old Man of the Mountain, the leader of a violent sect based in Syria who had allied with Saladin against the Christians. Richard was immediately rumored to have sponsored the attack because he had supported Guy of Lusignan. The politics of kingship in Outremer fell once more into crisis. A summer march on Jerusalem ended in failure. When Saladin poisoned all wells in Judea, strategic disagreements raged about whether an attack on Jerusalem was preferable to concentrating on southern Palestine, in order to disrupt Saladin's links with Egypt. Stalemate beckoned, with Saladin controlling Jerusalem and the Christians the coastal ports.

At the end of July Richard attempted a feint around Acre, hoping to convince Saladin that he had designs on Beirut. Saladin did not rise to the bait. In Richard's absence he launched a fierce attack on Jaffa. It was a brilliant success. The walls were mined and sapped with lethal skill, and on July 31 huge sections collapsed in a juddering landslide of stone and dust. The city was sacked by rampaging Saracens. It was a disaster: Jaffa was Jerusalem's port and an essential strategic stronghold for Christian maritime superiority.

On the night of July 31 Richard sailed into the harbor with a small fleet. He had sailed against the wind in utter desperation. A red awning covered the royal boat from which the redheaded king waded ashore, his red banner waving in the breeze. He led his men toward town, where Muslim flags flew over every quarter and the streets rang with shouts of "Allahu Akbar." As some of his crew built a beachhead from scavenged wood, Richard led a charge against the town.

The attack was fearsome and unexpected. Against absurd odds, Richard's men cleared Jaffa of the Muslim invaders, scattering them with crossbow fire, and drove them inland. A few days later, when they returned to the devastated city, they were again repulsed, this time by a hedgehog formation of knights firing crossbows. Once again Richard won a victory that had seemed impossible, cementing his legend in the East. It was the final military engagement of the Third Crusade.

The war was becoming unbearable on both sides. Richard wrote to Saladin warning that if fighting continued much longer, "you and we together are ruined." The two sides had nothing more to throw at each other but diplomacy. A three-year truce was finally agreed to on Wednesday, September 2, 1192. Saladin kept Jerusalem but agreed to allow a limited number of Christian pilgrims access to the Holy Sepulcher. The Christians kept everything they held between Tyre and Jaffa. The True Cross remained in Saladin's hands.

Richard never met Saladin, and he never made his pilgrimage to Jerusalem. He sent a message to the sultan that he would return to conquer again, a challenge that Saladin manfully accepted, writing back that he could think of no king to whom he would sooner lose his empire. But Saladin had less than a year to live. He died from a fever on March 4, 1193, in Damascus. He had been the most feared and respected Muslim leader of his age. Although a man capable of extraordinary butchery and cruelty, Saladin was also conspicuously generous and concerned for the plight of the poor. He died with no possessions to his name other than a few coins, having given everything else away. Despite Richard's best efforts, Saladin's rule had seen the reconquest of Jerusalem and virtually every crusader city in the Holy Land, save the narrow strip of Christian territory remaining between Jaffa and Tyre.

In October 1192 Richard set sail for Europe. He must have left with great trepidation. For all he knew, his throne might have been usurped by his brother. Richard left behind the twenty-six-year-old Henry count of Champagne, his nephew, as king of Jerusalem. But this was a king with only part of a kingdom. Richard's crusade had been, by the harshest measure, a failure. And yet it had succeeded in one aspect: it had created the legend of the Lionheart.

An Unexpected Detour

In the late spring of 1193 Richard composed a song. It was a ballad of melancholy and abandonment, frustration and homesickness. Written in Occitan, the native language of Aquitaine, it became known, after its first line, as "Ja nus hons pris" and would survive for more than eight centuries. The lyrics of the two most famous verses are:

Ja nus hons pris ne dira sa raison
adroitement, se dolantement non;
Mes par confort puet il fere chancon.
Moult ai amis, mes povre sont li don;
honte en avront, se por ma reancon
sui ces deus yvers pris.
Ce sevent bien mi homme et mi baron,
Englois, Normant, Poitevin et Gascon,
que je n'avoie si povre compaignon,
cui je laissasse por avoir en prixon.
Je nei di pas por nule retracon,
mes encor suit ge pris.

No man imprisoned tells his story
rightfully, as if he were not sorrowful;
but for comfort he can write a song.
I have many friends, but poor are their gifts;
shame on them, if for my ransom
I must be two winters imprisoned.
It is well known by my men and my barons,
English, Norman, Poitevin, and Gascon,
that I do not have the poorest companion
whom I would leave to remain in prison.
I don't say this for their reproach,
but still, I am imprisoned.

Richard composed this lonely song in the imperial palace of Hagenau, a great fortified hunting lodge on the Moder River. The magnificent building had been erected by Frederick Barbarossa and was now held by his successor, Henry VI. It was filled with precious jewels and the great treasure of the Holy Roman Empire—but its most valuable cargo was the English king.

Richard began his return home from his crusade only to find his name blackened across Europe. His efforts in the East might have been appreciated by those who remained with him until the end, but for many of the allies who had returned before him, Richard was proud to a fault, overbearing, and ripe for a fall. He had rejected the French king's sister in humiliating circumstances. He had deposed the ruler of Cyprus, who was related to several other important European nobles. He had refused to share the spoils of war with Leopold of Austria, having had the ducal flag torn down during the sack of Acre. It was widely rumored that he had sponsored the murder of Conrad of Montferrat. Almost every major prince in Western Europe incubated some reason to hate him, and as he returned from Outremer, it soon became clear to him that there were few safe territories in which he could now travel; this included the lands of the emperor Henry VI, who was now in alliance with King Philip. Richard's trip back from the Holy Land had therefore followed a very different course from his outward journey. His first port of call was Corfu, where he learned that his enemies had cut off virtually every sea route and landing point between northern Italy and the southern tip of Iberia. Almost every path back to his kingdom meant heading through hostile territory.

With the November seas turning rough, Richard and a handful of trusted lieutenants hired galleys and headed north. They were shipwrecked off the coast of Istria, in the Adriatic. A long land route home through Central Europe beckoned before Richard could reach the territories of his sympathetic brother-in-law, Henry the Lion duke of Saxony, in northeastern Germany. Almost every step of the way would take them through hostile territory. The small party disguised themselves as pilgrims and set out on foot. But the most famous crusader king in Europe could not travel unrecognized. Three days into the journey, fifty miles from Vienna, they were spotted and denounced. Richard was arrested and delivered as a prisoner to Leopold duke of Austria. In February 1193 Leopold sold him to Emperor Henry VI, for a fee of half the ransom the emperor could raise for the captive king. He was held to await charges, which included causing Conrad of Montferrat's death and betraying the Holy Land by treating with Saladin.

As he sat trapped in the emperor's court, Richard was treated with caution but not cruelty. The rules of aristocracy meant that he was essentially under house arrest; it would have been highly irregular to throw a king into a dungeon. Richard was a crusader, and his imprisonment was technically forbidden by the pope, a point that his diplomats made in furious terms in Rome. But Richard was imprisoned nonetheless, as surely as his mother had been by his father and his great-uncle Robert Curthose by his grandfather Henry I. It would have played on his mind that his mother had been a prisoner for fifteen years and that Curthose had died in prison, after three decades' incarceration. How long would he share their fate?

Back in England, Richard's brother John wanted nothing more than to see his rival kept forever in an imperial prison. It gave him a free run at the Crown, and John, as ambitious and ruthless as any Plantagenet before him, needed no prompting. In January 1193 the twenty-five-year-old John paid homage to Philip II in Paris for the bulk of the Plantagenet dominions and agreed to marry his brother's spurned bride Alice, now thirty-two. Then he went back to England and attempted to raise a rebellion.

Fortunately for Richard and for England, there were more sensible heads in a country used to coping with an absent king. To prevent an invasion in support of John's bid for power, Eleanor of Aquitaine and Walter of Coutances manned the coastal defenses, newly threatened by sea from the lands in Flanders that Philip had rushed so enthusiastically back from crusade to claim. William the Lion king of Scotland, respecting an absent crusader's plight and mindful of Richard's past generosity, refused to rise up against the absent king. Hubert Walter, Richard's companion on crusade, who was elected archbishop of Canterbury after Richard had nominated him from captivity in March, presided over a great council at which it was generally recognized that the king was in grave need of assistance.

In March Richard was put on trial by the emperor. He spoke to the assembled magnates and courtiers with such magnificence, dignity, eloquence, and grace that he moved many to tears and won friends among the local nobility. William the Breton wrote that Richard "spoke so eloquently and regally, in so lionhearted a manner, it was as though he were seated on an ancestral throne at Lincoln or Caen." When Philip II tried to have him transferred to the French court, Richard consulted the rebellious nobles of the Rhineland, who bordered the Holy Roman Empire and the French kingdom, reconciled them to the empire, and kept himself at the imperial court by the cunning of his diplomacy. Although reports reached him that Philip's forces were overrunning Normandy, taking the great castle at Gisors and besieging the ducal capital of Rouen, he did not panic but sent reassurances to his supporters in England, maintaining the vital impression that release was not far away.

But release was an expensive option and one that would strain his coffers to the limit. Already hard-pressed by the demands made to fund the crusade, Richard's dominions were now subject to a brutal 25 percent tax on income and movables. The great nobles were to contribute personally to the king's ransom. Monasteries and churches around England learned to beware the heavy footsteps of royal servants as they approached to demand wool, crops, and valuable plate. As the chronicler Ralph de Diceto recorded, "the greater churches came up with treasures hoarded from the distant past, and the parishes with their silver chalices. . . . Archbishops, bishops, abbots, priors, earls and barons [contributed] a quarter of their annual income; the Cistercian monks and Premonstratensian canons their whole year's wool crop, and clerics living on tithes one-tenth of their income." The pockets of the Church and subjects alike were ruthlessly tapped, under the watchful eye of Eleanor and the royal justiciars. It was testimony to the value placed on the legitimate kingship of a proven warrior that Richard's kingdom rallied to fund his extortionate ransom, while all but ignoring his brother John's increasingly unbecoming attempts to snatch power for himself.

But even with such a mighty effort, it took more than six months to raise Richard's ransom. Throughout the autumn he languished at the emperor's pleasure, while legends of the captive Lionheart spread throughout Europe. Years later tall tales would circulate of Richard's favorite minstrel, Blondel, walking the Continent in search of his master, finally recognizing his prison cell from afar when he heard the refrain of a song the two of them had composed together. This story was the product of a later age, but Richard does seem to have kept his spirits high in captivity, appearing bright and cheerful to visiting diplomats, even as his treacherous brother strove to seize his kingdom.

On February 4, 1194, Richard was released. He paid one hundred thousand marks for his freedom, gave hostages (including the archbishop of Rouen and two of Henry duke of Saxony's sons) as guarantee for fifty thousand more, and was persuaded by his mother to submit to a piece of ungentlemanly brinkmanship from Henry VI, who late in negotiations demanded that Richard release the English Crown to the emperor and promised he would then grant it back to him as a vassal of the empire. It was a wild price to pay, a true king's ransom. But it meant freedom at last, after a year and six weeks in captivity. By now the empire was fraying at the edges. According to the chronicler Roger of Howden, Philip II wrote urgently to John to tell him the news. "Look to yourself," wrote the king; "the devil is loose."

Richard landed at Sandwich, in Kent, on March 20; he had been gone nearly four years. Three days later, wrote Ralph de Diceto, "to the great acclaim of both clergy and people, he was received in procession through the decorated city [of London] into the church of St. Paul's." It was a joyful homecoming. But Richard could not afford to linger over grand welcomes. He had plenty of work to do.

Return of the Lionheart

On April 17, 1194, Richard emerged from his rooms at the priory of Winchester Cathedral dressed in the finest royal regalia of kingship. He wore a heavy crown on his head and the great ceremonial robes that he had last donned at Westminster in 1189. Just as at his coronation, three earls processed before him carrying swords. One was King William of Scotland, in his capacity as earl of Huntingdon: the Lion walking before the Lionheart.

From the priory Richard walked to the cathedral church, surrounded by the great earls and knights of England. Inside the cathedral, Eleanor, now bent with age but still politically acute, and her ladies waited to witness the king in his splendor. Outside, crowds of people gathered to watch. Here was the hero of the Holy Land, the bête noire of Europe's princes. Lined by the strains of warfare and captivity, Richard was back in his kingdom, making a show of might.

This was an official crown wearing, a public occasion almost as great in its solemnity as a full coronation. It was a habit that the Norman kings of England had kept up but that had fallen into disuse under Henry II. It was not Richard's choice to resurrect the tradition; he was persuaded by his leading advisers, who recommended the ceremony as an important and highly visible way to reassert royal authority. Richard, usually impatient of ritual and public posturing, chose on this occasion to pay kingship its due.

He then spent the spring of 1194 consolidating his control. He had squashed the flickering embers of John's revolt within days of entering the country, laying siege to the castles of Tickhill and Nottingham, hanging disloyal rebels, and announcing himself the returned king to all who set eyes upon him, confiscating vast swaths of English estates from his feckless brother and his supporters, casting out of office a large number of sheriffs and leasing their positions to new, loyal men whom he trusted to keep order and the royal coffers filled.

From captivity Richard had written a letter to London appointing his crusading ally Hubert Walter archbishop of Canterbury and chief justiciar. An outstanding administrator and famous for his bravery and courage on crusade, Walter was the nephew of Henry II's exchequer, Ranulf Glanvill, and probably the greatest in a long line of medieval royal servants. Rich, generous, pious, and ambitious, he had made his way in life through practical legal and administrative training rather than formal education. He had been a faithful, effective servant to Henry II and a successful diplomat on Richard's behalf in Outremer. When Richard was taken captive, Walter was the first English subject to reach him and the first to begin the process of negotiating his release. Richard had appointed him archbishop of Canterbury by letter from prison, and Walter had repaid him by rallying up political support to prevent John from fatally damaging his absent brother's kingship. Now Walter was promoted to the post of vice-regent. Again, he did not let Richard down. Royal and ecclesiastical business flowed smoothly through his hands. His reforms of England's judiciary, its exchequer, and its chancery made government more profitable, available, and efficient. He was widely trusted; his word was as good as the king's itself.

With Walter at the head of royal administration, Richard was confident that he would not be starved of cash when he returned to France on campaign. Even after the demands made on England by the ransom, spare capacity was still found. Richard raised a great deal of money from the sale of offices, either to new men or to existing holders who were sometimes put out to learn that they would have to pay again for positions they already occupied. Walter personally led a sweeping judicial tour of England. This was partly with the aim of restoring law and order following John's rebellion, but he also paid meticulous attention to the state of royal manors and lands, as well as feudal rights, such as wardships, custodies, and escheats (inheritances due to the Crown). Local knights were appointed to maximize all sources of royal revenue in the shires, which could be sent back to the exchequer for accounting. Walter also oversaw the establishment of a new system that supervised, recorded, and regulated moneylending by England's Jews, a matter of concern to royal finances because unpaid Jewish debt passed to the Crown when the lender died.

All these measures helped reinforce the sense, introduced under Henry II, that the royal government was settling ever deeper and more uniformly into local society. Not that this was Richard's primary concern. Hubert Walter's financial policies were necessary simply because Richard had already demanded more revenue from his kingdom than any other king before him. It is testament to the wealth of England (and Normandy, whose coffers began to swell during the late 1190s) that these demands were met without insurrection or constitutional crisis. One of Richard's greatest feats as king was to impose financial sacrifices while retaining the trust of the great men of the kingdom. The sums he demanded may have been fed into the insatiable maw of siegecraft and bloody warfare, but they were never wasted.

Richard set sail from Portsmouth for Barfleur in Normandy on May 12, 1194. Before he left, he granted Portsmouth a charter and began the process of building a town and palace that would transform a quiet coastal village into the most important military port on the south coast—a conduit for treasure, men, and weapons as they were funneled to the Continental war. Then he boarded the lead ship in his fleet and left his kingdom. For the next five years of his life he spent nine or ten months a year in Normandy and the rest of his time in Aquitaine, Brittany, and Anjou, engaged in a war against Philip II for the very soul of the Plantagenet empire in France.

When Richard reached Barfleur, the town erupted into celebration. It was a triumphant sight: the returning duke at the head of a fleet of one hundred ships, with siege engines and flags, armor and soldiers, horses, knights, mercenaries, and royal servants. There were scenes of dancing and singing, triumph and feasting. William Marshal, the faithful soldier who had known almost half a century of Plantagenet rule, had never seen anything like it. "When the king arrived in Normandy, all his people, as soon as they saw him come, made him fine gifts and spoke fine words to him. He had folk tripping and dancing gracefully around him all the time. . . . Such a great, dense overpowering crowd of joyous folk that . . . you could not have thrown an apple in the air and seen it land. . . . The bells rang out everywhere, and old and young formed long processions, singing as they walked: 'God has come with all his might, now the King of France will go away!'"

But amid all the celebration, Richard was troubled. His enemy was strong. When Philip returned from crusade, part of his assertion of French control over Flanders had included directly seizing the rich county of Artois. This had significantly increased his wealth and power, and the French king had pressed his advantage where it hurt: in Normandy. Not since his grandfather Geoffrey Plantagenet had conquered Normandy in the 1140s had the duchy faced so severe an assault. With the treacherous connivance of John and the switched allegiance of lords whose lands straddled the

French-Norman borders, Philip had overrun great swaths of territory, including the Vexin, much of western Normandy, and the seaboard lordships of Arques and Eu. These, along with his new territories in Flanders, allowed the Capetians for the first time to threaten the English coast by sea. Elsewhere, John had granted away vital castles in Touraine and disclaimed overlordship in Angoulême, the most troubled part of Aquitaine. While these did not affect Norman security directly, they provided unwelcome distractions far from the main theater of war, which Philip could stir up whenever he wished to distract Richard's attention.

The most serious loss was the castle at Gisors, in the Vexin. Gisors was one of the finest castles in all France, a fortress to rival those at Dover and Chinon. Its huge octagonal wall surrounded a cylindrical keep and a stone motte. It bristled with heavy defenses, as befitted its vital strategic position between the rival capitals of Rouen and Paris. From this castle the dukes of Normandy had been able to control and defend the most important marchland in Western Europe. Now that it lay in Philip's hands, the tables were turned. All over the Plantagenet empire a half century of border security had been undermined by the venal hand of John.

After all that his brother had done to erode the empire, it would have been natural if Richard had considered him a lifelong enemy. But he did not. As soon as he arrived in Normandy, John came to his court and threw himself at his brother's feet, begging forgiveness. William Marshal recalled the scene that spoke of both the compassion and the disdain with which Richard regarded his brother: "The king lifted up by the hand his natural brother and kissed him, saying 'John, have no fear. You are a child, and you have had bad men looking after you. Those who thought to give you bad advice will get their deserts! Get up, and go and eat.'" The king had just been presented with a salmon and ordered it cooked for his delinquent brother.

Why did Richard forgive John? Roger of Howden, a Yorkshireman and chronicler who knew royal family politics at first hand, having accompanied the king on crusade, suggests that the reconciliation was engineered by Eleanor of Aquitaine. She realized that the family had been strongest when it fought together rather than against itself. On her advice, Richard accepted that his twenty-seven-year-old brother was devious and cowardly but considered him a better ally than enemy. As soon as Richard had bestowed forgiveness, John showed the value of his treachery. He made for the town of Evreux, which he had been holding for Philip, and had the French garrison killed before declaring that he was now holding Evreux for the English king. Eleanor, assuming that her work was finally done, retired in splendor to the family abbey at Fontevraud, near Chinon. She was seventy-two years old.

Richard did not linger long at court. He knew that the contest against Philip would be a long and hard one. William Marshal described it as a "fierce and dangerous war," which "hung in the balance for some time." Richard's armies were made up of a combination of knights doing feudal service, vicious Welsh mercenaries, units deploying Greek fire, an exotic smattering of Saracen fighters, large numbers of siege machines, and the usual bands of crossbowmen and archers. His basic policy was to keep armies in the field under his personal command, while paying large sums to an alliance of princes around the French borders to maintain a united front against Philip.

Philip deployed greater resources than any of his predecessors to chase Richard up and down the borders of his territories. Siege followed siege; alliances shifted, and knights from both sides engaged one another with a ferocity that bordered at times on the comical. Marshal described one battle in which he fought his way alone onto the battlements of the castle of Milly, so exhausting himself in the process that he eventually disarmed the castle's constable by sitting on him.

The winter of 1195–1196 belonged to Richard. He sacked the vital port of Dieppe, which had been granted by Philip to his ally the count of Ponthieu, and disarmed Philip's attempt to lay siege to Issoudun, in Berry. In the subsequent peace, Philip abandoned all claims to Plantagenet territory except the Norman Vexin and a clutch of particularly sensitive border castles. More important, he gave up his alliance with Toulouse, finally ending the long and tiresome proxy war that had been waged in the southwest of Aquitaine for four decades. This reshaped the politics of an entire region at a stroke and showed that Philip's priorities were becoming clear. He had no immediate wish to break up the Plantagenet empire in the south or to threaten England. His eyes were on Normandy and the Vexin. Philip was prepared to use whatever means he could to push the dukes of Normandy permanently out of the Vexin. In 1196 his fortunes changed when he managed to gain custody of Richard's nine-year-old nephew Arthur of Brittany.

Arthur was Henry II's only legitimate grandson in the male line. His mother, Constance, had given birth to him shortly after her husband, Richard's brother Geoffrey, had died. Aside from John, Arthur was the only natural heir to the Plantagenet possessions should Richard die childless. So in early 1196 Richard sent an imperious message to Constance, demanding that she bring Arthur to his court in Normandy. When she refused, Richard invaded Brittany. The Bretons, who had never taken kindly to Plantagenet invasions, promptly packed Arthur off to the French court.

Philip now held a trump card. Richard's relationship with his wife, Berengaria of Navarre, was not close. She had produced no children in six years of marriage. In the same period a generation earlier, Eleanor of Aquitaine had given Henry II two sons and three daughters. Richard was separated from his wife for longer stretches than his father, but to have left the succession dangling so long smacked either of carelessness or of physical deficiency. (The old tale that Richard was more interested in his male friends than in his wife has been roundly discredited.) In any event, Arthur spent several months at the French court and was acquainted with Philip's young son Louis, who was about his age. Philip had discovered another useful wedge to drive into his rival when the time was right.

By the summer of 1197, however, Richard's fortunes had risen once more. His policy of buying the loyalty of Philip's neighbors was proving highly successful, and the war had turned in his favor. Arthur was returned to Brittany following Richard's withdrawal, and Constance began to involve her son in the government of the duchy. Richard undermined a dangerous alliance between Philip and Baldwin count of Flanders by imposing a strict embargo on valuable Anglo-Flemish commerce. He survived a bad wound in the knee by a crossbow bolt during a siege of Gaillon, the French stronghold in the Vexin. Construction was under way on a new forward base in Normandy: the vast, luxurious palace, town, and castle at Les Andelys known as Château Gaillard.

Château Gaillard (Saucy Castle) was Richard's greatest pride and soon became his favorite residence. Towering high on the rock of Andelys, just five miles from Gaillon, this huge, round castle was a statement of defiance: a stake driven into the ground deep inside the Vexin; a monument to Richard's martial legacy. Perched hundreds of feet above a fully realized town and palace, which included a river port, a system of bridges, and luxurious quarters in which the Plantagenet king could hold court, it took just two years to build (Henry II's reconstruction of Dover Castle, by comparison, had taken more than a decade) and drained more money from Anglo-Norman coffers than every other castle-building project of Richard's reign. It was said that while Château Gaillard was being built, blood rained from the skies. Château Gaillard formed one end of a defensive line that ran from the new military base at Portsmouth through Rouen to Les Andelys. Communications could run safely from Normandy to England, allowing English sovereignty to operate smoothly even with the king entrenched in the Vexin.

In July 1197 Richard finally persuaded Baldwin of Flanders to break away from Philip; by the autumn the tilt in power had led Philip to sue for a year's peace. While the truce was in effect, yet another boon fell Richard's way, as the contacts he had made with German princes during his imprisonment bore fruit. The emperor Henry VI died suddenly during a military campaign in Sicily, and in February 1198 the imperial electors were persuaded to appoint Richard's nephew Otto—son of his sister Matilda and Henry the Lion of Saxony—to the throne. Otto had been brought up at Henry II's court in England, and having been appointed count of Poitou in 1196, he was closely tied to the duchy of Aquitaine. He could be counted on for support. With the tide now tugging so powerfully in Richard's direction, Philip began to lose allies to the east and west. Noblemen all across France judged that the duke of Normandy and Aquitaine was once again in the military ascendance. As quickly as they had abandoned Richard during his years in captivity, they now flooded back to him.

Baldwin of Flanders attacked Philip in Artois, opening a second front, and Richard harried the French troops as they moved around the Vexin. In September he launched a surprise attack against Philip's army at Gisors. According to William Marshal, Richard led the attack personally, bellowing, "God is with us!" as he "rode at them just as a ravening lion, starved of food, runs at its prey." As the French army scattered, a bridge collapsed under the weight of the knights trying to cross it. King Philip was fortunate to be pulled alive from a ford. "When they had pulled the king out of the water—he had been very frightened for his life—he declined to stay at Gisors . . . for he feared his enemies very much," wrote Marshal, cheerfully.

Richard was now almost totally dominant throughout the Vexin. Philip held little more than Gisors, and this former Norman stronghold was overshadowed by the new fortress at Les Andelys. It was clear to the French king that the time had come to settle with his rival. As soon as Christmas was over, on January 13, 1199, Philip and Richard met to thrash out the terms of a long-term truce. The papal legate Peter of Capua initially arbitrated the negotiations, hoping to reconcile the two kings and expedite the launch of a new crusade under a new pope, Innocent III. But it was clear during the bad-tempered discussions that Richard bore a great fury against the Church for abandoning him during his imprisonment and for sitting by while Philip threatened his absent lands. Richard sought from Philip a peace that would return every single possession that had been taken from him. Philip was prepared to agree, saving the return of the castle of Gisors, which he hoped to secure by a marriage alliance. Negotiations dragged on into March.

At the end of March, although it was Lent and war making was technically forbidden, a revolt led by the count of Angoulême and the viscount of Limoges broke out in the south. Richard went unhesitatingly to put it down and led a company of men in attacking the castle of Châlus-Chabrol.

It was not a large castle: inside it were forty men and women, of whom only two were trained knights. They were barely equipped for battle or siege, lacking both numbers and munitions. As he examined the castle's defenses, Richard would no doubt have considered that a short siege would suffice to break the defenders' resistance.

Richard's army brought all the usual terrors: men with swords and crossbows galloped through the countryside, burning the homes and farms of nearby villagers before laying siege to the castle itself. Engineers dug tunnels, under the cover of crossbow fire, which flew at the battlements of the castle, keeping defenders pinned down, unable to disrupt the sapping of the walls on which they stood. The rumble of masonry occasionally imperiled those working closest to the walls. But they kept digging, weakening the will of the besieged as surely as they undermined the strength of the stone defenses.

For three days they dug and fired. For three days the small garrison resisted. For three days Richard camped near his men, watching over them, directing them, drawing on all his experience to bring the castle to quick submission. In the gloom of the evening of March 26, he left his tent to inspect the state of the defenses. He was armed with a crossbow, an oblong shield, and an iron helmet, but he wore no other armor. The battlements of the castle were all but deserted in the gathering dusk.

But not entirely. As Richard looked up, he saw a flicker of movement.

A lone body popped up above the ramparts. It was a man later identified by the contemporary English chronicler Ralph de Diceto as one Peter Basilius. He was carrying a crossbow in one hand and a frying pan from the castle's kitchens in the other, as a makeshift shield. Brave in the face of unbeatable odds, the hapless Basilius loosed a single bolt in the direction of Richard's party.

Richard was used to being in the line of fire. From Jaffa to Gaillon, he had stood before hostile forces, trusting in his training, his instinctive feel for the battlefield, and the professionalism of the men around him. He had led men from the front many times before and dodged countless arrows and bolts. He lived for the thrill of battle and took deep pleasure in the noble pursuit of combat. Pathetic as his enemy was here, Richard was filled with admiration for the makeshift courage he saw above him. Characteristically confident under attack, he took time to applaud the indomitable defender before ducking out of the way of his bolt. But the delay was fatal. Whether Richard's reactions were slowing fractionally or pride finally conspired against him, he failed to move in time. The bolt struck him in his left shoulder and sank to a depth of around six inches.

Richard did not cry out. He was a king and a leader. He could not afford to offer succor to the castle's defenders or to worry the men around him. With a wooden shaft sticking out from his shoulder, he simply returned to the royal tent.

When he arrived, it was dark. Richard would have been in considerable pain. The bolt had not severed a major blood vessel and had missed his heart, but it was deep in his body nevertheless. Richard tried to yank the bolt from his shoulder, but as he did so, the wooden shaft snapped, leaving the barbed point buried deep inside his body.

Professional help was required. A surgeon was summoned. Great care was taken to keep the king's injury a secret. By firelight the surgeon tried to take out the wicked shard of metal from the royal shoulder. He dug deep into flesh, widening the wound, searching for the embedded barb. Eventually the bolt was removed, and the wound was bandaged up.

But a darkened medieval battlefield was no place to perform surgery. Soon the wound festered, and during the days that followed, infection set in.

Sickness began to spread throughout Richard's upper body. It was clear what lay ahead. Medieval soldiers did not recover from infected wounds so close to their hearts. And Richard was a soldier to the last.

He remained in his tent, where his condition continued to be a closely guarded secret. He did not leave his quarters, and only four of his fellow soldiers were allowed to enter his presence. The chronicler Ralph of Coggeshall heard rumors that during his confinement Richard ignored the advice of his doctors and behaved "without control." Later another legend of the Lionheart sprung up, to the effect that the king spent his final days on earth having sex with local youths. It is unlikely that this was true, for Richard was dying of gangrene. One of the few people to be told about the severity of the king's sickness was his mother, Eleanor of Aquitaine. As Châlus-Chabrol finally fell, a messenger was dispatched to Fontevraud to tell the aging duchess that her favorite son was gravely ill. Eleanor rode hard to his side and was at the camp when, on April 6, 1199, Richard the Lionheart forgave the brave defender with the frying pan and crossbow and died. His heart was taken to Rouen, to be interred next to his brother Henry. His body was taken to Fontevraud, along with the crown and the splendid costume that Richard had been so impatient about at his coronation. He was buried at his father's feet, the exact spot where his journey as a king had begun.

Lackland Supreme

A dark spring night was settling in on Saturday, April 10, 1199. Hubert
Walter archbishop of Canterbury was in Rouen preparing himself for
bed. The next day was Palm Sunday, the celebration of Jesus's triumphant
entry into Jerusalem. This was a time of contemplation for England's primate, a hero of the Holy Land and a man who had come close to the city of
Jerusalem himself. It was late when a visitor, William Marshal, was announced. He wanted urgently to see the archbishop. It was a visit that Walter had been dreading for days.

The two men were party to secret information. They, along with a tiny
handful of trusted servants, knew that King Richard had been badly injured at Châlus-Chabrol. They had been waiting for news of his condition,
hoping against the worst, but preparing for it too. Walter knew that for
Marshal to visit in person at such an hour could not bode well. Marshal's
biography records the words they exchanged that evening.

"Come now," said Walter as Marshal approached. "Give me your news!"
But his face must have betrayed extreme misgiving.

"I can tell you it's not good, my dear lord," said Marshal.

King Richard was dead. It was disastrous news for both men. As news
leaked across the Continent of the shocking death of the forty-one-year-old
king, his subjects and rival leaders braced themselves for massive upheavals,
knowing that the political map of Europe would begin rapidly to change. So
much of the Plantagenet resurgence of the late 1190s was owed directly to
Richard's personality, his leadership, and his mastery over Philip II of France.
Richard's burning mission, to fight until Philip was put out of every quarter
of his empire, was the cornerstone of his kingship and the thread that bound
all those who followed him. The truce between the houses of Plantagenet and
Capet was as much a personal settlement between the two kings as a political
settlement between two great powers. With Richard gone, all this was
thrown into jeopardy. As Archbishop Walter put it that night, chewing over
the consequences of the dramatic news, "All prowess is extinguished."

The two men talked together as the night grew late. Richard's death
made no sense. Had he been punished for his greed? For lust? Was God

angry? It was impossible to know. The archbishop and the king's loyal knight could only imagine what the future might hold.

Richard had died without a legitimate heir and was estranged from his wife at the time of his death. He had been entirely reckless with regard to the future, making no clear provision for the succession during his lifetime. This was even more problematic because unlike his father, Richard had inherited the Plantagenet lands en masse. It looked more now like one large imperial patrimony than it had in the 1180s, when Aquitaine, Anjou, and the Anglo-Norman realm might have been split up among different claimants. Since Richard's crusading days it had generally been accepted that if this empire was going to be inherited by one man, there were two possible candidates: his brother John and Arthur of Brittany, his twelve-year-old nephew. Early in his kingship Richard had favored Arthur as heir, but according to the information that reached the chronicler Roger de Howden, he named John as his successor on his deathbed. It is quite likely that this decision was made on Eleanor of Aquitaine's advice.

To Marshal and Walter, however, the issue of right in the succession was far from clear. As they stayed up into the night, deep in political speculation, Marshal, a feudal statesman of indissoluble loyalty to the Plantagenets, argued in favor of John. Walter disagreed. Marshal was of the view that Arthur lacked good advice. He called him "unapproachable and overbearing." "If we call him to our side, he will do us harm and damage," Marshal said. "He does not like those in our realm. My advice is that he should never be king. Instead, consider the claim of John: he seems to be the nearest in line to claim the land of his father as well as that of his brother."

This was hardly an incontestable claim. Did the son of a king's older brother (in Arthur's case, this was Henry II's third son, Geoffrey) trump the claim of a king's younger brother? Lawyers and writers disagreed. Customs varied across Europe, and quite frequently the issue was still decided according to the personal suitability of the individuals concerned. Certainly Hubert Walter could not give an irrefutable defense of Arthur's claim in the dead of that April night. But he gave Marshal one dire warning, based not on the law of succession, but on his assessment of John himself. "This much I can tell you," he said. "You will never come to regret anything you did as much as what you're doing now."

John did not inspire confidence. This was perhaps his defining characteristic. Neither princes nor bureaucrats were fully inclined to believe him or to believe in him, and frequently this was with good reason. His career up to that point was pockmarked by ugly instances of treachery, frivolity, and disaster, from his earliest, unwitting involvement in dynastic politics as John Lackland, his father's coddled favorite, until his covetous behavior during his brother's long captivity. John's behavior during the latter years of Richard's reign had been broadly unimpeachable, but it did not take much to recall how appallingly he had acted while Richard had been out of the country. He had rebelled against Richard's appointed ministers, interfered with ecclesiastical appointments, undermined Richard's justiciar, William Longchamp, encouraged an invasion from Scotland, spread rumors that his brother was dead, entreated the king of France to help him secure the English throne for himself, paid homage to Philip for his brother's Continental lands and given him almost the whole duchy of Normandy, attempted to bribe the German emperor to keep his brother in prison, and was almost single-handedly responsible for the feeble state in which Richard had found the Plantagenet lands and borders on his eventual release from captivity.

Unsurprisingly, then, John was still thought by many to be untrustworthy. Contemporary writers commented on his unpleasant demeanor, in dark contrast with his brother's brilliant glow of chivalry. Like Richard and Henry II, John was already known for his tough financial demands and fierce temper; he was thought to be cruel, and he tended to make vicious threats against those who thwarted him. Unlike Henry and Richard, however, he was also weak, indecisive, and mean-spirited. Several writers noted that John and his acolytes sniggered when they heard of others' distress. Very early in his life he was thought by the northern English chronicler William of Newburgh to be "nature's enemy."

On his brother's unexpected death in 1199, John could not be at all certain of a smooth accession. He knew that Philip II would support Arthur's rival claim. John's first action therefore was to seize the royal treasure at the castle of Chinon. He was right to do so, for as he rode on to visit his brother's tomb at Fontevraud and pay his respects to his widow, the winds of opinion in the Plantagenet heartlands were billowing behind Arthur. On Easter Sunday the barons of Anjou, Maine, and Touraine—the beating heart of the empire created by Henry II—declared loyalty to Arthur, at a stroke cutting off Normandy from Poitou and the rest of Aquitaine. At Le Mans, his father's birthplace and dearest city, John was turned away by the garrison and nearly trapped by Philip's and Arthur's armies.

Only in Rouen, where the rules of ducal inheritance were more clearly in favor of a brother over a nephew, did John meet with something like a welcome. On April 25, 1199, he was invested as duke of Normandy with a crown of golden roses placed on his head. This, at least, was a triumph, for to lose Normandy would have been a sorry failure indeed.

The redoubtable Eleanor, now seventy-five years old, led the movement to secure her son as heir in Aquitaine. She had despaired of John's behavior in the early 1190s but was ultimately loyal to her children. The wife of two kings, she would do all in her power to see to it that she was the mother of three. Now she deployed an army under the famous mercenary captain Mercadier, harrying forces loyal to Arthur of Brittany and helping secure John's succession in the face of stern opposition. In England, meanwhile, Marshal turned his belief in John's legitimacy into action. He sent envoys to convince the English barons to take an oath of fealty: it should be obvious, they argued, to those who had interests on both sides of the Channel that John, already invested as duke of Normandy, was a better choice to safeguard their positions. So with the support of Hubert Walter and Geoffrey Fitz Peter, the justiciar, John was accepted as king. But as Marshal, so ardent a supporter in that first night's conversation, later recalled, "Neither the Gascons nor the men of Limousin, the men of Poitou or Anjou, or the Bretons agreed to it at all, for they had no love for his overlordship."

John Softsword

In mid-January 1200 the old king of France met the new king of England on the border between their lands. There were only two years between them in age, but they were separated by a world of experience. John, who was now thirty-two, had been a king for eight months; Philip II, by contrast, had ruled France for just short of twenty years. Christmas had passed, and a truce that had been arranged to discourage warfare during the holy season had held. Now came the first meeting between the two kings since John's accession. They talked for a long time about the truce they were making and embraced warmly. It must have felt to John as though he were being pulled into the warm fold of kingship. But Philip must have known that here, at last, was a Plantagenet rival whom he could hope to dominate. His experience with John ran deep. They had gone to war beside and against each other already—but never on equal terms. During their long history together John had always been the child, the younger brother, the supplicant; Philip, the king and the judge.

The deals John had been ready to make to feel the weight of a crown on his head while his brother had been in captivity had suggested that John hankered for power but had a stunted idea of what wielding authority truly entailed. This was a man who would blink first in a negotiation and who would allow his prerogatives to be chipped away without a serious fight.

John had been crowned king by Hubert Walter at Westminster Abbey eight months earlier, on May 25, 1199. Little time was afforded for a magnificent ceremony, as had been the case in the past. The new king had been showered with gifts and reverence, but the whole thing smacked of a necessary formality rather than a pageant to be reveled in. John could not, nor did he wish to, stay very long in his new kingdom. The anointing and ceremony were precursors to a difficult defense of Normandy, Anjou, and the soft points of his new dominions' borders. Within a fortnight of his coronation John had embarked for the Continent. The situation in Normandy was already urgent, and he needed allies. Philip had backed Arthur of Brittany, and Anjou, Maine, and Touraine were all under attack from the combined French-Breton forces. The middle swath of the Plantagenet territories, which joined the duchy of Normandy with that of Aquitaine, risked being overrun.

Soon after arriving at Dieppe, John had renewed the alliances Richard had so carefully cultivated with the counts of Flanders and Boulogne. That autumn he marched against Philip in Anjou. Here John managed to achieve a great coup. William des Roches, the most powerful baron in the county, who was leading the rebellion there on behalf of Arthur's claim, suddenly switched sides. Messages of support for the new English king had filtered through from both the emperor Otto IV and from Pope Innocent III, and it seemed to des Roches that the tide was now in John's favor.

When des Roches clashed with the French king over a castle in Maine, a convenient rift was opened. Des Roches met John in Le Mans to formalize his change of allegiance. He brought with him a brilliant tribute: Arthur of Brittany and his mother, Constance, ready to make their peace. In theory this should have removed Philip's reason to fight. But that would depend on John's ability to make peace with his nephew. He could not. Constance and Arthur approached John's court with more trepidation than des Roches did. They simply did not trust him to do right by them. On September 22 they went through the formalities of official submission. But as night fell, they absconded and fled back to Philip's court.

This, then, was the situation when John and Philip met on their borders in January 1200. Arthur had submitted to John but was in Philip's hands, a latent threat. Furthermore, many of John's allies were abandoning him for the Fourth Crusade. The counts of Flanders, Blois, and Perche and the marquis of Montferrat all announced during a tournament in Champagne in November 1199 that they were taking the cross. Baldwin of Flanders had doubled the insult by subsequently negotiating peace with Philip, removing John's ability to fight on two fronts in Normandy. And so, five months after their January embrace, John and Philip put their seals to the Treaty of Le Goulet, ostensibly cementing a permanent peace.

Looking back on the Treaty of Le Goulet, the chronicler Gervase of Canterbury recalled the gossip of pilgrims and traders. John's detractors, Gervase remembered, nicknamed him Softsword. Gervase himself disagreed, thinking that war-weariness and financial exhaustion had made peace prudent, but there was no doubt that John's concessions at the very outset of his reign struck some as ill advised. Even as the treaty was sealed, one northern French writer, Andreas of Marchiennes, looked with contempt on John's "sluggish" pursuit of a war that Richard had fought with manly vigor. Andreas was of the view that at Le Goulet John had signed away his right to the castles for which "the whole war had been fought."

Philip had agreed to recognize John as lord of most of the Continental lands held by his brother and father, but the peace terms were skewed heavily toward France. The whole of the Norman Vexin, with the exception of Richard's massive Château Gaillard, was to remain French. So too would Evreux, another vital border county between France and Normandy, and Issoudun, Graçay, and Bourges, in Berry. These may have seemed like small sacrifices to John, but as Richard and Henry II had realized, it was sometimes from such small concessions that great troubles arose.

Ever since 1156, when Henry II first paid homage to Louis VII, the Plantagenet kings had accepted that in theory they held their Continental lands from the French Crown. But this had remained, broadly, a formality. With the Treaty of Le Goulet, John turned it into feudal reality. In return for Philip's acknowledgment of his rights, John agreed to pay twenty thousand marks as a succession duty. This was a vitally important concession, formalizing a relationship of dependency. Philip also littered the Treaty of Le Goulet with instructions appropriate to a more imperious lord-vassal relationship. John was forced to renounce his alliances with Flanders and Boulogne not just as a gesture of peace but as a recognition that they were first and foremost Capetian vassals and loyal to the French Crown before the English. Only Aquitaine, still technically held by John as his mother's heir, was excluded from the treaty.

There were many good reasons for John to have conceded so much at Le Goulet. His brother had subjected his realm to some of the most severe financial demands in its history. How long would heavy taxes levied on barons and Church alike be sustainable? How many more Château Gaillards would be required to keep the French king out of the Vexin, a small strip of land with more strategic than economic importance? How long could England bankroll the mercenaries necessary to keep Normandy on a permanent defensive footing? How could John hope to sustain his brother's system of alliances when all around him friends were disappearing on crusade?

The tempting answer to all these questions lay in the agreement John sealed in May 1200. England's new king had the appetite for power but not for a fight. Thus, in the first five months of the thirteenth century, John granted away a position that had taken his brother, father, and grandfather almost one hundred years to establish. It would be easy to dismiss the wags overheard by Gervase of Canterbury who laughed at John Softsword—they knew not the troubles of a king—but it would soon be clear that much greater trouble lay ahead.

Triumph and Catastrophe

On July 29, 1202, a large party of knights rode noisily up to the walls of Mirebeau Castle, just south of Chinon. There were more than 250 of them, a substantial force, with an intimidating purpose. They had come to capture Eleanor of Aquitaine. The old queen was seventy-eight—old enough, she might have reasoned, not to be troubled by the depredations of enemy armies. But below her, amid the melee of riveted helmets, chain-mail armor, crossbows, swords, and lances, she could pick out a familiar face, that of her sixteen-year-old grandson, Arthur of Brittany. The adventures of her life were not yet over.

Arthur's reasons for wishing to capture his grandmother were simple: she was a valuable prisoner in the war for succession, which he continued to wage against his uncle.

Elsewhere among the besiegers was Hugh de Lusignan, who had reason to hate Arthur's rival with a passion. Two years previously, King John had swept abruptly into Angoulême, the county that neighbored Hugh's, and stolen his young bride, Isabella of Angoulême, from under his nose. Isabella had been betrothed to Hugh in a pact that was designed to unite two of the most important families in Aquitaine. But in August 1200 John had seized the twelve-year-old girl and married her himself in Bordeaux. It was a shameful episode for the Lusignans, which pushed them into open opposition and hostility to his rule. Since then John had done all in his power to provoke the Lusignan family and remind them that he had sided with their rival, the counts of Angoulême. He had taken countless opportunities in the two years since his marriage to put the Lusignans in their place: attacking their men and castles in counties as far apart as La Marche and Eu and summoning them to his feudal court to demand, unsuccessfully, that they fight a judicial duel against his royal champions.

John's high-handed behavior had driven them into the willing arms of Philip II, who spent the first two years of the thirteenth century amassing a large and powerful army. By the spring of 1202 he was ready to turn it against King John. Appealing to the Treaty of Le Goulet, which had established John as his feudal vassal, Philip had decreed that the English king should forfeit all his Continental possessions. He paired the Lusignans up with Arthur, whom he now knighted, betrothed to his young daughter Marie, and acknowledged as duke of Brittany and Aquitaine and count of Anjou and Maine. Then he sent the Lusignans and his new protégé off to attack John's lands in Anjou.

Eleanor, who was not well, tracked political developments with alarm from her sickbed. It did not please her to realize that she would be a target for her grandson's new friends. And sure enough, they had come to find her at Fontevraud, the lavish monastery that served as her retirement home. She had been there for a year or so, recuperating since completing the final diplomatic mission of her career—a long journey to northern Spain, where she had selected from her daughter Eleanor's children with Alfonso VIII of Castile a wife for Philip II's son Louis: Princess Blanche of Castile. When she was given notice of the approach of Arthur's and Hugh de Lusignan's forces in advance, she fled Fontevraud for Poitiers, but they caught up with her at Mirebeau. Her one hope, as hostile knights stalked the castle walls, was that rescue might come from the north. On her flight from Fontevraud, Eleanor had found time to compose an urgent note to John, who was in Normandy, organizing the defense of his frontier castles from Philip's armies. It would take a miracle for him to reach her before the castle's defenses fell, but miracles were all that Eleanor had.

As his mother surveyed the enemy army with trepidation at Mirebeau, John, using recruiting officers in England, was in Le Mans assembling a mercenary army. Throughout the summer his army of paid cutthroats had been swelling. Now, in late July, it was sufficient to the task of taking on Philip in the north and Arthur and the Lusignans in the south.

It was always remarked of Henry II, usually by his exasperated enemies, that he was capable of popping up like a jack-in-the-box wherever and whenever he was least expected, no matter where in his empire he might be. It was this superhuman ability to flog his horse and his armies at speed across the vast Plantagenet territories that had lain at the heart of his success. Now, summoning up the spirit of his father, John traveled the eighty miles that separated Le Mans from Mirebeau in less than forty-eight hours, a punishing pace even for lightly armed men.

They arrived at Mirebeau on the evening on July 31 to find that Arthur and his men had already forced their way into the walled town. Clearly they expected an assault from John because they had blocked up all but one of the town's gates with great mounds of earth. "Securely they awaited the king's arrival, confident in their multitude of proven knights and serjeants," wrote Ralph of Coggeshall. But their confidence was misplaced.

As John raced from Le Mans, he collected William des Roches, who had defected to his side from Arthur's camp in 1200. Des Roches struck a deal with the king. As seneschal of Anjou, the king's chief administrative officer in the region, he knew Mirebeau well. He agreed to lead the attack on the town and castle on the understanding that if Arthur was captured, des Roches would have a guiding voice in his treatment. It was a deal John was happy to make. As they camped before the earthed-up walls of the town, des Roches planned an attack for daybreak.

At dawn Hugh de Lusignan's brother Geoffrey was enjoying a breakfast of roasted pigeons when a vicious assault on the one working gate to the city took him by surprise. John's men surrounded the town, and before long they had battered down the gate. Heavy street fighting ensued, led by the indomitable des Roches, who lost three horses from under him as he led charge after charge against the town gates. Seeing the strength and unusual vigor of their opponents, the rebels fled for the safety of the castle. But they were unable to hold out. Under des Roches's ferocious leadership John's men completed a stunning rout, and Eleanor was freed from the castle and told that Arthur, Hugh and Geoffrey Lusignan, "and 252 of the worthiest knights" had been captured.

It was the most complete and striking victory won by forces under an English king since Richard's relief of Jaffa in 1192. At a stroke, John had decapitated the resistance in Aquitaine and captured Arthur. John's illustrious prisoners were paraded, heavily manacled, through the streets along the road to Normandy, a public warning of the consequences of rebellion. Arthur and Geoffrey Lusignan were taken to Falaise in Normandy, and Hugh de Lusignan was kept in solitary confinement in Caen, under heavy guard. Many of the rest of the prisoners were shipped to English strongholds such as Corfe Castle, the bleak fortress that loomed over the Purbeck Hills, in Dorset. Their imprisonment would be miserable and lonely.

Arthur's incarceration was especially grim. Falaise, a large Norman castle with a square keep, was the birthplace of William the Conqueror and closely connected with the duchy's former capital in Caen. Behind the castle walls the sixteen-year-old Arthur was kept in ghastly conditions. The well bred could generally expect less punitive conditions than the poor and indigent, but medieval prisons as a rule were bleak, dangerous, and lonely. And John's prisons were more dire than that. According to William Marshal, a connoisseur of the rules of war and chivalry, John "kept his prisoners in such a horrible manner and such abject confinement that it seemed an indignity and a disgrace to all those with him who witnessed his cruelty."

Arthur was a high-grade feudal pawn. His captivity under John became one of the most notorious political imprisonments of the thirteenth century. With John still childless, Arthur was heir presumptive to the English throne, and his claim to the Plantagenets' Continental domains rivaled that of John himself. He came from the wild Celtic fringe of mainland France, an area that had claimed to be the birthplace of the legendary King Arthur, after whom the young duke was named. Both his status and his closeness in blood to John ought to have afforded him a certain degree of protection. Knowing his value to Philip, Arthur must have calculated that his uncle could not do him any serious harm without suffering severe consequences. But John did not play by the rules of the time. Despite his success at Mirebeau, he was growing ever more obsessed by the notion that treachery lurked in every corner of his empire. "The king's pride and arrogance increased," wrote Marshal. "They so blurred his vision that he could not see reason."

We do not know how much access Arthur had to news of John's actions during his early months of captivity, but if any word slipped through, he would have known that as he festered at John's displeasure, the whole of Normandy was rotting around him, riven with treason and discontent. Everywhere it was suddenly remembered that Normans and Angevins were supposed to be enemies. The loyalty that Richard had inspired by his personal leadership was ebbing fast, and support for John's rule was crumbling.

Though Arthur was walled off from the world, the effects of his imprisonment spead far and wide. Grumblings grew that John was unchivalrous in his treatment of his captives. Certainly he was behaving badly toward his allies. In September 1202 William des Roches, who had led the storming of Mirebeau on condition that he should have a say over Arthur's fate, was cut out. "The king . . . never kept his agreement with the lord des Roches," wrote Marshal. "[And] as a consequence of this ill-treatment des Roches later crossed over to the King of France's side. The King made a major blunder in not trusting him."

Losing the support of William des Roches was a bad mistake, made worse when des Roches took another valuable ally from John's side: Aimery de Thouars, whose support had only barely been kept by the determined agency of Eleanor of Aquitaine. De Thouars and des Roches were not natural allies, but John contrived to unite two enemies in common opposition to him. Together the two men began raiding Anjou. A month after they abandoned the English king, they led the capture of Angers itself. John clung on in Anjou until December 1202, but it was impossible to resist the surge of rebellious defections to Philip's cause. Piece by piece, turn by turn, Anjou was wrenched from John's hands until all that was left of the Plantagenet heartland was a handful of loyal castles.

As Anjou teetered on the brink, the rebellion spread to Aquitaine. Early in 1203 John released the Lusignans from prison. He hoped that if he offered them the hand of friendship he had so haughtily failed to extend two years previously, they would rally to his cause in northern Aquitaine. They did not. John had taken plenty of hostages as guarantees of his subjects' good behavior, but on release they immediately rebelled against his rule. John had neither the feel for the ways of the south nor the long experience necessary to keep the duchy in order, and its most powerful residents neither feared nor trusted him.

By the end of 1203 John's worries were spiraling out of control. "He saw his marches and land getting worse by the day as a result of war, and Frenchmen who had no love for him and pillaged his land . . . with the connivance of the turncoats who had gone over to their side," wrote Marshal. When he retreated to Normandy in December, John garrisoned his castles with mercenaries, further alienating the local population, as the same mercenaries plundered local towns and monasteries for supplies and riches.

The more John lost friends, the crueler his rule became. When twenty-five prisoners tried to break out of Corfe Prison in England, they were surrounded and had their food supply cut off. Almost all of them starved to death rather than yield to the king. John was far away from Corfe at the time, but the atrocity was nonetheless done in his name.

Early in 1203 John sent instructions to the royal servant Hubert de Burgh, who was serving as Arthur's jailer, demanding that he should blind and castrate his prisoner. Fortunately for Arthur, de Burgh felt a pang of conscience and could not carry out the grisly sentence on the sixteen-year-old, who pleaded for pity. Fearful at having disobeyed the king's instructions, de Burgh then leaked word that Arthur had died of natural causes. The Bretons burned with rage at the idea that their scion had been murdered and swore retribution. As soon as the reaction became clear, de Burgh tried to backtrack, revealing that Arthur was alive after all. But it was too late; the damage had been done. Attacks against John in Brittany had been given a firm moral justification.

How anyone could have believed that Arthur would serve John's purposes better if he were blind, castrated, or dead is uncertain. But logical thought was not always a priority for the English king. John was almost frantic with worry. As Anjou fell to his enemies in January 1203, he nearly lost his queen, Isabella, when rebels surrounded her at Chinon Castle. She had to be rescued by a band of mercenaries.

In the spring of 1203 John was overrun. Philip and his allies held Brittany and dominated almost all of Anjou, Maine, and Touraine. The freed Lusignans pressed John's forces deep into Poitou, where his mother was now too frail to organize the defenses. The French hammered relentlessly at the border fortresses of Normandy, a duchy in which it was said that no man could be trusted any longer to stay true to his word for even a week. All around, allies were scuttling for cover. John was deserted by the count of Alençon, who abandoned him for Philip's cause two days after dining with John. "Count Robert ... behaved disgracefully, for after the King had ... given him some of his wealth, and kissed him on the mouth, the very same day the count laid him low," wrote Marshal.

John was paralyzed by the immensity of the task and his own indecision. He still held Arthur, although more by luck than by judgment. He had his throne in England and a reasonable grip on lower Aquitaine. But nothing else was certain. John could neither direct an effective resistance nor inspire anyone else to do the same. All he could do was sit behind his ever-receding lines and hope for the best.

Lackland Undone

It was the Thursday before Easter, a mournful time for all Christians. King John was drunk and angry. As he sat down to his dinner in Rouen, he was surrounded by invisible enemies and oppressed by dark thoughts. He trusted almost no one and could not ride safely around his own duchy without fear of ambush or attack.

Also in Rouen that night was Arthur of Brittany. Arthur was not enjoying a debauched dinner that evening. He had been transferred from Falaise after the debacle of his rumored mutilation and had languished in a dungeon in Rouen ever since. William de Briouze, an immensely powerful and wealthy nobleman whose estates stretched across the Welsh borders, had escorted the prisoner to his king. Briouze was a close ally of John's; it was he who had captured Arthur at Mirebeau. Knowing the mood of his king when he delivered up the young duke, he claimed that he would no longer answer for Arthur's safety.

Briouze's fears were well founded. After dinner on Maundy Thursday, John's drunkenness took a turn for the belligerent. We will never know what he was thinking. The best witness we have claims he was possessed by the devil. Certainly he must have appeared a terrifying specter to all who saw him as he made his way, drunk, to Arthur's cell. Although we cannot be totally certain of the facts of that terrible night, it is highly likely that John entered the prisoner's cell and killed the young man with his own hands, before tying a heavy stone to his nephew's lifeless body and throwing it into the river Seine, where it was later retrieved by a fisherman. The nuns of Notre-Dame-des-Prés afforded Arthur a Christian burial in secret, for fear of John's wrath.

If it was possible to visit greater sacrilege on the festival of Easter, then no English king ever did. But John did not appear to have much remorse. In fact he seems to have taken comfort from his nephew's death. He sent a letter to his mother soon afterward, with a cryptic message containing the words "the grace of God is even more with us now than [the messenger] can tell you."

But John was wrong. The grace of God was about to abandon him, with disastrous consequences. Normandy, Brittany, and greater France had been swirling with rumors of Arthur's fate for months. The news of his death would not become fully accepted at Philip's court until 1204, but even while it was only a foul rumor, the duke's murder placed John in an impossible position. In all subsequent negotiations with Philip II, the French king had a trump card. "No peace until you first produce Arthur" was the refrain. And now, even if he had wanted peace, John could do no such thing.

As the summer of 1203 unfolded, Philip took advantage of John's perilous position—trapped in Normandy between angry Bretons and rebellious Poitevins in the south, while the French king's own armies pushed in from the east. John continued to base himself in Rouen and sallied back and forth between the city and the eastern front. At neither was the news ever encouraging. Philip gamboled throughout Plantagenet territories as he pleased. He was able to take a boat all the way down the Loire—the artery through what should have been the heart of Plantagenet holdings—in perfect safety.

In such a climate, Norman morale began to dissolve. Castles along the border capitulated as soon as Philip approached. John lost Conches, then Vaudreuil with barely a whisper. The knights garrisoning the latter disgracefully did not even bother to mount a proper defense. The Norman defenses were eroded with the ease of melting sand castles. At the end of August the French army rumbled toward the greatest castle of them all: Château Gaillard.

Richard's prized citadel was built to be unbreachable. But now Philip's forces massed around the fortress, which towered on an enormous cliff, with the Seine sweeping around a bend below. They blockaded the river, hoping to starve the enemy into submission. One night at the end of summer John attempted to break the blockade with a flotilla of supply boats and an accompanying commando force of mercenaries. Led by William Marshal, John's men attacked in the warmth of the late-summer night. But luck cruelly deserted him. As the rowers struggled with the current of the Seine, they lost step with the land army on the riverbank, and the massive invasion fleet was picked off in staggered waves by the French defenders until the river ran red in the darkness.

This was the end of John's serious attempts to save Château Gaillard. The siege lasted until March 1204, but John did not try to break it again. Instead, he made a violent but useless attempt to distract Philip on the

Breton front, burning the town of Dol. But the overriding sense during the autumn of 1203 was that John's grip on power was unraveling. Gossip spread that he spent all his time in bed with his teenage wife, dismissing demands to raise himself for a proper defense of Norman independence with the insouciant words "Let be, let be, whatever he takes now I will one day recover." William Marshal watched bewildered as the king took to riding aimlessly about the countryside, disappearing from his court without a word and touring the back roads of his own duchy, for fear of meeting traitors on the highways.

When Christmas 1203 approached, John left Normandy for the last time. Despite having promised that he would stay in his duchy and fight on for a year, in early December he made private preparations to send his baggage train back to England. Before dawn on December 5 he rode hard from Rouen to Bayeux via Caen. As he set sail for Barfleur Harbor with his queen beside him, John passed the rock that had killed the drunken revelers aboard his great-uncle William the Aetheling's *White Ship* in 1120. That tragedy had been the catalyst for a bloody civil war in England for more than half a century of Plantagenet dominance over France, from Rouen to Toulouse. Now, as John's more sober crew steered clear of danger and pulled strongly toward Portsmouth, that window of mastery was closing. Behind him in Normandy a few remaining loyalists fought on, hoping to hold out against Philip's relentless advance. John promised to return to their side, but he never did.

Of the vast dominions conquered by Henry II and defended by Richard I, a ragged core remained. Barring isolated castles and pockets of loyalists, John had lost most of Normandy, Anjou, Maine, and Touraine. He was the most despised man in Brittany. He retained nominal control in Poitou and the rest of Aquitaine only because of the residual loyalty that the nobles of the duchy felt toward his mother. To reconquer what had been lost from a resurgent, vastly enriched French empire under a king who had handsomely earned his nickname, Philip Augustus, was a task that would have daunted John's father and brother at the height of their considerable powers. John himself was totally inadequate for the task. The best he could do was flee the embers of his collapsed Continental empire with his tail between his legs. It was a dismal way to go.

PART III

Age of Opposition
(1204–1263)

When a bad man has the advantage, cruelty and
outrage are the consequences.

—William Marshal

Salvaging the Wreck

England froze. In 1204 the country was struck by a cruel winter that suspended life and crushed hope. In London the Thames filled with ice so thick that men and women crossed from the south bank to the north on foot. In the fields the ground was so hard that it could not be plowed until the end of March. Winter crops were destroyed by the cold, and vegetables were dug up by the starving when they were little more than seedlings. Prices soared as famine racked the country. The cost of oats rose tenfold in a year. There was widespread misery and suffering. The word on the street, recorded by Ralph of Coggeshall, was that God had punished King John by taking Normandy from him, and now the punishment was being extended to England.

John had been marooned in the kingdom for a year. It had not been an easy time. Although his court was characteristically gay and lively, amused by indulgent feasting and the chivalrous entertainments of the young men who were known as the king's bachelors, no one could fail to notice the hardship that lay all around. Rumors sped around that England was about to be invaded from France. It was said that Philip Augustus had found a convenient excuse to attack in the form of claims held by the counts of Brabant and Boulogne to English lands that had been taken from them during Henry II's reign. Philip's appetite to crush the Plantagenets was thought to have no limits; John's ability to lose his inheritance, to know no end.

The threat of invasion was taken seriously. At a great council held in January 1205 John ordered every man over the age of twelve to enter into a sworn pact to defend the realm and preserve the peace. Failure to take the oath was to be counted by local constables as an admission of treachery. It was decreed that those who failed to act to defend the realm in the event of an invasion were to be punished by permanent disinheritance or perpetual slavery. In the freezing ports no ships were allowed to leave without written permission from the king.

It is easy to understand why such fears took root. The collapse of the Plantagenet cause in France had been fast, dramatic, and painful. The duchy of Normandy had not survived John's departure and was now wholly

Philip's, subsumed into the French kingdom for the first time in living memory. Anjou, Maine, and Touraine were all but gone, save for a few islands of loyalty at the fortresses of Chinon and Loches, held by good men surrounded by the French. The absent John's name was blackened in all parts of the French kingdom, as word began to circulate freely that Arthur of Brittany had been murdered.

The situation was only a little better in Aquitaine. On April 1, 1204, Eleanor of Aquitaine had died. She had lived to the extraordinary age of eighty, passing her dying moments at the abbey of Fontevraud. To her last day, decrepit but defiant, she continued to buttress her son against impossible odds in her duchy, granting land and privileges to loyalists and shoring up the Plantagenet cause even while living as a habited nun.

In accordance with the will she had made in 1202, Eleanor was buried beside her husband, Henry II, and her favorite son, Richard I, in the chapel at Fontevraud. Three members of the twelfth century's most charismatic and influential family now lay at rest together, at far greater peace in death than they ever were in life. The effigy on Eleanor's tomb still stands, as remarkable as the woman it immortalizes. It was made to capture her in the magnificent prime of her adult life, her eyes closed but a book open in her hands. It was—and still is—an image of great intellectual power.

The nuns of Fontevraud paid Eleanor their respects in an obituary in which she was thanked for opulent gifts that she had made to the abbey—of gold, silver, jewels, and silk. The nuns also observed, somewhat obsequiously, that the queen had "brightened the world with the splendor of her royal progeny." Given the careers of Henry the Young King, Geoffrey duke of Brittany, and John king of England, this was not wholly believable. Yet Eleanor had been a magnificent queen whose influence had straddled three important reigns and who had loved and guided her sons even when they behaved unwisely.

Without his mother's guiding hand, John had little hope in Aquitaine. Already he had offended numerous barons by his marriage to Isabella of Angoulême and his clumsy management of the duchy's delicate politics. No right-minded lord there would pay homage to the English king as his mother's successor, for fear of dispossession by the ascendant king of France. As soon as Eleanor's death was known, many lords who had accepted her authority scrambled to make their peace with Philip. The French king advanced in triumph on Poitou, the county from which all Aquitaine was ruled, during the summer of 1204. Simultaneously John's brother-in-law Alfonso VIII of Castile invaded Gascony, in the southwest of Aquitaine, claiming that it was his by right of his wife, John's elder sister Eleanor. The last corner of the Plantagenet empire in Europe creaked and crumbled.

All this was dismaying for John. As winter's death gripped England in the first months of 1205, it looked very much as if all of the holdings his family had accumulated within the kingdom of France might soon be gone. It was not enough simply to cower in England and defend the coast, and John must have realized that his public reputation, never particularly high, was at a nadir from which it might never recover if he did not act swiftly. He would have to make a stand. Men like the Melrose chronicler were recording for posterity that he had "ignominiously lost his castles and lands across the sea."

So in the summer of 1205, as invasion fears began to subside, John began preparing for a huge assault on France, directed from two points of attack. A fleet from Portsmouth would beach on the Norman coast and reconquer the duchy from the west, while a second expedition from Dartmouth was to undertake a simultaneous advance on Poitou. This force would be commanded by John's illegitimate brother William Longespée earl of Salisbury, a man of about the same age as John, of high military reputation and experience, and a good friend of the king, with whom he passed many happy hours at the gaming table.

To effect his plans, John ordered the largest military mobilization since Richard had embarked on crusade. He would preside over a massive expansion of royal sea power. Richard had been the first Plantagenet king to amass a significant English naval force, mobilizing large numbers of boats in 1190, building another seventy vessels to patrol the Seine in 1196, and founding Portsmouth as the great naval town to link England with Normandy. John now carried this further. Forty-five warships had been built to patrol England's coasts in 1203–1204; to expand the naval force any faster would require different means. In 1205 John simply seized all the shipping vessels that his constables deemed convertible for war. Even if a vessel was only large enough to carry a few horses, it was appropriated from its owner and amassed for the nascent royal navy.

To fill the warships, there was a drive to muster men and matériel. Thousands upon thousands of horseshoes, nails, crossbow bolts, and arrowheads were struck. Pig carcasses were salted, and great sides of venison rumbled on carts down to the coast. The national coinage was recommissioned. New silver pennies, stamped with John's image, flooded the country. Everyone handling one in receipt of payment for a service rendered to the war effort would have looked upon his king's face: his hair curling about his ears, his beard cropped short, and his eyes, even in the simple minted likeness, bulging out at the holder, daring that person to defy him.

Many of these coins were used to recruit mercenary soldiers: sailors and men-at-arms who were transported to the coast as midsummer approached. Perhaps a quarter of a year's revenue was pumped into military preparation, funding the vast human cargo that was loaded onto the great ships that floated in The Solent. According to the English chronicler Ralph of Coggeshall, it was the largest English army ever assembled and the greatest collection of ships in a single English port.

Here, at last, John was acting with purpose. If England was busy, however, it was not entirely united. Although John proved he could assemble a vast army, he was hamstrung by the changing mood of the English barons. John's invasion preparations may have resembled a crusade muster, but the cause did not move hearts with quite the same fervor. When Normandy had been threatened in earlier years, there was a clear interest among the English magnates in supporting the king. Henry II had been careful to pursue the Norman habit of keeping his barons' cross-Channel estates intact. He had retained the political integrity of the Anglo-Norman realm by making sure that the great lords remained truly Anglo-Norman—with interests and lands that spanned both territories and gave them a self-interest in assisting the king to keep them together and defend them from external threats.

John's loss of Normandy, however, profoundly changed a status quo that had existed for nearly 150 years. Forced to decide whether they wished to keep their lands in England or in Normandy, most barons made a choice in 1204 and threw in their lot with one king or the other. They ceased almost overnight to become Anglo-Normans and pledged their allegiance either as English subjects or as French. The Channel became a divide, rather than a causeway, between kingdom and duchy. A few great lords, like William Marshal, came to private arrangements with both kings for the security of their lands in both kingdoms. They were in an equally ambiguous position: some had paid homage to Philip for their Norman lands and to John for their English. It was impossible to go to war with either lord without betraying their promise to the other.

So when John arrived in Portsmouth to inspect his marvelous fleet in 1205, he found his English barons unwilling to come with him and fight. There was a furious argument at Porchester Castle between John and Marshal. The king accused Marshal of acting treasonably in coming to terms with Philip; Marshal gave a grand speech in which he presented himself as betrayed by the king and warned his fellow barons that the king planned to disinherit him and "will do [the same] to all of you once he becomes powerful enough."

Even if the rest of the barons had been prepared to trust in John's character as a general, they were now deeply unswayed by the prospect of fighting either for Norman lands in which they had no interest or against a king in Philip whose wrath was potentially as great as John's. As the mood turned sharply against setting out for the French coast, Marshal and Hubert Walter begged the king not to cross the Channel. Walter listed some practical reasons: Philip was massively more wealthy and militarily stronger; John had precious few safe houses on the Continent and was relying on an alliance with Poitevins, who were a naturally treacherous race; the king should not leave England undefended when Philip's nobles had designs on invasion themselves; and England had no heir should John meet his end on the battlefield.

It amounted to a mass mutiny, in the most humiliating circumstances imaginable. The whole invasion force at Portsmouth was now useless, for without the barons who were to provide leadership and their own private resources, there was no hope of retaking Normandy. John was beside himself with rage. The king put to sea for a couple of days, sailing up and down the coast in the fruitless hope that he might shame or persuade the barons into changing their minds. It was to no avail. Salisbury's expedition from Dartmouth successfully crossed the Channel to reinforce the garrison of La Rochelle, but for the most part all the preparations of 1205 had come to nothing. Across the Channel Philip went about his business, going merrily into territories that his father could only have dreamed of visiting. The fall of Chinon and Loches in the summer meant that the whole of Touraine was now in French hands. It had been another disastrous year.

While it would scarcely have been possible to repeat the fiascoes of 1204 and 1205, it is still to John's credit that in 1206 he experienced an upturn in his fortunes. Instead of being cowed by the failure of his invasion, he adjusted his sights. He spent the winter of 1205 sending chests of treasure to various potential allies across the Channel and the spring of 1206 touring the north of England, attempting to personally charm the barons of Yorkshire, Cumberland, Cheshire, and Lancashire into supporting his military endeavors. In April 1206 another large expedition set off from England, this time aiming for Poitou. John was at the head, supported by the barons he had either bribed or coaxed into following him. Arriving at La Rochelle in June, he led an army around the lower coastal regions of France and recovered parts of Aquitaine: regained the Saintonge, strengthened his hand in his wife's county of Angoulême, and reversed the gains that Alfonso VIII had made in Gascony. Toward the end of summer the king allied himself with the powerful Poitevin baron Aimery de Thouars, and marched north toward Anjou. There they received word that Philip II, who had preferred to assure himself that Normandy was secure, was raising an army of his own. Not willing to let a whole summer's gains be undone by defeat, John backed away, and in October 1206 he agreed to a two-year truce with Philip.

It had been a moderately successful campaign. Still, the fact remained that John now ruled over England, the Channel Islands, and a reduced coastal rump of Aquitaine, a mere slice of the great territories he had inherited. He was a king of England who, unlike his predecessors, would be forced to remain in his kingdom. As John learned to rule England, the realm discovered what it meant to have a restless, aggressive Plantagenet king permanently in its midst.

They found him a busy overlord. John wanted to know his kingdom intimately, and he was always on the move. This was not entirely novel, for itinerant travel was a matter of kingly necessity, and very few areas of the English countryside could accommodate a king and his vast court for long. But even by royal standards, John was a restless traveler. He rarely stayed anywhere for more than a few days, picking his way from royal castles and hunting lodges to palaces and manors, resting awhile before moving immediately on.

John cared more for luxury, finery, and display than Henry II had. He took regular baths in an age when this was not the general fashion, and the bachelors of his household were given to displays of courtly ostentation. Yet fundamentally the king's household was a cavalcade of carts and packhorses, stretching out for hundreds of yards as the court rumbled through the countryside. Everything was portable: finely dressed servants carried bed linen and precious plate, heavy pouches of coin, the valuable books John enjoyed reading, and well-guarded caches of precious jewels. John's chapel could be unpacked by the roadside, as could his dining room. The great snaking caravan train moved twenty or so miles every day, churning up muddy roads and drawing openmouthed spectators as John called on his subjects and enjoyed their generous hospitality.

John's royal progress was a magnificent spectacle. And while its presence would have lain heavy on the shoulders of the Englishman who had to bear the burden of royal hospitality, the approach of the royal court also came with some advantages. For under John the court was not simply a traveling circus. It was also a judicial circuit.

Everywhere he went, John thought of lawgiving. His tutor as a young man had been Henry II's chief justice and one of the leading legal thinkers of his age, Ranulf Glanvill. As a result, John was deeply interested in the role of a king as supreme judge. He engaged with the law and sat in legal judgment with unprecedented zeal. He took a close personal interest in the smallest, meanest cases. And his law was much in demand. He traveled with professional justices in tow and sat with them as they heard the cases that were waiting in the localities for the king's law to arrive and decide them.

We have some extraordinary images of John's court touching the lives of ordinary people in the early thirteenth century. The beneficiaries of his judicial intervention were many and varied. He gave reprieve to a little boy who had accidentally killed a friend by throwing a stone. He dismissed a case against a mentally deficient man who had confessed to a crime of which he was clearly innocent. He threw himself into the minutiae of cases that touched in only the slightest degree on his royal prerogative or interest. He was concerned for the plight of the poor.

All this was highly unusual and marked a significant departure from the behavior of previous English kings. Henry II had been a great legalist, but he had been interested primarily in expanding royal jurisdiction and devolving the judicial aspects of English kingship during his long absences. Richard, simply by virtue of the fact that he spent almost no time in England during his reign, had followed suit. By contrast, King John was fascinated by the great machine of law and government. He was a hands-on king, closely involved in day-to-day governance and keen to intervene in person wherever he could, from disputes between the great barons to stone throwing between boys.

Of course John could not run government and the legal system single-handed. Hubert Walter, the archbishop of Canterbury and veteran administrative servant, had died from a septic carbuncle on his back in July 1205, and John had—according to several chroniclers—declared: "Now for the first time I am king of England!" With Walter gone, the king gathered around him a new set of advisers and officials. Some were brought over from the lost Continental territories. Men like Peter des Roches, Peter de Maulay, Falkes de Bréauté, and Girard d'Athée were noticeable for their foreign names and manners, which reminded Englishmen that their king was not a native prince, even if he was now restricted to the realm. But there was not a wholesale takeover of government by foreigners. English-born men retained high posts; they included the justiciar Geoffrey Fitz Peter, the treasurer William of Ely, and the chief forester Hugh Neville.

After 1206 the overriding aim for all those men, and for John too, was simple: they needed to raise money. John was going to require vast sums of cash, both to fund his own armies of mercenaries and to pay a network of Continental allies to oppose Philip. It promised to be a more expensive task than it had been for any of his ancestors.

Both Henry II and Richard I had had an advantage in fighting their wars against the Capetian Crown: both were generally defending their lands rather than conquering them afresh. The cost of manning Richard's defensive lines along the Seine and paying his allies in Germany and Flanders might have been punitive, but they were borne in part by Normandy and the rest of the Continental dominions. This was a luxury John did not have. If he had any hope of regaining his inheritance, he would have to rely primarily on his English revenues.

John set about the task of exploiting those English revenues with a vigor that was evident to all. The hostile chronicler Roger of Wendover spread stories that John was a tightfisted man who gave lousy tips to those who helped him. This was largely slanderous, but it demonstrated the popular view that the king was a miser obsessed with scraping every penny from his subjects. For indeed there were piles of pennies to scrape. As John traveled England, he would have seen everywhere the signs of its prosperity, even after the heavy tax burdens of Richard's reign. The early thirteenth century was a period of booming development in trade and industry, as well as monetary inflation originating in European silver from newly discovered mines, which had been flooding the country with coin since the 1180s.

In 1207 John made his first serious move to tap this wealth. On goods, revenues, lands, and property he levied a thirteenth—a tax of one shilling in every mark—on the whole country's movable goods. It raised an astonishing amount of money for the royal coffers: £57,425, or more than two years' revenue. There had been a steady series of experiments with this sort of tax during the previous two decades, but the thirteenth was an extraordinary success, which emphasized both the wealth that existed in England and the Crown's ability to tap into it through a well-organized system of royal administration. Although John did not know or plan it, the thirteenth was to form the tax model on which all the regular income of medieval and Tudor England would be based.

Direct taxation of the wealthy was only part of his drive to exploit the revenues of his realm. For John, the most obvious way to accrue greater profit from kingship was through the legal system. In this, he used two interlocking tactics. The first involved the simple profits of justice. When Henry II had established a deep and penetrative system of royal justice and government, by which the royal law was easily accessible throughout England, and the role of the royal sheriff was the most important position in local government, it had not been done for the pure love of administrative reform. Rather, there was a clear understanding that justice was a profitable enterprise. The royal chancery made money from selling writs. The Crown prospered handsomely from the fines and forfeitures of property that were the result of criminal convictions in the courts. The eyres—large itinerant courts of justice—that traveled the country both restored law and order and brought in a great deal of money to the Crown, and the accompanying forest eyres (dealing specifically with crimes committed in the king's forestland), which aggressively asserted the rights of the Crown over the extensive forestland that stretched across England, were pure profit-making enterprises.

A whole series of forest eyres were sent out between 1207 and 1210 as John squeezed thousands of pounds in total from counties in which forestland had been encroached or wild beasts hunted without royal permission. A total of £8,738 was brought in solely from forest eyres during those years—more than double what had been realized in 1198–1201. It was both a sign of the efficiency and extent to which the Crown could use justice to squeeze out profit and a mark of John's newfound determination to exploit his royal rights to new levels after the loss of Normandy.

The second way in which John used the law to profit was far more political and eventually caused him far more problems. He used it as a direct tool by which to both tax and control the great barons of England.

Justice in the royal courts may have been widely available, but it was ultimately subject to the king's discretion. To have the king's courts launch an investigation into a private matter would come at a cost, and John was fully prepared to charge high fees. At every stage of a legal case wealthy litigants could offer the king large bribes for favorable judgments or stays of procedures. A typical fee charged by John in 1207 was a thousand pounds and fifteen palfreys from one Gerard de Furneval for peace in a legal case being pursued against Nigel de Luvetot. Hundreds and thousands of pounds changed hands as litigants bid for particular outcomes to trials and actions. Not all the proceeds reached the king directly—plenty was taken by his ministers—but there was a period of rapid inflation of judicial payments during John's reign that amounted to a vast system of justice for sale. This was in some senses the way of the world, but the spiraling costs under John made it a more and more onerous system in which to operate.

Alongside this was a rapid inflation in the costs of what are now known as feudal incidents. England's political society was built on a complex system of bonds between lords and their vassals, in a hierarchy topped by the king and his barons. In theory, the king guaranteed the internal and external safety of his subjects, and they honored him with allegiance and customary payments for certain privileges. The most common of these payments were for the great rituals of aristocratic family life: an eldest son knighted, a daughter married, or a son coming into his father's inheritance. The fines—or reliefs—paid to the king for these privileges were held to be established by custom, and the king, in swearing his coronation oath to uphold the customs of the realm, had agreed to abide by them or to keep within the bounds of reason when deciding who should pay what.

A king could also exercise certain privileges of kingship. He could auction off an aristocratic widow or heiress to the highest bidder or else take a payment from a widow so that she would not be forced to remarry. A child who came into his inheritance before the age of majority (twenty-one for boys) would not be allowed to control his lands; rather, the king could take charge of them himself in the form of a wardship, or else he could sell the right to control and profit from a wardship to another of his subjects.

In the course of a lifetime a great magnate might run up a massive debt to the Crown for his feudal dues. Frequently, however, this debt remained notional, and it was never fully called in by the Crown. It might be paid in installments or not paid at all, depending on the king's lenience. It was a form of financial bond between king and subject.

John, in his mood of financial need following the loss of Normandy, saw the system of fines and reliefs as a great potential source of wealth and power. The generally accepted relief for inheriting the estates of an earl was one hundred pounds. In some cases John charged seven times that sum. He began to demand faster payment of debts; hundreds or thousands of pounds were now called up in payment over a fixed schedule. The penalty for failing to make payments was the seizure of lands.

In 1207 the first major forfeiture occurred when John seized the lands of the earldom of Leicester, which had been vacant since the death of the fourth earl, Robert Beaumont, in 1204. Instead of honoring the right of inheritance of Beaumont's daughter Amicia and her husband, John took the estates into his own hands and confiscated the revenues, citing as his reason the nonpayment of debt. It might have been legally plausible, but if one of the fundamental duties of a king was to protect the property of his subjects, John was doing precisely the opposite.

This, then, was the king that the realm of England came to know in the years immediately following John's loss of Normandy. The systems of government did not change in any substantial way, but the demands of the king in charge of them grew very much more urgent. Nor was there any sign that they would soon abate. On October 1, 1207, the nineteen-year-old queen, Isabella of Angoulême, gave birth to a baby boy at Winchester Castle. It was the first Plantagenet son to have been born since John himself, forty years previously. He was named Henry, after his illustrious grandfather, once lord of Normandy, Anjou, Maine, Touraine, and Aquitaine. There could have been no greater signal of John's intentions: to raise the money he required to take back all that his own father had won. England had little choice but to follow him.

A Cruel Master

The Plantagenets were often likened by the chroniclers of their times to devils: kings who wielded immense power, but who could also be unnaturally cruel. In this respect John was no different from the rest of his family. Yet even by the standards of his age, the grip that the king exerted on his realm between 1208 and 1211 was severe and overbearing. During these years, as John's confidence soared, he exerted his royal mastery over every aspect of life in England. As he matured as a king, he not only fulfilled his dream of amassing the greatest hoard of treasure held by any king of England before him but also extended the power of the Crown over Scotland, Wales, and Ireland, ruthlessly impoverished and exiled families that opposed his rule, extorted vast sums of money from England's Jews, and—most spectacular of all—faced down the pope in a battle for supremacy over the Church.

The period of John's cruel mastery was heralded on February 15, 1208, when an ominous sign loomed in the sky. Men and women looked up with awe and foreboding into the darkness as, according to Roger of Wendover, the moon appeared "first of a blood red color, and afterward of a dingy nature." It was a lunar eclipse, and like all celestial signs, it had a powerful effect on the medieval mind. The eclipse was seen as a portent of evil, and within five weeks the portent was fulfilled. The church bells of England fell still, and thanks to a fierce and lengthy argument between the king and Pope Innocent III, the realm was placed under papal interdict. The disagreement between John and Innocent had fairly mundane origins, but it spiraled quickly into a matter of international importance. It concerned power, precedent, and preeminence. Its effects reached down into the lives of every man and woman and child in England.

It all began in 1205, when Hubert Walter's death, shortly after John's aborted invasion of Normandy, left the archbishopric of Canterbury vacant. John was determined that it should go to a man of his choosing: John de Gray bishop of Norwich, an experienced legal clerk, judge, and occasional diplomat who had served as John's secretary and lent the king money pawned against royal jewels during the retreat from Normandy.

The election protocols to Canterbury were disputed, however, and John found that he could not gift such a high ecclesiastical office without a fight from the Church. The chapter of clerics at Canterbury, who claimed an ancient right to elect the new archbishop, opposed Gray in favor of their own man, the subprior Reginald. In December John went in person to browbeat the chapter into electing Gray. When news of this reached Rome, it enraged Innocent III, a dogmatic reforming pope who believed strongly that he had ultimate sovereignty over each of Europe's kings. He overturned Gray's election in March 1206, rejected Reginald's candidacy, and put forward his own candidate, Cardinal Stephen Langton, a theologian and scholar with a pious demeanor, a talent for writing hymns, and a reforming instinct that pleased Innocent. In Rome on June 17, 1207, the pope consecrated Langton as archbishop of Canterbury.

When John heard that Langton had been elected his new archbishop, he flew into a rage. He sent furious letters to Rome, dark with promises to stand up for his royal rights until his death and threats to embargo all travel to the papacy from his ports. When this made hardly any impression upon Innocent, John expelled the monks of Canterbury from England, declared Langton an enemy of the Crown, and took the possessions of the See of Canterbury into royal custody. Innocent responded, on March 23, 1208, by placing the whole of England under interdict.

A papal interdict was supposed to be a grim sentence. It forbade almost all church services from being held, effectively withholding God's offices from an entire people. Numerous European kingdoms suffered such a sentence during the twelfth and thirteenth centuries, for it was a standard weapon used in any dispute between a pope and a king. Innocent himself had previously issued interdicts against both Norway and France. The sentence was indefinite and could last as long as the pope's displeasure prevailed. So from the spring of 1208, silence descended on John's realm as all church services ceased. The rhythm of life was suspended. Only confession, anointing of the dying, and baptism of children were permitted. Elsewhere church doors were boarded shut, and priests sat idle. Marriages took place in porchways, and the dead were buried outside the walls of towns, in ditches by the roadside, with no priest standing by. England was placed in a form of ecclesiastical Coventry.

John's reaction was worthy of his father. At first he was angry: upon hearing of the interdict he was said to have gone nearly mad with fury, blaspheming and cursing at the presumption of popes, swearing by God's teeth that he would pluck out priests' eyes and clip their false tongues. Yet John was also a pragmatist, and the day after the interdict was proclaimed, royal officers swept England, seizing clerical property in the king's name. Barns and parks, fields and fishponds, all were taken by John's agents, leaving the English clergy not just idle but impoverished. Sheriffs and administrators were put into place to manage the property in the king's name, and county committees were appointed to assess clerical wealth and pay the clergy a small living allowance during their time out of work. Two weeks later he started permitting dispossessed clergy to buy back their property, on onerous conditions. Clergy who wished to have their lands and property free from direct royal interference were forced to hand over large portions of their revenues to the king.

By these ingenious methods, John collected vast sums from the English Church during the five years of its estrangement from Rome and enjoyed himself while doing it. Perhaps his most inventive scheme was to take hostage and ransom back his clergy's wives, concubines, and mistresses. Since plenty of churchmen had babies in their houses, it was a price that many of them had no choice but to pay.

It seemed that the sentence that was intended by Innocent to put the fear of popes into King John had in fact swelled the royal coffers. Yet one did not laugh in the face of the pope with impunity. The personal cost to John of his amused disregard for the interdict was the most severe that the Church could apply to him. On January 1209 Innocent began proceedings to excommunicate him. By November of that year the sentence had been passed. It was now not only John's kingdom but the king himself who was officially exiled from the Church.

To excommunicate a king was a very severe sentence because it tacitly encouraged other Christian kings to attack England without fear of papal condemnation. Yet excommunication, a fate that even Henry II had avoided after Becket's murder, seemed to do little to discountenance John. No invasion came. The worst that happened was a mass exodus of English bishops, many of whom went into exile overseas. And even this was hardly a burden on John's kingship; as bishoprics and abbacies fell vacant, their profits reverted to the Crown.

So another sentence passed lightly over John's head. After a while the only real effect of the interdict and excommunication was a moderate inconvenience to ordinary Englishmen and a massive financial penalty on the English clergy. John's income from the interdict amounted to something in the region of twenty thousand marks a year, perhaps as much as three times what was raised by the Saladin tithe of 1188.

As the interdict crisis established John's temporary supremacy over the Church, he was vigorously exploring other ways to impose himself on others of his neighbors and subjects. At Christmastime 1209–1210 he turned his attention to the Jews, who held a monopoly on moneylending and were a very small but extremely rich group within England. Legally the Jews were the king's personal chattels, and it was only by royal protection that they could live and work. John tapped their wealth initially with a tallage of sixty-six thousand marks, a vast sum that was extracted with extreme prejudice. Throughout England, Jews of both sexes were persecuted. According to the chronicler Walter of Coventry, they were "seized, imprisoned and tortured severely, in order to do the king's will with their money; some of them after being tortured gave up all they had and promised more."

None of this was conceptually new. In 1187 Henry II had taken a quarter of the Jews' chattels for a crusading fund. After Richard's coronation, mobs whipped up by crusading fervor had burned and plundered London's Jewry, leaving its inhabitants slaughtered in the street. But even by the standards of the day, John's measures were harsh. He made heavy demands on individual Jews and backed up the demands with horrible violence. In Bristol one Jew refused the king's demands. He was imprisoned, and his jailers began smashing his molars out. According to Roger of Wendover, "the king ordered his agents to knock out one of [the Jew's] cheek-teeth daily, until he paid ten thousand marks of silver. . . . [A]fter they had for seven days knocked out a tooth a day with great agony to the Jew, and had begun the same operation on the eighth day, the Jew . . . gave the said sum to save his eighth tooth, even though he had already lost seven."

This was a measure of the cruelty to which John could sink. The next year he began his most notorious vendetta of all, the hounding of the Briouze family. This was a pursuit that united all of John's instincts and policies: his thirst for wealth, his interest in establishing direct royal power over the Celtic fringe of Britain, and his fierce hostility toward some of his richest and greatest subjects.

William de Briouze was a baron of ancient Norman stock, whose royal links stretched back to the Conquest. His wife, Matilda, was also of noble lineage. Together they built up the Briouze line into one of England's greatest families and established a power base in the Welsh marches, where they shared an important role with men like William Marshal earl of Pembroke in keeping the native Welsh subdued and English power strong.

William de Briouze had been near many of the important events of Richard's and John's reigns. He had served at Châlus during the campaign in which Richard had been killed. He was a near-constant companion to John during the early years of his reign. John had farmed out Welsh policy to Briouze and men like him, granting them baronies in Wales and the marches and encouraging them to expand their lands through military conquest. Briouze had been granted landed rights around Limerick, in Ireland, and paid a handsome yearly fee for the right to pursue an inheritance there. The family also held property in Surrey, Hertfordshire, and Devon and two valuable priories seized under the interdict. Briouze's second son had been appointed bishop of Hereford. The result was that after a decade of John's reign, Briouze was a very significant baron, who had acquired vast tracts of land and many wardships, castles, and manors. He had also acquired secrets, and his closeness to the king in Normandy in 1203 meant that he was probably one of the few who knew what had really happened to Arthur of Brittany.

By 1208 John had started to see Briouze less as a valuable servant who had been well rewarded and more as a potential troublemaker who was providing less than his financial due to the Crown. In the course of his career Briouze had, like most other barons, run up huge debts to the Crown. He had accrued large feudal fines and fees in exchange for his titles and inheritances, amounting to well over three thousand pounds, payable in installments to the royal exchequer. In March 1208 John began calling in the debt in its entirety. According to Roger of Wendover, John's demands for repayment were accompanied by demands for hostages. When royal messengers were sent to collect them from the Briouze family home, William's wife, Matilda, "with the sauciness of a woman," sent the royal messengers packing with the shrill cry that John had done away with Arthur and would most likely do the same for her sons. According to Wendover, Matilda shouted that the king had "basely murdered his nephew . . . whom he ought to have kept in honorable custody!"

This was, to say the least, impolitic, and it earned the Briouze family John's undying rancor. For the next three years he foreclosed on the family's debts and began to remove them from office and positions. In a public letter later written to justify his actions, the king explained to the realm that he was pursuing the family "according to the custom of England and the law of the exchequer," but it was a campaign of sustained legalized malice. William de Briouze was sacked as bailiff of Glamorgan and replaced by a foreign mercenary John had brought back from the Continent. Castles at Hay, Brecon, and Radnor were taken back into royal hands. On the pretext of recovering debt, John allowed mercenary soldiers to raid Briouze lands; he compounded the misery by sending the Briouzes a bill for the expense. The Briouzes attempted to retaliate by attacking the castles that the king had seized from them, but that simply put them further outside the law. John made life so dangerous for them that in early 1209 the family was obliged to flee across the Irish Sea and take refuge in Leinster with William Marshal.

Marshal had been created earl of Pembroke at the beginning of John's reign, but he and the king had never really been able to work with each other. Since his quarrel with John in 1205, Marshal had been out of favor. He was now one of a number of exiles from John's court who, by the end of 1209, were living in Ireland. Marshal welcomed the Briouzes with all his chivalrous kindness, and others followed the example. There was widespread sympathy for the family in Ireland, and they were sheltered by various of the great lords there, who attempted to keep them safe until peace could be made with the king in England.

John, however, was not in a peaceable mood. He had no desire to be brought to an accommodation with the Briouze family. Rather, the fact that they had successfully escaped the clutches of his law focused his mind on subjecting Ireland to stricter control by the English Crown. He would not tolerate the existence of a haven for dissenting bishops (many had fled to Ireland during the interdict) and persecuted barons, and in the summer of 1210 he began to muster an invasion, amassing hundreds of ships at Pembroke.

News of the massive invasion fleet spread quickly across the Irish Sea, and some of the exiled barons made their peace before John's arrival. William Marshal wrote that he "well understood what the King's designs were, that is that his sole aim was to find an opportunity to do him harm, and without cause." He crossed to England and submitted. Marshal then turned around and accompanied John on his campaign in Ireland. The campaign pursued two main strategies. "He made and ordained English laws and customs, appointing sheriffs and other agents to govern the people of that kingdom according to English laws," Marshal explained. "After this the king proceeded in great force, and took several of the fortresses of his enemies." During a fearsome military progress that lasted little more than two months, John destroyed most of his enemies in Ireland and reduced the opposition to a rump.

The Briouzes were understandably terrified. Left with nowhere to hide in Ireland, Matilda and her eldest son fled from Ulster to Scotland. Yet there was no respite from John's power. In August 1209 the king had marched a large army to the Scottish borders and imposed the humiliating Treaty of Norham on the aging king William the Lion. Scotland was no longer a bastion of resistance. Matilda and her son were captured and handed over to the English king. William de Briouze meanwhile escaped to France and lived out the rest of his years as an outlaw, albeit one who now shared the full story of Arthur's death with the horrified French court.

It was a measure of the Briouzes' extreme fear of what fate would befall them at John's hands that when she was captured, Matilda offered the king the outlandish sum of forty thousand marks to ransom herself and her son. For once John was not interested in promises of vast wealth, and in any case it was obvious that Matilda did not have forty thousand marks to give him. He sent his captives either to Windsor or to Corfe Castle. They would not survive the year.

One of the Briouzes' greatest crimes was to know too much. They held the secret of Arthur's death, and it was no surprise that they were terrified of meeting the same fate. Their concerns were well grounded. Before the end of 1210 Matilda and her son had been starved to death in jail. It was said that when the dead bodies of mother and son were found, they were huddled together against their cell wall. Matilda's son bore toothmarks on his body. Mad with starvation, his mother had tried to eat him.

This was what happened to those who crossed King John. By the end of 1210 he had unambiguously stamped his might across England. Silent church bells reminded a fearful people that they lived in a godless realm under an excommunicated king. Toothless Jews and dead wives bore testament to John's ruthlessness. In ten years he had swelled the royal treasury with so much wealth that a national coin shortage was developing. Scotland and Ireland had been cowed into a new respect for the might of the English Crown. In 1211 John was to lead two massive armies into Wales against the dominant prince Llywelyn ap Iorwerth, otherwise known as Llywelyn the Great. After a series of decisive victories, John imposed humiliating terms of peace on the Welsh. In Britain, if not in France, John's authority was cemented by his achievements on the battlefield. As Walter of Coventry wrote, "in Ireland, Scotland, and Wales there was no man who did not obey the nod of the king of England—a thing which, it is well known, had never happened to any of his forefathers." Unfortunately for John, he would soon fall prey to the fate of his predecessors.

Beginning of the End

Peter of Wakefield, a Yorkshire hermit, had a reputation across the north of England as a simpleton who ate a staple diet of bread and water and could predict the future. It was said that Christ had appeared to him three times, twice at York and once at another nearby town, Pontefract. The Savior had taken the form of a child, held in the hands of a priest, who had said to Peter, "Peace, peace, peace," and instructed him on the way to live a more virtuous life.

In 1212 a new vision came to Peter. The king's reign, he said, would end before the next anniversary of his coronation, Ascension Day in May 1213. According to Roger of Wendover, the hermit would exclaim: "[A] vision has revealed to me that the king shall not rule more than fourteen years, at the end of which time he will be replaced by someone more pleasing to God."

In an age when superstition was rife and rumors could be powerful, Peter of Wakefield's prophecy caught like wildfire. When it reached the king, he laughed at the story, but as he brooded on it, he became alarmed. He had Peter of Wakefield arrested and dragged to court to explain himself. According to Wendover, the king questioned Peter personally, asking "if he should die on that day, or how he would be deprived of the throne of the kingdom." The hermit replied: "Rest assured that on the aforesaid day you will not be king; and if I am proved to have told a lie, do what you will with me."

Needing no encouragement, John sent Peter to Corfe Castle and put him into the custody of William d'Harcourt, "who loaded him with chains and kept him imprisoned to await the event of his prophecy." But even with Peter in prison, Roger of Wendover recorded that his declaration spread far across England, "so that almost all who heard it put faith in his words as though his prediction had been declared from heaven."

The year 1212 should have been a time of triumph. John's expedition to Ireland had been a success: he had managed to keep the most belligerent native kings in check, thanks to the many hostages he had taken and the numerous now-Anglicized lordships and bishoprics he had created. Success in Ireland had been matched by the unprecedented extension of English mastery over the Welsh. An aggressive program of castle building had been initiated to secure the gains made in northern Wales and throughout the western marches. John had won far more territorial advantage in Wales than either his father or his great-grandfather, and he had humiliated the native princes. The court had been swelled by young Welshmen taken as security against rebellion.

When the king of the Scots, William the Lion, fell ill and began to suffer plots against his rule, John pressed his advantage. He granted his goodwill in exchange for hostages and promises of vast cash payments, then knighted William's twelve-year-old son and heir over dinner on Easter Sunday 1212 and provided the boy with mercenaries to defeat Guthred MacWilliam, a rival for the Scottish throne. The English Crown was preeminent over the British Isles.

Unsurprisingly, after five years of extraordinary success on the battle-field, John's confidence was returning. This was helped by the fact that he was now vastly rich. Even discounting the windfall revenues earned from Jews and the interdict, he had managed to more than double his annual income since the loss of Normandy so that it now regularly exceeded fifty thousand pounds a year. Although his reign had seen a period of rapid inflation, he was still richer in cash terms in 1212 than his brother Richard had been before the Third Crusade, with as much as two hundred thousand pounds in cash stockpiled in various English castles. Buoyed by his success, John felt ready to take the fight for Normandy back to France. He was rich enough to contemplate reviving Richard's successful foreign policy of bribing Philip's neighbors into a grand anti-Capetian coalition. Diplomatic approaches were made to former allies such as his nephew, recently restored as the emperor Otto IV, and Reinauld count of Boulogne. Mountains of silver pennies were spent recruiting mercenaries and fitting out an army.

But as John's preparations for an invasion moved forward in the summer of 1212, his hold over his kingdom began to weaken. It began in northern Wales, where John's castle building had provoked the remnants of the Welsh resistance to band together against his rule. As forty towns around England received demands for men to serve on the Continent, John was suddenly faced with guerrilla attacks upon English border castles from the woods and hills of inland Wales. English knights and soldiers were brutally beheaded, and acrid smoke blew up from burning towns. The Welsh rebels slew and looted wherever they could, then melted back into the countryside.

The rebellion in Wales was the first serious challenge to John's authority since 1205. Its scale was such that he was forced to abandon his Continental plans and muster his army at Chester to deal with the border threat. In August, to relieve his frustration, he hanged twenty-eight Welsh hostages from the town gibbet in Nottingham. But the situation was worse than he thought. William Marshal recorded how even as the last feeble kicks of the dying men shook the scaffold, anonymous letters arrived in Nottingham warning that "if the king persisted with the war which he had begun he would either be slain by his own nobles or delivered to his enemies for destruction." Some of John's barons, it seemed, were plotting to murder him and install a new king in his place. John had frequently acted as though he were under attack; now he had good reason to believe he really was.

The prime suspects in the plot to kill the king were Eustace de Vesci and Robert Fitzwalter. De Vesci had been active in royal service since the days of Richard the Lionheart, and John had used him as an agent in negotiations with the Scots because he had extensive landholdings in Northumberland and Yorkshire and knew the wild border country better than most. His grievance with John was obscure, but an almost certainly scurrilous tale was spread that the king had attempted to seduce his wife. De Vesci was more likely typical of a set of northern barons who objected to John's harnessing of England's wealth to fund his Continental aims. As soon as it was clear that the plot had been uncovered, de Vesci fled over the border to take refuge in Scotland.

Fitzwalter, by contrast, was a powerful figure in northern Essex and the city of London. He claimed—probably spuriously—to be aggrieved because the king had attempted to forcefully seduce his eldest daughter, though it is likely that his grievances ran deeper and fed into the patchwork of private disgruntlements and quasi-constitutional disquiet that was beginning to be shared by many English barons who opposed John's aggressive style of kingship. When John learned of the plot, Fitzwalter escaped to France. Only one unlucky plotter, an exchequer official called Geoffrey of Norwich, fell into the hands of the king. Unsurprisingly, he died in prison.

The plot uncovered at Nottingham unleashed in John a renewed paranoia. The letters he had seen at Nottingham indicated that John not only had cause to fear his external enemies—Innocent III, Philip II, the rebellious Celts—but was confirmed in his suspicions that treachery abounded among his own barons. Victory turned quickly to distrust and dismay. Within a month of his discovery of the plot, he had disbanded his Welsh army altogether and, accompanied by his mercenaries, was on his way back to London. Royal castles across the north were put on armed standby. Long trains of soldiers and munitions plowed up the roads north during the autumn of 1212 as John put the upper half of his kingdom on a civil war footing. Ever on his guard, he sent letters to all his barons demanding that they deliver him a hostage for their good behavior, frequently one of their sons or younger relations, whose lives were then at the king's mercy. From the summer of 1212 on, the chroniclers recorded, John took an armed bodyguard everywhere he went.

How had relations between John and his barons reached such a nadir? The simplest explanation is that England was suffering from weary overfamiliarity with an ever-present king. The realm had known John at greater length and more intimately than any other Plantagenet monarch, and many of his barons found his energetic personal rule difficult to adjust to. He was unlikable and cruel, and his pursuit of the Briouzes had scandalized aristocratic values and opinion. But cruelty was no cause for rebellion. Henry II and Richard I had been cruel, and their reputations had never suffered so badly. Henry II had hanged Welsh hostages by the score; Richard had slain men in cold blood at every end of Christendom.

John's problems were exacerbated by his paranoia. He was so sly and secretive that he developed a complex code—so complex that he himself sometimes forgot it—which he used when sending out orders that he wished not to be carried out. His treatment of men like William Marshal and the Briouzes inspired no confidence in other barons. He was under no obligation to be friends with his barons, but to treat them with kisses and patronage before starving their wives and sons to death smacked of a dangerous instability. If John could not treat his favorites well, what chance was there for those outside the royal confidence?

And yet there was more to the problem than weaknesses in the king's character. A rift between the Crown and the English barons had been growing since Henry II's reforms. Serious questions remained to be settled about the nature of royal government in its entirety. Royal authority had been massively and systematically extended as England was rebuilt from the ashes of the civil war between Stephen and Matilda. Now it was visible everywhere. In the mid-twelfth century one in five English castles had been in royal hands. Thanks to half a century of castle building and confiscations, by 1212 nearly half of England's castles flew the royal standard above their keeps. The massive expansion of the common law and royal involvement in judging even the humblest cases, which reached an apogee under John, had taken royal power into the shires at the expense of baronial power. There were only a few places, such as the palatinate of Chester, where the royal writ did not run.

Royal officials were increasingly lowbred men and foreigners with professional skills, who were seen to be accumulating significant power in areas that had in recent memory been subject to baronial control. Under John, no senior household official or great officer of state was drawn from the ranks of the barons. From the outside, these officials looked like an ill-born clique. The increased use of mercenaries in the royal armies further reduced the role of the barons and weakened the sense that royal military expeditions were joint ventures between king and nobles.

For the most part, this brought great advantage to ordinary English freemen. Government under John continued to become more professional. People could protect their property and dispose of it as they chose thanks to the royal law. They could challenge their social superiors before royal courts. They were sold a brilliant and quasi-divine image of kingship as handed down from God; at Christmas in 1207 John invested heavily in the glorious pageantry of kingship, wearing his grandmother Matilda's imperial crown and holding a scepter and a golden rod, dressed in purple silk decorated with gold embroidery. When compared with the fractured kingdom of the civil war, divided between warring barons and rival monarchs, King John's England looked—and was—united and strong.

The main losers were the barons. This group of 160 or so men and their families had lost the most territory when England and Normandy were wrenched apart in 1205. They dealt most often with John in person, and their experience of government was therefore colored by his caprice, cruelty, and financial greed. For these men, kingship was both a system and a personal relationship. Its operation relied on the goodwill of a single man. As Henry II's justiciar, Richard FitzNigel, wrote, "To some, the king does full justice for nothing, in consideration of their past services or out of mere goodness of heart; but to others . . . he will not give way either for love or money." With a king of John's nature, this inherent contradiction was dramatically magnified. Barons found their power eroded from below by the advance of royal law and justice, but they were attacked from above when John chose to deal inconsistently and arbitrarily with them.

John, with his legalist's mind and lofty view of his position, saw little contradiction between his role at the head of an ever-growing government of process and systems and his feudal position as master of his barons, whom he could dispossess and punish entirely as he chose. This personal means of governing his barons allowed him to squeeze them financially, invoking his right as their lord to seize their property and impose massive fines on them for feudal customs or transgressions. He saw it as his right to settle arguments and legal cases between individual barons, or between barons and himself, by personal judgment, taking informal counsel with his close advisers or else through the exchequer, where he himself determined the outcome of the case. This, to his mind, was the privilege of kingship. And indeed none of it was novel in conception—merely in scale. But it was not a view that his barons embraced.

This, then, was the situation at the end of 1212. John was still desperate to launch his reconquest of Normandy and had begun to commit himself financially to the foreign alliances that were necessary to see it through. He was pursuing his aims against a background of growing discontent at home. It would require heroic degrees of leadership, skill, and luck to reclaim the lost lands without pushing the increasingly disgruntled English political community into full revolt.

To Bouvines

The first great naval victory in English history was won against the French fleet on May 30, 1213. Two days earlier five hundred ships had put out to sea under the command of John's half brother William de Longespée, the earl of Salisbury. After crossing the Channel and raiding his way up the Norman coast, Salisbury had reached the Flemish coast and sailed into the Zwyn, a tidal inlet that provided the sea route to the great coastal trading cities of Damme and Sluys.

The ships bristled with arms and men, English knights and foreign mercenaries paid for with the vast stores of coin John had amassed since 1204. As they sailed up the Zwyn toward Damme, they met with an extraordinary sight: a vast array of French ships, some beached, some bobbing in the harbor, all waiting to be filled with a force to invade England. There were reckoned to be seventeen hundred ships, fully kitted out and ready for war. The harbor creaked with menace.

For months it had been rumored that Pope Innocent III, stung by John's continued insouciance in the face of interdict and excommunication, had declared the king deposed, and Philip had readied himself to execute the sentence. (Papers of deposition had in fact been prepared in Rome but were never published.) Philip had begun to consider England a possible appanage for his son Louis and had spent months preparing his invasion fleet. The evidence of his deadly intent now lay before Salisbury's eyes.

The English commander wasted no time. English units piled at once into the harbor, attacking the poorly defended French fleet, cutting adrift hundreds of ships loaded with corn, wine, flour, meat, and vital parts of the French military arsenal. Other soldiers ran ashore and raided beached ships for their valuable supplies before setting fire to the timber frames. Black smoke shot up into the air as pitch blazed in the water.

Although Philip was not present in the town for the attack, he arrived soon afterward to a scene of scorched catastrophe. "It was a very bitter thing for the King of France to see his ships at sea burning and belching forth smoke, as if the very sea were on fire," wrote William Marshal. "King Philip, out of his mind with rage and in a black mood, had the remaining ships in his navy burned to cinders in a fit of rage and depression." It was a brave and vital victory that destroyed the French threat to the English coast for several years to come.

Unbeknownst to Philip, Salisbury's destruction of a fleet designed to carry out a papal sentence, was done with the full backing of Innocent III. Before he launched his naval attack on France, John had bowed to the mounting tide of pressure and, in an attempt to reduce his list of enemies and weaken Philip's cause, decided to make peace with Rome. Among those who counseled him to do so was Marshal, now once again an important royal adviser. A legate, Pandulph Masca, was sent from the pope to negotiate terms, and John had met with Pandulph in Dover just days before Salisbury's fleet set sail.

There, in the presence of England's barons, the king had sealed a charter giving over his kingdoms of England and Ireland in feudal vassalage to the pope. At a stroke, England had been transformed from a chilly outcast on the edges of Christendom into a papal fief, along with other European kingdoms including Sicily, Poland, Sweden, Denmark, Portugal, and Aragon. "The kingdom is become a royal priesthood and the priesthood a kingdom of priests," wrote Innocent when he heard the news. John had apparently been duly rewarded with the awesome victory at Damme.

Reconciliation with Rome was a process, however, and not an event. Six weeks after Damme, on July 20, John stood on Morn Hill, outside Winchester, and looked down on the splendid city below. His fine robes of colorful silk and satin shone in the summer sun, as did those of his courtiers and their thoroughbred horses. Winchester was alive with color and activity as Stephen Langton, an archbishop of Canterbury at last allowed to tend his flock, made his way in a great ecclesiastical procession across the Sussex Downs and into the ancient city. Minutes later John and Langton took part in a public ceremony of reconciliation, complete with tears, incense, and kisses of peace and promises by John that he would love and uphold the Church.

John paid handsomely for this reconciliation, both in the fines he had agreed to pay the pope and in the fall in income he had accepted when he gave up his exploitation of vacant ecclesiastical posts. But the prodigal son had returned, and John was now much in favor at Rome. This, combined with Philip II's loss of his navy, encouraged John to throw everything into another attempt at regaining his Continental possessions.

He began to plan a massive invasion, scheduled to land in Poitou and push north during the spring and summer of 1214. It was vital that he convince his barons to go with him. But the northern barons, led by Eustace de Vesci, now uneasily reconciled with the king, refused to serve, claiming they could not afford to do so. Faced with baronial intransigence for a second time in his reign, John flew into a predictable rage. This time, unlike in 1205, he would not be deterred from his ambition. He spent autumn 1213 preparing the ground for an invasion under what he described in a letter to his sometime ally Aimery de Thouars as "an unbelievably large force."

John's exploitation of his feudal dues and the profits of justice mounted wildly in the months before the invasion. He levied scutage—a tax substituting cash payments for the barons' feudal obligation to provide knights to serve in the king's army—at three marks per knight's fee, the heaviest rate ever recorded. The reliefs and fees on feudal incidents became astonishingly high. William FitzAlan was charged ten thousand marks for succession to the FitzAlan barony. John de Lacy paid seven thousand marks for the honor of Pontefract. Widows were being charged up to one thousand pounds to keep their dowries and not be forcibly remarried. The greatest sale of all was the offering of twenty thousand marks from Geoffrey Mandeville, who paid the sum for the hand in marriage of Isabel countess of Gloucester. Isabel carried the dubious distinction of having once been married to John, before he discarded her in 1199 to wed Isabella of Angoulême. She was a rich heiress in her own right, but the sum charged to Geoffrey for her marriage was still astronomical. And these were not notional debts: Geoffrey was expected to pay for his queenly bride in four installments over nine months.

The cash raised did not lie idle. John's money began flooding the Continent, and he built a coalition around the support of his nephew the emperor Otto IV. The counts of Holland, Boulogne, and Flanders joined the resistance to Philip in northwestern Europe. The plan was to trap him in a pincer movement between two forces: the first, under Salisbury, would attack Philip from Flanders; the second, under John, would move up from Poitou to strike from the south. In February 1214 John sailed from Portsmouth for La Rochelle, in a galley laden with precious gemstones, silver, and gold and carrying numerous English nobles, as well as Queen Isabella and John's five-year-old second son, Prince Richard. This was no whimsical campaign. It was to be the glorious recapture of John's birthright.

The campaign started well. Throughout the spring John employed a combination of diplomacy and siegecraft to secure Poitou and its environs. Peace was made with the troublesome Lusignan family, who had been so slighted back in 1202, when John had whisked his queen, Isabella of Angoulême, out from under their noses: to bring them back to favor, a marriage was arranged between John's daughter Joan (born in 1210) and Hugh de Lusignan's son and heir. In early June, with Poitou successfully secured, John moved on to Brittany and took Nantes by siege. Angers, in the heart of Anjou, swiftly opened its gates. With Philip reluctant to join battle, John was showing that the spirit of Plantagenet bellicosity lived on.

Then disaster struck. John was besieging the castle of La Roche-aux-Moines on the border between Poitou and Brittany in the company of some of his Poitevin barons when he heard that Philip's twenty-six-year-old son, Prince Louis, was approaching at the head of an army. John decided that the moment was ripe for a pitched battle. Yet his allies suddenly lost faith. The Poitevin barons who had accompanied him for months fulfilled their reputation for inconstancy. They simply upped and ran, refusing to risk battle with the house of Capet. With a speed that belied the painstaking and expensive diplomacy with which John had built his coalition, the southern alliance melted away. Instead of fighting Prince Louis, John could only retreat before his advance and take cover back where his expedition had begun, in La Rochelle.

Despite the humiliation of this retreat, John could still hope that the northern allies in his pincer movement would show their mettle. While he waited in La Rochelle, on July 27 the northern coalition assembled under Emperor Otto IV's fluttering banner of the dragon and golden eagle and made ready for the destruction of the French king on a plain near the village of Bouvines.

The army that took to the field against Philip at the battle of Bouvines was a typical medieval affair—loud, violent, and disorganized. Each leader had his own men and his own standard, and such grand strategy as existed was fairly rudimentary. Cavalry charges were the main weapon used by either side. At times the battle would have resembled the melee of the tournament field, but with added intent. Men carried heavy lances and pounds of chain mail, which could suffocate its wearer to death if he fell awkwardly in the churned mud of the field. Bloodcurdling screams and the sickening crunch of heavy metal piercing into human flesh, grunts of effort and the thick, gurgling breath of the dying, would have raged all around, as hand-to-hand fighting left the plain at Bouvines gouged and bloodstained.

The English troops rallied around the earl of Salisbury's blue banners with yellow lions rampant emblazoned upon them. They fought bravely on the right flank. The leaders from both sides were at the center; both Otto IV and Philip were unhorsed during the fighting. The battle raged for three long hours, first in favor of the imperial troops and then, as the fighting wore on, tipping toward the French.

The French were victorious in the end. Their cavalry charges, led by some of the finest knights in Europe, gradually overwhelmed the patchwork of coalition forces arraigned against them. Otto and Philip led their knights in a melee, which was settled decisively in the French favor. Otto was protected manfully by a group of Saxon knights, but eventually he had no choice but to flee the battlefield, narrowly escaping capture as he galloped off. The counts of Flanders and Boulogne and the earl of Salisbury were less fortunate. They were all taken prisoner and escorted back to Paris, where the citizens and students of the university danced and sang in the streets for a week to celebrate the famous victory.

Far away in La Rochelle there was no dancing. Only despair greeted the news that the coalition had given its all and lost. John had invested everything in the campaign of 1214, and he had been beaten. He was forced to sign a five-year truce with Philip in the autumn, at a price that was rumored to be sixty thousand marks. Financially the king was ruined. He had spent all he had on war preparations and had cut off his main source of fast cash by reconciling with the Church. His military reputation was trampled back into the mud. After Bouvines, John the commander was all but finished.

The Magna Carta

When John returned to England after his defeat at Bouvines, he was weaker than he had ever been before. Victory and the recovery of a large portion of the Plantagenet lands might have justified his extortions, just as Richard I's glorious achievements in Outremer and France had made good the expense of his crusading fund and king's ransom. But John returned to England discredited. The only patch of territory in mainland France that remained loyal to the English Crown was Gascony and the area around Bordeaux, a pitiful rump of what had once been the sprawling duchy of Aquitaine. A beaten king, John returned to his realm a dangerously vulnerable figure.

Baronial disquiet, which had been bubbling up since 1212, now burst into the open. The feeling growing among a broad coalition of English barons was that John's methods must somehow be constrained, that the king who had wielded his powers and prerogatives so mercilessly should now be brought under some sort of control. The unfathomable question was what sort of bell could be tied to the cat.

Two meetings between king and barons during the winter of 1214–1215 failed to resolve their differences. In January 1215 John met with about forty dissatisfied barons in London, where he stalled for enough time to write to Rome and place the case before his new feudal overlord, the pope. During the spring both sides wrote to Innocent III. The barons submitted demands that John should be made to obey the Charter of Liberties that had been issued by Henry I on his coronation in 1100. They proposed that the king should be forced to stand by his own coronation oath to observe good law and exercise justice and argued that demands for English barons to pay scutage or provide armed men to fight on the Continent were unfair and illegal. John's papal envoys thought the king, as a reconciled son of Rome, ought not to be troubled by rebellions from his subjects, a position that was strengthened when John took the cross on March 4. As a crusader he was now explicitly protected from attack by fellow Christians.

That the barons chose to appeal to the spirit of Henry I's charter was illuminating. The Charter of Liberties, which had been confirmed by Henry II in 1154, promised (among other things) that the king would not plunder Church property or charge outrageous fees for inheritances, marriages, and widows' remarriages, nor would he abuse wardships or extend the royal forest. These were all requests that could fairly be directed at King John, but the choice of Henry I's charter also demonstrated that the barons viewed their grievances as part of a grand scheme of Plantagenet government dating back more than a century. It was a reasonable position for the barons to take, but their arguments were ignored. Innocent appointed Archbishop Langton to mediate between king and barons and held legal hearings on the dispute in Rome. There, rather than attempt to arbitrate the dispute fairly, Innocent found wholly in favor of his vassal, the crusader king John. Innocent wrote to the English barons insisting that they should pay their scutage and cease making demands of the king. It was a blunt judgment that did nothing to address the serious political disquiet in England. The only possible outcome was civil war. On May 5, 1215, a group of rebels formally defied John, renouncing their homage and fealty, effectively rejecting him as king of England.

The barons who opposed him were led by the plotters of 1212: Eustace de Vesci and Robert Fitzwalter, who styled himself by the magnificently pompous title of marshal of the army of God. De Vesci was the foremost of a group of northern barons including William de Mowbray, Richard de Percy, and Roger de Montbegon lord of Hornby in Lancashire. The northerners were a tight-knit group, bonded by marriage, kinship, and territorial proximity; all had personal cause to dislike John in particular and Plantagenet government in general. Around these rebel leaders was a band of magnates from East Anglia and the home counties, which included most prominently Richard de Clare earl of Hertford, and his son Gilbert, and Geoffrey de Mandeville earl of Essex and Gloucester. Other barons included Robert de Vere earl of Oxford, Henry de Bohun earl of Hereford, and William Marshal's son, William the Younger. Plenty—in fact almost all—of the rebellious barons opposed John on grounds of self-interest, and some, like Fitzwalter, were simply unscrupulous and belligerent. But the rebels were also bound together by the germ of an ideology, a sense that the government was in need of fundamental reform.

Once they had renounced their homage, however, very little reform could take place without recourse to bloody warfare. On May 10 John wrote to the rebel barons stating that he "would not arrest or disseise them or their men nor would he go against them by force of arms except by the law of the land and by judgment of their peers in his court." He made personal overtures to those whom he had dealt with particularly severely during the buildup to the Poitou campaign. He offered to submit to arbitration by a panel of eight barons, chaired by the pope himself. His terms were rejected, and on May 12 John ordered the confiscation of rebel lands. There was now no escaping the fact that England was, for the first time since 1173, at war with itself.

The third week of May saw a dash for London between the earl of Salisbury, who had been released from prison following the defeat at Bouvines, and a group of rebel barons, led by Fitzwalter. They raced through the dark of night to reach the capital, which was crucial to the symbolic and strategic control of England. London was an economic powerhouse, a city of culture and prosperity. Its great stone walls protected the city, with William the Conqueror's Tower of London in the east and Baynard's castle in the west. Its skyline prickled with scores of little church towers, like needles around the central spire belonging to the vast wooden-roofed cathedral of St. Paul's, perched proudly on top of Ludgate Hill. London was a hub of trade and of political power. Holding the city had been essential to King Stephen's survival against Matilda, and in the spring of 1215 it once again became the key to controlling England.

On May 17, a quiet Sunday morning, the rebels reached London, emerging as the sun was still drying the dew from the city's rooftops. The bells in the church towers were clanging with their fat, metallic call to morning worship as the seven gates in the city walls were cranked open to allow forces hostile to the king of England into the capital. "The rich citizens were favourable to the barons," wrote the chronicler Roger of Wendover, who lived and worked at St. Albans in Northamptonshire. "And the poor ones were afraid to murmur against them." By the time Salisbury reached the city it was too late. Guards loyal to the barons manned the city gates. Inside the walls, scribes were compiling documents to be sent to all earls, barons, and knights thought still to be faithful to John, demanding that they abandon "a king who was perjured" and come over to the rebel side. With London, the rebel barons had their wedge. John's hopes of crushing resistance to his rule were over.

Yet they could not be said to have won. John might have lost the confidence of a large swath of his barons, but he was still legitimately the king, backed by the pope. He could in theory still dispossess and outlaw his enemies. The rebels wished to reform government, not so as to depose or fundamentally hobble kingship but to bring it within what they regarded as reasonable bounds. They wanted to force the king to govern peacefully and fairly within the law, yet they were doing so by breaking the law. It was a situation of deep complexity for both sides. So, as the rebels camped in London, and John took his court upriver to Windsor, the roads and waterways between the two were well trodden by messengers from both sides, attempting to find a way in which the proud king could be cajoled into putting his seal to a document that answered some of his rebels' demands.

After a month of wrangling, a solution emerged. Sometime between June 10 and 15, baronial envoys agreed with the king that a document now known as the Articles of the Barons could form the basis for a final negotiation of a peace. This list of forty-nine points set out what the barons hoped to achieve from King John. It concerned issues of justice and feudal precedent, such as the well-argued matters of how much should be charged for wardships, inheritances, and widows; scutage payments and the obligation to serve in armies outside the realm; and the extent of the royal forests. The articles formed an agreed schedule for detailed negotiation, and several more days of hard and detailed bargaining ensued. Eventually another document was agreed upon by June 18, when John's chancery sent out writs commanding his officers in the shires to stop making war on his enemies. The following day, at Runnymede in Berkshire, barons started renewing their homage to John, who wore the regalia of Empress Matilda to emphasize the ancient status of his kingship. In return, John, his allies, and selected rebel barons swore oaths to obey the terms of an agreement that is among the most famous in English history, the Magna Carta.

The term "Magna Carta" means, simply, "great charter." Read today, the document of 1215 seems to reflect a difficult compromise: it was an agreement that neither side quite welcomed. On the one hand, it granted sweeping rights: "the English Church shall be free . . . the city of London is to have its ancient liberties." On the other, it was full of highly exact statements of English custom: clauses laid out the specific conditions under which a scutage could be levied on the kingdom, where bridges should be built, and the laws concerning Jewish debts. It agreed on one hundred pounds as the fee for an earl's or a baron's inheritance, and one hundred shillings for a knight's. On the matter of wardships, the king promised to take "no more than reasonable revenues, reasonable customary dues, and reasonable services," although what was "reasonable" was undefined. It was promised that "a widow shall have her marriage portion and inheritance forthwith and without any difficulty after the death of her husband; nor shall she pay anything to have her dower" and also that "no widow shall be forced to marry so long as she wishes to live without a husband." The king promised that "no scutage or aid shall be imposed in our kingdom unless by common counsel . . . except for ransoming our person, for making our eldest son a knight and for once marrying our eldest daughter."

Whereas many of the clauses in the charter were formal terms pertaining to specific policies pursued by John—whether with regard to raising armies, levying taxes, impeding merchants, or arguing with the Church— the most famous clauses aimed at a deeper elaboration of the rights of subjects to set out the limits of central government. Clause 39 reads: "No free man shall be taken or imprisoned or disseised or outlawed or exiled or in any way ruined . . . except by lawful judgment of his peers or by the law of the land." Clause 40 is more laconic: "To no one will we sell, to no one will we deny or delay right or justice." These clauses addressed the whole spirit of John's reign and by extension the spirit of kingship itself. For the eleven years in which John had resided in England, his barons had tasted a form of tyranny. John had used his powers in an arbitrary, partisan, and exploitative fashion and had used the processes of law deliberately to weaken and menace his noble lords. He had broken the spirit of kingship as presented by Henry II back in 1153, when he traveled the country offering unity and legal process to all.

Defining the appropriate limits to the powers of a king—and, by extension, his government—was no easy task. Neither was ensuring, once it was defined, that the king stuck to its terms. The Magna Carta ended with a security clause, providing for a council of twenty-five named barons to make war on the king if he broke the terms of the agreement. This was nothing more than a contractual basis for civil war. Stating that a king should govern according to the law and making sure that he did so were, it turned out, quite separate matters. These questions would lie at the heart of every major disagreement between king and country for centuries to come. And in the fierce, tense atmosphere of 1215, finding an agreement was to prove impossible.

As a peace treaty—for this is what it was—the Magna Carta was an immediate failure. There was a brief moment of hope on June 19, when the homage and oaths were made, the twenty-five "security barons" were elected, and a substantial number of rebels agreed to the terms of the charter as the basis for peace. "The king satisfactorily restored justice everywhere, lifting the sieges which he had begun," wrote Walter of Coventry. The production line began, and "a copy of the charter was circulated around the towns and villages and all who saw it agreed to it." But not all the barons accepted the charter of liberties as drafted, and some chose at once to rebel. "Certain from across the [River] Humber went away and renewed hostilities," the chronicler continued.

The Magna Carta sparked debate everywhere, and it was quite unacceptable to one man above all others: King John. In less than two months John secured an annulment of its terms from Innocent III, who wrote in a wonderfully bombastic dispatch that "we utterly reject and condemn this settlement and under threat of excommunication we order that the king should not dare to observe it and that the barons and their associates should not require it to be observed: the charter . . . we declare to be null, and void of all validity forever." The war resumed, and this time it escalated. Before the end of the year Philip II of France had declared John's Crown forfeit, citing a "trial" in which John had been found guilty of killing Arthur of Brittany. Preparations were made for the French king and his son Prince Louis to invade England on the invitation of the barons and depose the tyrant king.

The French landed in Kent on May 14, 1216. Prince Louis found London waiting for him. "He was accepted with all alacrity and happiness, and they performed homage," wrote Walter of Coventry. Ignoring a papal interdict and excommunication levied on him by the papal legate, Cardinal Guala Bicchieri, Louis then advanced to Winchester, before heading back to the southeast to besiege Henry II's massive gateway fortress at Dover.

As John moved about the country, attempting to lay siege to rebel towns and evade the enemies who wished to depose him, he grew desperate and disconsolate. Crossing the Wash in Lincolnshire that autumn, he misjudged the tide and lost much of his baggage train. According to Ralph of Coggeshall, "he lost . . . his portable chapel with his relics, and some of his packhorses with many household supplies. And many members of his entourage were submerged in the waters of the sea and sucked into the quicksand."

During this desperate journeying John contracted dysentery, and throughout October he grew gradually weaker. By the middle of the month he was being carried on a litter. When his party reached Newark in Nottinghamshire, he was attended by the abbot of Croxton, who was a doctor. It was to no avail: John died on October 19, 1216, his country invaded and his royal authority utterly diminished. His body was not taken to Fontevraud, where his mother, father, and brother were buried. Rather, he was buried at Worcester Cathedral, near the altar of St. Wulfstan, the eleventh-century Saxon bishop who had been canonized earlier in John's reign. For the first Plantagenet to have spent more time in England than out of it to be buried in an ancient Anglo-Saxon city was perhaps fitting.

To writers like Walter of Coventry, the problems of John's reign were obvious. "John was indeed a great prince but scarcely a happy one," he wrote. "Like Marius, he experienced the ups and downs of fortune. He was munificent and liberal to outsiders, but a plunderer of his people, trusting strangers rather than his subjects. . . . [H]e was eventually deserted by his own men and in the end, little mourned." William Marshal was more poetic. As John sank into his final illness, he wrote, he was racked with pain. "Death, that great harrier, that wicked harsh creature, took him under her control and never let him go until he died." It was an appropriate way for England's most remorseless king to end his life.

John's reputation is as one of the worst kings in English history, a diabolical murderer who brought tyranny and constitutional crisis to his realm. The legends of Robin Hood began to circulate in their earliest forms toward the end of his reign, stories in which a hero who has been dispossessed and badly treated by the king's corrupt agents takes his bloody revenge on his enemies. The subject of badly wielded authority lay at their heart. John's name has over the years been associated with the worst evil of these stories, and he has been written off as a monster, a failure, and a devil. But was anything he did truly more grotesque than some of the deeds perpetrated by his much-lauded brother Richard or his father? Probably they were not, yet John's reputation suffered far more than theirs.

In the most sympathetic analysis, John's greatest crime was to have been king as fortune's wheel rolled downward. He had all of his family's most ruthless instincts allied with none of their good fortune. He presided weakly over the loss of Normandy, and once the duchy was lost he twice failed to win it back. He did not inspire men to great deeds with the force of his personality, yet it is fair to wonder if Henry II or even Richard might have regained Normandy from the position that John occupied in 1204. It is easy to see why he trod the path he did between 1207 and 1211, and aside from his paranoid pursuit of personal vendettas it is hard to see what any other king in his position would have done differently. For four deceptive years John was master not only of his kingdom but of the English Church, England's Celtic neighbors, and a powerful system of justice and government that offered some protection for the lesser men of the kingdom against their lords, even if it was turned mercilessly toward the needs of the Crown. He failed to realize in good time what problems he was making for himself by dealing with his barons not as partners but as creditors, whom he could treat with cruelty and disdain.

As it was, a disastrous civil war, capped by a French invasion, was John's immediate legacy to his family. In 1215 the Magna Carta was nothing more than a failed peace treaty. John was not to know—any more than the barons who negotiated its terms with him would have done—that his name and the myth of the document sealed at Runnymede would be bound together in English history forever. Yet this, in the long run, was the case. The Magna Carta would be reissued time and again in the years immediately following John's death, and interpreting this intricate document on the limits of the powers of a king would be at the heart of every constitutional battle that was fought during the thirteenth and fourteenth centuries. As Henry III struggled to regain the rights and territories that his father had lost, the great charter gradually came to define the terms of engagement between king and community. When it was reissued in 1225, the Magna Carta was nailed to church doors and displayed in town squares across England, gaining legendary status as a document whose spirit stood for the duty of English kings to govern within the laws they made. That, in a strange way, was John's legacy. Perhaps the most ruthless legalist ever to reign as English king would have appreciated the irony.

Securing the Inheritance

Henry III was nine years old when his father died, and he was crowned in a hurry. The ceremony was a West Country affair that took place in Gloucester Abbey, a safe haven behind loyalist lines. Beneath the great nave of the Norman abbey church, a reduced smattering of ecclesiastical and lay lords watched uncertainly as the bishops of Winchester, Worcester, and Exeter carried out the anointing and placed a simple lady's coronet on the child's head. There was little pageantry and no regalia, for all the sacred robes and effects of a full coronation were at Westminster, which was controlled by the rebels. This was an expedient, heavily simplified ceremony designed to transfer what was left of John's authority to the young boy.

Henry was the elder of John's two sons (his younger brother, Richard, was just seven), and even as a young child he had been notable for his serious countenance and manner of speaking. He was to grow up to be deeply pious—devoted to all manner of cults, particularly that of the Virgin Mary—and such a voracious hearer of the Mass that it sometimes interfered with his ability to conduct government business. The young king stood in Gloucester Abbey and, in a fragile voice, swore before the great altar that he would observe honor, peace, and reverence toward God and the Holy Church and its ordained ministers all the days of his life; that he would give his people justice; that he would abolish bad laws and customs and observe the good.

How realistic were these promises? Certainly Henry had to make them, for they were the sacred oaths of a king. But a truer reflection of the authority that kept England from collapse was evident when the child paid homage for England and Ireland to the pope, represented in person by the papal legate, Cardinal Guala Bicchieri. He swore an oath to put the realm under the protection of the Church and a few men of God.

Ninety miles away Westminster was held by Philip II's son Louis. Castles across the country were manned by garrisons of French knights, invited to England by the rebel barons, who wished to elect a new king from the house of Capet rather than suffer under a fourth Plantagenet king. The baleful end to John's reign had left England fatally divided. Once again the succession had become not simply a question of legitimacy but a trial of strength.

All those in the abbey church's sparse crowd would have realized that this was a dreadful way to start a reign. No boy had been king since the time of Aethelred, in the days before the Conquest. And the precedents from that reign were miserable indeed: Aethelred had presided over a time of Viking raids and invasions and had been deposed for a year. Grim times were ahead if England was to be thrown back into Saxon chaos.

A few men remained devoted to avoiding that fate. Henry III was fortunate to have around him a group of supporters committed not to seizing power for themselves but to maintaining the fragile office of kingship. On his deathbed John had begged for the elderly William Marshal earl of Pembroke to become his son's guardian. Now well into his seventies, Marshal had accepted the task at first with knightly reticence and then in typically grandiloquent style, declaring that "if all the world deserted the young boy, except me, do you know what I would do? I would carry him on my shoulders. . . . I would be with him and never let him down, from island to island, from land to land, even if I had to scavenge for my daily bread." Notwithstanding his weakness for a dramatic turn of phrase, it was not just to the solemn nine-year-old Henry's advantage that such an attitude should prevail among a few good men in England. The king, if he was ever to take office fully, would need officers committed to restoring his authority. The future of his kingdom depended on it.

The other key men around the new king included Peter des Roches, John's former justiciar and bishop of Winchester. Des Roches had crowned Henry, and despite his widespread unpopularity in the country at large, he was to become Henry's tutor and mentor, on and off, for the next two decades. Then there was Guala, whose presence in the royal camp gave papal legitimacy to the cause. Finally there was Hubert de Burgh, the Norfolk-born loyalist who had served John for more than a decade. Appointed as the new justiciar, de Burgh presented an acceptable face of government to those who mistrusted "aliens." These men would form the core of a working coalition whose first and most urgent task was to defend against the invasion and resolve the crises that engulfed the realm.

The rebellious northern barons had a dangerous leader in Prince Louis; he and his allies had captured and held castles all over England. Many were garrisoned by foreign mercenaries. Louis had broad control over the southeast, and French ships patrolled the Channel. The only way to rid the realm of the French was in battle.

Henry's fate was decided at Lincoln. It was the last and perhaps the greatest military engagement of William Marshal's long and distinguished life. Having assembled 400 knights and 250 crossbowmen from all parts of the kingdom in Newark after Whitsun in 1217, Marshal marched his men straight to Lincoln. He arrived on May 20 to find that Louis's forces had entered the walled city and were besieging the castle. The French prince himself was farther south, besieging Dover, and the count of Perche was in command at Lincoln, surrounded by the bulk of the rebellious English earls. The French knew that Marshal was arriving, but they dithered and could not agree on a strategy. As they procrastinated, Marshal addressed his knights with a speech to rival that written by Shakespeare for Henry V. "These men have seized and taken by force our lands and our possessions," he said. "Shame on the man who does not strive, this very day, to put up a challenge. . . . If we beat them, it is no lie to say that we will have won eternal glory for the rest of our lives."

The rhetoric must have had some effect. Marshal took charge of his loyal knights, telling them to be ready to slit their own horses' throats if they needed to take shelter behind the carcasses in the open plain that lay before the northern entrance to the city. Bishop des Roches commanded the crossbowmen, and Ranulf earl of Chester one group of knights, but they could only watch with awe as Marshal led a direct frontal cavalry attack on the city. The old man was so desperate to join battle that he almost forgot to put on his helmet before he charged the enemy. When he adjusted his armor and led the first charge, he plowed into the French defenders with such force that he punched a hole three lances deep in their lines. If this was the last chance to save the dynasty he had served all his life, then he was determined to give it his all.

Six bloody and brutal hours of fighting ensued. It was a grisly, awful scene: the air filled with the deafening clang of weapons upon helmets, lances shattering and flying in splinters into the air, limbs crushed and severed by blows from swords and maces, and sharp daggers plunging into the sides of men and horses alike. They fought through the city until the streets heaved with blood and human entrails. "The noise," recalled Marshal, "was so great that you would not have heard God thunder."

At the end of the fighting, the French were roundly defeated. Almost every major rebel baron was captured, and the count of Perche died when a spear was thrust through his eye and into his brain. When the news of the loss reached Prince Louis in Dover, he immediately raised his siege, made for London, and began to think of terms for withdrawal.

But the war would not end before the French suffered worse humiliation. In August they were beaten at sea when Hubert de Burgh commanded a resounding naval victory at Sandwich over French troops led by the pirate captain Eustache the Monk, who later became the subject of his own Robin Hood–style outlaw romance. The English showered the French with arrows and blinded them by throwing quicklime downwind, to burn out their eyes. Eustache the Monk was captured hiding in the ship's bilges. He was offered a choice: beheading on the side of a siege engine or on the ship's rail. It is not recorded which fate he chose.

This was enough for Prince Louis. Henry's regency government had shown its mettle on the battlefield, and the French prince was happy enough to pocket a bribe and leave. Thus was the greatest external threat to the English Crown in a century averted.

After leading the heroic charge at Lincoln, William Marshal served as regent of England for more than two years. He reached the distinguished old age of seventy-three before his health began to fail him, but in the spring of 1219, after a life of devoted service, he died. For many in England this was a matter of great dismay, for Marshal was as close to a nonpartisan figure as existed, a loyal critic of the Crown who had been unwavering in his support of Plantagenet kingship but never afraid to criticize when he believed that the kings were behaving improperly or ruling badly. Marshal's life story was interwoven with all the great kings of his age: Henry II, Henry the Young King, Richard I, John, Louis VII, Philip II, and latterly, in battle, the future Louis VIII. He had been an able regent, and without his guiding hand and sureness of principle, the world looked set to be a more turbulent place.

In the days before he died Marshal dealt with many things, not least his children's futures and his wish to be invested as a Knight Templar in fulfillment of his crusader's vow. Most important of all, he thought of Henry III's future and how best the child king should be educated to ensure the prosperity of his kingdom. As he lay suffering, he called for the twelve-year-old king and took him by the hand. He told him that he wished him to be passed into the care of the new papal legate, Pandulph, who had replaced Guala in 1218, and then exhorted the king to lead a better life than his father.

"I beg the Lord our God that, if I ever did anything to please him, that in the end he grant you to grow up to be a worthy man," Marshal said. "And if it were the case that you followed in the footsteps of some wicked ancestor and that your wish was to be like him, then I pray to God, the son of Mary, that you die before it comes to that."

"Amen," the king replied.

By the time Marshal died, Henry III was old enough to be consulted on matters of governance and had been given his own seal to ratify decisions made on his behalf. Yet if he had an awareness of the stiff realities of government, that did not mean that he was trusted to take on the business of rule for himself. For as long as he remained a child, there would be faction and uncertainty.

Marshal was replaced by a triumvirate, with Pandulph, Peter des Roches, and Hubert de Burgh all having a hand in reconstructing England's battered administration after the ravages of civil war. But after Henry's second, more magnificent coronation in 1220—this time in the grander surroundings of Canterbury—des Roches fell from grace and eventually departed for the Holy Land. Thereafter de Burgh dominated. Throughout the 1220s Henry clung to the justiciar for advice and leaned on him as he set about rebuilding royal finance and directing campaigns to subdue internal rebellion by truculent barons and Welsh aggression under Llywelyn the Great of Gwynedd.

De Burgh did his best to contain Llywelyn by leading a military expedition to the west, while he attempted to increase the king's ravaged finances by squeezing royal sheriffs to produce more income from their shires. Yet kingship without a mature king remained a ship captained by committee, and any realm under a minority smacked of weakness. When Philip II died in 1223, his thirty-five-year-old son—England's erstwhile invader—became Louis VIII and determined almost at once to attack the English Crown's position in Poitou.

After the domestic disturbance of the early years this was the first real foreign crisis of Henry's reign. The critical blow fell in the summer of 1224, when the citizens of La Rochelle heard the thunderous approach of a French army before their walls. The new and energetic king of France wheeled his siege engines against them from the land; with a weak and still-impoverished young king of England on the other side of the Channel it was not surprising that the townsmen surrendered almost immediately, selling their allegiance for French coin.

Poitou itself had been held precariously ever since John's ill-fated sally in 1214. Losing La Rochelle removed a vital English foothold on the Continental coast and put Channel shipping into serious jeopardy. As the chronicler Roger of Wendover explained, "[La] Rochelle is . . . where the kings of England and their knights usually land for the defense of those districts; but now the way was closed to the king."

Meanwhile, Hugh de Lusignan, who had married John's widow, Queen Isabella, and was thus now technically Henry's stepfather, overran most of Gascony. The already truncated English rump of Aquitaine was reduced to Bordeaux and a few coastal towns. All that was left of the Plantagenet Continental possessions was in danger of being lost for good.

Recovering Gascony and Poitou was a matter of urgency for de Burgh and the young king. Family pride depended on it. But what promise did it hold for anyone else? Merchants did good business in the wine trade, but they were not political men. No English baron had a stake there. Thus the need to recover Poitou and Gascony raised fundamental questions about the means by which the English Crown could finance war on the Continent. The refusal of John's barons to join his various expeditions had touched off a crisis that ended with the promulgation of the Magna Carta and civil war. How could de Burgh and Henry convince the same class that now, eleven years later, it was in their interest to fight for land where they had no financial stake?

This, in a nutshell, was to be the central dilemma of kingship for the rest of Henry's long reign. Although he had not really known any of his royal ancestors, Henry felt keenly the historical burden of restoring their prestige, a task he saw as expressed through the defense of what was left of the Continental empire, the expansion of power back into the old lands of central and western France, and building influence on the fringes of Henry II and Richard's empire in Germany, Sicily, and Castile. Yet these were precisely the burdens that, under John, had been felt to be intolerable to the political community of England. In 1224–1225 the new regime needed urgently to restate the case for restoring the Plantagenet empire.

The solution came by two routes. The first was to appeal to fear. Wild rumors circulated that with the Channel full of French shipping and a hungry new Capetian king on the throne, England was under threat of another invasion. If Continental reconquest was of little interest to the English barons, then defense of the coast was a worthy rallying cause. Hubert de Burgh played on the invasion scare for all it was worth and succeeded in making it—in the short term at least—a valid reason for national military expenditure.

The second line of attack, which was to matter far more in both the political history of Henry's reign and the constitutional development of Plantagenet kingship for nearly two centuries afterward, was to seek to heal the wounds of John's reign by reissuing the Magna Carta. It was granted to the assembled lay and ecclesiastical lords of England in a great council in January 1225, as a political exchange for the grant of a tax of one-fifteenth part of England's movables. That the reissue of the charters represented a quid pro quo between king and political community was unmistakable, to Roger of Wendover at least: "All the assembly of bishops, earls, barons, abbots, and priors . . . gave . . . that they would willingly accede to the king's demands [for a fifteenth] if he would grant them their long-sought liberties."

The Magna Carta had been issued twice—in 1216 and 1217—since its original promulgation in 1215. In 1217 it had been accompanied by a Charter of the Forest, which limited the king's rights over the swaths of royal forestland that stretched across England and allowed ordinary people the rights of grazing animals, digging ditches, and other vital agricultural privileges. Previously, forest law had been onerous and hugely resented by landowners. Royal forests were not just areas of woodland but included pastures and even parts of farms and villages. Resisting the creep of the special law that governed these lands meant confronting the most powerful arm of kingship on the ground. Committees of men were appointed to physically walk the boundaries of the royal forests and provide reports on their extent.

The 1225 reissued charters were, in the long run, far more important than the original versions that had been foisted upon John at Runnymede and given to the country by William Marshal in the aftermath of a bloody civil war. Together they formed a grant that was to change the course not just of Henry's reign but of the English kings and queens to come. No longer an ad hoc collection of liberties asserted hotchpotch, the charters became a symbolic statement of political principle.

On February 15 and 16, 1225, packets of orders were sent to every county sheriff in England, ordering them to proclaim and observe the charters and carry out new surveys of the forest boundaries, while also making provision for the assessment and collection of a tax that would unlock tens of thousands of pounds for an expedition that—for all its advertisement as a means to protect the coasts—was essentially a private royal expedition of reconquest.

In immediate political terms the tax was wildly successful, raising forty-five thousand pounds, far more than the minority government had managed to raise by feudal levies. The money enabled Henry and de Burgh to muster a well-equipped summer expedition to relieve Gascony. It was led by the king's younger brother, Richard (by now a vigorous young man of sixteen, who had been raised to the rank of earl of Cornwall as a birthday present at the beginning of the year), accompanied by the forty-nine-year-old statesman, military veteran, and royal uncle the earl of Salisbury.

The expedition, richly equipped and led by a seasoned soldier, was a success. The English came fast and fought hard, driving back the French and preventing them from overrunning the last parts of Aquitaine. Salisbury soon found that he could not retake Poitou in a single campaigning season, but his efforts secured Gascony and its valuable wine trade for the English Crown, establishing a dependency that was to last for more than two centuries. It was a high point of Henry's minority.

Yet the territorial and trade gains were arguably of less significance than the bargain that was struck at home. As English royal flags fluttered above Gascon castles, copies of the two great charters flew around the kingdom across the Channel. Royal lawyers scratched their heads and wondered how they could find gaps in the charters and ways to maintain royal prerogative wherever possible. But the genie was out of the bottle. The charters were revered wherever they landed. It swiftly became obvious that a constitutional bargain had been struck. Henry's administration had begun a process by which military expeditions would be financed at the expense of detailed concessions of political liberties, written up in the form of charters that were distributed far and wide across the realm. The deal had been struck by an assembly of barons, bishops, and other magnates that, if it could hardly yet be called a parliament, was an early iteration of what became one. The feudal prerogatives of kings and their rights over their subjects were now a matter for debate and discussion. This was a compact that would endure for the rest of the Middle Ages, which would define the future of English kingship and lay the seeds of distant political rebellion overseas.

Kingship at Last

Henry's minority could, and perhaps should, have come to an end in 1225, when he turned eighteen. The reissue of the Magna Carta would have marked a clean break with his father's reign and a point from which decisively to launch his own. This would have proved especially advantageous when, in November 1226, Louis VIII, aged thirty-nine, died of dysentery, and the long minority of his son, the twelve-year-old Louis IX, began.

But 1225 did not mark a clean break. Nor did January 1227, when a nineteen-year-old Henry declared himself fully of age at a council in Oxford. Although the king began to build up his own household, independent of his advisers, he was far from competent in the exercise of power. He was pulled in two directions, particularly with regard to France. Henry attempted to raise money for the reconquest of Normandy and Poitou in 1228 and 1229, while simultaneously wriggling where he could out of the obligations of the charters that had been promulgated in 1225. But it was clear that real power still lay with de Burgh, whose reluctance for war on the Continent damped the king's enthusiasm and that of his brother Richard earl of Cornwall. Henry's attempts to invade Normandy in 1229 and 1230 were dismally unsuccessful; de Burgh's caution prevented the major offensive required to match the king's ambition.

This slothful progress toward adulthood and independence was a reflection of the king's character. Henry was from his earliest years vague and somewhat guileless. He had vision but not the ability to put his ideas into practice or the stomach for headstrong personal government that had been common among even the worst of his ancestors. With de Burgh clinging to power in his position as justiciar for life and Henry lacking the strength and self-confidence to grasp the reins of government, an uneasy status quo continued for the best part of another decade. It was not until 1234 that Henry shook off the men he had inherited from his father's reign, and it took a crisis of the utmost gravity to induce him to do so.

Having grown up without a father, Henry was excessively drawn to paternal figures and had an infuriating tendency to take the last, rather than the best, piece of advice given. He had inherited the Plantagenet temper, and there were numerous occasions during his reign when he flew into rages with his friends and ministers, hurling violent abuse at them and occasionally trying to brain them with nearby objects. During one fit of temper he tried to attack Hubert Walter with a blunted sword. Yet he could rarely stay angry with his advisers long enough to remove them, and as a consequence, they continued governing on his behalf for an unseemly length of time.

The longer de Burgh's hands stayed clamped on the levers of power, the deeper into malaise Henry's reign subsided. While the justiciar enriched himself with wardships that gave him the profits of major estates, Henry suffered the political consequences of petty squabbling between his justiciar, de Burgh, and leading young barons who should have formed a loyalist core around the new king, in particular William Marshal's son Richard and his own brother, Richard earl of Cornwall, who were provoked into revolt in 1231.

De Burgh's regime was self-serving and at odds with the king's own aims in government, but things grew far worse in 1231 with the return from crusade of Henry's onetime tutor Peter des Roches bishop of Winchester. The overbearing des Roches had no intention of allowing de Burgh to run England for his own profit and saw to it that he maneuvered himself swiftly back into a position of royal influence. Henry was briefly torn between the two men, both of whom had exercised formative paternal influence on him but who could never work together. In the end, des Roches won out. In July 1232 a violent quarrel broke out at Woodstock between Henry and de Burgh, which ended with the twenty-four-year-old king accusing his mentor of a bewildering array of crimes, including poisoning the earl of Salisbury and the earl of Pembroke, both of whom had recently died (almost certainly through no fault of de Burgh's). The deposed justiciar was tried in London before his peers, an unmistakable nod toward the demands of the Magna Carta and the new political reality, and was sentenced to perpetual imprisonment in Devizes Castle.

Des Roches now dominated Henry and his government. Henry briefly delighted in the precious jewels and trinkets he had confiscated from de Burgh and enjoyed a rare period of solvency: in September 1232 des Roches secured for him a tax to pay for a campaign in Brittany, and in 1233 the government laid a savage tally on the Jews. But to the country at large, nothing had changed. Des Roches's rule was no advance on what had preceded it;

Henry I laments the loss of his son and heir William the Aetheling in the *White Ship* disaster of 1120. Henry's failure to produce another legitimate male heir resulted in nearly twenty years of civil war in England—known appropriately as "The Shipwreck."

Henry II in dispute with Thomas Becket. The disastrous failure of the friendship between king and archbishop resulted in the most shocking murder of their age and the subsequent creation of a cult of national sainthood around Becket. (akg-images/British Library. Ms. Cotton Claudius D.II, fol.73, 14th century)

Eleanor of Aquitaine was the wife of two kings and the mother of two more. Brave, resilient, and proud, she remained a cunning and active politician well into her seventies. (Peter Newark Pictures/The Bridgeman Art Library)

Geoffrey Plantagenet, father of Henry II, was described by John of Marmoutier as "admirable and likable . . . he excelled at arguing . . . [and was] unusually skilled at warfare." The best of his descendents shared at least two of these qualities. (The Art Archive/Musée de Tessé, Le Mans/Kharbine-Tapabor/Collection CL)

n deo suscepto meus es.

Images like this of Richard the Lionheart (*left*) jousting with Saladin during the Third Crusade became a widely repeated symbol of Plantagenet family lore and English history during the thirteenth and fourteenth centuries. In fact, despite their mutual admiration, the two great warriors never met in person. (The Art Archive/British Museum)

A French chronicle depicts the fall of Acre in 1191, one of Richard I's most significant victories during the Third Crusade. The city was in Christian hands for precisely one hundred years, and Edward I visited Acre in the 1270s. (Scala, Florence/ Heritage Images)

The Magna Carta was a peace treaty that failed to end the civil war between King John and his barons. Nevertheless, the principles of justice and government it evoked would be central to every political crisis of the Plantagenet age.

(The Print Collector/HIP/Topfoto)

Simon de Montfort is hacked to pieces at the battle of Evesham in 1265. De Montfort's prickly opposition to Henry III has given him the reputation as the father of English parliamentary democracy.

(The British Library/HIP/Topfoto)

Edward I, a legal reformer and Hammer of the Scots, was the most physically intimidating of the Plantagenet kings. Tall and fierce tempered, it was said that he once scared a man to death. Here, seemingly in a milder mood, he addresses his court. He holds a sword of conquest while tonsured clerks take note of his utterances.

(akg-images/British Library, Ms. Cotton Vitellius A. XIII, fol.6v)

Château Gaillard: the magnificent castle built on the Seine by Richard I to protect the Norman border with France. Supposedly unconquerable, it was taken from John by Philip II Augustus in 1204 during the fall of Normandy. (© Eye Ubiquitous/Superstock)

Edward I built a ring of expensive fortresses to enforce his conquest of Wales. Conwy was completed in 1287; the castleworks and town fortifications cost around £14,500. In 1399 Richard II met the earl of Northumberland at Conwy to negotiate the relinquishing of the Plantagenet crown to Henry Bolingbroke. (© Buddy Mays/Alamy)

Edward II never grasped the art of kingship. He was mocked and feared in equal measure and surrounded himself with loathsome favorites, including Piers Gaveston and Hugh Despenser the Younger. His tomb (pictured) is in Gloucester Cathedral rather than in the Plantagenet mausoleum at Westminster.

(© Angelo Hornak/ Corbis)

Isabella of France, queen consort of England, was known as the She-Wolf of France. Her father and all three of her brothers were French kings. With her lover Roger Mortimer, she helped topple her husband Edward II from the English throne, and then ruled England for three years in the name of her son Edward III. (Mary Evans Picture Library)

The Wilton Diptych shows Richard II as he saw himself: divinely anointed and protected by the saints, including the Virgin Mary, St. Edmund, St. Edward the Confessor, and John the Baptist. (© The National Gallery, London/Scala, Florence)

Medieval naval battles were rare and, when they did occur, chaotic. Nevertheless, the battle of Sluys in June 1340, depicted here, was one of the first English successes in the Hundred Years War.

(White Images/ Scala, Florence)

Edward III wearing the blue robes of the Order of the Garter. This band of brothers bound England's aristocrats together in the cause of war under a code of knightly chivalry and reduced the political pressure exerted on Edward by the outrageous cost of his campaigns in France.

(© The British Library Board, Stowe 594, f.7v)

Edward III's third surviving son, John of Gaunt duke of Lancaster, loomed large in the reign of his nephew Richard II. A divisive character in his life, his death in February 1399 prompted his son Henry Bolingbroke's invasion of England and the final fall of the Plantagenet Crown.

(Private Collection/The Bridgeman Art Library)

the bishop was even less popular and more overbearing an influence than de Burgh, and he brought with him hated followers who had blighted John's reign. England needed kingship in person and not by proxy. Yet for two more years it got further partisan rule by an overbearing minister. To secure his position, des Roches rid the court of his opponents and set about building himself and his followers up with lucrative royal offices, castles, and lands. According to Roger of Wendover, under des Roches's guidance Henry "exiled his nobles and barons without judgment of their peers, burning their villages and houses, cutting down their woods and orchards, and destroying their parks and fishponds." The principles of the Magna Carta were trodden underfoot. This did nothing to improve relations between the king and Richard Marshal, who rebelled twice in 1233, sparking a minor civil war and throwing Henry's attempts to campaign against rebels in Wales into disarray.

It was clear to all that the situation was untenable. According to Roger of Wendover, by June 1233 Henry's magnates were beginning to talk of deposing him. In a great council at Westminster held in February of the following year the English bishops implored the king to rid himself of des Roches and his pernicious henchmen and stand on his own. Henry agreed, but then, as became his way at times of crisis, he took fright at the prospect of imposing his will on his realm. Instead of sweeping the deck and installing new ministers, he vanished from Westminster for more than a month on a tour of the holy shrines of East Anglia, praying to the holy fragment of the True Cross in the monastery at Bromholm, the shrine to the Virgin Mary at Walsingham, and other favorite monasteries. Richard Marshal and Llywelyn of Wales were in rebellion, yet the king was on a pilgrimage.

In April 1234 Richard Marshal died from his wounds after a battle in Ireland, and Henry was—wildly and erroneously—accused in some parts of having had him murdered. By May the crisis in government had grown so acute that the English bishops, led by the new archbishop of Canterbury, Edmund Rich, were threatening to excommunicate him. Henry finally shook himself into action. With some regret he ordered des Roches to retire to his diocese and took control of government for the first time. He was not keen to rule, but it was clear that if he did not do so, he would very swiftly find himself in the same dire circumstances as his father. At a great council held at Gloucester directly after des Roches's fall, Henry acknowledged that his ministers had failed to abide by their agreement to afford barons who were accused of crimes "judgment by their peers." He reversed some of the arbitrary land seizures undertaken by des Roches and committed himself once more to the spirit of the Magna Carta by promising to take important decisions only after consultation with great councils of his magnates. Out of the crisis Henry emerged, however unwillingly, as a king in keeping with the spirit of the realm, in which consensual observance of the principles of the Magna Carta was now esteemed above all other things.

Curiously, at the same time as he took on the mantle of kingship it also became clear that Henry was undergoing a form of spiritual transformation. As his realm erupted in protest and he found himself confronted by overbearing ministers, rebellious barons, and truculent Welshmen, Henry, deeply wounded and confused by the upheaval, looked into English history for the inspiration he hoped would help him finally become a king worthy of the name. He found it not in the example of his uncle or grandfather but in the life story of one of his more distant ancestors, the last of the Anglo-Saxon kings, St. Edward the Confessor.

Edward, whose childless reign had ended in 1066, immediately resulting in the succession wars between Harold Godwinsson and William the Conqueror, was not a king much venerated in Plantagenet England. He had been canonized in 1161, thanks to the offices of Henry II, but there was no great cult around him, and John's request to be buried alongside St. Wulfstan at Worcester, rather than St. Edward at Westminster, showed that there was little special sentiment attached to his example. Yet to Henry, delving into the past in search of a new father figure to prop him up, St. Edward the Confessor seemed to be an alluring role model.

The history of Edward's reign looked to Henry rather like his own. Like Edward, he had come to power amid a time of civil war and popular oppression. Like Edward, he had to some extent been betrayed by his ministers (just as de Burgh and des Roches had manipulated Henry for their own ends, so the Confessor had been undone by the treacherous Earl Godwin). Edward had endured the tribulations of kingship and ascended to heaven accompanied by St. John the Evangelist. Pertinently his laws that were held up as the ancient models for good kingship were cited in Henry I's Charter of Liberties. King John himself had sworn to adhere to the laws of King Edward when he was released from his excommunication by Stephen Langton in 1213. Edward the Confessor was an appealing model for a devout and well-meaning young king.

From 1234 onward Henry began to devote himself to the cult of Edward the Confessor with ever-growing zeal. He studied his life and legend, began to order images painted of famous scenes from the saintly life in Westminster and his other palaces, observed his feast day, October 13, with ever more fanatical zeal, and referred in charters to "the glorious king Edward," whom he regarded as his "special patron." Henry would seek to follow his example for the rest of his life.

Although devotion to saints and the archetype of the pious king was well established in the medieval mind, there was something rather extreme about Henry's growing adulation. Nevertheless, no one could complain of the effect it had on him. From 1234 Henry III was at last an adult king governing in his own right, committed to the spirit of the Magna Carta. It was what the realm had been demanding for years.

The man who emerged from this long road out of childhood was a peculiar specimen. Henry was about five feet six inches in height. He was said to have a drooping eyelid, which gave him a crooked solemnity to match his somewhat ponderous character. He was noticeably pious, even in an age when the fashion among kings was for asceticism and ostentatious religiosity. (Henry's counterpart, Louis IX of France, was fanatically devout, planning magnificent church-building projects such as the sublime Ste.-Chapelle, and thrusting himself into a burgeoning market for holy relics: in 1239 Louis was to pay the astonishing sum of 135,000 livres to Baldwin II of Constantinople for the Crown of Thorns and a fragment of the True Cross.) The holy competition between Western kings was a game of spiritual trumps, and Henry was determined to be among the holiest kings in Christendom.

Henry was not as physically or personally arresting as his forebears, but he was self-consciously given to greater displays of kingly magnificence than any of them. Perhaps the greatest artistic patron of all of England's medieval kings, he transformed the great centers of courtly life with paintings and buildings that celebrated the virtuous antiquity of kingship. Walls and windows burst with his favorite historical scenes and figures. St. Edward the Confessor was everywhere, but so too were Lazarus and Dives, the Four Evangelists, the keepers of King Solomon's bed, and military saints like St. Eustace, who was painted to stand guard over the king's bed at Westminster. Henry also commissioned paintings of Alexander the Great, the siege of Antioch, and images of his uncle Richard the Lionheart's legendary deeds in the Holy Land. He was becoming a masterly propagandist, with a deft grasp of history and an instinct for broadcasting the divine magnificence of kingship. He spent an average of three thousand pounds a year—a tenth of his revenue—on building. His right-hand man in constructing the image of kingship was a goldsmith called Odo, and, from 1240, Odo's son and successor Edward of Westminster, whose role as melter of the exchequer and keeper of the king's works included making all the gold cups, crowns, dazzling vestments, beautiful candles, and fine jewels with which Henry loved to surround himself.

In January 1236, having carefully sought the permission of a great council to marry, the twenty-eight-year-old Henry finally took as his queen the twelve-year-old Eleanor of Provence. On the face of it, his choice of bride was somewhat eccentric. He had previously been engaged to Joan, the heiress to the county of Ponthieu; but the French court had fiercely objected to the prospect of an English king's marrying into a county on the northern French coast, and the marriage alliance had fallen apart. Henry had turned next to Eleanor, the second of four daughters born to Ramon-Berengar IV count of Provence, whose eldest daughter, Margaret, was already married to Louis IX. Like Henry's famous grandmother Eleanor of Aquitaine before her, Eleanor of Provence brought with her the influence and interests of a vibrant southern French culture. Controversially, she did not bring the promise of any landed territory in France, but what she lacked in land she made up for in connections, not just to the French court through Margaret but to the Holy Roman Empire and the papacy through her mother's family. Eleanor's mother, Beatrice of Savoy, had five brothers, all of whom were extremely skillful diplomats with alliances and contacts throughout Europe. The counts of Savoy, also known as Savoyards, controlled the northern passages into Italy and as such were in the thick of the violent diplomatic struggles between the Holy Roman Emperor Frederick II and the papacy. Henry's keen interest in the politics of the Holy Roman Empire had been shown when he married his younger sister Isabella to Frederick in 1235. His own marriage to Eleanor now reinforced his links. Even if Plantagenet kingship was to be restricted to England and Gascony, Henry was determined to stay firmly involved in the complex power politics of Europe.

Henry knew that the eyes of Europe would be upon his wedding ceremony in Canterbury on January 20, 1236, and on the new queen's coronation, which took place six days later. "Whatever the world could afford to create pleasure and magnificence were there brought together from every quarter," wrote the chronicler Matthew Paris, who was close to Henry's court. London was filled to bursting with the great men and women of England, servants, hangers-on, and crowds desperate to glimpse the king's wedding. "The whole city was ornamented with flags and banners, chaplets and hangings, candles and lamps, and with wonderful devices and extraordinary representations, and all the roads were cleansed from mud and dirt, sticks and everything offensive," wrote Paris. "The citizens . . . went out to meet the king and queen, dressed in their ornaments, and vied with each other in trying the speed of their horses."

A highly competitive spirit took hold as archbishops, bishops, abbots, earls, and the citizens of England's ancient cities laid claim to their rightful ceremonial duties. From roles as prestigious as crowning the queen and bearing the ceremonial sword of St. Edward the Confessor to more modest ones, such as waving a stick at onlookers who pressed too close and arranging the cups on the dinner table, every act within the pageant dignified its actor and bound all together in a communion of kingship. At the end of it all, Henry had a bride who provided him with a direct connection to European high politics, a confirmation of his manhood, and a grand occasion to direct England's peers and paupers in enthusiastic demonstrations of their loyalty. He celebrated his nuptials by taking his new queen on a summer trip to Glastonbury, to see King Arthur's supposed burial site.

This was enough on its own to excite the realm, but Henry and Eleanor's marriage was followed by another that proved equally important to the history of the reign. In January 1238 the rising star of the court Simon de Montfort was sensationally married to Henry's twenty-three-year-old sister, Eleanor of Leicester. The princess was not merely the youngest child of John and Isabella of Angoulême but also the widow of William Marshal the Younger, late earl of Pembroke and eldest son of the king's onetime regent. On her first husband's death, the sixteen-year-old Eleanor had sworn a holy oath of chastity before Edmund Rich archbishop of Canterbury. Now, wooed by de Montfort, she had chosen to break it.

De Montfort had arrived in England in 1230, pursuing a claim, through his grandmother Amicia de Beaumont, to the earldom of Leicester. A charismatic, highborn Frenchman, he was only two years younger than the king, whom he impressed and eventually intimidated with his shrewd political and literary mind, military brilliance, formidable social connections, and religious fanaticism. Simon de Montfort was a difficult man: obstinate and consumed by ambition, he wore a hair shirt, ate and drank frugally, and stayed up late in saintly devotions. Although they were roughly the same age, de Montfort would become yet another paternal figure to whom Henry could look up with childish admiration. It did not take him long to become the king's close friend and one of his closest counselors. Nevertheless, his sudden marriage to Eleanor shocked the realm.

Eleanor was by some measure the most valuable bride in England. She came with royal access, landed power, and high status. Although Henry had consulted a great council of barons and prelates before both his own marriage and that of his sister Isabella, Eleanor was given to de Montfort without consultation, and the couple was married in secret. This seemed to run contrary to all the principles of consensual government that Henry had promised on his assumption of full kingship, and it caused outrage among the English nobility, both lay and ecclesiastical.

The barons objected that de Montfort's marriage would upend regional and national power structures, bringing him a vast income and lands throughout southern England to add to the lands he had inherited in the earldom of Leicester. The bishops, for their part, were perplexed that Eleanor was allowed to remarry after having taken a vow of chastity. General outrage was so severe that a political crisis erupted in which Henry's brother Richard earl of Cornwall allied himself with Gilbert Marshal (the new earl of Pembroke) and the earl of Winchester and led yet another armed rebellion against the king, which took six months to defuse.

Fortunately for Henry, he tended to make peace with his troublesome brother rather quickly and the crisis passed. De Montfort was secured in his position as royal favorite and brother-in-law and traveled to Rome to seek approval from Pope Innocent IV for his marriage. Shortly after his return, in November 1238, Eleanor de Montfort gave birth at Kenilworth Castle to the couple's first child, a boy whom the couple named after the king.

In the meantime Henry's new young queen was joined at the royal court by a crowd of Savoyards, including three of her diplomat uncles: Peter, Thomas, and Boniface of Savoy. Peter and Thomas of Savoy would do much to influence public policy during their time in England. Impressed by the elegance, experience, and well-connected worldliness of the Savoyards,

Henry was generous with his patronage. Thomas, who had inherited the county of Flanders, was in little need of royal generosity, but Peter was knighted in 1241 and granted the lordship of Richmond in Yorkshire. Three years later his younger brother Boniface was invested as archbishop of Canterbury, having been elected to the position in 1240 after the death of Edmund Rich. As Henry dispensed landed titles, Eleanor busied herself tying together English and Savoyard families in marriage, adding a new flavor to certain quarters of the English aristocracy. Not everyone liked it, but on the whole the Savoyards brought more to England than they took.

In mid-June 1239 the sixteen-year-old queen Eleanor gave birth to the first royal child. The king had been sleeping with her since their marriage (indeed Henry's life had been saved two years earlier when a knife-wielding maniac had broken into the royal bedroom only to find the king absent, in bed with his fifteen-year-old wife), and it was a source of great joy that she finally bore him a boy to continue the family line.

When news broke that the queen had given birth to a son, there was wild celebration throughout the palace of Westminster. The clerks of the royal chapel sang *Christus vincit, christus regnat, christus imperat* (Christ conquers, Christ reigns, Christ rules), and when news reached London, there was a citywide street festival. Henry was exacting about the joy he expected of his subjects. This was the first Plantagenet heir to be born in three decades. When messengers returned bearing gifts of congratulation from the great nobles and bishops of England, the king inspected his haul. Presents that were not deemed worthy of the occasion were returned with a demand for something better.

What would the boy be called? Plantagenet family tradition might have suggested Henry, John, Richard, William, or even Geoffrey. But Henry III had something more exotic in mind. He decided that his son would be named Edward, after his beloved Confessor. It was a bizarre choice of name for a Plantagenet prince or indeed for any aristocratic child born in England during the thirteenth century. It would have sounded odd and archaic to well-bred ears. But Henry had a vision of kingship that wound together historical narratives of Plantagenet conquest and the saintliness of the ancient kings. Like William the Aetheling before him, Lord Edward, as the child grew up to be known, was to embody both England's ancient past and its future and bring a distinct new identity to Plantagenet kingship.

At Queen Eleanor's churching, a religious ceremony carried out to celebrate a woman's recovery from childbirth, a furious argument blew up between the king and de Montfort; it was to have unforeseen but deadly repercussions for both parties. Ever since his rapid elevation, de Montfort had been in some financial difficulty. It had cost him handsomely to buy his brother Amaury out of his half share in the earldom of Leicester, and in 1237 he had taken the cross, which brought with it more expense. His wife had a reputation for high extravagance, and all in all he was finding his position as the king's brother-in-law to be somewhat beyond his means. He had borrowed two thousand pounds from Thomas of Savoy in 1239 and pledged Henry's name as a guarantor without first consulting the king. Henry took exception to this, and at the churching ceremony he exploded in anger. There were probably other reasons, including simmering resentment on Henry's part of the political cost he had been made to pay for allowing de Montfort to marry his sister, but shifting suddenly from a position of lavish generosity to white rage, Henry berated de Montfort and Eleanor, now pregnant for the second time, and accused Simon of having seduced his sister before their marriage. The king was so furious that his pregnant sister and former friend were forced to flee England.

Effectively banished, de Montfort decided to make good on his crusader's oath. Richard earl of Cornwall lived up to his uncle and namesake's reputation by leading a crusade to Palestine between 1239 and 1241, and de Montfort joined enthusiastically. The Barons' Crusade, as it was known, was quite successful, and in alliance with Theobald IV of Champagne, Richard managed to recover Galilee and refortify Ascalon. As her husband fought the infidel in Outremer, Eleanor de Montfort retired to Brindisi, in southern Italy, where she was sheltered by her brother-in-law Frederick II.

When de Montfort returned from the East in 1242, he found Henry in a confident mood, ready to welcome him back into royal favor. Henry had taken advantage of a succession dispute in Wales between two sons of Llywelyn the Great, supporting Llywelyn's son Dafydd as the new ruler of Gwynedd and forcing him to pay homage at Gloucester, thereby establishing the superior authority of Plantagenet kingship. As with his father before him, supremacy at home had encouraged Henry III to think again of his territorial claims overseas, and he was planning a military expedition to Poitou. There was little enthusiasm among the magnates, who refused to permit him to levy the taxes he would need for a grand conquest, so Henry required all the money and talent he could gather to launch what amounted to a purely private invasion. He was grateful to have his brother-in-law, now a skilled and experienced general, back in his service.

In the end the expedition to Poitou was a disaster: the English army was small and underfunded, accompanied by a paltry two hundred knights, regularly betrayed by supposed Poitevin allies, and completely outwitted by Louis IX. Simon de Montfort fought with distinction, but it was in a hopeless cause. Henry III suffered a string of humiliating losses, during the course of which he was shown up as the worst general his family had ever produced. The campaign caused yet another quarrel with his brother Richard, to whom Henry had promised Gascony as a reward for his valiant service in a losing cause, before reneging on the queen's advice. At Saintes, de Montfort was overheard likening Henry to Charles the Simple, the tenth-century Carolingian king of France whose military failings were such that he was eventually imprisoned by his own subjects. Even if they were outwardly reconciled, it was clear that de Montfort and Henry were unlikely to remain at peace for long. Indeed it seemed increasingly unlikely that any of Henry's large and varied extended family would see their holy but hapless king through many more untroubled years.

Holy Kingship

Tapers flickered in the king's chamber throughout the night of October 12, 1247. It was the eve of the feast of the translation of St. Edward, now the holiest king in English history and the namesake of Henry's eldest son. The king knelt, deep in prayer. He had been fasting on a pauper's diet of bread and water and was preparing himself, with a sleepless night of devotion, for a ceremony of profound, solemn divinity.

Henry had purchased from the nobles of Outremer a delicate crystalline vessel containing a portion of the blood of Christ, which was said to have been collected from Jesus as he suffered the agonies of the Passion. It fitted well into the royal relic collection, which already contained a stone marked with the footprint of Jesus, left just prior to the Ascension. On the feast of St. Edward, Henry himself would now present his latest gift, which to his mind rivaled Louis IX's Crown of Thorns as the greatest Christian relic in Western Europe, to the community of Westminster Abbey.

For once he had something to celebrate. In a rare moment of peaceful collaboration, his brother Richard was overseeing the production of a reformed coinage that would restore faith in the debased English currency and earn a tidy profit for both the treasury and his earldom of Cornwall. Better still, after a period of renewed rebellion following Dafydd ap Llywelyn's submission to Henry in 1241, a coalition of Welsh princes had in April 1247 once more come to terms with the English Crown, accepting Henry as their feudal overlord and extending English rule farther and deeper into Wales than at any time since his father's reign. Meanwhile the royal family continued to expand; in May Henry had married two of the queen's relatives to two of his royal wards, the earl of Lincoln and the lord of Connaught. This drew two significant baronial families directly into the royal orbit.

When dawn broke on that October morning, all the priests of London assembled beneath the giant wooden spire of St. Paul's Cathedral dressed in grand ceremonial attire with surplices and hoods, their clerks arranged around them, carrying symbols and crosses. Hundreds of tapers gave a steady glow to the dark autumnal morning. They awaited their king.

Henry arrived, dressed humbly, in a poor cloak without a hood, a simple penitent whose mean dress was accentuated by the finery of his attendants. He entered the cathedral and emerged carrying the little crystal vial above his head, both hands fixed around it, both eyes trained upward to this exquisite relic and on to the heavens beyond. Thus he began his procession on foot along the road from London to Westminster.

It was a tiring business. The king was drained by a night of sleepless fasting, and the potholes and bumps in the road threatened constantly to bring him to his knees. But at some level, such was his love of ostentatious piety, he welcomed the discomfort. He had been drawn to the pageantry of royal devotion all his life, ever since as a thirteen-year-old he had watched with awe at the Trinity Chapel in Canterbury as St. Thomas Becket's remains had been transferred to a golden, bejeweled coffin. His mind may have wandered back to that day as he processed with the holy blood, two assistants supporting his aching arms as they held his prize aloft.

Before reaching the doors of Westminster Abbey, the procession would have heard the commotion awaiting them. Songs and tears and exultations to the holy spirit rang from the abbey church. It was in the early stages of a massive rebuilding project, begun in 1245 to redevelop it in the French Gothic style. Some forty-five thousand pounds would be spent to ensure that the abbey church mimicked and rivaled the great French churches of Ste.-Chapelle, St.-Denis, and Reims. Slender, soaring columns were to be added, with pointed windows and stained glass; the weight was to be borne outside the walls by flying buttresses.

The king, deep in his devotions, did not stop when he first reached the church. He carried on, the vial held above his head as before, and made a circuit of the church, then the nearby palace, and finally his own royal chambers. When this tour was complete, he returned to the church and presented the priceless gift to God, to his beloved Edward the Confessor, to the church of St. Peter at Westminster, and to the community of the abbey.

This lavish spectacle was the high point of Henry's royal pageantry. Before his assembled English knights, nobles, and bishops he carried off a triumphant scene that would have been the envy of Louis IX's and Frederick II's sophisticated courts. The bishop of Norwich later gave a sermon pointing out the preeminence of Henry's relic above any other relic in Europe: "The cross is a most holy thing, on account of the more holy shedding of Christ's blood made upon it, not the blood-shedding holy on account of the cross."

He added, according to Matthew Paris, "that it was on account of the great reverence and holiness of the king of England, who was known to be the most Christian of all Christian princes, that this invaluable treasure had been sent by the patriarch of Jerusalem . . . for in England, as the world knew, faith and holiness flourished more than in any other country throughout the world."

Here, then, was Henry's vision of kingship. It was a holy office that redrew the lineage of the royal family back to pre-Conquest times. Like Henry I, the king was knitting his own rule to ancient Saxon lineage, celebrating its English origins as well as its Continental sophistication.

But there was more to the ceremony than a simple affirmation of genealogy. Henry's kingship was made a matter not merely of right and conquest but of divinity. Here was the king as minister, not at war with his church, as had so often been the case under his father and grandfather, but enriching and protecting it. Here was Henry the intercessor, Henry the pilgrim, Henry the benefactor. He spoke to England's soul and to its history.

After the ceremony Henry cast off his pauper's costume and donned a glittering garment made from precious cloth, woven with shining metal thread, and decorated in gold. With a simple golden crown on his head, he knighted his half brother William de Valence and several others of his Poitevin and Gascon nobles. The priest-pilgrim king thus became the chivalric lord.

Though there were plenty outside the walls of Westminster who had grave doubts about the likelihood that Jesus's blood had survived the thirteen centuries since it was spilled on Calvary, Henry's pious ceremony was very much of the moment, an autumnal version of the spring feast of Corpus Christi, which had been established as a yearly festival by the bishop of Liège the previous year. It was also impossibly grand, as the chronicler Matthew Paris was at pains to point out in the eyewitness account that the king commissioned him to write. But was it politically effective?

The answer, alas, was no. Despite his masterly creation of a new dynastic myth over the course of the 1240s, as the fifth decade of his reign approached, Henry began to experience a succession of troubles, mostly of his own devising, which combined by 1258 to cause the most severe political crisis in England in half a century.

In May 1247 Simon de Montfort had been persuaded not to leave Western Europe for a second crusade. He was sent instead to shore up a troublesome region of Henry's overseas dominions, Gascony. After the failure of the Poitou expedition of 1242–1243 Henry had to reinforce that part of the French mainland of whose loyalty he could still be reasonably certain. De Montfort was thus sent to Gascony as a royal lieutenant, with sweeping powers to govern quasi-independently and protect the king's interests against the incursions of the numerous threatening powers close to the Gascon borders: France, Castile, Aragon, and Navarre.

De Montfort took to his new role with rather too much relish. Given almost total freedom of action in rebel country, far from the center of English royal government, he performed at first admirably, building a diplomatic shield around the borders of the duchy thanks to alliances with the great lords of the region. But before long he had run short of money and began collecting enemies. The Gascon nobles, led by the intractably rebellious Gaston de Béarn, refused to submit to his high-handed rule. Resistance was dealt with severely. De Montfort confiscated land, destroyed buildings, and, worst of all, cut vines—a terrible punishment in a land whose main source of income was from wine. By 1252 Gascony was in uproar.

Henry, despairing, recalled de Montfort to face trial before the royal council. It was a fractious affair, with hurt feelings on both sides. The accusations leveled were severe. The Gascons called him an "infamous traitor," guilty of extorting from the people and imprisoning and starving to death his enemies. According to Matthew Paris, de Montfort was acutely affronted by the aspersions cast upon his character. When he first heard of the Gascons' accusations, he raged to Henry: "Is it, my lord king, that you incline your ear and your heart to the messages of these traitors to you, and believe those who have often been convicted of treachery rather than me your faithful subject?"

Henry blithely responded: "If everything is clear, what harm will the scrutiny do you?"

As de Montfort's case came to trial before Henry's sympathetic barons, both parties let their emotions run away with them. After an incensed monologue denouncing Henry's fecklessness in giving credence to Gascon complaints, de Montfort demanded of the king: "Who could believe that you are a Christian? Have you never confessed?"

Henry coldly replied: "I have."

In a bitter retort recorded by Matthew Paris, de Montfort then said: "But what avails confession without repentance and atonement?"

To damn so devout a king before the great and good of England was ill advised. Although the royal council found in the earl's favor and he was returned briefly to Gascony, his very presence there was by now a cause for rebellion. Henry was forced to go to Gascony in person, subdue it with lavish expenditure, and fit it out for his son to take over as an appanage. And in due course, when Lord Edward was married to Eleanor of Castile on November 1, 1254, in the abbey of Santa María la Real de Las Huelgas in Castile, Henry granted the duchy to his son as a wedding gift, bringing to a close a disastrous period in its administration.

As part of the settlement Henry paid off de Montfort's contract as lieutenant. But the king's bitter words to his former friend summed up the simmering feeling that endured for the next decade: "I never repented of any act so much as I now repent of ever having permitted you to enter England, or to hold any land or honors in that country, in which you have fattened so as to kick against my authority."

Henry's vision of a restored Plantagenet patrimony, rejoining Normandy, Anjou, and Aquitaine to the English Crown, was close to his heart from the moment he assumed his majority, but any real attempt to realize that ambition lay far beyond his budget. While Louis IX was able to pay 150,000 livres for his Crown of Thorns and raise 1,000,000 livres in a crusading fund, Henry III struggled to amass enough coin to launch a simple cross-Channel invasion force every four or five years.

There was simply no escaping the fact that in comparison with both his ancestors and his rivals, Henry was poor. The means he derived from his estates in England and the profits of government, justice, and trade may have been adequate to his needs when carefully managed in peacetime— indeed during the periods of his reign when Henry was not pursuing his inheritance his revenues looked positively healthy—but they were never fit for the task of fighting major wars to conquer foreign territory.

Henry did his best to mask this unpleasant fact. His motto, which adorned the wall of the Painted Chamber in Westminster, was *Ke ne dune ke ne tine ne prent ke desire*, roughly translated as "He who does not give what he loves does not get what he wants." He wished to cultivate the image of the free-spending prince whose magnanimity brought bountiful reward. He had a passion for precious stones and shimmering metal. He invested heavily in his architectural projects and freely indulged his love of collecting art and jewels (although he ended up having to pawn much of his treasure in the 1260s). Like Louis IX, he traveled in style, made lavish donations to his favorite institutions and shrines, and had his daily masses celebrated by priests in gloriously decorated vestments. He stockpiled gold—the rising currency of Europe—in his personal chambers, living among stacks of ingots, gold leaf, and gold dust. But unlike Louis, whose annual income at more than seventy thousand pounds was nearly twice the English king's, behind this facade Henry faced a deep structural problem with royal finance.

Because he could not raise enough money by his own devices to launch successful foreign campaigns, Henry relied on ad hoc raids on marginal groups such as Jews and on the taxes he could now obtain only through negotiation with his greatest subjects. We have already seen how, with the compact of 1225, Henry had established a principle of quid pro quo with regard to political concessions in exchange for taxes. By the late 1240s this relationship had matured, and the great men of England had begun to view their meetings with the king as a legitimate and customary venue in which to air their critiques of government policy. The meetings gained a formal name when Henry III adjourned a law case to a "parliament" in 1236.

Between 1248 and 1249 four of these prototypical parliaments refused Henry a grant of tax to fund Simon de Montfort's conquest of the old Plantagenet lands. As well as refusing to grant money, they also made loud complaints about widespread corruption in local government. Henry was reduced to raising funds by selling royal treasure, carrying out a ludicrous second recoinage in 1257, in which gold rather than silver was issued as currency, and borrowing heavily from powerful nobles, including his brother Richard. Since he met stubborn resistance to taxation from his barons, Henry was forced to squeeze other, less regulated sources of income. He concentrated on revenue streams that drew more heavily on the pockets of his knights and lower-born subjects.

Repeated, heavy tallaging of the Jews became ever less profitable during the 1250s. Henry's traveling royal courts attempted to take up the slack and began to concentrate more heavily than ever on milking the profits of justice. Sheriffs—frequently foreign-born, centrally appointed officials parachuted into the shires to oversee royal government—became noticeably more rapacious in their efforts to raise money. Ignoring the shameful and unbalancing effect this had on governance in the localities, Henry would grant multiple shrievalties to his followers, leading them to press heavily for money on people to whom they were neither connected nor accountable. Meanwhile feudal exemptions were widely sold by the Crown, leading to an unpredictable and uneven level of royal exactions in the localities. Much of this ran directly against the spirit, and at times the letter, of the Magna Carta.

As the 1250s progressed, Henry's government once again began to chafe. Problems were raised by factions at court and by one faction in particular, a group of the king's relatives who had recently arrived at court and were known collectively as the Lusignans.

The Lusignan brothers—William and Aymer de Valence—were Henry's half siblings through his mother Queen Isabella of Angoulême's second marriage, to Hugh X de Lusignan. They had revolted against Louis IX during Henry's ill-fated Poitou campaign of 1241–1242, and the French king held a fierce grudge against the family. William, Aymer, their brothers Guy and Geoffrey, and their sister Alice had arrived in England in 1247. Henry received them with much acclaim and fanfare, knighting William at his great Westminster ceremony on October 13, 1247. The king's partisan generosity caused widespread resentment, tinged with xenophobia. William de Valence, as well as his belting as a knight, had also been granted marriage to Joan de Munchensi, the granddaughter of the first William Marshal, and had thus come to be lord of Pembroke and plenty of other manors and castles in Wales and the borders. Aymer meanwhile became bishop-elect of Winchester, while Guy and Geoffrey were granted wardships and money. More important, however, as friends of the king they were frequently protected from royal justice.

The Lusignans were a clique. They arrived together and were planted into English life en masse, much as the queen's Savoyard uncles had done when they arrived in the 1230s. They were, however, considerably harsher and more unpleasant in their conduct than the queen's cousins, and there was significant tension between the two groups. The Lusignans were seen as haughty, ill mannered, violent, proud, contemptuous, and quarrelsome. Even in a society regularly punctuated by violence, they managed to attract attention for their unpleasantness. A dispute between Aymer and the queen's Savoyard uncle Boniface archbishop of Canterbury resulted in an armed band of Lusignan supporters ransacking Lambeth Palace, stealing money, silver, and plate, and hotfooting it with hostages to their castle at Farnham. The king, who relied on the Lusignans for cash loans, did not punish them satisfactorily for this or other misdemeanors. Indeed quite the opposite was true: in 1256 Henry gave an order that writs against his favorites should not be acted upon. It was a serious failure of government and unsurprisingly was viewed as a direct violation of the clause in the Magna Carta that forbade the denial or delay of justice.

By the mid-1250s the king was seen by the barons at court and by much of the country as dominated by his new favorites at the expense of good governance. As a group of barons later wrote to the pope, "if anyone brought a complaint and sought judgment against the Lusignans . . . the king turned against the complainant in a most extraordinary manner, and he who should have been a propitious judge became a terrible enemy."

Henry's undue leaning toward his cousins was undermining what was increasingly being seen, from the baronial side at least, as his basic duty: to provide accessible, ready, reasonably evenhanded justice. He was corrupting public authority to favor private interest. Mild-spirited as he was, in the language of classical political philosophy, the king was becoming a tyrant. Worse still, he was growing delusional. The final problem of the 1250s, which illustrated both the scope of Henry's vision of kingship and the reach of his awesome folly, lay on an island far from the borders of England, Sicily.

When Henry decided to take the cross in 1250, a significant shift in his foreign policy followed. Having spent his entire reign attempting to build anti-French alliances in the East, particularly with Emperor Frederick II, to whom he had married his sister, he now shifted tack and dreamed of sending a vast army east to assist with the recapture of Jerusalem. The city, reclaimed for the Christians by Frederick II during the Sixth Crusade in 1228, had in 1244 been invaded and almost wholly razed by fierce Khwarezmian clans from farther east. Louis IX had taken up the crusading mantle in 1248, and Henry determined to join him. In the short term, this had allowed him to collect a crusading tax, but it was no cynical financial trick. Pious Henry, who decorated his palaces with paintings of Richard the Lionheart fighting a supposed duel with Saladin (the two men, of course, never met), genuinely imagined the glory that would be showered upon him if he revived his family's crusading tradition.

Unfortunately, Henry's fanciful plans had to compete with his real obligations in Gascony, which devoured his time and, more important, his money. Although he amassed substantial funds through clerical taxation, by 1255 almost all had been sunk in restoring order across the Channel. Yet the king's crusading ambition remained undimmed. Rather than give up his ambition, he readjusted his sights, from Outremer to somewhere closer to home. In 1254 Pope Innocent IV began to hawk the theoretically vacant crown of Sicily around the princes of Europe, claiming that as the feudal overlord of the island, its Crown was in his power to award. Henry saw an opportunity. He could reclaim a far-flung former Plantagenet land, a project that would combine his enthusiasm for crusading with his ambition to restore his inheritance.

Henry's aunt Joan—daughter of Henry II and Eleanor of Aquitaine—had been queen of Sicily during the 1180s and a prisoner of King Tancred II during the 1190s. Richard I had freed her on his journey east to the Third Crusade, then conquered the island to teach Tancred a lesson. Since then the kingdom had been drawn into the interminable wars between the emperors and the papacy, a strategic pawn in the power struggle that engulfed Italy and Central Europe for decades. In 1254 Henry sent emissaries requesting that the kingdom should be granted to his second son, Edmund, and his request was granted enthusiastically via the papal legate in March of that year.

Had Henry III been richer, less beset by other problems, and a more competent military strategist, securing Sicily for his second son might have been a realistic task. Unfortunately, he was instead a naive fantasist with a penchant for impossible schemes. Richard earl of Cornwall, troublesome but far wiser than the king, had been offered the Crown of Sicily in 1252. He had flatly refused it, telling the papal nuncio: "You might as well say, 'I will give or sell you the moon; climb up and take it.'"

Nevertheless, from 1254 Henry's crusading plans morphed into an obligation to fund the conquest of Sicily in the name of the pope. In May 1255 it was made official. A parliament was astonished when, on St. Edward's Day, October 13, 1255, the assembled magnates were told that in pledging to undertake the Sicilian expedition, Henry had incurred debts to the new pope, Alexander IV, of 135,541 marks. It was a mind-boggling sum of money, perhaps three times as much as Henry could hope to raise from clerical taxation and ironically not far off the 150,000 marks that Richard I had been forced to pay to escape imprisonment after the Third Crusade.

With this vast and entirely fanciful fortune, the barons learned, Henry was to fund an army that would march through France to Sicily, using the Alpine passes that Henry controlled thanks to his Savoyard connections.

From southern Italy an amphibious invasion would be launched against the island, and its Crown seized. Clearly, this was ambitious considering Henry's mediocre history of generalship. To make things worse, Henry had agreed that if he defaulted on his obligations, England would be placed under interdict and he would be excommunicated.

It was a mess. And yet Henry brimmed with confidence about his new cause. He made a great show of the official announcements connected with the scheme. He accepted Sicilian clergy into the realm. Thinking he had gained a useful ally in his Sicilian project, he celebrated when his brother Richard was elected king of the Germans in 1256 and installed the following year. Most preposterously, in March 1257 Henry presented his twelve-year-old son, Edmund, supposedly now the king of Sicily, to his assembled—and stunned—magnates and prelates. The boy was wearing full Apulian costume.

The truth was that no aspect of the Sicilian venture was even remotely realistic. "The nobility of the kingdom grieved at being reduced to such ruin by the supine simplicity of one man," wrote Matthew Paris. This new "crusade," far from appealing to his nobles, led to Henry's finding himself despised for his reckless adventurism. The magnates would have no part in paying for his scheme and pointed out on every possible occasion its long list of problems. But Henry had sworn an oath, which he was much less inclined than his father to break, that he would conquer this faraway island with very little practical value.

By 1257 the country was growing deeply skeptical about Henry's ability to rule. His coffers were empty. The Lusignans were loathed. He was committed to his Sicilian madness, on which he had mortgaged his kingdom and his immortal soul, with no way of making his payments. The pope, Alexander IV, was making ominous, albeit probably not entirely sincere, noises about executing the sentences of interdict and excommunication. And in 1258 Henry's barons, summoned to a parliament in Westminster in the hope that they might miraculously help pay for the Sicilian project, arrived in a radical, reforming mood.

If any scene summed up Henry's state of mind in the fortieth year of his reign, it was that which in 1256 he had had painted in the wardrobe at Westminster, a very personal room in which the king's head was washed and in which he spent some of his most private hours. It was a scene in which a king was rescued by a pack of dogs from a plot made against him by his own men. As a child Henry had seen his father's realm invaded. He had seen as a boy king in 1216–1217 his own barons turn against his family and beg a French prince to be their king. Now, four decades later, with the English barons once again mutinous, it was clear that those terrible memories were coming back to haunt him. Henry had finally proved himself his father's son.

The Provisions of Oxford

It was early in the morning on April 30, 1258, when a large body of nobles, knights, and their followers approached the king's hall at the palace of Westminster, armor clattering and swords clanking against their sides. At the head were four men: the queen's uncle Peter of Savoy; Richard de Clare earl of Gloucester; Roger Bigod earl of Norfolk; and Simon de Montfort earl of Leicester, who was fast becoming Henry's bête noire.

The men would have been up since dawn, nervous with anticipation for the confrontation that lay ahead. As they approached the door to Henry's magnificent hall, they would have known that their message would be profoundly unwelcome. They were ostensibly there to give the king a reply to his recent request for aid with the Sicilian crisis. But really they came determined to detach him from the pernicious Lusignans and to address a political crisis that could no longer be ignored. They were bonded together in a pact of mutual alliance to "help each other . . . against all people, doing right and taking nothing that we cannot take without doing wrong, saving faith to our lord the king of England and to the Crown."

England had sunk into a miserable condition. Respiratory disease swept through the country in the summer of 1257, before torrential rain killed the autumn crops and a hard winter prevented the cultivation of land for the spring. Disease and pestilence galloped through the country, and thousands starved in the villages. "Dead bodies were found everywhere, swollen and livid, lying by fives and sixes in pigsties or on dunghills or in the muddy streets," wrote Matthew Paris.

When the earls and their followers had been summoned to parliament three weeks earlier, rebellion was ripping through Wales led by the formidable prince of Gwynedd, Llywelyn ap Gruffudd; the papal envoy Arlot continued to bluster about excommunication and interdict if the Sicilian debt was not settled; and the Lusignans had broken free of any pretense of control. At the start of April men loyal to Bishop Aymer of Winchester had killed a follower of the influential noble John FitzGeoffrey, and Henry had refused to punish the perpetrators. As parliament convened in Westminster to answer yet another request for royal finance, it was generally agreed that the king was powerless to discipline the criminal faction that dominated his court.

What occurred on April 30 was recorded in the annals of Tewkesbury Abbey, a continuous chronicle charting the history of the monastic institution and the country at large, whose author probably heard it from an eyewitness. "As the third hour [midmorning] approached, noble and vigorous men, earls, barons, and knights went to the court at Westminster," wrote the annalist. "They placed their swords before the entrance to the king's hall, and appearing before the king, saluted him as their lord king in devoted manner with fitting honor." These were no rebels. They presented themselves to Henry as friends of the English Crown and all that it ought to stand for. But Henry could not see past their armor. The swords might be resting by the door, but it was hardly an encouraging sight when a group of powerful nobles approached the throne dressed for warfare.

"What is this, my lords?" he asked. "Am I, wretched fellow, your humble captive?"

"No," replied the earl of Norfolk. "But let the wretched Poitevins [i.e., the Lusignans] and all aliens flee from your face and ours as from the face of a lion, and there will be 'glory to God in the heavens and in your land peace to men of goodwill.'"

Henry may have been shocked, but he could not have been entirely surprised. Hostility toward the Lusignans was nearly universal, and it is likely that the men who stormed into his presence had the covert backing of the queen. Hugh Bigod said he spoke for all the magnates in England when he said the king ought to swear to obey their counsels; both Henry and Lord Edward ought to swear on the Gospels that they would be bound by the consideration of a panel of twenty-four barons, half elected by the king, and half by the magnates; Henry should promise not to attempt to impose any taxes; and he should hand over the royal seal—the ultimate tool of government—to a responsible person whose identity would be decided by the twenty-four. The twenty-four would then elect a continual council of fifteen to guide the king's hand on matters of day-to-day government, while a parliament would meet three times a year and appoint royal ministers.

These were extraordinary demands, but on that April morning there seemed to be no way around them. The collective political will of the barons was impossible to resist. That same day Henry and his son Edward swore on the Gospels to do as Bigod asked. After a decade of mounting catastrophe, kingship was to be performed by committee, its essential functions placed in the hands of the barons.

And yet, as the experience at Runnymede of the barons' forefathers had shown, the king might consent to new restrictions on paper, but these were often difficult to enforce in practice. Henry, like John before him, wriggled after the fact, attempting to exploit his right to appoint half the committee of twenty-four by packing it with Lusignans. Yet his efforts foundered: he could not find even a dozen men of sufficient status and rank who still supported his kingship. Eight weeks later, at Oxford, another parliament was convened. The town bristled with the vicious weaponry of knights loyal to either side, all there supposedly en route to a campaign in Wales, but actually there in case full-blown civil war should erupt. At Oxford Henry's resistance collapsed. He was presented head-on with a litany of his misdeeds and was accused of failing to observe the Magna Carta. "When parliament opened, the proposal and unalterable intention of the magnates was adopted, most firmly demanding that the king should faithfully keep and observe the charter of the liberties in England," recorded Matthew Paris. "They moreover demanded that a justiciar should be appointed to dispense justice to those suffering injury, with equal impartiality toward rich and poor. They also asked for other things touching the kingdom for the common good, the peace and the honor of the king and kingdom alike."

Henry and Edward swore another oath to abide by the barons' reforms, but the Lusignans adamantly rejected all calls for them to give up lands and castles awarded to them by the king. They were told in no uncertain terms what to expect if they continued to resist. According to Matthew Paris, "the earl of Leicester [Simon de Montfort], addressing himself to William de Valence, who was blustering more than the others, replied, 'Know for certain and make no mistake about it, you will either give up the castles which you hold of the king, or you will lose your head.'" Horrified, the Lusignans fled Oxford to the safety of Aymer's diocese of Winchester. They were formally expelled from the country later in the year, but in the meantime parliament broke up, in the words of the same chronicler, "uncertainly and inconclusively."

The barons' proposals at Oxford had been drawn up in close consultation with knights drawn from across the shires of England, and a wideranging program of reform was issued. It sought not only to regulate central government but to address the serious issues of corruption at the county level. The measures were known as the Provisions of Oxford and were almost as wide-ranging as the far more famous charter sealed at Runnymede. The provisions allowed for four knights in each county to investigate abuses by royal officials and established a panel of twenty-four to oversee government of the realm. Hugh Bigod was appointed justiciar by the magnates, and all the major royal officers—from the treasurer and chancellor to the sheriffs, bailiffs, escheators, and castellans who exercised royal power in the shires—were to be appointed by parliament.

On October 18, 1258, proclamations were sent in the king's name to the people of England and the king's subjects in Ireland, telling them of the new order that had been established and their duty to obey it. The knights who had assembled at Oxford never made it to Wales, as the war there was abandoned. That this was a national program of reform was emphasized by the fact that the proclamations were written in French, Latin, and English, declaring: "Know ye all well that we will and grant that that which all our councillors, or the greater part of them, that were chosen by us and by the community of our kingdom, have done and shall do for the glory of God and in loyalty to us, for the benefit of the country in the judgment of the aforesaid councillors, be firm and lasting in all things always without end. If any man or men oppose we will and command that all our loyal subjects hold them deadly foes." A further proclamation, confirming the procedure by which the four knights of each shire appointed under the Provisions of Oxford should go about the business of investigating corruption by royal officials, followed two days later.

Both these proclamations were in Henry's name, but the reality was that government had been removed from his hands. His barons, backed by the knights who had forced their own interests into the provisions, were now firmly in charge. Henry's friends were expelled from the country, and for the next three years, government proceeded by the rule of the magnate council, with baronial envoys taking over the negotiations for peace in Wales and France and attempting to persuade the pope to forget the whole sorry Sicilian business. Simon de Montfort came to the fore as an abrasive voice in the center of politics—not quite a regent but the dominant voice in the new regime.

Henry, as he tended to do in moments of crisis, disappeared into religious devotion. After Oxford he toured his favorite shrines at St. Albans, Bury St. Edmunds, and Waltham Abbey, mourning his beloved three-year-old daughter, Katherine, who, having been born severely disabled, had died the previous year. In the king's absence, baronial reform continued apace. The Provisions of Westminster, issued in October 1259, laid down a far-reaching program of reform in law and government and set the schedule for an eyre to systematically investigate abuses by royal officials. By the end of 1259 Henry had been reduced to a dithering irrelevance.

On December 4, 1259, a fifty-two-year-old Henry III knelt amid the gnarled trunks and wind-stripped branches of the apple trees in the orchard of Louis IX's luxurious Parisian palace. Before him stood the French king, seven years younger, the saintliest monarch in Europe. The two deeply devout men were about to transact one of the most sacred acts of kingship. It had taken Henry a long time to reach Paris, and it might have taken him longer yet as he had tried to stop at every church on the road to Paris in order to hear the Mass. Even Louis had tired of the English king's compulsive behavior and had expedited his approach by having as many of the churches shut as possible.

Seldom jovial, Henry III was now very solemn indeed. His council of barons had made a peace with France despite the obstructions of Simon de Montfort, who held a personal stake in continued hostilities, and Lord Edward, who at twenty years old opposed any diminution of the Crown's authority. The peace came with one mighty and onerous term: Henry was compelled to pay liege homage to Louis, renouncing once and for all his claims to empire and acknowledging that he held his remaining lands as a peer of France, rather than as a king in his own right. English kings had paid forms of homage before, of course—Henry II had done so in the first stages of his conquest in 1156 in order to secure Louis VII's support against his rebellious brother Geoffrey, and John had paid homage for Normandy before becoming king to strengthen his plot against Richard—but neither of those ceremonies had approached the one-sidedness of Henry III's submission.

As the ceremony progressed, the archbishop of Rouen read aloud the terms of the Treaty of Paris. His voice echoed around the orchard. Henry renounced all that remained of his claims to rule the lands that had been held by Henry II and Richard I: Normandy, Maine, Anjou, and Poitou. In the south he was to be confirmed only in his right to Gascony and his wife's interests farther inland, areas including the Saintonge and Agenais, to the north and east of Bordeaux. In a hollow show of gratitude for his reduced status, Henry promised to pay Louis fifteen thousand marks and to supply the French king with funds to support five hundred crusading knights for two years. Thus was the king of England accepted into the roll of the French aristocracy: no longer a prince below God but a duke below his lord, the French king.

The party that gathered to witness this ceremony stood just a few hundred yards away from some of the holiest relics in the West: Ste.-Chapelle held both the Crown of Thorns and a fragment of the True Cross. But even the holiness and magnificence of the surroundings could not obscure the fact, as he knelt before the French king, that Henry was finally bringing to a close a great chapter of English kingship.

Henry went to his grave believing himself to be a Norman and an Angevin. But the world could no longer pretend that English kings were connected in any meaningful sense to the cities of Le Mans and Angers, Rouen, or Tours. Even the remaining slivers of the duchy of Aquitaine, fiercely and proudly independent of France, were acknowledged to be a fiefdom. Henry's barons had seen to that. Geographically, politically, and feudally, in an orchard a few hundred yards from the True Cross, the Plantagenet empire was finally pronounced dead.

The trend across Europe over the course of the thirteenth century was of consolidation. Louis IX completed the work begun by his grandfather Philip II, extending French sovereignty from Flanders to Toulouse. The fluid condition that had existed in the twelfth century now creaked into shape. The Sicily debacle illustrated that the age of Plantagenet dominion, when kingship and kinship stretched from Scotland to Outremer, was no longer affordable, either financially or politically. England's horizons had narrowed.

The Treaty of Paris was in some senses a result of the fundamental shift in the nature of royal rule that had evolved during the first forty-three years of Henry's reign. Frequent reissues of the Magna Carta and the Charter of the Forest, granted in return for funds to fight overseas, reset the boundaries and rules of kingship, forming the basis for a new compact between Crown and political community over how the country should be ruled. It was a process propelled by Henry III's doomed and fanciful ambitions to reclaim his Continental territories, which set him continuously at odds with his barons, codified in their ultimate act of legal rebellion, the Provisions of Oxford. What had once been a firmly hierarchical structure of monarchy and nobility became more of a partnership, in which kingship was knitted into the fabric of English governance, universal but beneath an increasingly abstract law, susceptible to correction by the political community if it strayed.

Henry was described in many ways by his near contemporaries. He was flattered by Pope Alexander IV in 1258 as *Rex Christianissimus* (a most Christian king). But it was Dante's description that stuck: *vir simplex* (a simple man). He projected himself with all pomp and magnificence as a glorious king, but in fact he was weak, a man with an eye for art but no feel for politics, who was never able to operate successfully in rapidly changing times. His penchant for schemes beyond his talent for execution led him into dire financial and political trouble. Although surrounded by talented individuals, he was susceptible to taking the wrong advice from the wrong people at the wrong time. His lack of good sense and judgment meant that he was never able properly to extricate himself from the messes he landed himself in. And when crisis came, the *Rex Christianissimus* would generally disappear to tour his favorite shrines. Born without a father, abandoned by his mother, never able to grow up watching another king rule, all his life dominated by others, Henry was from the start a poor candidate for the Crown, an office that required supreme self-belief as well as self-discipline.

Oddly, when the occasion called for it, Henry could play the public part of high priest immaculately and with apparent enjoyment. He understood the way kingship should look, even if he was at a loss to know how it should work. The gold coins produced in one of his great years of crisis summed it up. Wildly inappropriate as currency, they glittered with the image of Henry as Edward the Confessor, the embodiment of England's ancient monarchy and a national saint in the making. They also attempted to rank English kingship alongside the majesty of the imperial Crown, which traded in gold augustales. Henry thought big, and he created a cult of royalty manifested in stained glass and wall friezes and the stunningly redeveloped palace and abbey at Westminster and countless royal houses, including the palace at Clarendon near Salisbury. Henry was an incredibly powerful propagandist for his dynasty. That was his most valuable legacy.

Yet after 1259 in many ways he was irrelevant. He was old and broken, humiliated and overmatched by circumstance. As de Montfort and the barons attempted to rule in the king's name, the locus of royal power shifted gradually but inevitably from Henry to his twenty-year-old son, the aggressive, soldierly Lord Edward. Edward would not be king for more than a decade, but he was most decidedly the future of the Plantagenet family, if indeed that illustrious family was to have a future at all.

The Battle of Lewes

Shortly after dawn on May 14, 1264, a small army stood in quiet array high on the downs outside the town of Lewes, in Sussex. Their numbers were slight, but they were zealous. They had crept through thick woodland in the dead of night to claim their ground. Now they were prepared for that most unusual of medieval military engagements: a pitched battle.

The army comprised just a few hundred cavalry, accompanied by several times that number of foot soldiers and servants. As the morning sun climbed through the sky, they looked down upon the enemy. It was far greater in number. Before them, along a front that stretched the better part of a mile between Lewes Priory and the castle nearby, was a royal army packed with more than one thousand armed knights, equipped as if for a Welsh invasion, attended by thousands of infantry and led by royal princes in foul and bloody mood, hell-bent on vengeance against rebels who had defied royal rule for too long. They had derided offers to negotiate: the rebels could have peace, they had said, if they presented themselves with nooses around their necks, ready for hanging.

The small rebel army was led by the fifty-six-year-old Simon de Montfort, who, lame with a broken leg, had been wheeled to the battlefield on a cart. Six years on from the Provisions of Oxford de Montfort remained an implacable enemy of the king. In 1262 Henry had obtained a papal bull freeing him from the obligations of the provisions, and de Montfort had briefly left the realm, only to return in 1263, raising rebellion at the head of a baronial coalition, convinced that war was now the only way to force Henry III to govern according to the vision laid out at Oxford. Since then he had stoked the fires of antiroyal sentiment wherever he could. Now he surrounded himself with young aristocrats in awe of his military reputation and his willingness to take on a king whom hostile writers characterized as depraved, debauched, and ruinous to the kingdom. The war had begun well, and the rebels had succeeded in capturing much of southern England, but in January the tide had turned toward the royalists. Henry and Edward had summoned a powerful army in Oxford and deployed it against de Montfort's rebel forces in a series of sieges. By Easter royalist forces had squeezed the rebels out of everywhere but London. Now de Montfort was preparing for a final showdown at Lewes.

It was a desperate move. No pitched battle had been fought in England for nearly fifty years. In comparison with the staple tactical set pieces of siege and plunder, battles were wasteful, uncertain, and chaotic. So strenuously did medieval commanders avoid them that few, if any, of the knights on either side had ever fought in one. But with two armies facing each other on the edge of the downs, it was clear that a moment of reckoning had been reached. De Montfort's men, with white crosses pinned to their clothing, were zealous. The mood in the royal camp was vigorous and uncompromising, a reflection in part of the spirit of its leader, Edward.

In the six years since rebellion against his father had broken out, Lord Edward, who was just under a month short of his twenty-fifth birthday, had seen more than his share of violence and difficulty. He had watched his father writhe against de Montfort's attempts to shackle and reform the Crown and had seen him suffer the disintegration of his royal prerogative as the opposition barons, aiming to control the royal household and persecute members of the royal family whose influence they judged pernicious, forced legislation upon him.

Edward had frequently changed his position with regard to reform. In 1258 he had sided with his Lusignan relatives. The following year he had allied with the reform party. Between 1260 and 1263 he had flipped his allegiance another three times. But by 1264 Edward was a die-hard loyalist.

Edward's view of his enemies was broadly captured by the writer of the "Song of Lewes," who noted that under de Montfort's influence "the degenerate race of the English, which used to serve, inverting the natural order of things, ruled over the king and his children." A letter sent in Edward's name to de Montfort's army on the day before the battle accused the earl of being a "perfidious traitor, the falsehood of yourself," and promised the rebels that "from this time forward we will, with all our mind and our strength, wheresoever we shall have the means of doing so, do our utmost to inflict injury upon your persons and your possessions." Surrounded by the warlike marcher lords—hard-bitten barons from the Welsh borders—whom he had befriended during his youth, Edward took command of the division on the right flank of the army, which stood before Lewes Castle, where he had been lodging. His uncle Richard earl of Cornwall, who had returned to England following a collapse in his position as king of the Germans, was at the head of the central division; Edward's father, the king, commanded the left flank, before the priory.

Facing Edward's division stood a rebel band of Londoners. These were not fighting men. To Edward, they were an unforgivable rabble who had gravely insulted his mother, the queen, by pelting her with rubbish from the streets of the city the previous year. When battle began, with an almighty roar, Edward's cavalry charged the Londoners.

Edward led his charge with the aggression that characterized a seasoned horseman with a love of the melee. He had spent several years abroad during his youth competing in the fashionable tournaments held by the European aristocracy. Now the melee was real. Such was the strength of his attack that his men easily scattered the opposing division's cavalry, driving them back across the valley to the banks of the river Ouse. They caused havoc among the rebel lines and proceeded to chase the routed Londoners for several miles across the Sussex countryside, killing and maiming all they could reach. By the time Edward's men regrouped and returned to the battlefield it was past midday. Judging by their own success, they expected to see the rest of the rebels slaughtered or imprisoned. Instead they gazed upon a scene of utter devastation for the royal cause.

By leaving the lines to chase the rebels' left flank, Edward had tipped the scales of battle against the royal army. Henry's central division had been driven back by the charges of the rebels behind the walls of the priory. Richard earl of Cornwall had pushed the division on the royalist left hard against the enemy, but on reaching high ground, he had found himself surrounded and had been forced to take cover from his enemies in a windmill. Edward returned to the battlefield to hear raucous rebel songs and taunts being hurled toward his uncle in this makeshift castle and to learn that his father was also surrounded and effectively defeated.

The king's forces had suffered a humiliating defeat. The only pragmatic solution was a negotiated surrender; indeed de Montfort threatened to behead the captured aristocrats, including Richard earl of Cornwall, if such an agreement was not forthcoming. This was a token both of his seriousness and of the frightening degree to which English politics had disintegrated: no aristocrat had been executed in England since William I had beheaded Earl Waltheof in the eleventh century. In return for allowing Henry to remain free and titular king (a necessity for both sides, in order to prevent a degeneration into total anarchy), de Montfort demanded that

Edward and his cousin Henry of Almain, eldest son of Richard earl of Cornwall, be handed over as prisoners.

The peace that was hammered out on the day of the battle was known as the Mise of Lewes. The political terms reinstated, in modified form, the Provisions of Oxford and called for many of Edward's marcher lord allies to appear before parliament for judgment. Several political questions were deferred to French arbitration, and Edward and Henry of Almain went to prison. Henry remained king but was no longer free to pick the staff of his own household. He was now, more than at any time in his reign, a puppet king. The power behind the throne lay not with a broad baronial coalition but squarely in the hands of Simon de Montfort.

From Imprisonment to Evesham

The year 1264 was the lowest point thus far for the Plantagenet dynasty. After the battle of Lewes, the king was taken to London at liberty but disempowered. Queen Eleanor was exiled, plotting unsuccessfully in France to raise an invasion force to retake the kingdom. Lord Edward, Henry of Almain, and Richard earl of Cornwall were imprisoned under close guard at de Montfort's pleasure—first at Dover Castle and subsequently in Wallingford. England remained unsettled, violent, and poorly ruled. Civil war continued to flare in the aftermath of Lewes, and the chronicles of the time teem with stories of burning countryside, castles besieged, and coasts guarded for fear of foreigners arriving to plunder the fractured land.

De Montfort did not—nor could he have been expected to—find the form of quasi kingship thrust upon him a straightforward affair. He was a private lord attempting to take control of a public office. Although he controlled the king and the great seal, his mandate to govern came from the fact that he had defeated his own lord in battle. He was by his very nature a divisive figure. Edward had forged close personal bonds with the marcher lords—men like Sir Roger Mortimer of Wigmore, Roger Clifford, and Roger Leybourne—and all were set implacably against de Montfort's rule. Their numbers soon began to swell as the angry young nobles who had fought with the earl at Lewes slowly began to drift away. In the aftermath of victory they found that de Montfort's administration solved nothing. Government was just as partisan as, if not more so than, it had been when Henry was in league with the Lusignans. Whether in the name of imposing security or in the interest of aggrandizing his family, de Montfort divided the spoils of victory unfairly, awarding to himself and his two elder sons, Henry and Simon the Younger, lands, territories, and castles taken from the royal party.

Most aggrieved by this was Gilbert de Clare, the twenty-year-old earl of Gloucester. Clare had been deprived of his inheritance during the king's resurgence in 1262, which had driven him into rebellion with de Montfort. He had fought with tremendous distinction on the rebel side at Lewes and was rewarded with a role in government that befitted the massive landed power that the Gloucester estates gave him throughout England. But he soon developed deep reservations about de Montfort's autocratic rule. He disapproved of his use of foreign knights, and he had particular reservations about keeping Edward in prison. De Montfort attempted to allay these concerns by releasing Edward from physical captivity in March 1265, but he did so with prohibitively onerous conditions: Edward was deprived of most of his royal lands, which were grabbed by the de Montforts, and furthermore, although he was no longer to be locked in a castle cell, he remained sentenced to perpetual escort by de Montfort's son Henry. By the beginning of 1265 Gloucester and many others like him had begun to fear that the de Montforts had designs on far more than reform of the realm: they were thought now to be aiming at the Crown itself.

In February 1265 Gloucester left de Montfort's court and traveled west to his Welsh estates, claiming that they were being ravaged by Llywelyn ap Gruffudd. He refused to attend a tournament in April, and by the end of May it was clear that he had abandoned de Montfort's cause entirely and had begun plotting with the loyal marcher lords to free Edward and advance the royalist cause.

On May 28 Edward, who had been permitted visitors under the more relaxed conditions of his supervision order, went riding in Hereford, at the heart of marcher country. He was accompanied as usual by his minder cum jailer, Henry de Montfort, but the group of knightly friends that joined him also included Gloucester's younger brother Thomas de Clare. Edward left for the expedition in a buoyant mood, as if all the problems that beset him lay lightly on his shoulders. As the young men rode, they began to play a game: each was allowed to try out every horse, to determine which of the animals was the fastest.

As amusing a game as this was, it had a more practical purpose: it allowed Edward to find the mount best suited to a dash for freedom. When he found it, he lost no time. Digging his heels into its side, he shouted to his captors: "Lordings I bid you good day! Greet my father well, and tell him I hope to see him soon and release him from custody!" And with that, he galloped expertly into the distance, accompanied by a handful of friends who were in on the plan. They picked up Sir Roger Mortimer, who was hiding in the woods nearby. Together they rode to Mortimer's castle at Wigmore, then on to Ludlow, where Edward met Gloucester and swore to him that if they could rid the realm of de Montfort, he would restore good old laws, abolish evil customs, expel aliens from the realm, and entrust government to native Englishmen. This promise was almost exactly what the barons who had stormed into his father's presence at Westminster in 1258 had demanded. Finally, Edward had found his middle ground.

The accord between Edward and Gloucester formed the basis of a new royal coalition, composed of returned royalist exiles under William de Valence and the marcher lords who had never seen de Montfort's rule as much more than another version of Hubert de Burgh's and Peter des Roches's grasping administrations. They would fight on their own territory, the marches. As de Montfort scrambled for an army to resist the resurgent royalists, Edward's men set up their defenses. They destroyed every crossing to the Severn, limiting the field of battle by cutting off most of England and trapping de Montfort on the western—Welsh—bank.

Throughout the summer a showdown loomed. De Montfort, who still held the king, was chased around Wales by Edward's army; he played for time, requesting foot soldiers from Llywelyn ap Gruffudd, while his son Simon raised a reinforcing cavalry from the east. But the de Montforts were on the defensive, pursued by a coalition renewed in its vigor by the presence of the bellicose prince.

On August 1 the royalists attacked young Simon at Kenilworth. The army was billeted in the great Midlands fortress, while Simon himself lodged in the nearby priory. Believing that Edward's men were at a safe distance in Worcester, Simon's men were unprepared for attack. They did not realize that Edward and Gloucester had spies among them, including a female transvestite called Margoth. At dawn, while Simon and his men were sleeping—or in Simon's case, awake but not yet dressed—hooves sounded outside the priory. The young man saved his skin by rowing naked from the scene of the assault and taking refuge in the castle, but many of his knights showed no such improvisational common sense. They, along with their banners, were captured by the royalists.

When the elder de Montfort heard that his son's reinforcements had been attacked, he was shaken. A crisis was now imminent. There was a scramble to unite the two branches of the army and to escape the territory in which they were penned. De Montfort finally found a place to ford the Severn and pushed east toward Worcester. Edward's army was no more than a few miles away. On the night of August 3 de Montfort moved once more, this time south to Evesham.

The next day de Montfort's men paused for breakfast at Evesham Abbey, positioned in a loop of the river Avon. Above them, the skies were dark and pregnant with rain. A thunderstorm was brewing. A lookout was stationed on the tower, watching through the gloom for the approach either of Edward or of the younger Simon's army. Three hours after dawn the cry went up from the ground. Simon the Younger's banners had been spotted in the distance. The day was saved.

Or was it? From high in the tower, the lookout shouted fatal news: this was not Simon approaching, but Edward's army, marching under the banners stolen at Kenilworth.

De Montfort raced to the lookout tower to watch Edward's men approach, red crosses pinned to their armor in imitation of the white crosses worn by the rebel army at Lewes. Impressed by their discipline and the well-drilled advance, the earl declared in typically grand style: "By the arm of St. James, they are advancing well. They have not learned that from themselves, but were taught it by me." This was not simply the arrogance of a commander; de Montfort knew that he was outmaneuvered.

Escape was impossible. On the south bank of the Avon, Mortimer led a detachment that blocked escape via the bridge. Trapped in the river's loop, de Montfort's men watched as Edward's army moved into their positions, commanding the high ground of Green Hill, to the north of the abbey. De Montfort's men faced the royalists defiantly. They were outnumbered by three to one. Their only chance was to rely on the fact that they had the captive King Henry at the center of their forces and hope that this inspired some caution among Edward's men. Everything now came down to this. De Montfort and his men awaited the onslaught.

They did not have to wait long. As the thunderclouds broke above them and a violent storm drenched the battlefield, Edward's men attacked.

Both sides fought conspicuously bravely in cold, soaking conditions. De Montfort threw himself into the fight with as much aggression as he had shown at any time during his long career, but the numbers, combined with the superior generalship of Edward and Gloucester, overwhelmed him. He watched as his young knights were dragged from their horses and stabbed to death. His son Henry was slaughtered, and his son Guy captured. The king, whose armor identified him as a Montfortian, was wounded in the fighting. He escaped death only by bellowing his name to the knight who would have killed him.

There would be no reprieve for de Montfort himself. A twelve-man hit squad independent of Edward's main army stalked the battlefield, their sole aim to find the earl and cut him down. In the end it was Roger Mortimer who found him and thrust his lance deep into the earl's neck, killing him where he stood. The body was then mutilated in sickening fashion. News reached the mayor and sheriffs of London that "the head of the earl of Leicester . . . was severed from his body, and his testicles cut off and hung on either side of his nose; and in such guise the head was sent [as a trophy] to the wife of Sir Roger Mortimer at Wigmore Castle. His hands and feet were also cut off and sent to divers places to enemies of his, as a great mark of dishonour to the deceased; the trunk of his body, and that only, was given for burial in the church of Evesham [Abbey]." Within weeks a rather improbable cult of sainthood had grown up around de Montfort's grave, and miracles stemming from both the earl's burial site and the battleground where he was slain were reported.

At the end of the day the battlefield lay strewn with highborn cadavers, proud men lying dead in the summer rain. De Montfort, his son Henry, and key rebel allies such as Henry Despenser, Ralph Basset, and Peter de Montfort were all killed. Many more were captured and wounded. The king had been returned, joyfully, to his son Edward, and he was sent to recuperate in Gloucester and Marlborough castles, where he busied himself in typical fashion, restoring altar plates.

Power in England shifted toward yet another quasi king. This time, however, it was a prince of the blood royal. Lord Edward, who had for so long swung between the competing factions in England's mid-century crisis, now moved closer than ever before to the political center. He was not king yet, nor was he even the dominant voice in English government. But the heir to the throne had proved himself, during the fourteen months that divided Lewes and Evesham, to be a pragmatic politician and a fierce soldier.

The Leopard

The young prince who moved into the spotlight in the 1260s was considered an enigma by many of his contemporaries. He had grown up in England and had been intimately involved in the political turmoil of his father's reign. While some men thought he had performed with valor, others considered him an odious, treacherous turncoat. Matthew Paris wrote that "Edward was a man of lofty stature, of great courage and daring, and strong beyond measure," but there were also notorious stories of a foolish youth whose supporters invaded priories at Wallingford and Southwark without permission, mutilated strangers they passed by the road, and stole food from the ordinary people of England, a prince who was glamorous and fond of the tournament but by instincts frivolous and cruel.

Edward was physically very striking. Although he had been a sickly child, as an adult he stood a head above his fellow men at six feet two inches; it is clear why he was later nicknamed Longshanks by the Scots. He was broad chested and powerful, his physique a testament to many long hours spent on the tournament field, where he had competed since he was seventeen. Edward had been married at fifteen to Eleanor of Castile, two years his junior, and proved to be both a virile father and a doting husband. In temperament he was a ferocious soldier, rather like his famous great-uncle Richard the Lionheart, whose image was painted all over the palaces and hunting lodges of his childhood. He had blond hair, a droopy eyelid inherited from his father, and the Plantagenet temper in perhaps its most potent form. It was said that in a fit of rage he once actually frightened a man to death. He had shown during his escape from the de Montforts and on the path to Evesham that he was an inspiring leader of men as well as a skillful and vengeful conqueror, who would not hesitate to impose brutal violence on the vanquished.

His reputation, then, was mighty but not wholly enviable. Edward's slippery course through the political crises preceding the Barons' War had earned him a reputation as a shifty politician. Yet the fact that he had flipped his allegiance numerous times in the struggles between his father's party and the reformers was less a reflection of duplicity than a statement of the profound confusion he had felt as a result of his closeness to both his mother's Savoyard relations and his father's Lusignan favorites. Nevertheless, it would not be easily forgotten. During the course of the war Edward had frequently broken his word in order to wrest political or military advantage. At the siege of Gloucester in 1264, a landmark engagement on the way to Evesham, he had relied on the chivalry of a surrounding rebel army to escape imprisonment, then promptly broken a sworn truce to hold the town's citizens to ransom.

The young Edward was therefore known to both his supporters and his detractors not as a lionheart but as a leopard, fierce but changeable. A song written in praise of him around the time of his coronation described him as "warlike as a pard, sweet as a spikenard." And the author of the pro–de Montfort "Song of Lewes" elaborated on the theme: "He is a lion by his pride and ferocity; by his inconstancy and changeableness he is a pard, not holding steadily his word or promise, and excusing himself with fair words."

The first demand placed on Edward following the victory at Evesham was to aid in the process of healing his father's divided realm. Evesham might have killed and scattered the de Montforts, but the realm was still in a state of civil war, and the role of men like Edward, his brother Edmund, and loyalists such as their cousin Henry of Almain, who had been sent abroad by his baronial jailers and therefore missed the battle of Evesham, would be vital in reestablishing royal governance. Their task was not easy. Pockets of rebellion remained all over the country. In September 1265 Henry III made a highly divisive statement at a Winchester parliament, declaring that all Montfortian rebels were to be permanently disinherited and their land distributed to men who had proved their loyalty to the Crown.

A student of his own family's history would have pointed Henry III toward his grandfather Henry II's contrasting efforts to cauterize the wounds of a divided kingdom in the 1150s or the efforts at reconciliation after the Great Revolt of 1173–1174. Then the king had settled his troubled realms by offering justice, peace, and reconciliation to the barons who had defied him. Henry III now did the opposite: he refused to accommodate those who had rebelled. This ruined nearly three hundred families in a stroke. Rather than settle the realm, it merely encouraged disaffection among the losers and revenge among the royalists, which in turn prolonged the war against Henry's rule.

Edward's part in the aftermath of Evesham was characteristically ambiguous. He had wept after the battle at the loss of so many lives, and in the days that followed he acted with clemency when leading Montfortians approached him begging not to be disinherited for their part in the rebellion. Yet despite his better instincts, when Henry III announced the terms of revenge, Edward and his supporters opened their arms for reward, and the prince was by his father's side for much of the questionable retribution that took place during the autumn of 1265. In London he accepted a share of the spoils when Henry ruthlessly dispossessed disloyal citizens; a number of Edward's supporters received rebels' confiscated houses, and Edward took custody of a valuable prisoner in the shape of the mayor.

As land and property changed hands across England, many of the dispossessed rebels found themselves in the woods, living outdoors in guerrilla bands that would have resembled those from the popular ballads of Robin Hood. The main center of Montfortian resistance was at Kenilworth Castle, but by Christmas 1265 pockets of revolt were breaking out all over England; Edward was kept on the move helping snuff out the flames of resistance. The distressed rebels had come to be known as the Disinherited, and as Edward took charge of numerous operations against them, he came to realize that conciliation was a more powerful tool than sheer bloody-minded aggression. In December he found one group of rebels camped out in the marshlands of Axholme, in Lincolnshire, and convinced them to surrender without bloodshed. Afterward he joined Roger Leybourne in subduing the Cinque Ports (the collective name for five towns on England's southeastern coastline: Hastings, Sandwich, New Romney, Hythe, and Dover). Edward tempered his ally's capable but violent siegecraft with promises of pardons and liberty in exchange for submission.

Unfortunately, Edward was swimming against a powerful tide, dragged by Henry III's misguided desire for revenge. By Easter 1266 there were rebellions across a central belt of England, from East Anglia to the Midlands, and military action once again became the only feasible solution. Toward the end of May, at Alton Wood, in Hampshire, Edward crowned a victory over a rebel band by fighting their leader Adam Gurdon, an experienced knight, in single hand-to-hand combat. Although the political significance of this duel was limited, it became one of the more memorable events of the civil war. The two men did battle in a forest clearing, watched by Edward's supporters, who were cut off from him behind a ditch. The tale of this glamorous fight was embellished during later years, and it was said that Edward had been so impressed with Gurdon's martial skill that he had given him favor and fortune once the fight was over. The truth is that Edward beat Gurdon into submission, hanged his rebellious friends, then gave the defeated knight to his mother, the queen, from whom Gurdon had to buy back his freedom and possessions at an onerous price.

Slowly, though, the royalists grew more secure, and by the middle of the summer they could make their advance on the great castle at Kenilworth, a vast fortress that had been fortified by King John and subsequently by Simon de Montfort with the intention of making it impervious to siegecraft. It was defended by huge walls and fortifications and a massive man-made lake and garrisoned by more than one thousand men. Cracking the defenses was likely to take months of dirty, technical engineering work. Trebuchets and huge wooden siege towers with gantries from which archers could fire were brought in, and the site, overseen by Edward's younger brother Edmund, teemed with miners and engineers. Special barges from Chester were used to try to storm the castle across its water defenses, and the food supplies of counties across the Midlands were severely drained as the besiegers maintained a full feudal muster outside the fortress walls. Yet it was an effort in which Edward the soldier had little part to play. He remained on duty stamping out isolated rebellions in East Anglia and enjoying the summer with his wife, who gave birth to their first boy on July 14. The couple rather provocatively named the child John.

After months of expensive, draining effort, it became clear that Kenilworth could only be starved into submission, a painful process that could take more than a year. With the Disinherited still causing problems all over England, conciliatory tactics were once more foisted upon the royalists. The wisest political head among them was that of the papal legate Ottobuono, who alongside Henry of Almain led a committee to produce a peace that would bring the rebels out from the stinking fortress and reconcile them with the royalists who had been awarded their lands and possessions. Together they produced the Dictum of Kenilworth. Set out in forty-one clauses, the dictum was formally addressed from England's leading loyalist bishops and barons to the king, the realm, and the Holy Church. It defended the king's right to "freely exercise his lordship, authority, and royal power without impediment or contradiction" but asked him to "appoint such men to do justice and give judgment as do not seek things for themselves but things which are of God and justice." After the obligatory request that the king obey the Magna Carta and the Charter of the Forest, the dictum went on to set out the means by which rebels who had followed de Montfort could be rehabilitated and restored to their lands—"that the course to be followed is not disinheritance, but redemption." It allowed the Disinherited to buy back their confiscated lands or what portions of them they could afford, albeit at the severe rate of between five and seven times the land's value, payable to the royalists who had been granted the lands since confiscation. These were hardly generous terms, but they at least provided a mechanism for restoring peace. The dictum was given and made public in front of the castle walls on October 31, 1266. The garrison in the castle, dirty, freezing, and starving, surrendered in the middle of December.

It was an important step toward peace, which had been achieved by consensus and negotiation rather than the bloody grind of military force. There was a brief moment of crisis in the spring, when the earl of Gloucester invaded London to protest the fact that the Disinherited were being forced to pay their entire fines before they were allowed to enter into their confiscated properties. But danger was averted thanks to the interventions of Ottobuono, who persuaded England's better-off barons to pay into a distress fund to assist the Disinherited, and of Richard earl of Cornwall, who negotiated an amendment to the Dictum of Kenilworth allowing rebels to return to their lands at once rather than at the end of their terms of repayment. As Gloucester was persuaded to withdraw from the capital and Henry made his way in, it was clear that the process of bringing peace to the kingdom had truly begun.

With Henry and Edward now in a firmly conciliatory mood, the Dictum of Kenilworth was followed in September 1267 by the Treaty of Montgomery, which brought peace with Wales by conceding vast feudal power to Llywelyn ap Gruffudd. The Welsh prince had been allied with de Montfort and had made great headway in establishing his power over Gwynedd during the turbulent years of the Barons' Wars. Rather than being forced into a humiliating peace, Llywelyn was now granted extensive control and territory in northwestern Wales, in return for a tribute of twenty-five thousand marks. The price to Edward of this was immense, for it effectively gutted his personal power beyond the marches. This was a situation that he would take much trouble to reverse later in his reign, but for the sake of peace in 1267 he gritted his teeth and consented.

Two months later the final plank of rehabilitation and reform was put in place when the Statute of Marlborough was issued, again with Edward's approval, if not his detailed involvement. The statute was a vast and influential set of legal provisions touching on areas of government that had been under discussion since 1258. Marlborough recognized in its preamble that "the realm of England, oppressed of late by many tribulations and unprofitable dissensions, needs amendment of its laws and legal rules so that the peace and tranquillity of its people may be preserved." The statute that followed touched in its twenty-nine detailed chapters on a wide range of legal matters, from the jurisdiction of courts and the supremacy of royal justice in matters of land disputes to wardships, charter repeal, and communal fines. The language was highly technical, concerning procedure, precedent, and jurisdiction. It was not a statute of fundamental principle like the Magna Carta, but it began a long process of statutory reform that would carry on until the end of the century.

For Edward, twenty-eight years old and approaching the prime of life, the world was still a place for making war rather than law. Paradoxically, now that the realm was beginning a long process of healing, it had less to offer him. Peace had been made both with the rebel barons and with the Welsh, and Henry III had settled back into making expensive plans for a new tomb for Edward the Confessor at Westminster Abbey, to which the saint's body would be transferred on October 13, 1269. This left few opportunities for the prince and his friends to further their military reputations. Edward, his brother Edmund, and his cousin Henry of Almain jointly sponsored an edict allowing tournaments to be held in England, but this was still not quite enough to sate their appetites for military adventure. If Edward wished to continue his soldierly career, he would have to look farther afield, to the Holy Land.

Ever since 1267 King Louis IX had been planning a new crusade, due to leave Europe in 1270 with the aim of beating back the advances of the Mamluk sultan Baybars, who had pushed deep into what remained of the Christian states in Outremer. This, for Edward, was a field of war in which he could gild his reputation. Deeply intoxicated by the promise of glory in the East, he scraped together cash from whatever sources he could in an effort to fit out a crusader army. This included taking a seventeen-thousand-pound loan from Louis IX himself, repayable from the revenues of Bordeaux. After Easter in 1270 Edward and his fellow would-be crusaders succeeded, with the utmost effort, in convincing the knights of the shire gathered in a highly skeptical parliament to grant them a crusader tax. The price was a renewal of the Magna Carta and a limitation on Jewish moneylending, which gave the shire landowners enough respite from debt to be able to afford their contributions to Edward's adventure. From the end of May, England sprang into action, and Edward prepared to depart. He submitted to arbitration to settle a long-running and bitter dispute that had blown up between himself and Gilbert earl of Gloucester. He put his lands into trust under a committee headed by his uncle Richard earl of Cornwall, and since his wife, Eleanor of Castile, was determined to come on crusade with him, he also named Richard guardian of his three young children—John, aged four, Henry, aged two, and the baby called Eleanor. Finally, on August 20, 1270, the royal crusading party set sail from Dover, leaving the cares of England far behind them, and headed toward the dusty lands of the East.

PART IV

Age of Arthur
(1263–1307)

Now are the islanders all joined together,
And Albany reunited to the royalties
Of which king Edward is proclaimed lord.
Cornwall and Wales are in his power,
And Ireland the great at his will ...
Arthur had never the fiefs so fully.

—*The Chronicle of Peter Langtoft
of Bridlington*

King at Last

Edward's crusade started under a cloud. He traveled to the Holy Land via a familiar path: through the south of France to Sicily, graveyard of his father's ambition, with the intention of moving on to Outremer via Cyprus. Before he had even reached Sicily, however, he discovered that the crusade as a pan-European venture had begun to unravel. Louis IX's army was traveling several weeks ahead of Edward's, and when Louis passed through Sicily, he met up with his younger brother, Charles of Anjou, who had succeeded where Henry III had failed and claimed the Sicilian throne. While Edward was still marching through France, Charles managed to convince his brother Louis to divert his mission from Outremer to Tunis, where various enemies of Sicily were hiding from justice.

The French set sail assuming an easy victory, but just days after landing on the North African coast, Louis IX died of a plague that swept through the French army. In shock, Charles led the crusade back to Sicily, only for the majority of the French fleet to be smashed by a storm while in harbor at Trapani. Edward, Henry of Almain, and the rest of the English arrived in Sicily in November 1270 to find the French in utter disarray. They wintered on the island, hoping that the spring might bring better fortune, but they were helpless when, in January 1271, Louis's timid twenty-five-year-old son, now King Philip III, decided that Providence was against the French and, leading his men overland through Italy back to Paris, turned for home.

Edward, however, was determined. When spring arrived, he sent Henry of Almain back to ensure that the new French king did not attempt to threaten his lands in Gascony, then set out with his remaining men for Outremer. They arrived in mid-May.

Just more than a year later Edward found himself in the heart of the labyrinthine politics of the Middle East. Christian Outremer had dwindled almost into oblivion. Frankish rule was in a parlous way. Despite Richard earl of Cornwall's efforts to reinstate control over Jerusalem during the 1240s, and Louis IX's massive expenditure fortifying the city of Caesarea at the same time, most of the great cities of Christian Palestine had since fallen to Mamluk invaders. Caesarea and Jerusalem were in infidel hands.

So too were Antioch and the supposedly impregnable crusader fortress the Crac des Chevaliers, whose soaring walls had resisted the hammering of trebuchets but which had fallen to trickery. What remained of the kingdom was ruled from Acre, a demoralized city surrounded by hostile country and dreading any day the arrival of a Mamluk army thousands strong beneath its walls.

It was clear from the outset that Edward's crusade was never destined to be much more than a sortie into a hopeless battlefield. The Christians were done for, and the days of great triumphs before the walls of the most spectacular cities of the Middle East were over. The main enemy to the Muslim forces of Palestine was now no longer the Frankish knights of the West but the terrifying Mongol horsemen who attacked them from the north and east. Edward and his companions found not a vast war to be joined but a diplomatic jigsaw to be puzzled over.

Yet Edward stayed for more than a year, organizing sorties into Muslim territory, exchanging letters with the Mongol leader, Abagha Khan, in Marageh, a city some seven hundred miles from Acre, and welcoming the occasional arrival of fresh troops from the West, including a party led by his brother Edmund. He was determined to make the best of his crusade.

On the evening of June 17, 1272, his thirty-third birthday, Edward lay in bed with his wife in his private chambers in Acre. As he drifted into sleep, he had much to contemplate. His small band of men had suffered horribly from heat and dysentery. The Mamluk leader Baybars had vastly superior forces and supplies. Hugh III, the titular king of Jerusalem, was more inclined to peace than war and the previous month had signed a ten-year peace with Baybars, which restricted Edward's hopes of glory still further. Edward had been furious when the treaty was agreed to. He had refused to become a party to it; quite likely he was still brooding over this as he fell asleep.

What happened to Edward that evening soon became the stuff of legend. As he slept, a messenger arrived claiming to be a renegade diplomat, a turncoat from Baybars bearing lavish gifts and ready to give up his own side's secrets. Whatever message he gave Edward's servants and guards must have sounded both urgent and convincing, for they woke the sleeping prince and asked him to meet his visitor. Edward staggered out of his sleeping chamber and met the man while still wearing his nightclothes.

As it transpired, the messenger wished to give Edward a very special birthday gift: a deathblow. Edward's position as the only nonsignatory to the peace deal had made him a dangerous presence, whom Baybars wished to be rid of. The messenger rushed at Edward with a dagger, attempting to stab him in the hip. But Edward, no mean fighter, was up to the task. "The Saracen met him and stabbed him on the hip with a dagger, making a deep, dangerous wound," wrote the chronicler known as the Templar of Tyre. "The Lord Edward felt himself struck, and he struck the Saracen a blow with his fist, on the temple, which knocked him senseless to the ground for a moment. Then the Lord Edward caught up a dagger from the table which was in the chamber, and stabbed the Saracen in the head and killed him." In hand-to-hand combat, there were few who could match the long-limbed Englishman.

Nevertheless, when he rose from his opponent's dying body, Edward realized that the blow he had received was a serious one. As attendants rushed to the scene, it was feared that the weapon might be poisoned. Legend has it that Eleanor of Castile tried to suck the venom from her husband's wound, though as it turned out, the dagger was almost certainly poison free.

There was still a real risk of infection, though, which could lead to the same sort of agonizing gangrenous death that Richard I had suffered at Châlus-Chabrol. Edward was saved from a similar fate by a more skillful surgeon, who cut away the rotting flesh that festered around his wound. He took his time to recuperate before he and Eleanor of Castile, together with their young daughter, Joan, who had been born in Acre, departed Outremer for Europe in late September. They stopped in Sicily on their way home, before traveling to the Italian mainland for Christmas. It was there that they were met by English messengers bearing sad news. Henry III had died in November, aged sixty-five, following a short illness. After a magnificent funeral, he had been buried in the tomb vacated by Edward the Confessor's recent translation. After one of the most remarkable apprenticeships in his family's eventful history, Edward I was now king.

He took his time returning to England. Trusting the government of his kingdom to ministers such as Robert Burnell, Edward stayed abroad to enjoy the fruits of his glamorous crusader reputation. He joined in French tournaments, paid homage to Philip III for his French lands, and settled the rumblings of rebellion in Gascony. Then, during the dog days of summer, he sailed for England, his coronation day set for Sunday, August 19, 1274.

Edward alighted at Dover on August 4, setting foot on home soil for the first time in nearly four years. He returned to a country that had waited patiently for him and that now acclaimed him in style. There had been plenty of time to prepare for his arrival. Edward was the first king to be crowned in more than half a century. There was a whole new royal family to welcome. At the coronation Queen Eleanor was in the early stages of her tenth pregnancy with a daughter, Margaret, who would be born in 1275. After the long and troubled reign of Henry III, here was a brand-new generation of royal power and people to welcome.

The citizens of London, despite or perhaps because of their acrimonious history with Edward, used the occasion to produce a festival of show and wealth. "When Edward thrives, behold!" wrote one enthusiastic Londoner. "He shines like a new Richard!" Unfortunately, no detailed accounts of the ceremony survive, but it is known that the city was draped in gold cloth and that there was pageantry and mass celebration in the streets as the king and his entourage rode into the city. Edward most likely processed from the Tower of London to the palace of Westminster on the day before his coronation, before staying overnight in the Painted Chamber, richly decorated with biblical images and scenes from his family's history.

The abbey would have been packed with magnates from England and its neighbors as Edward processed toward a giant wooden stage at the crossing of the church. They would have watched him make an offering at the altar of two gold figurines, one of St. Edward the Confessor and another of St. John the Evangelist. Then he made the same coronation oath that his ancestors had sworn. In what was now time-honored fashion, Edward promised to protect the Church, to do justice to all men, to abolish evil customs, and to protect the rights of the Crown. Unlike many of his predecessors, as Edward swore these things to a packed abbey, he meant every word.

Edward's first priority was the oath he swore to protect the rights of the Crown. Almost as soon as celebrations were complete, royal servants began a survey of royal rights in England that was conducted on a gigantic scale—comparable only to the Domesday Book of William I's reign. It was known as the Hundred Rolls inquiries because it concentrated on the hundreds, the smaller subdivisions of the English shires, which were used for administrative and judicial purposes at a local level. Between November 1274 and March 1275 every hundred in England received a visit from royal commissioners, who put detailed questions before local juries "about the lord king's rights and liberties which have been taken away and the excessive demands of the sheriffs, coroners, escheators and other of the lord king's bailiffs and of any other bailiffs whosoever appertaining/belonging to the lord king in any way, in the third year of King Edward's reign 1274–1275." This, at least, was the purpose laid out in the text of the enrolled returns that collated the information that the commissioners gathered.

The Hundred Rolls inquiries were massively wide-ranging and extremely detailed. They were the first great project undertaken by Edward's new chancellor, Robert Burnell, now the bishop of Bath and Wells and a trusted, highly capable diplomat. Burnell had governed England during Edward's absence on crusade, and he was to oversee much of the governance and administrative reform of England until his death in 1292. The commissioners he appointed collected vast amounts of material, ranging from examples of appalling abuses of power (beatings, torture, and illegal imprisonment by royal officials cropped up in some places) to comical, harebrained schemes (the sheriff of Essex was accused of having plotted to release flying cockerels carrying incendiary bombs over London during the troubles in 1267). They produced far more information about wrongdoing and royal rights than could manageably be dealt with, and even when a general eyre was sent out to punish the crimes uncovered, it was clear that the king could not successfully prosecute every deviant royal official in the land. Still, the keen investigations into wrongdoings conveyed the message to everyone in England that the new king was deeply committed to shaking out the corruption among royal officials that had blighted Henry III's reign and that had so animated the knightly class in particular.

The point of the Hundred Rolls inquiries was more their symbolic value than their practical use. They showed that Edward had learned lessons from the baronial reform programs of the 1250s and had taken to heart the spirit of the Provisions of Oxford. By adopting and expanding the program under the royal banner, Edward made an immediate statement about his reign: he would be the king who remedied ills of his own accord.

Although he did not share his father's instinctive dislike of political reform, Edward shared with him an extraordinary capacity for spending money. He had returned from the Holy Land with debts amounting to more than one hundred thousand pounds, much of which was owed to

Italian bankers. Simply to manage a debt of this magnitude would require political consensus and financial innovation. And given the ambitious plans that Edward would shortly unveil for an even more expensive and ambitious foreign policy than his father's, he would need the community of the realm behind him. Legally, financially, and politically, England and Britain were to be transformed. The first area of transformation would be Wales.

A New Arthur

One of the greatest popular crazes in thirteenth-century Europe was for the legends of King Arthur. Reflected in the art, literature, and tourist industry of the day, Arthurian lore had the power to excite, inspire, and entertain men and women everywhere from Sicily to Scotland. Few men were more excited by the stories and supposed relics of Arthur than the new king, Edward I.

The legend of Arthur—for we now know that Arthur belongs chiefly to the realm of imagination and not to history—had been a part of European literary tradition since the early ninth century, when stories were exchanged of a native Briton who rose to become king and fought against both Roman and Anglo-Saxon invaders. Down the centuries his legend had been re-molded and translated to suit the cultures that took an interest in it until, in the 1130s, the author Geoffrey of Monmouth inserted a vivid and dramatic account of Arthur's life and reign into his wildly successful book *The History of the Kings of Britain*. Geoffrey's Arthur was a pious Christian king who fought valiantly against pagans, Saxons, and Romans alike, driving invaders out of native British lands, uniting the British kingdom, conquering Ireland, Iceland, parts of Germany, and Orkney, and subduing Norway, Aquitaine, Gaul, and the Balkan kingdom of Dacia. He was the heroic, munificent king of a British kingdom that was the envy of the world. Geoffrey related that in Arthur's time "Britain had arrived at such a pitch of grandeur, that in abundance of riches, luxury of ornaments, and politeness of inhabitants, it far surpassed all other kingdoms. The knights in it that were famous for feats of chivalry, wore their clothes and arms all of the same color and fashion: and the women also no less celebrated for their wit, wore all the same kind of apparel; and esteemed none worthy of their love, but such as had given a proof of their valour in several battles. Thus was the valour of the men an encouragement for the women's chastity, and the love of the women a spur to the soldier's bravery." Romance, chivalry, and beauty abounded in this knightly paradise, and it was not hard to see why the stories appealed to the late-medieval barons, knights, and ladies who heard them.

As they were distributed, retold, and embellished by other writers, Geoffrey of Monmouth's stories, dressed up as a genuine history of the British Isles, began to be thought of as actually true. By the time Edward was born, there was a booming trade in Arthuriana, and a healthy industry had grown up around King Arthur's imagined memory. When Glastonbury Abbey burned down in 1184, Henry II had encouraged the monks to broadcast the fact that they had "discovered" the tomb of Arthur and his queen, Guinevere, buried beneath the ruins. Arthur had originally been a Welshman, and it was a matter of faith among the Welsh that he would return to liberate them from the English; now he was conveniently revealed to be English and dead, and the brothers at Glastonbury Abbey encouraged paying tourists to come inspect the skeletons that they had supposedly found. During the course of the twelfth century the legend became a potent part of English aristocratic culture, and tournaments known as Round Tables were held to award prizes for gallantry and good jousting. It was no surprise, therefore, that Edward, a young man with conventional noble tastes, was since his youth as enthralled by Arthur as his peers, or indeed that when he married Eleanor of Castile, he had whisked her off on their honeymoon to see the tomb at Glastonbury.

For Edward, however, the myth of an Anglicized Arthur was more than just a matter for entertainment and courtly discussion. It was a mental template for his whole approach to kingship. Just as Henry III had fixated upon Edward the Confessor as his guide, inspiration, and savior, so Edward I was to see the world through the prism of his own particular version of Arthurianism. It was as convenient a myth for him to cleave to as the Confessor had been to his father, for his problems were Arthur's in mirror image. Arthur, to put it crudely, had been a Welsh king whose mission was to crush the English. Edward, in 1277, faced the opposite task.

In the summer of 1277 Edward assembled his first great army. More than fifteen thousand men, equipped with horses, supplies, and vicious weaponry, advanced along the coast road from Chester into North Wales. Above them fluttered a multiplicity of banners and flags marking out the various components of the feudal host. They rumbled toward Gwynedd to root out and crush the "rebel and disturber of the peace," Llywelyn the Last prince of Wales.

This was a national army, agreed upon by Edward, his magnates, and an assembly of the knights of the shire at one of the twice-yearly parliaments he held almost every Easter and Michaelmas from the start of his reign until its end. On or around November 12, 1276, the English had declared war upon Llywelyn, determined to stamp on this troublesome prince in the name of security and stability for the kingdom. Edward had been unable to raise more than a handful of his household knights when he had made the journey to Outremer, but he found that with the support of his barons and knights in parliament behind him, he could take the whole might of England to war against the Welsh.

Wales had been a constant problem for the Plantagenets. As every English king since the Norman invasion had found, to control or even to pacify Wales was a task that required immense resources, time, and will. Ever since King John's advances against the Welsh during the brief period of his British mastery, English power beyond the marches had been slipping away. Llywelyn the Great was effectively sole ruler of Wales from his power base in the northwestern province of Gwynedd until he died in 1240. Subsequently, during the Barons' Wars, his grandson Llywelyn ap Gruffudd, later known as Llywelyn the Last, had allied with de Montfort to take further advantage of the English Crown's weakened position. The Treaty of Montgomery, sealed as Henry's realm was being pacified in 1267, had cemented Welsh gains. In fact the Treaty of Montgomery was, from Llywelyn's point of view, one of the great treaties in Welsh history: Llywelyn was acknowledged as prince of Wales in his own right, with direct control over Gwynedd and feudal lordship over almost every other lord in Wales. The Treaty of Montgomery was irksome to Edward for many reasons. Personally it had compelled him to give up land of his own in Wales. And viewed in the context of kingship, it represented a damaging loss of the Crown's rights.

This alone might have justified a war of reconquest, but throughout the early 1270s Llywelyn piled on further provocations. He invaded English baronies in Shropshire and the marches, antagonizing important marcher lords, including Roger Mortimer and Humphrey de Bohun earl of Hereford. In 1270 Llywelyn invaded Glamorgan, causing a rift with his erstwhile ally, Gilbert earl of Gloucester. At home Llywelyn quarreled with his brothers, imprisoning one, Owain, and forcing the other, Dafydd, into exile at the English court. But Llywelyn himself refused to go anywhere near Edward's presence, despite repeated requests that he do so. Neither would he pay the English Crown the fifteen thousand marks due to it under the terms of the Treaty of Montgomery.

In a final, fatal act of overreach, in 1275 Llywelyn gave Edward an indisputable casus belli. Having reached his fifties without producing an heir, he began negotiations to bring Eleanor de Montfort to Wales. The daughter of the late Simon de Montfort, Eleanor was a potent symbol of the damage the Welsh had done to the royal family by their alliances during the Barons' Wars. She had been betrothed to Llywelyn in 1267 but was living in exile in France. In 1275 she was married to the Welshman by proxy, and at the end of the year she set out from the Continent to meet her husband. It was an impressive litany of provocation, and Edward felt compelled to respond. He headed off Eleanor by having her ship captured in the Bristol Channel and imprisoning the good lady at Windsor. But preventing a marriage between the Welsh prince and Simon de Montfort's daughter was not enough. Edward needed to put Llywelyn firmly back in his place.

Edward invaded Wales in 1277 and marched his army through the summer down the coast road from Chester. Shadowing the knights, soldiers, and supply wagons on their march along the coast was a fleet of ships that served both to blockade the Welsh from escape or reprovision via Ireland and to keep the enormous English army well supplied on its march west.

The whole campaign was supremely well organized. Edward's military companions managed the logistics. Crusading men such as Roger Clifford, Otto de Grandison, and John de Vescy combined with civil war veterans like William de Beauchamp, the earl of Warwick. They based themselves at Worcester and began to gather a terrifying arsenal with which to batter Llywelyn into submission. Confident that his long-standing allies were up to the job, Edward showed that he had something of his father in him. He allowed them to organize the war muster while he toured the shrines of East Anglia, praying before Henry's favorite relics and giving a passable impression of a man of peace.

But peace was not what was planned at Worcester. Hundreds of thousands of crossbow bolts were ordered from Gloucestershire. Warhorses were bought in the specialist markets in France; wheat and oats, ordered from the justiciar of Ireland. Vehicles were requisitioned from private owners all over England. The royal mints produced silver pennies to pay the many thousands of soldiers drafted to fight for England's security and the Plantagenet family's honor. It was a mark of Llywelyn's fractured authority that Edward's royal infantry included Welsh mercenaries.

More important even than the infantry, however, were the large teams of engineers engaged with the purpose of cutting a path through North Wales along which Edward's huge advance might be made. Guarded by crossbowmen and knights, bands of men from the English interior constructed a huge road along which the invading army could roll. They felled the thick, silent woodlands that overhung the regular routes to the mountainous heart of Gwynedd known as Snowdonia, clearing a way that was in places hundreds of feet wide, now rendered impervious to Welsh guerrilla tactics, which relied upon swooping out of the trees to slash and hack at an unguarded enemy before disappearing. At Flint, where Henry II had almost been killed by just such tactics, a great timber fortress was begun as a forward base of operations.

The whole effort was a magnificent achievement of military requisitioning, planning, and engineering. In pure numerical terms Edward's army was not as strong as the armies that had marched on Toulouse for Henry II or mustered for the Third Crusade under Richard I. But the campaign was conducted with deadly logistical intent to neuter Llywelyn's only fighting option. The Welsh prince could not hope to harry an army on the move by use of guerrilla tactics, for Edward's engineers had blown his cover.

The army marched deep into Llywelyn's territory. Throughout August they cut a path from Flint to Rhuddlan and then on to Conwy. As they ground their way into Gwynedd, they gradually cut off supplies and the movement of men, surrounding the Welsh and starving them into submission. At every main outpost they stopped and engineers began digging to create sites on which permanent castles could later be constructed.

Llywelyn fell back into the mountains. Edward pushed forward to the river Conwy and camped at Deganwy. This was deep into enemy territory, where Welsh regard for Plantagenet rule was starkly demonstrated by the silhouette of a ruined castle Henry III had once built on the spot.

Soon the lesser Welsh princes started fleeing Llywelyn's cause. The decisive blow was struck in early September, when English marines disembarked on Anglesey, occupied the island, and harvested the grain crop there, thus capturing the richest farmland in Wales and simultaneously emptying the granary of Gwynedd. It was enough to persuade Llywelyn that the English king was an opponent to be taken seriously. He surrendered within days and on November 9 agreed to a truce at Rhuddlan. He was allowed to keep Gwynedd, but virtually everything else was taken from him. Llywelyn submitted to a fine of fifty thousand pounds and abandoned his claims to the Four Cantrefs—the four small counties that bordered Gwynedd—and everything that Edward had seized on his march west. The disputes with his brothers Owain and Dafydd were to be settled, and in recognition of the supremacy of the English king over the Welsh prince, Llywelyn agreed to pay homage to Edward not only on his borders at Rhuddlan but back at Westminster, at the seat of English governance and power.

Llywelyn had been sorely beaten, and the treaty was, from Edward's point of view, a satisfactory way to end the expedition. To solidify the English position, castles were planned in Aberystwyth and Builth, Flint, and Rhuddlan. The English now had military outposts bristling on the outskirts of Welsh territory. The invasion had been an impressive success. Little did Llywelyn know that this was only the beginning.

The Final Stand

Edward celebrated Easter in 1278 with an eerie twilight ceremony at Glastonbury Abbey during which the supposed tomb of Arthur and Guinevere was opened. According to the local chronicler Adam of Domerham, the skeletons were found side by side, each in a casket with images and arms painted on the sides. The following day the piles of bones were moved to a grand new resting place in the abbey. This tomb was later destroyed in the dissolution of the monasteries, but the sixteenth-century antiquary John Leland described it as made from black marble with two lions at each end and an effigy of Arthur at the top. The ceremony fairly pulsed with messages about the new regime: on the one hand, the King Arthur whom the Welsh so venerated was dead, but he was to live on in Edward. As the king and queen venerated the bones in Glastonbury Abbey, they sought to stitch the myth of Arthur into the fabric of Plantagenet family lore. It was a well-contrived end to a brutally effective campaign.

In the aftermath of Edward's first victory over Llywelyn, he turned his attention to domestic affairs. His chancellor, Robert Burnell, was pressing ahead with the first stages of a sweeping program of legal reform, and three extremely wide-ranging statutes were passed in 1275, 1278, and 1279 (known respectively as the first Statute of Westminster, the Statute of Gloucester, and the Statute of Mortmain). They dealt with matters as diverse as rules on land tenure, ensuring free elections to parliament, and the right of all free men, rich or poor, to justice (Westminster); establishing a new system of eyres to travel the country investigating abuses of royal rights (Gloucester); and preventing land from being granted to the Church in order to avoid feudal dues and taxes (Mortmain). They marked the start of a legal revolution by statute, which continued for more than a decade.

The matter of the Church also began to vex the king. He was prevented from promoting Burnell to archbishop of Canterbury by Pope Nicholas III and had to accept the difficult and extremely pious Franciscan friar John Pecham as archbishop instead. Pecham was a highly principled ecclesiastical politician and a strict observer of the Franciscan rule. He refused all personal property (meaning that he had no income and was thus constantly in crippling debt to Italian bankers), insisted on extremely strict discipline from the English clergy, and believed that he had a divine mission to root out corruption and abuse in the Church, most notably among clergy who grew rich from pluralism, the practice of holding multiple benefices. His view on relations between Church and Crown was pithily alluded to in his official seal, which had an image of the martyrdom of Thomas Becket on the reverse.

Unsurprisingly, Pecham clashed numerous times with Edward from the very beginning of his tenure as archbishop. His stance on pluralism irritated the king, who gained a good deal of advantage from being able to give his clerks multiple lucrative posts in the Church as reward for their work. A long-running battle also flared up over the conflicting jurisdictions of royal and Church courts, a subject that had animated Becket against Henry II, and Pecham frequently expressed to the king his frustration at royal ministers' reluctance to help enforce sanctions against the (numerous) people whom he had excommunicated from the Church. In autumn 1279 a furious argument blew up over Pecham's demand that a copy of the Magna Carta should be hung in all of England's cathedrals and collegiate churches. He was eventually forced to back down, but not before further souring his relationship with the king.

Despite their equally strong characters, Edward and Pecham were diplomatic enough to ensure that their relationship never spilled over into murderous hostility. Despite significant political differences, they were generally on good terms and on some matters agreed wholeheartedly. One such was the character of the Welsh, whom both king and archbishop considered unreconstructed savages. It was as well for his survival that Pecham took such a view, for in 1282 Edward's war with Wales exploded once again, this time in an even bloodier form.

On the night preceding Palm Sunday in 1282 Llywelyn's brother Dafydd, a former member of the English court, appeared unexpectedly at Hawarden Castle, the residence of Edward's ally Roger Clifford, with a great forty-foot stone keep on top of its rounded motte. The Welsh prince had been expected as an Easter guest, but he turned up early, in company, and armed. In the dead of night, Dafydd led a band of men in storming the castle, seizing Clifford from his bed, and filling the corridors of the stone fortress with the stifled screams of men whose throats were slit in the dark. This was no Easter visit. It was a declaration of war.

Over the course of the next few days royal officials were tricked, grabbed, and held as hostages; castles in English hands were attacked and taken in lightning raids by bands of armed Welsh rebels; and the peace imposed by Edward at Rhuddlan disintegrated almost overnight as Wales was plunged into violence. The instigator on this occasion was Dafydd, but his brother Llywelyn's hand lurked close behind. The villain of 1277 had been welcomed into Edward's circle, allowed to marry Eleanor de Montfort in a ceremony at which Edward himself had given away the bride, and gently coaxed into the ranks of the Edwardian aristocracy. But he had never forgotten his family's heritage. And although he professed ignorance of the rebellion until it fully erupted, he had spent his time since 1277 moving quietly to reestablish his prestige among the minor Welsh princes.

Despite Edward's shrewd attempts to rehabilitate both brothers, in the early 1280s Dafydd and Llywelyn still had personal grievances with Edward, whose origins lay in the redistribution of lands seized after the first war. As their attitudes toward the English king hardened in the years following Rhuddlan, they adeptly spun their complaints into a wider argument about Edward's apparent desire to override Welsh law and customs.

After his victory Edward had imposed English law, customs, and administrative efforts harder on the Welsh than any Plantagenet king before him. Llywelyn and Dafydd suggested to their compatriots that in so doing, the English king was deliberately attempting to crush the spirit of the Welsh people. This argument was crystallized in a complex legal dispute between Llywelyn and his compatriot Gruffudd ap Gwenwynwyn over the *cantref* of Arwystli, a county to the southeast of Gwynedd. Llywelyn wished it to be judged under Welsh law; Edward pushed for it to fall under English jurisdiction. A dispute over an obscure parcel of land was effectively parlayed into a test case for the very survival of Welsh law and customs. The result was to produce a quite different Welsh opposition from that which Edward had faced at the beginning of his reign. In those days he had taken it upon himself to discipline a wayward neighbor. Now he faced a war of national identity.

The invasion blueprint he followed was similar to that which had proved so effective in 1277. Once more troops and engineers worked in tandem, tearing through the Welsh countryside and establishing building sites where they went. Military assistance, which was formalized as a call to the feudal host in May, was requested from the English earls. To carry the cost of the building works, large loans were raised with Italian bankers. Once more forces were mustered at Worcester and marched via Chester to Rhuddlan. Once more the Cinque Ports provided shipping. Once more marcher lords were relied upon to carry out private engagements in the south. The main body of the Welsh army was encircled in Snowdonia, and Anglesey was linked to the mainland by a giant bridge formed of forty pontoon boats, built to order by huge teams of Chester carpenters. The remaining outposts of Plantagenet dominion overseas were called upon for their support, and aid was sent from Ireland, Gascony, and Queen Eleanor's county of Ponthieu.

Progress was not so swift as it had been five years previously. The Welsh were in no mood to submit to another round of Edward's punitive treaty making. The king, for his part, was determined not to give an inch. The best offer he was prepared to make to Llywelyn, which the latter rejected out of hand, was to exchange Snowdonia for a rich English earldom. Losing Snowdonia would mean giving up land so valuable that Gerald of Wales had written during the previous century that "if all the herds in Wales were driven together, Snowdonia could provide them with pasture." It could not be granted to the English without destroying the territorial integrity of Gwynedd, the center of Welsh resistance and national identity. This Edward well knew. Pecham tried to arbitrate, but it was clear from the outset that the two sides were set for a bitter fight.

The Welsh fought valiantly, as was their way. Llywelyn orchestrated the war from the north, while Dafydd roamed more freely across the principality. (Their brother, Owain, had retired to his estates and took no part in the rising.) They achieved a significant victory in November 1282, when forces led by Edward's Gascon supporter Luke de Tany were ambushed near the pontoon bridge with Anglesey, and large numbers of knights drowned beneath the weight of their armor in a cold sea. But these losses were not enough to deter the English king from his task.

The English fought into the winter, reinforced by hundreds of men drafted over from Gascony. They squeezed Snowdonia hard, and in December Llywelyn, fearing starvation, tried to make a desperate sortie from his hideaway. He was ambushed at Irfon Bridge, near Builth, in the central marches, and slaughtered in battle on December 11, 1282. The accounts of his death are hopelessly confused, but he was probably run through with a lance before his prone, bloodied body was decapitated and his head was sent to London.

Llywelyn's death was the final blow to Welsh independence, struck on a freezing hillside surrounded by bare trees shortly before Christmas. The Welsh fought on under Dafydd until spring; but in April 1283 the final Welsh stronghold, Castell y Bere, was captured after a short siege, and in June Dafydd was betrayed and captured by Edwardian Welshmen. He was taken to Rhuddlan and then to Shrewsbury for trial in front of a Michaelmas parliament.

Edward delivered the severest punishment on Dafydd, a man he believed had betrayed his hospitality and lordship and was the scion of a family of traitors. Dafydd was hauled roughly to the scaffold and hanged as a common killer, but the punishment did not end there. Before he was dead, his intestines were slashed clean from his body with a butcher's blade and burned in front of him. His body was hacked into quarters and sent to four English cities. His head was sent to London and set on a spike at the Tower of London. It was a traitor's death. In London Dafydd was reunited with his brother; the two Welsh princes stared lifeless over England's largest city. Meanwhile the country for which they had given their lives was smothered beneath an ambitious building project. Edward was determined that his victory should be complete. To ensure that Wales would not rise again, he put into action the greatest castle-building program that Britain had ever seen.

The King's Castles

A medieval building site was a raucous, dirty, smelly place, a cacophony of clatter. For seven months of every year—between April and November, when the hard earth softened and the weather allowed for unbroken outdoor work—the castle-building season entered full swing. Wherever a major fortress was erected, the landscape around it was sculpted and transformed. Woodland was felled and leveled, stone cut and dragged into place; furnaces roared. Endless streams of carts arrived bearing giant logs and pieces of timber hewn in faraway forests. New roads and routes were trodden by innumerable artisans and laborers, carpenters and masons. Great piles of earth, thrown up out of the deep ditches that were dug as protection around the working site, rose against the horizon. Workers' campsites hummed with the reek and warmth of human bodies, piled close together, creating mounds of rubbish and filth as they labored in the hot summer sun.

Master James of St. George was the greatest castle builder of his age. He had met Edward in Italy, during the king's meandering journey back from Outremer to claim his Crown, and the king had not forgotten him. James came from a building dynasty; he had learned the art of masonry from his father and spent his youth working on castles for the counts of Savoy. They had built towns and castles across the Alps, tailoring their magnificent projects to the tastes and security needs of the demanding and wealthy nobles of northern Italy. Master James was a military engineer, a specialist in organizing and managing building sites rather than an architect, but his ability to carry out ambitious projects to exacting standards made him an invaluable servant to the kings and princes who were his clients. He knew the best experts in Europe for specialist skills, such as canal digging, and he had long experience building castles in difficult and dangerous Alpine terrain.

In 1278 Edward hired Master James for one of the biggest commissions of the age, a massive ring of fortresses designed to brand Plantagenet power deep into the flesh of the principality of Wales, altering both the landscape and the political makeup of the nation. Every Plantagenet king with the exception of Richard I had come to Wales, and all had departed having barely left a footprint. Edward I ended that trend emphatically. His two invasions cost him immense amounts of cash and political capital, and right from the start it was clear that he meant to enforce a settlement that would prevent the Welsh from ever rising in rebellion as an independent nation again. He intended to build such an imposing ring of castles around the heart of Gwynedd that the Welsh could not physically remove the English and would be confronted every time they looked to the horizon by a reminder of their subject status.

Edward and his advisers had a very clear vision of what they wanted from the castles. They were to be placed on strategically important sites and built to incorporate features of the best fortresses of northwestern France and the southern marches, two regions that had seen some of the heaviest and most prolonged warfare of the last century and that had accordingly developed the best defenses. The king corresponded directly in person with Master James, instructing him on the positioning of towers and moats, the fine details of gateposts, the type and color of stone and timber to be used, and even where he wanted the latrines to be located.

Most of the castles whose building was managed by Master James still stand. Some were extensive reworkings of castles already built. Others were new commissions. The earliest begun were at Flint and Rhuddlan on the northern border with England, Aberystwyth on the west coast, and Builth in the southern marches. All these were begun in 1277 as part of the limited settlement program undertaken after Edward's first Welsh invasion. The first three were attacked during the rebellion that prompted Edward's second invasion, during which time the half-built structure at Aberystwyth was badly burned and had to be started again once the war was over. By the time Aberystwyth came to be reconstructed, however, the building program had been extended in scope and ambition. Alongside Rhuddlan, Flint, and Aberystwyth, further castles were commissioned at Denbigh, Harlech, Conwy, and Caernarfon. (A final castle, perhaps the most magnificent of all, was begun on Anglesey, at Beaumaris, in 1295.)

The terrifying magnificence of Edward's castles is hard to overstate. They were, like all castles, visible symbols of the wealth, military might, and artistic sophistication of a conquering dynasty. But they also had

Arthurian overtones. Edward was not simply constructing military out-posts; he was wrenching at the national imagination of the Welsh, co-opting their legends and knitting them together with the Plantagenet myth.

The castles took many years to build, and in some cases, as with Caer-narfon, they were never completely finished. Some were pragmatic reforti-fications of existing structures, and thus worked within blueprints already set. But for the great fortresses of the north—the finest were Conwy, Caer-narfon, Harlech, and Beaumaris—Master James worked to a template of a keep surrounded by concentric walls, studded with towers and twin-towered gatehouses, and defended with a devilish innovation, the arrow slit. It was nearly impossible for the enemy to aim an arrow into an arrow slit, but a crossbow bolt could be quite easily fired out.

The architectural and historical influences brought to bear upon the Welsh castles were many and varied. Nowhere captured Edward's imagina-tion more than the building at Caernarfon, which was the site of an ancient Roman fort, Segontium, said to have been built by the emperor Magnus Maximus, whom legend held to be the father of Constantine. Caernarfon was built with multicolored masonry and octagonal towers rather than the round towers seen elsewhere in Wales. It took its cue from the angular walls of Constantinople and was awarded even greater historical signifi-cance by the supposed discovery, during the construction, of Maximus's remains, which were exhumed and interred in the town church.

In many cases Edward's castles were accompanied by new fortified towns, planned settlements designed to deepen the grounding of the garri-son in the locality and provide an income to offset the dazzling cost of building the castle. In an age of rapidly rising population, as the thirteenth century was, there was no shortage of English settlers and workers ready to head west for a new life in Wales, even if they would have to contend with the hostility of the conquered locals.

In the spring of 1284, during the early stages of work on Caernarfon Castle, Queen Eleanor was brought to the town, where she went into labor for perhaps the sixteenth time of her life. The couple had six surviving chil-dren: five girls, named Eleanor, Joan, Margaret, Mary, and Elizabeth, and a boy named Alfonso after his maternal grandfather. (At least eight other children, including the king's first- and second-born sons, John and Henry, had died in infancy.) On April 25 the queen gave birth to another son, who was named Edward after his father. The birth missed St. George's feast day by a couple of days, but the symbolism was otherwise perfect. A prince who shared his father's Saxon-Plantagenet name was delivered to the world at a town rich in ancient British history. The little boy, named Edward of Caernarfon, was a flag of conquest and a tool of propaganda. He was Eleanor's fourth son, and his birth was part of a narrative that drew on Arthur, Maximus, and the Britons of time immemorial. It was perhaps destiny that this child should ascend to his father's throne. And so it would transpire when the ten-year-old Alfonso died at Windsor in August 1284. Suddenly the four-month-old Edward became heir to the newly reimagined kingdom of Britain. With Wales conquered, myths created, and a new heir born, Edward's kingly vision was taking shape. All he had to do now was to pay for it.

The Price of Conquest

Stamping the legacy of conquest upon the Welsh was a project that required huge investment. The first Welsh war, it has been estimated, cost a relatively modest £23,000, but the second ran up a heavy price tag of around £150,000. Much of this went toward the castles built to secure victory, each of them worth between £14,000 (the eventual cost of the never-finished castle at Beaumaris) and £20,000 (for building Anglesey).

The investment was not all made in stone and timber. Edward imposed on Wales a conqueror's peace as severe as the Norman settlement of England. In keeping with the legal revolution beginning in England under Robert Burnell's supervision, the Welsh settlement was grounded in statutory law. The Statute of Wales, passed in 1284, overrode much of the native Welsh legal and administrative systems. Flint, Anglesey, Merioneth, and Caernarfon all became English-style counties with the administrative machinery of sheriffs and courts that formed the central nervous system of local government. English criminal law took formal precedence over Welsh custom and legal procedure. Edward came down hard this time on the Welsh princes: family after family was destroyed, their lands taken and inheritances confiscated. Loyal Edwardians were then parachuted in to hasten the process of Anglicization.

But for all the changes the conquest imposed upon Wales, its effect in England was no less extraordinary. The vast price of conquest abroad—even if only beyond the marches—put Edward under serious pressure to make sure that a political consensus was maintained at home. As a child of the Second Barons' War he had seen his father fritter away money on foreign policy only to reap the rewards in the form of rebellion from the political community that had begrudgingly paid for military expeditions. It was an experience he was determined not to repeat.

Clustered, therefore, around the wars of Welsh conquest was a huge program of English legislative and financial reform. Almost every area of English administration, justice, and financial regulation was addressed as Edward's government strove both to purge the machine of royal government of rogue agents and to reach its hand deeper into the shires. The program was the first great sweep of legal state building that had taken place since Henry II's day. Some of this was badly needed after the drift of Henry III's reign, but the willingness of Edward's government to engage with reform was also critical to the king's success in raising the eye-popping levels of finance required to pursue his ambitious foreign policy in the British Isles.

The key measures were the statutes, overseen by Burnell, whose role in designing the architecture of the new English state was no less fundamental than Master James's imprint on the castle-building program. The three statutes made before the second Welsh invasion (Westminster, Gloucester, and Mortmain) had begun the process. After the invasions the flood of legislation continued. The statutes of Acton Burnell (1283) and Merchants (1285) dealt with matters of debt. Westminster II (1285) was, like Westminster I, a wide-ranging piece of legislation whose fifty dense and detailed clauses set out new processes, rules, and writs for everything from the inheritance and alienation of land and the passing of land from dead men to their widows to the troublesome issues of false accusations of homicide and jury dodging by rich men who bribed sheriffs to avoid doing their service.

These legal reforms were not simply aimed at making land disputes and trade agreements easier to resolve for the kingdom's barons. Rather, they penetrated to the very lowest levels of society. The Statute of Winchester of 1285 revolutionized criminal justice at the village level, where it was believed that criminals were avoiding justice because juries unwilling to indict and convict their own people were shielding them from the full weight of the law. "Whereas every day robbery, homicide, and arson are committed more frequently than used to be the case," it read, "and jurors . . . would see the felonies committed on strangers pass unpunished rather than accuse the offenders, many of whom are persons of the same country . . . our lord the king to reduce the power of felons establishes a penalty in such case, so that for fear of the penalty . . . they shall henceforth not spare anyone nor conceal any felony."

The Statute of Winchester demanded that local communities take responsibility for flushing out felons. If a crime was committed and no criminal was produced, then the whole hundred would be punished collectively. It turned the whole system of law and order into a system where every subject had a responsibility to help keep the peace. "People living in the district shall answer for robberies and felonies committed in the district," said the statute succinctly. "In great towns which are walled the gates shall be closed from sunset to sunrise.... [A]nybody harbouring or otherwise lodging persons suspected of being... violators of the peace" would be punished as an accomplice to the crime.

Most visibly, Winchester left a stamp on the English landscape. Just as Edward's workmen had cut a vast path through the woodlands of Wales to facilitate his conquest, so now every commercial road in England was to be cleared for safety: "It is commanded that highways from one trading town to another shall be enlarged wherever there are woods, hedges, or ditches; so that there shall be neither ditches, underbrush, nor bushes for two hundred feet on the one side and two hundred feet on the other, where men can hide near the road with evil intent," read the statute. The mercantile arteries of England were turned into treeless highways to allow the free movement of goods and money about the realm.

Alongside the system of statutory reform, Edward's government was characterized by a drive to streamline royal finances. A recoinage in 1279 sought to rectify the currency from Henry III's reign, which was, according to Matthew Paris, "so intolerably debased by money-clippers and forgers, that neither natives nor foreigners could look upon it with other than angry eyes and disturbed feelings." Edward also instituted reform to the systems of royal bookkeeping. The Statute of Rhuddlan in 1284 arranged for old debts to be written off the pipe rolls on which government business was recorded, the processes for chasing up debts and fines from the royal courts were sped up, and royal commissioners were subsequently sent around the country to investigate debts owed to the Crown.

But even with these measures there remained a gaping deficit in royal finance. By 1289 Edward was relying heavily on foreign bankers' loans and a combination of regular taxes upon the lay and clerical population to top up his income. It was a sign of the political credit he had earned by virtue of his reform program that he could raise taxes of fifteenths on lay and clerical goods early in his reign and could continue to raise income this way for years to come.

In law, as in war, Edward was determined that his government should pursue radical and permanent policies that would cement his legacy long after his death. Only by this sort of active government could he hope to bind together a nation that would support him in his expensive foreign policy. Yet if his reforms were much needed and vital for the financial and political security of the Crown, there was a darker side too. A terrible stain upon Edward's transformation of his kingdom spread from his treatment of England's Jews.

The Expulsion of the Jews

On Tuesday, October 10, 1290, a group of poor Jews from London boarded a boat to sail down the Thames. In their hands they carried royal warrants of safe passage. On their coats they wore the yellow, book-shaped badges that the law declared they must wear to distinguish themselves from Christians. In their packs they carried all their worldly possessions. They were headed for the coast, and after the coast for the Continent. They knew they would never return to England.

The boat passed out of London and through the countryside that surrounded the capital. They were leaving behind a city in which it had been increasingly difficult to live, in which ever more strict and onerous laws had been passed against their people, preventing them from trading or earning or even from engaging with their Christian neighbors, as their ancestors had done quite freely. Their synagogues had been burned, their friends beaten or hanged, and hotheaded preachers had called for their conversion to Christianity. London was a city that no longer welcomed or wanted them. They had no choice but to leave.

They floated downstream. After many miles the river widened, and the Kentish landscape to starboard fragmented into islands and sandbanks. The open sea lay ahead. The tide was going out. Their captain, a Christian, turned the boat south, toward the Isle of Sheppey. As the tide grew lower and lower, he cast the anchor overboard and allowed the vessel to come to a rest on the exposed sand of the Thames estuary's ebb tide. Calling to his Jewish passengers, he explained that they could go no farther until the waters began to rise. Feel free to leave the boat, he told them; stretch your legs on the sandbank.

All the passengers took his advice, stepping out of the vessel and walking on the wet sand. They did not notice the tide coming back in.

The captain of course did notice. He and his crew knew that after ebb tide the Thames rushes back over the sands it has vacated, carrying all before it. He rushed to the side of his boat and clambered aboard. He shouted down to his Jewish passengers, who had wandered on the sandbanks and were now cut off from safety, telling them to call upon Moses, who had parted the seas for them once before, to do so again. Then the boat sailed off, with its passengers' stolen baggage still aboard. The Jews were swept away as the tide rolled in around them. Every one of them was drowned.

For their efforts, the captain and crew of the boat were later imprisoned. Their crime was one of the most heinous acts that accompanied Edward's expulsion of England's small Jewish community in 1290. It was not typical of what was generally a rather peaceful exodus, but it was a painful illustration of the callous cruelty that was aimed toward Jews by Europe's Christian people and governments during the thirteenth century.

By the time of Edward's reign England's Jewish population numbered around two thousand people, organized into some fifteen mainly urban communities and still living, as they had been in John's day, under the terms spelled out by the apocryphal laws of Edward the Confessor: "the Jews themselves and all their chattels are the King's." Yet since John's reign conditions had grown less and less welcoming. In 1240 three Jews were executed in Norwich for the supposed crime of having circumcised a five-year-old child, whom it was said they planned to crucify at Easter, in a case that prompted attacks on Jews and their property. In 1255 a Jew called Jopin was accused of having murdered an eight- or nine-year-old Christian boy by torturing him to death with a number of accomplices in a ceremony associated with witchcraft. A legend held that the boy's body would not sink in a stream or be buried in the ground; when thrown in a well, it was said to have emitted a sweet smell and a bright light. When Henry III visited Lincoln, he had ordered Jopin's death and had had ninety-one Jews rounded up and sent to London, where all were condemned to death; eighteen were executed before Richard earl of Cornwall intervened to spare the rest. Similar cases were recorded in London and Northampton in the 1260s and 1270s.

In 1269 Henry III had restricted the terms under which the Jews could trade and made blasphemy by Jews a hanging offense. When Edward returned from his crusade, he passed the Statute of Jewry (1275), which outlawed most forms of usury (or moneylending); restricted Jews to living in certain cities; imposed the yellow badge of shame, described as "in the form of two tables [i.e., religious tablets] joined, of yellow felt, of the length of six inches and of the breadth of three inches"; and levied an annual tax of threepence on all Jews aged over twelve. The queen mother, Eleanor of Provence, expelled Jews from all her lands at around the same time as the Statute of the Jews was proclaimed in England.

When Edward instituted harsh laws against coin clipping (the process of shaving the edges of silver coins and thereby accumulating the precious metal) and his justices began prosecuting offenders in 1278–1279, the Jews were subjected to a judicial massacre; although almost equal numbers of Christians and Jews were found guilty of coin clipping, ten times as many Jews as Christians were executed for their crimes. The head of every Jewish household in England was at some point imprisoned in the late 1270s on suspicion of coin clipping, and in a climate of legal terror there were frequent cases of extortion against Jewish families, as their unscrupulous neighbors threatened to report them for coin offenses. Further mass arrests and forced tallages continued during the 1280s. In 1283 Jews were excluded from the protection afforded to ordinary merchants, and in 1284 Archbishop Pecham issued a decree ordering that all of London's synagogues should be destroyed except for one. Two years later Pope Honorius IV demanded that the archbishops of Canterbury and York stamp out intercourse between Christians and the "accursed and perfidious" Jews.

None of this was unique to England. The thirteenth century was perhaps the most violently anti-Semitic of the whole Middle Ages. Kings across Europe enacted similarly oppressive measures against their kingdoms' Jews. Frederick II demanded that Sicilian Jews wear a blue T-shaped badge and keep their beards long. French kings since Philip Augustus had ordered French Jews to wear a wheel-shaped badge. Pogroms, massacres, ghettoization, discriminatory laws, persecution, and abuse were on the rise against Jewish people wherever they lived. Edward, obedient to his time with his aggressive, muscular, intolerant Christianity, was following the trend of a bigoted age.

Despite the rising tide of abuse and the legal hobbling of their trade, the Jews still remained England's de facto financial sector. Usury continued illicitly, and Jews traded in bonds of debt, by which loans were sold to speculators who could hope to inherit the lands against which the loans were secured if the borrowers defaulted. For obvious reasons, Jews were not popular with the landowning classes that fell into the default trap. By Edward's reign there was severe religious and political pressure upon the king to cripple Jewish trade once and for all. It was a pressure to which the king, at once conventionally pious and happy to advance any position that would fill his barren coffers, would easily bend.

Edward had profited personally from the presence of Jews in England.

His father had taxed the Jews collectively six thousand marks for his crusading fund, and between 1272 and 1278 Edward's exchequer attempted to raise more than twenty thousand pounds from them (albeit unsuccessfully). But Edward was also a crusader prince whose contempt for the rights of other religions was easily stirred. He was a conventional bigot, no more enlightened or unusual than his fellow Englishmen who, like Archbishop Pecham and Thomas de Cantelupe bishop of Hereford, were of the opinion that Jews should either convert or face persecution.

The immediate cause of the expulsion, as with so much in Edward's reign, was financial. Almost immediately after the settlement of Wales, the king had been compelled to go to Gascony to overhaul his rule in the duchy. He left England on May 13, 1286, and stayed there for more than three years, reasserting his feudal rights, establishing new towns, and codifying the ducal government. Gascony experienced a sweeping, ordered, and regulated Edwardian reform program, but of course this required expenditure. On his return from the duchy, Edward owed the Riccardi bankers of Lucca more than one hundred thousand pounds.

He arrived back in England on August 12, 1289, to find the political atmosphere highly charged. There were allegations of serious corruption against some of his foremost officials, including the two most senior judges in England, the chief justices of the courts of King's Bench and Common Pleas. His officials' searching probes into royal rights that had lapsed were causing irritation and unrest, and several English earls were muttering about the legitimacy of Edward's demands for financial assistance when he was outside the realm. In October Edward was compelled to write to every shire of England inviting anyone with a complaint against royal ministers or officials to bring it before his commissioners at Westminster. This was not a political environment in which to demand more money from a parliament without making major concessions.

Yet money was on Edward's mind, for he had begun to think once again of the possibility of returning to the Holy Land on another crusade. The Mongols had sent diplomatic messages inquiring about Edward's return to fight the Mamluks, and his trusted ally Otto de Grandison was already en route to the Holy Land on a reconnaissance mission. Negotiations were opening with the papacy to levy a crusader tax, but Edward would need to call extensively on the wealth of his barons and the country's lesser landowners if he was to fit out a more successful crusading mission than his first. Desperate for money and willing to accommodate any policy that would help him raise it, he turned to the logical conclusion of Plantagenet policy toward the Jews. The landowning classes wanted to be rid of them; Edward was ambivalent and perhaps even enthusiastic about the idea. He had expelled all the Jews of Gascony in 1287. Now he would do the same in England. It would buy him political capital, raise a popular tax, and perhaps bring in some income from the confiscated property of the departing Jews.

Thus, when England's nobles and knights assembled at Westminster in July 1290, a deal was struck. A tax was granted in exchange for the expulsion of the Jews. The Edict of Expulsion issued on July 18, 1290, commanded England's Jewish minority to leave the realm by November 1 on pain of death. The edict was distributed throughout the realm and read aloud in synagogues. The Jews put up no real resistance. They began to leave during the summer, and by the autumn they were mostly either gone or—in the case of those unfortunates who boarded ships like the one that sailed down the Thames on October 10—dead.

The Edict of Expulsion marked the end point of nearly a century of increasing hostility aimed against the Jews by Edward and his ancestors. For all the pain, dislocation, and misery inflicted on Jews who left England for an equally unwelcoming Europe, the expulsion was a populist move that proved spectacularly successful. As the two thousand or so Jews who had escaped death or ruin during the first eighteen years of Edward's reign were handed their passes to leave England, royal tax collectors worked on the Christian population that remained. England's delighted landowners, or those represented in parliament at any rate, had granted Edward a tax of a fifteenth on all movable goods. It yielded an astonishing £116,000, the biggest tax levied on England in the entire Middle Ages. "The people groaned inconsolably," wrote the Osney chronicler of its effect on the ordinary English folk. The Jews groaned all the louder as they dispersed throughout Europe, but no one was listening. Edward had once again shown his willingness to legislate and reform according to his needs.

The Great Cause and French Trickery

As the Jews left England in the autumn of 1290, all signs pointed to the likelihood that Edward would leave with them, on a crusade to reconquer lost territory in Outremer. With his tax collectors working the land, milking secular and clerical wealth alike, it seemed as though "the new Richard" were about to usher in another period of death and glory in the name of Jerusalem. Yet within months fortune had decreed that there would be no journey east and no new chapter in the story of the Plantagenet crusades. The rest of Edward's reign would be concerned with events far closer to home: a revived insurgency in Wales, a newly aggressive French monarchy with designs on throwing the Plantagenets out of Gascony, and, bloodiest of all, a new war with Scotland. "When all the Welsh tyrants were suppressed, the Scots raised their spears, armed with rags." This jaunty lyric to a popular song written in 1298 succinctly depicts the switch that occurred halfway through Edward's reign from making war on the Welsh to making war upon the Scots. The truth, as is often the case, was not nearly so neat.

In early September 1290 a fleet of boats set out from Bergen, on the southwestern coast of Norway, heading for Scotland. The cargo was precious: a girl no more than six years old, named Margaret. She was known as the Maid of Norway, but circumstance now dictated that she was to become the Lady of Scotland. On her slim shoulders rested the hope and security of a troubled nation. Margaret was the granddaughter of Alexander III, the Scottish king who had died in 1286. Alexander's death had plunged his realm into a state of confusion. There was no obvious heir to the throne. Although Alexander's wife, Queen Yolanda, had been pregnant at the time of the king's death, the child was stillborn, and they had no other children.

The failure of the Dunkeld family line spelled disaster for the kingdom. "Christ born in virginity, succour Scotland and remedy, that state is in perplexity," wrote the fourteenth-century chronicler Andrew of Wyntoun, reflecting decades afterward on the turmoil provoked in the kingless state.

Between 1286 and 1290 Scotland was in a state of suspended animation, ruled by a council of guardians who attempted to maintain the country until an heir could be found. They eventually settled on Margaret, whose transfer to Scotland was agreed on in the summer of 1290 after lengthy negotiations between the English and Norwegian courts and the magnates of Scotland. Since the rule of a little girl was no remedy for a constitutional crisis, the Scots had persuaded Edward she should be married to the English king's son Edward of Caernarfon, who was also six years old. The marriage would function as a dynastic union, knitting together the English, Scottish, and Norwegian royal lines. The Treaty of Birgham, sealed on July 18, 1290, confirmed the marriage alliance, guaranteeing "that the kingdom of Scotland shall remain separate and divided from the kingdom of England . . . and that it shall be free from subjection."

Margaret's journey from Norway was not an unusual or dangerous one. Links between Norway and Scotland were close, the kingdoms separated by a short stretch of the North Sea with regular trade routes. The stopping point between them was Orkney, an archipelago off the Highland coast whose earls owed joint allegiance to the Scottish and Norwegian kings. By the first week of September 1290 Margaret was at sea, and by the third week of the month she had landed at Orkney. Scottish and English diplomatic channels fizzed with news of her arrival, and English diplomats under Anthony Bek, the bishop of Durham, were sent into Scotland bearing precious jewels as gifts to mark the maid's arrival.

The English diplomats were never able to present the child with the rich gifts that Edward had intended for her. In the last days of September grim news filtered into Scotland from Orkney: Margaret had died on the island after a week's illness. The cause of her death is a mystery, but it probably derived from acute food poisoning triggered by eating rotten food at sea. With Margaret's death, the line of Dunkeld, which stretched back nearly three hundred years to the reign of Duncan I at the turn of the first millennium, was extinguished. Scotland was truly kingless. The effort to find a new ruler very nearly tore the kingdom apart.

From the first rumors of her death, letters and entreaties flowed between Edward's court and the great men of Scotland. A newsletter written by the bishop of the Scottish city of St. Andrews in the immediate aftermath of Margaret's death reveals that there were widespread fears of civil war. The magnates were arming themselves and preparing to fill the power vacuum with blood. Only a king with such resources and reputation as Edward could assist in preventing a descent into anarchy. "Let your excellency deign, please, to approach the Border to the consolation of the Scottish people and to staunch effusion of blood, so that the true men of the kingdom can ... set up as king him who by law should inherit," wrote the bishop. Without the sort of overarching authority held by Edward, he implied, there could be no legal process to decide upon the new king.

As news reached Edward of the maid's death, he was also told Queen Eleanor was suffering from a recurrence of a feverish illness she had first contracted in Gascony during a visit in 1287. She was traveling to meet him at Lincoln when she took to her bed on November 28, 1290, in the village of Harby in Nottinghamshire. Edward rushed to meet her and was by her side when she died. Eleanor was forty-nine years old; the couple had been married for thirty-six years, and she had borne him sixteen children.

Edward grieved very publicly for a wife of whom he wrote the following year, "we cannot cease to love." As Eleanor's body was brought back to Westminster in twelve stages, embalmed and stuffed with barley, Edward ordered that large tiered stone crosses surmounted with spires should be erected where her body lay. These Eleanor crosses were very public monuments of mourning inspired by the Montjoie crosses that had been erected for Louis IX of France. In addition, Edward lavishly sponsored masses to assist Queen Eleanor's soul on its journey through purgatory; six months after Eleanor's death the archbishop of York boasted to the king, somewhat improbably, that forty-seven thousand masses had been sung for his late wife's soul.

Edward took the utmost interest in supervising the Great Cause, the name given to the complex legal case that erupted among thirteen different claimants to the Scottish throne. The case lasted for two years and boiled down to a choice between John Balliol, the lord of Barnard Castle, in County Durham, and Robert Bruce, an aged nobleman who had served as sheriff of Cumberland and had accompanied Edward on his crusade. In a condolence letter written on the occasion of the maid's death, Edward described himself as a "friend and neighbor" to Scotland, but he saw the Great Cause as a clear opportunity to reinforce his influence in Scottish affairs. He believed firmly in the feudal rights of his Crown over the Scottish Crown, which had been asserted only sporadically during his dynasty's history. Edward, by contrast, would make every effort to demonstrate that he was the lord and master of all the British Isles.

The legal case that eventually found in favor of John Balliol was labyrinthine. Who was fit to judge the appointment of a king? The reluctant decision reached at last by the claimants to the throne was that submission to Edward was the only means by which they could answer the question. But that decision was not taken lightly or easily. A year had passed since the Maid of Norway's death before a conference was held at Norham Castle, on the border, at which Edward's overlordship was recognized by the Scots. By November 1292 the case had been settled, and on November 30 Balliol was inaugurated as King John of Scotland in the ancient capital of Scottish kingship, at Scone.

If Balliol thought that kingship would put him on a par with his "friend and neighbor" in the south, he was sorely mistaken. Edward had overseen the election of a vassal, not an equal. Henry II and John had been happy simply to have Scottish kings pay them homage, satisfying themselves with theoretical rather than practical power, and for many generations Scottish kings had enjoyed good relations with the English court, holding English earldoms (most notably of Huntingdon) and serving in English feudal armies. For Edward, however, this was not enough. He expected full and public submission, not only in ceremonial form but in fact.

Ten days before his inauguration Balliol had given his fealty to Edward, swearing in French that he held Scotland from the English Crown and that he would "bear faith and loyalty to you of life and limb and of earthly honor, against all folk who can live and die." On December 26 he had paid homage to Edward in front of twenty-three Scottish magnates.

This was not unusual, but in addition to the simple pageantry of kingship, Edward claimed as part of his overlordship a right to hear appeals against the Scottish king's legal decisions. This directly contradicted the state of affairs that had been envisaged in 1290 under the Treaty of Birgham, which, despite projecting a dual monarchy under Edward of Caernarfon and the Maid of Norway, had promised that "the rights, laws, liberties, and customs of the kingdom of Scotland in all things and in all ways shall be wholly and inviolably preserved for all time throughout the whole of that kingdom and its marches" and that "no one of the kingdom of Scotland shall be held to answer outwith [outside of] that kingdom for any agreement entered into, or for any crime committed, in that kingdom, or in any other cause." Times having changed, Edward saw fit to exercise his authority more vigorously. In a case involving the Scottish magnate Macduff of

Fife, who claimed to have been denied his succession rights to lands in northern Fife, Edward summoned John Balliol himself to appear before the English parliament of Michaelmas 1293. Balliol rejected the English parliament's right to hear appeals from Scotland, but under threat from Edward he backed down, withdrew his protest, and renewed his homage. It was a humiliation from which Balliol never recovered. The vassal king and all who observed his kingship soon realized that with such a forceful neighbor as Edward, the Scottish monarchy was hollow indeed.

Edward, however, was overreaching. It was all very well to stamp England's might on the kingdom of Scotland, but his uncompromising stance crushed Balliol between two irreconcilable positions. The Scottish king was expected to be a sop to Edward's Arthurian ambitions, while simultaneously standing up for the independence of the Scottish Crown. The effect would ultimately be to destroy Balliol's kingship and drive the whole of Scotland into fierce opposition to the English. Far from embedding his authority over Scottish affairs, Edward was driving the Scots into the arms of the French.

The Conquest of Scotland

The sea routes across the English Channel and along the Atlantic coast of France were major trading arteries during the thirteenth century, as merchants from the wealthy countries of Europe ferried goods between far-flung territories, risking rough conditions and the peril of the open seas to make profits in port towns and markets from Flanders to the Iberian Peninsula and beyond. Mercantile activity was constant, and traders of all nationalities rubbed regularly alongside one another. During the early 1290s, however, a fierce trade war broke out among various shipping merchants of England, Normandy, Flanders, Gascony, and Castile. It resulted in running battles and pirate raiding from the Cinque Ports to Lisbon, in Portugal. The seaways and estuaries turned dangerously violent as banners of war were raised and private naval battles spilled the blood of all nations into the sea.

The causes of the shipping war are now obscure. Trouble began with a scuffle in Normandy in 1292. It escalated during the following year until on May 15, 1293, a series of skirmishes were fought between private armies flying English and Norman banners. At this point the seriousness of the disorder demanded government intervention. Edward, who had little desire to be drawn into a national conflict by the activity of pirate traders, made every effort to appease. An English embassy was sent to France with the aim of arranging peace with Philip IV, who had acceded to the French throne at seventeen when his father, Philip III, died in 1285 after contracting dysentery during an invasion of Aragon.

Philip IV viewed Edward from much the same lofty position that Edward viewed the new king of Scotland. He was a handsome young man whose popular epithet—Le Bel (the fair)—he shared with Geoffrey count of Anjou, the founder of the house of Plantagenet. But this handsome demeanor masked a cold, inflexible personality. Dante called him "the Pest of France," and the bishop of Pamiers wrote: "He is neither man nor beast. He is a statue." During the course of his reign, Philip would persecute numerous groups and subjects that offended his authority. He tortured Knights Templar and suppressed their order. In 1306 he rounded up and expelled the French Jews (although they were invited back by Louis X in 1315 and remained in France until another expulsion under Charles VI in 1394). And in the notorious Tour de Nesle affair he had three of his daughters-in-law imprisoned for adultery while their supposed lovers were tortured to death in public. This was a man whose intransigence and capacity for ruthless cruelty exceeded even Edward's, and although Edward paid homage to Philip for Gascony in a lavish ceremony in 1286, France would once again prove too small for a Plantagenet and a Capetian king to cohabit peacefully.

It was ironic that Edward should be attempting to stamp his feudal lordship on John Balliol at the same time as Philip sought to humiliate him in Gascony. Using the shipping war as a pretext, Philip demanded that he be allowed to pass judgment on a number of Gascon citizens and officials who had been involved in violent attacks. When they were not delivered to him, he summoned Edward to appear before a French *parlement* shortly after Christmas 1293. Edward sent his brother Edmund earl of Lancaster to negotiate on his behalf. But Philip negotiated in bad faith. He told the English that if Edward publicly professed to renounce Gascony and hand over towns and fortresses, sealing the bargain by marrying Philip's sister, the eleven-year-old Margaret of France, the French would then hand back their Gascon gains and drop the summons for Edward to appear before the French parlement.

The English were spectacularly gulled. Why Edward or his envoys would be so naive as to trust in the unlikely promises of a new French monarch who was brazenly aggressive and expansionist is puzzling. Indeed so marvelous was it to the chroniclers of the time that they concluded the English king must have been so consumed by lust for the young French princess that like his grandfather King John, who had fatally undermined his Continental possession by his decision to seize the prepubescent Isabella of Angoulême, Edward was prepared to ignore his better judgment. But this explanation fails to allow for the fact that Edward was a hard-bitten politician, keen to explore any political position that would free up the diplomatic channels for his new crusade. Whatever the motivation, the English were fooled. The summons to the *parlement* was not withdrawn but rather renewed and repeated. When Edward refused to humiliate himself before Philip in precisely the fashion that he himself had recently humiliated John Balliol, England and France found themselves once again at war.

Marriage plans were shelved. Edward dragged out the old thirteenth-century war plans: he formed alliances and coalitions with princes to the north and east of France and plotted a direct invasion to defend and consolidate territory in the south. His diplomats, under Anthony Bek, began to negotiate with the king of Germany and the magnates of the Low Countries and Burgundy. Cash payments and marriage alliances were promised in exchange for cooperation against Philip. Meanwhile the muster went out for an English invasion force.

This plan had worked for Richard I but conspicuously failed for John and Henry III. It would prove little more successful for Edward because like many a ruler before and after him, he had grown dangerously overstretched. In October 1294 a force was sent to Gascony under the king's inexperienced nephew John of Brittany, but it was smaller than had been intended. Troops that were needed in France had to remain at home to keep order in Wales.

A month before John of Brittany set sail, a massive Welsh rebellion broke out under Madog ap Llywelyn, a distant relative of Llywelyn the Last's. Madog claimed to be the successor to Llywelyn's titles, but in reality he led a tax revolt against a heavy duty that had been levied on movable property in 1292. The final installment of the tax was being collected from Wales in September 1294, and it came along with a demand for Welshmen to go and fight in Gascony.

Madog joined forces with other minor Welsh princes. Cynan ap Maredudd, Maelgwyn ap Rhys, and Morgan ap Maredudd were not prominent native magnates, but Edward had effectively wiped out the top layer of Welsh nobility after the 1282 invasion, and there were few other choices. Madog's men attacked the new English castles across Wales. All the major new constructions held out, but it was still necessary for Edward to divert a great portion of the Gascon invasion force to Worcester, so that they could deal with the Welsh. This was a severe drain on his resources. Edward might be the most powerful man in Wales, but even before the French hostilities began, his hopes of mounting a swift and robust defense of his lands on the Continent were choking on the fruits of his mastery in the British Isles.

Edward's third Welsh invasion, which began as winter set in, was the largest of the reign. His men marched into Wales in December 1294, sticking to the old tactics of large assaults from Chester to Conwy by the royal army, while royalist lords launched semi-independent attacks through the marches in the south. There were minor setbacks during the invasion. The Welsh managed to capture a good portion of the English baggage train, and Edward was besieged during the winter in Conwy Castle, which was cut off from reinforcement by heavy floods. Here he was said to have refused his small ration of wine, insisting that it be divided equally among his men while he drank water sweetened with honey. It was a safe gesture to make because when the floods receded, the siege was easily relieved.

The spring brought victory for the English. On March 5 troops commanded by the earl of Warwick defeated Madog's men in a battle at Maes Moydog. "They were the best and bravest Welsh that anyone has seen," wrote one observer in a newsletter preserved in the Hagnaby chronicle. But faced with an English war machine confident in its methods and secure in its infrastructure, they had little chance of succeeding. After Maes Moydog, Edward felt comfortable in venturing out from Conwy to lead a tour of Wales; he mopped up the collapsing insurgency in a three-month journey around the principality. By mid-June 1295 Wales had been subdued and the rebel leaders captured.

Victory had once more come with very little serious opposition. But Edward had been forced to spend in excess of £54,000 on the campaign, with a further £11,300 spent on building Beaumaris Castle on Anglesey between 1295 and 1300. He had also lost precious time in his war for Gascony.

Time and money were now running pitifully short. Gascony desperately needed reinforcement, and the southern coast of England was attacked by French ships in August 1295: Dover was burned, and several people were killed. But when the king addressed his noblemen at parliament in Westminster that month, he encountered a maddeningly familiar attitude: about a quarter of the English magnates declared themselves completely unwilling to serve the Crown on an overseas invasion. The thirteenth century's great complaint rang as loudly in 1295 as it had in 1214: Gascony was the king's business, not England's.

Edward was furious. He imposed harsh financial sanctions against those who would not help him pay for the campaign in Gascony and ordered a fleet of new fighting galleys to bolster his coastal defenses. But panic was spreading. Rumors began to circulate that a full French invasion of England was already under way. A knight of the household, Thomas Turberville, was discovered to have been spying for the enemy. Watches were kept the length of the south coast, from Kent to Cornwall, as anxious men and women scanned the horizons for the flags and sails of a French fleet come to destroy the realm.

In desperation, Edward turned to a tactic that had always served him well in the past, concessions and consultation. At the end of November he called a vast assembly of barons and bishops, knights and burgesses, men of the shires, and representatives of the towns and cities to a parliament. It was the largest political gathering Edward had convened since he had plotted the Welsh invasion, and he came in a conciliatory mood, promising that no one should end up out of pocket on account of campaigning with the king. The writs that summoned the men to what was much later called the Model Parliament appealed to a sense of national danger: "The King of France, not satisfied with the treacherous invasion of Gascony, has prepared a mighty fleet and army for the purpose of invading England and wiping the English tongue from the face of the earth."

The whole of England, then, was called upon to come protect the kingdom from the perfidious French. But by the time the country answered the king's summons and parliament met, the Gascon cause had once again been overtaken by a crisis closer to home. No sooner had Edward restored his rule in Wales than his puppet king John Balliol was stripped of power in Scotland. War with France had once more to be postponed as Edward turned his attention elsewhere.

The war with Scotland sprang from many causes. Chief among them was the king's pride. Edward's desire to put his mark on the affairs of the northern kingdom went a long way beyond the assertion of his legal right. As the muster for war in Gascony began in the summer of 1294, he had issued a summons to John Balliol and eighteen other Scottish magnates to provide feudal military service against the French. The war with Wales prevented the summons from taking effect, but it was another example of Edward's rigor in applying his royal rights in Scotland rather than allowing their simple theoretical existence.

As Edward grew more belligerent, John Balliol's position in Scotland grew weaker. A man who could not resist Scotland's neighbor, the magnates concluded, was simply not a king. In 1295 they stripped Balliol of power and reestablished a twelve-man council to rule the country in his name.

It was a glaring failure on Edward's part not to realize that by bullying the Scottish king he would fatally undermine the entire office of Scottish kingship. Perhaps he really could not see the analogy between his treatment of Balliol and the demands being made on him by the French Crown in Gascony. Edward's inability to empathize with the pressures brought to bear on his opponents was the cause of most of the rebellions and crises of his reign. In 1295 he managed to drive together two enemies that were to remain in each other's arms for the following 365 years. In February 1296 the Scottish government ratified a treaty of friendship with France. The Auld Alliance was born.

Edward's army marched north toward Scotland in February 1296, with the intention of teaching his rebellious vassal kingdom a painful and lasting lesson for its impertinent alliance with the French. The king's arrival brought fuzzy border allegiances into focus. The boundary between Scotland and England was a political and not a cultural one; in a zone of changeable loyalties there was no clear and lasting border at which one crossed from one kingdom to another. But if the border was vague, the bloody consequences of war were very real.

As Edward approached with his army, the Scots sent raiding parties into Northumberland, terrorizing and destroying villages around Carlisle. The English preferred to wait until Easter's festivities were complete before joining battle. Their first assault was on Berwick-upon-Tweed, a border town in the northeast of England that had been endlessly disputed between the two kingdoms, partly because it was an excellent base from which to launch attacks either north or south, depending upon who held it. The battle of Berwick, like the short, decisive, and violent campaign it began, was a savage and bloodthirsty affair that would live long in the memories of song-writers and chroniclers on both sides of the national divide.

It took place on Friday, March 30, 1296, a month to the day after Edward had arrived in the Scottish borders, and it did not start well. As the tall, white-haired King Edward, not far from his sixtieth birthday, was busily knighting some young men in the customary prebattle fashion, the sea's gray horizon was daubed all at once with thick smoke belching from three English ships that had begun the battle prematurely when one ran aground near the town and was stormed and burned by jubilant Scots.

The streets of Berwick were soon painted with blood as Edward's army, captained by Robert Lord Clifford, a highborn soldier with extensive experience in the border region, advanced to the sound of trumpets. They slaughtered the men of Berwick in their thousands and were later accused by their enemies of having killed women and children too, including a pregnant woman who was said to have been hacked to pieces. The Scots had mocked the English as they made their preparations for war, but they did not mock them once the fighting began. They were ripped to shreds in the streets, the bodies too numerous to bury. Corpses were thrown down wells and tipped into the sea as the town fell victim to a hideous and terrible massacre. The chronicler Walter of Guisborough estimated that 11,060 people were slain before the clergy of the town managed to plead successfully for mercy.

After the battle the English diggers who built a large defensive ditch around the captured town were very cheerful. The ditch was eighty feet wide and forty feet deep, and the king had wheeled the first barrow of earth himself. It was a symbol of English strength and victory, and the workers sang a gleeful song as they worked. The chronicler Peter Langtoft recorded fragments of their verse:

> Scattered are the Scots
> Huddled in their huts
> Never thrive will they:
> Right if I read,
> They tumbled in Tweed
> That lived by the sea!

This was the manner of Edward's conquest of Scotland. Edward's army numbered around thirty thousand strong, and he marched it through the northern kingdom killing all who opposed him.

Mockery and insults flew. The Scots called the English "tailed dogs" because it was common knowledge in the Middle Ages that Englishmen had tails. But the English had something more powerful than gibes: a sophisticated war machine that the Scots failed utterly to match. After the rout of Berwick, Edward received a message from John Balliol renouncing his homage in bitter terms. News reports came from other parts of the border region of burning and slaughter in the fields of Northumbria. Scottish raiding parties apparently repaid English atrocities by burning two hundred schoolboys alive in a church.

A point was fixed for the next engagement when three prominent Scottish earls seized the castle at Dunbar, an ancient stone fortification perched on a rocky outcrop on the east coast of Scotland that had been a castle site since Roman days. Edward sent the earl of Surrey north to besiege it. When Surrey was attacked by forces sent by Balliol, the result was another humiliating rout for the Scots. The three earls in the castle garrison were captured, along with numerous barons, bannerets, and knights. Peter Langtoft wrote: "The Earls [were] sent to the Tower of London. . . . Others [were] sent to different castles two by two, mounted together on a hackney, some with their feet fettered in carts." It was a dismal way for prisoners to be transported and a potent symbol of the crushing defeat that Edward was inflicting on the Scots.

After Dunbar, Scottish resistance melted. The short and largely unhindered English campaign lasted twenty-one weeks. Edward paraded ceremonially about the kingdom, taking his troops as far north as Elgin and Banff. Much of the Scots' brittle defense must be ascribed to the weakness of John Balliol. In a process that was split over two dates and four locations—July 2 and 10, 1296, at Kincardine, Stracathro, Brechin, and Montrose—Balliol was publicly and ceremonially humiliated. His coat of arms was ripped from his tabard (or short overcoat), for which he earned the Scottish nickname Toom (empty) Tabard. He was sent to join the captive earls in the Tower of London. And most devastatingly of all, Edward's men took the government records from Edinburgh and all the Scottish royal regalia, including the sacred enthronement stone from Scone, and brought them to London.

The Stone of Destiny was carried south to Westminster Abbey and incorporated into a special Coronation Chair. Plantagenet power would henceforth be transferred through a piece of furniture containing Scottish kingship's most revered relic. Instead of installing a new king in Scotland, Edward decided that he would rule directly, as he did in Wales. Hoping that an English victory would place him on the throne, the heir and namesake of Robert Bruce, who had confronted Balliol in court for the kingship, had fought in Edward's army. Now he was contemptuously dismissed. "Do you think we have nothing better to do than to win kingdoms for you?" Edward asked him.

A gloriously reconstructed Berwick was to be the center of English power, beginning with a parliament held in the town, at which thousands of Scots traveled south to swear their fealty directly to Edward. A new network of English governance and administration was imposed under the direction of the earl of Surrey. As he handed over the seal of Scotland to Surrey, Edward joked: "A man does good business when he rids himself of a turd." The Scots had been clinically disposed of. At last, after two years of firefighting, Edward was once more ready to take the fight to France.

Crisis Point

Parliament met at Salisbury in February 1297. It met to face a king who was determined that after years of delay and distraction his war against Philip IV of France should finally be realized. That would take money, and money took consensus. "What touches all should be approved by all" was Edward's new motto when summoning gatherings of his political community. And what Edward demanded at parliaments now really did touch everyone in England.

The French situation required immediate action. After several years of diplomacy, Edward had stitched together a coalition of northern allies, which had been completed the previous month when the twelve-year-old count of Holland was married to Edward's daughter Elizabeth while the court was in Ipswich. Holland joined the king of Germany, various Burgundian lords, and the counts of Guelders and Flanders in coalition, and they could not begin their action against Philip too soon. Gascony was in terrible danger. On January 30 English forces under the earl of Lincoln had suffered a disastrous ambush and defeat between Bayonne and Bonnegarde. Urgent relief was needed.

Unfortunately for Edward the parliamentary gathering at Salisbury was hardly hungry for further glory. Rather, the mood he encountered was one of anger, exasperation, and stubborn refusal to cooperate in funding yet another expensive war.

England was racked by disaffection. Every estate had suffered Edward's onerous demands for war funding, and by the late 1290s spending had run wild. Even before the Scottish campaign was accounted for, recent war costs had amounted to something in the region of £250,000. Edward had incurred debts of at least £75,000 just in assembling his northern coalition on the Continent; the actual business of campaigning in France and Gascony was going to cost far more.

Edward's taxes had been regular and extremely severe. Massive customs duties, known popularly as the *maltote* (bad toll), were levied on wool, driving down the price paid by merchants to ordinary farmers and suppliers. Two heavy taxes had been raised in 1295 and 1296. Since 1294 royal officials had been seizing food and equipment in a program of forced requisition known as the prize (seizure). "Many were the oppressions inflicted on the people of the land," wrote the northern chronicler Walter of Guisborough. The financial exactions had hit the whole country hard, and the clergy were first to refuse to cooperate any further.

Since the death of Pecham on December 8, 1292, the English Church had been led by a new primate, Robert Winchelsea, a top-ranking intellectual and academic with a temper and sharpness of mind to match Edward's own. Using as his justification a papal bull, issued by Pope Boniface VIII, that condemned kings who taxed the Church, Winchelsea led the English clergy into outright refusal to grant Edward any financial assistance for his French campaigns. Edward flew into a fury, declared every member of the English clergy outlawed, and sent his officers across the country to seize their temporal property. "No justice was dispensed to the clergy . . . and clerks suffered many wrongs," wrote Walter of Guisborough. "The religious were also robbed of their horses on the king's highway and got no justice until they redeemed themselves and got the king's protection." It was a minor victory for Edward, but soon he was bedeviled by further resistance.

At the Salisbury parliament the king asked his magnates to fight in Gascony while he led the campaign in northern France. His brother Edmund, who had led an English expedition to defend the southern duchy in early 1296, had died the previous summer. Edward intended to attack Philip from two points, and this necessarily required a division of his forces. It was a tactic that had been suggested twice before, in 1294 and 1295, and on both occasions there had been pockets of discontent or refusal. Barons and knights could be persuaded to fight alongside the king, but to be sent to fight in a foreign land on their own was felt to be beyond both the call of duty and their legal obligation. In 1297 Edward was faced with mass desertion. Led by Roger Bigod earl of Norfolk and marshal of England, the magnates put it to him that he had no right to demand feudal military service of them in Gascony when he himself intended to fight in northern France. Bigod's argument was particularly pertinent because as he pointed out, in his office of earl marshal he was obliged to serve alongside the king, not independently of him. Walter of Guisborough recounted their exchange:

"With you will I gladly go, O King, in front of you in the first line of battle as belongs to me by hereditary right," he said.

"You will go without me too, with the others," Edward replied.

"I am not bound, neither is it my will, O King, to march without you," said the earl. Enraged, the king burst out, so it is said, with these words: "By God, O Earl, either you will go or you will hang!"

"By the same oath," replied Norfolk, "I will neither go nor hang."

Bigod had touched the heart of the matter: for all the king's might and will, he was bound by his own law, which stated clearly that his barons were not obliged to serve without him. Edward was furious, and he pressed ahead with his attempts to send aid to Gascony and plan a campaign in northern France. He impounded clerical property and called in all debts owed him by the lay magnates. For their part, some of the clergy and four of the most important nobles—the earls of Norfolk, Hereford, Arundel, and Warwick—dug in their heels and refused to cooperate with war preparations.

Parliament broke up in March 1297 and was recalled to meet in Westminster in July. By then Edward had made peace with Archbishop Winchelsea and some of the earls. It was agreed that he could levy a lay tax in return for a reissue of the Magna Carta and the Charter of the Forest. On Sunday, July 14, the king stood on a wooden stage outside Westminster Hall and spoke to large crowds of his subjects. He pleaded his case, acknowledged that he had made mistakes, but insisted that he acted only for the good of the country. The chronicler Peter Langtoft reports that he told his listeners: "I am castle for you, and wall, and house." Archbishop Winchelsea stood beside the king in tears, as Edward proclaimed that he was going to France to fight and asked everyone present to swear allegiance to the thirteen-year-old Edward of Caernarfon in his absence.

Not everyone was convinced. The earls of Norfolk and Hereford, who had been dismissed from their preeminent military offices of marshal and constable of England, remained intransigent. They began to compile a list of grievances, known as the remonstrances. In August, in belligerent desperation, Edward ordered another harsh tax on the Church and a general levy of an eighth of movable income and sent out orders for the seizure of fifty thousand pounds' worth of wool sacks from the country. He claimed that the measures were justified in parliament; his opponents snorted derisively that this "parliament" amounted to no more than "the people stood about in his chamber." On August 22 the opposition earls burst into the exchequer at Westminster to forbid the collection either of wool or of the eighth, and they raged against a king who they said was tallaging them like serfs. The country was slipping rapidly toward civil war.

With the realm seemingly on the brink of chaos, Edward left for the Continent. It was an extraordinarily bold move, but he was not prepared to wait at home while Gascony slipped from his grasp. He sailed for Flanders to begin the northern part of his French invasion on August 24, 1297.

His campaign, long anticipated, turned out to be a futile mess. Despite repeated promises, some of his expensive allies proved less than willing to fight. The king of Germany failed to send help, and Edward's sailors from East Anglia and the Cinque Ports proved happier to fight among themselves than to fight the enemy. Those Flemish allies who did play a part were defeated by Philip IV at the battle of Veurne the week before Edward arrived. Soon after landing on the Continent, Edward was pinned down in Ghent, where there were riots against his leadership. Not long after that, word came from the east that the king of Germany was abandoning the cause altogether. The coalition collapsed with all the speed, if not quite the same drama, as the unraveling of John's northern alliance at Bouvines more than eight decades before. It was expedient, as the autumn set in, to sue for peace. A truce was announced in October and cemented with an agreement for a two-year suspension of hostilities at the end of January 1298.

The peace with France might have heralded a much-needed period of stability and recovery from the demands of war. But once again events in Scotland intervened. While Edward was overseas, a rebellion had broken out against the earl of Surrey's Berwick administration. On September 11, 1297, a rebel Scottish army had routed forces under Surrey's command at Stirling Bridge, a brilliantly chosen battle site about one hundred miles north of Berwick, at a crossing of the river Forth. Surrey's leadership had been panicked, lazy, and ineffectual. He and his men were undone by an army led by William Wallace, a common robber and brigand, but a genuine popular hero, who had dismissed English negotiators before the battle with the words "Go back and tell your people that we have not come for the benefit of peace, but are ready to fight, to avenge ourselves and to free our kingdom."

Wallace's arrival at the head of the Scottish rebellion in 1297 briefly united the kingdom of Scotland. Wallace was knighted by his countrymen and declared sole guardian of Scotland in the absence of John Balliol. He led a movement dedicated to fighting to the death for the cause of reclaiming Scottish kingship from the southern usurpers. Meanwhile, south of the border, at York, Edward faced a May parliament. In a spirit of reconciliation he appeased the political community by promising inquests into ministerial abuse and agreeing to uphold the reissue of the charters that his son's regency government had granted the previous autumn.

Edward issued the Confirmation of the Charters, sealed on October 10, 1297, after news had filtered south of Wallace's victory at Stirling Bridge. The confirmation restated both the Magna Carta and the Charter of the Forest—now both documents of legendary status—and added several new clauses, including the abolition of the *maltote* duty on wool and acceptance that any future tax might be taken only with the "common assent of the realm." On the back of the confirmation, Edward's government had also agreed to stop treating the earls who had opposed him with his own deep-felt "rancour and indignation."

The May parliament met in the midst of what was already a highly militarized situation in the north. The exchequer had been moved north from London to York and was distributing funds to muster an army of more than thirty thousand at Roxburgh. They marched at the end of June. Problems with supplies meant that there was more wine than food; before long the Welsh and English contingents in the infantry were fighting each other. Without the naval support they had enjoyed in Wales, the vast armed force marched hungry as it pushed north. All the while William Wallace lay low somewhere in the Scottish hills, falling back and destroying crops and supplies as he went, drawing the English deep into the Scottish interior and waiting for his moment to confront them.

Edward was on the verge of falling back to Edinburgh when he learned that Wallace was camped at Callendar Wood, near Falkirk. He marched his army overnight to meet the Scots early in the morning of July 22, 1298. During a night spent in the open, the king's horse trampled him and broke two of his ribs. It was a painful reminder of the unpredictability of battle. Anthony Bek held a morning Mass as dawn's weak light broke on a misty battlefield. Across a patch of boggy ground they saw the Scots arrayed for battle before Callendar Wood, in highly defensive formation. Wallace had his men in four schiltroms, hedgehog formations with long spears bristling outward. Battle was destined to be fierce and bloody.

Edward attacked the Scots from two directions, splitting his battalions around the bogland in front. The earls of Norfolk, Hereford, and Lincoln led an attack from the west, while Anthony Bek struck from the east. The Scottish cavalry, not incorporated in the schiltroms, fled the battle. Meanwhile the English split the schiltroms open by firing arrows and crossbow bolts and throwing stones. Once the formations were broken, the Scottish defense disintegrated, and a fearful rout followed. As many as two thousand infantry were killed on the English side. Slaughter rained down upon the Scots.

The battle was a humiliation for William Wallace, badly denting his military reputation. But the escape of the entire Scottish nobility, as well as of Wallace himself, meant that despite the rivers of blood that fed the bog at Callendar Wood, it could not be counted alongside Dunbar as a total victory for the English. Weak, hungry, diseased, and divided, Edward's army was in no condition to keep the field. Tensions, which were exacerbated by Edward's division of captured Scottish estates, still existed between the king and the earls of Norfolk and Hereford. The best the king could do was to fall back to Carlisle, sending an unsuccessful manhunt deep into Scotland in search of the young earl and claimant to the throne Robert Bruce.

Relapse

Edward at sixty years old was tall and imposing, and all the more striking once his dark blond wavy hair had turned white. Always the archetypal virile knight, he continued to add to the large royal family when he finally married Philip IV's young daughter Margaret of France in 1299, fulfilling his obligations under the peace made in 1297. The seventeen-year-old Margaret became the first French queen of England, and she was a good companion for the energetic king. After their wedding at Canterbury she accompanied him back to Yorkshire, where in June 1300 a son was born. The boy, Thomas of Brotherton, was named after St. Thomas Becket, to whom Margaret had prayed during her labor.

A vast household was set up for Thomas and his brother Edmund of Woodstock, who was born the following summer. In keeping with the queen's extravagant love of fashion and jewels, the princes grew up in elaborate finery. As babies they slept in ornate cradles, draped in scarlet and blue. More than fifty servants attended their household, where they ate and lived well, learning the arts of noble life in the most luxurious surroundings that a doting old man, who had fathered fourteen times before, and an enthusiastic young woman with a feel for the extravagances of European aristocracy could provide. But although Thomas of Brotherton and Edmund of Woodstock grew up in luxury and comfort, they were not the most important of the royal children. That honor fell to Edward of Caernarfon, the eldest surviving son of Edward's first marriage to Eleanor of Castile.

In 1300 Edward of Caernarfon was sixteen years old, a fine age to begin adopting some of the responsibilities of kingship. For all the trauma of the 1290s, the boy reached the critical stage of early manhood at an easier time than his father had. Peace had been reached with France. Wales, his own principality, was largely subdued, with the ramparts of Master James's castles beginning to loom over the horizon as a symbol of permanent English mastery.

Among the barons there was still some discontent, but one major source of friction was smoothed in 1302, when a reconciliation was staged between Edward I and Roger Bigod, the earl of Norfolk. In its place, a series of highly complex disputes over jurisdictions and privileges developed between King Edward and his erstwhile friend and close adviser Anthony Bek, the bishop of Durham, who had been central to the pursuit of the Scottish wars. Edward confiscated Bek's lands in 1305 and showed that he retained the appetite to dominate any magnate, lay or ecclesiastical, who crossed him.

But Scotland still made trouble. English armies were raised to offer battle in 1300, 1301, and 1303, but the Scots had learned their lesson at Falkirk. They refused to fight, and Edward's capacity to impose a Welsh-style settlement on the northern kingdom was severely limited. There were successes: the young Robert Bruce, grandson of the claimant in the Great Cause, defected to the English in the winter of 1301–1302, and William Wallace was captured in 1305 and violently executed in London, and his tarred head was stuck on a spike on London Bridge. But Scotland still refused to submit. A new vision, new leadership, and new life were needed at the head of English government for the campaign to move on.

Was Edward of Caernarfon prepared for all this? Certainly the heir to the throne was a strong, athletic young man, who had inherited his father's capability on horseback. He was also a keen adherent of family mythology. In 1301 he commissioned a picture of the martyrdom of Thomas Becket for Chester Castle; the following year he received as a gift an illustrated life of Edward the Confessor.

These signs of respect for Plantagenet traditions were not enough to balance the growing fears that Edward of Caernarfon lacked the strengths that had made his father such a successful king. That he was not a man for tournaments suggested that Edward's love of the front line of military skirmishing had not passed on to his eldest surviving son. There were suspicions around court from 1300 that a young companion known as Piers Gaveston was creating a distraction inappropriate to the bearing of a Plantagenet prince. Gaveston encouraged a streak of brattish impetuosity in the prince that others found hard to bear. In 1305 the young Edward got into an argument with the king's chief minister, Walter Langton, in which he used such "gross and harsh" words to the treasurer's face that the king threw him out of the court for several months.

Worrying though these things were, nevertheless in 1306 it was clear that Edward of Caernarfon had to be thrust to center stage. Uproar broke out once again in the northern kingdom, this time occasioned by the vicious murder of John Comyn, the lord of Badenoch and erstwhile guardian of Scotland, who was stabbed to death in front of the altar at the Franciscan church in Dumfries. The murderer was none other than Robert Bruce. Having turned coat to join the English in 1302, in March 1306 he had himself crowned King Robert I of Scotland in Scone Abbey. The Scottish wars had begun once again.

As Edward made preparations to go to Scotland for yet another campaign, his health began to fail him. When Robert I was crowned, Edward I lay sick in Winchester. From late spring 1306 he was being transported by litter. Without delay, Edward of Caernarfon began to receive the accoutrements of power. He was granted Gascony in April 1306. At the festival of Whitsun (seven Sundays after Easter) he was knighted at Westminster, where he and three hundred other young men were belted as knights in a ceremonial passing of the torch to a new generation of Englishmen. The ceremony was known as the Feast of the Swans because after the meal Edward had a pair of golden swans brought before the assembly. The king promised, in Arthurian fashion, that he would not rest until he had avenged himself on Robert Bruce and that once he had been avenged, he would lay down his arms in Britain forever and travel to the Holy Land to fight the infidel. Young Edward agreed, swearing a similarly Arthurian oath that he would not sleep two nights in the same place until the Scots had been defeated. All the rest of the knights swore their oaths over the golden swans, and to demonstrate their seriousness, forces under the king's cousin Aymer de Valence were sent north to assert English justice once again over the rebellious Scots.

As he traveled once more to Scotland, Edward I knew he was getting old and that he had run out of time to finish the job of uniting Britain under one crown. The pursuit of Bruce over the next two years was to be among the most savage events of his life, in which earls, bishops, and women were imprisoned and executed in cruel and humiliating fashion. Yet it was not enough. While the old king's men struggled hard without success to bring Bruce to justice, his son and heir continued to disappoint him. Violent arguments raged between them, particularly over the son's inordinate favoring of Piers Gaveston.

On July 7, 1307, a Friday afternoon, Edward I died at Burgh-by-Sands, on his way north with another massive army. Death came, rather pathetically, as his servants attempted to lift him out of bed for a meal. He had been ill for many months, and despite a valiant attempt to mount his old warhorse and lead troops out of Carlisle at the end of June, he was physically shattered by a lifetime of warfare, uncompromising politicking, and energetic leadership. He was sixty-eight years old and a shadow of the man he had been even two years before. His son meanwhile was nowhere near the war zone, preferring the comforts of southeastern England, from which he had been forced to send his friend Gaveston into exile on the king's orders in May 1307.

In life Edward had been a leopard and a lion, a builder and a hammer. In death he passed into the realms of legend, like his hero, Arthur. He had done more to enhance the mastery and majesty of the Plantagenet Crown than any king since Henry II. He had established English mastery over much of the British Isles and defended what remained of the Plantagenet dominions overseas. He had overhauled England's law and institutions and regularly purged corrupt officials as the price for continued war finance. He had pandered to popular prejudice in 1290 by expelling the Jews. Although he had driven several of his great barons to the brink of armed insurrection, civil war had been averted, and the prestige and position of the Crown had never once slipped to the depths it had plumbed under his father.

Of course everything came at a cost. Edward had stamped his mark on Britain by nearly bankrupting the country and by exercising kingship with appalling cruelty and prejudice. He left the Crown with crippling debts of around two hundred thousand pounds. Even by the standards of the age, he could be a violent and coarse individual. England groaned and grumbled beneath the financial constraints he had imposed upon it. The Scots and the Welsh darkly resented the overlordship he had stamped on them from above. But it was not long before England grew bitterly to rue the leopard's passing.

PART V

Age of Violence

(1307–1330)

O calamity! To see men lately clothed in purple and fine linen appear now in rags and, bound in shackles, shut up in prison!

—*The Life of Edward II*

The King and His Brother

Y ou bastard son of a bitch! You want to give lands away? You, who never gained any? As the Lord lives, were it not for fear of breaking up the kingdom, you should never enjoy your inheritance!"

These, according to the inventive chronicler Walter of Guisborough, were the words hurled at Edward of Caernarfon by his father, Edward I, during one of their final arguments, in February 1307. According to Guisborough, the younger Edward had approached the king through an intermediary with a request to grant away the county of Ponthieu to his close friend, confidant, and fellow knight, Piers Gaveston. Ponthieu had been brought into the Plantagenet family by Eleanor of Castile, young Edward's much-mourned mother. In fury the old king had attacked his son, first with words and then with his hands, tearing out clumps of the young man's hair before throwing him, exhausted, out of the royal presence.

Was this story true? Certainly there were those who were prepared to believe it. Edward of Caernarfon was a curious young man. In some ways he was the image of his father: tall and athletic, a skilled horseman, a good-looking Plantagenet prince without his father's lisp or his grandfather's droopy eye. He was "a handsome man and strong in body and limb," wrote the author of the *Anonimalle Chronicle*. "But he fell short of the qualities and style of his father, for he was concerned not with deeds of chivalry or prowess but only with his own desires." Despite his regal good looks, it was clear from the very beginning of his reign that he was a very poor candidate for kingship.

This was a pity inasmuch as when Edward II acceded to the throne, he inherited a very advantageous set of conditions. His father's two most troublesome noblemen—the earls of Norfolk and Hereford—had recently died. The greatest remaining earls—Thomas earl of Lancaster and Gilbert earl of Gloucester—were Edward's cousin and nephew respectively. Archbishop Winchelsea of Canterbury was exiled as a result of a dispute with Edward I in 1306, and Walter Langton, the royal treasurer with whom Edward had clashed the previous year, was swiftly fired, deprived of his lands, and imprisoned. There was an imposing debt of around two hundred thousand pounds, but a competent king with the goodwill of his leading subjects would have been able to refinance it without too much difficulty.

Yet Edward was from his earliest months as king viewed with suspicion and hostility. Every aspect of his life seemed at odds with the office. In an age when chivalry and martial valor still formed a crucial part of the royal ideal, Edward was constantly portrayed as a degenerate. Many of the most poisonous chroniclers' pen portraits of him date from a time when disaster had struck his reign, but it was nevertheless commonly and contemptuously said that he was obsessed with such peasant activities as swimming and rowing.

Edward was accused by the chronicler Ranulph Higden of preferring the company of "jesters, singers, actors, carriage drivers, diggers, oarsmen, [and] sailors" to fraternizing with nobles and knights, and indeed sailors, bargemasters, and carpenters were recorded dining in the king's chamber at times during the reign. "If only he had given to arms the attention that he expended on rustic pursuits he would have raised England on high," bemoaned the anonymous author of *The Life of Edward II*, a contemporary history of the king's reign. A royal messenger once said that the king preferred thatching and ditching (countryside hobbies better suited to lower-class craftsmen than to princes of the blood) to hearing the Mass. Although other evidence suggests that Edward was conventionally pious and could hold his own in battle, he did not enjoy or hold tournaments, nor did he sponsor great chivalric occasions such as the Feast of the Swans at which his father had belted him as a knight. This lack of interest in the proper public conduct of kingship eventually reduced him to a figure of popular derision.

Edward also had a reputation for favoritism, and this was a great deal more damaging. He spent his entire adult life under the shadow of cronies with whom he fostered unhealthy obsessions. "The king dishonoured the good people of his land and honoured its enemies, such as flatterers, false counsellors and wrongdoers, who gave him advice contrary to his royal estates and the common profit of the land, and he held them very dear," wrote the Anonimalle chronicler. There were several such favorites during Edward's lifetime, but only one for whom his passion ran highest of all. From as early as 1300 Edward was dominated by one notorious individual in particular, Piers Gaveston.

Gaveston was a Gascon knight. He was slightly older than Edward and was probably placed in his household by Edward I following good service rendered on campaign with the old king in Flanders in 1297 and Scotland in 1300. According to the chronicler Geoffrey Baker, Gaveston was "graceful and agile in body, sharp-witted, refined in manners, . . . [and] well versed in military matters." He must have struck the elder Edward as a perfect model of knightly chivalry for his eldest son to follow.

It quickly proved otherwise. It was clear from very early on in their acquaintance that they shared a bond of unhealthy closeness, in which the pliable Edward was led by the nose wherever the clever, ambitious, and grasping Gaveston would take him. Gaveston was highly charismatic but insufferably arrogant, a trait that the author of *The Life of Edward II* called "intolerable to the barons and the main cause of both the hatred and the anger." His puffed-up pride delighted the king as much as it infuriated his contemporaries. "If an earl or baron entered [Edward's] chamber . . . while Piers was there, [Edward] addressed no one except Piers alone," wrote the same chronicler, who also suggested that "Piers was regarded as a sorcerer."

We will never know if Edward II and Piers Gaveston were lovers, whether in the sense that we would understand such a relationship now or on any other terms. It seems likely that they shared some bond of adoptive brotherhood, modeled perhaps on that of Jonathan and David in the Old Testament, in which "Jonathan made a covenant with David because he loved him as himself." Every major chronicler of the reign noted that Edward treated Gaveston as a brother, and the king referred to his friend as such in official documents. Perhaps there was a sexual dimension to the relationship as well, but if there was, it was not known at the beginning of the reign, when Edward was betrothed to Philip IV of France's daughter Isabella. A fiercely conventional king such as Philip would never have allowed his daughter to marry a sodomite and a heretic. And yet there was an intimacy to the relationship that scandalized their contemporaries, and it fell into a wider pattern of behavior that Edward's subjects thought of as abominable and unkingly.

This first became a matter of national importance in 1305, when Gaveston was banished from the young Edward's company as part of the prince's punishment for a bitter argument with Edward I's treasurer, Walter Langton. Although he was readmitted and knighted in the great ceremony that preceded Edward I's final Scottish invasion the following year, Gaveston absconded from the campaign with twenty-one other knights and disappeared overseas to take part in tournaments. For this indiscretion he was exiled from England on a pension of one hundred marks per year.

When Edward of Caernarfon learned that his father had died in Burgh-by-Sands and that he was now Edward II king of England, his first act was to recall Gaveston from exile, grant him the earldom of Cornwall, and organize his marriage to Margaret de Clare, the daughter of Gilbert earl of Gloucester and Joan of Acre, Edward's own sister.

This was an inordinately lavish promotion, more fit for a kinsman of the king. The earldom of Cornwall was one of the great Plantagenet titles, most famously held by Henry III's brother Richard, who in his day had been one of the senior noblemen in Europe, king of Germany, and count of Poitou. It brought with it lands not just in the southwest but in Berkshire, Oxfordshire, and Yorkshire. The annual income was around four thousand pounds. It was both a royal title and an award of enormous and significant power. To bestow it on a mere household companion like Gaveston was not merely overly generous but politically very dangerous.

The list of people who might be offended by Gaveston's promotion was long. Chief among them was Margaret of France, the dowager queen, who had understood from the late king that the earldom would go to one of her sons, Edward II's half brothers Thomas of Brotherton and Edmund of Woodstock. Despite their youth, either of these might have been expected to be placed in nominal charge of England's government when Edward went to France in 1308 to marry Philip IV's daughter Isabella. But they were not; that honor fell to Gaveston.

That the office of regent was one that traditionally fell to a senior royal official, a member of the royal family, or the queen did not trouble Edward. But it troubled all around him. Gaveston was manifestly not a Plantagenet. Nor was he a justiciar, a chancellor, or an archbishop. "Yesterday's exile and outcast has been made governor and keeper of the land," wrote the author of *The Life of Edward II*, in disbelief. But regent was not the zenith of Gaveston's rise, as the king's coronation set out to prove.

Edward II was crowned at Westminster on February 25, 1308, in a ceremony attended by the combined nobility of England and France. All crammed together into Westminster Abbey to witness the anointing of a new king, accompanied by his twelve-year-old queen, Isabella, whom Edward had married in Boulogne a month previously, in a shimmering ceremony attended by five kings and three queens.

The abbey church and the streets around were packed with participants and onlookers. (The crush was so intense that a knight and former seneschal of Ponthieu, Sir John Bakewell, was killed when a wall collapsed.) Inside the church the assembled nobility glittered in cloth of gold. The French had sent a magnificent delegation, including the counts of Valois and Evreux; Isabella's brother Charles (the future Charles IV of France); John duke of Brabant and his wife, Margaret, Edward II's sister; Henry count of Luxembourg (soon to become the emperor Henry VII); and many more besides. The English earls, barons, and knights of the shire packed alongside them to witness the most important political ceremony of all.

Silent, but present, were the remains of the old king. Edward I's newly constructed tomb was a smooth and austere box of black Purbeck marble, inscribed with the words EDWARDUS PRIMUS SCOTTORUM MALLEUS HIC EST. PACTUM SERVA (This is Edward the First, hammer of the Scots. Honor the vow). It was a cool reminder that kingship brought military responsibility. All who had promised to see out the vision of a reunited, Arthurian Britain were held to their responsibility and the oath that had been sworn at the Feast of the Swans.

The new king entered the abbey church wearing a green robe with black hose, walking barefoot along a carpet of flowers with his young bride beside him. Above the royal couple was held a great embroidered canopy, and in front of them processed the magnates and prelates of England. There was strict protocol to the order of procession, which invariably caused arguments at coronations. Each earl had a certain role to fulfill. At Edward's coronation the earls of Lancaster, Warwick, and Lincoln carried great swords; the king's cousin Henry of Lancaster carried the royal scepter; four other barons—Hugh Despenser the Elder, Roger Mortimer of Chirk, Thomas de Vere son of the earl of Oxford, and Edmund Fitzalan earl of Arundel—bore a board on which the heavy and luxurious royal coronation robes were placed.

Unexpectedly, among all these great men was Piers Gaveston, proceeding in pride of place directly before Edward and Isabella. According to the Annalist of St. Paul's, he was decked out like "the God Mars." Gaveston trumped the assembled nobles in their cloth of gold by wearing silks of royal purple, decorated with pearls. He carried the crown of Edward the Confessor, the most sacred item among all the royal regalia. This could not have been construed by the assembled nobles as anything but a vile insult.

Before the stunned congregation, Edward swore his coronation oaths in French rather than the traditional Latin. In a development of the coronation oath, the king promised to uphold both the laws of St. Edward the Confessor and also "the laws and rightful customs which the community of the realm shall have chosen." Under the king's father, parliaments had been held frequently and were forums for political dissent, discussion, debate, and negotiation. By including in the sacred coronation vows a nod to the developing role of the political community, the pageantry that day reflected the new political reality.

Yet it was Gaveston, not the new coronation oath, that occupied everyone's attention. At every juncture his presence offended the other nobles present. When the time came for the ceremonial fixing of the king's boots, Gaveston shared duties with the count of Valois and the earl of Pembroke, fixing the left spur to the king's heel. After Edward and Isabella had been anointed, as the king sat on the throne containing the Stone of Scone to receive homage from his magnates, Gaveston led the outward procession carrying the royal sword Curtana, which had been carried by the earl of Lancaster on the procession into the abbey. In a society ordered by hierarchy and sacred belief, these were grave offenses against protocol. As the pantomime unfolded, there were unseemly shouts of protest from among the congregation. But worse was to come.

Gaveston organized the feast that followed the coronation, and he made it a vulgar bid to award himself further glory. The walls of the banqueting hall were arrayed with rich tapestries. They were decorated not with the arms of Edward and Isabella but with those of Edward and Gaveston. For the new queen to be sidelined so blatantly was offensive to her visiting family, an insult that was deepened when Edward spent the entire banquet, at which the food was late and virtually inedible, talking and laughing with Gaveston and neglecting his bride. Even before the ceremony the young queen had written to her father complaining that she was kept in poverty and treated with dishonor. Here was a public demonstration of her ill treatment. To make things worse, it later transpired that Edward had given the best of the queen's jewels and wedding presents to his favorite.

The coronation was a disaster. It confirmed to the entire English political community, and to Isabella's family, that the king was dangerously obsessed with Piers Gaveston, in a fashion that was not only unbecoming but likely to bring political ruin. Edward could scarcely have found a better way to upset and alienate all who sought to support him.

It took mere days for the anger engendered by the coronation to spark a political crisis. With a parliament due to be held in April, there were rumblings that the magnates would come in arms, seeking to visit retribution on Gaveston for his behavior. In anticipation of trouble, the bridges over the river Thames were broken at the end of March, and the king took refuge in Windsor Castle. Within days of his coronation, Edward had expended every ounce of political capital and goodwill that a new reign customarily brought.

When a parliament met in April 1308, a group of magnates led by Henry de Lacy earl of Lincoln produced a series of three articles of shattering constitutional importance. "Homage and the oath of allegiance are more in respect of the crown than in respect of the king's person," they declared, drawing for the first time an explicit distinction between the king and the office he held. The magnates demanded that Gaveston be exiled from the kingdom and stripped of his earldom, writing that "he disinherits the crown and . . . impoverishes it . . . and puts discord between the king and his people."

This was no manifesto from a disaffected minority party but a clear signal of constitutional opposition, presented by virtually the entire English barony. The earls of Lancaster, Pembroke, Warwick, Hereford, and Surrey all supported the earl of Lincoln and made a show of armed aggression in Westminster to make it clear how serious they were. Archbishop Winchelsea, who had been absent from the realm during the coronation, was recalled to England by the king. As soon as he arrived, he sided with the barons, threatening to excommunicate Gaveston unless he left England by the end of June. Only one baron, Sir Hugh Despenser the Elder, stood by the king. Despenser was a trusted diplomat and an ardent loyalist who had paid a fortune—two thousand pounds—to marry his only son, known as Hugh Despenser the Younger, to the earl of Gloucester's sister in 1306. He would stick close to the king in years to come.

Despite such a slim show of support, Edward wriggled. It was obvious that Gaveston had to go and that he could not retain his earldom. But rather than comply directly with his opponents and send his favorite away,

Edward appointed Gaveston to the position of king's lieutenant in Ireland and awarded him castles and manors in England and Gascony with which to support himself. He accompanied Gaveston to Bristol and saw him off from England's shores with the utmost dignity.

Everything demonstrated by his father's career ought to have taught Edward II that the politics of English kingship were based on consensus and compromise. Barons were not naturally troublesome or opposed to royal authority, but they were exceptionally sensitive to the inadequate or inequitable operation of kingship and would act to take a grip on government if they believed that the king was failing in his task. Alas, Edward was unable to perceive this. He saw Gaveston's exile as a personal attack on a man he loved rather than as a political act undertaken for the good of the realm. Thus in 1308 he was concerned with nothing more than negotiating the return of his favorite. It would be a familiar pattern established over the following four years, one that brought England once more to the brink of civil war.

The King Restrained

It is hard to overstate the hatred that flared against Gaveston in the aftermath of the embarrassing coronation. To Edward it must have seemed unfounded. He appears genuinely to have considered Gaveston his brother and rewarded him accordingly with the lavish gifts and deep emotional bond that his feelings called for. The queen came a poor third in the relationship, to the intense chagrin of the French; but she was after all a child of twelve, barely ready to be either a sexual partner or a meaningful political figure. Fatefully, instead of following Gaveston's banishment to Ireland with a resolute effort to address the urgent needs of government, Edward bent his energies to the task of rescinding his favorite's sentence and petitioning the pope to annul Archbishop Winchelsea's suspended sentence of excommunication.

Edward was not a stupid man, and he realized that Gaveston could not be recalled without a charm offensive leveled at his magnates. A concerted drive to regain the favor of the leading earls and bishops was built around a reform program. Statutes were issued at Stamford in July 1309 dealing with purveyance—the forced purchase of provisions for the royal army—and the excessive powers of royal officials in the shires. In return Gaveston was allowed back into England and was regranted his earldom of Cornwall in August. The grant was witnessed by many of the most powerful men in England, the bishops of Durham, Chichester, Worcester, and London and the earls of Gloucester, Lincoln, Surrey, Pembroke, Hereford, and Warwick. However, the king's cousin Thomas earl of Lancaster, the earl of Arundel, and Archbishop Winchelsea were absent.

As soon as Gaveston was back, his intemperate behavior resumed. According to several chroniclers, he came up with offensive nicknames for a number of the other earls. He called the earl of Warwick "the black dog of Arden"; Gloucester was known as "whoreson," Lincoln as "burst belly," Lancaster as "churl," and Pembroke as "Joseph the Jew." Gaveston also upset the earl of Lancaster by having a Lancastrian retainer replaced in a royal office by one of his own men. His influence over the king remained powerful and extremely disturbing, not least because the country was supposed to be readying itself for a return to war with the Scots.

As 1309 unfolded, tensions grew. An army ordered to muster for Scotland in September did not materialize. Yet Edward's officials continued to exercise the rights to prizes and purveyance, using the food and supplies they seized to supply royal garrisons in the north. A tax of a twenty-fifth was also taken. The burdens were so severe that rumors of an impending peasants' revolt began to circulate.

Popular anger was focused through the magnates at a parliament in early 1310. There was a general refusal to attend Westminster unless Gaveston was dismissed from the king's presence. When Edward acceded to this request, *The Life of Edward II* records, parliament made urgent complaints that "the state of the king and the kingdom had much deteriorated since the death of the elder King Edward . . . and the whole kingdom had been not a little injured." Their complaints were summed up in a petition. Its authors pointed out that since 1307 Edward had been guided by evil counselors and that he had impoverished the Crown to such a degree that his ministers were forced to break their obligations under the Magna Carta by extorting goods and money from the people and the Church. Edward was accused of losing Scotland by his negligence and diminishing the royal possessions in England and Ireland.

This was a damning indictment. To blame the dire Scottish situation on Edward II overlooked the fact that the overstretched military position derived in large part from his father. But otherwise the complaints were justified. To fix the broken state, the petitioners in parliament demanded that "twelve discreet and powerful men of good reputation should be elected, by whose judgment and decree the situation should be reformed and settled; and if anything should be found a burden on the kingdom, their ordinance should destroy it." This was a bold and urgent step to take when a reign was still only in its third year. And it shows the concern with which the whole political community viewed Edward's leadership. The barons were not unreasonable men, driven by ambition and a desire to encroach upon royal power. In the main they simply wanted a strong, fair king.

If Edward was unconvinced at the beginning of the parliament, he was soon shown how seriously his magnates took the situation. *The Life of Edward II* records that they accused the king of breaking his coronation oath and threatened him with deposition if he failed to heed their demands:

"The united barons . . . [said] that unless the king granted their requests they would not have him for king, nor keep the fealty that they had sworn to him, especially since he himself was not keeping the oath he had taken at his coronation."

Edward realized that he had no choice but to bow to the popular demands. On March 20, 1310, a group of twenty-one ordainers—as the lords who were responsible for carrying out the reforms known as the ordinances became known—was elected and sworn in. It was a balanced panel of loyalists and reformers, which included the archbishop of Canterbury and many of the English bishops, along with every English earl except for Oxford, Surrey, and—unsurprisingly—Piers Gaveston earl of Cornwall. They agreed to publish their ordinances for the reform of the realm in September 1311.

In September 1310, eager to keep his distance from the ordainers in Westminster, who were busily—and to his mind impertinently—putting together a plan to reform his kingship, Edward made his way to the Scottish borders. He stayed until July 1311. He had nothing like the cohorts of soldiers that his father had taken north during the mighty campaigns of the previous decade, but an army of three thousand or so infantry and seventeen hundred cavalry was still a sizable force.

But he made no progress. Robert Bruce continued to evade open battle, preferring to skirmish and retreat. There were diplomatic exchanges between the Scottish and English kings, and Gaveston took a strong force to Perth with the intention of winning support through his military endeavor; but nothing was achieved. Eventually Edward ran short of money and supplies, failed to raise further troops either in Ireland or in England, and, having overseen a failed expedition, returned south in the summer of 1311. Robert Bruce invaded the north of England as soon as Edward left, causing much misery and damage. The king returned to Westminster to find a full program of political reform in action and his enemies strengthened in dangerous ways.

While he was in Scotland, several important men had died. Anthony Bek, the bishop of Durham, was one; more significant for the rest of his reign was the death of Henry de Lacy earl of Lincoln. Lincoln, who also held the earldom of Salisbury, was in many ways the elder statesman among the magnates. He was well known, vastly experienced, and respected. His death robbed English politics of an influential figure. It also altered the delicate balance of English aristocratic power.

Lincoln's daughter Alice was married to Thomas earl of Lancaster, the king's first cousin. Lincoln had no sons, so Lancaster inherited Lincoln's two earldoms when the old man died. This gave Lancaster a vast power bloc, which he would not hesitate to exploit. Even before Lincoln's death the thirty-three-year-old earl of Lancaster was a formidable figure. He already held three earldoms: Lancaster, Leicester, and Derby. His father was Edward I's brother Edmund; his mother had been a queen consort through her marriage to Henry I of Navarre; his half sister, Joan of Navarre, was queen of France. Lancaster was thus directly descended from both Henry III and Louis VIII of France. He was around six years older than the king, and the two had been close companions during their youth. Lancaster had supported the king through the tribulations of his early reign, but like so many of the other English barons, he had been forced into a reformist position by the behavior of Gaveston and the manifest abuses in government—particularly the onerous practice of purveyance. He had drifted out of the king's circle during the winter of 1308–1309 and was usually to be found far from Westminster on his northern estates, where he could play the role of the region's most powerful Englishman to his heart's content.

When Lancaster inherited the Lincoln estates, he became at a stroke the most powerful nobleman in England. The Lincoln inheritance boosted his income to eleven thousand pounds—almost double that of the next most senior earl, Gilbert earl of Gloucester—and gave him lands throughout the kingdom. He could raise vast private armies of retainers and wield power at both a national and a local level.

Like Simon de Montfort, another vastly powerful earl and Plantagenet kinsman, who had tormented Henry III, Thomas earl of Lancaster was an abrasive figure. Proud, spiky, and dogmatic, he tended to isolate himself from his peers and found it difficult to command the loyalty of his inferiors. He was a hugely unpopular landlord, who frequently broke the law against his tenants. He did not inspire devotion, and his lack of political judgment was a source of concern as he was elevated to the position of second most powerful man in England. Throughout his life Lancaster was the most zealous of the ordainers. He was heavily involved in preparing the schedule of the forty-one articles of reform that was presented to Edward at the end of August 1311 and promulgated to the country in November.

The 1311 ordinances were broad-ranging and exhaustive. They attacked familiar abuses dating back to Edward I's reign: purveyance and prize; the siphoning of customs duties to Italian banks in order to service debt; the king's right to go to war without consulting parliament. They placed Edward under heavy restrictions: he could not grant away his lands without the consent of the barons in parliament until his debts were paid off; revenues were to be paid directly to the exchequer rather than into the king's household; parliaments should be held once or twice a year with special committees set up to hear complaints against the king's abuses. Edward's entire administration, from his chancellor and treasurer to his county sheriffs, was to be appointed by committees.

Here was 1258 all over again. Government was effectively removed from a failing Plantagenet king and reimposed upon him in a strict and prescriptive way. How the ordinances were practically to be enforced against the will of a truculent and reluctant king was no clearer in 1311 than at any other time of constitutional crisis. Almost every previous attempt to reform an unwilling Plantagenet king had ended in civil war. Yet there was little option but to try.

One demand could be enforced: the exile of Piers Gaveston. As in 1308, the ordainers leveled another raft of attacks at Gaveston, who was now seen as a focal point for all the inadequacies of kingship. It was stated in the articles of the ordinances that Gaveston had "led the king astray," that he had "persuaded him deceitfully and in many ways to do wrong," and that he had "estrang[ed] the king's heart from his liege men." Gaveston was blamed for taking the country to war without the barons' permission. He was accused of having blank charters sealed "to the deception and disinheritance of the king and crown" and more generally of behaving "craftily, falsely and treacherously to the great disgrace and damage of the kingdom." For the third time in his life Edward was faced with an angry demand that his adopted brother Gaveston should be exiled—this time not only "from England but from Wales, Scotland, Ireland and Gascony, and from every land as well beyond the sea . . . subject to the lordship of the king of England, forever and without return."

Gaveston left England from Dover on November 3 and landed in Flanders, intending to seek the hospitality of the duke and duchess of Brabant, to whom Edward had written in advance requesting that they look kindly upon his exiled friend. Once again, however, the exile was short. At the end of November a second set of ordinances was issued, probably on the order of Lancaster and the earl of Warwick. These were aimed solely at purging the king's household of anyone connected with Gaveston. They backfired. The severity and provocative nature of the new terms succeeded only in making the king defiant. Humiliated and furious, he secretly recalled Gaveston after only a few weeks of exile. In early January 1312 the disgraced earl returned once more to England, arriving in Yorkshire just in time to meet his wife, Margaret, who had given birth to their first child, a daughter named Joan.

Almost immediately Edward began distributing notices to the country saying that he rejected the ordinances and confirmed that he had recalled Gaveston and restored him to his earldom. In late February Edward and Gaveston celebrated Margaret's churching. It was the last celebration that they would share.

Manhunt

The village of Deddington, in Oxfordshire, was arranged around a castle built shortly after the Norman Conquest by Odo bishop of Bayeux, the brother of William the Conqueror. It was familiar territory to Aymer de Valence earl of Pembroke, whose wife was staying just twenty-two miles away in the manor of Bampton when the earl arrived in the village on the evening of June 9, 1312.

He came with a notorious prisoner in tow: Piers Gaveston was captured. The king's favorite had been in custody since May 19, when he had surrendered to Pembroke, the earl of Surrey, and two other barons who were besieging him in Scarborough Castle. Pembroke held Gaveston prisoner in the name of the political community of England. He affected to take his duties seriously: during negotiations with Edward II that had taken place at York, the earl had agreed that he would forfeit all his property if any harm should come to Gaveston while in his custody.

The manhunt for Gaveston had been planned and put into action with a remarkable degree of cooperation among the great magnates of England. Within weeks of his arrival back in England the earls had mustered men right across England and Wales, under the pretense of organizing tournaments, "lest the country be terrified by the sight of arms," wrote the author of *The Life of Edward II*. The real reason for raising men was of course to make war upon the king and his loathsome favorite. The prime movers in the plot were Archbishop Winchelsea, who had excommunicated Gaveston; the earls of Lancaster, Pembroke, Hereford, Arundel, and Warwick; and two lesser barons, Henry Percy and Roger de Clifford. Others, such as the earls of Surrey and Gloucester, were aware of the plot and involved to a lesser degree. Each magnate had been charged with keeping the peace in a different part of the kingdom, while Pembroke and Warwick had formal responsibility for capturing Gaveston.

Pembroke, Surrey, Percy, and Clifford had eventually plucked Gaveston from his bolt-hole at Scarborough Castle after a short siege. Negotiations for his release had immediately begun with Edward and were set to continue nearer to London during the summer. Pembroke journeyed south with the captured earl and on a warm June night arrived in Deddington. In spite of his solemn oath to ensure Gaveston's safety, the earl made a curious decision that evening, announcing that he was leaving Deddington and going to visit his wife at Bampton. He would be leaving Gaveston to rest under a light guard.

Was this foolishness or treachery? Pembroke forever protested the former, but it was naive to leave the most hated man in England alone overnight when his enemies abounded. Within hours of Pembroke's departure the earl of Warwick had swooped into the village with a large party of men-at-arms. The man that Gaveston had scorned as the Black Dog was here to bite his tormentor. The author of *The Life of Edward II* gave the story a vivid hue:

> When the earl of Warwick had learned all that was happening about Piers, he took a strong force and secretly approached the place where he knew Piers to be. Coming to the village very early in the morning one Saturday he entered the gate of the courtyard and surrounded the chamber [where Gaveston was staying].
>
> Then the earl called out in a loud voice: "Arise traitor, you are taken." And Piers, hearing the earl, also seeing the earl's superior force and that the guard to which he had been allotted was not resisting, putting on his clothes came down from the chamber. In this fashion Piers is taken and is led forth not as an earl, but as a thief; and he who used to ride on palfreys is now forced to go on foot.

Warwick marched Gaveston from the village of Deddington in triumph, his retainers blowing trumpets to advertise the victory around the rolling fields of Oxfordshire. Crowds thronged around the parade, bellowing abuse at the fallen favorite. Gaveston was marched all the way to Warwick Castle, where he was thrown in prison as a traitor to the realm.

This was no renegade action from a single earl. Within a week of Gaveston's capture the earls of Lancaster, Hereford, and Arundel and their retinues of privately hired soldiers and servants made their way to Warwick, along with lesser barons involved in the plot. Pembroke, now showing genuine horror at his contemporaries' ruthlessness, protested to Lancaster that his vow to protect Gaveston was being torn up in front of him. He was dismissed with the advice that he ought in future to make his promises with greater care.

Lancaster, a royal earl and the most senior man present, from this point took overall responsibility for the fate of Gaveston. The prisoner was tried before a court assembled under Lancaster and Warwick's authority, accused of breaching the terms of the ordinances, which called for his exile. Clearly he was guilty: here was a man brought before a court assembled especially for his condemnation, operating under a law drafted specifically for his destruction.

Gaveston was sentenced to death. On June 19 he was taken from his cell and brought before Lancaster. Chroniclers described a pitiable scene in which the prisoner wailed for mercy. Instead of clemency, Gaveston was handed over to armed guards, who dragged him two miles north of Warwick to Blacklow Hill. At the top of the hill he was passed on to two Welshmen. Each dealt a deadly blow: one ran him through the body, and the other hacked off his head. Lancaster was shown Gaveston's severed head as proof that the ghastly deed was done. The body lay on the ground where it fell, until some Dominican friars collected the remains, sewed the head back onto the body, and took it to Oxford. The Dominicans were an order especially close to the king, whose members had taken an active part in his education and that Edward had patronized generously throughout his adult life. Therefore, for two and a half years the king's friend's corpse lay embalmed and dressed in cloth of gold in the Dominican house. That was as much as charity would bear: Gaveston died excommunicate and could not be buried on holy land. Even given Gaveston's insolence and his irresponsible career, this was a shocking way for the king's favorite to die.

Edward, when he discovered the fate of his adopted brother, was distraught. Rather than count his errors, he became ever more determined to resist the ordinances. He would never forgive his cousin Lancaster for his act of arrogant brutality, and a blood feud boiled between the two for the best part of the next decade.

And far from uniting England, Gaveston's death divided the political community. A permanent split was created among the barons: those responsible for Gaveston's murder were now permanently isolated from royal favor, while Pembroke and Surrey, who felt that they had been at some level deceived by Lancaster and Warwick, became unwavering loyalists.

For more than 150 years the Plantagenets had reigned in England by rule of law. Only in the most severe instances had great men died in the course of political and constitutional disputes: Thomas Becket by misadventure; Simon de Montfort on the battlefield; Arthur of Brittany in cold blood in his prison cell. Now a king's closest companion had been killed in calculated fashion on the order of another earl. For all his transgressions, Gaveston's death could not possibly be a just sentence under the laws of the realm. Rather, when he was run through and beheaded on Blacklow Hill, Piers Gaveston—a nobleman, whether his peers liked it or not—was murdered.

Kidnapping, violence, and murder were commonplace in medieval society, but they were not an acceptable part of the ordinary course of royal government except under the severest circumstances. Now violence had become a political tool in England. Pandora's box had been opened. As Edward and Lancaster moved toward implacable hatred, the Plantagenet family was in danger of tearing itself apart and taking England with it.

Promise and Disaster

To be in Paris during the summer of 1313 was to know the high delights of medieval France. At the beginning of June the whole population flocked in the city streets, and lodgings were crammed with countless noblemen, young knights, the aristocratic young ladies of Europe, and dignified visitors from foreign lands. Great crowds watched public performances, ceremonies, and processions. Colorful fabrics decked the streets, while the city bourgeois provided a fountain that sprayed wine into the air and was decorated with fabulous creatures: mermaids, lions, leopards, and mythical beasts. In a covered market in one part of the city an enclosed wood was built and filled with rabbits, so that revelers could amuse themselves by chasing tame animals. Open-air theatrical performances and musical recitals delighted the population. The French chroniclers averred that this was the most spectacular festival ever seen in France. It was a summer of great pageantry and celebration. King Edward II of England and Queen Isabella were at the heart of it all.

The king and queen of England had arrived on a state visit at the end of May, traveling with the earls of Pembroke and Richmond and other loyalists, including Hugh Despenser the Elder and Henry Beaumont. They had been invited to France to enjoy the honor of witnessing Edward's father-in-law, King Philip IV, knight nearly two hundred young men, including his sons Louis king of Navarre, Philip, and Charles. The ceremony had echoes of the great Feast of the Swans held by Edward I on the eve of his final Scottish invasion in 1306, at which Edward and all his new knights swore first to conquer Scotland and then to win back the Holy Land. But as in all matters, the French Crown determined to make the ceremony greater than anything before it, an occasion of unsurpassed glory and magnificence.

As the English party rode into Paris on June 1, they were greeted with huge acclaim and celebration. A series of six celebratory banquets was planned to mark their arrival, and the occasion was costing Edward handsomely: he had given his father-in-law nearly 100 oxen and 200 pigs, 380 rams, 200 pike, 200 carp, and 80 barrels of wine toward the feasting. At the banquet that the English were to host, Edward planned service on horseback inside tents thrown open for the public to gawp into. The banquet was to be lit even in daylight by hundreds of torches. He had hired famous minstrels and musicians to entertain the guests, and the king of Navarre's men had built a "castle of love" to provide amusement between courses.

Edward was weak and unpopular at home, but in France he was welcomed with reverence into the royal carnival. The writer of *The Life of Edward II* dismissed the first six years of Edward's reign as a betrayal of Plantagenet values, writing that the king had "achieved nothing praiseworthy or memorable, except that he has made a splendid marriage and has produced a handsome son. . . . How different were the beginnings of King Richard, who, before the end of the third year of his reign, scattered far and wide the rays of his valour." But in France, Edward was welcomed with the dignity befitting his connection to the king.

There were many causes for the English and French royal parties to celebrate together. Philip wished to mark a victory in a long dispute with Rome, which had ended with a French pope, Philip's childhood friend Clement V, moving the papacy to Avignon in 1309. (Popes remained at Avignon until 1377, marking a period which the Italian poet and scholar Petrarch called the Holy See's "Babylonian captivity.") The French king had also ensured the destruction of the Knights Templar, a crusading order of holy warriors whose vast wealth and moneylending ability had made them enemies throughout Europe. Pope Clement had condoned Philip's vicious persecution of the whole Templar order on the grounds of heresy and sodomy, in which hundreds of knights were tortured and killed. In 1311 the order had been officially disbanded under papal authority, and much of its wealth reverted directly to the French Crown. Moreover, peace between England and France over Gascony was open to arrangement, and Edward and Philip had made that most Christian of accords: an agreement to launch a new crusade against the Muslims of Egypt. On June 6 they took their crusading vows at Notre-Dame, where Edward became the sixth successive Plantagenet king to make the sacred promise.

How much life had improved since the previous June, when the murder of Gaveston had pushed the country to the brink of civil war. Although in public Edward lamented Gaveston's idiocy in falling into Warwick's hands, in private he had considered punishing Lancaster and his allies with a military campaign against them. Only counsel from those around him that civil war would allow Robert Bruce to invade from Scotland held him back.

It had taken six months to coax England away from the brink of insurrection and anarchy. But as Edward and Isabella joined the revelries in Paris, they both could reflect that things were on the mend. For a start, they were now parents. Queen Isabella had grown into her role as queen after Gaveston's death, aided by the presence of her aunt Margaret of France, the king's stepmother. She had been loyal to her husband through his troubles, and finally, on November 13, 1312, she had given birth to a son at Windsor. Resisting pressure from the French to name him Louis or Philip, the boy had been named Edward. According to a monk of St. Albans, the boy's birth had distracted the king from grieving for Gaveston. The queen had written to the citizens of London to announce the birth, and the news was greeted with great rejoicing in the streets of the capital. Edward of Windsor's birth had been a relief to all. The boy was made earl of Chester at the age of twelve days, and his existence gave a measure of stability to the regime. Edward II had followed the birth of his son by raising his twelve-year-old half brother Thomas of Brotherton to the rank of earl of Norfolk.

When Edward and Isabella returned from their lavish tour of France in mid-July, it seemed as though their greatest moment of crisis had passed. There was by no means an easy relationship between the king and his baronial enemies, who continued to despise a number of other royal companions, most notably Hugh Despenser, who had been virtually the only baron to have stood by the king and defended Gaveston until his death. Despenser was a rare figure among the barons, one prepared to see past the king's failings in order to further his career and wealth through grants of land, office, and title. His advocacy for Gaveston and his uncritical commitment to royal policy made him the object of some suspicion by Lancaster and his allies. Nevertheless, at a Westminster parliament in October peace between the two parties was formalized. Months of mediation by envoys from France and the papacy had been required to broker peace. But finally Edward agreed to pardon Lancaster, Hereford, Arundel, Henry Percy, Roger de Clifford, and their allies for Gaveston's death. In return, the barons agreed to pardon former allies of Gaveston like Despenser. The ordinances were not mentioned, nor did the barons demand that any ministers be removed. Gaveston and his supporters were no longer described as enemies of the king and kingdom. It was a step forward, if not quite full reconciliation.

More good news followed. At the end of November Edward obtained parliament's consent to wage war against the Scots. In December he went to France to seek his father-in-law's permission to secure a papal loan against the duchy of Gascony. He was successful, and the next spring twenty-five thousand pounds were received from Rome, allowing Edward to fund a large campaign in the north. Finally, it seemed, he was about to take up where his father had left off.

Edward's Scottish campaign began promisingly. On June 17 or 18 the king marched a formidable army out of Berwick. It was well equipped, well funded, and well stocked. The wagon train was said to stretch seven leagues (roughly twenty miles) from end to end, while ships hugged the coast to keep the army provided. The army was easily the largest that had been raised for fifteen years, since Edward I's Falkirk campaign of 1298. The earls of Gloucester, Hereford, and Pembroke, Hugh Despenser, and Roger de Clifford all brought large contingents with them, and there were thousands more knights and infantry both in the king's personal retinue and in the army at large. Missing were the earls of Lancaster, Warwick, Arundel, and Surrey, who sent the minimum number of fighting men for which they claimed they were obliged under law. They argued, falsely, that the campaign was not properly agreed upon in parliament: the true reason was that they feared that if Edward were victorious in Scotland, he would be capable of turning on them and their lands in England.

Edward marched his men fifty miles north from Berwick, and the thunderous approach of the English army gave the impression, according to the author of *The Life of Edward II*, that it was "quite sufficient to penetrate the whole of Scotland. . . . [S]ome thought that if the whole strength of Scotland had been gathered together, they would not have stayed to face the king's army." Unfortunately for Edward, that would not be the case. He arrived near Stirling on June 23 to find that Robert Bruce had camped a smaller army, consisting of five hundred light cavalry and no more than six hundred infantry, in the New Park, a leafy hunting ground on the road to Stirling. Half a mile away lay a stream known as the Bannock Burn, which regularly flooded the land around it, making it boggy and treacherous underfoot, conditions that Bruce's men had deliberately worsened by digging potholes in the ground that were disguised under piles of sticks and grass.

The battle of Bannockburn fell into two phases. The first, which took place on June 23, was a day of skirmishing between English and Scottish knights. Henry de Bohun, the earl of Hereford's nephew, challenged Robert

Bruce himself to single combat. He had his head split clean in two with a blow of the Scottish king's battle-ax and died on the spot. The twenty-three-year-old Gilbert earl of Gloucester then brought dissent in the English ranks by disputing the leadership of the vanguard with Hereford (who was constable of England). The vanguard was the foremost of the three traditional divisions of an army, and the honor of leading it was therefore substantial. But Gloucester gained little from winning the argument, as he was knocked from his horse in combat and was fortunate to escape with his life. In a separate engagement on the same day, English cavalry reconnoitering a siege at Stirling Castle were attacked by Scottish spearmen. Sir Thomas Gray had his horse killed under him and was captured, along with many other knights.

If this was an ominous beginning, it was soon compounded by further divisions among the English ranks. Gloucester argued overnight with the king: the earl believed that the troops, exhausted from the march north, urgently needed rest before carrying on the engagement with Bruce. Edward wished to fight on. He called the earl a traitor and a liar, and a furious argument erupted.

The following morning, as the armies drew up again for battle, Gloucester attempted to defend his honor. He began the fight hotheadedly and recklessly by charging the English vanguard at the Scottish infantry. But far from achieving a feat of chivalrous derring-do, Gloucester was surrounded and killed in a seething crush of horses and men. This was the cue for a general slaughter of the English cavalry by Scottish spearmen, arranged in hedgehog schiltroms, as they had been at Falkirk in 1298. On that occasion Edward I's archers had destroyed them with a deadly rain of arrows. But at Bannockburn, Edward kept his archers in the rear until too late, and his cavalry was run through on the sharp tips of Scottish spears.

As the battle turned into a chaotic massacre, Edward had to be dragged from the battlefield by the earl of Pembroke and Sir Giles d'Argentein, a man reputed to be the third-greatest knight in the Christian world. The king fought bravely as he retreated, smashing at Scottish attackers with his mace when his horse was killed. It took the combined strength of Pembroke and Sir Giles to remove Edward to safety and avert a catastrophic capture. But there was a sickening end even to the king's escape. Sir Giles, mindful of his knightly duty in the face of abject defeat, was hacked to pieces when he left the king and hurtled back into battle.

Edward and an escort of five hundred men left Scotland in a hurried naval evacuation from Dunbar. They left behind them thousands of doomed men. The Bannock Burn, the river Forth, and the boggy ground all around groaned with dead and dying Englishmen. The mud thickened with blood, seeping into the tiny crisscrossing streams that covered the battleground. Some of the greatest knights in Christendom were slain by Robert Bruce's army, butchered on the battlefield, or drowned attempting to cross the Bannock Burn or the river Forth. Besides Gloucester and Sir Giles d'Argentein, at least two hundred knights were killed, including Sir Roger de Clifford. The earl of Pembroke was very lucky to escape alive. Edward's privy seal was captured in battle. The earl of Hereford was taken prisoner by the Scots, as were numerous other high-ranking knights. As the English fled, the Scots pursued them across the border, their plundered belongings left behind. The author of *The Life of Edward II* lamented "so many fine noblemen, so much military equipment, costly garments, and gold plate—all lost in one harsh day, one fleeting hour."

But the gold plate and costly garments were not the principal losses. Although military tactics were turning at the beginning of the fourteenth century and infantry were beginning to hold sway over mounted knights wherever the two met, the loss at Bannockburn was still humiliating. Bruce was stronger than ever in Scotland and was free to open a military front in Ireland.

Edward II meanwhile was once again at a grievous disadvantage in his relations with the earls who had tormented him. Lancaster, Warwick, Arundel, and Surrey, having gambled on Edward's military incompetence by refusing to serve on the Scottish campaign, were now ascendant. Instead of a victorious king's swooping down to crush his domestic enemies, a humbled king was returning to face his demons. With the king's fortunes as low as at any time during his reign, the disgruntled barons were free to press their desire for reform upon him once again.

New Favorites

On January 2, 1315, the embalmed body of Piers Gaveston was buried at King's Langley, one of Edward's favorite residences. The manor house in Hertfordshire had belonged to his mother, Queen Eleanor. Edward had visited it as a child, and it had undergone extensive work and restoration to create a sumptuous residence for the family. The brightly painted halls were lit by large fireplaces, and beasts roamed grounds large enough to host tournaments. Within the parkland and vineyards that surrounded the main house there was a lodge known as Little London. It was a place of royal delights, and now of royal mourning, as the king's former favorite was finally given the monument Edward desired for him. Gaveston had almost certainly been absolved of his excommunication by the new and pliant archbishop of Canterbury, Walter Reynolds, and could now be transferred from his Dominican morgue to Langley's cold earth. His embalmed corpse was wrapped in cloth of gold that had cost the king three hundred pounds before being buried with honor in the presence of most of the bishops of England.

The English earls were less well represented. The attractions of a lavish wake at which at least twenty-three tuns of wine were drunk were not enough to gather Lancaster and his allies to watch as the man they had killed was finally laid to rest. Plenty of political tension still existed between Edward and his cousin's supporters; reconciliation was not likely to be helped along by the ghosts of 1312. The years that followed Bannockburn saw the king and the earl of Lancaster make efforts, ultimately fruitless, to coexist. Political recovery was marred by the intransigence and arrogance of the earl and the king's desire to retreat once more into a circle of men whom he trusted but whom the rest of the country found it hard to stomach.

The core members of the king's new cabal had come to watch the old favorite laid to rest. Chief among them were the two most loyal earls, Pembroke and Hereford. One was the king's savior at Bannockburn, and the other had recently been released from captivity under Bruce, having been exchanged for Bruce's wife, Elizabeth de Burgh, who had been taken prisoner by the English. Also attending were Henry Beaumont and Bartholomew Badlesmere, who had been one of the late earl of Gloucester's most important retainers and who was becoming an ever more influential baron in his own right, as well as more than fifty other knights and most of Edward's royal officials. But most important among all the party were Hugh Despenser and his son and namesake, Hugh Despenser the Younger.

"Whatever wickedness was perpetrated in the king's court proceeded from his counsellors," wrote the author of *The Life of Edward II*, and the remark was pointed toward the Despensers. The family had never wavered in their loyalty to Edward, and following Gaveston's death they moved to fill the gap he had left. Both demonstrated unquestioning commitment to the king and were rewarded by successive grants of land, power, and access that allowed them to act with immunity from the law. Hugh the Elder was as close a companion as ever, regularly accompanying the king on foreign visits and gradually accruing titles and castles in the west of England, while pursuing a bitter personal feud with Lancaster. The author of *The Life of Edward II* alleged that Hugh the Elder had "harmed many unjustly through his office; he has disinherited many great men and rich men." The same was true of Hugh the Younger, who was on the road to becoming an even closer friend and ally to the king than his father. These two men grew to have an ever more profound and destructive influence on Edward as his reign spiraled toward disaster.

Between 1314 and 1317 northern Europe suffered terribly as perishingly hard winters were followed by exceptionally wet summers. It rained hard and ceaselessly between May and October 1315, bringing flash floods that swept away villages, destroyed arable land—in some cases forever—and created massive lakes in low-lying parts of Yorkshire and Nottingham. Everywhere the downpour ruined the crops in the ground, plunging England into a state of appalling famine that lasted for two years. People starved in the countryside. Whole villages sank into beggary, as crop yields plummeted by more than 80 percent. People ate anything they could find: bird droppings, pets, damp and rotten corn, and on occasion human flesh. Mob violence broke out over scraps of food or the tiny yields of what few plants could grow in the waterlogged ground. Disease spread among sheep and cattle, destroying England's wool revenue and meat supplies and putting pressure on the military garrisoned near Scotland. Food shortages and sodden living conditions made life on the frontier hungry and unclean.

Against this unpromising background, England's magnates tried hard to establish a lasting political settlement. Parliament met shortly after Gaveston's funeral, and in an attempt to stabilize royal finance and address some of the corruption that was seen to be endemic in central and local government, the barons reimposed the ordinances, purged a number of royal ministers, replaced all the sheriffs in England, ordered the resumption of royal grants, and put pressure on Edward to hear petitions of grievance and complaint from the country at large. In some areas Lancaster and Warwick appeared to be willing to cooperate with loyalist magnates such as Pembroke and with ministers of the king's household.

Cooperation was crucial, because various matters of state and foreign policy had to be addressed. King Philip IV had died in 1314 and was succeeded by his son Louis X. A new French king required renewed diplomatic embassies to secure the status of Gascony. The Scots, emboldened by their success at Bannockburn and the deaths of several eminent lords of northern England, including the earl of Warwick, who died in August 1315, began to raid deep into English territory. Robert Bruce's brother Edward Bruce opened a new front in the war with Scotland when he led an invasion force to Ireland in May 1315. The threats to the borders were magnified by the weather and the famine, which prevented the English from putting an army in the field for any length of time. This in turn put intense pressure on Edward. In a parliament that met at Lincoln at the beginning of 1316, Lancaster was appointed head of the king's council, with a mandate to enforce the ordinances and reform the royal administration.

Lancaster unfortunately proved just as incapable of consensual governing as his cousin. The enforcement of the ordinances and the principle that the king should be checked and sanctioned by the collective will of the barons were the lens through which he viewed all government. But it was also, for Lancaster, an end in itself. Despite his bloody-minded insistence on republishing and reconfirming the ordinances, he had very little time either for Westminster or for the business of ruling. Easily slighted and highly suspicious of the king's favorites, whom he believed were plotting to murder him, he preferred to hold his own court in the north, posturing but doing very little in practical terms. The ordinances called for the repeal of royal grants and mandated that future patronage should be confirmed by parliament. Lancaster's dogmatic insistence on this was a constant reminder of the rift of 1312 and a factor in his growing isolation from the rest of the

English earls, several of whom remained deeply angry at the summary fashion in which Gaveston had been murdered.

Lancaster's quasi regency lasted for just a few months. From April 1316 he retreated to his lands in the north, basing himself at Pontefract Castle. In his absence Edward's new group of favorites grew in prominence and power, and among them, the Despensers began to be preeminent. Given the size of Lancaster's retinue and landholdings, he could not fail to be the dominant force in English politics, and his massive landed power in the north made him a critical figure in the Scottish wars. Yet he was unwilling to engage in governance beyond insisting that the king obey the ordinances that he so detested.

Edward for his part did little to appease his cousin. He showered his new favorites, including both Despensers, Hugh Audley, Roger Damory, and William Montagu, with royal grants and patronage, much of it in Wales and the marches. The lands of the late earl of Gloucester, who had left no sons when he was killed at Bannockburn, were parceled up and divided among Despenser the Younger, Audley, and Damory, who had each, at various points, married one of Gloucester's young heiresses. All five favorites became extremely rich in defiance of the ordinances, which demanded that the king take back past royal grants and have all new ones confirmed in parliament. Even those moderate barons like Pembroke and Hereford, who did not fawn on the king's person but supported him out of loyal principle, were placed on lucrative contracts to serve the king in peace and war. Rather than rely on the natural obligation of barons and lords to serve their king out of mutual self-interest, Edward was now effectively paying men to bind them to the Crown. He was making kingship a private rather than a public enterprise, creating a culture of ins and outs, and pushing his hostile cousin even deeper into opposition.

Crisis deepened throughout 1317. By the summer, when Edward took a sizable army north against the Scots, he found Lancaster gathering his own forces around a rain-lashed Pontefract. Under the cloud of impending anarchy, and with the king's authority implicitly undermined by Lancaster (and vice versa), disorder began to escalate. In September Louis Beaumont bishop-elect of Durham and two visiting cardinals were held up and robbed by Sir Gilbert Middleton, a knight belonging to the king's household, on their way from Darlington to the bishop's consecration. This event caused severe embarrassment to both sides. Once Edward had returned south,

Lancaster's retainers attacked castles belonging to the king's closest supporters.

As public authority evaporated, moderate barons like Pembroke and Badlesmere began to take desperate action to cling to peace. They offered private contracts to Edward's favorites; Roger Damory signed one such contract, in which Pembroke and Badlesmere promised to defend him from all men (in effect, from Lancaster) in exchange for Damory's undertaking not to pester the king for grants of land or anything else that might be prejudicial to the Crown. This was desperation. Royal authority could no longer be said to exist, and it was only thanks to the mediations of the English bishops, moderate royal counselors like Pembroke, Hereford, and Badlesmere, and envoys sent from the pope that war did not break out in 1317.

During the next three years the circle of favorites around Edward narrowed even further as he fell ever deeper under the influence of the Despensers and particularly Hugh the Younger, who was appointed chamberlain to the king's household in 1318, a role that gave him intimate and regular daily access to the king. It was no coincidence that the role had once been held by Gaveston. Despenser used his special favor with Edward to accrue ever-larger portions of the Gloucester estates in South Wales that he had inherited through his wife, and this brought him directly into conflict with other favored barons, including Roger Damory and Hugh Audley. Edward blithely permitted Despenser's aggressive pursuit of land, castles, and retained tenants in South Wales, causing relations even among his tight-knit group of favored friends to become poisoned and volatile.

Early in 1318 a tanner from Exeter called John Powderham appeared before the king at Oxford and claimed that he was in fact Edward I's son and that the kingdom of England belonged to him "by right of blood." He was accusing the king of being a changeling, placed in the royal crib at birth, and offered to fight him in single combat for the Crown. Powderham insisted he was the real king of England, and Edward an impostor. The man was clearly deranged, but his story stuck. According to various chronicles, the king was initially amused by the oddness of the claim and then extremely angry as rumors of Powderham's claims began to spread throughout England. Such was the misery of war, flooding, famine, and political disarray that the tale of scandal and mistaken identity found an audience entirely willing to believe it.

Powderham himself did not last long. Edward thought briefly of keeping him as an amusing fool, but the danger was too great. His parents were summoned for interrogation, and he was tried and hanged at Northampton on July 23. (During his trial he claimed that his pet cat had become possessed by the devil and incited him to his crimes. The cat was also hanged.) But was it possible that Edward was unduly tortured by thoughts of his own legitimacy? At around the same time as Powderham's story was traveling the country, Edward was under the spell of a fraudulent Dominican friar, Nicholas of Wisbech. Nicholas claimed to own a vial of holy oil that had been given to Archbishop Thomas Becket during his exile in France. Edward began to believe that if he was reanointed as king with this oil, not only would his political troubles pass, but he would be endowed with the virtue and power to reclaim the Holy Land from the heathen. Eager for a miraculous recovery, he made urgent requests to the pope in Avignon to be allowed a ceremony of reanointing. Even when one allows for the superstitious mind-set of medieval society, these were weird and wonderful events, which emphasized Edward's brittle political position and his gullibility. In the end a civil war was averted not through the divine intervention of the holy St. Thomas but through long and tiring political negotiation with the very real earl of Lancaster. Matters were resolved in August 1318 with the agreement of a formal peace between the king and his cousin: the Treaty of the Leake established a permanent royal council of sixteen (eight bishops, four earls, and four barons; Lancaster was not a member), and Edward once again agreed to observe the ordinances of 1311.

But this was as fragile a peace as any made before it, based as it was on principles that could satisfy neither side. Within four years it had failed. Between 1317 and 1321 England slid, unstoppably, into civil war.

Civil War

In May 1321 huge bands of armed men marched and rode through South Wales and the marches. They seized goods, plundered manor houses, broke down the fences of game preserves, and slaughtered the animals that ran within them. They murdered or kidnapped servants and guards who tried to stop them. They stole weapons and food and destroyed valuable charters and legal documents. They made off with mares and stallions, cattle and oxen, sheep, swine, wagons, carts, and plows. They broke into houses and smashed or stole valuable items; legal records later lamented the loss of a nutwood chessboard with crystal pieces, ivory ornaments, gold religious artifacts, and rich tapestries and clothes.

They flew the king's banner of arms, protesting their loyalty to the Crown. But these were not Edward's men. They were soldiers loyal to the marcher barons of the Welsh borders: the earl of Hereford, Roger Mortimer of Chirk, his nephew Roger Mortimer of Wigmore, Hugh Damory, Hugh Audley, Roger Damory, and many others. Many of these men were former allies, but now they did all they could to destroy the power and possessions of the Despensers, who, like Gaveston before them, were hated almost beyond reason. War, which had been averted for so long by the tireless efforts of England's moderate barons and churchmen, had finally broken out. Edward, once again under the influence of unscrupulous men, had alienated two vastly powerful elements of his country, the northern lords around the earl of Lancaster and the marcher lords of the west.

In the year leading up to the rebellion, Edward had shown some convincing signs of a capacity for strong kingship. Peace had been made with Lancaster in August 1318, followed in October by a superb victory in the war with Scotland. Forces under the loyalist earl of Louth had defeated and killed Robert Bruce's brother Edward in Ireland, at the battle of Faughart. This was the most significant military victory of Edward's reign. It removed at a stroke the Bruce effort to throw the Plantagenets out of Ireland and revive a Scottish high kingship of Ireland. It suggested that there was hope in the Scottish wars at large.

Then, in 1320, the king had visited France to do homage to the new

French king, Philip V, for Ponthieu and Aquitaine. When it was suggested by the French that he pay personal fealty to his brother-in-law, a move that would have implied a far more subservient relationship than mere homage, Edward stood defiant and gave a vigorous impromptu speech defending the rights of his Crown. He told Philip and his councillors that homage between the kings was done "according to the forms of the peace treaties made between our ancestors, after the manner in which they did it. . . . [N]o one can reasonably ask us to do otherwise; and we certainly do not intend to do so." Edward's visible anger stunned the French delegation into silence.

Moreover, these successes came against a background of seemingly genuine attention to kingship on Edward's part. Queen Isabella had produced a second son, John of Eltham, in 1316, and another daughter, Eleanor of Woodstock, in 1318. Edward was attending to the succession. He was also said to be rising early, paying heed to parliamentary business, and showing clemency in judicial matters. Nevertheless, his rule had slipped into the pattern of domination by favorites. And this time the favorites were not frivolous and arrogant playmates like Piers Gaveston. They were conniving, grasping enemies of the realm.

The rise of the Despensers had been steady between 1317 and 1321. They had gradually been accruing power in Wales and the marches. Despenser the Younger's power base was made up of lands and castles in the lordship of Glamorgan, which included Cardiff, Llantrisant, and Caerphilly, and its fierce expansion had upset almost all the lords in the region. The Despensers—and foremost Hugh the Younger—used their proximity to the king to ride roughshod over other lords' landed rights, swooping on territory in the marches and consolidating their already substantial holdings there. This did not merely rile those who found themselves without recourse to royal justice against the Despensers. It offended the marcher lords in general, who saw the traditional laws of the march overridden by a king blatantly favoring one man's private interest over the traditional balance of power in the region. Additionally, the Despensers began playing gatekeeper to the king, controlling access to him by the rest of the barons. The chronicler Adam Murimuth wrote that no one could talk to Edward without Despenser the Younger's listening in and replying freely on his behalf. Those who crossed the Despensers were liable to be deprived of land or possessions or else thrown into prison.

In late 1320 the dowager countess of Gloucester died, and her lordship of Gower, which was ruled from Swansea, was contested among the earl of Hereford, Roger Mortimer of Wigmore, and another marcher lord, John de Mowbray. Edward moved to seize it into royal hands and granted it out to Despenser the Younger. This was an award that was viewed with the utmost hostility by a large band of the marcher lords, including Hereford, Audley, Damory, and Roger de Clifford. It also upset the two Roger Mortimers—of Chirk and of Wigmore—with whom lasting enmity already existed. (Edward I's ally, an earlier Roger Mortimer, had helped trap and kill an earlier Hugh Despenser at the battle of Evesham.) When they complained to the king, he rejected their complaints outright, and Despenser accused them of treason. In early 1321 the marcher lords took matters into their own hands and began the invasion of the Despenser estates. War had begun.

Between the violent anger of the marcher lords and the general simmering hostility of Lancaster, who in 1321 was building a coalition of northern lords against the king, it was clear that once again Edward had succeeded in uniting the greater part of England's political community against his rule. Even moderate barons like Bartholomew Badlesmere and (briefly) the earl of Pembroke inclined to the opposition's side. In August 1321 a parliament at Westminster drew up a list of accusations against both Despensers and demanded their exile from England by the end of the month. This was ordered on the authority of the earls and barons of the realm with the assent of parliament, an authority that the opposition barons claimed overrode a king's resistance. Queen Isabella, who had given birth to the couple's fourth child (a girl named Joanna) at the beginning of July 1321, begged Edward on her knees to give way for the sake of the realm. He did so, and the Despensers were sent away. But Edward did not capitulate happily. As he agreed to his wife's plea, he swore vehemently that within six months he "would make such an amend that the whole world would hear of it and tremble."

It was with an ominous reference to an ancient part of Plantagenet family history that Archbishop Reynolds of Canterbury summoned an emergency council to meet at St. Paul's, in London, on December 1, 1321. In the summons he sent to his fellow prelates he stressed the urgency of the cause. The realm, which had once rejoiced in the beauty of peace, he wrote, was now in danger of shipwreck through civil war.

Shipwreck. The same analogy had been used by chroniclers more than

180 years previously, when England was torn apart between a pair of cousins in a civil war that lasted for the better part of two decades. Then it had been King Stephen whose authority was challenged by his cousin the empress Matilda. Now it was King Edward who risked losing his authority and perhaps his whole kingdom to rebels represented by his cousin Thomas earl of Lancaster.

The younger Despenser's exile lasted a matter of weeks. At the beginning of October he was recalled to England, where he met the king on the south coast, between Portsmouth and Southampton. Edward then struck his first blow of the civil war by besieging his former ally Bartholomew Badlesmere's castle at Leeds, in Kent. The king took personal command of the siege, and Edward was therefore directly responsible for executing a number of Badlesmere's men and sending his wife and children to the Tower of London.

Edward was not without allies. Despite the Despensers' unpopularity, there were those who feared the consequences of making war on the king more than trying to accommodate him. Among the earls Edward was supported by his two young half brothers, Thomas Brotherton earl of Norfolk, and Edmund of Woodstock earl of Kent, as well as the earls of Pembroke, Richmond, Arundel, and Surrey. Edward also held the command of an elite fighting force of household knights.

The opposition, whose members became known as the contrariants, split along complex lines. They were led by marchers—Hereford, the two Roger Mortimers, Badlesmere, and the former favorites Damory and Audley—and acted with the limited support of the earl of Lancaster, who held off joining the war until January 1322. Despite their lack of unity, the war began well when they captured the border towns of Gloucester, Bridgnorth, and Worcester in the autumn and winter of 1321. But in early 1322 they were struck a damaging blow: the two Roger Mortimers, who were suffering defections from their armies and attacks from Welsh lords loyal to Edward, surrendered to the king and were sent to the Tower of London. This defection began a process of collapse among the coalition: in February Maurice de Berkeley and Hugh Audley the Elder also surrendered. Edward confiscated Berkeley Castle from Sir Maurice, a decision that would return to haunt him.

For all his political stupidity, Edward could be a crafty tactician. As he continued to pick off his opponents, he pushed the marchers deeper and deeper into a state of panic. Suddenly the opposition was scrambling. The earl of Hereford, Hugh Audley the Younger, and Roger Damory joined forces with the earl of Lancaster in late January 1322, but by that stage the military initiative lay with the Crown. Edward began attacking Lancaster's castles in February and successfully took a number of them, including the fortress at Kenilworth that had played an important role during the thirteenth-century wars against Simon de Montfort. Throughout the campaign Lancaster leaked vital and close supporters. At least ten of his retainers, either unwilling to fight against their king or else fearful of their fate should Lancaster be defeated, changed sides.

Although the marches and the north of England inclined against him, Edward drew valuable support throughout 1321 and 1322 from the native lords of Wales, particularly from Rhys ap Gruffudd and Gruffudd Llwyd. The Welsh lords faced more regular threats from the English marcher barons than they did from the king, and they saw their opportunity in allying with Edward's cause to win valuable territorial gains from their neighbors.

Along with the military campaign, Edward was able to launch a brilliant propaganda offensive. In February 1322 treasonable correspondence came to light, proving that Lancaster had been negotiating with the Scots to form an alliance against the English king. The earl's moral case now collapsed, along with his military defenses. Edward had the incriminating letters published all across the country. Orders were sent to the archbishops, bishops, and sheriffs, instructing them to read in public the letters that showed Lancaster's treason as he lobbied the Scots to invade England in order to further a personal quarrel with the king. It was a fatal blow. Ten days after the letters were published, Edward and the earls loyal to him declared Lancaster a traitor to the realm and ordered the earls of Kent and Surrey to capture Pontefract Castle.

As the contrariants' war crumbled around them, inside Pontefract Castle panic broke out. There was a furious debate among the barons on whether they should stay and hope to withstand a siege or attempt to escape north toward Scotland. Lancaster himself agreed to abandon his stronghold only when Roger de Clifford threatened him with a sword.

The end came at Boroughbridge, in Yorkshire. As Lancaster and his allies attempted to make their way to Northumberland, they were intercepted by Sir Andrew Harclay, the warden of Carlisle Castle. Harclay had an army of four thousand men, and they routed the Lancastrian force. The earl of Hereford was run through with a spear during the fighting; the other nobles, including Lancaster, evaded capture for a few days but were rounded up as they attempted to flee the region disguised as beggars.

On March 21 Lancaster was transferred from prison in York back to Pontefract Castle, which stood captured by royal forces. He was greeted on arrival by the king, who sneered and insulted him. Then, according to the author of *The Life of Edward II*, Lancaster was imprisoned in a tower he had had built in anticipation of one day capturing Edward.

The following morning he was brought from his cell and charged before a panel of justices that comprised Edward, the two Despensers, the loyal earls, and one professional judge. "[He was] charged one by one with his crimes, and for each charge a particular penalty was awarded," wrote the author of *The Life of Edward II*. Lancaster was sentenced to be hanged, drawn, and beheaded. In recognition of his royal blood, the hanging and drawing were suspended, but so was Lancaster's right to reply to the charges leveled against him. "This is a powerful court, and very great in authority, where no answer is heard nor mitigations admitted," spluttered the earl, as his fate was sealed. Without any delay, he was led from his own castle and beheaded. It took the axman two or three blows to sever the head from the body of the greatest nobleman to have been executed in England since the Norman invasion.

To some there was a righteous symmetry about his awful fate. "The earl of Lancaster had cut off Piers Gaveston's head, and now by the king's command the earl of Lancaster has lost his head," wrote the author of *The Life of Edward II*. "Thus perhaps not unjustly, the earl received like for like, for as it is written in Holy Scripture, 'for with the measure that you shall mete withal it shall be measured to you again.'"

But this was not symmetry. It was a grotesque escalation of the murderous politics of a dysfunctional reign. More barons and earls died violent deaths under Edward II than in the five reigns that preceded his. Lancaster had defied his cousin on countless occasions. He had murdered the king's favorite, made war upon him, and connived with his enemies. But he was still a royal earl. His condemnation and summary execution did not so much right the wrong of Gaveston's death as worsen the crisis of violence and political anarchy that had begun with it. The civil war may have been over, but it was still fair to say that England was shipwrecked.

The King's Tyranny

The parliament summoned to York in May 1322 was advertised as an opportunity for a "colloquium" and "tractatum," a chance for the king to discuss and treat with his country. Summonses were sent far and wide. The Cinque Ports were granted parliamentary representation for the first time in recognition of the fact that they had harbored the Despensers during their exile, while the principality of Wales was similarly rewarded for assisting in the fight against the marcher lords. Yet despite this new inclusiveness and the language of consultation and peacemaking, Edward used the parliament for one clear end: to reward and rehabilitate the Despensers and to formalize the destruction of the late earl of Lancaster's whole program of reform.

Edward's revenge on the contrariants was nearly merciless. The gibbet in York, visible to everyone who attended parliament, held the bloated corpses of John de Mowbray, Roger de Clifford, and Jocelin d'Eyville, all lords of considerable renown and wealth, who were hanged in chains the day after Lancaster died. On April 14 Bartholomew Badlesmere, the moderate baron who had been a prominent peacemaker earlier in Edward's reign, was viciously executed in Canterbury. He was dragged through the streets, hanged, and beheaded, and his head was placed above the entrance to the city known as the Burgate.

More executions followed. Twenty other men were killed for their part in the rebellion against Edward's rule. The horror of Edward's revenge shocked the country. Gibbets were erected in London, Windsor, Bristol, Cardiff, and Swansea. The bodies of executed men swung in chains, bloating and decaying, for more than two years. Everyone who entered a major town between 1322 and 1324 might have shuddered at the sight of once-great men butchered and hung up like hogs. It was not surprising that Roger of Wendover, the author of the *Flores Historiarum* chronicle, wrote that the king "hated all the magnates with such mad fury that he plotted the complete and permanent overthrow of all the great men of the realm."

Perhaps surprisingly under the circumstances, the two Roger Mortimers, the marcher lords who had been involved in the initial attacks on

Despenser property, were sentenced to death but had their sentences commuted to life imprisonment. Maurice de Berkeley and both Hugh Audley the Younger and the Elder—once loyal lords who had been driven away from the king by hatred of the Despensers—were also imprisoned rather than executed. The Tower of London heaved with wellborn prisoners, while contrariants' families were deprived of their lands and property or imprisoned in castles across England and Wales.

The parliament convened at York in May 1322 tore up almost all the restrictions that Lancaster and his allies had attempted to impose on the king since 1311. The ordinances were repealed, save six so-called Good Clauses that were reissued in the Statute of York. The legal processes that had been started against the Despensers prior to the civil war were halted, and Lancaster's extensive lands began to be taken into royal hands. Various other items of parliamentary business, concerning trade regulation and legal procedures, were discussed and referred to the royal council, but it was clear to all who gathered at York that these were matters incidental to the king's revenge on his enemies.

There was a limited program by which those contrariants who survived the bloodletting could buy back their estates at extortionate prices, but in the main Edward distributed the confiscated possessions to his followers. Andrew Harclay was raised to a new earldom of Carlisle for his part in capturing Lancaster. The loyal earls of Pembroke and Surrey were given manors and lands that either had been confiscated from them by Lancaster in 1318–1319 or else were taken from Lancaster's own estates. The earl of Arundel was given lands confiscated from Roger Mortimer of Chirk, as well as the latter's title of justice of Wales. The king's half brother Edmund earl of Kent gained castles in the Midlands and Wales, and Edward's younger son, John of Eltham, although only six years old in August 1322, was given the Lancastrian castle of Tutbury.

Most heavily rewarded, unsurprisingly, were the Despensers. The sixty-one-year-old Hugh the Elder was raised to the earldom of Winchester with five separate grants of land to support his new rank, including the valuable lordship of Denbigh, in North Wales, which had been stripped from Lancaster. Hugh the Younger meanwhile received virtually all the lands (albeit not the title) of the earldom of Gloucester. He was restored to all the estates in Wales—Glamorgan, Cantref Mawr, and Gower—that had been raided and taken from him in the civil war, and over the next two years these western landholdings were linked up by the award of lordships in Usk, Is Cennen, Brecon, Chepstow, and Pembroke. He was de facto lord of South Wales, vastly wealthy, with an income of perhaps five thousand pounds a year, and now the trustee of almost unfettered royal power in the west. After 1322 the two Despensers and Edward controlled between them perhaps three-quarters of Wales.

If the Despensers prospered, so too did the king. Tens of thousands of pounds of revenue from confiscated lands and fines paid by disgraced nobles now flowed directly into his chamber. The York parliament granted him taxation amounting to more than forty thousand pounds for a war with the Scots, but a botched invasion in August and September 1322, in which Queen Isabella was almost captured, was swiftly aborted in favor of a thirteen-year truce. More than half the money raised for defending the northern border went unspent, and the coin was sent in large barrels for safekeeping in the Tower of London. More followed from a clerical tax, also supposed to fund a Scottish war. The king took a close personal interest in collecting money, and his coffers filled accordingly. The author of the *Brut* chronicle reckoned Edward to be the richest king since William the Conqueror.

Emboldened by the security of his riches, Edward now became a tyrant. It seemed to the country that he governed in alliance with the Despensers; the chronicler Thomas de la More wrote afterward that under Edward and the Despensers, England had three kings at once. The younger Despenser dominated the highest reaches of the state, sending covering letters with documents sealed by the king, involving himself deeply in affairs of state, and spreading a network of retainers and followers throughout county government.

Cruelty was rife. When the Scottish invasion failed, casual vengeance was taken upon a man who had only months previously found himself high in royal favor: when Andrew Harclay, the newly ennobled earl of Carlisle, was discovered to have opened independent negotiations with Robert Bruce in early 1323, he was hanged, drawn, and quartered as a common traitor. The hero of Boroughbridge was dead within a month of his greatest act of loyalty.

All the king's enemies were vulnerable. The earl of Pembroke, who had been conspicuously loyal between his roles in Gaveston's death and the attacks on the Despensers of 1321, was forced to swear an oath of allegiance to the king, guaranteed by his life, his lands, and his goods. He was broken politically and would die in 1324. Meanwhile Lancaster's young widow, Alice de Lacy, had been imprisoned in York Castle along with her mother following the earl's death. The Despensers threatened both women with burning if they did not surrender their estates in exchange for empty honorific titles and a small cash pension. Hundreds of others were affected in this way. Meanwhile Hugh Despenser the Younger built himself a hall of regal magnificence at Caerphilly Castle, spending vast sums on master craftsmen and the finest materials. He reveled in his position as the king's most trusted adviser, and his hand appeared everywhere in government.

Under his influence the period between 1322 and 1326 was characterized by grotesque cruelty. "The king's harshness has indeed increased so much today that no one, however great or wise, dares to cross the king's will," wrote the author of *The Life of Edward II*. "Parliaments, consultations and councils decide nothing. . . . For the nobles of the realm, terrified by threats and the penalties inflicted on others, let the king's will have free rein. Thus today will conquers reason. For whatever pleases the king, though lacking in reason, has force of law."

Edward had defeated his enemies and enriched the Crown. But he had not done anything to strengthen his rule. Indeed, by wielding his office solely in his own and his favorites' interest, he was simply making his overlordship worthless to all those who could not gain access to his justice or protection from his law. For all the magnificence that accrued to him in victory, he was fatally undermining his own reign.

Mortimer, Isabella, and Prince Edward

On the night of August 1, 1323, the Tower of London came silently to life. The Tower was full of Edward's political prisoners, and chief among them were two men from the marches, Roger Mortimer of Chirk, by now in his mid-sixties, and his nephew Roger Mortimer of Wigmore, who was twenty-six. These onetime contrariants had been imprisoned since they had surrendered to the Crown. They had been tried and condemned to death. Both had thus far escaped execution, but with an unpredictable king in the grip of the Despensers, who bore the whole Mortimer dynasty a grudge, they could not hope to live for much longer.

The Mortimers had been helpless as their lands in Wales and the marches were parceled up and awarded to their enemies. But they were determined not to suffer indefinitely. During the months of their imprisonment the younger Mortimer crafted an escape plan. As darkness fell on the night of August 1, the deputy constable of the Tower, Gerard d'Alspaye, slipped a sleeping draft into the drinks of the constable and the Mortimers' guards. Then he hurried to Roger Mortimer of Wigmore's cell, unlocked the door, and led the knight through the castle kitchens and onto the Tower's southern wall.

Once at the top of the wall, the two men unfurled a rope ladder. It rolled quietly down against the sheer stone toward the river Thames, directly below them, where several coconspirators were waiting in a boat. Mortimer and d'Alspaye slid down the ladder, climbed into their escape vessel, rowed across to the south bank of the river, and escaped on horseback to the south coast of England. Mortimer put to sea at Porchester and within days had taken refuge in France.

It was a brilliantly realized escape, and it threw Edward's court into a state of paranoia. An inveterate opponent of the king had fled from what was supposed to be the most secure fortress in the realm. Rumors reached the royal household that this was part of a wider conspiracy to seize royal castles and even to send assassins to murder Edward and the Despensers. From the autumn of 1323 onward spies across the Continent began to send reports back of plots and invasion attempts involving Mortimer. A devastating chain of events had begun.

Mortimer was welcomed to France by a new king. Charles IV had succeeded his brother Philip V in January 1322, becoming the fifth ruler in the seven years since Philip IV had died in 1314. Like all new French kings, he was eager to show the kings of England that he regarded their claims to the duchy of Gascony with a suspicion that bordered on hostility. When a violent dispute broke out over a French bastide (fortified town) built on English territory at St.-Sardos, in the Agenais, Charles used the ensuing quarrel as a pretext for an invasion of Gascony. The earls of Kent and Pembroke were sent to protest and were dismissed haughtily. Charles wanted to discomfit the English as much as possible. In August 1324 he moved thousands of troops to the borders of the duchy and began to besiege its major towns. Almost in a blink, England and France were once again at war.

Back in England the outbreak of war put Edward in a painful bind that exposed precisely why his aggressive, divisive approach to kingship could only lead to ruin. He could not trust his own subjects to obey his rule, for other than a small band of handsomely rewarded favorites, he had never given them reason to do so. He could—and did—arrest all Frenchmen in England and confiscate all lands held by French citizens, including the queen. But when he began to make plans to lead an army to Gascony in person, he faced a dilemma. Were he to leave England with an invasion force he would have to take with him most of the officials and magnates who were still loyal to him and trust in the regency of his eleven-year-old son and heir, Edward earl of Chester. That would leave England highly vulnerable to plots, rebellions, and invasion. If he left the Despensers behind him to keep order, he risked losing them the way he had lost Gaveston. Furthermore, he feared rumors of Roger Mortimer's plotting on the Continent and imagined that either he or the Despensers could be kidnapped if they happened across Mortimer's agents overseas.

Rather than cross the Channel, Edward sent more envoys to negotiate for peace. In the first instance he sent an embassy led by the bishops of Winchester and Norwich, the earl of Richmond, and Henry de Beaumont. When this failed, a diplomat of altogether higher status was sent: Queen Isabella. Both her two eldest brothers had been crowned king of France: Charles IV was the third and last. She had long enjoyed close links with her family, despite her involvement in the Tour de Nesle scandal of 1314, in which Charles's wife, Blanche, had been imprisoned for adultery and her alleged lover beaten to death in public. If anyone could appeal to Charles to end his aggression, reasoned Edward and the Despensers, it was his sister.

It proved to be a fatal decision. Although she had been staunchly loyal to her husband during the convulsions of his reign, the queen had been rewarded with little more than the same humiliation that she had suffered as an adolescent, when she was sidelined by Gaveston at her own coronation. She had been made to suffer roundly when war broke out: her lands had been confiscated, her servants exiled or imprisoned, and her maintenance payments from the king reduced and diverted via the younger Despenser. (She had written furiously to her brother Charles, complaining that she was treated like a maidservant.) On top of that, Despenser's wife, Eleanor de Clare, was detailed to spy on Isabella's correspondence. The queen had borne all this with public dignity, but she was clearly simmering with rage. "The queen departed very joyfully," wrote the author of *The Life of Edward II*. She was "pleased in fact to visit her native land and her relatives, pleased to leave the company of some whom she did not like." This was something of an understatement. Isabella could not leave the Despensers and her weak, unpleasant husband quickly enough.

A joyful reunion between the English queen and her brother took place at the end of March, and Isabella made her ceremonial entry into Paris on April 1, 1325, dressed in a black riding habit, checkered black boots, and a golden headdress. Her negotiating skills proved no more successful than any other English diplomat's, but she did her duty and extended the fragile truce that held in Gascony. With her work done she ought to have returned to England, but Isabella had no such intention. She spent the summer of 1325 in France, touring her brother's properties and waiting for her husband to make his long-awaited journey to France to pay homage to the French king at Beauvais.

She waited and waited. But Edward would not and could not be tempted from England. He could neither leave his kingdom nor be separated from the Despensers. And the prospect, in any case, of a demeaning ceremony at which he had to humble himself before the younger French king was hardly appealing. In the end the two sides compromised. It was agreed that young Edward of Windsor should be sent in his father's place. He would be granted Ponthieu and Aquitaine in his own right and would then travel to France to pay homage to the king in person.

This solution looked good to Edward II. But it looked even better to Isabella. Her son, now twelve years old, having been appointed duke of Aquitaine by his father, arrived in mid-September 1325 and paid homage for his new lands in a ceremony at Vincennes. With the crisis satisfactorily ended, Isabella and her son were expected to make a prompt return to England. But they adamantly refused to return to the troubled kingdom. In late November Isabella wrote to her husband explaining with venom the hatred and contempt in which she held the Despensers and stating in bald terms her refusal to return. The author of *The Life of Edward II* reported the contents of her letter. "I feel that marriage is a joining of a man and woman holding fast to the practice of a life together," wrote Isabella. "[But] someone has come between my husband and myself and is trying to break the bond; I declare that I will not return until this intruder is removed, but discarding my marriage garment, shall put on the robes of widowhood and mourning until I am avenged of this Pharisee."

It is more likely here that the queen referred to Despenser the Younger's intrusion into the political dimension of her marriage, rather than complained about a sexual liaison between Edward and Despenser. In any case, Isabella stayed in France, with her brother's satisfied support, taunting the king of England, who had so abused her, and drawing around her a coalition of disaffected English nobles and prelates. True to her word, she wore the black robes of mourning and a veil over her face. It was a powerful political statement of the injustice she had suffered and the rotten condition of the country from which she had exiled herself.

In England Edward raged. He wrote furious letters to his wife and instructed all the leading bishops of England to do the same, telling Isabella that her absence roused fears of a French invasion of England and accusing her of wishing "to destroy a people so devoted to you for the hatred of one man." But Isabella's heart was unmoved. She held his heir, and she was protected by her brother, the king of France. And she was about to make her extraordinary position even more distressing to her husband. As 1325 drew to a close, Isabella committed what to Edward was the ultimate sacrilege: she allied herself with the fugitive Roger Mortimer of Wigmore.

Endgame

The crossing from the Low Countries to England was rough. Storms blew up around the fleet of ninety-five ships, and they were tossed by powerful winds and violent waves as they made the journey toward the Essex coastline. For two days the fleet was scattered, but around midday on September 24, 1326, it was in sight of shore. The fleet dropped anchor in the mouth of the Orwell, on the Suffolk coast, and unloaded its cargo in haste. As each vessel was emptied of its men, horses, and supplies, it put swiftly back to sea and returned to the Continent.

The army that landed in the small East Anglian port was small. At its center were seven hundred Dutch and German mercenaries. With them came a party of English exiles, who included noble veterans of the battle of Boroughbridge, refugees from the harsh royal revenge that followed, and a number of prominent magnates who had left England during the tyranny of the Despensers and never returned. They included the king's half brother Edmund earl of Kent and John of Brittany earl of Richmond, two men who had been almost unwaveringly loyal throughout Edward's reign but who now, at last, had joined the opposition.

The leaders of the invasion were Queen Isabella of England; Roger Mortimer of Wigmore; and the heir to the English throne, Edward earl of Chester and duke of Aquitaine. The exiles had finally returned to England. But they did not come in sorrow and humble apology. They came to rid the country of the king and his favorites forever.

Queen Isabella and Roger Mortimer made an odd and scandalous couple. They met around Christmas 1325, and within weeks Isabella had taken Mortimer as her lover. Shortly afterward the couple began to live together quite openly, and they had appeared in public as a couple by May 1326, when Mortimer carried Prince Edward's robes at the coronation of Charles IV's third wife, Jeanne d'Evreux. (Charles's first wife, Blanche of Burgundy, had been imprisoned for her alleged adultery in the Tour de Nesle affair, and her marriage had been annulled; his second wife, Marie of Luxembourg, had been killed in a carriage accident in 1324.) Edward II had heard about his wife's betrayal by February 1326, when he stated angrily: "[T]he queen will not come to the king, nor permit his son to return, and the king understands that she is adopting the counsel of the Mortimer, the king's notorious enemy and rebel." Edward put pressure on Pope John XXII to censure the French king for harboring an adulterous couple, and Charles, under threat of excommunication, was obliged to order Isabella and Mortimer to leave France. Mortimer spent his time on the Continent establishing a network of allies, and the couple found a safe haven in the county of Hainault, in the Low Countries, where the count was sweetened by the betrothal of the young Edward to his daughter Philippa.

The support of the Hainaults enabled Isabella and Mortimer to raise their invasion force. The paranoia of Edward II and the Despensers had allowed them to land in safety. England was on a defensive footing, but it was marshaled against the wrong invasion. Edward was convinced that Charles IV was going to invade the south coast from Normandy. He was mistaken. Charles had no such intention.

When news reached London that Isabella and Mortimer had landed on the east coast, Edward was dining in the Tower of London with the younger Despenser. He was dismayed. The size of the force reported in Suffolk— probably no more than fifteen hundred men in total—was tiny. But the king rightly concluded that this meant the bulk of his enemies were already inside England. "Alas, alas!" the *Brut* chronicle has him exclaim. "We be all betrayed, for certain with so little power she had never come to land but folk of this country have consented." Like King John before him, Edward's violent paranoia had bred real treachery.

As news of Isabella and Mortimer's arrival spread throughout England, supporters flocked to her side. The Anonimalle chronicler preserved an open letter written in French to the citizens of London, which proclaimed that the queen came "with good intent for the honor and profit of the Holy Church and of our very dear lord the King and to uphold and safeguard all the realm." She offered a reward to any citizen who could help her "destroy sir Hugh Despenser, our enemy and all the realm's, as well you know." Copies of the letter were fixed to windows, and the sealed original was pinned on the Eleanor cross at Cheapside in London, a highly symbolic location for a queen's propaganda. Isabella was claiming the inheritance of the old king and his beloved queen, and she found a willing audience.

The Londoners rose in revolt on October 15. They dragged John Marshal, a close ally of the younger Despenser, from his house and beheaded him on Cheapside, the great thoroughfare through London. The bishop of Exeter, a former royal treasurer, was discovered seeking sanctuary in the porch of St. Paul's. Although he rode in full armor, he was dragged from his horse as he neared the north gate of the cathedral and taken to Cheapside, where the mutilated and bloody body of Marshal lay prone on the ground. The bishop's armor was wrenched from his body, and his head was cut off with a bread knife. Two of his attendants were also murdered.

Anarchy reigned. Every supporter of the realm—whether bishop, earl, judge, or lowly servant—began to flee for his life. Members of Edward's favorite monastic order, the Dominicans, disappeared into hiding. Offices connected with the Despenser regime and those who served it were plundered, burned, and smashed. The plaque erected by Thomas earl of Lancaster to commemorate the 1311 ordinances was put up again in St. Paul's for the first time since the earl's death.

Meanwhile Isabella was moving west. Edward and the Despensers had fled the Tower of London almost as soon as they learned of her arrival and headed for their power base in Wales, which had stood firm during the civil war of 1321–1322. They sent word ahead to their old allies Rhys ap Gruffudd and Gruffudd Llwyd to raise troops for the cause. With almost thirty thousand pounds to his name, the king was certainly rich enough to pay a large army to defend him.

By late October Edward and the younger Despenser were in Chepstow, on the western bank of the Severn estuary, while the earl of Winchester (the elder Despenser) was barricaded in Bristol Castle. The queen and Mortimer gave steady pursuit and were at Gloucester by the time the bishop of Exeter's head arrived for Isabella's inspection. As they moved through England, magnates gathered to their side. The king's other half brother, Thomas of Brotherton earl of Norfolk, joined their company, as did Henry of Lancaster earl of Leicester, the younger brother of the late Thomas earl of Lancaster.

On October 18 Bristol Castle was besieged by Lancastrian forces. The earl of Winchester tried frantically to bargain for his life, but neither Mortimer nor Henry of Lancaster was in any mood to spare a Despenser. After eight days of siege their army stormed Bristol Castle, and Winchester was brought out in chains.

While Bristol Castle lay under siege, Edward and the younger Despenser decided that their best chance of survival lay in fleeing to Ireland. With a small party of men-at-arms, they boarded a ship at Chepstow. But the wind was against them. Desperate prayers from a friar brought no succor, and after five days spent battling the angry sea, the royal party was forced to put ashore at Cardiff and flee for the grandly rebuilt and supposedly impregnable Despenser castle at Caerphilly.

As they were doing so, Isabella and Mortimer issued a statement at Bristol arguing that inasmuch as the king had left the realm, his son Edward should take control of government. The statement, preserved on the Close Rolls, cited the assent of prelates and barons, including the archbishop of Dublin, the bishops of Winchester, Ely, Lincoln, Hereford, and Norwich, the king's two half brothers, Henry of Lancaster, "and other barons and knights then at Bristol."

According to the statement, Duke Edward was chosen to lead the country "with the assent of the whole community of the realm there present . . . that the said duke and keeper should rule and govern the realm in the name and right of the king his father." The king was stripped of his authority, and it was given, albeit temporarily, to a fourteen-year-old boy entirely under the sway of the queen and her lover. He assumed his responsibilities on October 26.

The following day the elder Despenser was brought before a court headed by Sir William Trussel and deliberately styled on that which had convicted Thomas earl of Lancaster. He was charged with robbery, treason, and crimes against the Church and told that because in convicting Lancaster, he had constituted a court that did not recognize a defendant's right to reply, he would be treated in the same way. The cycle of quasi-judicial violence continued: Despenser was hanged, drawn, quartered, and beheaded on the public scaffold at Bristol. His head was sent to Winchester to be displayed in public.

To all around Edward it was clear that the game was up. Despenser's tenants in his Welsh lands bore him no love and refused to turn out to defend him. On October 31 the king's household deserted, leaving Edward and his favorite with a few retainers to protect them.

The king's actions grew increasingly panicked and desperate. He might have remained in Caerphilly a long time, for the castle was stoutly defended and well stocked. He had vast reserves of cash and jewels, as well as the great seal, the privy seal, and other appurtenances of government. But in early November Edward and Despenser left for the Cistercian abbeys at

Margam and Neath. At Neath they discovered that a manhunt was under way, led by Henry of Lancaster and a group of barons seeking personal revenge for wrongs they or their families had suffered during or since the civil war. The king, Despenser, and the royal chancellor, Robert Baldock, attempted to flee, probably along a high mountain path, toward the castle of Llantrisant. On the road they encountered the search party, which eventually captured the king and his remaining adherents as they cowered in a wood.

On November 24 the whole population of the town of Hereford assembled in the market square. Before them sat a now-familiar form of court, headed by Sir William Trussel, the man who had sent the elder Despenser earl of Winchester to the gallows less than a month previously. Before the court stood Hugh Despenser the Younger, a disheveled and sorry shadow of the man who had ruled England through the king. He had been brought to the town earlier in the day to the sound of drums and trumpets.

A large crowd had gathered to see the fallen favorite arrive, and they bayed and cheered as he approached on horseback, a crown of nettles on his head to symbolize his crime of accroaching royal power and his arms reversed on his tunic to proclaim his treachery. The front of his tunic bore a Latin verse from the New Testament: *Quid gloriaris in malicia qui potens est in iniquitate?* (Why do you glory in malice, you who are mighty in iniquity?) For almost a week before his transfer to Hereford the captive had been attempting to starve himself to death. But he was allowed no such easy fate. The crowd dragged him to the ground, stripped off his clothes, and scrawled biblical slogans on his skin. Then he was hauled before the court.

It was certain that the defendant would die and that he would die without the right to speak in his own favor. The earl of Arundel had been beheaded in Hereford a week previously, and there was no question that the king's favorite would join him in that fate.

Despenser's crimes were read out to the court. The list was exhaustingly long and included breaking the terms of exile, breaching the Magna Carta and the ordinances of 1311, killing, imprisoning, and tyrannizing the great and good of the realm, causing the king to fight in Scotland at the cost of thousands of men's lives, usurping royal authority, and attempting to fund the destruction of Queen Isabella and her son Duke Edward while they were in France. Sir William, sitting in judgment, condemned Despenser to the full and hideous death of a robber, traitor, and tyrant. He was to be hanged, drawn, and quartered, his entrails were to be burned before him, and he would be beheaded. "Go to meet your fate, traitor, tyrant, renegade," thundered Trussel. "Go to receive your justice, traitor, evil man, criminal!"

Along with his associate Simon de Reading, who had been tried alongside him, Despenser was roped to four horses and dragged through the streets of Hereford to the walls of the castle. There both men had nooses placed around their necks, and Despenser was hoisted onto a specially made fifty-foot gallows, designed to make punishment visible to everyone in the town. A fire burned beneath the scaffold, and it was here that Despenser's genitals were thrown after the executioner scaled a ladder and hacked them off with a knife. He was then drawn: his intestines and heart were cut out and also hurled down into the flames. Finally, his body was lowered back to the ground and butchered. The crowd whooped with joy as his head was cut off, to be sent to London, while his body was quartered for distribution about the country.

This was the fate of the most notorious traitor in England, another baron slaughtered in the orgy of violence that had engulfed the realm since Edward's accession. But what of the king himself? What to do with Edward was a vexing question.

Twenty disastrous years had demonstrated to all that the king was incapable of leading the country competently. Yet nearly 175 years of Plantagenet rule had been based on an evolving partnership between kings and the community of the realm. Kings had been threatened with deposition— John, Henry III, and Edward I had all been warned that they might be deprived of their thrones in moments of crisis—but the reality was quite different. The whole basis of English law and governance, which for the most part operated efficiently and to the advantage of the majority of English subjects, rested on an authority that stemmed ultimately from the Crown. The king was counseled by his advisers, and he consulted parliaments over matters of taxation and war; but he remained the source of all public authority and, in a properly functioning realm, the bulwark against anarchy. Who had the right to depose him and declare another man king? Who could speak for this higher authority? If the realm unilaterally deposed—or worse, killed—the king, was it not killing itself? What hope was there of order in a state where a king who upset a faction of his kingdom might be summarily removed?

These were all, to some degree, unanswerable questions. Yet everyone agreed on the practical reality: Edward had to be removed from power. To bolster the case against him, Isabella and Mortimer's propaganda machine ground into action. Adam Orleton bishop of Hereford was active in preaching that Isabella and her son had returned to England because the king and Despenser were sodomites and tyrants. The first charge is unknowable, but the second was undeniable. From this point on Edward's reputation as a degenerate homosexual began to run wild throughout contemporary chronicles.

As soon as the Christmas celebrations had finished, parliament assembled at Westminster to decide the king's fate. The queen could not even visit her husband in his prison at Kenilworth Castle, where he was held over Christmas 1326. Bishop Orleton reported that if Edward saw his wife, he was liable to kill her. Words later attributed to Orleton (although he denied them) were that Edward "carried a knife in his hose to kill Queen Isabella, and that if he had no other weapon he would crush her with his teeth." Edward utterly refused to travel from Kenilworth and engage with the proceedings, probably reasoning that without him present the parliament would lack legitimacy. But this was another misjudgment, and business carried on without him. The bishop of Hereford addressed parliament on January 12 and asked the assembly whether Edward II should continue as king or be replaced by his son. By the evening it was decided that he should be replaced, and a series of articles of accusation was drawn up.

The following day Roger Mortimer stood up in Westminster Hall and told the assembled prelates and lay nobles that the magnates collectively wished for the inadequate king to be removed from the realm. Westminster then heard sermons from the leading bishops of the realm, giving ecclesiastical weight to the decision that had been taken. The bishop of Hereford preached upon the text of Proverbs 11:14 ("Where there is no governor the people shall fall"). The bishop of Winchester used the phrase *Caput meum doleo* (My head hurts) to argue that an evil head spread evil throughout the body of the kingdom. Finally, the archbishop of Canterbury gave a sermon in French, using the popular medieval aphorism *Vox populi, vox dei* (The voice of the people is the voice of God). When he had finished telling the assembly that God had heard their prayers for a remedy to the evils of Edward's reign, he introduced the fourteen-year-old boy, Edward duke of Aquitaine, who was to be the new king. "Glory, laud and honor" was sung.

Later in the day oaths were sworn at the Guildhall to protect and uphold the honor of Queen Isabella and her son who would be king.

All that now remained was to convince Edward himself to concur with the wishes of the community of the realm and voluntarily relinquish his office. To that end, a delegation of twenty-four worthy men was sent to Kenilworth to confront him.

Henry of Lancaster and the bishops of Winchester and Lincoln were sent ahead of the rest of the group, and on January 20 they met the king and told him that his time had passed. Edward resisted. The chronicler Geoffrey Baker says that he was told that failure to abdicate in favor of his son would mean deposition. A new, non-Plantagenet king would be elected, and his entire bloodline, not merely his own person, would be removed from kingship. A tearful argument followed, and by the time the twenty-one remaining representatives of the realm arrived, Edward was so grief-stricken that he had to be held on his feet by Lancaster and the bishop of Winchester.

On January 24, 1327, London woke to proclamations that Edward had "of his own good will and with the common assent of the prelates, earls and barons, and other nobles and of all the commonalty of the realm, re-signed the government of the realm." A new king had been appointed. Edward duke of Aquitaine had become King Edward III, and the old king was reduced once more to Edward of Caernarfon. Sir William Trussel, the hanging judge of the invasion, had formally withdrawn homage on behalf of all the kingdom. Oaths were sworn to the new king. Any voices of dissent were momentarily drowned out by the clamor of the revolutionaries.

False Dawn

The boy king Edward III was crowned at Westminster on February 1, in a ceremony arranged at unprecedented speed. Royal authority had collapsed to a woeful condition under his father; the immediate priority for the new king and his minders was to reestablish it. Fortunately, since most of England's political community was in London at the end of January, it proved relatively simple to assemble them at Westminster at short notice to see Edward, along with three of Roger Mortimer's sons, knighted by the thirty-six-year-old Henry of Lancaster, brother of the late earl. Then, on the day of the coronation itself, Westminster Abbey filled with magnates and prelates to watch Archbishop Reynolds of Canterbury lower the large, heavy crown of Edward the Confessor, fitted with extra padding to ensure it did not topple off at some critical, ill-omened moment, onto the head of the fourteen-year-old king.

Edward swore the same coronation oath that Edward II had taken in 1307, including the novel fourth vow that his father had so conspicuously failed to observe: that he would "hold and preserve the laws and righteous customs *which the community of the realm shall have chosen.*" The new reign was then celebrated with a feast in Westminster Hall of wilder extravagance and luxury than would be seen again for another half century. The hall glittered with priceless cloth and precious plate. The royal throne was hung on every side with cloth of gold. The celebratory atmosphere served as a much-needed counterpoint to the miserable, bloody events of the previous year, and there was no mistaking the political message: the old king might have fallen, but the Crown itself remained supreme and magnificent.

Yet kingship was palpably not recovered. At fourteen Edward had reached the age of discretion, but he was not fit to rule in his own right. This presented an ambiguous state of affairs: a king too old to be a mere figurehead but not yet old enough to take the reins of power in both hands. Although he took control of his own household from March 1327, the real business of government very quickly fell to Queen Isabella, who controlled influence and access to her son, and Roger Mortimer, who performed a similar role toward the queen. It would not be very long before they too had perverted the principles of the royal office they were supposed to protect.

The first task of the new regime was to rehabilitate the outcasts of the previous reign. A parliament assembled the day after the coronation reversed the sentences of treason that had been passed on Thomas earl of Lancaster and his allies in 1322 and allowed for the proper inheritance of the family estates and titles, which were largely awarded to Henry of Lancaster. Mortimer was restored to his lands and titles and began an aggressive pursuit of other marcher territories, beginning with those belonging to his uncle Roger Mortimer of Chirk, who had recently died. None of this was very unusual, for Mortimer, like Henry of Lancaster, was fully entitled to reclaim what had been unfairly taken from him by Edward II and the Despensers. Yet there were signs very early that Isabella and Mortimer had just as grasping a mind-set as their forerunners.

Before Edward's coronation, during the chaotic bloodletting that preceded her husband's abdication, Queen Isabella had resumed all the lands of her dowry, worth some forty-five hundred pounds. When her son was crowned, she was awarded further estates, taking her landed income to twenty thousand marks, making her a greater landowner than any other magnate in England. This massive accumulation of wealth, combined with her access to the large stockpiles of treasure that had been amassed by her husband and the Despensers, rattled onlookers.

Of more immediate concern, however, was the queen's involvement in foreign politics. Here three urgent issues pressed the new government. Peace with Isabella's brother Charles IV of France had to be formalized, to protect the disputed borders of the beleaguered Aquitanian territories. Scotland required a show of force to subdue its impertinent natives, some of whom had led a successful assault on the English-held castle at Norham on February 1, the very day that Edward was crowned. Finally, Edward needed a bride, through whom to sire a new generation of princes.

Failure greeted almost every move. The terms of the Treaty of Paris, hastily agreed upon with the French Crown, reached the king in Lincolnshire in mid-April, and it was clear that they were designed not only to humiliate him but also to cripple his realm financially. English possessions in southwestern France were reduced to the Gascon coast between Bordeaux and Bayonne. Everything else would be controlled directly by the French king. The cost to Edward for retaining this tiny sliver of the former Planta-genet empire was a punitive bill of fifty thousand marks. It seems that Isa-bella and Mortimer recognized just how high a price they were being made to pay for peace because the detailed terms of the treaty were suppressed on the English side of the Channel. This represented a helpless acquiescence, an acceptance that England was too mired in internal discord to contem-plate reconquest in France.

When Charles died in 1328 without a direct heir, minimal effort was made to turn the situation to England's advantage. Although Edward was one of the three surviving grandsons of Philip IV and thus had a claim to the French Crown, only token protests were made when Charles's cousin Philip of Valois was crowned Philip VI, following a strictly male line of succession. (This later became known as Salic law.) Edward, whose claim to the French Crown was transmitted by his mother, traveled to Amiens in 1329 to pay homage to the new king for the rump of Aquitaine and the county of Ponthieu. This was hardly a sign that the English were prepared to use his dynastic claim as a bargaining lever for greater security in his Continental lands.

In Scotland things fared worse. Border raids continued from February into the summer, with bands of Scots crossing into northern England to burn and plunder as they pleased. At the same time as the terms of the Treaty of Paris were put before a disappointed Edward III in Lincolnshire, royal orders were heading north for an old-fashioned feudal muster of troops at Newcastle-upon-Tyne and York.

Edward and his mother traveled in late May to York, where they met with a band of five hundred Flemish knights under Isabella's Continental ally John of Hainault. This elite fighting unit made itself immediately un-popular with the citizens of England's second city by fighting with the En-glish troops, rampaging in violent disorder through the streets of York. Despite this unpromising beginning, Edward left Isabella in York in early July and set out for the Scottish border, aiming to meet the enemy, amassed under the veteran commander Sir James Douglas, and bring them to battle. The mission was a disaster: Douglas spent several weeks dodging his En-glish pursuers before abruptly changing tack at the end of the month. He fell upon the royal camp near Stanhope Park near Durham, scattering the king's attendants, and, according to one chronicle, rode to the middle of the royal encampment, "always crying 'Douglas!' and stroke asunder two or three cords of the King's tent." Several days later Douglas took his rampaging troops on a final retreat back into Scotland.

Edward was said by several chroniclers to have been so enraged at his own failure that he wept in fury. Well might he have done: the campaign ran through funds so quickly that the crown jewels had to be pawned to keep the English government solvent. By the Treaty of Edinburgh-Northampton (so called because it was sealed in Edinburgh by Robert Bruce in early 1328 and subsequently ratified by an English parliament held in May at Northampton), Mortimer and Isabella accepted that they could not afford to wage a war in the north. They settled with the Scots, disgracefully giving up England's claim to overlordship in Scotland for a paltry twenty thousand pounds. Scotland was recognized as a sovereign kingdom, ruled over by Bruce and his heirs and constrained by the border as it had been in Alexander III's time. Edward's six-year-old sister, Joanna, was betrothed and swiftly married to Bruce's infant son, David. This did little to obscure the fact that everything the English had fought for since Edward I's glorious war had begun in 1295 was forfeited in a stroke.

Edward's wedding at least was more certain. The alliance made with the count of Hainault before Isabella and Mortimer's invasion was honored, and the young Philippa of Hainault—born sometime between 1310 and 1315, so approximately Edward's own age—was brought over to London in late 1327. The couple were married at York Minster on January 26, 1328, in an opulent, gold-trimmed ceremony designed to demonstrate as surely to Edward's northern subjects as his coronation had shown his southern ones that royal power was not in decline. (That such magnificence could be afforded against a background of war-weary penury was thanks to the Plantagenets' generous Italian bankers, the Bardi family. The Bardis would learn their lesson some years later, when Edward's repeated defaults on his loans ruined them, a financial catastrophe that began the rise of the Medici family in Italy.) Marriage was one area of foreign diplomacy in which Isabella and Mortimer succeeded, although Isabella's wish to exercise the powers of queen consort meant that she would not allow the girl's coronation for nearly two years. Yet Edward's wedding came against the background of strange events closer to home.

During the night hours of September 23, 1327, the young king was woken in his chamber at Lincoln and told that his father was dead. Since

April, Edward of Caernarfon had been imprisoned in a dungeon in Berkeley Castle, Gloucestershire, and it was there that he had died two days previously, according to the messengers, from natural causes. Since the young king was pressingly engaged with parliamentary business related to the Scottish situation, plans to bury the old king were made for December. At the time of Edward's death very few people questioned the cause. Edward III certainly seems to have accepted that his father had died in unexceptional circumstances and organized a funeral for him. But as the years passed, a number of descriptions of Edward of Caernarfon's death circulated, beginning to suggest that there had been foul play. At first the king was said to have died from grief or illness or in some sort of pain. Soon, though, talk turned to the presumption of murder.

Three times during Edward of Caernarfon's imprisonment plots had been uncovered to release him from captivity: once in April, while he was imprisoned at Kenilworth, and twice, in July and September, during his captivity at Berkeley. The first two plots involved Dominican friars, but the third involved men from Wales, the most prominent among them Rhys ap Gruffudd, a longtime ally of Edward II, who had come to his assistance in 1321 and 1322 and been with him during his final flight in 1326. It began to be rumored that these repeated escape attempts had exhausted the patience of Isabella and Mortimer, and eventually Mortimer had ordered that the old king be slain in his cell. In October 1330 it was stated before parliament that Edward had been murdered. Two decades after Edward's death the well-informed chronicler Adam of Murimuth wrote that the king had been killed by a trick and that Roger Mortimer had had him suffocated.

As news of Edward's death spread and suspicions of murder strengthened, the supposed cause of death grew more extreme. A tradition grew up that he had been strangled before suffering the agonizing fate of internal burning, with a red-hot poker inserted via a "trumpet" device placed in his rectum. This has become the standard account of Edward's death because as its originators probably intended, there is a ghastly poetic symbolism in the emasculated, decadent, possibly homosexual king being buggered to death. It is almost certainly untrue. Nevertheless, it seems most likely that Edward was indeed murdered and that it happened on the orders of Roger Mortimer. The murderers were probably Mortimer's allies William Ogle and Sir Thomas Gurney, acting in alliance with the steward of the royal household, Sir John Maltravers, who was personally responsible for Edward's custody.

In any case, Edward of Caernarfon was buried on December 20, 1327. He was not buried with his grandfather and father next to the Confessor's tomb in the Plantagenet mausoleum at Westminster Abbey. Rather, he was interred at St. Peter's Abbey, in Gloucester, where Henry III had been crowned as a nine-year-old boy during the civil war of 1217. Perhaps it was appropriate that the only other royal figure to have been buried there was Robert Curthose, son of William the Conqueror, a man who might have been a king of England but who had instead been imprisoned for nearly thirty years at Devizes and Cardiff by his brother Henry I. Edward was buried in the underclothes he had worn at his ill-fated coronation in 1308, and he had the distinction of bearing on his tomb the first-ever royal effigy to be used in England, a tradition that continued for centuries after his death. If it was not quite a great royal farewell, it was still a surprisingly dignified end for a king who had besmirched the English royal line and suffered the most damning verdict imaginable in the articles of accusation published by his enemies in January 1327. These had described him as "incompetent to govern in person . . . controlled and governed by others who have given him evil counsel," and unwilling "to listen to good counsel nor to adopt it nor give himself to the good government of his realm." Eleven months on from his deposition all remained acutely aware that Edward II had "stripped his realm, and done all that he could to ruin his realm and his people, and what is worse, by his cruelty and lack of character he has shown himself incorrigible without hope of amendment, which things are so notorious that they cannot be denied."

But was the regime that had succeeded him really any better? The answer, more and more, appeared to be no. Concerns with Isabella and Mortimer's control over the young king went beyond their influence in foreign policy. At home their behavior increasingly seemed to mirror the acquisitive excess that had blighted the previous reign. By 1330 they had gone even further, and England plunged once more into the depths of murderous villainy.

As Mortimer grew confident in the queen's support, he soon found that he was as unable as a Gaveston or a Despenser to resist using his proximity to royal prerogative to enrich himself. He steadily accumulated territories throughout Wales and the marches, many of which had been confiscated from the traitors of 1326. At a series of tournaments held around England, Mortimer presided above Edward III in quasi-kingly fashion, holding Round Tables and parading himself as King Arthur, a nod to his Welsh ancestry. He reveled in his role as consort to the king's mother, and in a parliament held at Salisbury in 1328 he succeeded in his final ascent to the upper ranks of the nobility when he was awarded the extraordinary and novel title of earl of March.

So soon after the Despenser fiasco, this was wildly disruptive. On his watch England had suffered humiliation on two fronts of war and diplomacy; the king's young wife was still uncrowned; judicial "commissions of trailbaston" (brigandage courts), which had been sent out into the shires to deal with widespread violence and disorder, had collapsed; and the Crown, despite the treasure that had been inherited from the old king and the vast loans taken from the Bardi bank, was perilously close to bankruptcy. Yet the new earl of March was enriching himself to the point where he resembled another king. As disillusion grew with the new regime, England began to split once more into warring factions. Henry earl of Lancaster led the opposition, which by January 1329 threatened to turn to outright warfare. Suggestions sped around that the king, through his failure to take good counsel and govern reasonably, was in breach of both the Magna Carta and his coronation oath. War seemed so probable that a new set of armor was commissioned for Edward. Throughout almost the whole of 1329 the seventeen-year-old king was kept away from Westminster and London, prevented from taking command of government himself, coddled like a child by his rapacious mother and her lover.

Full civil war was mercifully avoided, but by the spring of 1330 Edward could be nannied no more. Philippa of Hainault was pregnant, a fact that demanded her coronation at Westminster Abbey in February. Simultaneously, very worrying rumors reached the ears of the court. It had begun to be said that Edward of Caernarfon, buried in Gloucester more than two years previously, was alive and at large. Stories of Edward II's supposed survival remain in currency to this day, active particularly in a tradition that has the former king escaping captivity and living out his days as a hermit in Italy. That they are unconvincing is neither here nor there; in 1330 the notion that the old king might return was a frightening prospect that haunted everyone who had been complicit in his abdication.

It is possible that one source of the rumors was the man responsible for the king's death. By 1330 the earl of March was more unpopular than ever before. It seemed highly likely that the French were about to annex what remained of Aquitaine, and Mortimer had made himself gravely unpopular by attempting arbitrarily to seize funds for the defense of Gascony from local communities and individual lords. He had many bitter enemies, not least Henry earl of Lancaster, but also the king's half uncles, Thomas earl of Norfolk and Edmund earl of Kent. While both had professed their loyalty to the Crown, Mortimer saw them as threatening to his own position as protector and governor of the king's person.

At the end of a parliament held in Winchester in March 1330, at which funds for the defense of Gascony were under urgent discussion, Mortimer launched an attack on the earl of Kent. As parliament was breaking up, Kent was suddenly arrested for treason and accused of plotting to make contact with his (supposedly living) half brother Edward II at Corfe Castle. The earl was dragged before a court set up hastily under Mortimer's presidency. He was charged with treason, incriminating letters were produced, and he was duly found guilty. He was summarily disinherited, his wife and children were sentenced to imprisonment in Salisbury Castle, and Kent himself was sentenced to death outside the walls of Winchester Castle. It was a mark of the savage, terrifying nature of Mortimer's decision that for some time no one could be found to execute the sentence. Eventually another prisoner at Winchester, responsible for cleaning the latrines, was given his freedom in exchange for hacking off poor Kent's head. Yet another earl had gone to his death—and this one of royal blood. Edmund was a son of Edward I and thus an even greater casualty than Thomas of Lancaster had been.

As parliament broke up and the king headed to Woodstock to join his wife for the birth of their first child—a boy named Edward, born on June 15—he was distraught. He had wished to pardon Kent but had been overridden by Mortimer. Edward III was a husband, a father, and a king, but another man ruled his realm, slept with his mother, and murdered his kin as he saw fit. The kingdom, beggared by his father, was approaching the point of total dissolution under Mortimer's cruel and greedy tyranny. Three disastrous years of misgovernment had brought as much calamity upon England as had been seen under the old king. The time had come for action. Edward III—desperate, daring, and not without courage—began to plot the recapture of his Crown. A bright new age of kingship was about to dawn.

PART VI

Age of Glory
(1330–1360)

Long live, therefore, the young Edward, and may he himself embody the virtues that enriched each of his forefathers separately. May he follow the industry of King Henry II, the well-known valour of King Richard, may he reach the age of King Henry [III], revive the wisdom of King Edward [I] and remind us of the physical strength and comeliness of his father.

—*The Life of Edward II*, on the birth of Edward III

Royal Coup

The plotters moved as quietly as they could through a secret underground passage deep in the bowels of Nottingham Castle. There were at least sixteen and perhaps more than twenty of them, heavily armed, mostly young men, loyal to their king and desperate for their own lives. Above them, the castle was settling down for the night, emptied of the day's visitors, who had returned to their lodgings in the town outside. The only sounds in the tunnel would have been stifled breath, the dull clank of moving armor, and the crackle of torchlight.

They were acting on urgent royal orders. Earlier in the day five of the conspirators in the tunnel and the seventeen-year-old king himself had been hauled before a suspicious panel headed by Roger Mortimer earl of March, the queen's lover, who had been controlling the government of England for three years. Spies had informed Mortimer that a group of men around the young king were planning an attempt on his life. All had strenuously denied it. All had left their interrogation knowing that they had to act.

The leader was William Montagu, twenty-nine years old, a knight-banneret in Edward III's household and a friend of the king's. He had accompanied Edward on recent business in France and had just returned from the papal curia at Avignon, where he had been sent to relay secret messages to Pope John XXII. Montagu was a soldier, a loyalist, a royal friend—just as his father had been to Edward II. He feared that the king's life was in jeopardy from Mortimer and had told the king that day that immediate action was essential. "It is better to eat dog than to be eaten by the dog," he had told the king, and Edward had heeded his advice, giving his assent to a plan that was destined either to be a suicide mission or to rescue the Crown.

Alongside Montagu crept four more of Edward's household companions: Edward Bohun, Robert Ufford, and William Clinton, also bannerets, and John Neville of Hornby, a household knight. These were brave men, ready to risk their lives for their lord on a violent, dangerous mission. Key to the mission was a sixth man, William Eland, "speculator" of Nottingham

Castle. A speculator was probably a watchman, in which case Eland knew the corridors and passageways of the fortress better than any man alive.

The tunnel through which Montagu and his men now stole was the only route into a castle to which Mortimer held the keys; the earl left them under the queen's pillow at night. The tunnel linked the riverbank outside with Queen Isabella's apartment at the heart of the castle. Eland had flouted his duties on October 19, 1330, and left unlocked the postern gate in the tunnel. Now he used his inside knowledge to guide the men through the darkness.

Nottingham Castle was rotten with treachery. Within the castle, coconspirators, including Edward's personal physician, Pancio de Controne, supplied alibis for the king to absent himself for the evening and may even have helped unlock the door that joined the secret passage to the castle keep. Eland and Montagu must have prayed, as they led their men up the spiral staircase from deep underground to the heart of the royal quarters, that their plot would not have been foiled by the time they reached the final door. If Mortimer had cracked any one of their allies, he might already have sent soldiers into the tunnel behind them. Death and ruin would await.

In the queen's hall, Isabella sat in conference with Mortimer, his two sons Geoffrey and Edmund, Simon Bereford, Sir Hugh Turpington, and Henry Burghersh bishop of Lincoln, discussing the best way to proceed against the men who, unbeknownst to them, had now left the tunnel and entered the castle keep, and were advancing on the meeting room with deadly intent.

As Montagu and his men burst into the apartment complex, they encountered Turpington, the steward of the household, who was ultimately responsible for the security that had now been breached. John Neville attacked and killed him. The noise drew the startled attention of those few household esquires posted as guards at the doorway of the hall. As the plotters burst in, they cut down two of the guards where they stood.

Mortimer ran, aiming for his chamber to collect his sword. But he and two of his advisers were captured and arrested, and the earl of March was deliberately kept alive to be tried as a traitor. Both of Mortimer's sons, as well as Simon Bereford, were also taken prisoner. According to the *Brut* chronicler, Bishop Burghersh forgot his ecclesiastical dignity completely. He made a bid to flee by running to the lavatory and trying to throw himself down the chute that evacuated human waste to the moat outside. As Montagu's men gave chase and eventually hauled the bishop from his squalid bolt-hole, Queen Isabella stood by the door of the hall, wailing into the darkness, calling for her son, who she believed was lurking behind the plotters.

By these dramatic means, the seventeen-year-old Edward III threw off his shackles and took personal control of the government. The day after the coup a declaration made to the sheriffs of England informed them that Roger Mortimer earl of March had been arrested and that Edward would "henceforth govern his people according to right and reason, as befits his royal dignity, and that the affairs that concern him and the estate of the realm shall be directed by the common counsel of the magnates of the realm and in no other wise."

After his arrest Mortimer was imprisoned and prepared for a grand trial before a parliament that met in Westminster Hall in November 1330. Bound, gagged, and humiliated, he was brought before the assembled peers of the realm. He was accused, according to the official parliamentary record, of having "usurped by himself royal power and the government of the realm concerning the estate of the king" and of having used his servant John Wray "to spy on [Edward's] actions and his words; so that, in such a way, our said lord the king was surrounded by his enemies so that he was unable to do as he wished, so that he was like a man living in custody." The long list of charges (Mortimer was accused of fourteen separate crimes) included alienating royal lands with the creation of his earldom, making war upon the earl of Lancaster and his allies, framing the earl of Kent for treason, and siphoning off royal funds, including the fee paid by the Scots for peace.

Most important, however, Mortimer was explicitly accused of Edward II's murder. "The said Roger by the royal power usurped by him ... ordained that [the old king] be sent to Berkeley Castle where he was traitorously, feloniously and falsely murdered and killed by him and his followers," reads the record. This was the first time that it was officially stated that Edward II had been murdered, and it was enough for Mortimer to be "drawn and hanged as a traitor and an enemy of the king and of the realm." In keeping with all the other noble killings that had taken place, Mortimer was not allowed to speak in his own defense. But with his traitor's death at Tyburn, on November 29, 1330, a gruesome chapter was closed.

Isabella, for her part, was not ill-treated. As the king's mother she was simply removed from power and pensioned off. She spent the next twenty-seven years of her life in magnificence and luxury at Castle Rising in

Norfolk, playing an important diplomatic role for the Crown and participating in her son's increasingly lavish ceremonial feasts and family celebrations.

With his daring sponsorship of a dramatic coup and a decisive seizure of power at the approach of his eighteenth birthday, Edward III gave promising signs that he had the character and capability to restore some sense of normality and order to a badly diminished realm. And indeed he did so. He showed early on a pattern of behavior that would underpin everything his kingship stood for: he identified a problem and took radical, even reckless action to solve it, aided by a close group of trusted supporters. This would prove to be an effective, intoxicating form of kingship. But it took many years of difficulty before Edward was recognized for what he was, perhaps the greatest of all the Plantagenet kings.

Glorious King of a Beggared Kingdom

In the aftermath of the Nottingham coup Edward was lauded throughout his land. He turned eighteen years old in November 1330 and was at last in sole command of his Crown and his destiny. His personal badge was the sunburst—rays of golden sunshine exploding from behind a thick cloud—and this was the impression that the young king wished his subjects to take as he stepped out from the cramping grasp of his mother's lover to rule the kingdom as his own man. The new king offered light, courage, and hope.

He marked the beginning of his reign with a series of tournaments, mainly held around London and the southeast. Here he presented himself at once as a knightly king, his court a center of revelry and fun, romance and martial competition. "This king led a gay life in jousts and tournaments and entertaining ladies," wrote the northern chronicler Sir Thomas Gray. Tournaments became a near-monthly feature of his reign, each one an occasion for the great men and women of the realm to dress up in splendid costumes, acting out roles as fierce animals, mythical beasts, and heavenly beings, rehearsing great stories from history and legend, and cavorting about dressed mischievously as friars, merchants, or priests. Large and keenly fought mock battles that took place both bonded the aristocrats who fought in them and provided valuable training for a time that was to be dominated, once more, by real warfare.

The king at the center of it all was a vigorous, athletic, enterprising young man. Most representations of him show a slightly delicate face, with a long, slender nose beneath wide, deep-set eyes and a flat brow. He had a high forehead and, in keeping with the times, wore throughout his adult life a long beard, described as "berry-brown" by a poem written in the mid-1350s. Thick, wavy hair hid his ears and stood out from beneath the fine hat or commander's helmet that he almost invariably wore. He was an exceptional horseman and a redoubtable warrior as well as a paragon of chivalric magnificence. He and Queen Philippa had a taste for the finest clothes, embroidered with slogans and quasi-cryptic royal sayings. Some of Edward's favorite mottoes later in his life included "It is as it is," "Hay hay the wythe swan/By Godes soule I am thy man," and "Syker as ye wodebynd"

(Strong as the woodbine). Queen Philippa's slogans included "Ich wynde-muth" (I wind myself [around you]) and "Myn biddeneye" (My bidding). The coin struck to commemorate Edward's coronation had featured a slogan that captured the king's lifelong confidence and ease in his own office: "I did not take; I received."

Outward show and pageantry were an essential skill for any king, but Edward had a better intuition for it than any of his predecessors—excepting only Henry III. He imported the finest gold cloth from the Far East, and his robes were decorated with exotic animals: leopards, tigers, pelicans, and falcons. He loved music, and as his court traveled, it rang with minstrels singing, drums and lutes filling the air with sound—the king at the heart of it all, laughing with joy at the spectacle he created. He kept a menagerie that included lions, leopards, a bear, and various apes and monkeys. He was as avid a huntsman as any king before him; of his forebears only Henry II could have matched the thrill Edward got from thundering on horseback through his parks, forests, and the English countryside, chasing down wild animals to shed their blood. The thousands of pounds he spent on sumptuous costumes and lavish entertainment for himself, his friends, and his family combined to create a vision of royal power that was worthy of celebration. In tune with his personal knack for charming the ladies of the court and striking up close, brotherly friendships with the men, Edward began from the earliest days of his personal reign to bind the noblemen and knights of England—the political class with whom all successful kings would cultivate a natural amity—to his rule.

Edward III was a conventionally educated young aristocrat, versed in the spheres of knowledge and culture that fitted his position. He spoke both English and the courtly language of northern France. Brought up surrounded by scholars such as Richard Bury (an Oxford scholar and churchman who turned government administrator and became one of the king's closest advisers), he had absorbed what they had taught him and was literate beyond the simple standard of being able to read in Latin and French: he was the first English king to leave us examples of his handwriting. He took his instruction on kingship from a variety of classic texts on governance known as the mirrors for princes—books by European scholars analyzing the great achievements and ignoble failures of rulers modern and ancient, which were designed to reveal sound principles of leadership to their readers.

Edward had been fascinated from his youth by the great heroes of history and mythology, and he was especially taken with a popular fourteenth-century literary staple, the lives of the Nine Worthies. (These consisted of three "good pagans"—Hector, Alexander the Great, and Julius Caesar—three great biblical kings—Joshua, David, and Judas Maccabaeus—and three great Christian kings—Arthur, Charlemagne, and Godfrey of Bouillon, the first king of Jerusalem.) He consciously studied the lives of kings and would try to imbue his own reign with their best qualities, while avoiding their failures. He was fascinated by the providential quality of history, with its ability both to foreshadow the events of his own life and to set the conditions for the lives of his descendants. His contemporaries, excited by the dash of his Nottingham coup, were eager to see him as fulfilling the prophecies of Merlin, and Edward did not discourage them, visiting Glastonbury in 1331 and inspecting the great tomb of Arthur and Guinevere, which his grandfather had commissioned. Indeed, of all his Plantagenet ancestors, Edward III reserved special veneration for Edward I, sending gold cloth to Westminster to deck his tomb, sharing his tastes for Arthuriana, and ensuring that the anniversary of the death of the Hammer of the Scots was never neglected. The leopard—Edward I's pejorative nickname during his youth—now became a symbol of Edward III's kingship, in its heraldic form of the lion *passant gardant*.

For all his finery, Edward understood that kingship was, more than at any time before, a sacred bond between king and realm. At some tournaments he liked to fight incognito, disguised as an ordinary warrior and competing shoulder to shoulder with his contemporaries and companions. In his taste for the legends of Arthur, he was careful not to emulate Roger Mortimer's arrogant assumption of the legendary king's role. During the 1330s Edward preferred to identify himself as one of the simple knights of the Round Table—most frequently Sir Lionel. Mortimer had been the first to assign him this role when at a tournament held in 1329 at Wigmore he had presented the king with a cup bearing Sir Lionel's arms. That Edward persisted in playing Sir Lionel, wearing the same arms at the tournaments he held throughout the 1330s and christening his third son, born in Antwerp in 1338, by the fabled knight's name, was a sign that he had not forgotten the values of enterprise and endeavor that had led him to overthrow Mortimer's rule. It was also, perhaps, a wry joke.

For the first seven years that followed the start of his reign proper in

1330, Edward got to know his realm. The near-ceaseless tourneying drew him close to the political community on both a symbolic and a social level. A fruitful marriage to Queen Philippa, which had produced the young prince Edward of Woodstock in 1330, yielded more children at regular intervals: Isabella of Woodstock was born in May 1332, Joan of the Tower in late 1333, William of Hatfield (who died young) in December 1336, and Lionel of Antwerp in 1338. But for all the young king's lusty grandeur, England was beset by troubles. The first three decades of the fourteenth century had been ruinous to the state of the realm and to public order. The Great Famine of 1315–1322 had caused widespread misery and death, and the turbulent politics that had dogged Edward II's reign from his coronation to his death had set the stage for lawlessness to thrive. In the Midlands the Folville gang, a corrupt gentry family from Leicestershire, took to large-scale violence and spoliation, murdering their political enemies with impunity and even taking traveling judges hostage. A similar gang, known as the Cotterils, operated in the Peak District. Various attempts at sending judicial commissions into the shires to restore calm and royal law had met with resistance and collapsed under the strain of endemic abuses of local power.

In response, Edward showed himself open to radical experiments with judicial reform. The itinerant system of the eyres—slow-moving traveling county courts whose circuits might take seven years or more—was outdated and unwieldy. Instead, Edward listened in the parliament of March 1332 as the chief justice, Sir Geoffrey Scrope, led a debate on reforming law and order. The system that eventually emerged was one in which permanent royal offices were created in the counties to regulate criminal disorder. The role of keeper of the peace (the predecessor of justice of the peace) sprang from this reform, and it was to these officials—backed by ad hoc royal commissions to deal with special cases such as those of the Folvilles and Cotterils, commissions of oyer and terminer (hear and judge), and sporadic local visitations of the Court of King's Bench—that the business of local peacekeeping would fall for the rest of the century. The system of English justice was institutionalized further than ever; no king would ever again ride as King John once had, sitting as judge where he chose and executing the judicial role of the Crown in person. Yet if the king as judge was fading away, the king as military captain was an idea that Edward determined should be stronger than ever.

His first target was Ireland. Not for 120 years, since John's expedition in

1210, had an English king set foot in Ireland; but violent disorder was rife, and the authority of the English king over the Anglo-Norman settler barons had crumbled almost to nothing. During the summer of 1332 plans were drawn up to send a massive invasion force across the Irish Sea to reestablish royal rule. Just at the point of readiness, however, they had to be abandoned. On August 11, 1332, at Dupplin Moor, near Perth, in Scotland, armies supporting the new Scottish king, Robert Bruce's son, David II (Edward's brother-in-law by marriage), clashed with rebel forces known as the Disinherited. These rebels were made up of Scots who had lost all they had at Bannockburn. They fought under John Balliol's son Edward and were supported by Edward's friend and ally Henry Beaumont, a grizzled veteran of every major Scottish battle since Falkirk in 1298.

The tiny army of the Disinherited, which may have been only fifteen hundred strong, a tenth of the size of the Bruce forces, won a stunning victory, killing numerous Scottish knights and earls. Balliol was proclaimed king at Scone on September 24, and Scotland sank again into utter disarray. Edward III abandoned his plans to invade Ireland and turned his attention to the northern border. At a parliament held in York in January 1333 he announced his intention to invade Scotland, shattering the truce established by the Treaty of Edinburgh-Northampton and reinvigorating the war for mastery that had stuttered so badly since the death of Edward I.

Between 1333 and 1337 the capital of England became York, as Edward took the whole machine of government north to let him focus on the war. His army combined household troops, feudally summoned nobles with their knights, and foreign mercenaries, including the Hainaulters who had fought during Isabella and Mortimer's ill-starred campaign. Regular soldiers were raised by array—a form of press gang by which conscripted men were paid a day wage once they set foot outside their home counties—and included hobelars (light cavalry), infantry that fought with spears and knives, and archers who rode on horseback before dismounting to fight. Mounted archers were to become the most tactically effective and dangerous element of English medieval armies, and during the course of his reign Edward was to rely on them as his elite units, raising their status in the army well above the rest of the rank and file. If they were not quite equal to the aristocratic cavalry, mounted archers nevertheless became some of the most respected and feared warriors in Europe during the fourteenth century. They, and the rest of Edward's armies, were fed and maintained in the field by the purveyance taken throughout the whole realm, a source of perennial grievance for English subjects.

Edward's campaign began in the spring of 1333. Throughout the summer his captains—among them William Montagu, Henry Percy, and Henry earl of Lancaster's son Henry of Grosmont, barons all roughly of the king's age and generation—assisted Edward Balliol in raiding across the border. Then the English laid siege to Berwick, before meeting the Scots in battle at Halidon Hill, two miles away.

The tactics used at Halidon Hill were those developed by Henry Beaumont at Dupplin Moor, and they were to serve Edward well during the course of his reign. Although his army was perhaps only half the size of that of the Scots, Edward took up strong defensive positions on the hill, with three divisions of dismounted men-at-arms, each flanked by dismounted archers. The king commanded the central division, Edward Balliol led the left, and the king's uncle the earl of Norfolk led the right, with the king's younger brother John of Eltham earl of Cornwall beside him. There would be no cavalry charges at the Scottish schiltroms; Bannockburn had taught the English that these were suicidal tactics. Rather, as the massed bands of Scottish spearmen advanced up the hill, the English bowmen loosed a vicious hail of arrows upon them, causing panic and terror, and scattering much of the Scottish advance before it even reached the men-at-arms. By the time hand-to-hand combat was joined the Scots were already tired and terrified. Edward and his men attacked the enemy bravely, and the king fought hand to hand against Robert Stewart, the seventeen-year-old grandson of Robert Bruce, who was steward of Scotland. The battle very swiftly became a rout, with Edward's and Balliol's men remounting their horses and chasing the shattered Scots from the field. By the time the battle was over, there had been another bloody slaughter of the finest Scottish nobles and knights, including six earls, whom the king had buried with chivalrous propriety.

Edward's victory at Halidon Hill was so complete that he was able to put Edward Balliol on the throne, reclaim Berwick for the English, and lay claim to large tracts of territory in the Scottish Lowlands. He spent the second half of 1333 back in the southeast of England, hunting and holding tournaments. Early in 1334 Balliol agreed to return Scotland to full dominion status, making the Scottish Crown once again a dependency of the English. It seemed almost indecently easy.

Of course it was not. Since 1326 Scotland had been in alliance with France, and by June 1334, when Edward Balliol performed liege homage to Edward in Newcastle, it was known that the French king, Philip VI, had snatched the deposed king David II and his wife, Joanna, from Scotland and given them sanctuary in Normandy, where they were ensconced in Château Gaillard, Richard the Lionheart's great fortress. In David's absence, Scottish resistance rallied under young Robert Stewart and John Randolph, the earl of Moray. Much of the winter of 1334 and the summer of 1335 Edward spent marching an army around the Lowlands in a violent, destructive tour of terror. This was repeated in July 1336 in the Highlands, where he burnished his chivalric legend by rescuing a group of ladies held prisoner at Lochindorb Castle. There was precious little chivalry to the rest of the brutal campaign, which was only marred for the English by the death from illness of Edward's younger brother John of Eltham in September. Edward's tactics—bloody rampages around enemy countryside, burning, looting, and killing with no greater strategic purpose than to demoralize enemy civilians—were exported to the Continent in later years, earning English soldiers a reputation as some of the fiercest in Christendom.

For all the terror inflicted on the Scots, however, a settlement did not emerge. Edward and his friends—particularly Henry of Grosmont, who was showing himself to be a robust and vigorous captain—were learning the business of war, but they could not compel the Scots to love a Balliol king by slaughter alone. At the heart of the problem lay the alliance between the rebellious Scots and the king of France. For Philip VI, Plantagenet actions in Scotland were bound tightly to the status of Plantagenet dominions in Aquitaine. As long as the English refused to accept full French sovereignty over Gascony, Philip would support the Scots in their own struggle for independence. By 1337 Edward had lost some of his interest in burning Scotland into submission. At the heart of his approach to kingship lay a desire to tackle problems directly and energetically. The problem in 1337 was no longer Scotland. It was France. A new theater of war tugged at him, irresistibly. The greatest conflict of the Plantagenet years was about to begin.

New Earls, New Enemies

When parliament met in March 1337, a hum of excitement and agitation settled over Westminster. There were reasons to be excited. Radical legislation was to be introduced to the country. A reform of the wool trade was planned. War loomed on two fronts. But more exciting than any of this, at least to observers of the parliament and lovers of the pageantry and show of Plantagenet kingship, was the impending creation of six new peers of the realm. Edward III had been king for a decade. He had ruled in his own right for seven of those years, during which time he had shown himself to be a willing friend to the aristocracy. At great tournaments he held, he had grown familiar with the wealthy fighting elite of the country, and it was to these sorts of men that he felt naturally closest.

There had been a general decline in the state of the aristocracy during the previous two generations. Edward I had been distrustful of nobility in general and correspondingly stingy with earldoms. His suspicions of the rights of nobles were never more obvious than in the Quo Warranto inquiries, when his justices quizzed the barons of the realm about their right to wield powers and jurisdictions that might be deemed to belong to the Crown itself. Edward II had been more inventive and liberal with the great landed titles, but he tended to save his key awards as gifts for his immediate favorites, rather than create families of great men who he feared would rival his authority. Edward II had made Gaveston earl of Cornwall, Andrew Harclay earl of Carlisle, Hugh Despenser earl of Winchester, and his half brothers earls of Norfolk and Kent; but of all these, only the earl of Norfolk lived past 1330. John of Eltham, who had been created earl of Cornwall in 1328, had died on campaign in Scotland and now lay at rest in Westminster Abbey.

Unlike his grandfather or father, Edward III believed that there was naturally a community, not a conflict, of interest between a king and his great subjects. At the March 1337 parliament Edward laid out this philosophy in clear terms. He told his assembled lords that "among the marks of royalty we consider it to be the chief that, through a due distribution of positions, dignities and offices, it is buttressed by wise counsels and fortified by mighty powers." Because England had seen a lessening in its pool of noble families headed by formidable earls and barons, he argued, "the realm has long suffered a serious decline in names, honours and ranks of dignity."

Edward announced to the realm that he was taking decisive action to establish a new generation of English nobles, with whom he could share both the prestige and the burdens of kingship. They all were men who had proved their service to him over the ten years of his reign and in several cases had been at his side since that daring raid on Nottingham Castle. Here were the natural boon companions of an ambitious young king, and they would soon be pressed into action alongside him.

Six earls were created in parliament. First among them was William Montagu, leader of the 1330 coup. Since that famous October day Montagu had been demonstrating to the king that he was both a valuable diplomat and a brave soldier in the wars against Scotland, during which he had lost an eye. He had already been rewarded with much booty, patronage, and land grants, but now Montagu was raised to the rank of earl of Salisbury.

His leading coconspirators from 1330 were similarly rewarded. Robert Ufford became earl of Suffolk, and William Clinton was made earl of Huntingdon, a title that had once been held by the Scottish kings. Meanwhile the scions of England's greatest families were given titles to reflect their status. Henry of Grosmont became earl of Derby. William Bohun, another veteran of 1330 and the Scottish wars, became earl of Northampton. Hugh Audley, a long-serving soldier and an early opponent of Roger Mortimer's, was awarded the earldom of Gloucester.

Edward and Philippa's eldest son, Edward of Woodstock, was a healthy six years old in March 1337. From Tudor times he became known by the title of the Black Prince for his (supposedly) black armor and diabolical soldierly reputation. In 1337, however, he was given a new title to reflect his importance as the heir to the throne of England. Edward III made him duke of Cornwall, the first time that the French title *duc* had been translated to England and a recognition that the status of the greatest royal earldom now had special, familial status. This was both a rapid regranting of the late John of Eltham's title and an implicit statement that never again would a lowly nobody like Gaveston hold so great a royal title.

A magnificent feast, at which hundreds of pounds were spent on food and entertainment, was given to celebrate the new peers. Twenty knights were also created, and everyone rejoiced in style, with separate courts held by Edward and Philippa.

This unprecedented creation of landed magnates was no fit of idle generosity on Edward's part. Rather, the situation in 1337 demanded it. The king needed military supporters with resources, mighty households, and an obligation to the Crown to fight. Not only was Scotland perpetually turbulent, but war with France was once again looming. This time, however, the terms and the stakes had escalated, and the personalities arrayed on either side were the most intractable, aggressive, and well matched since Richard I had faced off against Philip Augustus at the end of the twelfth century. The Plantagenet world was on the brink of a war that would last not merely for months or years but for generations.

The Hundred Years War Begins

On January 26, 1340, Edward III entered the Flemish city of Ghent with his entire household accompanying him, including his heavily pregnant queen, who was carrying the couple's sixth child in ten years. (The boy who was born on March 6 was John of Gaunt, his name an English variant on the name of the town.) A huge ceremony had been prepared for the king's arrival, and the large open square of the Friday market was being lavishly decorated in expectation of a large crowd. A platform was set up in the middle of the square, and all around it hung banners displaying Edward's royal coat of arms, but these were not the arms with which bystanders would have been familiar.

For 142 years, since the penultimate year of Richard the Lionheart's reign, Plantagenet kings had depicted their English sovereignty through three lions *passant gardant*—commonly known in heraldry as leopards—against a bright red field. Now there was something radically different about the royal arms. Rather than striding proudly across the whole coat of arms, the leopards had been quartered with the ancient arms of the French Crown, golden fleurs-de-lis against a blue field. Moreover, the French fleurs-de-lis took pride of place, displayed in the upper-left and lower-right corners of the coat of arms. It was a stunning alteration to a generations-old heraldic device. And it left in no doubt the message Edward was about to deliver to the crowd that assembled in the market square.

Edward walked out onto the stage and stood flanked by the great men of his court and the magistrates of the three most important towns of Flanders. Raising his voice to shout over the hubbub of the crowd, he called on the townspeople of Ghent to recognize him as the king not only of England but also of France. He demanded their obedience and took homage from various Flemings, including Guy of Flanders, half brother of the count. Edward reassured all those before him that he would respect their liberties and protect their mercantile rights. Then he gave the day over to a typically Edwardian celebration, a jousting contest.

This event, held in the packed marketplace of Ghent, marked the most profound reimagining of the Plantagenet Crown since Edward I had determined to make himself a modern-day Arthur. Edward's formal assumption of the royal titles and style of the king of France fundamentally changed relations between the two kingdoms in a way that had not been achieved even under Henry II. It also sparked an exhausting, seemingly endless period of hostility between the two realms that became known as the Hundred Years War.

The roots of the war can be found deep and tangled in the fabric of Plantagenet history and the politics of the fourteenth century. The traditional focus of disagreement between the French and English kings was a running dispute over the English kings' status as dukes of Aquitaine. This had been a cause of friction since 1259, when Henry III had agreed to the Treaty of Paris, doing homage to Louis IX for the duchy and abandoning the family claims to Normandy, Anjou, and the rest of the empire.

English and French interests had clashed repeatedly all across northwestern Europe over the course of the fourteenth century, and the French Crown was entering a new stage of aggressive expansion. French kings were determined to establish their rights, expand their borders, and spread the reach of their political power in a way that had not been attempted since the days of Philip II. This brought France into direct competition with English interests in trade battles in the Low Countries; in the matter of Scotland, which had been allied with France since 1295; and over control of shipping routes and trade in the Channel, where the English sent wool (and later cloth) across the sea passages to Flanders and brought wines back from Bordeaux. But beneath all these sources of mutual aggravation lay a more fundamental alteration in the status of the two crowns.

In France the death of Charles IV in 1328 and the accession of Philip VI had brought to an end the direct line that had reigned since the accession of Hugh Capet in 987, throwing open a new age of dynastic uncertainty in the kingdom. The young Edward's visit to Amiens to pay homage for his Continental possessions had suggested acceptance of Philip's claim and the principle that descent followed Salic law. Thanks to the violent politics that blighted the beginning of Edward's reign, his claim to the dual inheritance of France and England had been passed over with barely a whimper.

By the time Mortimer and Isabella had been removed from power, Philip was established as king of France, and it seemed beyond the means of the young king Edward to start demanding a revision to the French succession, not least because every campaigning season between 1333 and 1337 was taken up by expeditions to Scotland. Instead of hostilities, there had been cautious diplomacy between the two Crowns. Exploratory talks were held over a new crusade in 1332, but Philip's decision to support David Bruce in 1334 was unacceptably provocative.

Yet Philip was not alone in harboring fugitives. In 1334 Edward had given his protection to Robert of Artois, an aging but valiant fugitive from French justice, luckless enough to have slipped from being Philip VI's closest adviser and greatest friend to being his bitterest enemy. Robert was offered generous sanctuary by Edward, who valued his knightly bonhomie and military prowess, but in doing so he roused the infernal ire of the French king and nobility. A Flemish propaganda poem of the mid-1340s known as "The Vows of the Heron" blamed Robert for starting the war when he accused Edward of cowardice for failing to claim his rightful inheritance.

The poem claimed that at a decadent, amorous banquet Robert approached the king and presented him with a roasted heron, caught that day by his falcon. "I believe I have caught the most cowardly bird," the poet had Robert tell the king and his courtiers. "When it sees its shadow it is terrified. It cries out and screams as if being put to death. . . . It is my intention to give the heron to the most cowardly one who lives or has ever lived: that is Edward Louis [i.e., Edward III], disinherited of the noble land of France of which he was the rightful heir; but his heart fails him and because of his cowardice he will die without it."

Edward's immediate response, in the poem, was to swear oaths to "cross the sea, my subjects with me . . . set the country ablaze and . . . await my mortal enemy, Philip of Valois, who wears the fleur-de-lis. . . . I renounce him, you can be sure of that, for I will make war on him by word and deed."

"The Vows of the Heron" is pure propaganda, intended to paint Robert of Artois as a devious provocateur and Edward as a blustering, licentious aggressor. It graphically evokes the willing belief among its audience that these things were so. And indeed, it was Edward's harboring of Robert of Artois that provided Philip with his casus belli. In December 1336 Philip had sent envoys to Gascony to demand Robert's extradition. The request was refused, and within a year Edward had sent envoys to Paris to "Philip of Valois who calls himself king of France." The diplomats renounced the English king's homage; Philip's predictable and immediate response was formally to confiscate Ponthieu and Gascony. War had begun.

When Edward stood on the stage in Ghent in 1340, England and France had already theoretically been at war for three years. Much of this had been a phony conflict, as both sides maneuvered for allies and position. Edward had concentrated his war efforts on the Low Countries, where he paid the count of Hainault, the duke of Brabant, and other allies tens of thousands of pounds in bribes to form a grand alliance against the French king. This was a conventional, expensive tactic that Edward bolstered by purchasing the title of imperial vicar-general from the emperor Ludwig IV of Germany, a title that gave him full imperial rights over the lords of the Low Countries. The only significant fighting that had interrupted this costly diplomacy was in autumn 1339, when Edward brought an army to northern France to fight a vicious campaign in the border territories of the Cambrésis and the Vermandois. Philip meanwhile had sent troops deep into Gascony, advancing as far south as Bordeaux.

But these were preliminary skirmishes. The war escalated in 1340, when Edward made his formal claim to the French throne. This was to be something more than the traditional Anglo-French war. Granted, the struggle was still in essence that between a French king insistent on his rights and a Plantagenet lord of Aquitaine jockeying to offer as little deference as possible. English tactics followed a familiar pattern: bribing lords and princes in Flanders and on the eastern French border to create a military alliance in the north, while preparing an invasion force to campaign in the south. But by activating his dynastic claim to the French throne, Edward was about to change the whole terms of engagement between the French and English royal houses.

By October 1337 Edward had begun styling himself king of France and England in letters; three years later he made his claim explicit and public in the ceremony at Ghent. This was no longer just a war between lord and vassal. It was to be framed as a war of succession, in which only one man could be left standing.

Edward at Sea

As dusk approached on the evening of June 24, 1340, six months after he had declared himself king of the better part of Western Europe, Edward stood aboard his flagship, the cog *Thomas*, a large merchant-style vessel with a single square sail, and watched the sea offshore from Sluys, in Flanders, churn with the blood of tens of thousands of Frenchmen. He was wounded in the leg, but the injury was worth the pain. A fierce battle raged before him between the 213 French and Genoese ships of Philip VI's Great Army of the Sea and around 120 and 160 English sails, which had left East Anglia under Edward's own personal command two days previously. The English were murderously, brilliantly winning.

Edward had crossed the Channel to put an army ashore in Flanders. It was a desperate action dictated by extreme circumstance. Two months earlier his friends and allies the earls of Salisbury and Suffolk had been captured while fighting outside the town of Lille. Flanders was overrun by the French, and Queen Philippa had been taken hostage in Ghent. The Channel was patrolled by French ships that threatened to ruin the English wool trade, and for two years the southern coast of England had been plagued by French pirates, who had reduced the town of Southampton to little more than a smoldering shell.

Edward had been planning a large military invasion for some months. Inevitably, word of the preparations had reached Philip, and a huge French fleet, detailed to blockade the ports and prevent the English army from landing, had been gathered from the coasts of Normandy and Picardy. Now, looking toward the coast, Edward saw that the French were ordered in a tight position, their vessels anchored and chained together in three lines across the mouth of the river Zwin.

After a night spent anchored within sight of the intimidating masts and armored prows of the French fleet, Edward had directed his ships to approach the mouth of the Zwin at around 3:00 P.M. They came up from the southwest, with the sun and the wind behind them. As he moved into view, he must have felt a pang of anxiety, even fear. He was about to fight one of the largest naval forces ever assembled in the Channel. Failure would mean utter ruin.

In the first line stood some of the largest ships ever launched into the Channel, cogs carrying hundreds of men with crossbows bristling, including the *Christopher*, a giant ship stolen from the English some months earlier. Behind them bobbed the smaller ships; in the third line were merchant boats and the royal galleys.

The English attacking force at Sluys had sailed to France against the pleas and warnings of Edward III's ministers, led by Archbishop Stratford of Canterbury, who had warned him that the size of the French fleet meant certain death and destruction to the smaller English armada. Edward, stubborn and determined, had set out from the mouth of the river Orwell, leaving his advisers stung by a harsh rebuke: "[T]hose who are afraid can stay at home."

A medieval sea battle was much like a land battle. There was little maneuver or pursuit. When two navies came together, it was a collision, followed by boarding and a desperate, bloody fight at close quarters. Although some large weapons like catapults and giant crossbows were carried on board, by and large it was bolts and arrows and the violent smash of men-at-arms' maces and clubs that did the damage. "This great naval battle was so fearful," wrote the chronicler Geoffrey Baker, "that he would have been a fool who dared to watch it even from a distance."

The French, commanded by Hugues Quiéret and Nicolas Béhuchet, were undone by their decision to shackle their ships together in three ranks across the mouth of the Zwin, thereby sacrificing all mobility for what seemed like the security of close ranks. The two rows of vessels behind the front line were barred from fighting by the ships in front of them, and as the English attacked, the French found it impossible to evade a head-on assault.

The air filled with the blast of trumpets, the throb of drums, the fizz of arrows, and the splintering sound of huge ships smashing into one another. The English fleet attacked the French in waves. Each ship rammed into an enemy vessel, attaching itself with hooks and grappling irons as English archers and French crossbowmen traded hailstorms of vicious arrows and bolts. The bowmen took up high vantage points, either on the raised endcastles of the boat or on the masts, and when they had killed enough of the defenders, men-at-arms clambered aboard the enemy ship to mete out death and destruction at close quarters.

The French were trapped and slaughtered. "It was indeed a bloody and murderous battle," wrote Jean Froissart, the French poet and chronicler, whose account of the Hundred Years War was one of the great works of contemporary history in the fourteenth century. Froissart noted that "sea fights are always fiercer than fights on land because retreat and flight are impossible. Each man is obliged to hazard his life and hope for success, relying on his own personal bravery and skill." Between sixteen thousand and eighteen thousand French and Genoese were killed, either cut down on deck or drowned. Both French commanders died: Quiéret was killed as his ship was boarded, and Béhuchet was hanged from the mast of his ship.

The battle of Sluys was one of the greatest early naval victories in English history. The English and their Flemish allies cheered and celebrated the victory in disbelief. Almost the entire French fleet had been captured or destroyed, eliminating at a stroke much of the danger to English merchant ships in the Channel and Philip's ability to blockade the Continental coastline. The death toll alone on the French side was shocking. The English monastic chronicler Thomas of Burton wrote that "for three days after the battle in all the water of the Zwin . . . there seemed to be more blood than water. And there were so many dead and drowned French and Normans there that it was said, ridiculing them, that if God had given the fish the power of speech after they had devoured so many of the dead, they would thereafter have spoken fluent French."

Centuries later the Elizabethans and Jacobeans thought of Sluys as a historical precursor to the Spanish Armada. The sixteenth-century writer of the play *Edward III* (likely cowritten by Shakespeare, although the following passage is not thought to be his) imagined the aftermath thus:

> Purple the sea, whose channel filled as fast
> With streaming gore, that from the maimed fell,
> As did her gushing moisture break into
> The crannied cleftures of the through shot planks.
> Here flew a head, disseevered from the trunk,
> There mangled arms and legs were tossed aloft,
> As when a whirlwind takes the summer dust
> And scatters it in middle of the air.

Thus the battle of Sluys was later immortalized in English maritime history. But at the time it was only one victory amid a tide of discontent.

After three years of fighting, Edward's war with France had put greater strain on English government and royal finance than any military project since the Third Crusade. Sluys was a great victory, no doubt, but it came at great cost.

Edward's war was conceived on the grandest possible scale. The Lanercost chronicler estimated payments to Flemish and German allies from 1337 to 1340 at "one thousand marks a day, according to others, two thousand." This was an exaggeration—but not a wild one.

When he stood on the *Thomas* watching French ships burn in 1340, Edward had already spent four hundred thousand pounds on the war, much of it owed as debt to Italian banks—mainly the Bardi and the Peruzzi of Florence, although he also had substantial accounts with the Portinari of Florence and the Busdraghi of Lucca as well as with banks and merchants in the German Hanse and the Low Countries. At home the northern merchant William de la Pole organized even greater loans from syndicates of merchants from London and York, who advanced hundreds of thousands of pounds to the Crown. Although usury was still forbidden, Christian banks and merchants employed a variety of ingenious bookkeeping devices to hide the fact that interest on loans ran as high as 40 percent. Royal crowns and jewels stood as collateral against the loans, as did vast amounts of plate forcibly borrowed from English religious houses. The large debts Edward had run up throughout Europe were already beginning to cause him some political difficulties. Exactly a month after the French fleet was destroyed, the earls of Northampton, Warwick, and Derby were arrested in Brussels by creditors. They had stood guarantors of debts that were in default, and it was only with some difficulty that Edward had them released.

Back at home, England suffered for Edward's new war. The effects were felt at every level of society. Taxation was levied heavily and often; tenths and fifteenths were imposed on the country every year between 1337 and 1339, and a general ninth followed in 1340. The hated practice of purveyance was rife. Efforts were made to rig the wool market by selling monopolies on the trade to leading merchants, although the scheme eventually failed. Popular protest songs captured the discontent of the poor in their struggle to cope with Crown demands that squeezed harder than any before them. One poem, now known as the "Song Against the King's Taxes," complained that "such tribute can in no manner last long; Out of emptiness, who can give, or touch anything with his hands? People are reduced to such ill plight, that they can give no more; I fear, if they had a leader, they would rise in rebellion. Loss of property often makes people fools."

A rural laborer born in 1300 would have been lucky to reach his fortieth birthday at the time of Sluys. Had he done so, he would have lived through near-constant war on two fronts, seven years of the Great Famine coinciding with a period of plummeting wages, and onerous rates of taxation, while hearing rumors that Edward III rather enjoyed his expensive campaigns in Flanders as an excuse to hold lavish, wasteful, and costly tournaments. England would not feel the fury of a popular rising for another forty years, but in 1340 Edward's chronic need for cash had driven the country back into the sort of political crisis that had rocked his grandfather in 1297 and beset his father for the better part of his reign. His need for cash would soon pinch his progress in France and embitter many who remained at home.

Violent seas threw the king's boat about for three days as it stuttered from the coast of Flanders to the mouth of the Thames. It was the very end of November 1340, five months after the battle of Sluys, and with winter approaching, a Channel crossing was more dangerous than usual. But Edward was desperate and furious, ready to thrash England and his ministers with every ounce of his considerable energy. His war with France was floundering—short of money, short of glory, and short of allies—and Edward had convinced himself that the fault lay with the regency administration he had left behind, which was led by John Stratford, the archbishop of Canterbury. The king was convinced that he was being deliberately starved of the funds he needed to fight his war. "I believe that the archbishop wished me, by lack of money, to be betrayed and killed," he later wrote to the pope. His solution was to return from Flanders and to mete out severe punishment in person.

The boat reached London long after the city's regular nightly curfew on November 30, 1340, having that evening navigated a gray, turbulent Thames estuary so rough, said the author of the contemporary history known as the *Scalachronica*, that Edward himself "was in jeopardy of drowning." Around midnight the captain put into a wharf by the Tower of London. The drenched and grim-faced passengers disembarked by the flicker of torchlight. As they looked up, tired, cold, and wet, it was as if the whole Tower were asleep. There was no sound and no movement on the ramparts. The king's return was not expected. Although there should have been a close watch kept on the fortress after dark, no one saw them arrive.

That London's fortress stood apparently unguarded during wartime enraged Edward. He burst into the Tower, inspected it in fury, and began to make a list of men he wished brought before him: his treasurer and his chancellor and their department officials; his justices; the mayor of London and the London merchants who were supposed to be managing the wool trade; and, of course, the constable of the Tower, upon whose watch the capital's key strongpoint had been left so disgracefully unguarded.

Edward's anger was easy to understand. After three years of sporadic fighting, he was almost bankrupt. Sluys had been a great victory, but the months that followed saw a costly stalemate, as Philip VI sidestepped attempts to draw him into battle. He had dismissed the English king's eccentric offer of a personal duel or a staged battle between a hundred knights from either side, considering that a pudgy French king approaching his fiftieth birthday was no match for a virile twenty-eight-year-old Plantagenet, and he had nothing to gain and much to lose in a tournament with live bets on the outcome. This came as a personal affront to Edward. Two military operations that followed the offer, and attacks on the border towns of Tournai and St.-Omer, cost a great deal of money and manpower but led in every case to nothing but slaughter and retreat. *Chevauchées*—armed horseback charges through the countryside designed solely to cause terror and chaos among the local people—might gratify the soldiers who rode on them but yielded no strategic advances. The truce of Esplechin, which established peace everywhere from Scotland to Gascony and concluded a season of fruitless campaigning, was hardly the decisive blow he had wished for when he had declared war three years previously.

There was no doubt in Edward's mind that a chronic shortage of war funding was to blame for the English failures after Sluys. Edward was in massive arrears to his Flemish allies and could not fight on until they were paid the enormous sums they had been promised for their support. For this, he needed his ministers to extract cash from the realm in any way they could. From this sticking point erupted the gravest crisis of his reign.

On December 1, 1340, the morning after his tirade in the Tower, Edward embarked on a wholesale purge of his government. He began to dismiss his officials from the top and worked his way down. First to go were the chancellor and the treasurer; then the chief justice of common pleas (one of the two most senior judges in England) was arrested, along with four other judges, the constable of the Tower, and three leading English merchants. A number of exchequer officials were fired, and instructions were issued to the clerks who remained to provide a full audit of their recent transactions. Edward then arranged for tax receipts now to be paid directly into an emergency treasury at the Tower of London. Outside London Edward purged his customs officials and replaced about half the sheriffs and all the coroners and escheators, responsible for collecting royal revenues in the shires of England. A public judicial inquiry known as a commission of oyer and terminer (to hear and to decide) was established to travel from county to county, rooting out corruption with a license to hear complaints about abuses of power by royal officials stretching back to his father's reign.

Then Edward turned on his archbishop of Canterbury for revenge. Stratford was president of the regency council and thus, in the king's eyes, ultimately accountable for all the failings he perceived in English government. His brother Robert Stratford bishop of Chichester was the chancellor, whom Edward had already fired. In an angry exchange of letters and public accusations, he charged John Stratford with keeping money from him, obstructing tax requests in parliament, and abusing his authority.

Stratford was unmoved. To his mind, fault lay not with his administration but with the king himself, who made excessive demands on the country, heeded the advice of ignorant friends, and acted as a tyrant when he made summary arrests of his subjects and threatened the rights of the Church. He replied to Edward's letters in equally angry terms. He called his king a new Rehoboam, a reference to the biblical king who ignored wise counsel for the words of his young friends and thus oppressed his people.

It was a barbed comment. Rehoboam was famous for having told the people of Israel: "My father made your yoke heavy, and I will add to your yoke: my father also chastised you with whips, but I will chastise you with scorpions" (I Kings 12:14). And in case that was too cryptic for a king who spent more time at tournaments than in his study, Stratford spelled out the comparison. He accused Edward of breaking the Magna Carta and his coronation oath, warning him that "what happened to your father, sire, you know well."

Over Christmas and in early spring Edward held a series of typically lavish tournaments around the country; meanwhile a continuing public war of letters with Stratford included an astonishingly angry assault referred to by Stratford as the *libellus famosus* (notorious libel), in which the king upgraded his disparagement of the archbishop and accused him of treason.

This was dangerous. Edward was correct to perceive that there had been mismanagement in his absence, but to accuse an archbishop of Canterbury of treason was to risk incurring suspicions of tyranny. Stratford refused to be moved by the king's rage, denied most of the accusations made against him, and demanded the right to defend himself in parliament. The fuming king began to fill his letters to the archbishop with personal abuse. Stratford, in his heated opposition to the king, was aware of the precedent set by his predecessor Thomas Becket.

Matters came to a head when a parliament was called for March 1341. Using the pretext of nonpayment of taxes, Edward attempted to have his servants physically prevent Stratford from entering the Painted Chamber in the palace of Westminster, where parliament met. Meanwhile he allowed into the chamber a number of his household servants and advisers, who had no right to sit there. Stratford took up an indignant place directly outside the chamber door, holding his archbishop's staff and steadfastly refusing to move until he was admitted. For three days a standoff prevailed, until the earl of Surrey stepped in to mediate, telling the king: "Parliaments were not wont to be like this. For here those who should be foremost are shut out, while there sit other men of low rank who have no business to be here." Stratford was eventually permitted to enter the chamber, only to hear thirty-two charges of misconduct brought against him.

If Edward felt he had won, he was mistaken. During the debates that followed, it soon became clear that the wrathful king had overreached. The whole weight of national support lay behind the archbishop. A petition was presented showing that he had the backing of a number of the great magnates and prelates, the community of London, and the parliamentary commons. There was little a king who wished to keep his throne could do in the teeth of such opposition.

By May 3, 1341, Edward had been forced, humiliatingly, to climb down. The king was persuaded by the earl of Salisbury and other loyalists to take part in a parliamentary reconciliation with the archbishop and agree to a program of reform. Tax collectors were made accountable to parliament, and investigations were launched into purveyance. The king promised that in the future the great ministers of state—the chancellor, treasurer, and judges, the keeper of the privy seal, and the leading men of the royal household—were to be sworn in parliament, while lords and royal ministers should not be arrested and judged "except in parliament and by their peers."

Fortunately for Edward, this was the most peaceful end to a full-blown political crisis that had been seen in England since 1297. He vowed, in the sort of bombastic fashion that would have suited Henry II, that he would never appoint another churchman as a minister or indeed any man whom he could not hang, draw, and behead when he let him down. But this was grandstanding, and it ignored the momentous implications of the crisis of 1341 for both the French war and the future government of the realm. Edward's personal quarrel with his archbishop had thrown up a principle by which the activities of the Crown's leading officials could be scrutinized in parliament. A mechanism had been established that meant England could settle political crises without descent into bloody civil war.

Edward's grudging concessions earned him enough political goodwill to negotiate a new source of funding for his wars. Rather than having to collect taxes by levying a movables tax of a ninth and taking a forced loan, parliament had agreed to grant the king a direct tax on wool, one of England's major exports, which raised an astonishing amount of revenue. Nearly thirty thousand wool sacks were appropriated for the Crown to sell on; their value, of around £126,000, made this the heaviest tax to be levied on England since the end of King John's reign.

While all this took place, Queen Philippa was at the royal residence of King's Langley in Hertfordshire, where on June 5, 1341, she gave birth to another son. He was given a traditional English name, Edmund, and a tournament was held to celebrate the birth. The assembled nobles then traveled together to London to attend a series of war councils, to advance the next stage of the king's quarrel with France. It would not have escaped Edward's notice that his survival in the recent quarrel with Stratford had been assured by the fact that no great nobleman had risen up to oppose him, as Thomas of Lancaster and Simon de Montfort had done to his ancestors. Despite the stresses of Edward's difficulties in France, the onerous nature of his financial demands, and his own hardheaded behavior, Edward enjoyed an unusually strong relationship with the leading men of his realm. They would in time come to enjoy the rewards of that relationship together.

Dominance

In the heat of July 1346 the English army marched through the scorched landscape of coastal Normandy. All around it fields were lit up in ghastly orange by marauding bands of arsonists. Ghost towns and villages lay smashed, burned, and looted behind them, abandoned by terrified families. The roads inland teemed with refugees fleeing the maw of destruction. Thousands of unruly soldiers from England and Wales had poured ashore off a massive fleet of 750 ships in mid-July, led by the English aristocracy and gentry military men.

As they marched, they spread out over the fertile Norman countryside, fanning across a front twelve to fifteen miles wide to torch or pillage all that they came across. The summer air would have been thick with choking smoke and loud with the screams of villagers who had been too slow or too feeble to escape. As the army marched a few miles inland, two hundred English ships hugged the shoreline, provisioning the men on land and disembarking to destroy every settlement they sailed past, until one royal clerk estimated that everything within five miles of the coastline had been ruined or plundered.

This had once been Plantagenet land. Long ago, when John was on the throne, it had been raided and burned by the Capetian kings battling their way west. Now John's great-great-grandson Edward III was exacting his brutal revenge as he shepherded an invasion force of perhaps ten thousand men in the opposite direction: crossing the duchy of Normandy, heading for the Seine and the cities of Rouen and Paris.

Edward had suffered a setback in Scotland in July 1341, when David II had returned from Normandy to oust Robert Stewart, reestablishing the Bruce monarchy. Edward had eventually been forced to agree to a three-year truce in 1343. That he was not more bullish in the aftermath of his brother-in-law's restoration might have been surprising were it not for events across the Channel. In April 1341 Duke John III of Brittany had died, and Edward had been presented with an opportunity to pursue war with the French via a proxy conflict. The main focus of the war between the Plantagenets and Philip VI's new French royal house of Valois shifted to a succession crisis in Brittany, as Edward backed John de Montfort and Philip supported his cousin Charles de Blois. The war of Breton succession lasted, on and off, for five years. The logistical difficulties presented by fighting in northwestern France were considerable, and Edward suffered some significant casualties. Foremost among them was Robert of Artois, the first to encourage the English king to pursue his claim to the French Crown. Robert had subsequently become a trusted captain in Edward's armies; he died after complications from wounds sustained during an attack on the town of Vannes.

At some point between 1341 and 1343 Edward had commissioned a copy of William of Newburgh's history of Henry II's reign, which recalled the glorious days when kings of England had ruled Normandy, Maine, Touraine, and Anjou as well as Brittany and greater Aquitaine. The war, in Edward's mind, was gaining a greater purpose than simply safeguarding the status of his Gascon lands and Ponthieu. His ambition was growing, and he was now beginning to countenance a full turning back of the clock, to a time before the 1259 Treaty of Paris—before the loss of Normandy in 1204, even—when his ancestors had ruled over a mighty Continental empire. A new gold coinage issued in 1344 for use on the international exchange markets proclaimed Edward to all the merchants of Europe as "king of England and France." This was becoming more than simply a piece of tactical rhetoric.

In 1345, when peace talks over Brittany mediated by Pope Clement VI at Avignon collapsed, Edward escalated hostilities. A three-pronged attack was planned. William de Bohun, the earl of Northampton, led an army into Brittany. Henry of Grosmont earl of Derby, who was fast becoming the king's best friend and most trusted commander, led another, smaller expedition south, to Gascony, where he was appointed lieutenant of Aquitaine. Edward himself led a vast force of between fourteen thousand and fifteen thousand men across the Channel to Normandy. All in all, this was the most substantial military force that had been sent to France since John's attempt to retake Normandy in 1214.

The character of the English war effort had changed since 1340. Edward had dropped his old-fashioned strategy of alliance building in the northwest and direct invasion in the south. Alliances were too expensive; allies, too prone to defect. One of the casualties of Edward's exorbitant bribes had been the Bardi bank, to whose ruin the English king contributed when he failed to honor the massive debts incurred to his allies. By 1346 Edward's only remaining friends were the pro-English faction in Brittany and the Flemings. Every man sent to fight under the royal arms in 1346 came from England.

Thus the brutal men who landed with the king in St.-Vaast-la-Hougue, on the Norman coast, on July 12, 1346, spoke in the same mother tongue. Their battle cry was "St. George!" (The French cried "Montjoie St.-Denis!") They had various specialties. Perhaps half were archers trained in their home villages to fire a deadly longbow with some accuracy. Others were engineers, miners, diggers, clerks, or servants. Many had been pressed into compulsory service, and some were criminals pardoned for their crimes in return for serving in the field. All were equipped and supplied with a huge wealth of supplies and weapons compulsorily purchased in a fearsome war drive. They brought with them thousands of white-painted bows and arrows and more food than they could eat before it rotted.

The army was instructed by Edward not to molest the local people, or to rob shrines and churches, or to commit wanton arson. The king commanded restraint, lamenting what a royal proclamation called "the wretched fate of . . . his people of France." But this was a vain hope. Edward had brought with him many old and accomplished soldiers, heading professional companies of mounted archers, hobelars, and men-at-arms, but the king could by no means claim to dispose a uniformed, well-drilled army. Such was the unprecedented size of the invasion force that it included a sizable element of press-ganged infantry, poorly equipped and undisciplined villagers stirred up back in England by royal propaganda denouncing Philip VI and the French people as spies and aggressors who wished to invade England, convert the population to French speakers, and incite the Scots to invade the north. No instructions on earth could prevent them from tearing Normandy to pieces like a pack of distempered dogs.

The army marched through the countryside, slaughtering and brutalizing as it went. Flags and lances bobbed overhead. The rear guard was marshaled by Thomas Hatfield, the warlike bishop of Durham. The king commanded the middle. The vanguard was nominally led by Edward's eldest son, Edward, prince of Wales and duke of Cornwall, who came generations later to be known as the Black Prince. He was sixteen years old, tall and striking, already a brave young man in his father's mold. He had been knighted as soon as he landed from the ship, alongside some other young men of the campaign: William Montagu, son of the earl of Salisbury, and Roger Mortimer, grandson of Queen Isabella's former lover. The earls of Northampton and Warwick rode at the Black Prince's side to guide his hand.

The buildup to Edward's invasion had been cloaked in secrecy. Very few men had known the destination of his vast army before its departure from the English coast. Philip VI had received information that the king intended to make for Gascony, to reinforce Henry of Grosmont (now raised to the earldom of Lancaster after his father's death in 1345) in resisting the siege of Aiguillon, deep in the southwest, at the confluence of the rivers Lot and Garonne. Philip's son John duke of Normandy was leading the siege; thus, when Edward's main invasion force landed at St.-Vaast-la-Hougue, they found it largely undefended.

The army reached Caen on July 26. After brief negotiations with the garrison of the castle, they stormed the rich residential suburb of the city, leaving twenty-five hundred corpses lying torn and bleeding in the streets and sending the richer citizens back as prisoners to England. Then they marched along the south bank of the Seine for a fortnight. The French army was belatedly moved into a position to defend against the invasion; it broke the bridges across the river to prevent the English from crossing it and shadowed the invaders along the north bank.

By August 12 the English were within twenty miles of Paris. Panic broke out in Europe's largest city as the Parisians realized the impact that such a violent and depraved army would have upon their lives and livelihoods. Philip's government was compelled to call in fifty men-at-arms to attempt to keep the peace. Throughout the city and suburbs buildings were barricaded and doors battened shut as the people prepared for street-to-street fighting. In the distance, downriver on the Seine, smoke was seen pouring from the towns of St.-Cloud and St.-Germain-en-Laye. The English were not far away.

Philip VI sat with his advisers in St.-Denis and floundered. On August 16 the English rebuilt the bridge over the Seine. Desperate to keep them at bay, Philip offered a pitched battle on a plain four miles south of Paris, and the French army marched to the allotted battleground. But instead of marching either south to give battle or east to besiege Paris, the English headed sharply north, toward Flanders, in an attempt to join forces with a Flemish army that was in the field near Béthune. They marched north for more than a week, pushing so hard that the exhausted infantry wore through their shoes and foraging parties left the countryside stripped and bare of all food and supplies. When they reached their intended rendezvous, the English found that the Flemish army had given up and gone home. It was a blow because the detour had given the French a chance to regroup. Philip's eldest son, John duke of Normandy, had abandoned Aiguillon in mid-August and marched rapidly north to defend his beleaguered duchy. The road to battle had been joined.

The English and French finally met before a forest between the villages of Crécy and Wadincourt on Saturday, August 26, 1346. The English were arrayed in two lines of infantry and men-at-arms in their impressive plate armor, who fought dismounted from their horses. The Black Prince commanded the front line, with Warwick and Northampton. The king drew up the troops, laughing and joking with them as he did so; then he took his place commanding the rear guard. On either side of the foot soldiers were two huge blocks of archers, dismounted from their horses and surrounded by baggage carts to protect them from cavalry charges. The archers would decide the fate of what became a famous battle.

The French arrived at Crécy in dribs and drabs, but they comfortably outnumbered the English. Philip VI may have had twenty-five thousand men in the field, including large numbers of Genoese mercenaries. The English had no more than half that. The French king arranged his men in three battalions: crossbowmen at the front, with two divisions of cavalry behind them, flanked by infantry.

The sides shouted curses at each other and waited for their commands. At around five o'clock in the evening, it began to rain. Against the deafening rumpus of bugles and drums a signal was given, and the French crossbowmen and English archers began to loose their volleys. The English arrows were lethal: fired at a rate of five or six per archer per minute, they fell from the sky like a blizzard. The crossbow bolts of Philip's Genoese mercenaries meanwhile were fired at less than half the rate and fell short of their targets. Here was the vital difference between the sides, an advantage that played out for much of the Hundred Years War: the longbow was the deadliest weapon in the field.

King David II of Scotland may have told Philip VI about the devastation that English longbows had inflicted at Halidon Hill, but if he had, the lesson was not passed on. The French cavalry, so long the pride and scourge of Europe, saw the crossbowmen in front of them falter and took their faltering for cowardice. As the cavalry chased on the heels of the stricken crossbowmen, they too were thrown violently from their horses by the sickening thud of deadly white wood and metal. Arrow shafts buried themselves deep into human flesh and horseflesh, creating a writhing, screaming chaos of rearing animals and dying, terrified men.

As the arrows whipped through the air, so Edward ordered another, novel assault. For the first time on the battlefields of France, cannon fire was heard. The English had brought to the field several cannons, primitive devices that used gunpowder to shoot metal bolts and pellets wildly and in the general direction of the enemy. They were not so deadly as the longbows, but with the whistle of arrows punctuated by the ungodly roar of cannon blasts, the demented battle cries of men-at-arms in the melee, the agonized screams of terrified horses and men dying with their limbs severed and intestines spilled, the drums in the background and trumpets screaming into the evening, the battlefield at Crécy would have sounded like hell itself.

The hero of the battle was afterward judged to be the Black Prince, who fought valiantly in his first armed conflict, slashing at armed men, cutting down horses, and bellowing instructions to the troops around him. At one point he was felled and his standard-bearer had to commit an act of utter desperation, dropping his flag momentarily to help the stricken prince to his feet. Thus Froissart relayed the tale that has since entered the corpus of English legend. As the fighting escalated, the prince feared his men were falling too fast around him and sent word to his father that he required help.

"Is my son dead or felled?" asked Edward, according to the chronicler.

Informed that the prince was not dead but faced difficult odds, Froissart has Edward reply: "Return to him and to them that sent you here, and say that they send no more to me for any adventure . . . as long as my son is alive . . . they suffer him this day to win his spurs."

Several hours of fierce, bloody fighting routed King Philip and his allies. Their cavalry charges were skillfully made. Their horsemen regrouped and recharged with enormous bravery and accomplishment at each turn. But they were as helpless against the dismounted English positions as Edward II's cavalry had been against the Scottish schiltroms at Bannockburn. The French king lost thousands upon thousands of men: 1,542 knights and squires were found dead by the English front line, and the losses among the ordinary soldiers were innumerable. Many important nobles allied to Philip's cause lost their lives; they included the blind king John of Bohemia, who emulated Sir Giles d'Argentein, the tragic hero of Bannockburn. Hearing that the French were losing, the sightless king, certain that he would be cut down, asked to be led into the thick of battle. His body was found lying roped to the comrades who courageously undertook the suicide mission of leading him into the melee. Besides King John, two dukes and four counts were killed. They all were given honorable burials by the victorious English.

Crécy was a landmark moment in the history of the medieval military. The new, more professional means of recruitment and radically revised field tactics that had been developing since the 1330s were proved not just against the Scots but against the full might of the French army. Edward sent proud news of victory back to England, boasting in a letter to parliament that "the whole host of France has been laid low." The news very swiftly spread across the country, via a network of Dominican friars whom the royal government at home employed as traveling newsmen. Crécy was a thundering, wonderful victory. It offered tangible return for all the hardships faced by the English people, who had paid for their rampaging army. It offered massive propaganda value, bolstered further in October, when forces under Ralph Neville, Henry Percy, and William Zouche archbishop of York routed a massive Scottish invading army at Neville's Cross in County Durham. Four Scottish earls were captured, and the marshal, chamberlain, and constable of Scotland died. The earl of Moray, a senior Scottish nobleman, was killed in battle. Almost the entire military leadership of Scotland was removed in a single day, and King David II was captured and brought to England, where he remained a prisoner for eleven years.

So 1346 was a very good year for English military power, yet it did not settle the war. For at the heart of Edward's tactics lay a paradox: although his army had inflicted a crushing defeat on the combined forces of the French king and his son, it had in no way endeared the people of Normandy to English lordship or won favor for an English king over a French one. And while he severely discomfited Philip VI, the duke of Normandy, and their allies, Edward's victory at Crécy did not destroy French military capability or curb Philip's overall political power.

So the two sides remained in the field. For the rest of the summer the earl of Lancaster continued to command action around Gascony. Sir Thomas Dagworth won a brilliant victory in Brittany, where he defeated and captured Charles de Blois at La Roche-Derrien. Meanwhile, in September 1346, Edward and the Black Prince began a brutal and terrible siege at Calais, which lasted until October 1347.

The siege of Calais was in some ways an even greater military occasion than the battle of Crécy. Almost twenty-six thousand men took part; it was the largest English army to take the field during the entire history of the Hundred Years War. Every English earl, with the exception of four who were elderly or infirm, was present at some point during the siege. The financial demands placed on England to maintain this massive army for more than a year were extraordinary and included numerous new goods and export taxes that spurred widespread grumbling at home. Victory at Crécy, however, had transformed Edward's status. The chronicler Jean le Bel wrote that 1346 had shattered the image of the English, recasting them from an ignoble race into the finest and most knightly people on earth. As the English camped outside the walls of Calais, the national gathering of magnificent soldiers served simultaneously as a pageant of chivalry and a hostile invading army.

Inside the town, meanwhile, the townsfolk grew so desperate and hungry that they began to chew the leather from their saddles. They held out for a year, during which Philip VI tried to goad the English into leaving Calais by bringing his armies close enough that they might be lured into a pitched battle. Eventually, in October 1347, when it became clear that the English could not and would not be removed, a deputation of citizens, wearing nooses around their necks to symbolize their utter subjection, emerged to surrender to Edward. In a choreographed show of chivalric might, Edward allowed Queen Philippa to plead successfully for clemency. The bedraggled supplicants were spared, but their town was seized and was to remain in English hands for more than two centuries. The king and his companions returned to England as conquering heroes.

The years 1346 and 1347 saw some of the greatest and deadliest fighting in Plantagenet history. But beyond these scenes of heroism and cruelty, resistance and privation, another, far more destructive form of death was gathering on the fringes of Europe, spreading down from the Asian steppe and entering Europe via its trading ports with the East. It traveled at a speed that even the deadliest army in Christendom could not match. By 1347 the plague was coming, and it could not be stopped.

The Death of a Princess

The English summer of 1348 was wet, but in defiance of the weather England fairly blazed with glory. The king had returned in October in triumph. Calais had been taken, and French advances in Gascony were stemmed. Philip VI had been humiliated on the battlefield and in diplomatic meetings that resulted in a yearlong truce. The Scots had been smashed. The royal family and the country celebrated in style. Pageantry and festivities had been in full swing since Christmas, when the court had dressed in outlandish masks and costumes. Aristocratic revelers paraded before one another disguised as rabbits, dragons, pheasants, and swans, while the king and his knights dressed in great green robes and peacock feathers. Once Christmas was over, a calendar of tournaments was organized. Jousts and romantic plays and games were held at Reading, Bury St. Edmunds, Lichfield, Eltham, Windsor, Canterbury, and Westminster between February and September.

At each tournament the king paid close attention to the glamour of the spectacle. Always it was lavish, with the royal family appearing in fine robes of purple, dazzling with pearls and diamonds sewn in intricate patterns on their sleeves and chests. Occasionally it was surreal. At one tournament the king dressed as a giant bird; at another he decked his team out in matching blue-and-white uniforms, perhaps to recall the fleur-de-lis he had appropriated from the French arms. At Lichfield he fought under the arms of one of his veteran knights, Sir Thomas Bradeston, a lavish chivalrous display of faux humility and comradeship. A love of chivalry and showmanship lay at the heart of Edward's whole being, and he made sure to parade his famous prisoners in high style: King David II of Scotland and all the captive nobility of Paris were given fine clothes and bathed in the warm munificence of the king's generosity.

Edward's large royal family was maturing even as it continued to multiply. Although Edward was only thirty-five and Queen Philippa two years younger, they already had nine children. They ranged from Edward of Woodstock, who, at eighteen, was now a war hero and a warrior to his bones, to

William of Windsor, a babe in arms, born in June, who would not live to adulthood.

Edward of Woodstock, the Black Prince, basked in his father's affections, stepping into the vacuum left after the death of William Montagu earl of Salisbury following a jousting match in 1343. For the time being, he was the only one of the king's sons of martial age, and he had played both a political and a military role in the French wars. Lionel of Antwerp was nine, John of Gaunt eight, and Edmund of Langley seven. (One further boy, Thomas of Woodstock, would be born in 1355.) The king and queen also had four girls: Isabella (sixteen) and Joan (fifteen) had grown up in the same household as the Black Prince, along with their cousin Joan of Kent; Mary and Margaret, three and two respectively, were toddlers in 1348.

Having begun his drive for European glory by adopting a claim to the French throne, Edward had in the late 1340s begun to add another strand to his strategy: he planned to knit the family deeper into the fabric of European aristocracy by contracting dynastic matches for his children. No Plantagenet king since Henry II had sired so many children who grew to adulthood. Although Lionel of Antwerp had been betrothed at three to an heiress of the earldom of Ulster, Edward saw opportunities further afield for his children—particularly the girls.

So it was that as the tournament season reached its peak in August 1348, his second daughter, Joan, prepared to take her leave of the family and begin a new life as bride to Peter, son of King Alfonso XI of Castile. The Plantagenets had roots in Castile: Henry II's daughter Eleanor had been married to Alfonso VIII, and their granddaughter, also named Eleanor, had returned to England as the beloved queen consort to Edward I. It was an illustrious marriage for the fifteen-year-old Joan, and preparations for her departure were made with appropriate ostentation.

Joan was dispatched from Portsmouth with four heavily armed ships to carry her attendants and belongings. Her wedding dress gives us a clue to the astonishing splendor in which she was expected to represent her dynasty: she was to be married in a gown made from 450 feet of rakematiz, a thick silk interwoven with strands of golden thread. Her first port of call was Bordeaux, where she was to disembark before traveling south to Castile. Aboard the ships were a talented Spanish minstrel sent as a prewedding gift by the groom, two senior royal officials, and one hundred royal archers. There may have been a truce in operation, but the Channel and Gascony were still war zones.

The mayor of Bordeaux, Raymond de Bisquale, stood at the harbor, waiting anxiously for his guests to arrive. The moment Joan's ships hove in sight he issued a dire warning to the passengers and crews. The town was in the grip of a deadly plague. It was not safe for the royal party to disembark.

Everyone on board the ships would have heard of the disease that had swept, in little more than three years, from the Asian steppe to the heart of Europe. The Continent was already reeling from its effects. The French called it *la très grande mortalité*. The English translated it as "the huge mortalyte." It was unfortunately an accurate description of the disease that historians since the sixteenth century have called the Black Death. Its coming, against the background of the vicious Valois-Plantagenet war, transformed medieval lives and minds. Tens of thousands had been killed by war along the villages of the Seine, among the vineyards of Bordeaux, before the forest of Crécy, and in front of the gates of Calais. The Black Death would annihilate millions, with no regard for where it found them.

Already the plague had ripped through Cyprus, Sicily, the Holy Land, and the Italian states. It reached France through Marseille during the winter and spread north and south at an unstoppable pace. It slashed south through Aragon toward Castile and north to Rouen and Paris. Philip VI fled the capital, but his queen, Joan the Lame of Burgundy, died of the plague on September 12. Black flags were raised over villages as the disease reached them; warning off visitors was the only precaution.

The royal party had come from a country as yet untouched by the scourge that had ravaged the rest of Europe. They brushed Mayor Bisquale and his warnings aside. The English party believed God had granted them so many victories since 1340; perhaps the princess and her advisers also believed they might be spared this latest threat. They landed in Bordeaux and disembarked to the town. In mid-August one of the party, Andrew Ullford, a veteran of Crécy, contracted the disease that had been sweeping across Western Europe at a pace of two and a half miles a day since the autumn of 1347. While Edward's family enjoyed the glorious carousal of the tournament life, Ullford lay in the Château de l'Ombrière and suffered the grim descent into death shared by millions of other Europeans. A typical plague victim developed large, tumorlike buboes on the skin; they started the size of almonds and grew to the size of eggs. They were painful to the touch and brought on hideous deformities when they grew large. A bubo under the arm would force the arm to lurch uncontrollably out to the side; sited on the neck, it would force the head into a permanently cocked position.

The buboes were frequently accompanied by dark blotches, known as God's tokens, an unmistakable sign that the sufferer had been touched by the angel of death. Accompanying these violent deformities, the victim often developed a hacking cough that brought up blood and developed into incessant vomiting. He gave off a disgusting stench, which seemed to leak from every part of his body—his saliva, breath, sweat, and excrement stank overpoweringly—and eventually he began to lose his mind, wandering around screaming and collapsing in pain.

Ullford died on August 20, his fate sealed from the moment he walked into a plague zone. Other members of the royal party were quick to succumb. On September 2 Princess Joan died. She never wore her beautiful wedding dress or reached her husband in Castile. Instead she died a bloody, stinking death at fifteen years of age, on the cusp of womanhood. She had only a small measure of relief in dying a virgin and not a pregnant wife; expectant mothers invariably gave birth during their death throes.

September 1348 was a grim month for Edward III. Word reached England that his daughter was dead around the same time that the Black Death began to grip the southern counties. Then he heard the news that his baby son, William of Windsor, was also dead, at only three months. The infant was given a full state funeral, a dignity never afforded to Joan, whose body was mysteriously lost in Bordeaux and never recovered.

To lose two children in a month was heartbreaking for the king and queen. But there was little time for personal grief, as the realm was cast suddenly and violently into a state of utter devastation and despair. The Black Death tore through the population. It leaped from its entry point—a ship that docked at either Southampton or Melcombe Regis (now part of Weymouth), in Dorset, and brought the first cases to England—to Wiltshire, Hampshire, and Surrey. On October 24 the bishop of Winchester wrote that the plague had made a "savage attack on the coastal area of England" and that he was "struck with terror" at the thought of the disease's spreading.

But spread it did. Between 1348 and 1351 many villages lost between one-third and one-half of their populations, the devastation of the plague coinciding with a terrible murrain among sheep, to add to the misery. The chronicler Henry Knighton wrote that "there was no memory of death so stern and cruel since the time of Vortigern, King of the Britons, in whose day, as Bede testifies, the living did not suffice to bury the dead." Settlements particularly weakened during the floods and the Great Famine of 1315–1322 were wiped out completely. The great death spared no one by virtue of faith or class. From princesses like Joan to beggars who bled and vomited to death in the streets, there was no avoiding it. Edward might destroy the armies of Philip VI, but he was helpless against those of the bacterium *Yersinia pestis*.

The Order of the Garter

On April 23, 1349, St. George's Day, Edward was hosting a tournament for the knights of the realm. The Black Death was ravaging his country, but the king would not be distracted from his favorite pastime. He hosted a festival of jousting and prayer at Windsor, in the castle where he had been born and where he was planning a series of elaborate building works to begin the following year. The twenty-five men invited to the jousts were largely veterans of the French wars. They included the Black Prince, the earls of Lancaster, Warwick, and Devon, Roger Mortimer (who would soon regain his grandfather's title as earl of March), William Montagu's son, also called William, who was now the new earl of Salisbury, and other royal companions and comrades.

The form of the tournament had been fixed in advance. The knights would divide into two teams of thirteen and ride against each other until one side was victorious. On this occasion there was added spice. The earl of Salisbury and his steward, Sir Thomas Holland, were riding on opposite teams. These two were in the unusual position of being married to the same woman, Edward's cousin Joan of Kent. Joan, a radiant twenty-year-old of royal blood, had grown up with the Black Prince. She was a granddaughter of Edward I's, and Froissart called her "the most beautiful woman in England."

Joan's father, the earl of Kent, had been executed on the orders of Roger Mortimer when she was just two. She had been adopted by Queen Philippa and had grown up in the royal household, where she met Holland. She had married him in secret when she was about twelve years old, and the marriage had apparently been consummated. But since the nuptials had not been carried out under proper permissions or perhaps because the relationship was genuinely clandestine, Joan had subsequently been given in an arranged marriage to Salisbury while Holland was away fighting on the Continent. When Holland returned, he claimed her publicly, and Joan found herself in an awkward situation because both men professed to be her legal husband. She preferred Holland, but personal preference was not the determining factor in unions between the great families of the medieval aristocracy. The case was heading to the pope for settlement; it was eventually decided in November 1349 for Holland. In the meantime the rivalry between Joan's two "husbands" was fierce.

With Joan a dazzling heroine preparing to watch her rivals clash in battle, the stage was set for an exciting spectacle. But there was more to single out this tournament, for this was the occasion on which Edward III had determined to launch a knightly institution that came to be known across the world. The tournament at Windsor marked the formal institution of the Order of the Garter, England's most exclusive knightly club and one of Edward's most brilliantly realized acts of royal propaganda.

The king, like his grandfather Edward I, was captivated by the Arthurian legend, with its heroic deeds, fearsome military reputation, and famous gentleness toward women and the stricken. Like his grandfather, he was determined that Plantagenet kingship should absorb and reflect the great values of the Arthurian world. In January 1344, as the Breton phase of the war with Philip was under way, he had held a tournament at Windsor to inaugurate a knightly society of the Round Table. The chronicler Adam Murimuth wrote that the king "made a great supper at which he began his Round Table and received the oaths of certain earls and barons and knights whom he wished to be of the said Round Table." Then, Murimuth says, the king issued instructions that a "most noble house" should be added to Windsor Castle, "in which the said Round Table could be held at the time appointed." This noble house was to be made of stone, two hundred feet in diameter, perhaps with a tiled roof around the outside in the fashion of the later Elizabethan Globe Theatre. In the first year of construction £507 17s. 11½d. was spent. No expense was to be spared in the pursuit of Arthuriana. In 1345 Edward bolstered his project by ordering a search for the body of Arthur's supposed ancestor Joseph of Arimathea.

As war escalated in the mid-1340s, the Round Table project ran short of cash and stalled. The cost of the fighting in Brittany compelled all funds to be diverted to waging war. Five years on, however, Edward had not abandoned his ambitions to form an exclusive brotherhood through which he could bind the elite knights and noblemen of his realm to the Crown. Throughout the tournament season of 1348 the king had been toying with the idea of creating an Order of the Garter. At Windsor in 1349 he formalized the idea and fixed the membership of the order.

The garter was an odd item to symbolize what was in essence a club for men of war. The story was spread that the idea came spontaneously, when the countess of Salisbury dropped her garter, a decorative garment worn on the thigh, during a dance, and Edward picked it up, saying, "*Honi soit qui mal y pense*" (Evil to him who thinks evil of it) and thus coining the order's motto. But this tale is apocryphal and probably muddles an allusion to Joan of Kent's scandalous marital situation with a saucy account of the royal court's romantic licentiousness. Edward's parties were famously louche, and this story found a willing audience among sniffy monastic types who saw decadence and scandal at the English court and shook their heads in disapproval.

It is more likely that the idea of the garter came from Henry of Grosmont earl of Lancaster, hero of the English war effort in Gascony and Calais, who had sported garters—then a knightly accoutrement and only later an item of female dress—in his dandyish youth. The king had also worn garters encrusted with pearls and gold to tournaments at the beginning of his reign, in 1333 and 1334. By the time the order was founded, Lancaster was thirty-nine and Edward thirty-seven. Perhaps the emblem of the garter served two purposes: an allusion to the knightly prowess they saw in their earlier selves as well as an in-joke about their wild youthful days.

Whatever the case, Edward was following European fashion: orders of knights were founded throughout the mid-fourteenth century, following the example of Alfonso XI of Castile, who formed the Order of the Band in 1330. In the 1350s Emperor Karl von Luxemburg of Germany formed the Society of the Buckle, and Count Amadeus of Savoy, the Company of the Black Swan. In the 1360s King Louis of Sicily founded the Society of the Knot, and John II of France the Company of the Star. Thereafter the trend proliferated.

So the Order of the Garter was founded on St. George's Day, with solemn oaths sworn by the twenty-six founding members to hold a celebration on the same day each year, together if possible. Any member not able to attend at Windsor was to celebrate in the same fashion wherever he was in the world. The society formed a sacred bond; it was determined that new members could not be added until an existing member had died. Great soldiers like Sir Thomas Dagworth, Sir Walter Manny, and the earls of Northampton and Huntingdon were not among the original twenty-six knights. All were in France when the founding tournament was fought, and they would have to wait for their membership, in Huntingdon's case until 1372. Dagworth died before he had the chance to receive the order's famous robes.

The Order of the Garter struck many contemporaries as crass and insensitive. At a time when England was ravaged by the Black Death and impoverished by the financial demands of war, to a chronicler like Henry Knighton it seemed the height of callousness for the king to indulge in carefree tourneying. But for Edward, the order had a purpose beyond simple enjoyment and indulgence. Every Plantagenet king since John had been prevented from defending his foreign territories by knights and earls who chafed at the duty to serve abroad. Edward had been lucky to win victories that partly justified the massive expense and human cost of fighting in France. He knew his family's history. If God withdrew his favor and victories slowed, the realm would soon demand a good reason to bear arms overseas.

The answer lay in making foreign service a badge of honor, not a tiresome holdover from the days of feudal service. Knighthood was expensive, uncomfortable, and perilous, so Edward would have to knit the knightly community of the realm around him by giving it a new sense of exclusivity. The Order of the Garter gave Edward a new caste through which to celebrate and reward knightly chivalry. It was a means of binding the king and his sons to the men they would lead into battle on the Continent for decades to come. The exotic French motto reminded all who aspired to membership that aristocracy was a pan-European brotherhood. Having been forced to abandon his plans for a Round Table house at Windsor, Edward now gave orders to establish a college church in the town. The chapel, within the College of St. George, would be the order's spiritual and ceremonial home. Work began in 1350, after a delay while the court waited for the worst ravages of the Black Death to recede, and it took seven years to complete, incurring as great a cost as some of Edward I's greatest Welsh castles. Sixty-five hundred pounds were spent at Windsor between 1350 and 1357, almost all of it on the chapel. To give the chapel a truly holy mystique, Edward gave it the Cross of Gneth, a fragment of the True Cross taken from Llywelyn the Last during the final conquest of Wales in 1283.

For centuries afterward St. George's Chapel stood for the intoxicating blend of martial prowess, spiritual devotion, romantic gentility, and lavish ceremony cultivated by Edward and his companions. Edward combined the flair for visual and architectural magnificence of Henry III with the fearsome military capability of Edward I. Truly this was a high point of the Plantagenet family's history: visionary propaganda from a superbly assured king.

Decade of Triumph

During the early years of his life and reign Edward III had cast himself in the Arthurian pageantry of his court as Sir Lionel, the humble knight of the Round Table, a comrade in arms who would fight shoulder to shoulder with his men. By the 1350s his achievements had overtaken his humility, and the king began to be represented as Arthur himself, ruling his glorious kingdom from the new Camelot, which was Windsor. The king had spent almost unimaginable sums of money on his wars, and they had brought him glory and prestige that reverberated across Christendom. England's prosperity was bound tightly to its fortunes in war. Edward reminded friends and rivals of the new military order by flying the arms of St. George wherever possible. The red cross fluttered on the masts of his naval fleet, led by the cog *Thomas* and supported by dozens of other ships, which patrolled the Channel. He added St. George to the great seal of England alongside the Virgin Mary. In 1348 Edward felt sufficiently secure in his resurgent kingship to reject an approach by the electors of the German states to become the next Holy Roman Emperor.

Relations with France and Scotland were now at the king's command. The English court teemed with wellborn hostages; King David II of Scotland and the counts of Eu and Tancarville led a large and valuable group of French and Scottish prisoners. Despite the ravages of the Black Death and the uncertainty it cast over large-scale military campaigning, Edward pursued both. Frequent sallies were undertaken across the Channel, some under his own command, others under trusted lieutenants like Henry of Grosmont earl of Lancaster, who led a small expedition to Gascony during the winter of 1349–1350.

On December 24, 1349, as the court was beginning its Christmas celebrations at Havering, in Essex, Edward III received alarming news: Calais was about to be betrayed to the French. With no time to raise an army, he enlisted his eldest son, Edward, and a small company of trusted soldiers and sailed at once and in the utmost secrecy for France. By January 1, 1350, Edward's crack force was at Calais and had gained clandestine access to the town. Before dawn the next day a treacherous Italian mercenary raised the

French flag above the citadel of Calais, the signal for a band of French knights to storm in through the town gates. The king was waiting. He and his men fell upon the invaders, advancing under the arms of Sir Walter Manny while Edward passed himself off as a simple knight to avoid detection and capture. Fierce hand-to-hand combat broke out in the streets of Calais as the king and his men battered their enemies back, shouting, "Edward and St. George." Within hours Calais was saved. The story of its defenders' daring and glamorous mission added to the burgeoning body of folklore attesting to the bravery of Edward III and the Black Prince.

On August 22, 1350, Philip VI died. He was succeeded by his son John II, the duke of Normandy, who had fought against Lancaster in Gascony and led men into battle at Crécy. His accession as king coincided with a yearlong truce between the kingdoms, and during the summer of 1350 Edward turned his attention to another one of England's Continental rivals: Castile. The realm in the north of the Spanish peninsula was also ruled by a new king, Pedro I, "the Cruel," and Edward was quick to talk up largely baseless rumors that Pedro wished to invade England. In actual fact, he was engaged in a form of trade war. Castilian ships sailed through the Channel on their way to trade wool in Flanders and made a vexing habit of attacking English ships on their way. For Edward this was pretext enough. As the sun was setting on August 29, 1350, a large English fleet of around fifty cogs met a fleet of more than twenty larger Castilian galleys in the waters off Winchelsea, a few miles east of Hastings on the southern coast of England. The English ships were commanded by the king, the Black Prince, and the earls of Lancaster, Northampton, and Warwick. Together they drew the willing Castilians into a bloody sea battle.

Although the design of ships had improved in the last hundred years, medieval naval tactics in the rough seas north of the Mediterranean remained primitive, particularly when compared with those of the land armies, with their dismounted men-at-arms and mounted archers. The art of fighting actions in open water still amounted to little more than a waterborne melee. Edward's boats charged at the Castilian galleys like battering rams, as his men threw sharp grappling irons on the end of ropes or chains, designed to embed themselves in the sides of the ships and prevent them from sailing freely. Parties of knights then tried to forcibly board the enemy vessels, slay the sailors, and throw their bodies into the churning waters. Little attention was paid to the tactics of maneuvering ships in formation or of attacking at a distance. Battle was given at close quarters and leaned heavily on chance.

At Winchelsea this was very nearly fatal for the king. Amid the blast of trumpets and shouts of pain and rage, his cog was seriously—ultimately fatally—damaged when it crashed into a galley. Only by fighting his way aboard and taking command of the enemy ship amid a hail of arrows and iron bars thrown down by Castilian defenders did Edward escape drowning. Meanwhile the Black Prince's ship, jousting at another Castilian vessel, was damaged just as seriously, and the prince was rescued only by the arrival of Lancaster's ship. Finally, as darkness fell over the Channel, an enemy ship very nearly succeeded in towing away an English vessel carrying many members of the king's household; one enterprising royal servant had the presence of mind to creep aboard the galley and cut through the halyard to bring down the sail and stop the galley from escaping with its valuable booty. Eventually, despite their escapades, the English won the day, capturing numerous galleys, destroying others, and hurling hundreds of stricken sailors into the pitiless sea, where they drowned. In later years the battle of Winchelsea became known as *Les Espagnols sur Mer* (the Spaniards in the sea).

It was a matter of great fortune that Edward and his captains and lieutenants emerged unscathed, but good luck was something that the king of England often banked on during his dazzling military career. The Castilian fleet was effectively put out of the Channel for years to come, while Edward's fleet established its hegemony, escorting merchant ships back and forth between Bordeaux and the thriving English ports of Bristol and London and the south coast.

The king celebrated his victory by giving thanks at Thomas Becket's shrine in Canterbury, then headed to his northern estates to hunt. His lieutenants meanwhile returned to France to skirmish their way around the fringes of Aquitaine. The truce between England and France had expired, and several spectacular victories in Brittany and Gascony had left Edward effectively in charge of Aquitaine, Brittany, and the area around Calais by autumn 1352. In Scotland a power vacuum in the absence of David II allowed English lords to extend their reach into the Scottish Lowlands. For the next eight years Edward busied himself in the quest to make his dominance permanent.

As military plans were made for an invasion of Scotland, Edward retained a firm grip on the government of England. The first wave of the Black Death had thrown England's labor economy into tumult, and the effects were worsened as the plague returned in waves throughout the 1350s, 1360s, and 1370s. Hundreds of thousands of workers died, and as a result, wages threatened to soar; that would prove damaging, if not disastrous, to the class of knightly landowners who sat in Edward's parliaments, granted his taxes, and served as royal officials in the localities. The Crown, as the greatest landowner in England, would suffer similar losses should the cost of estate management rise too sharply. Reacting promptly to the threat, Edward instituted in 1349 the Ordinance of Laborers, which was ratified in parliament as the Statute of Laborers in 1351. The labor laws set rigid schedules for wages for every class of worker imaginable, which kept them artificially deflated. "Saddlers, skinners, white-tawers, cordwainers, tailors, smiths, carpenters, masons, tilers, shipwrights, carters and all other artisans and labourers shall not take for their labor and handiwork more than what, in the places where they happen to labor, was customarily paid to such persons in the said twentieth year [1347] and in the other common years preceding," read one typical clause of the statute. "If any man take more, he shall be committed to the nearest jail." Lords were granted the right to compel laborers—whether legally free or unfree serfs—to serve them, while prices of foodstuffs were similarly kept down: "butchers, fishmongers, hostlers, brewers, bakers, pullers and all other vendors of any victuals, be bound to sell . . . victuals for a reasonable price," read the statute.

The Statute of Laborers was enforced with some vigor by the same class of men it was designed to protect. Commissioners were appointed to investigate excessive wages and prices, and for decades afterward their appearance in the localities to investigate breaches of the law and to fine offenders created a simmering class resentment between shire elites and the lower orders beneath them. This effect was redoubled by the fact that the labor commissions were one part of a radical overhaul of the whole system of local lawkeeping, for which England's political classes had been waiting nearly half a century. Instead of relying on large, irregular circuits of judges touring the country, Edward began to use smaller, regular bodies made up of leading local landowners. They sat both on peace commissions (as justices of the peace, or JPs—the heirs to the keepers of the peace, who had been established earlier in the reign) and on a raft of other local commissions, most notably those to enforce the labor laws. The sense that royal government was coalescing in the hands of a self-interested political class would cause violent social tension in later decades. In the short term, however, Edward's swift action to deal with the most obvious economic effects of the Black Death secured him the confidence of the class on which he relied heavily for war funding.

With peace at home, Edward was able to concentrate on pushing toward a lasting settlement with France and Scotland. Part of the problem there was that Edward was not entirely certain what a perpetual peace should look like. He clung proudly to his dynastic claim to the French Crown, but it was increasingly obvious that this was a lever by which to move negotiations in favor of a reconstituted Plantagenet empire. At peace talks held in Guînes in 1354 Edward proposed to renounce his claim to the French throne in exchange for full English sovereignty over Aquitaine, Poitou, Anjou, Maine, Touraine, Limoges, and Ponthieu, even before disputes over the lordship of Brittany, Normandy, and Flanders were settled. Subsequently, at a magnificent peace conference held under papal authority in Avignon during the winter of 1354–1355, Henry of Grosmont, raised in 1351 to the rank of duke of Lancaster, and the earl of Arundel began negotiations from an even more aggressive position, demanding English control over Aquitaine, Poitou, Maine, Touraine, Anjou, Angoulême, Normandy, Ponthieu, Quercy, and Limousin.

It was hardly surprising, in the face of these onerous demands and Lancaster's bullish negotiating tactics, that the peace talks collapsed. John II's envoys argued that to grant away such vast swaths of France would put the king in breach of his coronation oath. Both sides prepared for the resumption of war, and by the autumn of 1355 Edward had two large invasion forces organized, one under his own command and another under that of his son the Black Prince. The goal was to teach John II the same lessons his father had learned at Crécy and Calais in 1346 and 1347.

Of the two armies that sailed for France in late 1355, only the Black Prince's stayed very long. The king landed at Calais in late October, unsuccessfully petitioned John II to meet him in battle, and, scornful of the French king's refusal to fight, returned to England by November 12. For the rest of the winter he concentrated on leading troops in a terrible chevauchée around the Lowlands of Scotland, inflicting such misery on the local people and putting so much of their land and property to the torch that January 1356 became known as the Burned Candlemas.

Yet the devastation caused in the Lowlands could not compare with that wreaked upon southwestern France by the Black Prince and his companions. Throughout the spring of 1356 it became clear that a showdown between John II and the English was inevitable. The Black Prince had wintered at Bordeaux, and the frontiers of English Aquitaine were littered with armed companies, some in the pay of the prince, others released from army service and operating as freebooters. In May another English force under the duke of Lancaster was sent to Normandy. It wreaked havoc in several important Norman towns before retreating from John's reach. There was widespread disgruntlement among the French aristocracy, and the king was beginning to face open opposition from his cousin Charles "the Bad," king of Navarre and count of the Norman province of Evreux, who wished to depose John II and place his eldest son, the dauphin, also called Charles, on the throne. Charles the Bad was arrested in April 1356 for his impertinence, but his brother Philip of Navarre crossed to England in August, held talks with Edward III at Clarendon, and paid liege homage to the English king as "king of France and duke of Normandy." The pressure on John to make a decisive move against the English was becoming intolerable.

The moment arrived on September 19, 1356, in fields outside the city of Poitiers, traditionally the most important city in the duchy of Aquitaine. The Black Prince's army, consisting of six thousand to eight thousand English and Gascon men, was split as was now conventional into three divisions, with the prince commanding the middle. The French outnumbered the English-Gascon army by perhaps as much as two to one. Nevertheless, the English were well drilled and organized, in contrast with John II's undisciplined and fractured army. Although the French had learned some of the lessons of Crécy and were preparing to deploy their men-at-arms on foot in a defensive formation rather than waste them in suicidal cavalry charges, they lacked the leadership to turn their numbers to their advantage. As the prince's men traversed the French front line, two French commanders were goaded into attack. Traditional cavalry charges were sent against the English van and rear guards. They were slaughtered as they tried to cut through the the thick hedges that lay between them and their enemies.

It was the beginning of a day of unparalleled carnage for the French, one that ended in a defeat unrivaled until the battle of Agincourt in 1415. During heavy fighting they lost more than two thousand men, including the duke of Bourbon, the constable of France, one of their two marshals, and the carrier of the oriflamme, the sacred red battle standard of the French army, which was said to have been dipped in the blood of St. Denis. Countless French noblemen were captured; they included the king's youngest son Philip, the archbishop of Sens, numerous counts, the other marshal, and—most disastrous of all—John II himself. The English lost no more than a few hundred men and took prisoners worth hundreds of thousands of pounds. It was the most crushing defeat ever inflicted by a Plantagenet prince on a French king, and it crowned forever the glorious military legend of the Black Prince. A banquet was given at the English camp following the victory; the legions of French prisoners were toasted and honored with the greatest chivalric deference by the prince and his noble captains. John II was lauded as a great king who had fought more bravely than any other man on the field. But beneath the knightly courtesy, the political reality was clear: France was in crisis, while the English, who began to refer to the Black Prince informally as King Edward IV, were ascendant. The hostages taken at the battle of Poitiers were sent back to the king in England, who began to plot their ransom, a deal that would finally achieve the aim of reestablishing the lost Plantagenet empire in France.

By January 1358, following long and complex peace negotiations, John II's ransom was set at four million gold ecus—an impossible £666,666—a ransom that, even allowing for inflation, made Richard the Lionheart's look puny. Alongside it was a draft Treaty of London, along much the same lines as the failed Treaty of Guînes. Edward's price for abandoning his claim to the French Crown was to be sovereignty over Aquitaine, Saintonge, Poitou, and Limousin in the south, and Ponthieu, Montreuil, and Calais in the north. The treaty might have been sealed by both sides had events in France not sharply deteriorated: during the chaos that followed King John's capture, radical reformers chased the dauphin from Paris, and Charles of Navarre, now freed from prison, offered a deal to the English in which France would be partitioned, with Edward taking the Crown and around two-thirds of the realm's territory. In the summer of 1358 a mass popular rebellion known as the Jacquerie—*les Jacques* was a contemptuous aristocratic nickname for peasants—tore through northern France, with the aim of destroying noblemen and knights, whom the peasants blamed for betraying the realm. Chroniclers reported ghastly atrocities as ordinary men and women took bloody revenge on their social superiors. One chronicler, Jean le Bel, records peasants killing a knight and roasting him on a spit, gang-raping his wife, and force-feeding the unfortunate lady and her children the roasted flesh of their husband and father.

Another French chronicler, Jean de Venette, left a vivid description of the countryside during the late 1350s. He described the area of his birth near Compiègne, which had been ruined by relentless English attacks:

> The vines in this region . . . were not pruned or kept from rotting. . . . The fields were not sown or plowed. . . . There were no cattle or fowls in the fields. . . . No wayfarers went along the roads carrying their best cheese and dairy produce to market. . . . Houses and churches no longer presented a smiling appearance with newly repaired roofs, but rather the lamentable spectacle of scattered smoking ruins to which they had been reduced by devouring flames. . . . The pleasant sound of bells was heard indeed, not as a summons to divine worship but as a warning of hostile intentions, in order that men might seek out hiding places while the enemy were yet on the way. . . . Every misery increased on every hand, especially among the rural population. . . . Yet their lords did not . . . repel their enemies, or attempt to attack them, except occasionally.

By November 1358 Edward was no longer convinced that peace was the best option. He began to plan for a third massive invasion and was only temporarily dissuaded by the personal pleas of his prisoner John II, who petitioned him successfully for a second draft to the Treaty of London. In this the king's ransom remained at four million ecus, but the list of territories to be awarded to the Plantagenets in full sovereignty now included Normandy, Anjou, Maine, Touraine, and Boulogne, along with the overlordship of Brittany.

As the hundredth anniversary of the Treaty of Paris approached, Edward was pressing for its final obliteration and a return to the heyday of Henry II's and Richard I's supremacy over Philip Augustus. Unsurprisingly, the second draft Treaty of London was utterly rejected in Paris. In summer 1359 invasion plans were made; in October the king, the duke of Lancaster, and the Black Prince led an army of around ten thousand men, split into three divisions, out of Calais and southwest toward Reims. It was the most provocative target they could have picked: Reims held the cathedral where French kings had been crowned since Louis I in 816. The town was just a few days' march from Paris; if it should fall to the English king, he would certainly have himself crowned as Edward I of France.

Fortunately for the French, Reims was stoutly defended. Edward abandoned his attempt at a siege in January 1360, after spending just five weeks before its walls. He negotiated an alliance with the duke of Burgundy and set out for Paris, in the hope of drawing the dauphin into a pitched battle. Wisely, the dauphin refused to be tempted into following two previous generations of Valois kings and risking his freedom and sovereignty against English men-at-arms and archers. He stayed in Paris, a city that even a buoyant Edward could not hope successfully to besiege, and in April the English king was forced to march his army, weakened by plague and tired from several months in the field, back in the direction of Brittany. As they marched back west, they were caught outside Chartres in a powerful thunderstorm, which destroyed a large part of the baggage train. Hailstones large enough to kill horses fell from the sky in a day so ghastly it was later dubbed Black Monday. For once, fortune had turned against the king of England. There was to be no Crécy or Poitiers in 1360; instead peace talks were opened in the village of Brétigny on May 1. Seven days later they had concluded. Edward accepted a treaty by which he took sovereign control of Aquitaine, Poitou, Saintonge, and Angoumois in the south and Ponthieu, Montreuil, Calais, and Guînes in the north. He gave up his claim to the French throne, Normandy, and Brittany and reduced John II's ransom to three million ecus. John agreed to stop supporting the Scots against the English, and Edward to cease aiding the Flemings who regularly rebelled against France. Normandy, Maine, Anjou, and Touraine all remained part of the French kingdom. It was not the grand reestablishment of Henry II's empire that had once seemed possible; but it was a triumph nonetheless.

Edward returned to England in time for Christmas in 1360, to proclaim and celebrate the peace, the achievement of almost everything for which he and his allies had fought for twenty-three long years. Parliament was called in January 1361 and duly ratified the peace. On St. George's Day at Windsor Castle in 1361 Edward's sons Lionel of Antwerp, John of Gaunt, and Edmund of Langley were all admitted to the Order of the Garter in recognition of their service in the wars. (Edward's youngest son, Thomas of Woodstock, born in 1355, had been the nominal regent of the realm during the king's more recent absences.) The country was given over to celebrating the apparent end of a long and costly war.

In France the mood was bleak. King John had been released on December 5, 1360, to return to France and raise his ransom, for which the first-ever gold franc (the franc à cheval) was minted. But the realm was devastated, overrun with English mercenary companies that had been disbanded from Edward's armies and were now in need of occupation. They found this chiefly in inflicting continued misery on the inhabitants of Brittany and the southwest, capturing villages and castles before selling them back to their unlucky inhabitants. While England basked in triumph France lay ravaged, crippled for a generation by John II's ransom, and territorially dismembered. A high point in Plantagenet history had been reached. What was astonishing was the speed with which fortune's wheel turned, and the age of glory fell spectacularly apart.

PART VII

Age of Revolution
(1360–1399)

My God, this is a strange and fickle land.

—Richard II (according to Adam of Usk)

The Family Business

On November 13, 1362, Edward III celebrated his fiftieth birthday. As he faced old age, he could feel proud of his achievements. He was phenomenally rich, a powerful and famous king who had shaped England in his own image: legal, cultural, military, and aesthetic. If he was riding toward the twilight of his years—the life expectancy for Plantagenet kings was around sixty—he was doing so in style.

He and Queen Philippa lived in splendor and luxury. Enriched by the massive bounty and the large ransom payments he had won from the French, Edward led a truly regal existence. The king's and queen's households were merged in 1360, in recognition of the fact, after the Treaty of Brétigny, that the king would no longer be traveling around makeshift camps on the Continent. Thousands of pounds were spent on tournaments and jewels, falcons and dogs, fine clothes and lavish living. As the fortieth anniversary of Edward's accession approached, his court spent one of the first protracted intervals of peacetime in an endless round of feasting and partying.

Much of the vast royal treasure was spent overhauling the king's residences. Windsor Castle was the showpiece. Directed by his talented, humble-born new minister William of Wykeham, the king spent vast sums (eighty-five hundred pounds a year in the mid-1360s) redesigning Windsor as a monument to martial kingship and courtly love. Old buildings were torn down, and vast, luxurious new royal halls, chapels, and chambers were built in their place. Vaults and marbled cloisters connected splendid apartments. (Queen Philippa alone had four personal chambers under construction: one for sleeping, a chapel for prayer, a third decked with mirrors, and a fourth for dancing.) And this was only one of the royal homes, to be lived in when the king and queen were not at their leisure in any number of splendid palaces and hunting lodges dotted about the Thames Valley and the New Forest.

Edward was not entirely self-indulgent. He thought a great deal of his people and the way they regarded him. Another severe wave of the Black Death returned to Europe between 1361 and 1364 and was particularly deadly to children. Amid this general misery, it befitted the king to try to make life a little easier for his traumatized subjects. The public celebrations of his birthday therefore centered on a meeting of parliament dominated by knights, burgesses, and citizens and were orchestrated in a spirit of high royal generosity. The parliament heard large numbers of petitions and sought to remedy as many complaints and grievances as possible. A Statute of Purveyance was finally granted, drastically limiting the most pernicious royal practice of requisitioning in wartime by limiting the forced purchase of food and goods to the king, queen, and heir. Royal purveyors were now known as buyers, and they operated under a strict code of conduct. This was an easier concession for Edward to make in peacetime than in wartime, to be sure, but the fact that he made it suggested that he understood and was sympathetic to the hardships of his subjects.

During the course of Edward's lifetime, there had been an important shift in the fabric of life in his kingdom. The language of the realm was moving away from French and toward English. The native tongue, once considered a rude, barbaric dialect unfit for wellborn mouths to speak or administrators to use, was now becoming commonplace. The king spoke it. All the aristocrats of the age understood it. Traveling minstrels singing the newly fashionable English ballads of Robin Hood did so in the native tongue. Rising dons like John Wyclif, who was beginning to impress his colleagues at Oxford University in the early 1360s, came to translate the Bible into English, and in turn this led to the rise of Lollardy, a heretical movement in which personal interpretation of scripture and the teachings of the Church was aided by their availability in the mother tongue. The age of the first great English vernacular poets—Geoffrey Chaucer, William Langland, John Gower, and the *Pearl* and *Gawain* poet—was dawning. In recognition of all this, Edward used his fiftieth birthday parliament to usher in a new age of English speaking. The Statute of Pleading formally changed the spoken language of parliamentary address and arguments in the royal law courts from French to English. (Records were still to be kept in Latin.) It was another populist statute, designed, as it said, to remedy a situation in which "the people which do implead ... in the king's court ... have no knowledge or understanding of that which is said for them or against them by their Serjeants [lawyers] and other pleaders."

Finally, Edward turned his mind to his family. Now that he was fifty, it was time to look after the next generation. His final act in the birthday parliament was to honor his adult sons with lavish new titles and roles, setting them up to take the helm of the mighty land of England when he was gone. Nine of his twelve children had reached adulthood. By 1362 six of them were still alive. Young Joan had died in plague agonies during the Black Death, and when the second wave of the plague came back to England in 1361, it killed two of her sisters. The Children's Plague wiped out around a quarter of England's young people, including the seventeen-year-old princess Mary and fifteen-year-old princess Margaret. Only one daughter remained: Isabella, who was approaching her thirtieth birthday. She had hotheadedly refused to marry a Gascon lord proposed by her father and had withdrawn herself for good from Edward's diplomatic plans, refusing to marry for anything but love.

Despite the truculence of his last surviving daughter, Edward could still boast five healthy Plantagenet princes, and all but the seven-year-old Thomas of Woodstock were handsomely rewarded in 1362. The eldest, Prince Edward, heir to the throne and the finest soldier in England, had quite scandalously married his first cousin Joan of Kent. According to the writer known as the Chandos Herald, who was a servant of Prince Edward's best friend, John Chandos, Joan was "a lady of great worth . . . very beautiful, pleasing and wise." Not everyone was so kind, and indeed the marriage was very much for love rather than political gain. Joan had been married twice before. She already had five children by Sir Thomas Holland, and her other former husband, the earl of Salisbury, was still alive. She was addicted to jewels and finery and brought no beneficial foreign alliances. The marriage was set to afford the Black Prince the dubious status of being the first Plantagenet king to be married to a divorced mother since Henry II had wed Eleanor of Aquitaine. The union was also technically forbidden by the Church because first cousins were well inside the prohibited degrees of consanguinity.

Nevertheless, Prince Edward had been well rewarded by his father. At the time of his wedding he was earl of Chester, duke of Cornwall, and prince of Wales, and his income exceeded eight thousand pounds. Since he and Joan had married, they had been living just south of London at Kennington, in a brand-new palace designed by the master mason Henry Yevele, who would become the most brilliant builder of the age. Shortly before the king's birthday, Edward awarded them a new home. He settled the duchy of Aquitaine on his eldest son, who had won the greatest battle of the age at Poitiers on its northern borders. With this gesture the king was sending an unequivocal message: the Black Prince was ready to switch from leading campaigns to running a powerful fiefdom, and his time for kingship would arrive shortly. Edward and Joan moved to the duchy in February 1363 and based their household mostly in Angoulême and Bordeaux.

Edward had plans for his other sons too. He had read William of Newburgh's twelfth-century chronicle of early Plantagenet history, and now, as his birthday approached, he began to put into place his own version of the grand familial strategy that Henry II had conceived for his own children two hundred years earlier. Each one was to be awarded a landed inheritance in a different corner of Europe.

On his birthday itself, which fell on November 13, Edward came to the final day of parliament with his third and fourth sons, John of Gaunt and Edmund Langley, and proceeded to bestow marvelous new titles upon them. Parliament records give us a laconic clue to the magnificence of the ceremony. "And then the chancellor said to the great men and commons that our lord the king had discussed with some of the great men how God had truly blessed him in many ways, and especially in the begetting of his sons who were of legal age, and he therefore willed their names and honor to increase; that is to say, that his son Lionel [of Antwerp], then being in Ireland, should be named . . . duke of Clarence. . . ." Lionel was abroad, but John of Gaunt and Edmund Langley were present, and they received their honors in person: "And then our said lord the king girded his said son John with a lance, and put on his head a fur cap, and on top a circle of gold and precious stones, and named and made him duke of Lancaster, and gave him a charter of the said name of duke of Lancaster. And then he girded his said son Edmund with a lance, and named and made him earl of Cambridge, and gave him a charter of the name of earl of Cambridge."

Duke of Clarence, duke of Lancaster, earl of Cambridge: these were grand titles indeed. And each of them bore a notional responsibility for a different corner of the Plantagenet dominions.

Lionel of Antwerp's title was rather novel. The duchy of Clarence was an Irish title that brought with it lands on the west coast. (The name Clarence referred to the Clare family from which the lands were inherited.) When joined to the earldom of Ulster, which Lionel held by virtue of his marriage to Elizabeth de Burgh, the countess of Ulster, the new duchy of Clarence formed the greatest power bloc in Ireland. By the time his title was announced in parliament, Lionel was already in Dublin, having been appointed lieutenant of Ireland in 1361 and given 50 knights, 300 men-at-arms, and 540 mounted archers, with provision to raise more troops in Ireland. His destiny was marked out: he was to expand and maintain Plantagenet power in the wild Irish west. He was the first Plantagenet prince to set foot in Ireland since King John.

John of Gaunt meanwhile was raised to duke of Lancaster to replace Henry of Grosmont, Edward's friend and general who had died (probably of plague) in 1361. Gaunt had married Grosmont's daughter Blanche of Lancaster at Reading Abbey in 1359, and on his father-in-law's death he had inherited in its entirety one of the largest and most important networks of estates in England. He thus brought back into the immediate royal family the inheritance of Edward II's nemesis, Thomas of Lancaster, which played a vital role in maintaining order and security in the north of England.

Edward III had demanded on numerous occasions during the 1350s and 1360s that his third son be recognized as heir to King David II of Scotland, who had been released from prison in 1357 but struggled beneath the burden of his onerous ransom obligations. Whether the demand was posturing at the negotiating table, a mere feint to induce the Scots to pay their king's ransom, is debatable. But early in the 1360s it seemed that if the Black Prince took care of Aquitaine and Lionel guided policy in Ireland, John of Gaunt was to be groomed for a role that would see him overseeing Scottish defense and affairs. With Thomas of Woodstock little more than an infant, that left just Edmund Langley. The king's fourth son was earmarked for one of the most important spheres of foreign policy, Flanders and the Low Countries.

In November 1361, when the duke of Burgundy died, he left as his widow a twelve-year-old girl, Margaret, the daughter of Louis of Male count of Flanders. She was heiress to the counties of Nevers, Flanders, Rethel, Burgundy, and Artois as well as the duchies of Brabant and Limbourg. Together these lands formed a massive, potentially independent power bloc that, combined under the leadership of a single ruler, might be used to counterbalance the might of the French Crown. With its rich trading towns Flanders offered a treasure trove for whoever could acquire it.

As soon as the duke of Burgundy's death was known, Edward began to negotiate in secret for Margaret's marriage to his son Edmund. Like the Black Prince and Joan of Kent, Edmund and Margaret were related within the prohibited bounds of consanguinity, having a common ancestor in Philip IV of France. This made matters complicated because the marriage would require permission from Pope Urban V, a Frenchman based at Avignon, who could not be relied on to favor English interests over those of the king of France. But Edward III was not put off by the challenge. He made the twenty-one-year-old Edmund earl of Cambridge and awarded him control over the northern French counties of Ponthieu and Calais, to give him a standing interest in the region, and embarked on a diplomatic campaign of huge energy and cunning that occupied much of his time and energy.

Thus Edward celebrated his fiftieth birthday: with great laws, parliamentary gifts, family ennoblement, and the launch of a dynastic plan for his large, if diminished, brood. He appeared to anticipate and desire territorial expansion on the part of each of his four mature sons without offering the potential to bring them into conflict with one another, a problem that had blighted the final decades of Henry II's reign. If Edward III learned anything from his reading of William of Newburgh's histories, it was that eagle chicks left in the same nest would soon come to vicious fighting.

And indeed the decades that followed would prove that his children had far more brotherly loyalty than Henry's. Unfortunately, while fraternal relations were strong, the streak of good luck Edward had enjoyed in the 1350s was about to run out.

Unraveling Fortunes

The year 1369 was very bleak for Edward III and his family. It was a year of almost unrelenting failure and loss as death followed death, sickness piled upon sickness, and everything that had shone with such glory in the 1350s suddenly seemed to be fading away. The king and queen spent much of their time in the 1360s with their combined household at their hunting lodges in the New Forest, avoiding Westminster and slowly descending into old age. Edward took solace in the comforts of his wife's servant Alice Perrers, a girl in her early twenties with a seductive voice and a sharp eye for advancement. She bore the king his first illegitimate child in 1364 and used her position as his mistress to carve out more privileges for herself at court.

Edward used his time at home wisely. He continued to host great state occasions, as he did in 1364, when the kings of Scotland, France, and Cyprus were all entertained in London at once. He oversaw a program of domestic reforms, as new legislation was passed to empower justices of the peace to administer law and order in the shires. Parliaments also passed sumptuary statutes, which regulated what different ranks of society could wear and forbade the lower orders from wearing more luxurious types of furs, cloaks, or shoes. The efforts to settle the Plantagenet empire on the surviving royal children in a coherent way continued.

Yet against all this ran a current of decay. Careful though his plans were, spending the 1360s at far greater ease had not left Edward rested. From the middle of the decade his health was declining. In 1364 John II of France died at John of Gaunt's Savoy Palace, just outside the walls of London. Repayments on John's massive ransom ceased, and the kingdom of France had a chance to rally under the leadership of a new Valois king, Charles V. The new king was determined to topple the English and was fortunate enough to find a highly skilled general to assist him. Bertrand du Guesclin was a veteran of the protracted wars of Breton succession; he had fought against the English for more than two decades, facing down no lesser men than Henry of Grosmont duke of Lancaster. Over time he became the scourge of the English and a master of guerrilla tactics and attritional campaigning, grinding the life out of English invading armies.

The first theater in which war resumed was not northern France or Aquitaine, where the English had enjoyed so much recent success. Instead the French managed to draw England—through the ambitions of the Black Prince—into a complex and sapping proxy war fought in the hot, disease-ravaged territories of Iberia. A struggle for the Castilian throne erupted between two sons of Alfonso XI, the bastard Henry of Trastámara and the incumbent king, his half brother Pedro the Cruel. The chronicler Thomas Walsingham described Pedro as "a vile evildoer and a tyrant," and his name in the Spanish peninsula was synonymous with cruelty and bloodshed.

Pedro had inherited the throne from his father in 1350 and switched his realm's allegiance from its long-standing alliance with France to England, which he had begun to court in 1362. When Charles V inherited the French throne, it suited him well to punish the Castilian king for his abandonment. Taking on Pedro would supply him with an opportunity to reclaim some military initiative; perhaps more important, it offered the hope that the many free companies of violent mercenaries that had been roaming and terrorizing the French countryside would now be drawn away to a new and profitable war in the south. Their presence in France—particularly around Brittany, Normandy, and the Loire Valley—had for years been a source of disorder. Independent bands of discharged soldiers took control of castles, manors, and churches, which they used as bases for a military occupation of the surrounding area. They stole, murdered, burned, and raped with abandon. Then, once an area had been reduced to destitution, they moved on to inflict misery on the next. Their presence was viewed by many Frenchmen as a punishment sent from God. It was viewed by the new king as an impediment to any sort of stable government. And so, when an opportunity presented itself, Charles threw his support behind Henry of Trastámara, sponsoring a bid to depose Pedro. In 1366 this drove the king out of Castile and up into the arms of the Black Prince, who met him in the border town of Bayonne. The prince received Pedro as a friend and promptly engaged England in the new war.

As was usual with the Edwardian wars, fighting for the throne of Castile proved wildly expensive. The Black Prince had been levying a series of somewhat unpopular *fouages* (hearth taxes) on Aquitaine since his arrival in 1363, which did nothing for the unity of his new duchy and the warmth with which his rule was received. In 1366 he boldly agreed to shoulder the entire cost of invading Pedro's kingdom and expelling the French. In return Pedro gave over his two daughters, Constance and Isabella, as collateral against repayment of the £276,000 expedition. (The girls later married the Black Prince's brothers John of Gaunt and Edmund of Langley, respectively.) But the notion that a country as small and poor as Castile would ever have the means to cover its share of the costs of war should have struck the prince as improbable.

The campaign started well. On January 6, 1367, as the army was mustering, Princess Joan gave birth to Edward's second son (his first, Edward, was born in 1365). The boy was born in Bordeaux and named Richard, after the Lionheart, Eleanor of Aquitaine's most successful son. His baptism was attended by what the Canterbury chronicler William Thorne described as three "magi": King Pedro, King James IV of Majorca, and King Richard of Armenia. Three kings at court and a child born on Twelfth Night: these were seen as signs that the baby boy was marked out for great things. It was an auspicious way for his father to start on a campaigning season.

With his brother John of Gaunt alongside him, Prince Edward led an army of Gascon subjects and paid mercenaries over the Pyrenees, down past Logroño, to the banks of the river Najerilla, where Henry of Trastámara was waiting. The Black Prince was at the height of his military powers, and at Nájera he was aided by Henry, who ignored a letter from Charles V explicitly warning him of the dangers of standing to fight the English. Its army, wrote the French king, included "the flower of the chivalry of the world." Indeed it did. Sir John Chandos, Stephen Cusington, and the Poitevin nobleman Guichard d'Angle were formidable captains, and during the descent from the Pyrenees, the Black Prince knighted two hundred soldiers among his ranks.

When these knights, old and new, emerged from the mountains to the plains near the town of Nájera, Henry of Trastámara panicked. Instead of avoiding battle, he took up defensive positions against the river and prepared to engage, the one thing Charles V had explicitly warned him to avoid. Early in the morning of April 3, English divisions surprised Franco-Castilian forces under Henry and du Guesclin, attacking them on the left flank and causing chaos. Under a now-familiar English assault of heavy longbow fire and fierce attacks by dismounted men-at-arms, the Franco-Castilian force was routed and then driven back to the river by cavalry charges. At least five thousand men were slaughtered or drowned. Henry fled for his life, but du Guesclin was captured, along with almost every other nobleman on the Franco-Castilian side.

Tactically it was the best of Prince Edward's victories, even if the glittering cast of hostages did not quite reach the heights of those collected at Poitiers in 1356. The Black Prince had once again shown himself to be agile, ruthless, and brave in the thick of battle. But if the military victory was complete and glorious, the political and personal consequences of Nájera were little short of catastrophic. Although he had retrieved his throne, Pedro the Cruel was unable to raise the money to pay back his savior. This left Prince Edward effectively bankrupt and now under extreme pressure from the Gascon lords who demanded their wages. Even with the sale of Pedro's jewels and the ransoms of valuable hostages taken at Nájera, there was no way the costs of war could be met.

Worse yet, in the heat of the Spanish summer, infection and disease swept through the English ranks. The Black Death was not at its most severe in 1367, but Edward's soldiers suffered from other illnesses, including widespread bouts of dysentery, which accompanied them as they withdrew back to Bordeaux. The great were afflicted as harshly as the poor. Sometime around the battle of Nájera, the Black Prince contracted a serious disease—possibly dysentery, but perhaps malaria or more likely dropsy—that lingered and confined him to bed for long stretches for the rest of his life. When he returned to Gascony, a preacher gave a sermon comparing him to the Son of God. "No one should flatter even the greatest prince to his face like that," Edward later reflected as sickness racked his body. "Fortune may strike him down at any moment and all his famous deeds will then be forgotten and reduced to nothing."

After the Nájera campaign the Black Prince was never the same again. The dual consequences of his broken health and bankruptcy were disastrous for the government of Aquitaine and for the broader English position in France. Pedro of Castile had kept his throne, but he would not pay a penny for this privilege. Although hostages like du Guesclin realized valuable ransoms, they were but a tiny fraction of the overall debt. Prince Edward's only solution was to levy further harsh taxes on Aquitaine. These antagonized the local lords, and in 1368 they appealed against his rule to

Charles V, as "sovereign lord of the Duke and the whole duchy of Aquitaine." The appeals were a none-too-subtle request for the French king to strike up war against the English in France once again. Charles required little encouragement. In late 1368 French troops massed on the borders of Aquitaine. By the spring of 1369 hundreds of towns had joined the appeal against Plantagenet rule, and large areas of the principality were overrun.

Meanwhile, in Castile, Henry of Trastámara regrouped. In March 1369 he murdered his half brother Pedro in a tent with a dagger. Soon afterward he signed a treaty with Charles providing for a large war fleet to sail on the Gascon coast. Panic spread not only around the coastal towns of Gascony but up to southern England, where a new threat to the Channel was once again perceived. The futility of the Castilian campaign was now painfully exposed. Prince Edward was too sick to regroup and defend his lands against the resurgent French. By 1370 he was making preparations to return with his wife and children and what was left of his army to England. He came back a broken man in January 1371.

His family's fortunes had not fared well in his absence. Lionel of Antwerp, the duke of Clarence, had found his task in Ireland as arduous as had every prince who had attempted to bring English customs and order to the region before him. His first wife, Elizabeth de Burgh, had died in 1363, leaving him with a daughter, Philippa. By 1366 he had abandoned the job of managing Ireland as a lost cause. Edward III had arranged a new marriage, a purely mercenary arrangement, to the thirteen-year-old Violante Visconti, a Pavian heiress and member of the famous Visconti dynasty, the warlike lords of Milan and scourge of their neighboring Italian city-states. Lionel and Violante had a magnificent marriage before the doors of Milan Cathedral and celebrated in great style for several months afterward. The poet Petrarch was said to have been a guest at one great dinner given by the couple. But the high living proved fatal to Lionel. Within months of the marriage he had become sick, and on October 17, 1368, at Alba, in Piedmont, he died. His body was eventually returned to England for burial at Clare Priory in Suffolk.

Queen Philippa too was declining. She dislocated her shoulder in a hunting accident in 1357 and never fully recovered. From 1365 on she could not move about easily, and by 1367 she was relying on litter and barge to travel. On August 15, 1369, she died, with Edward and their teenage son, Thomas of Woodstock, by her side. The king held her hand and wept bitter

tears. The girl who had arrived in England four days after Edward II's funeral had grown up to see her husband and their family rise from puppets
of the Mortimer-Isabella regime to become Europe's most feared dynasty.
She had lived a fabulously rich and lavish lifestyle: Froissart, whom she patronized and knew well, claimed in his history that her dying wish to the
king was that he settle her debts to foreign merchants. Nevertheless, she
was highly regarded throughout England as a literate, pious, stable, and well-
grounded figure who had exerted considerable influence for the good on
her husband and sons. She was admirably connected to the noble families
of Europe and brought glamour and chivalry to the court with foreign
knights, whom she integrated into English society with unprecedented success. Thomas Walsingham called her "a most noble woman and most constant lover of the English." Philippa had been a great companion to her
husband and a dutiful mother to their many children. Her loss left Edward
distraught.

The king was in poor health himself. From the middle of the decade he
had begun to rely ever more heavily on expensive surgeons and doctors, the
lot of a man in his sixth decade of life. As his family and friends dropped
away around him, Edward began to sink into a closed household life. He was
outliving the era of his greatest victories. Yet the time had come to fight once
more. Indeed, against the onslaughts of Charles V, war was the only response that Edward knew how to give. In a parliament of 1369, the records
state, "it was agreed by all the prelates and magnates and commons of the
shires of England . . . with the assent of the whole parliament, that the King
of England should resume the name of King of England and of France, as he
held it before the peace." Peace with France was formally abandoned. The
sickly, grieving Edward had somehow, with the help of his beleaguered eldest son, to raise his country for a new round of war.

The Good Parliament

The chapter house of Westminster Abbey filled with purposeful occupants. It was April 29, 1376, the second day of parliament. For three weeks the majority of England's magnates had been making their way to Westminster from every corner of England to sit in their capacity as the parliamentary lords. They were joined by men of the shires, knights and gentry who now filled the chapter house as the parliamentary commons.

The previous day all of parliament had met together. The ailing king had come up from Havering to attend the opening ceremony, but that was the last they would see of him. John of Gaunt represented him for the rest of the proceedings, sitting with the other lords in the Painted Chamber at Westminster Palace. The commons took their place at the abbey chapter house, a large, octagonal stone building where the monks sat every day to pray, read, and discuss a chapter of the rule of St. Benedict. The chapter house was a relic of Henry III's extensive reworking of Westminster Abbey in the troubled 1250s, building work undertaken when his brother-in-law Simon de Montfort had done so much damage to Plantagenet rule in the name of reform. It was a magnificent building. The floor was tiled with figures of kings and queens, the Plantagenet royal arms, and an inscription proclaiming the beauty of the chapter house and the munificence of its royal builder: "As a rose is the flower of flowers, so this is the house of houses, which King Henry, friend of Christ and the Holy Trinity[,] dedicated . . ." Now King Edward's commons tramped across the tile-paved floor and took their seats on the tiers of stone steps that followed the walls. Above their heads, light poured through stained glass windows decorated with heraldic symbols intended to remind all who saw them of the power of Plantagenet kingship. But the commons had not come to venerate royal history. They came to summon the spirit of de Montfort and call upon their king to correct his stricken country.

The years that followed the resumption of war between England and France had seen indignity after indignity heaped upon the realm. No one could ignore it. Militarily there had been a catalog of disasters. In the opening period of the new war the English sought to carry on where they had left off in 1359. But they ran into a more forthright enemy, a lack of leadership, and a chronic shortage of good luck. A *chevauchée* under the veteran knight and freebooter extraordinaire Sir Robert Knolles in 1370 ran disastrously short of cash and was disbanded six months into a proposed two-year campaign. That same year the ailing Black Prince was joined by his brothers John of Gaunt and Edmund earl of Cambridge as he tried to stem French attacks over the borders of Aquitaine. It was a futile effort. There was no love for English lordship, and city after city simply opened its gates to the French when they arrived. In mid-September 1370, when Limoges surrendered to the duke of Berry, the Black Prince took violent revenge, sacking and burning the town as punishment. Froissart may have embroidered his account and exaggerated the number of deaths by some tenfold, but he captured the horror of the sack: "The Prince, the Duke of Lancaster, the Earl of Cambridge, the Earl of Pembroke, Sir Guichard d'Angle and the rest entered the city on foot with their companies and their hordes of hangers-on. All of them were equipped for evil.... It was heart-rending to see the inhabitants throwing themselves to the ground as he passed, crying out 'Mercy, noble lord, Mercy!' He was so enraged that he heard them not. No one listened to their appeals as the invaders ran through with their swords everyone they found in their way.... Three thousand people, men, women and children, died on that day.... And the looting did not stop until the whole city was stripped and left in flames." It was a pathetic sight: the Black Prince carried around on a litter, commanding the deaths of innocent people in a fruitless, spiteful revenge. This sorry massacre was his last significant contribution to the war. By 1371 Prince Edward, a broken man too ill to make any more contributions to war or government, was back in England.

Two attempts were made the following year to invade Aquitaine by sea. One fleet, under the earl of Pembroke, was captured; another, departing from Calais under the king, was forced back to port by adverse winds. It was the last campaign the king attempted to lead in person. When it failed, he retreated into seclusion, his mind and body faltering. The principality of Aquitaine had shrunk to little more than a narrow strip of English territory along the coast.

The war effort and the realm were now under the effective command of John of Gaunt, who was in no sense the military equal of his father or eldest brother. In Brittany the Anglophile duke John de Montfort was forced out of his own land into exile at Edward's court. A *chevauchée* carried out under

Gaunt's personal command in 1373 was thwarted by the Fabian strategy of the French, who refused to give battle, allowing the English to wear themselves out. The Channel teemed with pirates. For many, particularly London's superrich wool traders, the threat to shipping routes had become so acute that they were chartering private fleets in self-defense. The English claim to the French throne was as hollow a legal fiction as it had been at any time since the 1340s. All that was left was to sue for peace. A yearlong truce was agreed to at Bruges in 1375.

The commons that sat in the chapter house were as familiar with these failures as everyone else in the realm. After all, it was to the commons that repeated requests for taxation to fund the fruitless campaigns had been addressed. The Anonimalle chronicler records that when the parliament began, the chancellor, Sir John Knyvet, described "how the realm of England was in peril and on the point of being destroyed by its adversaries . . . wherefore Sir John asked on the king's behalf aid and succour against his enemies." The king, he said, wanted a tax of a "tenth from the clergy and a fifteenth from the laity." The truce made at Bruges would run out within a year, and fighting must resume. It was a familiar story.

But foreign failures were only a part of it. There was a growing sense that the assertive, charismatic kingship of Edward's reign was giving way to a power vacuum. "Little by little all the joyful and blessed things, good fortune and prosperity decreased and misshaped," wrote the chronicler Thomas Walsingham later. The king and his eldest son were sickly and incapacitated. Edward's household had ceased to be a center for chivalry and was peopled instead by rapacious hangers-on, none more despised than Alice Perrers, the king's mistress. She had scandalized public opinion the previous year when she had ridden from the Tower of London to a tournament at Smithfield dressed as the Lady of the Sun, arrayed in magnificent finery, all of it purchased by the aged king. Meanwhile in the localities there was a developing crisis of law and order. Divisions erupted between some of the leading magnates. The bishops were unhappy as John of Gaunt had agreed, in exchange for papal mediation at the peace of Bruges in 1375, to allow papal taxation of the English clergy for the first time since the 1340s. Corruption abounded. To raise quick cash from Italian merchants, licenses were being sold to avoid the Calais Staple, the designated marketplace for trading English wool, where taxes were applied by the government. Other merchants were either loaning the government money at extortionate interest rates or else buying up government debt at discounted rates and cashing it in, a practice that provided short-term liquidity to the Crown but allowed profiteering among the wealthy. London seethed with tensions between factions of merchant guilds and foreign traders. Government was collapsing both at the center and in the localities. It was a time of crisis.

Thus, when the commons met, they were in a restive mood. Various interest groups—merchants, knights, county gentry—shared a common sense that it was their duty to counsel and correct the king and his government. They knew they had the power to do so, for without their grant of funds, war could not continue. They began by promising oaths of mutual support in the chapter house, after which they presented their grievances about corruption and misgovernment in a single lengthy petition. Then they elected as their speaker Sir Peter de la Mare, the steward of the earl of March. During the ten weeks in which parliament sat in session—the longest parliament that had ever been held—they put forward a remarkable series of reforms and legal processes aimed at reforming royal government and restraining those they felt were corrupting it. Almost every day between the opening of what became known as the Good Parliament on April 28 and its dissolution on July 10, 1376, brought forward shocks to the realm.

De la Mare was a prominent member of the Hertfordshire knightly class, who had served as sheriff for the county and had raised troops for the earl of March during a campaign to Ireland in 1373. He was articulate, courageous, politically astute, and well connected with the lords in parliament. And it was to the lords, led by John of Gaunt, that de la Mare presented the commons' long list of grievances in early May, with a request that a committee of twelve lords be established to meet with their representatives to discuss means by which the realm might be repaired.

The bargaining tool that de la Mare wielded throughout the Good Parliament was an old one. Without reform, he repeatedly and consistently told John of Gaunt and the committee of the lords, there could be no grant of taxation. But in pressing for a direct involvement in the detail of reform, de la Mare and the commons in 1376 occupied a more central role in government than had ever been achieved in the past. In 1341, during the last serious political crisis, the debate had been played out between the lords and the king, while the commons played only a very minor role in the background. In 1376 they came directly to the fore.

Given the urgent need of the Crown to refinance the war before the Treaty of Bruges expired, there was little that Gaunt could do but listen. He heard a chorus of complaints about royal policy, centering on the corrupt activities of a number of people close to the increasingly senile king. After lengthy deliberations, formal accusations were made in full parliament against three in particular: Lord Latimer, a veteran soldier serving as chamberlain of the king's household; Richard Lyons, a wealthy merchant and royal counselor who had advanced a great deal of money to the Crown; and the king's mistress, Alice Perrers, who had amassed land, wardships, and jewels that had belonged to Queen Philippa and whose bewitching grasp on the king was such that Thomas Walsingham wrote that she "had such power and eminence in those days that no-one dared to prosecute a claim against her." The first two were denounced for financial corruption and avoiding the Calais Staple, while the commons demanded that Alice Perrers be removed from the king's company. By the end of May more accusations had been leveled: against Lord Neville, steward of the royal household, and three more merchants.

John of Gaunt could do little, in the face of such serious accusations, other than play for time. He adjourned parliament briefly and let his father know that serious problems were brewing and that many of those in the royal household were about to be arrested. According to the *Anonimalle Chronicle*, "the duke sent certain lords to announce to [Edward] the advice of the commons and the assent of the lords, that he should be counseled to banish from his presence those who were neither good nor profitable . . . and the king benignly told the lords that he wished entirely to do what would be for the profit of the realm . . . [and] that he would willingly act by their advice and good ordinance." It was a remarkably timid response. The lion that had roared in 1341 was reduced to a mouse.

All those accused by the commons were brought to trial before parliament in June 1376. When Peter de la Mare was asked who brought charges against the accused, he replied that they did so "in common." Thus the process of impeachment before parliament was born. Latimer was accused of a whole compendium of crimes in Brittany, including extorting money from the king and neglecting the duchy's defense. He was also accused of embezzlement of war finance on a grand scale, along with many other crimes. He was convicted and imprisoned. Lord Neville was dismissed, Lyons forfeited goods and land, and Alice Perrers was told to stay away from court at the risk of banishment (although within months she had been pardoned and returned to Edward's side). A council of nine was appointed to advise the king.

It was a clean sweep of government undertaken with the best intentions, and it would have unforeseen long-term consequences. As the impeachments were taking place in parliament, on Trinity Sunday, June 8, 1376, a week short of his forty-sixth birthday, the Black Prince died. Even as he lay bedridden, the warring factions of the Good Parliament had battled for his support. Indeed he had been sent a large barrel of gold by Sir Richard Lyons in an attempt to win his support against the commons. (When he refused it, Lyons sent it to the king, who accepted, saying: "He has offered us nothing which is not our own.")

"Thus died hope for the English" was the sad verdict of Thomas Walsingham following the death of the Black Prince. And indeed it felt to many in 1376 that when Prince Edward died, England had lost the last of its great heroes. The Black Prince had been behind what many Englishmen ranked as the greatest victories their realm had ever known: Crécy, Poitiers, Nájera, and the sack of Limoges. His body was buried with elaborate military ceremony. His will had requested that he be buried at Canterbury beside Thomas Becket, rather than at Westminster. The specifications for the occasion were precise: "When our body is taken through the town of Canterbury to the priory, two destriers covered with our arms and two men armed in our arms and in our helms shall go before our body, that is, one with our whole arms of war quartered, and the other with our arms of peace with the badges of ostrich feathers, with four banners of the same suit: each of those who carry the said banners shall have on his head a hat with our arms. He who wears the arms of war shall have an armed man by him carrying a black pennon with ostrich feathers." It was a soldier's passing. His tomb was decked in the symbols of the Holy Trinity, for which he reserved great reverence, and decorated with his armor, symbols of his military power, and his motto, *Ich dien* (I serve). In his later life, blighted by illness, the prince had become morbid, depressed by the fact that his warrior's spirit could not overcome his fragile flesh. His will requested that a French poem be inscribed around his tomb in Canterbury Cathedral, warning others of the same perils:

Such as thou art, sometime was I.
Such as I am, such shalt thou be.
I thought little on th'our of Death
So long as I enjoyed breath.
But now a wretched captive am I,
Deep in the ground, lo here I lie.
My beauty great, is all quite gone,
My flesh is wasted to the bone.

The loss of the prince struck a devastating blow to Edward's regime. With his death he catapulted to the center of English politics the last of the Plantagenets, a nine-year-old boy called Richard of Bordeaux.

New King, Old Problems

Richard of Bordeaux appeared before the assembled lords and commons in the Good Parliament. Several hundred men cheered for him and demanded that he be given titles and honors. On every side sat sumptuously dressed magnates, solemn bishops and abbots, merchants decked in fine robes and jewelry, and knights of the shire looking on expectantly. There were old, wise, and rich men in abundance. It could not have escaped young Richard that all these people were clamoring for him and him alone. For the new heir to the throne, it was an extraordinary way to begin public life.

This was June 25, 1376, just over two weeks since his father's death. The Good Parliament was still in full session, attempting to purge the king's household and to bring to justice the men it blamed for mismanaging the war. Sir Peter de la Mare courageously took the fight for reform directly to John of Gaunt. With the Black Prince's death, that battle was being played out against new and burning questions: What would happen when the old king followed his eldest son into the grave? Who would guarantee the security of the Plantagenet succession?

With Prince Edward dead, as his eldest surviving son Richard of Bordeaux was the next in line to inherit the Crown. That much was clear. What was not clear was whether he would be allowed to do so in peaceable fashion. The child was nine years old. It was virtually certain, with Edward III reduced to gibbering infirmity by a series of strokes, that the future king's reign would begin with a long minority of the sort that had been seen only once in England since the Norman invasion. Every student of English royal history would have recalled that Henry III's minority had been blighted by a French invasion and a long and damaging civil war. They might also recall that Edward III's much briefer minority between 1327 and 1330 had been dominated by the grasping and equally disastrous regency of Roger Mortimer and Queen Isabella.

It was widely feared, particularly in London, that John of Gaunt had designs on the throne for himself. This was unfair. Gaunt, although he was an unsubtle politician and a ruthlessly ambitious magnate, almost certainly had no intention of usurping the young heir to his father's Crown. He was at his core a loyalist. But this was not the perception among many of those in Westminster in 1376. The commons had demanded that young Richard of Bordeaux be brought before them in order that as the official records put it, "the lords and commons might see and honor Richard as true heir apparent to the realm." Anxiety and desperation must have fairly hummed in the air as Richard appeared before his future subjects.

While he stood before them, Simon of Sudbury, the sixty-year-old archbishop of Canterbury, rose to address the lords and commons together. The king, he told them, had briefed him to speak on his behalf. According to parliamentary records, he said "although the very noble and powerful prince my lord Edward, recently Prince of Wales, was departed and called to God, nevertheless the prince was as if present and not in any way absent, because he had left behind him such a noble and fine son, who is his exact image or true likeness."

As Sudbury brought his speech to a close, a great clamor erupted from the commons, which asked "with one voice that it might please [the king] to grant to Richard the name and honor of Prince of Wales," just as his father had done. They were told that such was the king's prerogative alone. But Richard, like the men around him, would have known that he would soon be raised to all the titles and honors that befitted his new station.

Almost a year later to the day, stupefied by a series of strokes, barely able to speak, Edward III died, alone but for a priest. Thomas Walsingham wrote that Alice Perrers took the rings from his fingers before taking leave of him for the last time. One of his last public appearances was before a deputation of Londoners, who came up the river Thames to his palace at Sheen and found him trussed up in cloth of gold and physically pinned into his chair in order to be held upright. The king slipped finally out of consciousness on June 21, 1377, following a reign of just over fifty years. He was sixty-four years old.

The old king was laid to rest on Sunday, July 5, in one of the most lavish funerals ever held in England. The procession lasted three days and cost thousands of pounds. Almost the whole of London and Westminster was draped in black cloth and lit by thousands of solemn torchbearers, dressed all in black. Archbishop Sudbury presided as the dead king's body, draped in red samite emblazoned with a white cross, was placed inside a coffin and interred in Westminster Abbey next to his wife, Queen Philippa. During the interment a knight entered the abbey church and presented a sword and shield as an offering. At Windsor another ceremonial sword was placed above the royal stall in St. George's Chapel. Then the fortunes of England and the Plantagenet family were catapulted into the hands of his grandson. The whole country looked to Richard.

His coronation took place just over a week later, on Thursday, July 16. The crowds who had come to London for the solemnities of the royal funeral now watched as the city was transformed into a throbbing hub of brightness and hope. As Adam Houghton, the bishop of St. David's, would proclaim in an address to parliament, Richard had been sent to England by God, just as Christ had been sent to earth to redeem the people. The streets of the capital were so packed that during the royal procession from the Tower to Westminster on the evening before the coronation John of Gaunt had to cut his way through the throng with his sword. In Cheapside, the main east-west thoroughfare through the city, a conduit flowed with wine for three days, a dark purple river that led up to a large mock castle at the western end of the street. In the turrets of the castle sat little girls of Richard's own age, dressed all in white as if to represent the sense of rebirth and purification that came with the accession of the first new king for half a century.

Richard, at the heart of the procession, soaked up the adulation of the masses. Next to him rode his tutor and father figure Sir Simon Burley, the loyal soldier who had fought alongside his father in Aquitaine, who had served at Nájera and during the sack of Limoges. Richard had known him all his life, and he had been closely involved in the young king's upbringing for several years before the coronation. He would have prepared the prince for the ceremonial process of his coronation. But he could not have prepared him for the sheer noise and excitement with which the people clamored in the street.

At ten years old Richard stood before all the people of his realm and swore a solemn oath to uphold the laws and customs of his ancestors, protect the Church, do justice to all, and uphold the laws that his people had "justly and reasonably" chosen. Then he was presented to the whole abbey for its acclamation. This was a reversal of the usual process, by which the people would cheer in advance of the oath swearing. It was arranged to make the clear point that this was a king who acceded by the right of his family to rule and not by the election of the masses. Once the cheers had subsided, Richard, concealed from the eyes of the congregation by a golden cloth, was anointed with holy chrism. Oil touched his bare skin at the hands, chest, shoulders, and head, sanctifying and separating him from all other men. He was handed the scepter, sword, and ring of kingship before being crowned by Archbishop Sudbury and the earl of March. It was an awe-inspiring experience for a young boy to go through. And it planted in Richard's mind the certain knowledge that he was a king by right of God. He was carried out of the abbey raised aloft on Sir Simon Burley's shoulders. There was such a commotion around him that one of his shoes fell off.

This was characteristic of the experiences of his early years. On public occasion after public occasion he was cheered and honored as a Christlike savior of a troubled people. There were repeated calls from the kingdom's great men for obedience to the new king; the day after the coronation Bishop Brinton of Rochester gave a sermon demanding that everyone obey Richard for the safety of the whole kingdom. In his household he was constantly cast in his father's image, surrounded by his father's old companions and exhorted to become the king that the Black Prince had never been allowed to be.

Yet cheerful as the realm was to have a new king, it also had immediate and desperate requirements of him. England was in acute peril, plagued by an escalating crisis of security. As the chronicler known as the monk of Evesham wrote:

> In this year . . . there was a complete collapse of peace negotiations [with France]; for the French refused to keep the peace unless an agreement highly favourable to themselves could be reached. . . . During this same period, the Scots burned the town of Roxburgh. . . . Afterward, the French landed in the Isle of Wight on 21 August: when they had looted and set fire to several places, they took a thousand marks as ransom for the island. Then they returned to the sea and sailed along the English coastline continuously until Michaelmas. They burned many places and killed . . . all the people they could find. . . . It is believed that at this time more evils were perpetrated than had been caused by enemy attacks on England during the previous forty years. [During a battle with French pirates at Lewes] one Frenchman was captured . . . who, on the point of death . . . declared, "If the English had made the duke of Lancaster their king, they would not now be invaded by Frenchmen as they are."

What could a boy king do against this?

The answer was very little. England required an arrangement that would allow the realm to govern itself while its savior grew up from a child into a fully formed king. The natural precedent to follow would have been from the reign of Henry III, when William Marshal had been appointed to the regency. But the only natural candidate for such a post in 1377 was John of Gaunt. Although he had been reconciled with the commons in parliament, there was still a great deal of suspicion of his motives and abilities. In February 1377, when he had intervened at the trial in London of his protégé the radical scholar John Wyclif, Gaunt's heavy-handed behavior had prompted riots in the capital. His capacity to vex and frighten made him an unpromising candidate for an official role in the new government.

Instead England settled on a fudge. From his coronation onward, Richard was held to be ruling as a king in his own right. A pretense of competence was established. A series of continual councils of twelve great men was appointed to advise him, but writs and charters were given under Richard's own seal. Conciliar government was carried out in his name, but power was also exercised from his household. The men closest to him were former retainers and servants of the Black Prince, such as Sir Simon Burley, Sir Guichard d'Angle (raised to the earldom of Huntingdon after the coronation), and Aubrey de Vere. It was by no means a perfect arrangement; but the south coast was in danger, and in France and Aquitaine there were severe threats to the two most important English coastal outposts, Calais and Bordeaux. To defend the realm, and the dwindling parcels of Plantagenet lands on the Continent, it was imperative that government begin to function fast. One pressing need was to find enough money to fight the French. Raising taxation from the whole country was vital. Unfortunately, it was also the route to one of the most extraordinary outbursts of popular rage that England would ever experience.

England in Uproar

The Great Revolt—or the Peasants' Revolt, as it is more commonly called by historians—was England's first great popular rebellion. It began as a series of village riots in Essex and Kent during late May and early June 1381. As royal tax inspectors and judges moved around the counties, inspecting low returns from a poll tax levied in parliament in November 1380 and collected the following spring, they were met with violent resistance. Royal officials were murdered, and the sheriffs of Essex and Kent were snatched in kidnap raids.

As the resistance movement built momentum, bands of mounted rebels gathered and began to tour the major towns of Kent, looting and burning official records in Maidstone, Rochester, and Canterbury. They were drawn from the ordinary folk of the villages and led by the "better sort" of yeomen—parish priests, village constables, and well-off farmers. They targeted lawyers, royal servants, and particularly odious local landowners, but they also acted with restraint and some political sense; an order was issued, according to one chronicler, "that no one who dwelled near the sea for the space of 12 leagues should come with them, but keep the coasts of the sea from enemies."

By mid-June the Kent rebels had a leader, Wat Tyler. It was rumored later that he had served in the French wars, but of his real biography we know almost nothing. He was aided by John Ball, a renegade Yorkshire priest with links to the movement known as the Lollards, who were highly critical of Church authority and dogma. Ball had been imprisoned on numerous occasions by Archbishop Sudbury for preaching heretical and seditious sermons outside churches on Sundays. He used catchy rhymes and popular slogans to spread a vision of a classless society in which lordship was abolished and land and goods were held in common. His most famous couplet was "When Adam delved and Eve span, who then was the gentleman?"

As the Kent and Essex rebels sacked their counties, they were also in touch with groups of disaffected Londoners. The city of London had been riven by faction and feuds for much of the 1370s. There were multiple hatreds between rival merchant groups and guilds, between native merchants and foreign traders, between supporters and opponents of the Oxford scholar John Wyclif, who was in many ways the father of Lollardy, and more generally between the apprentice classes and their rich masters. At the invitation of the Londoners, on June 11 the rebels set out for the capital. The Kent rebels approached from the southeast via Greenwich and Blackheath; the Essex rebels made their way from the northeast via Mile End.

Throughout this time Richard II was at Westminster surrounded by his household advisers, several earls and merchants, and a number of his family members, including his mother, Joan, his half brothers Thomas and John Holland, and his cousin John of Gaunt's young son Henry Bolingbroke. During the early stages of the rebellion the king's advisers sent men-at-arms into the shires to attempt to bully the rebels into submission. They were chased away, and some of them were killed. Belatedly, the government realized the scale of the uprising. Archbishop Sudbury panicked and resigned his position as chancellor, giving back the great seal. The royal party moved to the Tower of London for their own safety. They sent word to the rebels to meet them. On Wednesday, June 12, the Kent rebels, numbering in the tens of thousands, reached Blackheath, where they camped overnight. At one point on that evening the fourteen-year-old king sailed down the Thames for a conference with his people at Rotherhithe, but his advisers panicked when they saw the size of the crowds on the riverbank, and the party turned back.

This infuriated Wat Tyler and his men, who claimed that they had risen in loyalty to their king, to purge his court of evil counselors. "The commons had a watchword among themselves in English," wrote the Anonimalle chronicler. "[It was,] 'with whom hold you?' and the response was, 'With king Richard and the true commons,' and those who could not or would not so answer were beheaded." Denied their moment to parley with their adored monarch, the rebels flew into a rage and burned Southwark that evening. The next day, Thursday, June 13, they convinced sympathizers in London to lower the drawbridge at London Bridge. They piled, howling with delight, into the city, and paraded down the Strand, the moneyed suburb that lay between London and Westminster, which was dotted with palaces and mansions. The finest palace of all was the Savoy, John of Gaunt's magnificent London residence. The rebels piled over the walls, set fire to the outbuildings, and went about destroying the palace. Rebels ran through the building, smashing everything they could and dragging fine possessions out to a bonfire in the street. The palace was destroyed with barrels of gunpowder found in the cellars.

That same day the Temple—the lodgings and power base of many of the capital's lawyers—was ransacked by Londoners, and piles of legal records were burned in the street. Prisons were sprung across the city while notorious crooks who had been living at liberty were hunted down and beheaded by kangaroo courts. Flames licked the evening sky as a day of targeted rioting ended in debauchery and drunkenness, with pillaged wine barrels rolled into the street and broken open.

On that first night Richard stood dolefully on a turret in the Tower and gazed down at the ragtag army of his subjects who had camped out in the fields below the fortress walls. As London burned, he and his advisers were effectively terrified prisoners in the Tower. Although there had been similar risings in Europe during the second half of the fourteenth century—the Jacquerie in France in 1358 is the worst example—the king's advisers had been caught quite by surprise at the ferocity with which the ordinary people of London and the southeast had risen. Disorder was also breaking out as far afield as York and Somerset, with some of the worst taking place in Cambridgeshire, Hertfordshire, Suffolk, and Norfolk. England, which had only four years ago risen almost as one to acclaim its new king, seemed now to be descending into a godless anarchy.

What had driven the people of England to such paroxysms of rage? On one level, it was very easy to say. Three poll taxes had been levied between 1377 and 1381, a revolutionary experiment in taxing the wealth of communities that had never been taxed directly before. Instead of property and land being assessed, a levy was laid on people themselves. Although the second of the three poll taxes had allowed for graded payments according to social status, with the rich paying most and the poor least, the first and third levies were flat-rate and obviously regressive taxes, which hit the badly off far harder than the wealthy. At first the taxes had provoked disgruntlement, but this swiftly turned to outright fury as commissioners appointed to investigate widespread evasion were accused of heavy-handed tactics.

The poll taxes tapped a deeper root of resentment that had been building in England's towns and villages since the middle of the century. The Black Death had returned again to England in 1379, in an epidemic that eventually lasted for four years. The effect of this, coming on top of the first wave, in 1348 and 1349, and the Children's Plague during 1361 and 1362, was to cause the entire structure of medieval society to creak and change. Labor, once abundant in an overpopulated realm, became scarce and expensive. To combat the threat to landowners, Edward III's government had passed restrictive labor legislation, setting limits to wages and punishing anyone who took or received more than the legal day rate for anything from mowing fields and reaping crops to mending roofs and shoeing horses.

These laws were enforced by local legal commissioners, many of whom were drawn from the same ranks of wealthy county gentry that benefited from the labor laws. They punished the better-off peasants who paid their neighbors to work as well as the workers, whom they convicted of taking illegal wages. There was abundant work for lawyers and Crown officials in ensuring that county elites retained their privileged position. Men who served on labor commissions often also served as sheriffs, MPs, and justices of the peace. There was a real sense that a whole corrupt political class was oppressing ordinary Englishmen. Serfdom was dying out as an institution in the late fourteenth century, but it seemed to many of those who rebelled in 1381 that it was giving way to a new and equally oppressive system, by which lawyers and justices kept the rural poor in just as deep a misery as they had suffered when they were bonded to the land.

Poll taxes that hit the poor hardest; labor legislation that prevented them from earning a reasonable wage; the hideous fear of plague; a miserably failing war, in which families based in Essex and Kent experienced at close hand the dangers of French pirate fleets patrolling the Channel; general fear that the young king who was supposed to be England's savior was being corrupted by evildoers in his household: this all was sufficient in 1381 to kindle a rebellion that shook England to its foundations. Quite how much of the root causes of the rebellion Richard understood as he stood in the Tower of London and watched England burn we cannot know. He did, however, feel himself spurred into action: as a king, and a Plantagenet king at that. The dispersal of the Peasants' Revolt showed that in this pale-faced boy of fourteen, there was a streak of great personal courage and an appetite for leadership. It also scarred him for the rest of his life.

The events were almost impossibly dramatic. On the morning of Friday, June 14, Richard convinced a large deputation of rebels to leave London and go to the fields of Mile End, where he promised he would meet them to discuss their demands. Once they did so, a royal procession made its way through the still-tumultuous city to a conference. Richard rode out accompanied by his half brothers (from his mother Joan of Kent's marriage to Thomas Holland); his young uncle Thomas of Woodstock, now earl of Buckingham; the earls of Warwick and Oxford; William Walworth mayor of London; the veteran soldier Sir Robert Knolles; and various others. His mother, Joan of Kent, rode behind them in a gig. She was a popular figure in the city and generally acted as a conciliatory political influence during the minority, but even she was powerless before the mob. All around them sounded shouts and cries from agitated rebels and townsmen, but the royal party pushed steadily on to Mile End. Behind them in the Tower they left Archbishop Sudbury, Treasurer Hales, and several royal servants whom they knew the rebels wished to kill. The plan was to use the royal absence as a diversion and allow the marked men a window to escape by river.

The plan failed. As the frightened men in the Tower tried to board a boat by the Tower gate, they were spotted by an old woman on the riverbank, who raised the alarm, forcing them to retreat back into the fortress. At Mile End, meanwhile, Richard granted the rebels everything they asked. He commanded that charters be distributed guaranteeing that there would be no return to serfdom, that labor would be free, and that every man could rent land for a maximum of fourpence per acre. He also naively agreed that Tyler and his men could be free to hunt down all the traitors they desired and bring them to him for judgment.

This sealed Sudbury's and Hales's fates. Having failed to escape from the Tower, they were dragged out and murdered when the mob broke in. Their heads were put up on poles and paraded around London before being stuck up on London Bridge, where for several days they perched above the entrance to the city, Sudbury's red bishop's miter nailed crudely onto his skull. Eight others died in the same way; they included John of Gaunt's personal physician and John Legge, a member of Richard's personal bodyguard. Gaunt's son Henry of Bolingbroke, who was also in the Tower, escaped capture and death at the rebels' hands only when a resourceful soldier hid him in a cupboard, a fateful decision that was to have a profound impact on the kingdom's future. The sound made by the mob, wrote the chronicler Thomas Walsingham, was not "like the clamor normally produced by men, but of a sort which enormously exceeded all human noise and which could only be compared to the wailings of the inhabitants of hell."

After the fall of the Tower, London descended into chaos. On Cheapside, where just a few years ago the street had run with wine, now a wooden chopping block was set up, and the ground was soaked with the congealing blood of men and women murdered by the crowds. In St.-Martin's-in-the-Vintry, the bodies of more than one hundred Flemish traders were piled lifeless in the streets. They had been dragged from sanctuary in a church and murdered by a mob whose idle hatred for foreigners was stirred by the perception that the Flemings received special privileges from the government. All around there was a general orgy of murder, looting, and rapine. Targeted disorder soon gave way to general rioting. "This went on throughout the day and the following night, with hideous cries and horrible tumult," wrote the Anonimalle chronicler.

By Saturday it was clear that drastic measures were required. The holiest part of the Plantagenet mausoleum, St. Edward the Confessor's shrine at Westminster Abbey, had been violated when a group of rebels dragged out the disreputable warden of the Marshalsea Prison from his hiding place and took him as a prisoner to Cheapside, where he was beheaded. A rumor had started that Wat Tyler and John Ball intended to burn the whole of London down, capture the king, and make him the figurehead of their new order, in which there would be no lordship but theirs.

The king and his shrunken pool of advisers took refuge at the Wardrobe in Blackfriars, a well-stocked arms store, and concocted another desperate plan. As charters continued to be pumped out by scribes at Chancery, granting freedom from lordship to the people of England, word was sent to the rebels in London that the king would meet them again at the tournament fields beyond the city at Smithfield. Richard steeled himself for the most dangerous moment in his young life with prayer at the Confessor's shrine, where hours earlier, rebel hands had seized another victim. When he arrived at Smithfield, in midafternoon, he had Walworth, the mayor of London, close by his side. Walworth and Knolles had put word out to the loyal men of the city that they would be required at some point soon. A battle was anticipated.

Richard came face-to-face with Wat Tyler in one of the most bizarre meetings in Plantagenet history. The rebel leader appears to have been drunk on success after a weekend of lordship over all of London and by extension the realm. He surprised Richard by shaking him roughly by the hand and telling him to "be of good comfort and joyful, for within the next fortnight you shall have 40,000 more of the commons than you have now, and we shall be good companions."

These were startling words to a boy who had been anointed king by an archbishop now dead at the command of this ruffian. But Richard kept his composure. According to the Anonimalle chronicler, who wrote what was probably an eyewitness account, he conducted negotiations with Tyler in person:

> The king asked him what were the points he wished to have considered, and he should have them freely and without contradiction, written out and sealed. Thereupon the said Wat rehearsed the points which were to be demanded; and he asked that there should be no law but the law of Winchester [a demand for a return to central policing as it had operated under Edward I, rather than by local gentry sitting as JPs, as developed under Edward III], and that there should be henceforth no outlawry in any process of law and that no lord should have any lordship but that it should be divided between all men [i.e., that all social and legal hierarchy should be abolished] and except for the king's own lordship. He also asked that the goods of the Holy Church should not remain in the hands of the religious, nor of parsons and vicars and other churchmen, but that the clergy . . . should have a sufficient sustenance and the rest of their goods should be divided among the parishioners. And he demanded that there should be only one bishop in England . . . and he demanded that there should be no more bondmen in England, no serfdom or villeinage, but that all should be free and of one condition.

It was an extraordinary set of demands, a manifesto so revolutionary that it verged on madness. But Richard, attempting to appease Tyler as he had done at Mile End, again agreed "that [Tyler] should have all that could be fairly granted, saving to himself the regality of the Crown. And then he commanded him to go back home without further delay. And all this time that the king was speaking, no lord nor any other of his council dared nor wished to give any answer to the commons in any place except the king himself." Richard had shown composure well beyond his years.

When Tyler demanded a flagon of water and spit rudely at the king's feet, it prompted one of the royal party to insult the rebel leader. A fight broke out, and in the melee Mayor William Walworth drew his dagger and thrust it deep into Tyler's side, mortally wounding him. Then the mayor left the scene to rouse the city militia under Knolles to put the rest of the rebels to flight.

Now came Richard's crowning moment. Tyler's army was arrayed on the other side of Smithfield from the negotiations, but it was clear to them that something had gone badly wrong. Tyler mounted his little horse and rode back toward his men, crying treachery. As he fell to the ground before them, half-dead, they realized that they had been tricked. "They began to bend their bows and shoot," wrote the chronicler. Richard, understanding that something had to be done, shocked his own party by spurring his horse and riding straight out to the rebels, declaring that he was their captain and their leader and that they should follow him.

It was a moment of astonishing courage and quick thinking, worthy of Edward III, the Black Prince, or any of his most illustrious forebears. Overwhelmed by his majesty, the rebels bowed to their king. As he distracted them, the city militia began to arrive. They surrounded the rebels at Smithfield and herded them out of London with minimal bloodshed. The day was saved, and to a very large degree it was the fourteen-year-old boy king who had saved it. Revolution had been averted, if only for a while.

Return to Crisis

Richard at fourteen had shown the mettle of a king. He would show soon that he could also summon the wrath of a king. He played a prominent role in the bloody judicial retribution exacted against the rebels following the revolt. Richard may have presented himself as the rebels' friend during the crisis at Smithfield, but as soon as order was restored, his instinct was for fierce and merciless revenge. His famous words on tearing up charters in front of rebels who had come to him pleading for restitution were: "Villeins you are, and villeins you will remain; in permanent bondage, not as it was before, but incomparably harsher. . . . While by God's grace we rule over this kingdom, we shall strive . . . to keep you in subjugation, to such a degree that the suffering of your servitude may serve as an example to posterity!" It was cruel—vindictive, even—but decisive too. All in all, his actions during the crisis of 1381 boded well for the fourteen-year-old.

They showed also that he was coming toward an age when he could start governing in his own name. The continual councils that had been a feature of the first years of his reign had ceased after three years, and government now was carried out directly from the king's household. From May 1381 onward the records show a noticeable rise in royal orders coming from the king himself—or at least sealed with his signet, expressing some measure of personal approval.

At fourteen he was able to marry, and he did so with no delay. His bride was Anne of Bohemia, the sister of Wenceslas IV, the king of Bohemia and the emperor-elect. Richard was persuaded to take her as his wife after a three-year campaign by Wenceslas and Pope Urban VI, which had convinced the English court that it would be a propitious marriage. Anne's sister was queen of Hungary and Poland, and her aunt Bona had been married to King John II of France. More important, however, was the role of Richard's marriage in wider European politics.

Since moving from Rome in 1309, the papacy had been under French protection in Avignon and a succession of French popes had been elected. In 1377, however, Pope Gregory XI, a Frenchman, had moved the papal curia back to its spiritual home in Rome. His tenure there was short-lived, and when Gregory died on March 27, 1378, rioting had erupted in the turbulent Eternal City, with a mob demanding that an Italian be elected his successor. Urban VI, who had been born Bartolomeo Prignano in the kingdom of Naples, was duly installed as pope. This proved intensely dissatisfying to a number of French cardinals, who fled Rome for Avignon once again after Urban's election and elected their own pope, Robert of Geneva, who became known as the antipope Clement VII. For the next thirty-nine years there were two popes in Europe, one in Avignon and the other in Rome. The period is now known as the Western Schism.

The result of the schism was to draw ever-clearer fault lines across the Continent. Richard's marriage to Anne of Bohemia cemented his kingdom's place in the dispute. It made very clear that like the German and Italian rulers, England would follow the Roman pope, Urban VI, and oppose the French antipope, who was supported by, among others, France, Scotland, and Castile. If there had been any hope of bringing to an end the ruinous state of mutual hostility between England and France, the Western Schism dashed it.

Richard's marriage was also a financial burden on the overstretched treasury. Richard's new brother-in-law, King Wenceslas, was broke. Had Richard married an Italian princess, he might have received a substantial dowry. But instead of profiting from his marriage, he found he was expected to loan Wenceslas fifteen thousand pounds to seal the alliance. It was poor business indeed, and when Anne was married and crowned in January 1382, Londoners expressed their disapproval of the alliance by tearing down a sheet bearing the royal arms crossed with the imperial arms that decorated a fountain in the city.

They were a strange, fragile couple. The Westminster chronicler described Anne as "a little scrap of humanity." Richard was blond and radiantly boyish, with slightly protruding eyes and the long, mournful face that was so characteristic of the later Plantagenets. He did not grow a beard, and despite an emerging propensity for violent tantrums when he felt his royal dignity was under threat, he had a shy, stammering manner of speaking. Nevertheless, when the fourteen-year-old Anne arrived in England in December, it was the start of a loving relationship. Over the years the king proved truly devoted to his new wife.

Around these two wispy teenagers an elegant, extravagant royal court began to congregate. Even as a young man Richard was developing a taste for the finery of kingship. He adopted his grandfather's and father's taste for pageantry and courtly spectacle, although he was never to share their enthusiasm for riding in tournaments or throwing himself directly into the melee of battle. His would be far more of a visual, aesthetic kingship, in which public manifestations of divinely anointed authority and elaborate forms of ritual came to the fore. At Eltham, King's Langley, and Sheen, the royal palaces were reworked with beautiful private bathrooms, ballrooms, and sophisticated kitchens and spiceries serving the very latest in rich, delicate, and heavily spiced food. Richard, Anne, and their courtiers followed the very latest in fashion: the men in tight hose and codpieces, with jeweled, high-collared robes and expensive doublets; the women wearing fitted gowns, exquisite jewelry, and shoes so long and pointed that they had to be supported by garters joining them to the knees. Their court was designed to radiate the magnificence of Edward III's court, and it ran up debts with just as much alacrity.

As the household developed its own style, it slowly began to change in personnel too. Old companions such as Sir Simon Burley remained close to the king, but some of the older servants of the Black Prince gave way to a younger crowd of chamber knights, men like John Beauchamp, James Berners, and John Salisbury. At the heart of day-to-day government was Michael de la Pole, a former servant of the Black Prince's, who was in his early fifties and had initially been placed in the household at parliament's request. De la Pole's father had been a wealthy merchant and a key financier to Edward III, and he found great favor with Richard too. But the real darling of Richard's court was Robert de Vere, the young earl of Oxford. De Vere was only five years older than Richard, and his closeness to the king aroused some of the same suspicions and grievances that had accompanied the rise of another royal favorite, Piers Gaveston. The scathing chronicler Thomas Walsingham would accuse de Vere of having used black magic to manipulate Richard and implied that there had been a homosexual relationship between the pair.

That is unlikely. But what was clear was that Richard, like every young king, intended to have his own men. This meant a creeping isolation for the older heads and particularly for the king's uncles: John of Gaunt duke of Lancaster, Edmund Langley earl of Cambridge, and Thomas of Woodstock earl of Buckingham. The older magnates found that Richard and his circle frequently treated them with disdain bordering on hostility. Grants of land

and castles to favored knights cut across the established lords' local power structures. Meanwhile Richard's personal immaturity and petulance alienated several of his most senior noblemen.

This was not simply a matter of disgruntled personalities. Although every king had the right to choose his advisers, he would come under intense criticism if his alienation of powerful and experienced men led to a general diminishing in public order and foreign success. In Richard's case, this was precisely what happened, but when the earl of Arundel criticized the king's rule in the Salisbury parliament of 1384, Richard turned white with anger and, according to the Westminster chronicle, told Arundel that if "it is supposed to be my fault that there is misgovernment in the kingdom, you lie through your teeth! You can go to the Devil!" On another occasion, a year later, he had a furious argument with Archbishop Courtenay of Canterbury. When Courtenay upbraided him for the poor conduct of government, Richard drew his sword and tried to attack the archbishop. He was only prevented from doing so by his uncle Thomas earl of Buckingham.

These were obviously unbecoming actions for a king. His irresponsibility in rewarding his friends for doing very little grated in many parts of the realm. But his forebears had learned that the political community would tolerate the king's friends so long as they did not seem to be damaging England on the battlefield or using their position to seize other magnates' property. In the first case, however, Richard was unfortunate. The war was turning unstoppably toward the French during the 1380s. As his court flourished with new men and splendid pageantry, so the position across the Channel collapsed.

To call English prospects on the Continent dim during the early 1380s would be an understatement. Compared with the heyday of Edward III, they were downright embarrassing. Only Calais and a thin coastal strip of Gascony remained in English hands. The Channel was plagued by French and Castilian ships, while what passed for the English navy rotted in port. Trading was so perilous that wool revenues hit rock bottom. The situation was so dire that London's citizens considered a scheme to build a giant chain across the Thames to protect the city from burning raids. The death of Charles V in 1380 and the accession of his son Charles VI lulled French aggression briefly, but the new king was equally determined to kick the English out of the Continent. Without a king like Edward III, committed to war and with a vision of how to achieve victory and unite the realm behind the effort, the English war machine splintered into disarray.

Differing strategies emerged. For John of Gaunt, the future was Castile. He had married Pedro the Cruel's daughter Constance of Castile in 1372 as part of the deal making preceding the battle of Nájera. (His brother Edmund Langley married Pedro's younger daughter Isabella at the same time.) When Pedro died without male issue in 1379, Gaunt formally claimed the throne for himself. Thereafter he believed in "the way of Portugal," English conquest through Iberia. His brothers supported him, but it was essentially a private, dynastic focus that drew Gaunt ever further away from the center of politics in the 1380s and did not help the national interest one shred.

For most Englishmen, the path of warfare lay in Flanders. It was closer to home, and the fortunes of the trading cities of northwestern Europe had real significance for the English wool trade, which remained central to the nation's economy and a vital source of royal revenue. Moreover, the county of Flanders was under direct threat from Charles VI's uncle the duke of Burgundy, who aimed to conquer the rich trading cities one by one. In 1383 the warlike Bishop Despenser of Norwich, who was the grandson of Edward II's favorite Hugh Despenser the Younger and who had played a major role in putting down the 1381 revolt in East Anglia, launched a "crusade" to Flanders, by which he aimed to use papal license to protect the territories from falling to the duke.

Alas, despite ample funding and parliamentary approval, the mission was badly equipped and returned to England a dismal failure. By 1385 Flanders had fallen. It seemed increasingly clear that the best route out of France for the time being was to sue for peace. The dream of rebuilding the ancient Plantagenet empire, let alone of uniting the French and English Crowns, was over.

In 1385 Richard was eighteen. He was no pacifist, but he was highly unenthusiastic about the idea of launching another offensive in France, fruitless and expensive as it would be. Although all three of his uncles—Gaunt, Buckingham, and Cambridge—urged him to commit to more fighting, Richard was inclined to listen to those like his chancellor, Michael de la Pole, who counseled caution. Had he wanted to fight, it was most unlikely that parliament, skittish in the aftermath of the Peasants' Revolt, would have granted the necessary taxation to do so. That summer he led an expedition to oust French garrisons from Scotland. It was a pragmatic option. The king could lead the nobility, demonstrate his capability on the battlefield, and bolster military confidence without running up too heavy a bill.

What followed was a fiasco. Richard marched north with an army that included almost the entire nobility, all the English bannerets, and around fourteen thousand men. When they reached the Scottish border, he marked the occasion by raising Edmund Langley from earl of Cambridge to duke of York and Thomas of Woodstock from earl of Buckingham to duke of Gloucester. He also raised de la Pole to the earldom of Suffolk and his friend de Vere to the wholly unprecedented position of marquis of Dublin. In a stroke, de Vere outranked all the other English earls and stood virtually on a par with the royal dukes. "Just as the sky is rendered clear and bright by the stars, so dignity makes not only kingdoms but kingly diadems shine with its light," Richard later told parliament.

But the bolstered prestige did little for Richard's military prospects. As his army advanced, the Scots declined to give battle. They retreated into the hills, wasting the countryside as they went. It was the same tactic that had reduced Edward III to tears of frustration in 1328. The Scots dodged the English advance, slipped south, and burned Carlisle. The English reached Edinburgh in mid-August, found that they were starving and had no one to fight, and fell back to Westminster within three weeks. It was a feeble expedition, which achieved nothing.

By the time parliament met in October 1386, the mood of the country was mutinous. The list of grievances was long. English foreign policy was in the doldrums. Royal finances were parlous, and there was mounting hostility toward Michael de la Pole's competence in managing the king's money. John of Gaunt had left the country in high dudgeon, having been deeply unsettled by the snub given to his advice during the Scottish campaign and also by rumors of plots by the chamber knights to assassinate him. Across the Channel, Charles VI was said to be raising a forest of masts at Sluys, the largest invasion armada ever aimed at England. Advice given to parliament directly following the failed Scottish invasion had been utterly ignored. An unusual memo to the king included an ominous suggestion that Richard should "attach to himself persons of estate, of probity and of honor, and to associate with them and eschew the company of others; for if he does this, great good and honor will come to him, and he will win the hearts and love of his people. But if he does the opposite, then the contrary will happen, to the great danger of himself and his realm, which God forbid." The king's response to this particular note is not recorded. But the official parliament rolls record his response to similar requests made while the parliament was sitting. It is laconic but telling: "The king will do as he chooses."

What precious little taxation had been granted was now utterly wasted, while the impoverished king had seen fit to raise up his friend de Vere once more to the position of duke of Ireland. This gave him plenary powers and a rank that put him fully on a par with Richard's royal uncles: de Vere became the first duke not of the royal blood. (Henry of Grosmont, the first duke of Lancaster, had at least been Edward III's cousin.) Comparisons with Gaveston's award of the royal earldom of Cornwall were hard to ignore.

It was clear to everyone who attended what came to be known as the Wonderful Parliament in October 1386 that the country was suffering a crisis of leadership. The attacks came as soon as parliament opened. When Michael de la Pole earl of Suffolk stood before the assembled masses to open the parliament and announce the king's plans to lead an invasion of France, the commons erupted in complaint. They blamed Suffolk squarely for mismanaging the king's money and spending it in ways other than those stipulated by parliament, for allowing the English navy to fall into disrepair, and for failing English allies in Ghent by refusing to send them aid, which had resulted in the loss of Ghent to the duke of Burgundy. He was also accused of misappropriating funds and sources of royal income for his own personal gain. In general, the earl was reviled as the figurehead for all the inept advisers around the king, and the commons demanded that he be removed from his position and impeached on numerous charges of incompetence and negligence. They refused to go any further with parliamentary business until this was done.

Now the king's true colors emerged. Richard was a married man who had led his country on campaign. Outraged by the commons' impertinent demands, he refused to come to Westminster and sent a message from his manor at Eltham saying that he would not dismiss so much as a scullion boy from his kitchen on parliament's say-so. In an attempt at mediation, his uncle Thomas of Woodstock, newly duke of Gloucester, and Thomas Arundel bishop of Ely were sent to Eltham to negotiate face-to-face.

They found the king in a shrill and belligerent mood. When they tried to reason with him, he berated them. The chronicler Henry Knighton recorded the details that reached him of their conversation: they said to Richard that if a king refused to come to parliament "by his own irresponsible resolution," then parliament could dissolve itself after forty days. This drove Richard into a rage. It was clear that his uncle and the bishop had touched a streak of deep paranoia within him, developed no doubt through the experiences of his youth. "We have long been aware that our people and commons intend to resist and to rise against us," he shouted at them. "And in the face of that threat, it seems best to us to turn to our cousin [the king] of France, and seek his support and aid against our enemies, and better to submit ourselves to him than to our own subjects."

With an invasion fleet less than one hundred miles away, Gloucester and Arundel exclaimed in a state of disbelief: "The king of France is your chiefest enemy, and your kingdom's greatest foe." They reasoned with Richard, pleading that he should "think how your grandfather, King Edward III, and also your father Prince Edward, in his name, sweated and laboured all their lives in heat and cold, in tireless endeavor to conquer the kingdom of France ... remember too how ... peoples too unnumbered withstood in that war death and the danger of death, and how the commons of this realm have poured out ungrudgingly their goods and possessions and uncounted treasure to sustain the war." It was finally only after a veiled reference to Edward II's deposition ("your people ... have an ancient law which not long since, lamentably, had to be invoked") that the king was shaken out of his fit of pique and forced to accept that his government had to be reformed.

Cowed, Richard eventually came to Westminster. There he had to watch in ignominy as the Wonderful Parliament expelled Michael de la Pole and the treasurer, Sir John Fordham, from their posts and set up a commission to hold office for a year. It was to audit the royal finances, take control of the exchequer, and exercise authority to use the great and privy seals. In effect, it took government totally out of Richard's hands. The king, now nineteen years old, was reduced once again to a state of boyhood, his kingship as good as revoked. It was almost more than his proud young heart could bear.

Treason and Trauma

Just over a year after the Wonderful Parliament concluded its business, on December 20, 1387, Robert de Vere, the duke of Ireland, moved cautiously through the winter fog heading for Radcot Bridge, near Chipping Norton, in Oxfordshire. He had with him several thousand men recruited in and around the king's earldom of Chester. The countryside he moved through was thick with his enemies. Danger truly lurked around every corner.

He was riding hard southeast to meet the king in London. The Plantagenet Crown faced yet another crisis. Far from being repaired in the aftermath of the Wonderful Parliament of October 1386, relations between the king and his leading subjects had completely broken down. De Vere was heading for London in the knowledge that very soon England would erupt into violence. Richard was once more at the mercy of his subjects, who were rising in revolt against his rule and in particular against de Vere's influence. De Vere knew that he was riding against time. The combined armies of some of the most powerful noblemen in England had been sent out to capture him. Enemy companies fanned out across England, occupying not just the villages of the Cotswolds through which he now picked his way but the whole of the Midlands; everywhere west of Northampton was seething with hostile forces. It would not be long before they arrived.

How could things have sunk to this point? The answer lay largely with Richard. His response to the reforming council imposed upon him at the end of the Wonderful Parliament had been both petulant and severe. Humiliated and aggrieved, the king had spent the first few months brooding in his hunting lodges of the Thames Valley. Full of resentment and anger at the way he had been treated, he had left London in February 1387 defiantly to undertake what one chronicler called his "gyration," a tour of the realm during which he avoided the inspections and interferences of the council and assessed just what support he had in the country at large.

The tour had lasted nine months. He had traveled from Beverley to Shrewsbury and concentrated for the most part on the northern and northwestern Midlands, close to his royal principality of Chester. He had taken with him his friends de Vere and Michael de la Pole, and as they traveled,

Richard began to formulate a plan to reassert his authority once the council's term expired. He noted that his magnates now mobilized support by retaining personnel and paying them for their loyalty; in exchange for regular cash payments they wore their lords' distinctive badges and often uniforms, protected their interests, and fought for them if required. As earl of Chester he could do something similar. He could create a permanent power base of retained men whom he would have no cause to fear, with no concern that they would turn on him and no dread of the public chastisement that his supposedly natural supporters—the lords and commons of his royal realm—had heaped on his shoulders. A plan had formed. Richard would effectively set out to build himself up as a powerful private landed magnate as well as king.

During the summer of 1387 Richard also began to explore the legal means by which he could reverse the work of the Wonderful Parliament. Twice in August he had gathered together in secret the leading judges of the realm, headed by the Cornishman Sir Robert Tresilian, who as chief justice of the King's Bench was one of the two most senior judges in England. Richard questioned them about the ordinances by which he was bound. Their verdict, browbeaten out of several of the judges with threats of death, was published in the form of judicial rulings, which stated that "the statute, ordinance and commission made in the last parliament" was "derogatory to the regality and prerogative of our said lord the king." Moreover—and here it is easy to discern Richard's deceptively forceful hand—when the judges "were asked what punishment they deserved who compelled or forced the king to the making of the said statute, ordinance, and commission . . . they replied unanimously that they were deserving of punishment as traitors."

This was a fateful reply. The specter of treason had haunted Edward II's reign; it was the irredeemable charge that had justified the murders of Piers Gaveston, Thomas earl of Lancaster, Edmund earl of Kent, and Roger Mortimer earl of March. In an effort to prevent such bloody misery from ever again afflicting England, Edward III had passed the Treason Act of 1351, which limited the definition of the crime to attacks or plots on the lives of the king, the queen, and their eldest son, rape of the king's eldest daughter, murder of the chancellor, treasurer, or chief justices, or making war against the king in his kingdom. Now Richard was blowing the definition of treason wide open once again. A traitor was no longer someone who tried to kill the king, his family, or his most senior officials. It could be anyone who attempted to reform the realm or regulate the royal household. The judges, pressed by the king, had agreed that all those who had constrained him in 1386 could be considered traitors. Traitors too were any who ignored a royal command to dissolve parliament, impeached a royal minister, or reminded Richard of the fate of his great-grandfather Edward II.

The opinions of the judges were terrifying in their implications. When Richard returned to London in November 1387, it was clear from everything that there were now only two likely outcomes to the summer's activity: a judicial bloodbath or civil war. And civil war was what de Vere was preparing for as he hurried south through Oxfordshire.

He himself was the casus belli. During the king's gyration a new opposition, whose specific aim was to kick out de Vere and all others like him from the king's company, had gathered. They were known as the lords appellant, for on November 14 Thomas duke of Gloucester, along with the earls of Arundel and Warwick, had made a formal approach to the king "appealing" (or formally indicting) those around the king whom *they* thought guilty of treachery. The list of the accused contained five names: Alexander Neville archbishop of York; Michael de la Pole earl of Suffolk; Robert Tresilian chief justice; Nicholas Brembre, merchant, former mayor of London, and loyal hero of the Peasants' Revolt; and Robert de Vere duke of Ireland.

The king, furious at the presumption of the lords, had attempted to raise troops. But he failed. The county sheriffs would not recruit men for him, claiming that all the commons supported the appellants. The Londoners, to whom Richard appealed directly, refused to rise in his name. De Vere's Cheshire army was the only hope.

And so, as he marched his force through the damp wintry countryside, de Vere knew whom to fear. Gloucester, Warwick, and Arundel were loose, and they had picked up two useful allies, John of Gaunt's son Henry Bolingbroke, who now held the title of earl of Derby, and Thomas Mowbray earl of Nottingham. These five made a formidable team. They had supporters among many leading London families and knights and gentry across England. Their armies spread like fingers around the Cotswolds, preparing to wrap themselves tightly around de Vere.

On the morning of December 20 de Vere fought a small skirmish against the duke of Gloucester's supporters somewhere near Bourton-on-the-Hill, his first encounter with appellant troops. In a confused battle, many of de Vere's Chester men deserted. Later that day, probably at Burford, another skirmish took place against the earl of Arundel's men; de Vere's lieutenant Sir Thomas Molyneaux was killed. It was therefore in some desperation that the duke pushed his men on toward Radcot Bridge, where he was hoping to cross the river. According to the chronicler Henry Knighton, he believed that "if he had been able to cross the bridge it would have kept him safe from his enemies." Fighting his way south of the Thames, he calculated, was the only way to make it safely to Richard in London.

But he was out of luck. As he led his men toward the pointed stone arches of the twelfth-century bridge, he found that he had been beaten to his mark. At either side of the crossing stood armed men and archers wearing the livery of Henry earl of Derby. Turning, he saw Derby himself coming up from his rear, with a large body of soldiers. De Vere was trapped. There was no choice but to give battle.

As trumpets blasted and the royal standard was hurriedly unfurled, there was a general mumbling among the troops that fighting was uneven and unwise. "They were too few in comparison with the enemy," wrote Henry Knighton, "nor dared they affront so many of the lords and nobles of the whole realm."

De Vere panicked. If he was captured, there was no telling what his fate might be. A cycle of violence had begun, and it was unlikely that he would merely be exiled from the king's presence. He had to save his skin. He charged his men toward the bridge in an attempt to cross, but when they reached the bridge, they found that barriers had been erected and the road was broken in three places. It would be impossible for more than one horse to cross at a time. "We have been fooled," cried the duke, and, changing horses, he attempted to flee alone down the riverbank.

But looming in front of him was an even worse fate. As Henry earl of Derby approached him from behind, the duke of Gloucester himself was coming up ahead. De Vere had only one option left. He gambled on his life. "Spurring his horse, [he] cast off his gauntlets and his sword, and plunged into the Thames," wrote Knighton. "And thus [he] escaped with wonderful daring." As de Vere fled, eventually sailing for refuge in France, his men promptly surrendered.

Richard spent a somber Christmas in Windsor. On December 30 he met the five triumphant appellants at the Tower of London. They marched in with five hundred heavily armed men, closing the gates behind them. The meeting was stormy. The appellants castigated Richard for his behavior. They produced damning correspondence between the king and de Vere and accused him of wanting to use the king of France against his own subjects. They demanded that the five men they had accused be brought to justice and that the king's household be purged. When Richard proved truculent, they threatened to depose him, suggesting that they had already chosen his successor. (One chronicler suggested that they told the king he had been deposed already and that only a dispute between Gloucester and Derby over which of them should inherit the throne had prevented them from enacting the deposition.) Richard was forced to give in to their demands and call a parliament at which a new settlement could be thrashed out.

Parliament opened at Westminster on February 3. Lords and commons gathered together in the White Hall at Westminster, which was richly painted with a series of scenes from the life of Edward I. (Whitehall remains the name of the bureaucratic heart of British government.) The king took his seat before the assembled estates and prepared to hear the worst. Then, according to the chronicler Thomas Favent, "the most noble five appellants . . . with a numerous throng, entered the hall together, arm in arm, wearing cloth of gold, and after staring at the king bent the knee to him in salutation. There was a mass of people filling the hall, even to the corners."

Over the days and months that followed detailed legal arguments were put forward against the accused servants of the Crown. The initial list of charges alone took more than two hours to read aloud. They were accused of giving treasonable advice to the king, offering to sell English castles in France back to the French king, and stealing money from the royal coffers for themselves. Somewhat embarrassingly, four of the five accused had absconded and were tried in their absence. Only Nicholas Brembre, the former mayor, was present, and his trial began a fortnight after parliament opened.

The verdicts, however, were the same whether the accused were present or not. Archbishop Alexander Neville of Canterbury, the duke of Ireland, the earl of Suffolk, and Sir Robert Tresilian were all found guilty of treason in their absence. The duke, earl, and judge were sentenced to be drawn through London and hanged as traitors and enemies of the king. The archbishop was eventually sentenced to exile. All four men were to be disinherited. Brembre was present at parliament and protested his innocence on all charges, which in his case included allegations of illegally executing prisoners in London's jails, accroaching royal power, resisting the appellants, and forcing the citizens to swear oaths of allegiance to the king against his enemies. He offered to fight his accusers in judicial battle; but the request was not allowed, and he was condemned to a traitor's end: dragged on a hurdle to Tyburn before being hanged, drawn, and quartered. He recited prayers for the dead all the way to the gallows.

And more drama followed. Archbishop Neville, Robert de Vere, and the earl of Suffolk had all managed to escape overseas, but Tresilian had not. Six days after he was formally condemned in parliament, a strange figure was spotted spying on the proceedings at Westminster from a nearby rooftop. The house was raided, and inside, cowering under a table, was Sir Robert, the hanging judge and scourge of the rebels of 1381. He was dressed in beggar's rags and wore a thick false beard, but his distinctive voice betrayed him. Cries went up of "We have him!" and Tresilian was dragged from his hiding place to parliament, leaving his wife swooning behind him and screaming himself for the sanctuary of Westminster. But sanctuary was denied him. Tresilian was dragged in short order on a hurdle to Tyburn and forced up to the gallows platform, whinnying in terror. When his clothes were cut off, all could see that he had covered his body in protective charms. There was a dark irony to a judge's relying on superstitious trinkets to ward off the noose. Tresilian was hanged naked; in the end he was put out of his misery when his throat was slit.

But the appellants were not finished there. Once they were done with Brembre and Tresilian and had condemned the other three appellees in absentia, parliament launched a bloody purge of Richard's household. Proceedings began against many more of those who surrounded the king and were deemed to have led him astray. By May, Richard's beloved tutor Sir Simon Burley, as well as his household knights Sir John Beauchamp, Sir John Salisbury, and James Berners, had all been tried and sentenced to a traitor's death. Dozens died in a wild bloodbath aimed at wiping out anyone whom the appellants viewed as being connected even in the slightest way with Richard's hapless regime. The judges who had advised Richard that the ordinances of the Wonderful Parliament were treasonous were now themselves also sentenced to die; only at the end of the parliament were they spared and sent off to live in exile in Ireland.

Richard sat through nearly four months of state trials and saw his friends and allies hauled off one by one to be hanged, disemboweled, and beheaded. He was forced to preside over the parliament and became increasingly desperate as it proceeded. When Burley's time came, the king argued so violently with Gloucester that a fight almost broke out. Richard begged desperately for the old man's life, as did the queen, who went down on her knees to the three leading appellants. Indeed Burley's case to live was supported by several more moderate earls, including Edmund Langley duke of York, and even the two lesser appellants, Henry earl of Derby and Thomas earl of Nottingham. But at the Merciless Parliament, there was no escaping death and destruction. Burley was executed, just like all the others. Richard, at twenty years old, had seen enough humiliation to last a lifetime.

The Reinvention of Kingship

The five or six years that followed the Merciless Parliament were remarkably calm for Richard II. Many of his closest friends had been either exiled or killed by the appellants, but once the purging was over, England settled back into a state of curious peace. The appellants had achieved everything they set out to do. Richard had been brought to heel. There was not much left to fight for, on either side.

Evidence seemed to suggest that Richard had taken on board some of the lessons of the time. He appeared, outwardly at least, to be trying harder to rule effectively. On May 3, 1389, he made a dramatic scene at a meeting of his great council. Sitting himself before the members, he interrupted a session of the council by asking all those assembled how old he was. They replied, accurately, that he was now twenty-two. Richard then launched into a speech whose tone was reported by several chroniclers. According to Henry Knighton, he said: "It happens I have spent some years under your counsel and rule, and I give great thanks to God and then to you because you have governed and sustained both my person and my inheritance. . . . Now however, by God's care, we have attained the age of our majority, and are indeed already in our twenty-second year. Therefore we desire and will the freedom to rule . . . and to have our kingdom . . . to choose and appoint to those posts our officers and ministers, and so freely remove those who are now in office."

According to Thomas Walsingham, Richard then commanded the archbishop of York, Thomas Arundel, to resign the chancellor's seal. "The king collected it in a fold of his dress, and suddenly rose and went out; and after a short while he came back and sat down again, and gave the seal to William Wykeham, bishop of Winchester, although he was very reluctant to take it. And he created nine other officials . . . using in all things his own judgment and authority. The duke of Gloucester and the earl of Warwick . . . he removed from his council."

This could have been a disaster, but it was not. Richard set about governing with a good deal more responsibility than he had before. He asserted his right to choose his councillors and those who gave him more informal advice, but he also accepted that he was bound to listen to the advice of experienced men like Wykeham, who had been his grandfather's chief minister during the 1360s.

He was aided by the return from Castile of John of Gaunt, with whom he was reconciled and who now became a staunch supporter of the regime. Gaunt allayed tensions between Richard and the former appellants, threw lavish hunting parties for the king and queen, and took to walking arm in arm with the king whenever he could. The king proclaimed his gratitude toward his eldest uncle outwardly by wearing Gaunt's livery collar, two interlinked S shapes. In 1390 he granted him palatinate (that is to say, quasi-royal) powers in the duchy of Lancaster, which would be entailed on his male heirs. Furthermore, the king awarded Gaunt the duchy of Aquitaine for life. This was a significant break with Plantagenet tradition: Aquitaine had been the inheritance of the king's eldest son and heir since the thirteenth century. Its altered status gave Gaunt a vested interest in finding peace with France.

Gaunt rejoined the king's council in March 1390, and an agreement was drawn up stipulating that all decisions with financial implications had to be approved by all three of the king's uncles. Richard apparently accepted this, and a new state of consensus was reached, through which the king and the political community began to work together once again. As a result, the royal finances recovered to a state of good health (royal revenue rose by 36 percent between 1389 and 1396), and parliament ceased to be a battleground among king, lords, and commons and reverted to its proper function as a forum for discussions about royal government.

If Edward III's court had celebrated chivalry and war, Richard's celebrated the magnificence of the anointed king. New and grandiloquent forms of address were popularized. Whereas in the past English kings had been addressed as "my lord," now titles such as "Your Highness" and "Your Majesty" were introduced for the first time, in mimicry of styles fashionable in France. Written addresses were even more pompous and theatrical, such as "most high and puissant prince" and "your high royal majesty." The hostile Walsingham called these "not human, but divine honours" and "strange and flattering words hardly suitable for mere mortals."

Richard's court became a center for literary and artistic ideas, and some of the great writers of the age worked under the royal watch. Richard's interest in letters was transient, and he did not commission much literature himself, but his court was at the heart of the invention of England's native tongue as a language of high literature. John Gower, the great London scholar, claimed that he wrote his *Confessio Amantis*—a huge, complex love poem of more than thirty thousand lines—at Richard's personal request after meeting the king on a barge in 1386. The *Confessio* was written in English and published in its first version in 1390 with a dedication to the king and Geoffrey Chaucer, whose *Canterbury Tales* was also written during his period of association with Richard's court. The aged French chronicler Froissart visited the English court and presented Richard with a collection of French poems; Sir John Clanvowe wrote elegant lyrics, and Edward duke of Albemarle, the son of Edmund duke of York and thus Richard's cousin, translated a famous French hunting textbook into English. Even the soldierly courtier Sir John Montagu was praised abroad, by none other than the brilliant female Venetian writer Christine de Pisan, for his appreciation of literature and skill as a poet.

The king was a generous patron of artists and architects. By the 1390s Henry Yevele, the master builder of the fourteenth century, was an old man in his seventies. He had been most productive under Edward III, but in 1393 he embarked on his most famous work for Richard: the reconstruction of Westminster Hall. He raised the walls and added a huge hammer beam ceiling and ceremonial cathedral-like entrance. High in the hall he placed a series of white harts (Richard's personal badge; a hart was a mature stag deer), while thirteen statues were commissioned of the kings of England from Edward the Confessor to Richard himself, emphasizing the continuity of English kingship into the Plantagenet era.

Slightly later Richard took receipt of the *Wilton Diptych*, a haunting and beautiful painting depicting the king being presented to the Virgin and Child by three saints: Edward the Confessor, the Saxon child king St. Edmund, and John the Baptist. Richard's obsession with Edward the Confessor was nearly as strong as Henry III's. Whereas warrior kings such as Edward I and Edward III favored legendary soldiers like King Arthur and St. George, Richard saw himself as a prince of peace, a quality for which the Confessor was praised by the chroniclers. In 1395 the king altered the royal arms, quartering the fleur-de-lis and lions *passant gardant* with the arms of the Confessor.

The *Wilton Diptych* is full of cryptic symbolism: references to Richard's ancient Anglo-French lineage are intertwined with unmistakable signs of his literal belief in his anointed divinity. The very angels surrounding the Virgin wear the badge of the white hart as though they were personally retained to protect the king. On the reverse of the diptych there is a larger painting of a hart, reclining with a chained crown around its neck.

Yet beneath this celebratory, magnificent outward reinvention of kingship there were signs that Richard himself, calmer and apparently more reasonable, was not quite a king transformed. Over the course of the early 1390s he actively recast his rule in a far more authoritarian, personal style. Kingship was not about the Crown and its representation of public authority; it was about Richard himself. Knights and esquires across the counties of England began to receive the king's white hart livery. Many of them were men who already served in the royal administration. The king did not trust the machinery of his public authority; he felt he had to tie people to himself personally, visually, and ceremonially, as their private lord.

On great public occasions there was sometimes a spiteful edge to Richard's ceremony. When he fell out with the citizens of London in 1392 over the provision of a loan, reconciliation demanded pageantry on the scale of a full coronation. King Richard and Queen Anne processed through the streets in splendor, while the city guilds stood at obsequious attention. They were lavished with gifts: boys dressed as angels awarded them golden crowns; a gold table was presented to them at the Temple; a great service of thanksgiving, which included a procession to the shrine of Edward the Confessor, was held at Westminster Abbey. For months afterward the Londoners were still sending gifts professing their great favor to the king; at Epiphany 1393 Richard received a camel, and the queen a pelican.

This sort of genuflection was in one sense part of kingship. But the most successful Plantagenet kings—Henry II, Richard I, and Edward III—had tended to mix roughly with their subjects rather than set themselves aloof. Henry II had abjured the regality of kingship in favor of riding in a makeshift camp and making light with all who came before him. Edward III fought incognito against his own knights at tournaments and emphasized the role of the commons in governance. Even King John, a markedly inglorious king, had sat as a judge in cases involving the meanest wretches in his realm. Richard, however, seemed determined to amplify his singularity and superiority through court spectacle.

By the middle of the decade there was something decidedly pathological about the king's desire to be venerated. He had always been a fragile, suspicious soul, and it now appeared his grasp on sanity was slipping. On June 7, 1394, Queen Anne died at Sheen. She was twenty-seven. She had been Richard's constant companion for years, and he loved her. Distraught with grief, he ordered that the palace where she died, on which he had spent vast sums renovating as their home, be ripped down. Then he swore a melodramatic oath, declaring that for a year he would not set foot inside any building, save a church, in which he had spent time with his late wife. His concern for ceremonial was so intense that he delayed her funeral for two months so that the right sort of wax torch could be brought over from Flanders. But this was more than just grief. Anne's death seemed to trigger a return to the violent petulance of his youth. Richard summoned all his magnates to London for the funeral on July 29. The earl of Arundel arrived late, and when he came before the king, Richard hit him so hard in the face that he fell to the ground bleeding.

This was not the only funeral at which the king's behavior seemed odd. Robert de Vere died in exile in France in 1392, after being wounded by a wild boar. His embalmed body was eventually brought back to England in November 1395. Many of the English magnates refused to attend this reinterment. Those who did watched as the king ordered his friend's coffin to be opened, so that he might place gold rings on de Vere's cold dead fingers and gaze on his face—three years expired—one last time.

After Anne's death and de Vere's burial, Richard grew more and more obsessed with Edward II. He encouraged the monks of Gloucester Abbey, where Edward was buried, to commemorate the murdered king every year, and in 1395 he petitioned the pope to have his great-grandfather canonized. That same year he commissioned a strange epitaph for his own tomb at Westminster; it read: "He threw down all who violated the royal prerogative; he destroyed heretics and scattered their friends." This might have been read as a reference to Richard's vigilance against the Lollards, Christian reformers who followed the teachings of John Wyclif, but there was something potentially sinister about it too.

Like the ancestor he wished to canonize, Richard never truly understood the nature of successful kingship, which lay in balancing his public authority and the needs of the kingdom with his private wishes, friends, and tastes. His very reverence and pity for Edward II, a king who had brought nothing but disunity, violence, corruption, and bloodshed to his realm, spoke volumes about his understanding of a king's duty. The fact that he felt the need to retain his own public servants spoke of a deep-seated paranoia that had been with him from the earliest age.

But there was another motivating instinct in Richard's personality, which dominated the final years of the fourteenth century and which sat very uneasily with the king's self-perception as a man of peace. That was his unquenchable thirst for revenge.

Richard Revenged

After the savage turmoil that racked the first decade of his reign, Richard spent much of the following decade restoring some degree of confidence in his rule. Indeed for the first part of the 1390s government ran smoothly in partnership between king and council. Parliament did not attempt to purge the executive or humiliate the king. Royal revenues increased. In 1394 Richard led a seven-month expedition to Ireland, taking numerous young nobles and seven thousand men, to achieve what he called in a letter "the punishment of our rebels there and to establish good government and just rule over our faithful lieges." The venture was highly successful. Richard achieved more in Ireland—in the short term at least—than any king since Henry II.

In March 1396 a twenty-eight-year truce was finally concluded with France; it was cemented by a marriage agreement: Richard was to wed Charles VI's seven-year-old daughter, Isabella, with a handsome dowry of eight hundred thousand francs. When the bride was handed over in late October 1396, Richard and Charles met in Ardres, not far from Calais, to celebrate their agreement in a field studded with ornate tents, brimming with jewels and gifts: golden model ships, horses with silver saddles and pearl collars. The two kings posed as the saviors of Christendom because with England and France no longer at war, it was speculated that a single pope might now be elected to end the continuing Rome-Avignon schism. There was talk of launching a new crusade, this time against the Turks. It seemed to Thomas Walsingham that England was finally "basking in peace and the hope was for an entirely prosperous future on account of the magnificence of the king."

On January 6, 1397, Richard turned thirty. It was a significant age: the final milestone in his long journey to manhood. At long last the king had arrived. Or had he? There had been a few ominous signs that even at the height of his success, Richard remained deep down an acutely troubled king, hypersensitive, painfully insecure, and prone to outbursts of violence and bloody rage whenever he felt threatened. One of the first signs of acute paranoia came during the peace negotiations with France. The king wanted, in drafts of the pact, to bind Charles VI to provide military aid against the people of England if he thought it was necessary. This did not make it into the final agreement, but it was disturbing nonetheless. Richard had screamed at the bishop of Arundel and his uncle Thomas earl of Gloucester in 1386 that he would invite a French invasion if necessary to secure his throne. Here was an indication that the thought had never really left him.

More obvious signs of discontent bubbled up during a parliament held in January 1397. It had been convened in the aftermath of the truce with France, when it was made clear to the king that some did not share his joy at the new dispensation. There were mutterings, emanating chiefly from the duke of Gloucester, that—as Froissart put it—"the people of this country want war. They can't live decently without it. Peace is no good to them." Others complained that a seven-year-old queen was of no use to a thirty-year-old king who had not yet produced an heir; and there was disgruntlement over the epic scale of the celebrations at Ardres, which may have cost as much as fifteen thousand pounds, the budget of a decent-size military invasion. When Richard asked parliament for money to aid the French king in an expedition to Milan he was coldly rebuffed. He became agitated and addressed parliament to defend the policy in person. When a petition, ostensibly written by "Thomas Haxey, clerk," was put before him, complaining about the rogue activities of royal officials, the poor state of the Scottish border, his continuing habit of private retaining in the shires, and the "great and excessive" cost of the king's household, Richard flew into a rage and had Haxey arrested and sentenced to a traitor's death. (The sentence was later rescinded on account of Haxey's clerical status.)

All these signs suggested that in early 1397 the king, who described himself later in the same parliament as "entire emperor of his realm of England," was feeling a growing indignation about having his imperial magnificence traduced. Nothing irked Richard so much as to suffer outspoken criticism. Never was he so dangerous as when backed into a corner.

By July 1397 the most senior three of the appellants who had opposed the king a decade earlier once more found their relations very tense. Gloucester had positioned himself as the leading noble critic of the French truce and was generally to be found holed up in his castle at Pleshey, conceiving (according to Froissart) "such a hatred for the King that he could find nothing to say in his favor." Warwick meanwhile had been thoroughly isolated from politics for some years; Richard had ensured that two high-profile legal disputes had been turned against him. Arundel had long been isolated, following numerous quarrels with the king and with John of Gaunt. He had begun to skip council meetings as his disapproval of the king mounted. In retrospect, it should have come as little surprise to all of them when Richard suddenly decided to come after them.

An arrest party set out for Pleshey Castle after dinner on July 10, 1397, with Richard at its head. Well-armed men whose white hart liveries identified them as his faithful retainers, they rode hard through the dead of night. They were on a singular, very important mission: to take the king's uncle the duke of Gloucester into custody. Behind them in London they left the earl of Warwick imprisoned in the Tower. He had been Richard's dinner guest, and at the end of a convivial feast the king had risen, ordered the earl arrested, and had him thrown into prison. Now it was the duke's turn.

At daybreak they arrived before the high stone walls of the fortress. They were prepared for a confrontation, but it quickly emerged that the duke had only a skeleton staff with him. The king's men far outnumbered his, and it was therefore with ease that they marched into the fortress. Richard greeted Gloucester as "fair uncle." Then he had him arrested and taken away under armed guard to a ship that would transport him to a prison in Calais.

This was the culmination of a coup carried out with all the speed and efficiency of Edward III's arrest of Roger Mortimer in 1330. Within the space of twenty-four hours—and with no prior warning—Richard arrested all three of the senior appellants of 1386. Gloucester and Warwick were taken by the king in person. Arundel was persuaded by his brother the archbishop of Canterbury to turn himself in, and Richard had him sent to the Isle of Wight. The appellants had been abruptly and bewilderingly punished. And the kingdom was, in the words of Thomas Walsingham, "suddenly and unexpectedly thrown into confusion." For the next two years England trembled under the tyranny of Richard II.

In the aftermath of the coup a series of royal proclamations explained that the three lords had been arrested for "offences against the king's majesty" but denied that these were offenses relating to 1386. Few believed that this was true. Naturally, all manner of theories abounded. The chroniclers of the time recorded their own suspicions. The French author of *Chronicque de la traïson et mort de Richart Deux roy Dengleterre* heard that there had been an appellant conspiracy against Richard, John of Gaunt, and the duke of York. Thomas Walsingham claimed that Richard believed that he was about to be elected Holy Roman Emperor but that the electors wished to be convinced he could discipline his own subjects before granting him dominion over hundreds of thousands more. Others, like the chronicler Adam of Usk, simply disbelieved the king's proclamations and wrote that Richard harbored a long-held grudge against his former enemies and had merely been biding his time until he was politically ready to revenge himself. Whatever his motivations, it was remarkable how quickly Richard simply brushed his enemies aside. After their arrests on July 10, 1397, it took just three months for the king to rid himself entirely of his old foes.

When parliament opened on September 17, 1397, its members were packed with Ricardian loyalists, and proceedings were held under military guard. Because Westminster Hall was being refurbished, the meeting was held in a large, open-sided wooden structure. The commons and lords filed in under the glare of three hundred of Richard's Cheshire archers. Inside, they found the king sitting high upon a throne, from which, according to the monk of Evesham, he could "deliver his judgements" and preside with "greater solemnity than any king of the realm ever had before."

When the chancellor, Bishop Stafford of Exeter, stood up to give the opening sermon, he told the assembly that the government had embraced a new doctrine. He took as his theme Ezekiel 37:22: "There shall be one king over them all." It was an ominous beginning. As he warmed to his subject, Bishop Stafford announced to the assembly that "if the king were to be powerful enough to govern, he must be in full possession of his regalities, prerogatives and rights." Then a general pardon was issued, from which it was announced that fifty people, "whom it would please the king to name," were excluded. But Richard did not name them. Instead, he invited anyone who thought he had anything to apologize for to seek the royal pardon in person. In the year that followed, five hundred individuals applied for and received the royal pardon. Richard was forcing his enemies to step forward and name themselves. Those who were pardoned had to pay heavily for it.

A month before parliament opened, Richard mirrored the events of that year by approving a new appeal of treason against his three enemies lodged by seven noblemen (Richard's Holland nephew and half brother, the earls of Kent and Huntingdon, and the earls of Somerset, Nottingham, and Salisbury, along with Thomas Lord Despenser and Sir William Scrope). Most of these men later claimed to have acted under duress. But their appeal was used to full effect. Led by a handpicked speaker, Sir John Bushy, whom Walsingham described as groveling before Richard "as if praying to him," the packed, intimidated parliament repealed the act establishing the council, along with the pardons extended to Gloucester, Arundel, and Warwick in the aftermath of the Merciless Parliament. Several days later Archbishop Arundel of Canterbury (the earl's brother) was removed from his post and sentenced to exile.

During all this, John of Gaunt presided over parliament as lord high steward. It was a cruel role for the aging duke to play, but he had his own interests to think of. He was in poor health, and since his absence in his duchy of Aquitaine between 1394 and 1396 he had been sidelined from politics. Now he relied on Richard's favor to protect his eldest son, the former appellant Henry Bolingbroke earl of Derby, as well as to legitimize the bastard children he had fathered by his long-standing mistress and eventual third wife, Katherine Swynford. Gaunt, wearing a robe with a scarlet hood, did his duty. On Friday, September 21, he stood by the king as the earl of Arundel was brought before parliament for trial. He was formally accused of treason for his actions in 1386, while the new appellants danced around and shouted abuse at him. "Your pardon is revoked, traitor," Gaunt told his old enemy, before pronouncing him guilty of treason and sentencing him to death. "Where are the faithful commons?" demanded Arundel, looking bitterly around him. Then he told Speaker Bushy: "I know all about you and your crew, and how you got here." It did him no good. He was led out of parliament and beheaded with a sword on Tower Hill. His head came off with one stroke of the sword, and it was said that the torso stood on its own for as long as it took to recite the Lord's Prayer.

Thomas Walsingham wrote that the earl of Arundel haunted Richard as a ghost, "threaten[ing] him with indescribable terrors." If so, it did not bend him from his purpose. The following Monday it was Gloucester's turn. Here was a doleful spectacle indeed, as another English king angled for the execution of a duke of royal blood. Thomas Mowbray earl of Nottingham had been sent to Calais to accompany the duke back to parliament. Now he entered a hushed assembly and delivered some astonishing news: the duke was dead.

What Nottingham did not tell parliament was that the duke had been murdered at Calais, on his (and ultimately the king's) direct orders. He had been taken from his prison cell to a house where he had been suffocated with a feather bed, probably on the night of September 8, nine days before parliament had opened.

Nottingham read out a political confession in which Gloucester admitted to numerous crimes relating to the events of 1386, including a dubious admission that the appellants had agreed for several days to depose the king, before renewing their homage when they could not decide which of them should take Richard's place. The confession ended with a plea that the king should "accept me unto his mercy and to his grace . . . though I be unworthy." Even in death, he was afforded no such mercy. He was posthumously condemned as a traitor.

On Friday, September 28, it was Warwick's turn. When he came before parliament, he broke down in tears, blaming others for his involvement and howling for the king's mercy. It was a pathetic sight, a weak old man crying for his life. After pleas from various other lords, Richard condemned him to life imprisonment on the Isle of Man and forfeiture of all his lands and goods. The enemies of 1386 were finally undone. A new political order was about to begin.

By redistributing the numerous lands forfeited by his vanquished enemies, Richard created a huge new class of high nobility. The two appellants who had escaped punishment were John of Gaunt's son Henry of Bolingbroke earl of Derby and Thomas Mowbray earl of Nottingham. They were raised to duke of Hereford and Norfolk respectively, while Mowbray's grandmother Margaret of Brotherton became duchess of Norfolk in her own right. Edmund duke of York's son Edward became duke of Albemarle. Richard's nephew Thomas Holland earl of Kent became duke of Surrey, and the king's half brother John Holland earl of Huntingdon became duke of Exeter. John Beaufort, who was earl of Somerset, was raised to marquis of Dorset. And four new earls were created: the king's friends and courtiers Ralph Neville, Thomas Despenser, Thomas Percy, and William Scrope became the earls of Westmorland, Gloucester, Worcester, and Wiltshire respectively. All this represented a massive shift of property, power, and wealth. It had been a bewildering fortnight.

On September 30 parliament closed with a ceremony mimicking the end of the Merciless Parliament, as the lords swore before the shrine of the Confessor to uphold everything that had been done. Richard sat enthroned, magnificent and absolute. The country trembled before him. As John Gower, one of his few literary protégés, wrote in disgust, "During the month of September, savagery held sway by the sword."

Richard Undone

Coventry buzzed with excitement. Since daybreak on Monday, September 16, 1398, the tournament green at Gosford, just outside the town, had been filling with knights and nobles, bishops and visiting foreign dignitaries, and ordinary onlookers. Large, intricately decorated tents were manned by smartly dressed esquires in bright liveries of all colors, decorated with silver buckles and armor, their weapons gleaming dangerously by their sides. A rare event, one that had caught all England's attention, was due to take place at nine o'clock that morning. Two dukes of the realm were to undergo trial by battle in front of the king. By the end of the day either Henry Bolingbroke duke of Hereford or Thomas Mowbray duke of Norfolk would probably be dead. The victor would be vindicated. It was to be one of the great chivalric occasions of the age.

Bolingbroke and Mowbray had been allies in 1386, when they had joined the appellants to challenge the king. They had retained favor with the king in the purge of 1397, avoiding the fates of Gloucester, Arundel, and Warwick and profiting handsomely in the distribution of land and titles that followed. Now, however, they were mortal enemies. A fierce dispute between them had spilled over into accusations of treason made before the king in parliament. Richard, in his magnificence, had decided that the only way to settle the quarrel was in armed combat.

The argument was deep rooted and complex. It centered on an allegation made by Bolingbroke at a parliament in 1398. The duke had told the king and the assembled lords that Mowbray, shaken by the actions of Richard's revenge parliament, had warned him that the two of them were soon to be "undone" for their initial support of the appellants. According to Bolingbroke, Mowbray had told him that their pardons were worthless and that plots, stemming from the king himself, existed to kill both Bolingbroke and his father, John of Gaunt, reverse the pardons given to Thomas of Lancaster in 1327, and take the entire duchy of Lancaster into royal hands. These were serious allegations. Either Mowbray was trying to turn powerful lords against the king, or he did indeed believe that Richard was planning to wipe out the whole house of Lancaster, removing Gaunt and his son from the Plantagenet succession and thereby seizing another one of the greatest inheritances in England for himself.

In actual fact the dispute ran deeper. A factional split was emerging at Richard's court between those nobles affiliated with Gaunt, Bolingbroke, and the house of Lancaster and those who viewed the Lancastrians with suspicion, hostility, and jealousy. It now seems likely that it was Mowbray, rather than Richard, who had countenanced their deaths. Richard strongly suspected that his cousin Bolingbroke was telling the truth and imprisoned Mowbray in the royal wardrobe. But the charges could not be proved. And because Mowbray disowned them in the strongest possible terms, refused to be reconciled with Bolingbroke, and demanded that a trial by battle be held, that was the course the king had chosen to follow.

Thus Coventry was alive with nervous tension, feverish spectators, and the armed retainers of the kingdom's greatest lords, all keen to see who would emerge alive from the latest grisly drama of Richard II's despotic reign.

At nine o'clock Bolingbroke rode out to Gosford mounted on a white courser, the giant horse's saddle decorated in blue and green velvet embroidered with gold swans and antelopes. He was accompanied by six liveried attendants and wore brilliant plate and mail armor, which he had acquired at great expense from Gian Galeazzo Visconti duke of Milan. He carried a long sword, a short sword, and a dagger, and his silver shield had painted on it a bright red cross, the arms of England and St. George. He announced to the constable and marshal of England that he had come to "prosecute my appeal in combating Thomas Mowbray, Duke of Norfolk, who is a traitor, false and recreant to God, the King, his realm and me." He swore his oaths, had his weapons checked and blessed, and was given a small portion of food and wine with which to sustain himself during a battle that might last until sunset. Then he pulled down the visor on his helmet, signed himself with the cross, took his lance from an attendant, and rode forward to his pavilion, decorated all over in red roses, to wait for Mowbray.

Next came the king, amid much fanfare from his heralds. Richard was dressed magnificently, as usual, and accompanied by his large private army of Cheshire archers and men-at-arms. The air bristled with violent intent as Sir John Bushy, Richard's loyal speaker of the commons, announced to the crowd that no one should so much as touch the wooden lists that surrounded the tournament field on pain of having his hand chopped off. Then the duke of Norfolk arrived, clad in red velvet with silver lions and mulberry trees on his horse. He swore his oaths and went to his own pavilion. As he rode through the barriers, he cried: "God speed the right!"

The time had come for battle. The dukes' lances were measured, and the pavilions were rapidly dismantled behind them, to leave the lists open for combat. Each man mounted his horse. The constable and marshal retreated. Justice would now be served. Bolingbroke advanced toward his rival. Mowbray stood stock-still. Everyone waited for the first blow to be struck.

Suddenly, Richard stood up, shouting, "Ho! Ho!" Everyone stopped, stunned. There was a great commotion in the crowd as each duke was sent back to his tent, with his lance confiscated. And there they sat for two hours, as the king retreated into private deliberation. At length Bushy stepped forward once more and announced to the crowd the king's verdict. The trial was over. There would be no combat. Indulging his compulsion to acts of high drama and majesty, Richard had decided that both men were to be banished from the realm, Bolingbroke for ten years (later reduced to six) and Mowbray for life.

The chronicler Thomas Walsingham called the period between 1397 and 1399 Richard's "tyranny," and he was right to do so. The full force of royal might and prerogative, which was supposed to exist for the protection of the king's subjects, was turned against them for the enrichment of the king. With the aborted trial of Mowbray and Bolingbroke, Richard's theatrical absolutism, which had begun in 1397, reached its peak. Plantagenet rule had been founded on the protection of land, property, and wealth. Drunk on his own authority, Richard, like Edward II before him, turned kingship on its head.

Surrounding the king was his Cheshire retinue: knights, squires, and archers who wore the livery of the white hart and took salaries by the day to do what ought to have been their natural duty of protecting their king. Richard went everywhere with thuggish archers and men-at-arms, who spoke to one another in their broad northern dialect and addressed the king by the familiar name of Dycun—Dickon. Barrel-chested guards waited outside his chamber at night bearing massive battle-axes, saying to him: "Dycun, slepe sicurly quile we wake." According to Adam of Usk, a Lancastrian supporter but a writer with good sources, the Cheshire men committed brutal crimes with impunity: "wherever the king went they stood guard over him . . . committing adulteries, murders and countless other crimes." Richard went everywhere with a big fierce greyhound by his side, which had belonged to the earl of Kent before his death. Richard's actions were hardly those of a king. Constantly on his guard, constantly menacing his people, he seemed more like an overbearing private magnate, at war with his entire realm.

In the summer of 1397 the king had begun to demand forced loans from his subjects. Letters stamped with the privy seal were sent into the shires demanding specific amounts of money. The names of the lenders were left blank. Richard's officials simply issued these form letters of legalized theft to anyone they identified as rich enough to pay. Around the same time the king also began to compel his subjects to put their seals to charters in which they pledged their lives and property unreservedly to him. In the event that they should fall into royal disfavor, these charters could be used to ruin men in an instant. As the king's paranoia grew, he even demanded "blank charters," clean sheets of paper on which a subject was forced to affix his seal, which could be used, as Walsingham put it, "so that whenever he wished to make attacks on [sealants] he might have the means to attack them individually." There could have been no more flagrant way to breach the Magna Carta, that hallowed founding document of the English polity, which was renewed customarily at every parliament.

Here was Richard at his most powerful, spinning a web of financial liability and terror. Whole counties and cities were made to buy their pardons from the royal wrath for extortionate sums, forced to guarantee their good behavior at the cost of thousands of pounds. A "general pardon" was issued to the realm in 1397 for rather vague collective offenses against the king's majesty, but it was made conditional upon Richard's receiving customs revenues for life. The new dukes of Albemarle and Kent (Richard's cousin and nephew) were given license to use the laws of treason to hunt out enemies of the king. Richard seemed to believe that his vengeful hand was bringing his realm to peace. In 1397 he wrote to Albert of Bavaria that the "avenging severity" that had "been meted out to the destruction and ruin" of his enemies had brought "to our subjects a peace which, by the grace of God, may last forever."

Nothing could have been further from the truth. Far from pacifying the realm, his rule of terror, enforced by a swelling private retinue, was forcing it into a state of incipient civil war. As the king built up his retainers, so did his lords. His mass redistributions of lands caused serious disruption to local power structures. His habit of retaining men-at-arms wherever he went cut into his magnates' territorial orbits and destabilized shire communities, which were keenly balanced by loyalties to local magnates. Richard's behavior was at times psychopathic and intimidated even his own courtiers. One vivid report recalled how "on solemn occasions when, by custom, he performed kingly rituals, he would order a throne to be prepared for him in his chamber on which he liked to sit ostentatiously from after dinner until vespers, talking to no one but watching everyone; and when his eye fell on anyone regardless of rank, that person had to bend his knee toward the king."

The whole atmosphere of terror shook his people into a restless state. It was not just the aristocracy: There were outbursts of popular rebellion and dissent too. A rising of Oxfordshire yeomen in March 1398 threatened to kill the king and nobles; a simultaneous outbreak in Berkshire sought to ambush the king as he passed through the county. And while most of the new nobility, who owed their whole position to Richard and stood to lose it all in the withering heat of his glare, professed their loyalty to him, that loyalty was paper thin.

Quarrels, feuds, and plots between Richard's nobles were allowed to flourish. And so it was that the Bolingbroke-Mowbray dispute, which brought out so many aspects of Richard's tyranny, had become a moment of national drama, the high point of which was the king's restatement of his own absolute power of judgment over life and death. When Bolingbroke left London to begin his six-year term of banishment in October 1398, the streets were lined with sorrowful citizens, proclaiming (according to Froissart) that "this country will never be happy until you return." This was just the popularity that Richard feared in others and one of the motivating factors in Bolingbroke's banishment. None of them could possibly have realized just how soon the king's cousin would be back.

On February 3, 1399, John of Gaunt died at Leicester Castle. He was fifty-eight and was buried with what Adam of Usk called "great pomp" at St. Paul's Cathedral in London, after a slow procession through the English countryside, his cortege surrounded by black-clad mourners. The king visited his uncle on his deathbed, and a later story was put about that before he died, Gaunt showed Richard the ulcers around his genitals as a somewhat superfluous warning against lechery.

Gaunt had not been universally popular during his long life and career, but he had led a life of adventure and loyal service to the Plantagenet family during some very trying circumstances. He had headed great armies and splendid embassies. He had fought long and hard to have himself crowned a king in Spain, an effort that yielded him no crown, but he had raised two of his daughters to become queens consort of Portugal and Castile. At home he had fought equally obdurately to protect the rights of the Plantagenet Crown during the last years of Edward III and of the duchy of Lancaster during Richard II's reign. He had been an early sponsor of the radical theologian John Wyclif and a key figure in London's fractious politics. Most important, he had built up an unparalleled landed inheritance, worth well over twelve thousand pounds a year. Whoever inherited the duchy of Lancaster would also inherit Gaunt's position as by some distance the richest and most powerful magnate in England, superseded only by the king. It was inevitable that as Richard built up his vast landed power bloc, he should come into conflict with the duchy of Lancaster. And indeed great expanses of the Midlands were riven with conflict as the king's and John of Gaunt's spheres of private influence overlapped, and competition grew for retainers.

It was to Henry Bolingbroke, Gaunt's eldest son, that his death meant most. For Bolingbroke was heir to the whole duchy of Lancaster, and that made him, by 1399, a terrifying specter to his cousin Richard II. After the aborted duel at Coventry, both Bolingbroke and Mowbray had left England. Mowbray, who was stripped of his duchy, had decided to go on a pilgrimage to Jerusalem and had died of the plague in Venice. But Bolingbroke, whose exile was generally held to be unfair, had gone to the court of Charles VI in Paris, where he was made welcome and could monitor the situation in England from close at hand. What he saw was a king striving to conquer his own country. One by one the great and ancient English lordships were falling into the hands of Richard and his cronies. Lands and castles that once belonged to Warwick, Gloucester, Arundel, and Norfolk had all reverted to the king. In 1398 Roger Mortimer fourth earl of March and Richard's possible heir through the female succession of Lionel of Antwerp had been killed in Ireland. His son Edmund was a young boy, and thus the March lands too had reverted to the king in wardship.

After Gaunt's funeral, Richard went to King's Langley, the favorite residence of Edward II, the place where Piers Gaveston's body had been laid to rest, and where Edward had brooded on revenge over his own Lancastrian nemesis. By the time he reached King's Langley, he had made a fateful decision. According to his loyal servant Sir William Bagot, Richard declared that he would sooner restore the heirs of Gloucester, Warwick, and Arundel than allow Bolingbroke back into England. Bagot sent a message to Bolingbroke, advising him that he was now the king's "full enemy." Richard convened a council in Westminster on March 18, in which he formally annulled Bolingbroke's right to inherit the duchy of Lancaster and sentenced him to perpetual banishment.

The ultimate land grab was complete. Everything that Gaunt had feared in his final years had come to pass. In the spring of 1399 great swaths of his inheritance were doled out to key Ricardian supporters: Lancaster, Tutbury, and Kenilworth went to Thomas Holland duke of Surrey; the Welsh lands to John Holland duke of Exeter; Leicester, Pontefract, and Bolingbroke itself were granted to Richard's cousin the duke of Albemarle. Most of the rest remained in royal hands, its vast revenues now pouring straight into the treasuries Richard was building up in royal castles. To everyone in England it was now clear, as Walsingham put it, that Richard had banished his cousin not for the quarrel with Mowbray but "because it was a good opportunity of seizing the duke's property." Richard was no king; he was a wanton thief. With this last land grab he had sealed his own fate.

When news of his disinheritance reached Bolingbroke in Paris, it could hardly have come as a surprise. He had known Richard all his life and had been at close quarters during every crisis of the realm, hidden in a cupboard in the Tower of London during the Peasants' Revolt of 1381 and standing on both sides of Richard's long-running war with the appellants. He knew that the king was not a man to be trusted. He might, however, have been surprised by the other news that reached Paris around the same time: the king was preparing to lead a second invasion of Ireland. He would be taking his supporters and much of his private retinue across the Irish Sea, leaving England unguarded for months.

It was too good an opportunity to miss. Richard had enemies in both England and France, and Henry made contact with all of them. His first ally was Thomas Fitzalan, the former archbishop of Canterbury, whom Richard had stripped of his office and exiled at the same time as Fitzalan's brother the earl of Arundel was executed. The Arundels and Lancastrians might not always have seen eye to eye, but they were united in their hatred of the king. In England they made contact with the disaffected Henry Percy earl of Northumberland and Ralph Neville earl of Westmorland. Henry was convinced by what he heard from these men that an invasion in pursuit of his inheritance would find favor among enough other lords to make it feasible.

Richard left for Ireland at the end of May and landed on June 1. He must have known that an invasion was possible or even likely because he took with him his crowns and regalia—the essential tokens of Plantagenet kingship—as well as Henry of Monmouth, Bolingbroke's son. He also took most of his loyal nobles and large numbers of men-at-arms and archers and, with them, set about bringing various Irish chieftains to heel.

Unimpeded by a French government disabled by the recurring insanity of Charles VI, Bolingbroke left France at the end of June. On July 4, 1399, he landed near Ravenspur, at the mouth of the Humber River. He disembarked with a tiny contingent of no more than one hundred men, hardly a fearsome invasion. But the moment he landed, wrote the Kirkstall chronicler, "a great multitude of knights and squires came to him." They included a broad coalition of northern earls and knights, including Harry "Hotspur," Northumberland's son, who was reputed to be the finest knight in England.

Now Richard's kingdom, so long bullied and blackmailed, simply melted into Bolingbroke's arms. The author of a sympathetic account of Richard's last years known as the *Chronicque de la traïson et mort de Richart Deux roy Dengleterre* wrote that "there was no good mother's son who did not go to the duke and offer him both his services and his goods." All England rang with news of Bolingbroke's arrival. The government left behind by Richard was headed by Edmund Langley duke of York—uncle to both Bolingbroke and the king—and served by royal favorites, including Sir John Bushy and Sir Richard Scrope. They attempted to muster a loyal army at Oxford in mid-July, but as the Midlands surged to Bolingbroke's side, they were forced to pull back, ever farther west. Adam of Usk estimated that Bolingbroke raised one hundred thousand men. For once a chronicler may not have exaggerated.

Richard returned to England at the end of July and attempted to raise an army of his own in South Wales. But Bolingbroke was already at Bristol, and word was flooding across the border from England that virtually the whole country was abandoning the king. Disguising himself as a Franciscan friar, the king, along with a few colleagues, left the men he had mustered in the south and rode north across Wales to Conwy, where the earl of Salisbury was raising a loyalist army. When he arrived, there was further disappointment. The earl's forty-thousand-strong army was deserting in droves and carrying off the king's belongings—gold and silver, jewels, good horses, and fine robes.

By the beginning of August Bolingbroke was almost the undisputed master of England. As Richard sat helpless in Conwy Castle, praying to God and the Virgin Mary for intervention and telling friends that he hoped the king of France would come to his aid, the kingdom demonstrated just how little loyalty it owed him. On August 5 the principality of Chester, the very heart of Richard's power, sued for peace. On August 9 Chester Castle surrendered to Henry's army with not even a show of resistance. Although the duke commanded that there should be no massacre of the Cheshiremen, there was still sufficient looting and devastation for Adam of Usk to find Coddington Church, where he attempted to celebrate Mass, emptied of everything but the doors and broken chests.

Richard was undone. His allies the duke of Albemarle and the earl of Worcester rallied to Bolingbroke's side. His half brother the duke of Exeter and his nephew the duke of Surrey were taken prisoner. Bolingbroke, citing his authority as the steward of England, sent the earl of Northumberland to Conwy Castle to bring Richard in. The terms were abhorrent to a king still possessed by dreams of his own regality. He was summoned to appear of his own free will at a parliament in which Bolingbroke would sit as "chief judge" of England and at which five of his allies would be tried for treason: the dukes of Exeter and Surrey, the earl of Salisbury and the bishop of Carlisle, and Richard Maudelyn. The king flew into his customary rage, ranting that he would have his opponents put to death: "There are some of them," he said, "whom I will flay alive." But he had no choice. He had to accompany Northumberland.

Richard and Henry met face-to-face at Flint. Although the king was now clearly the duke's prisoner, they went through a charade of noble courtesy. Bolingbroke bowed low to the king; Richard addressed him as "fair cousin of Lancaster." According to the author of the *Traïson et mort*, who was an eyewitness to this encounter, Bolingbroke then told Richard that he had returned to England "before you sent for me" because "you have not ruled well these twenty-two years . . . and therefore with the consent of the commons, I will help you to govern it."

"Fair cousin, since it pleases you, it pleases us well," said Richard. Then he formally surrendered himself to his cousin. He and Salisbury were given two very poor horses to ride, and they set out with Bolingbroke, under armed guard, for Chester. The castle was no longer the military stronghold of a paranoid king but his prison.

Richard Alone

On September 21, 1399, the earl of Warwick's brother Sir William Beauchamp went to visit King Richard, now a prisoner at the Tower of London. Sir William was accompanied by Adam of Usk, who noted in his chronicle that the visit happened to fall on the second anniversary of Arundel's beheading. Beauchamp and Usk, hearty loyalists to the Bolingbroke cause, came with what the latter called "the specific intention of ascertaining [Richard's] mood and behavior."

Richard had been imprisoned in the Tower for nineteen days. His young wife, Isabella, was in Bolingbroke's hands too, kept in honorable confinement in Sonning, in Berkshire. The king had been moved on his cousin's command from Chester Castle at the end of August and had arrived in London on September 2. Although he was confined to apartments rather than in a dungeon, his visitors still found him in dismal mood; deprived of his regular servants and surrounded by Lancastrian spies, the diminished king was finally alone. Even his greyhound was gone, having abandoned him while the king was in South Wales.

Richard was understandably miserable. There could have been no more evocative place than the Tower for the duke to place him. The royal prison was the very fortress in which both had taken refuge during the great rebellion in 1381, when Henry had only narrowly escaped capture and certain death. Richard must have recalled childhood memories of looking out over the smoldering city of London from a lonely window at the top of the Tower and seeing his whole country risen in uproar. Now he was back, and although the realm was no longer in the grip of peasant anarchy, it had once again turned against his rule.

As he sat down to dinner with his guests, Richard "began to discourse dolefully," wrote Usk. "My God, this is a strange and fickle land," said the king, "which has destroyed and ruined so many kings, so many rulers, so many great men and which never ceases to be riven and worn down by dissensions and strife and internecine hatreds." Then he started enumerating sad stories of previous English kings undone by their people. Usk heard him recount "the names and histories of those who had suffered such fates, from the time when the realm was first inhabited." It was a pathetic sight: a king who reveled in the ancient tales of his ancestors' deeds now found history repeating itself, with himself as the victim.

"Seeing . . . the troubles of his soul," wrote Usk, "and seeing that none of those who had been deputed to wait upon him were in any way bound to him, or used to serving him, but were strangers who had been sent there simply to spy on him, I departed much moved at heart, reflecting to myself on the glories of his former state and on the fickle fortune of the world."

Usk did not detail which tales of royal misery Richard had recounted, but it is not hard to guess at whom he might have mentioned: his hero, Edward the Confessor, who had suffered several rebellions and died in the aftermath of a Northumbrian revolt; King John, the first of the Plantagenets to have his royal prerogative forcibly circumscribed by the will of the barons; Henry III, who was made a prisoner of his own barons; Edward II, whom he had tried to rescue from the ignominy of history.

In his own way, Richard had been a worse king than all of them combined. Like the Confessor, he had considered his own divinity above the practical necessity of having children to continue his royal line. Like Henry III, he had obsessed over holy rituals, while allowing English conquest in France to collapse. Like John, he had tyrannized his people. Like Edward II, he had antagonized the house of Lancaster, stolen land from his nobles, tainted politics with treason, and proved himself incorrigible over the lengthy course of a reign in which he had been offered many chances to reform his ways. More generally, he had listened to the counsel of unworthy advisers and attacked and plundered his subjects' property, rather than defend it. He had built himself up as an antagonistic private lord, rather than fulfill his higher duty to be a source of public authority. He had believed that kingship was about prestige and magnificence instead of leadership. And he had ended up with nothing.

Nine days after Usk dined with the king, on Tuesday, September 30, the lords of England gathered with an assembly of the commons at Westminster Hall. It was a parliament in all but name, although without the king's authority it could not claim full parliamentary status. An empty throne, draped with gold cloth, stood at one end of the hall. Richard remained in the Tower of London. Richard Scrope archbishop of York stood up and read a statement to the assembly. Richard, he said, had agreed to resign the Crown on the ground of his own inadequacy. Thomas Arundel, now restored as archbishop of Canterbury, stood and asked if the people would accept this. According to the official record, each lord agreed. Then the commons shouted their assent.

Had Richard really resigned? Certainly it seems that he had no choice. The official record was made to give the impression that he had given up his Crown willingly, saying that he had "asserted in his abdication [that] he was worthy to be deposed." But the *Traïson et mort*, a loyal source, suggests otherwise. It records a fierce argument between Bolingbroke and Richard, which took place one evening before the "parliament." The latter swore and cursed and demanded to see his wife, while Bolingbroke refused to release him from the Tower or to do anything else without parliamentary process. According to the *Traison et Mort*:

The king [was] in great wrath, but he could not help himself, and said to the duke that he did great wrong both to him and to the crown.

The duke replied, "We cannot do anything til the parliament meets."

The king was so enraged by this speech that he could scarcely speak, and paced twenty-three steps down the room without uttering a word; and presently he broke out thus: ". . . you have acknowledged me your king these twenty-two years, how dare you use me so cruelly? I say that you behave to me like false men, and like false traitors to their lord; and this I will prove, and fight four of the best of you, and this is my pledge." Saying which, the king threw down his bonnet.

It made no difference. The assembly that met to agree to the king's deposition moved rapidly through a new and unprecedented legal process. They listened as thirty-three articles of deposition were read out by the bishop of St. Asaph. The articles were a litany of Richard's failings, from the start of his reign to his tyrannical last days. They covered his "evil rule" in the 1380s; his destruction of the appellants ("against whom the king was extremely indignant because they wished the king to be under good rule"); his raising of an army against the people under de Vere; his use of the "great multitude of malefactors" from Cheshire against his own subjects; the extortionate selling of pardons; falsification of the parliamentary record; the denial of justice to Bolingbroke; misuse of taxation and loans; a refusal to "keep and defend the just laws and customs of the realm"; numerous counts of extortion and deception; removal of the crown jewels to Ireland; breaches of the Magna Carta; and a general, withering clause that simply stated that "the king was so variable and dissimulating in his words and writings, especially to popes and rulers outside the realm, that no one could trust him."

After reading the articles, the bishop of St. Asaph passed the sentence of deposition. Then Bolingbroke rose from his place in the parliament, crossed himself, and claimed the realm as his, saying in English: "In the name of the Father, Son and Holy Ghost, I, Henry of Lancaster, challenge this realm of England and the crown with all its members and appurtenances, as I am descended by the right line of the blood coming from the good lord King Henry III, and through that right that God of his grace has sent me, with the help of my kindred and my friends to recover it; the which realm was on the point of being undone for default of governance and undoing of good laws." He pulled out Richard II's signet, showed it to the people, and took Archbishop Arundel's hand in his own. The archbishop of Canterbury led Henry Bolingbroke up toward the golden throne at the front of the hall. Henry knelt and prayed before it. When he opened his eyes, the archbishops of Canterbury and York took an arm each and seated him on the throne. The great hall of Westminster roared with the acclaim and applause of the lords and commons.

The air in the hall vibrated with the cries of the people of England. The noise rounded upward, toward the hammer beam ceiling built by Henry Yevele at such lavish royal expense. It swirled around the decorative white harts that skirted the walls, and rebounded off the statues of the thirteen kings who had ruled England between Edward the Confessor and Richard II. And it reverberated in the ears of the first king of a new dynasty: Henry Bolingbroke, who would become the first king of the house of Lancaster.

A new king had been elected. Or looked at another way, the Crown of England had been abruptly seized. On October 1, 1399, Richard II was formally and ceremonially stripped of his allegiances and his Crown. Within four months he would be dead, having starved in prison at Pontefract Castle. Meanwhile Henry duke of Lancaster was crowned Henry IV of England on October 13, the feast day of Edward the Confessor. The choice of date was intended to make a point about the new king's own royal blood. But it could not conceal the bare facts. After eight generations and 245 years of rule, the unbroken succession of the Plantagenets had ended. Great magnates might now wrestle for the Crown among themselves. Richard II, by his folly, his greed, and his terrible, destructive misapprehension of virtually every aspect of kingship, had cast everything he had inherited onto the bonfire of history.

A new age of English kingship had begun.

Epilogue

At the time of his usurpation, Henry IV was likened by his staunch supporter Archbishop Arundel to Judas Maccabaeus, the popular biblical hero who had led God's chosen people in rebellion against their oppressors, driven the iniquitous out of Jerusalem, and repurified the Temple. It was a pointed analogy: like Henry, Maccabaeus had risen up to lead his people thanks to a blend of personal valor and military genius. He was a king who had earned his status by his righteousness rather than by birth alone.

The beginning of Henry's reign brought with it an intense propaganda drive, intended to emphasize the new king's sanctity as well as his pragmatic suitability for office. Not only was he crowned on St. Edward's Day 1399, but he was anointed at his coronation with the vial of holy oil that had supposedly been given to Archbishop Thomas Becket by the Virgin Mary and that had subsequently come into the possession of the new king's grandfather, Edward III's great war captain, Henry of Grosmont. At the feast that celebrated Henry's coronation there was a pointed edge to the arrival in Westminster Hall of a knight, Sir Thomas Dymock, who claimed to be the king's champion and who announced to the assembled guests that if anyone disputed Henry's right to be king of England, then "he was ready to prove the contrary with his body, then and there." No one rose to the challenge.

If Henry's approval as the new king of England seemed indisputable, then Richard's death, four months after his deposition, was inevitable. Adam of Usk marveled at the speed with which the old king had fallen, "cast down by the wheel of fortune, to fall miserably in the hands of Duke Henry, amid the silent curses of your people." He addressed Richard rhetorically when he wrote that had the king been "guided in your affairs by God and by the support of your people, then you would indeed have been deserving of praise." Indeed, to judge by the ease and speed with which Henry Bolingbroke took the throne, there was little general mourning for Richard.

Nevertheless, like Edward II, Richard alive presented a focus for plotting by the fallen favorites of the old regime. In December 1399 a plot was hatched by a group of former loyalists led by Edward earl of Rutland (Richard's cousin, who had been stripped in parliament of his duchy of Albemarle); John Montagu earl of Salisbury; and Richard's half brother John Holland and nephew Thomas Holland, who had also been demoted respectively from their duchies of Exeter and Surrey. The conspirators planned to storm Windsor Castle on the feast of Epiphany, January 6, 1400—Richard's forty-third birthday—disrupting the Twelfth Night celebrations, kidnapping the new king and his son Prince Harry (who had been made prince of Wales, duke of Aquitaine, Lancaster, and Cornwall, and earl of Chester), and subsequently setting the old king at liberty. However, fortune had long deserted Richard and his partisans; the plot was betrayed and easily disrupted. Neither Henry nor the prince was captured, and the rebels scattered across England, attempting unsuccessfully to raise popular rebellion as they went. Thomas Holland and the earl of Salisbury were beheaded by angry townsmen in Cirencester; John Holland was beheaded by popular demand at sunset at Pleshey (on exactly the spot where the earl of Gloucester had been arrested by Richard in 1397); and Sir Thomas Despenser, another conspirator, was killed by the commons at Bristol. Far from a popular rising in favor of the old king, there was spontaneous and widespread rage at the efforts of his former allies to disrupt the English polity once again.

The failure of the Epiphany plot prompted Richard's final demise. The former king had been sent to serve his sentence of life imprisonment at Pontefract, and according to Thomas Walsingham, when he "heard of these unhappy events, his mind became disturbed and he killed himself by voluntary fasting, so the rumor went." The more sympathetic author of the *Traïson et mort* suggested foul play, claiming that the king was killed by one "Sir Piers Exton," who staved in the king's head with an ax. It is most likely that the truth lies somewhere between the extremes and that Richard was deliberately starved on the orders of the new king's regime, which could no more tolerate his presence in the realm than Roger Mortimer had been able to suffer that of Edward II in 1327. Adam of Usk laid the blame for Richard's death by starvation on one "Sir N. Swynford" (most likely Sir Thomas Swynford, a knight of Henry's chamber).

Certainly, once Richard was dead—probably on St. Valentine's Day 1400 and certainly by February 17—Henry IV was at pains to show his cousin's corpse to the country. Richard's emaciated body was transported from Pontefract to London with the face visible to all. The body lay in St. Paul's Cathedral for two days, before it was transported for burial at the discreet royal residence of King's Langley in Hertfordshire.

Richard's deposition and Henry's accession were viewed with some bewilderment by contemporaries. The metaphor of the wheel of fortune used by Adam of Usk seemed particularly apt. When the old king had cast Bolingbroke out into the wilderness and enjoyed the heyday of his tyranny, he had seemed to be the mightiest of all his line. Yet within months his entire reign had collapsed and he was dead. God's providence was indeed a wonderful thing. But Richard's fall was not entirely a matter of divine caprice. It was widely recognized that he had brought his misfortune upon himself by his atrocious behavior, his violent misrule, and his choice of poor company and counsel. He had neglected his realm in favor of enriching himself, and he had repeatedly treated his coronation oath, the Magna Carta, and the dignity of parliament with contempt. He had made it easy for Henry, his nearest heir in the male line, to take his Crown from him by appealing to the oldest principle of Plantagenet kingship, the principle that had been at the core of every moment of political and constitutional crisis since 1215: the king should govern within his own law and with the advice of the worthiest men in his kingdom.

Despite the best efforts of the new regime to legitimize itself and argue the case for removing the old king, the Crown never fully recovered from the trauma of Richard's deposition. Unlike Edward II, Richard had been replaced not by his undisputed heir but by a nobleman who claimed sufficient royal blood to seize the throne and did so to some degree unilaterally. Henry may have been the closest heir by the male line, but Edmund Mortimer, the great-grandson of Lionel of Antwerp via his daughter Philippa countess of Ulster, had arguably a better claim in blood. Henry IV was not Edward III, the son of a discarded king. He was one cousin among several, all with competing claims in blood. A Rubicon had been crossed. The wars that erupted from the middle of the fifteenth century, known now as the Wars of the Roses, began as political wars, but, thanks to the unanswered questions raised by Henry IV's usurpation, they later became wars of Plantagenet succession, which were settled only by the accession of a king, Henry VII, who was barely a Plantagenet at all. (Indeed, after Henry VII had legitimized his usurpation of the throne with a wealth of pageantry attempting to demonstrate his descent from Edward III, he and later his son

Henry VIII set about murdering and destroying every surviving member of the English aristocracy with a trace of Plantagenet blood.) Richard's deposition had marked the beginning of this baleful end.

In some ways Henry IV's accession threw the English monarchy back to a near-forgotten age. Not since Henry II had displaced Stephen's son Eustace as heir to the English Crown in the 1150s had the royal succession so obviously combined blood right with the principles of election and the blunt political reality of a power grab. No royal dynasty would ever again hand down the Crown with such security and ease for as many generations as the Plantagenets did between 1189 and 1377.

Of course Richard's deposition did not turn the clock back to Norman times. The Plantagenet family's legacy was profound, for by 1400 England had changed unrecognizably from the Anglo-Norman realm that had existed during the mid-twelfth century.

The office of kingship was utterly transformed. By 1400 the king was not just the most powerful man in the land, with the prerogatives of legal judgment, feudal tribute, and warfare on behalf of the realm, but an office-holder whose awesome rights were matched by awesome responsibilities bound by a complex constitutional contract with the various estates of the realm. Whereas the Norman kings (and the Saxon kings before them) had occasionally granted their subjects limited and extremely vague charters of liberties and governed in accordance with custom, the Plantagenet years had seen the growth of a highly refined political philosophy that defined the king's duties to his realm, and the realm's to the king, and a huge body of common law and statute that governed the land. The king was still the source of universal authority in the realm, but his power underpinned a sophisticated system of justice and lawgiving.

Under these changed terms of rule, the king's actions and his personal will still mattered immensely. The personalities of individual kings had profoundly shaped their reigns and their worlds, as had the personalities of their immediate relations—wives, brothers, children, and cousins. In that sense, politics remained fundamentally unpredictable and unstable. Yet the Crown was also now distinct from the king, and the machinery and philosophy of royal rule were more separate from the person of the king than at any time before. Each successive Plantagenet king had been more tempered than the last by a system of institutions that drew a broad political community into government. Parliaments, including elected representatives of county society, rather than just the great barons and ecclesiastical magnates, reserved the right to grant taxes and expected that their grievances would be heard and remedied in exchange for the privilege. Government could be scrutinized, inadequate ministers could be impeached, and ultimately a king might be removed from office; even the most capable and successful of the later Plantagenet kings, Edward I and Edward III, experienced uncomfortable moments of crisis in 1297, 1341, and 1376. Parliaments, as well as the battlefield, would become the forums for much of the political upheaval that followed during the fifteenth century.

Away from parliament, the Plantagenets had given England a complex and deep-seated system of royal government in the localities. The business of government was no longer the exclusive preserve of churchmen and clerks attendant on the king and the great magnates dominating their own territories. It was carried out by a combination of trained, bureaucratic professionals at Westminster and laymen in the shires who were drawn from the community but worked on behalf of the Crown. Judges and lawyers, clerks and accountants, sheriffs, bailiffs, coroners, and escheators were drawn from middling ranks of men whose birth might now lead them to expect a professional career as much as a military one. As a result, the political community, which under Norman rule had comprised a handful of the greatest bishops and barons, had expanded so far that even the better class of peasants, men and women such as those who had rebelled in 1381, felt that they had a stake in royal government and the right to voice their disgruntlement in surprisingly sophisticated terms. The principles of the Magna Carta, whose successive reissues had been pinned to virtually every church door in the realm during the thirteenth century, had permeated the consciousness of men of all classes and backgrounds. When Jack Cade's rebels rose against Henry VI's administration in 1450, it was evident that the English lower orders had a more keenly developed sense of their place in the English polity than at any previous time in history. Whereas Norman England had been little more than a colonized realm, ruled from above and afar, the England created by the Plantagenets had become one of the most deeply engaged and mature kingdoms in Europe.

The symbolism of kingship too had evolved. The country now had two national saints: St. Edward the Confessor and St. George. Together they exemplified the two faces of Plantagenet kingship: the pious, anointed, sanctified king and the warrior with God on his side. Earlier English saints, such as St. Edward the Martyr and St. Edmund, were now largely forgotten, as St. Edward and St. George were woven skillfully into the narratives of English history, the fabric of the great buildings, and the iconography of kingship. Both saints continued to exert a powerful hold on the English imagination. St. George, in particular, became emblematic of English military glory. "Cry 'God for Harry, England and St. George,'" wrote Shakespeare, looking back on the reign of Henry V and the zenith of English fortune in the Hundred Years War. With those words, the cult that Edward III had encouraged and given form in the Order of the Garter was immortalized in the national imagination.

The two Plantagenet saints sanctified the two key centers of English kingship. Edward the Confessor's glorious tomb at the heart of the remodeled Westminster Abbey was the very hub around which the Plantagenet family mausoleum had been built. Interestingly, access to this mausoleum was not an automatic privilege of royalty. Edward II, despite being named after the Confessor himself, had led too egregious a life to die as a king. As punishment for his shameful reign he had been interred apart from the rest of his family at Gloucester Abbey. Likewise, Richard II's body was initially banished from Westminster. The superb double tomb with Purbeck marble base and copper effigies that he had commissioned in 1395 held only the corpse of Anne of Bohemia. Richard was buried at King's Langley, the resting place of that great villain Piers Gaveston. It was not until Henry V's accession in 1413 that Richard's body was moved to Westminster, belatedly to lie beside his wife and the Confessor at whose tomb he had prayed for protection before facing Wat Tyler's rebels at Smithfield in 1381.

If the royal tombs at Westminster were where St. Edward was most venerated, then the Garter Knights Stalls in St. George's Chapel at Windsor were where the more recent national saint received his celebration. (The chapel, rebuilt by Edward IV, later became an alternative burial place to Westminster for English monarchs.) Edward III's creation of the Order of the Garter, dedicated to St. George and the honorable code of martial chivalry, reinvented the relationship between the soldierly king and his leading noblemen. It provided a spiritual, honorific narrative for the bitter and ravaging wars that Edward and his sons had waged against France. St. George had to a degree supplanted even the mythical King Arthur as the hero of English conquest. Undoubtedly the cult of Arthur, a popular hero effectively stolen from the Welsh under Edward I, had been developed in the

Plantagenet years, and Arthuriana had risen from a staple of popular story-telling to a reliable trope of royal pageantry. (Popular stories had developed, for their own part, with the rise of outlaw ballads such as the rhymes of Robin Hood.) But the cult of St. George, as it had been developed during Edward III's reign, was more potent still. While Arthur gave Edward I an imaginative reason for conquering Wales and subjecting Scotland, the banner of St. George had served an even more useful end: uniting in common purpose the king with his nobles and the knightly classes and finally enthusing England with the cause of war across the Channel. This feat had eluded every other Plantagenet king since 1204, when John had lost Normandy and the Anglo-Norman realm had begun its painful, permanent partition.

St. Edward and St. George were not the only saints who rose to prominence during the Plantagenet years. Around them was a clutch of other heroes, whose memories were considered blessed, even if they were not all formally canonized. These were the great men who had fallen in opposition to the kings. At Canterbury, St. Thomas Becket's tomb was the lucrative center of England's finest pilgrimage site. The shrine to the cantankerous archbishop murdered under Henry II was steeped in blood and lore, and its holiness rivaled that of many of the Continental sites that lay on the pilgrimage roads between the Ste.-Chapelle in Paris and Santiago de Compostela in Galicia. Beginning with Henry II himself, successive Plantagenets came to St. Thomas's shrine alternatively to pray for fortitude and to give thanks for victory, and the site remained a place of the utmost holiness until 1538, when Henry VIII ordered it destroyed during the dissolution of the monasteries. The shrine was cast down, and Becket's bones were thrown in a creek. Today only a small candle and a plaque mark the holy site, although Becket's name is still one of the most famous in English history, and his murder remains one of the great events in the English historical canon. He is certainly more famous today than the other great Plantagenet opponents, Simon de Montfort and Thomas earl of Lancaster, although in both cases miracles were associated with their remains and shrines.

The legacy of each of the Plantagenet kings depended largely on his success in battle, and it was through their military accomplishments that the dynasty left its stamp on England. Just as English government and political culture had changed during the Plantagenet years, so too had almost every aspect of military strategy and tactics. Henry II, Richard I, and John had much in common with their Norman predecessors; the art of war was the art of siegecraft. The great engagements of the twelfth and early thirteenth centuries took place almost exclusively before the walls of castles and fortified towns. Henry II's largest deployment of the combined troops of his Plantagenet dominions took place, albeit unsuccessfully, before the walls of Toulouse in 1159; Richard I made his name storming Acre and Jaffa, before meeting his death at another siege, in Châlus-Chabrol. John lost Normandy because he failed in his daring attempt to retake Château Gaillard in 1203 from Philip Augustus; his attempt to defeat Philip in a pitched battle, when his allies rode against the king of France at Bouvines in 1214, was the defining disaster of his reign. Three eventful years later the Plantagenet dynasty was saved from obliteration by Philip's son Prince Louis at another siege, when William Marshal stormed the town of Lincoln in the name of Henry III and drove the French back toward the Channel.

From the middle of the thirteenth century, however, pitched battles had begun to replace sieges as the decisive means by which the English made war. Battles were initially the necessary recourse of beleaguered Plantagenet kings whose reigns had dissolved into civil war: Simon de Montfort was hacked brutally to death at the battle of Evesham in 1263, and Thomas of Lancaster was beheaded following his defeat by his cousin Edward II in 1322. From the late thirteenth century onward English kings began to rely far more frequently on the art of the pitched battle to engage their enemies abroad too. Edward I's armies stunned Scotland with victories at Falkirk and Dunbar; Edward II was undone at Bannockburn. Edward III learned much about the art of war from his humiliating defeat at Stanhope Park in the miserable summer of 1327. He was revenged at Halidon Hill in 1333, and thereafter an English array on a battlefield became one of the most terrifying sights imaginable.

The military innovations that developed in Edward III's reign—his use of dismounted men-at-arms to fight at close range and of mounted archers to disrupt cavalry charges and rain sharp death on infantry—earned him some of English history's most famous battlefield victories. The Hundred Years War gave England a sense of military parity with France that characterized relations between the realms deep into the Napoleonic era. The names of Crécy and Poitiers still ring through the ages, and the revolution in military tactics was later crowned by Henry V's astonishing victory at Agincourt on St. Crispin's Day in 1415, when the image of the indomitable

English archer was cemented. The importance of these fearsome bowmen in the development of English myth, lore, and legend is impossible to overstate. English archers riding into battle beneath the cross of St. George and the quartered leopards of England and fleurs-de-lis of France; kings of England fighting hand to hand with the French on enemy soil; the Black Prince earning his spurs at Crécy: these remain iconic images in English history, romanticized by generations.

The battle of Crécy, which was fought as the idea of the Order of the Garter was percolating in Edward III's mind, began the military career of the Black Prince and a period of English military supremacy that has been admired ever since. So much of England's royal iconography, particularly that connected with the Order of the Garter, stems from Plantagenet military triumphs in France. We should not forget, either, the potency of the myths and memories connected to Richard I, the Lionheart of the Third Crusade. The term "crusade" still has acute political resonance for Christians and Muslims attempting to live side by side in the twenty-first century. It is unhistorical but extremely tempting for modern rhetoricians to reach back and view our present culture clash as an extension of the wars that were waged between Richard and Saladin more than eight hundred years ago. But in their own time the crusades were vitally important, extending English royal horizons to the plains of the Middle East, and allowed English kings to play their role on the most prestigious military stage of them all.

Out of the Plantagenets' military legacy emerged too the foundations of the relationships between England and the rest of the British Isles, which have largely endured ever since. Before the Plantagenets, only the mythical King Arthur had ever been said to hold dominion over Wales, Ireland, and Scotland as well as the kingdom of England. Yet this goal of a unified Britain under English mastery was conceived and very nearly realized by Plantagenet kings from Henry II onward. It was Henry who first made Scotland a kingdom under English control, as revenge for William the Lion's involvement in the Great War of 1173. Edward I went further, receiving the humiliating homage of a Scottish king and removing the sacred Scottish coronation stone from Scone Abbey to form a solid base for his coronation chair at Westminster, where it sat for seven centuries until its return in 1996. Yet as Edward and his grandson Edward III discovered, Scots never could be compelled to love English kingship, and indeed the hostility that was aroused by brutal Plantagenet campaigns north of the border has never truly abated. The cause of Scottish nationalism is rooted in the events of the thirteenth and fourteenth centuries, and if Scots nationalists should this century achieve their aim of cutting their ties with the British union, it will feel for many like the long culmination of a historical process that began in the high Middle Ages.

In Wales too the mark of the Plantagenets remains nearly indelible. The ring of castles built by Edward I from the 1280s still stands; they are monuments of a long-ago conquest that remind the inhabitants of North and West Wales of the struggle for mastery that took place and that set many of the conditions of relations between Wales and England to this day. No less long standing are the grievances of the Irish against English conquerors. For some, the beginning of the long and troubled history of Anglo-Irish relations goes back to the papal bull *Laudabiliter*, granted in 1155 by the only English pope, Adrian IV, to the first Plantagenet king, Henry II. Of all the Plantagenet kings, only Henry II, John, and Richard II ever set foot in Ireland, and none with especially laudable consequences. Yet they did enough both to establish the idea of English dominion across the Irish Sea and to arouse the consequent violent resistance of the affronted native Irish. This was only the beginning of a story that has yet to end, but it was a beginning nonetheless.

Besides all this, the Plantagenets changed England in very obvious ways. The realm was not simply constituted differently in 1400; it looked different. Eight generations of builders and patrons of the arts had transformed the English landscape. The Plantagenets had established grand castles, palaces, and hunting lodges. They had employed the great artists and architects of their age. Westminster, Windsor, and the Welsh castles were the most obvious, but during two and a half centuries of rule the realm had also matured in myriad other ways. London was transformed; the capital had expanded rapidly and was well on its way to becoming a major international trading center. At Dover the massive fortress rebuilt by Henry II during the later years of his reign loomed over the white cliffs, daring any Frenchman to invade. A golden age of cathedral building had seen Gothic spires and flying buttresses erected across the realm. Brick building had been reintroduced to the realm for the first time since the Romans left. New towns and ports had sprung up, most of them before the population collapse that accompanied the Black Death. Portsmouth was the military town established by Richard I, but others, such as Harwich (given its charter in 1238 by Henry III) and Liverpool (established by King John in 1207), had flourished under royal patronage too. At the same time, the population collapse of the fourteenth century had seen many villages abandoned, though to say that this was attributable to the direct influence of the Plantagenet kings would be to overstate the case.

Finally, Plantagenet England now *sounded* English. When Henry II first landed on the wintry coasts of England as a young man in the chilly 1140s, he would have had the most basic, rudimentary understanding of the native language. Certainly he would not have regarded it as a very useful tongue for important conversation. No one of any worth or merit would have spoken English to him. The languages of Henry II's court were Norman French and perhaps the langue d'oc spoken by Eleanor of Aquitaine and her southern French attendants. The language of official record was Latin.

This state of linguistic affairs continued until relatively late in the Plantagenet years and, in some senses, beyond, for French remained the most sophisticated courtly language, best suited to the mouths of aristocrats, and Latin was an important language of record for courts and government departments. But by the fourteenth century English was rallying. Edward III's Statute of Pleading, given in celebration of his fiftieth birthday in 1362, at a parliament that marked the highest point of English medieval kingship during the whole of our period, had made English the language of proceedings in royal courts and parliaments. The stock of the rude native tongue had risen accordingly. By Richard II's reign, Geoffrey Chaucer, John Gower, William Langland, and the *Gawain* poet (among others) were transforming English from a language for dolts and serfs into a language fit for poetry and scholarship. In time English was to become not only a language of princes and kings but the preeminent language in the world.

When Richard II's body was carried from Pontefract to London, it marked both the dismal end of a dynasty and the beginning of a new and troubled century in English history. Richard's deposition and his agonizing death had truncated the direct line of kings that had begun with Henry II, and it had brought shame upon his realm. Yet it also marked the end point of a period of transformation, development, and growth, a time during which England had emerged as a vibrant and confident nation. During 245 years of turbulent rule, the Plantagenets had forged England in their own image. They had changed a lightly governed, brittle, and easily fractured realm into one of the most powerful and sophisticated of the age, and what is more, they had stamped their mark forever on the English imagination.

Further Reading

This note offers a starting point for readers who wish to know more about some of the more important themes and characters discussed in this book.

Anyone wishing to research the lives of English kings or of any key figure in British history should begin with the *Oxford Dictionary of National Biography*, now available online for a subscription fee at oxforddnb.com. (Many libraries and institutions provide free access.)

Another useful online source is *British History Online* (british-history .ac.uk), a hub that gives access to many valuable primary and secondary sources and government records. Again, many libraries will have free access. Particularly useful here are the Parliament Rolls of Medieval England (also accessible at sd-editions.com/PROME/home.html).

For readers wishing to sample the primary sources of the period, a very useful starting place is *English Historical Documents*, general editor David C. Douglas, particularly vols. 2, 3, and 4, which between them cover the period 1042–1485. A detailed guide to the building works of the period can be found in *The History of the King's Works*, by H. M. Colvin (2 vols., 1963).

Part I: Age of Shipwreck (1120–1154)

A useful general study to the early period is *England Under the Norman and Angevin Kings*, by Robert Bartlett (2000). For Henry I, the standard biography is C. Warren Hollister's *Henry I* (2001).

The best recent discussion of Matilda's life is to be found in *She-Wolves: The Women Who Ruled England Before Elizabeth*, by Helen Castor (2010). The last full biography is Marjorie Chibnall's *The Empress Matilda: Queen Consort, Queen Mother, and Lady of the English* (1993). Also worth consulting on Matilda and every other English queen in the period is *Queens Consort: England's Medieval Queens*, by Lisa Hilton (2008). For the other side, see David Crouch, *The Reign of King Stephen* (2000) and Edmund King, *The Anarchy of Stephen's Reign* (1994).

Revealing chronicles are *The Ecclesiastical History of Orderic Vitalis*, ed.

and trans. Marjorie Chibnall (1968–1990), William of Malmesbury's *Historia Novella*, trans. K. R. Potter, ed. Edmund King (1998), and the *Gesta Stephani*, ed. and trans. K. R. Potter (1976).

Part II: Age of Empire (1154–1204)

As a complete portrait of the Plantagenet founder, *Henry II*, by W. L. Warren (1973), remains to be surpassed, although it is best read with an eye on *Henry II: New Interpretations*, ed. Nicholas Vincent and Christopher Harper-Bill (2007). *Eleanor of Aquitaine*, by Ralph V. Turner (2009), is the latest biographical study of the first Plantagenet queen consort. Also see *Eleanor of Aquitaine: Lord and Lady*, ed. Bonnie Wheeler and John Carmi Parsons (2003). The latest biography of Henry's troublesome archbishop is *Thomas Becket*, by John Guy (2012). For sources on Becket's life and death, see *The Lives of Thomas Becket*, ed. and trans. Michael Staunton (2001). For Henry's legal reforms a useful account appears in *A History of English Law Before the Time of Edward*, by Frederick Pollock and F. W. Maitland (1968).

    Richard I, by John Gillingham (1999), is the standard biography of the Lionheart. Richard's adventures in Outremer are summarized and contextualized in *The Crusades*, by Thomas Asbridge (2010). A comparative biography, *Lionheart and Lackland: King Richard, King John, and the Wars of Conquest*, by Frank McLynn (2006), is strong on Richard's wars with Philip II. *King John*, by W. L. Warren (2nd ed., 1978), tries to balance John's flaws with his administrative achievements. Older, more damning biographies include *John Lackland*, by Kate Norgate (1902), and *John, King of England*, by J. T. Appleby (1959). All should be read alongside *King John: New Interpretations*, ed. S. D. Church (1999). For a broader overview of the Plantagenet wars in Britain and Ireland, *The Struggle for Mastery: Britain 1066–1284*, by David Carpenter (2003), is essential. For the significance of the loss of Normandy, see Daniel Power, *The Norman Frontier in the Twelfth and Early Thirteenth Centuries* (2004). The most recent biography of John's French nemesis is *Philip Augustus: King of France 1180–1223*, by Jim Bradbury (1998).

    English Historical Documents, vols. 2 and 3, contain lengthy extracts from chroniclers, including William of Newburgh, Walter Map, and Gerald of Wales. *The History of William the Marshal*, ed. A. J. Holding, trans. S. Gregory, historical notes by David Crouch (3 vols., 2002–2006), is a tub-thumper worth reading at length. Roger of Howden's chronicle is in English translation as *The Annals of Roger de Hoveden*, ed. H. T. Riley (1853). An insight into government and administration is Richard Fitz-Nigel's Dialogue of the Exchequer, published as *Dialogus de Scaccario and Constitutio Domus Regis*, ed. and trans. Emilie Amt and S. D. Church (2007).

Part III: Age of Opposition (1204–1263)

The classic study of the revolt against John is *The Northerners: A Study in the Reign of King John*, by J. C. Holt (1961). *Magna Carta*, by the same author (2nd ed., 1992), is a brilliant technical study of the charter and contains full texts from 1215 and 1225. John's role in justice is examined in *The King and His Courts: The Role of John and Henry III in the Administration of Justice, 1199–1240*, by Ralph V. Turner (1968). John's mistreatment of the English Jews is dealt with in *The English Jewry Under Angevin Kings*, by H. J. Richardson (1960), and put in historical context in *Trials of the Diaspora*, by Anthony Julius (2010).

Henry III is one of the few English monarchs lacking a modern biography in the Yale series. Readers should use *Henry III and the Lord Edward: The Community of the Realm in the Thirteenth Century*, by F. M. Powicke (1947), *The Minority of Henry III*, by D. A. Carpenter (1990), and the collection of essays in *The Reign of Henry III*, by the same author (1996). Henry's obsession with his royal ancestors is discussed in "King Henry III and Saint Edward the Confessor: The Origins of the Cult," by D. A. Carpenter, *English Historical Review* 122 (2007). Also important is *Peter des Roches, Bishop of Winchester 1205–38: An Alien in English Politics*, by Nicholas Vincent (1996). For the wars of the 1250s and 1260s, see *Simon de Montfort*, by J. R. Maddicott (1994). Lord Edward's early involvement in political crisis is narrated very well in Marc Morris, *A Great and Terrible King: Edward I and the Forging of Britain* (2008); for Edward's political education before his accession, see "Edward I and the Lessons of Baronial Reform," *Thirteenth Century England* 1 (1986).

Roger of Wendover's Flowers of History, trans. J. A. Giles (1849), is valuable on John's struggles with the barons. Matthew Paris, who continued Wendover's chronicle, was close to Henry III's court; his writing is published in Latin as *Matthaei Parisiensis, Monachi Sancti Albani, Chronica*

Majora, ed. H. R. Luard (7 vols., 1872–1873). Correspondence of Henry's court is collected in *Royal and Other Historical Letters Illustrative of the Reign of King Henry III,* ed. W. W. Shirley (2 vols., 1862–1886). Papers relating to the war with de Montfort are collected in *Documents of the Baronial Movement of Reform and Rebellion 1258–1267,* ed. R. F. Treharne and I. J. Sanders (1973). Contemporary poems and sources from the age of opposition are collected in *Thomas Wright's Political Songs of England,* ed. P. Cross (1996).

Part IV: Age of Arthur (1264–1307)

See *Edward I,* by Michael Prestwich (1988), and *Edward I,* by E. L. G. Stones (1968), for comprehensive biographies. Edward I's obsession with King Arthur looms large in *A Great and Terrible King,* by Marc Morris (2008), and is considered in detail in "Edward I: Arthurian Enthusiast," by R. S. Loomis, *Speculum* 28 (1953). For Edward's castles, see "Master James of St. George," by A. J. Taylor, *English Historical Review* 65 (1950) and *Castle: A History of the Buildings That Shaped Medieval Britain,* by Marc Morris (2003). For individual castles, see *The History of the King's Works,* by H. M. Colvin, ed. (2 vols., 1963).

For Edward I and Wales, see *The Age of Conquest: Wales 1063–1415,* by R. R. Davies (2000), and the same author's *Domination and Conquest* (1990). On Scotland, see *The Kingship of the Scots, 842–1292,* by A. A. M. Duncan (2002), and *Under the Hammer: Edward I and Scotland 1286–1306,* by F. Watson (1998). The process of English lawmaking by statute, which also developed in Edward I's reign, is important to the long-term processes described in *From Memory to Written Record,* by M. T. Clanchy (2nd ed., 1993). For Edward's most difficult year, see *Baronial Opposition to Edward I: The Earls and the Crisis of 1297,* by Michael J. Hodder (1976).

The original architect of Arthuriana can still be read: Geoffrey of Monmouth, *History of the Kings of Britain,* ed. L. Thorpe (1966). The laws of Edward's reign are collected in vol. 1 of *The Statutes of the Realm,* ed. A. Luders, T. E. Tomlins, J. France, W. E. Taunton, and J. Raithby (1810). Papers relating to the Great Cause are collected in *Edward I and the Throne of Scotland 1290–1296: An Edition of the Record Sources for the Great Cause,* ed. E. L. G. Stones and G. G. Simpson (2 vols., 1977). For sources concerning Edward's government under attack, see *Documents Illustrating the Crisis of 1297–98 in*

England, ed. M. Prestwich (1980). A noncontemporary but valuable Scottish chronicle perspective on Edward's wars is *Scalacronica by Sir Thomas Gray of Heton, Knight,* ed. J. Stevenson (1836).

Part V: **Age of Violence (1307–1330)**

Edward II, by Seymour Phillips (2010), is the new standard biography, which complements *King Edward II,* by Roy Martin Haines (2003). Additional aspects are considered in *The Reign of Edward II: New Perspectives,* ed. Gwilym Dodd and Anthony Musson (2006). The end of the reign is discussed in *The Tyranny and Fall of Edward II 1321–1326,* by Natalie Fryde (1979). The king's folly and his nemesis are considered respectively in *Piers Gaveston, Earl of Cornwall,* by J. S. Hamilton (1988), and *Thomas of Lancaster,* by J. R. Maddicott (1970). On his later favorites, see "The Charges Against the Despensers, 1321," by Michael Prestwich, *Bulletins of the Institute of Historical Research* 48 (1985).

Context is given to Edward's reign in *The Fourteenth Century,* by M. McKisack (1959), and *Plantagenet England, 1225–1360,* by Michael Prestwich (2005). For biographical information on Edward's wife, see "Isabella, the She-Wolf of France," by H. Johnstone, *History,* new series, 21 (1936–1937). For theories of Edward's survival, see *The Greatest Traitor: The Life of Sir Roger Mortimer, Ruler of England 1327–1330,* by Ian Mortimer (2003), and "The Death of Edward II in Berkeley Castle," by the same author, *English Historical Review* 120 (2005).

The essential chronicle for the period (referenced in the text as the "Life of Edward II") is *Vita Edwardi Secundi,* ed. and trans. Wendy R. Childs (2005). *The Chronicles of Lanercost, 1272–1346,* trans. Sir Herbert Maxwell (1913), is good on the war between Edward II and the Bruce family. *Peter Langtoft's Chronicle,* ed. T. Hearne (2 vols., 1725), is also very useful. Other contemporary chronicles are extracted and translated in *English Historical Documents,* vol. 3, ed. H. Rothwell (1975).

Part VI: **Age of Glory (1330–1360)**

Edward III is the subject of a fine new biography, *Edward III,* by W. Mark Ormrod (2011), as well as another very readable recent work, *The Perfect King: The Life of Edward III, Father of the English Nation,* by Ian Mortimer

(2006). Also see essays, particularly on military development, in *The Age of Edward III*, ed. J. S. Bothwell (2001). *Edward, Prince of Wales and Aquitaine*, by R. Barber (1978), examines the life and career of the Black Prince. Also see *John of Gaunt: The Exercise of Princely Power in Fourteenth-Century Europe*, by Anthony Goodman (1992).

The best guide to the opening phases of the Hundred Years War is found in *The Hundred Years War I: Trial by Battle*, by Jonathan Sumption (1990), and the same author's *The Hundred Years War II: Trial by Fire* (1999). On the 1341 crisis, see "Edward III's Removal of His Ministers and Judges, 1340–1341," by Natalie Fryde, *Historical Research* 48 (1975). For an example of disorder in England during the early years of Edward's reign, see "The Folvilles of Ashby-Folville in Leicestershire, and Their Associates in Crime," by E. L. G. Stones, *Transactions of the Royal Historical Society*, 5th series, 7 (1957). *The Black Death: An Intimate History*, by John Hatcher (2008), is one of the best recent books on the 1348 population crisis. For an introduction to Edwardian chivalry, see *The Order of the Garter, 1348–1461*, by Hugh E. L. Collins (2000).

The supposed origins of Edward's French wars can be read in *The Vows of the Heron*, ed. J. L. Grigsby and N. J. Lacy (1992). *Froissart's Chronicles*, trans. G. Brereton (1978), is a vital, vivid (if erratic) chronicle of the wars and their context and follows the model of the *Chronique de Jean le Bel*, ed. J. Viard and E. Deprez (2 vols., 1904–1905). A monastic perspective comes from *The St. Albans Chronicle: The "Chronica Maiora" of Thomas Walsingham*, ed. and trans. J. Taylor, Wendy Childs, and L. Watkiss (2003).

Part VII: Age of Revolution (1360–1399)

The Good Parliament, by George Holmes (1975), details the events of the opposition movement in 1376. *Shaping the Nation: England 1360–1461*, by G. L. Harriss (2005), provides essential context, overview, and analysis of domestic and foreign politics. *Richard II*, by Nigel Saul (1997), is the key biography of the last Plantagenet. *Richard II and the Revolution of 1399*, by Michael Bennett (1999), focuses tightly on the last years of the dynasty.

On declining English fortunes in France, see *The Hundred Years War III: Divided Houses*, by Jonathan Sumption (2009). *Summer of Blood: The Peasants' Revolt of 1381*, by Dan Jones (2009), narrates the great popular rebellion and its aftermath. "Richard II and the Vocabulary of Kingship," by

Nigel Saul, *English Historical Review* 60 (1995), examines Richard's ideas of kingly majesty. "The Tyranny of Richard II," by Caroline Barron, *Bulletins of the Institute of Historical Research* 41 (1968), shows how Richard oppressed his people in the final years of his reign; his removal from the throne is charted in "The Deposition of Richard II and the Accession of Henry IV," by B. Wilkinson, in *English Historical Review* 54 (1939).

The documents relating to Richard's deposition are to be found in *English Historical Documents*, vol. 3 (see above). Sources concerning the great rebellion and much else about Richard's reign can be found in *The Peasants' Revolt of 1381*, by R. B. Dobson (2nd ed., 1983). Other chronicles of Richard's reign include Thomas Walsingham (see above), *Knighton's Chronicle, 1337–1396*, ed. G. H. Martin (1995), and *The Chronicle of Adam of Usk, 1377–1421*, ed. and trans. C. Given-Wilson (1997). The sympathetic *Chronicque de la traïson et mort de Richart Deux roy Dengleterre*, published by the English Historical Society (1846), gives many personal details of Richard's deposition.

Index

Index

Index